Living in the USA

Cultural Contexts
for Reading and Writing

Kathleen Shine Cain

Merrimack College

ALLYN AND BACON

Boston   London   Toronto   Sydney   Tokyo   Singapore

Editor in Chief, Humanities: Joseph Opiela
Editorial Assistant: Brenda Conaway
Production Administrator: Rowena Dores
Editorial-Production Service: Tara L. Masih
Text Designer: Claire Seng-Niemoeller
Cover Administrator: Linda Dickinson
Manufacturing Buyer: Louise Richardson
Composition Buyer: Linda Cox

Library of Congress Cataloging-in-Publication Data
Cain, Kathleen Shine.
    Living in the USA : cultural contexts for reading and writing /
Kathleen Shine Cain.
        p. cm.
    Includes index.
    ISBN 0-205-14877-8
    1. Readers—Social sciences. 2. United States—Social conditions—
Problems, exercises, etc. 3. Pluralism (Social sciences)—
Problems, exercises, etc. 4. Minorities—United States—Problems,
exercises, etc. 5. English language—Rhetoric. 6. College readers.
I. Title.
PE1127.S6C35 1994
808'.0427—dc20   93-20933
                                                                        CIP

This book is printed on
recycled, acid-free paper.

Acknowledgments

Chapter One
    David H. Hackworth, "This Was No Riot, It Was a Revolt" from the May 25, 1992 issue of *Newsweek*. Copyright © 1992 by Newsweek, Inc. All rights reserved. Reprinted by permission.

Acknowledgments continued on page 620, which constitutes an extension of the copyright page.

Printed in the United States of America
10 9 8 7 6 5 4 3 2 1   98 97 96 95 94 93

Contents

❖ Chapter 1 ❖
Introduction: Reading Actively, Writing Critically 1

❖ Chapter 2 ❖
Cultural Identities 63

❖ Chapter 3 ❖
A Sense of Home 155

❖ Chapter 4 ❖
From Generation to Generation

❖ Chapter 5 ❖
Educational Opportunities   327

❖ Chapter 6 ❖
Finding Meaning in Work   425

❖ Chapter 7 ❖
A Woman's Place   *501*

❖ Chapter 8 ❖
Living on the Edge   *561*

A Note to Instructors

THIS BOOK, which is designed to be used in introductory writing and critical thinking courses, focuses on culture in its broadest sense. Culture certainly refers to race and ethnicity, but it also reflects the values, beliefs, and behaviors of groups based on their age, gender, socioeconomic position, sexual preference, and situation in society. Thus, in addition to material on several racial and ethnic groups, *Living in the USA* includes writings by and about working-class writers, homeless people, gays and lesbians, and prisoners. The readings, most of them anthologized here for the first time, have been chosen not only for their cultural significance but also for their contemporary flavor—the majority were written within the past ten years. Readings also represent a wide variety of genres and styles: In addition to traditional academic essays, there are newspaper and magazine articles, short stories, poems, a play, selections from personal memoirs, and oral histories. Several writers are represented by more than one selection, affording students the opportunity to gain a clearer impression of a writer's perspective and style.

Organization of the Book

Chapter 1 includes extensive discussion of the critical reading and writing process, complete with examples of student responses to a sample selection. The section devoted to reading instruction shows students how to interact with the text even before beginning a selection, and it continues to emphasize engagement with the text as students read. The section on writing instruction shows students how to move from informal, private responses to formal, public pieces—the former designed to explore responses to a text and the latter to communicate the writer's position. The sample selection and the three readings included at the end of Chapter 1 constitute an abbreviated chapter focusing on several topical issues with which students will almost certainly be familiar. These selections, grouped under the title "A Collage of American Issues," are designed to introduce students to the reading and writing process in two ways: First, they offer a glimpse of several problems facing U.S. citizens today, and second, they provide sample student responses to the apparatus. A series of exercises in this chapter allows students to practice the reading and writing process on their own.

The remaining chapters in the book are arranged to acquaint students with different cultural perspectives on a variety of issues:

Chapter 2, "Cultural Identities," immerses students in issues of multiculturalism through exploring the various identities found among those who call themselves Americans.

Chapter 3, "A Sense of Home," asks students to consider what home means to individuals and how social problems can alter one's understanding of home.

Chapter 4, "From Generation to Generation," offers reflections on how people from different generational perspectives address every-day issues and social concerns.

Chapter 5, "Educational Opportunities," examines the myth of equality in education as well as exploring related educational issues.

Chapter 6, "Finding Meaning in Work," presents selections by writers concerned with the benefits and frustrations of working in a capitalist economy.

Chapter 7, "A Woman's Place," focuses on the various roles women play in today's society.

Chapter 8, "Living on the Edge," provides a glimpse of those who live at the limits of mainstream society and beyond.

Apparatus

The apparatus is designed to involve students actively in their reading from the beginning. Chapter introductions acquaint students with topics that make up the focal points for the selections, while head-notes provide both biographical information on authors and contextual information on the selections. Before starting to read a selection, students are asked to write in their journals about the issue(s) it addresses; they are then given suggestions for focusing their annotations of the text. Each selection is followed by three categories of response: Focused Freewriting, Guided Responses, and Shared Responses. Instructors may use all three types of responses or choose from among them.

Focused Freewriting requires students to freewrite about the selection, choosing their own focus or using one of the focal points provided. For instructors who wish more structured responses from their students, the Guided Responses category offers traditional discussion questions similar to those found in many readers. These are not comprehension questions; rather, they ask students to draw inferences from their reading and to respond to those inferences. Finally, instructors who want to emphasize collaborative activity can ask students to explore a related issue in groups through Shared Responses. In these exercises students take their own journal entries and form small groups to discuss what they've written, analyzing individual responses and sometimes trying to reach consensus.

Formal writing assignments are found at the end of each chapter. As with the individual selections, instructors may choose the more open-ended categories Generating Ideas, Possible Topics, and Focusing Responses or the more structured Guided Writing Assignments. When choosing from the list of possible topics, students may generate their own ideas for an essay by reviewing their annotations and other written responses. The guided assignments, on the other hand, provide students with a focus for their written responses. The emphasis in these end-of-chapter assignments is synthesis, with each writing assignment asking students to make connections between two or three of the readings. Writing assignments also offer students the opportunity to explore different forms of writing. They may be asked to compose a letter to the editor, write a proposal, make up a conversation between two authors or characters, write in the voice of an author, or compose a conventional essay. Finally, for students who wish to explore issues further, guidance for choosing a subject or ready-made Research Topics is offered.

Course Goals

Students who work their way through the readings in *Living in the USA* should come away with both an appreciation of the complexity of American society and a respect for its various cultures. In addition, the integration of the reading and writing processes throughout the book should provide students with strategies for making meaning of their reading that will serve them throughout their college careers and beyond. Just as the content of the selections encourages students to question their assumptions about what constitutes American culture, the apparatus helps them question what they read. Taken together, the selections and the apparatus offer students the opportunity to become critical readers of—and writers about—the many texts they will encounter throughout their lives.

Acknowledgments

I owe a special debt of gratitude to the three students who worked through the sample chapter of this text: Jane Estrella, Dave Michaud, and Isa Perez spent many an hour cheerfully reworking material every time I reshaped the first chapter. My students and the tutors in the Merrimack College Writing Center also deserve credit for continuing to teach me about the critical thinking and writing process and about the benefits of collaboration. Invaluable research assistance was provided by Deborah Carlisle-Burger, and clerical assistance by Martha Heinze. For her help with revising I thank MaryKay Mahoney.

Several reviewers offered invaluable advice and suggestions: Irene Brosnahan, Illinois State University; Ray Dumont, University of Massachusetts at Dartmouth; Stephen Hahn, William Paterson College; C. Jerial Howard, Northeastern Illinois University; David Jolliffe, The University of Illinois at Chicago; Eunice L. Jordan, Eastern Michigan University; Floyd Ogburn, University of Cincinnati; and Dawn Rodrigues, Colorado State University.

The folks at Allyn and Bacon were tremendously supportive: Brenda Conaway's calm, competent hand kept the project on track, while her soothing, sympathetic voice kept me on an even keel. Joe Opiela often helped me see the forest when the trees kept blocking my vision. Rowena Dores and Tara Masih expertly guided the book through the production process.

I'd like to thank my husband Jim for that smile when things went well and that willing shoulder when the going was rough. And, finally, Shannon—what can I say, kiddo? You make it all worthwhile.

———— ❖ ————

For my parents Catherine and Dan Shine

with thanks

for the stories that sustained us

on all those trips to Chinatown

A Note to Students

THIS BOOK WILL INTRODUCE YOU to a variety of perspectives on American culture—probably more than you ever knew existed. In the past you may have heard the term *culture* used in a narrow sense, referring to a group defined by race, ethnicity, or perhaps religion. A broader definition of culture, however, includes any group that shares certain beliefs, values, and behaviors. Culture is defined broadly in *Living in the USA*, so within its pages you'll hear from people representing different races and ethnic groups, political camps, socioeconomic classes, sexual orientations, and ages—you'll even encounter a pair of hermits. Some selections will present opinions that seem foreign to you; sometimes you'll find ideas or positions in a selection unacceptable, perhaps even offensive. On the other hand, some readings will probably echo your world view. All selections, however, will provide you with an opportunity to think critically about the issues addressed. If you channel those thoughts into constructive written responses to the selections, you can enhance not only your reading and writing abilities but also your appreciation of the rich variety of cultures found in the United States.

Introduction

Reading Actively, Writing Critically

THE READINGS IN THIS BOOK challenge you to become an active partici-
pant in the conversations about culture found in these pages. This
opening chapter features advice on how to take part in that conversation, complete with examples showing how particular students have
engaged in active reading and critical writing.

Each selection in the book contains guidelines for reading actively
and writing critically; in addition, each chapter ends with suggestions
for writing critically about relationships between selections. For each
selection in the book, you will be asked to engage in active reading
through the following activities:

- · taking prereading notes
- · annotating (making notes as you read)
- · summarizing the selection
- · doing focused freewriting about the selection
- · responding to "guided responses" questions about the selection
- · sharing responses in small groups.

As you may have noticed already, all of these activities involve both
reading and writing. Even before you begin to draft a formal piece of
writing, then, you will have filled many pages with informal writing.
Most of this informal writing, which forms the link between your
reading and formal writing, will take place in a *reader's journal*. Keep-

ing this journal will help you understand and respond to the readings, as well as provide you with topics on which to write formal pieces. This chapter illustrates how three students—Jane Estrella, David Michaud, and Isa Perez—responded to several readings.

These students were chosen because of their backgrounds and abilities; they represent at least part of the cultural range of contemporary college students, and their academic records are exemplary. Jane is an English major from East Providence, Rhode Island, a heavily Portuguese-American community. Although she grew up speaking English at home, much of the conversation in her neighborhood is still conducted in Portuguese. David, looking for a more meaningful career, left a lucrative position as a sales manager and returned to college for a degree in English and psychology ten years after earning his associates degree in business. He is of Canadian American descent. Raised and educated in the Dominican Republic, Isa came to the United States with her family after she graduated from high school. Her experience at a primarily white, middle-class college has made her active in international students' affairs, and she is majoring in international business. All three students have demonstrated a keen ability to read actively and write critically.

KEEPING A READER'S JOURNAL

There are many ways to keep a reader's journal. Sometimes a journal involves only summaries and personal responses to readings; sometimes it consists of responses to questions found in the book or presented by an instructor; sometimes it contains a combination of the two. As you become more comfortable with active reading, you will probably develop your own journal-keeping strategies. As you read each selection in this book, you'll be asked to use your reader's journal for prereading notes, freewriting, answers to "guided responses" questions, and observations on related issues. You may also make notes in the journal as you read and summarize each selection after you've finished it. The journal allows you to record your part of the conversation with the author and with other students reading the text.

Prior to reading, you'll record thoughts about the author and the subject, as well as any questions you have about the reading. As you read, you'll make notes in your journal and/or the margins of the text. After you read, you may write a summary of the selection and you'll freewrite and/or write answers to the "guided responses." Finally, you'll record your observations on issues related to the text and use that journal entry as the basis for a group discussion.

All of this writing will help you not only to understand the selection better but also to clarify your responses to it. As you write, you often discover things you didn't realize you knew, and you will frequently be able to work through questions and problems you have with the selection. Ultimately, your journal writing lays the groundwork for your more formal responses to the readings, such as essays, proposals, and letters. The examples from student journals provided throughout this chapter demonstrate just how important the reader's journal is to the active reading and critical writing processes.

READING ACTIVELY

What is active reading? Sometimes called *critical reading*, *active reading* involves a lively dialogue between reader and writer. An active reader considers the author's ideas, makes observations, asks questions, analyzes the author's perspective in relation to those of others, forges connections between different selections—in general, *responds* to what the writer is saying. That response can take many forms, but it almost always means understanding fully what the author is saying, measuring the author's ideas against the reader's own experience and understanding, evaluating the author's ideas, and articulating other perspectives on the topic. The explanations that follow should help you focus on the basic elements of active reading, which generally fall under three headings: *taking prereading notes, making notes on your reading,* and *summarizing*.

Taking Prereading Notes

A reader who dives into a selection without first thinking about what he or she is preparing to read is adopting a passive role. An active reader, on the other hand, begins to interact with the author even before reading the first word. The first step in active reading is to put you on more equal terms with the author by reminding you what you already know about the author or the subject and by providing you with questions to help focus your reading. This process, called *prereading*, involves two different activities: *reviewing prior knowledge* and *asking questions*.

Reviewing prior knowledge Simply put, prior knowledge is what you already know that is relevant to the selection you're reading. Rarely do people read something about which they have no prior knowledge, but readers sometimes tend to look at authors as experts, believing everything the author says regardless of what they, the readers, may already know about the subject. If you call up your prior knowledge, however, you can measure the author's ideas against your own instead of blindly accepting what is presented on the page. Perhaps you've read something before by this author or have heard the author's name in another context. Perhaps you're familiar with the subject of the selection. In either case, you can use your prior knowledge to help you interpret what you read. In addition to considering what you already know, you may also want to begin thinking about the relevance of a selection to your own experience and understanding. No matter how irrelevant prior knowledge may seem at first, it may come in handy in making the material meaningful to you. Regardless of the extent of your general knowledge or the nature of your personal experience, drawing on prior knowledge offers a unique perspective from which to consider a selection. For example, even before you read David H. Hackworth's "This Was No Riot, It Was a Revolt" (p. 10), you had probably heard a good deal about the Los Angeles riots of April 1992 that followed the acquittals in the first trial of the police officers involved in Rodney King's beating. You can use that knowledge to help you understand the selection and make judgments regarding its conclusions. In this book, each reading is preceded by a headnote that offers some biographical information about the author, a few comments about the reading, and suggestions for taking notes on your prior knowledge of the topic.

Asking questions Most students are afraid, at one time or another, that their questions will sound stupid to others—especially to an instructor. Granted, it's sometimes difficult to ask a question in front of an entire class, but when you're in the privacy of your own reading space, who cares how stupid the question may seem? Nobody's there to hear it but you, and most "stupid" questions, as you will discover through reading and discussing your reading with others, are not stupid at all. In fact, you should be asking questions throughout your reading and beyond it in your discussions of the selection; but often it is the initial questions you ask that help you make sense of what you're reading. It may be precisely one of those questions that will alert you to an important idea in the selection you're about to read.

Sometimes your questions will be about the author of the work and his or her approach to the subject. While it is not necessary to have biographical information before reading a text, such details often offer some insight into the mind behind the material. The headnotes before each of the selections in this book are therefore designed to provide information to help answer some of your preliminary questions. In addition to biographical material, the headnote also contains a few comments on the selection itself. Those brief comments are designed simply to fit the selection into a context, not to tell you what to think about the topic.

Beyond making you think something about the author and the topic, however, asking questions before reading can help you focus your attention as you read. That is precisely what David Michaud did when he read "This Was No Riot." Dave discovered all he really needed to know about Hackworth from the biographical note, and in following the guidelines for prereading notes, he was able to uncover his prior knowledge of the issues addressed in the article. Recording his response to the guidelines caused Dave to pose two questions of his own about the article.

Below is the headnote for David Hackworth's article, followed by an exercise to acquaint you with the process of taking prereading notes. The exercise is followed by Dave Michaud's notes.

This Was No Riot, It Was a Revolt

DAVID H. HACKWORTH

DAVID H. HACKWORTH, *currently a member of* Newsweek *magazine's editorial staff, was educated at Santa Monica Community College and Woodbury College. From 1946 to 1971 he served as a career officer in the United States Army, where he won over 100 military awards. He has written two books,* Vietnam Primer *(1983) and* About Face: The Odyssey of an American Warrior *(1989). In this article, which originally appeared in* Newsweek *on May 25, 1992, Hackworth offers a military perspective on the Los Angeles riots that followed the initial acquittal of the four police officers accused of beating Rodney King. Noting the similarity of the riots to insurgencies he had seen in Korea and Vietnam, the author suggests that a program loosely based on Franklin Delano Roosevelt's Civilian Conservation Corps may hold the only hope for urban survival.*

Before reading the selection, write in your journal about your response to the King beating, the officers' initial acquittal, and the riots that followed. Did you consider the beating an isolated incident or an indication of deeper problems in society? What was your reaction to the verdict? Which view of the riots—e.g., that they provided an excuse for lawless people to go wild or an inevitable explosion of pent-up rage at urban blight—did you support?

As you make notes on your reading, you may want to focus on the history Hackworth provides, his analogies, or the details of the program he advocates.

❖ Exercise 1   Read the headnote for "This Was No Riot" and respond in your journal to the guidelines for prereading notes. If possible, make additional notes about your prior knowledge and pose a question or two. As you discuss your responses in small groups, compare your reactions with other group members and with David Michaud's notes (below), noting similarities and differences. Dave's prereading notes:

> I remember watching the videotape of the King beating on television and feeling truly horrified at what I saw. I felt sick— sick and numb. Each time they showed the tape, I grew more and more aware of what this meant, of what the greater ramifications of the incident were. I sat on the couch and wondered if I, or someone I know, might someday suffer the same brutal attack. I remember feeling helpless, not only about what I saw, but about society in general. Have we truly lost control? Isn't this a democratic country where the people, the general populous, make the decisions—the rules? Or have we lost our power as a voting public to second-rate militarists who get their jollies victimizing innocent people? Watching the video, I lost my comfortable sense of security and my respect for the so-called great nation of ours.
>
> It wasn't until the police officers were put on trial did I even consider racial issues and the problems of urban America. This was the "system's" chance to make a statement and not only show its compassion for the urban citizen, but to also demonstrate a notion of truth within the judiciary. However, as angry as I felt toward the acquittal and the recurring memory of the beating, the riots that followed muted my concerns. I forgot my anxiety for King . . . I forgot my anger toward the police officers . . . I was no longer thinking about racial tension or urban relief or public unification—I just felt rage. I wanted to hurt back all those doing the hurting. I wanted to punish all those who demonstrated unecessary violence toward innocent victims. Two wrongs don't make a right. Innocent people are not the enemy. Its one thing to organize and show anger, its quite another to hurt and kill innocent people out of blind emotional hatred. Something needs to be done alright: every city is a potential powder-keg, and every powder-keg is connected by a network of easily-lit fuses. I'm very anxious to read Mr. Hackworths article. Perhaps a journalist with military experience can offer me a different perspective on the events of that fateful day in LA.

Notice that while Dave certainly makes some thoughtful observations and is obviously articulate, he's simply recording his observations in a private journal and not preparing them for formal presentation. His notes contain misspelled words, incorrect punctuation, faulty sentence structures, clichés, and a mix of formal and casual language. Of course, such problems would be edited out of a public piece of writing. But the point of journal writing is simply to put ideas down on paper. As long as you can understand what you've written, you need not concern yourself with mechanics in your journal.

Making Notes on Your Reading

Prereading activities provide you with a perspective from which to approach the selection. Once you begin reading, you will want to maintain your active role by responding to the material as you read it. Of course you must grasp what the author is saying before you can make any significant response. Thus the first stage in making notes on your reading involves *skimming*. When you skim, you take mental notes on the text. After skimming, you take pen in hand and begin *annotating* the text.

Skimming   Truly active reading almost always means reading a selection more than once. If possible, it's useful to *skim* a selection before picking up a pen for more intensive reading. When you skim a text, you don't pause to understand complex ideas or mentally argue with the author's positions; you simply try to get a sense of what's in the selection. A reader skimming a text is like a hiker reading a trail map. The map does little more than point out landmarks and describe terrain, but it gives the hiker a sense of familiarity—and confidence— before setting out on the trail. Skimming a text provides the reader with a similar sense of familiarity. By reading titles, subtitles, introductions, first sentences of paragraphs, section titles, and conclusions, you, the reader, become acquainted with the work—its main idea, language, organization, evidence, and other features. During this reading you can form a general impression of how the author presents her- or himself to the reader, what the author believes about the topic, and what approach the author uses to address the audience. If there are any difficult sections in the selection, skimming will alert you to them. While skimming may seem at first glance a rather passive and superficial activity, rest assured that this initial assessment of the selection will serve you well once you begin your annotations. Skimming a selection makes you far more able to look at it critically on closer reading, and gives you a sense not only of what the author has to say but of what you may have to say to the author.

Annotating the text   As you read the essay more closely, you will want to make notes. What most readers do as they read closely is to *annotate* the text, underlining significant words, phrases, and passages, as well as writing observations and questions in the margins. Sometimes you will find yourself underlining passages (brief ones) that simply "grab" you. That's fine. If a passage is compelling, then it is surely worth remembering, and it may help you to understand the material better. When you underline such passages, you may also want to make a brief marginal note indicating why you think it's compelling. These notes can help you respond more fully to the selection in subsequent readings. You may also find your pen drawn to sections that make you think—perhaps a segment in which the author offers a viewpoint that you've never considered before or one that presents a reasonable explanation of an opinion with which you disagree. Again, marginal notes added to your underlinings will jog your memory in subsequent readings.

Undoubtedly, you will find other, more practical reasons for underlining passages or making marginal notes. Annotations are especially useful in creating an *outline* of sorts to help you understand the author's ideas and responses.

As you read, you will begin to notice ideas central to the author's purpose. Frequently such ideas come at the beginning of a paragraph, but not always. Look for statements that are broader in scope and presented more emphatically than the ideas found in surrounding statements. Often central ideas also summarize previous or following statements, answer questions presented previously, or offer conclusions drawn from evidence in the essay. Underlining or highlighting such statements and making marginal notes about them will help you compose an outline of the selection.

Annotating a text, however, is not an activity designed simply to help you outline the author's ideas. It also affords you the opportunity as a reader to *talk back* to the author. Thus when you find yourself questioning the author's conclusions, disagreeing with his or her arguments, or remaining unconvinced by the evidence, you should note these responses in the margins. You may, for example, want to make marginal notes of questions about the author's positions, either because you don't fully understand a particular position or because you disagree with it. Such questions will remain in your mind as you continue reading, helping you formulate your response to the entire selection. On second and third readings you may find yourself reformulating or answering your original questions. You may even find yourself writing down counterarguments or noting evidence that refutes the author's position.

The more you read, the more you will find yourself annotating selections. Reading what one author says about a particular issue will remind you of what another has said about the same issue; evidence offered by one author may even be refuted in the work of another. Extensive reading will also help you to formulate independent positions and thus write annotations offering a response based on your own experience and reading.

Truly active readers thus become fully engaged in the works they are reading; as noted earlier, the active reading process is much like a conversation between author and reader. Active readers, like people engaged in conversation, do not hesitate to respond to the author at every opportunity.

At first you may be uncertain about what to annotate, but rest assured that the more active reading you do, the more comfortable you'll be with how and when to annotate the text. (As you discuss your annotations with fellow students, you'll also discover that each reader responds to a text differently.) Often it helps to focus on specific images, issues, or ideas as you annotate a text. To this end, the headnotes include possible focal points for you to keep in mind as you make notes on your reading. For example, the headnote for David Hackworth's "This Was No Riot, It Was a Revolt" (p. 5) ends with the following advice for those who seek a focus for their annotations:

> As you make notes on your reading, you may want to focus on the history Hackworth provides, his analogies, or the details of the program he calls for.

A word of caution: Underlining or highlighting significant passages is fine as long as you don't overdo it. When you begin to review a selection, and especially when you begin to write about it, you don't want to look at pages and pages underlined from top to bottom. If you underline too much, you defeat the purpose of the exercise. Remember, underlining should be reserved for *selected* important passages.

Below is an exercise designed to acquaint you with the process of annotating a text. It is followed by the complete text of David H. Hackworth's "This Was No Riot, It Was a Revolt" and sample annotations from Isa Perez.

❖ Exercise 2   Glance over your prereading notes for "This Was No Riot"; then, as you read the selection, annotate the text based on the guidelines provided in the headnote (p. 5). Underline significant passages and make marginal notes; then compose a brief outline of the selection in your journal. Once you have completed the selection, work in small groups to compare one another's—and Isa's—notes and outlines, noting similarities and differences between annotations.

THE FIRESTORM THAT SWEPT down Normandie Avenue and spread through Los Angeles two weeks ago was no aberration. The kindling was in place long ago. I know. Los Angeles is my hometown. It's part of me. The anger of the young blacks and Hispanics was already festering on the streets in the 1930s and '40s when I grew up. I was a poor white. My grandmother stood in dole lines with black and Hispanic mothers. I wore the same "relief clothes." I ate the same "welfare food" and suffered the same shame. As a teen, I ran with a mixed-race gang, and we all had trouble with the law. Many ended up in prison, many others died. Those that escaped—like me—did so through military service.

Each year since, the conditions have gotten worse; now they're near terminal. Today the grandchildren of my black and Hispanic friends live in squalid conditions resembling those of undeveloped countries. They have no jobs, no hope and no trust in the establishment's authority. The government is not their friend, but their enemy.

I've seen similar despair and resentment on the faces of Yugoslav guerrillas in Trieste after World War II. I saw it among Korean insurgents in 1950, and again in the five long bloody years I fought guerrillas in Vietnam. What all of these disadvantaged young people had in common was a blind dedication, a belief in the efficacy of sheer violence to achieve a kind of rough justice. In Los Angeles the result was two days of rage that left some 50 dead, more than 2,300 wounded, 17,000 arrests and $1 billion in charcoal carnage.

The politicians called it a riot. So did the press. But soldiers call this kind of fighting something else: insurgency, or Low Intensity Conflict (LIC), as the army's training manuals say. Washington seemed to recognize this when it sent elements of the crack Seventh Infantry Division, the army's top LIC fighters, from Fort Ord to Los Angeles along with the California National Guard. Many thinkers on warfare believe LIC will be the principal form of combat in the future. Higher levels are too costly in blood and treasure. In most cases—the Gulf War was an exception due to Saddam Hussein's military ignorance—the destructiveness is its own deterrent. So the most ancient form of warfare is now the most contemporary, in Los Angeles no less than Lima. And it's not just Los Angeles, says police Sgt. Mike Schott of North Richmond, Calif.: "Our cities are not a powder keg waiting to explode, but they're like a slow fuse burning all the time. Daily there are race crimes: Shootings, beatings and violence. L. A.'s flame just got higher. People noticed. But believe me, it's ongoing everywhere. Day and night."

Let's not overstate the comparison. LIC operations in Southeast Asia, or Latin America have been premeditated. They seek not rough justice but well-defined political goals. The Los Angeles insurgency was spontaneous. It lacked organized leadership. It had no battle plan. Many of the participants were simply opportunists on a looting spree. But things may not stay that way. Already the two main warring youth gangs, the Crips and the Bloods, have pledged to join forces against the police. This could give inner-city rage both leadership and a command infrastructure. Overall, the city has maybe 1,000 gangs, with an estimated total of 110,000 members. These gangs are well armed, with everything from submachine guns to hand grenades. Even now, many police officers believe that inner-city duty is similar to combat. With the daily doses of danger from sniper fire and ambush, they become hardened like shock troops in an occupation zone.

American police are not equipped, either mentally or physically, for counterinsurgency. For that matter, neither are most regular army troops. Of the 48 insurgencies Americans have fought since the end of World War II, the score stands: Insurgents 48, United States 0. Vastly superior firepower is irrelevant to such struggles. As the Palestinian *intifada* shows, urban uprisings are especially difficult, with their house-to-house, block-to-block battles. The government force suffers heavy casualties and property undergoes mass destruction. And in any case, a free society cannot survive through force.

First step: As the smoke clears over L. A., a battered city we had to defend from ourselves, perhaps the two-day war we had here at home will focus us on what we are defending and what our priorities are. We can collapse the Iron Curtain and restore the Emir of Kuwait to his throne, but Americans are not free to walk in safety on the streets of their own cities, nor are inner-city Americans given opportunity and a decent standard of living. As retired U. S. Army Col. Carl Bernard, an eminent authority on revolutionary war says, "The mistrust, despair, hopelessness of our inner-city minorities need to be defused, and then eliminated."

Peace is possible. But throwing money at the problem won't make it go away. The first step is to learn from past insurgencies and overcome the hopelessness that separates the people from the government. This takes leadership. And I have a nominee: Gen. Colin L. Powell. He would follow the example of George C. Marshall, who was detailed to the Civilian Conservation Corps during President Roosevelt's war on poverty in the 1930s and later rose to become the army's chief of staff and eventually secretary of defense. In tandem with other military leaders and minority-group role models, Powell could assemble a cadre of people, perhaps from the active and retired ranks of the armed forces, where officers and NCOs have spent the last 20 years solving multiracial problems. This cadre could be organized in a job-training and reconstruction corps to lead our disenchanted youth of all races on a campaign to rebuild themselves, our crumbled roads, swaying bridges, and to tear down the Third World ghettos and rebuild them into modern cities. In the active ranks many of these leaders are being phased out of the military because the cold war is over. What better new war for them to fight? They would win—and win back an important part of our society.

Isa's annotations and notes:

This Was No Riot, It Was a Revolt

DAVID H. HACKWORTH

Non-Black, non-Hispanic lived same type life in LA—unique and different perspective (not a racial issue) Analysis emphasizes more on typical urban neglect, poverty, despair, rather than on racial discrimination.

WHAT?? inner cities like underdeveloped countries? Children see govt as an enemy not ally? Could be—look at Lawrence.

THE FIRESTORM THAT SWEPT down Normandie Avenue and spread through Los Angeles two weeks ago was no aberration. The kindling was in place long ago. I know. Los Angeles is my hometown. It's part of me. The anger of the young blacks and Hispanics was already festering on the streets in the 1930s and '40s when I grew up. I was a poor white. My grandmother stood in dole lines with black and Hispanic mothers. I wore the same "relief clothes." I ate the same "welfare food" and suffered the same shame. As a teen, I ran with a mixed-race gang, and we all had trouble with the law. Many ended up in prison, many others died. Those that escaped—like me—did so through military service.

Each year since, the conditions have gotten worse; now they're near terminal. Today the grandchildren of my black and Hispanic friends live in squalid conditions resembling those of undeveloped countries. They have no jobs, no hope and no trust in the establishment's authority. The government is not their friend, but their enemy.*

common bond—"belief in the efficacy of sheer violence to achieve a kind of rough justice"—riot an indication of "bottled up" anger, frustration, bitterness accumulating for years. They've been discarded, neglected, locked out of opportunities offered to mainstream society.

I've seen similar despair and resentment on the faces of Yugoslav guerrillas in Trieste after World War II. I saw it among Korean insurgents in 1950, and again in the five long bloody years I fought guerrillas in Vietnam. What all of these disadvantaged young people had in common was a blind dedication, a belief in the efficacy of sheer violence to achieve a kind of rough justice. In Los Angeles the result was two days of rage that left some 50 dead, more than 2,300 wounded, 17,000 arrests and $1 billion in charcoal carnage.

Military perspective: LIC approach, ancient form of war implemented again.

The politicians called it a riot. So did the press. But soldiers call this kind of fighting something else: insurgency, or Low Intensity Conflict (LIC), as the army's training manuals say. Washington seemed to recognize this when it sent elements of the crack Seventh Infantry Division, the army's top LIC fighters, from Fort Ord to Los Angeles along with the California National Guard. Many thinkers on warfare believe LIC will be the principal form of combat in the future. Higher levels are too costly in blood and treasure. In most cases —the gulf war was an exception due to Saddam Hussein's military ignorance—the destructiveness is its own deterrent. So the most ancient form of warfare is now the most contemporary, in Los Angeles no less than Lima. And it's not just Los Angeles, says police Sgt. Mike Schott of North Richmond, Calif.: "Our cities are not a powder keg waiting to explode, but they're like a slow fuse burning all the time. Daily there are race crimes: shootings, beatings and violence. L.A.'s flame just got higher. People noticed. But believe me, it's ongoing everywhere. Day and night."

Comparison: inner-city violence a flame.

Let's not overstate the comparison. LIC operations in Southeast Asia or Latin America have been premeditated. They seek not rough justice but well-defined political goals. <u>The Los Angeles insurgency was spontaneous. It lacked organized leadership. It had no battle plan.</u> Many of the participants were simply opportunists on a looting spree. But things may not stay that way. Already the two main warring youth gangs, the <u>Crips and the Bloods, have pledged to join forces against the police. This could give inner-city rage both leadership and a command infrastructure.</u> Overall, the city has maybe 1,000 gangs, with an estimated total of 110,000 members. These gangs are well armed, with everything from submachine guns to hand grenades. Even now, many <u>police officers</u> believe that inner-city duty is similar to combat. With the daily doses of danger from sniper fire and ambush, they <u>become hardened like shock troops in an occupation zone.</u>

gangs could
organize
themselves—
real war.

American police are not equipped, either mentally or physically, for counterinsurgency. For that matter, neither are most regular army troops. <u>Of the 48 insurgencies Americans have fought since the end of World War II, the score stands: Insurgents 48, United States 0.</u> Vastly superior firepower is irrelevant to such struggles. As the Palestinian *intifada* shows, <u>urban uprisings are especially difficult, with their house-to-house, block-to-block battles.</u> The government force suffers heavy casualties and property undergoes mass destruction. And in any case, <u>a free society cannot survive through force.</u>*

"A free society
cannot survive
through force"—
history shows this
type of violence
undermines society.

First step: As the smoke clears over L.A., a battered city we had to defend from ourselves, perhaps the <u>two-day war</u> we had here at home will focus us on what we are defending and what our priorities are. We can collapse the Iron Curtain and restore the Emir of Kuwait to this throne, but <u>Americans are not free to walk in safety on the streets of their own cities, nor are inner-city Americans given opportunity and a decent standard of living.</u> As retired U.S. Army Col. Carl Bernard, an eminent authority on revolutionary war, says, "The mistrust, despair, hopelessness of our inner-city minorities need to be defused, and then eliminated."

We have to do here
what we've done
overseas.

Learn from past/ reconstruction in infrastructure/new leadership—but can Colin Powell really be effective in inner cities? Not sure . . .

Peace is possible. But throwing money at the problem won't make it go away. The first step is to learn from past insurgencies and overcome the hopelessness that separates the people from the government. This takes leadership. And I have a nominee: Gen. Colin L. Powell He would follow the example of George C. Marshall, who was detailed to the Civilian Conservation Corps during President Roosevelt's war on poverty in the 1930s and later rose to become the army's chief of staff and eventually secretary of defense. In tandem with other military leaders and minority-group role models, Powell could assemble a cadre of people, perhaps from the active and retired ranks of the armed forces, where officers and NCOs have spent the last 20 years solving multiracial problems. This cadre could be organized in a job-training and reconstruction corps to lead our disenchanted youth of all races on a campaign to rebuild themselves, our crumbled roads, swaying bridges, and to tear down the Third World ghettos and rebuild them into modern cities. In the active ranks many of these leaders are being phased out of the military because the cold war is over. What better new war for them to fight? They would win— and win back an important part of our society.

Summarizing

I mentioned earlier that Isa Perez's annotations actually sketched out a brief outline of the Hackworth article. Preparing such an outline can be tremendously helpful in understanding a selection and in formulating your response to it. Whenever you annotate and outline a text, you would be wise to make a summary of it based on your annotations and outline.

What is a summary? Put simply, it is a brief restatement, in your own words, of the author's main ideas. Summaries come in varying lengths, but they should always be considerably shorter than the original, containing only the text's major elements and eliminating minor points and details. Perhaps the most effective way to compose a summary is to restate briefly the main points of each section of the text. Taken together with the central idea of the selection, these statements constitute a summary. (Careful annotations will provide you with these statements.) When writing a summary in your reader's journal, you need not be concerned with style—you may wish to list the statements one after the other or to integrate them into a paragraph or two. The form doesn't really matter: What matters is that you capture the author's main ideas. Below is an exercise designed to acquaint you with the process of summarizing, followed by Isa's summary of "This Was No Riot."

❖ Exercise 3   Using your annotations and outline as guides, compose your own summary of Hackworth's article. Working in small groups, compare one another's—and Isa's—summaries, discussing similarities and differences. Isa's summary:

> David Hackworth suggests that rather than looking at the LA riots in racial terms, perhaps a military comparison would be useful. America's inner cities are like underdeveloped countries, in which children see government as an enemy, not an ally. Like kids in underdeveloped countries, LA kids seem to believe in violence as a way to get justice and vent bottled up anger, frustration, and bitterness. The riots could be considered "low intensity conflict"; in fact, gangs could easily organize themselves and wage real war. If they do, government force won't be the answer—history shows us that. What needs to be done is what we've done overseas, that is, have active and retired military personnel organize inner-city people to rebuild their communities. This approach would help both the inner cities and the military.

READING ACTIVELY

Take prereading notes in a journal:
· review prior knowledge
· ask questions
· respond to guidelines
Make notes (annotate) as you read
· skim entire selection
· highlight significant words, passages
· underline main ideas
· question, comment on author's ideas
Summarize
· focus on main ideas
· use your own words
· record only author's ideas

Notice that Isa's summary relies heavily on her annotations, and that she keeps to the main points of the article. She eliminates her observations about Hackworth's background and some elaborations on inner-city frustrations. Nor do her personal observations enter into the summary: She makes no mention of her own city, Lawrence, and doesn't question the author's observations. A summary is designed to encapsulate the author's ideas, not what the reader thinks of them.

WRITING CRITICALLY

Once you have read a selection actively, you're ready to respond to it in writing. (Of course, as you compose written responses to the selection, you'll find yourself rereading sections of it, often adding new annotations.) Written responses can be either *informal* or *formal, private* or *public.* In this book, the responses you write in your journal after reading individual selections are informal and are considered part of the active reading as well as the critical writing process. This informal writing is both private and public: private in that it reflects your personal responses to the author, public in that you will share some of those responses in group discussions with your fellow students. Assignments at the end of each chapter ask for more formal, public responses designed to present to an audience your conclusions about the ideas in the readings.

A note on audience The selections in this book were written with certain audiences in mind. Some originally appeared in publications geared toward specific audiences—educators, residents of particular urban areas, and members of racial or ethnic groups, for example. Articles from a magazine such as *The Progressive,* for example, will normally reflect liberal thinking, while articles from *Time* or *Newsweek* are written from a more moderate perspective. As you read the selections, you should be aware of the audience for which they were written so that you can respond accordingly. When you begin writing critically about the readings, keep in mind the audience for which they were written. You may want to address that same audience in your response, or write with a broader audience in mind. Although most of what you write in this course will be read primarily by your instructor and your fellow students, you may find yourself moved enough by a topic or reading to draw up a proposal for action, or to write to a newspaper or public official. If you are aware of your readers' attitude toward the issue, you'll be better able to make your case persuasively.

Informal Responses

The *informal responses* come first because they help you formulate the conclusions you'll use to compose the more formal responses at the end of the chapter. These informal responses have two purposes: first, to continue the thinking process that began with prereading notes, annotations, outlines, and summaries; and second, to prepare you to communicate your ideas to others. In this book informal responses come under two headings, Focused Freewriting and Guided Responses. You are also given the opportunity to develop responses in small groups through the section Shared Responses.

Focused freewriting   Some of you may have done freewriting in high school writing courses. When you do *focused freewriting,* you choose one general topic and write about it nonstop for a specified time or length (usually five to ten minutes or one page). The important thing to remember about freewriting is that almost anything goes. You don't worry about grammar, punctuation, sentence or paragraph structure; you don't even worry about wandering off the subject. You write what comes to mind. From this material you can often discover ideas that you never realized you held or find subjects for more formal written responses. Ordinarily you'd choose the topics on which to focus your freewriting. But since many of you may be unfamiliar with the process, possible topics are provided after each selection. Here are the suggested topics for focused freewriting on "This Was No Riot," followed by an exercise designed to acquaint you with the freewriting process. The exercise is followed by Dave Michaud's freewrite on one of the topics and Jane Estrella's freewrite based on her own notes.

> Consider as possible focal points the suggestion that the Los Angeles riots were not an isolated incident, the despair of inner-city residents, a personal experience with urban or racial tension, or one of the topics you've identified in your journal.

❖ Exercise 4   Choose one of the suggested topics for your focused freewrite on "This Was No Riot, It Was a Revolt." Write nonstop for ten minutes. Compare your freewrite with those of other group members, as well as with those of Dave and Jane. Discuss the reasons that people chose certain topics for their freewrites. Dave's freewrite:

> The LA riots probably illustrate the rage and frustration felt by urban residents across the nation. No longer can we ignore the plight of urban America—too many of use have closed our eyes to these areas—so many or us are the first to com-

plain about that "horrible part of town," or "those terrible looking buildings," or "those disgusting people" but so few are ready to acknowledge these complaints as cold and inhumane. Come on, prejudice isn't just a disavowal of a race or a people, its a disavowal of someone's way of life, their predicament, urban America is not some vague-notioned place its not just a mess that "someone should take care of someday." Urban America is a geographic neighbor to just about everybody, containing fellow citizens—no, fellow human beings, with the same inalienable rights as suburbia and rural America—but they're closer to third-world people than they are to the rest of us!

We have to share ownership of urban problems. Jesse Jackson made good sense when he talked awhile ago about all the money spent on Japan and other countries and how much it costs to keep kids in the criminal justice system. We need to aim these funds on education, thats were the ownership comes in we need to educate those trapped in the smoldering coals of urban depravity, but we also need to educate those who are free and comfortable enough to look in from the outside and scoff instead of understand. It's this kind of partnership thru education that can cement the first building blocks necessary to forge a new America—a single unified public each able to appreciate the other's culture and ethnicity.

Jane's freewrite:

When I first read the title I was kind of confused—isn't a riot the same as a revolt? But when he talked about underdeveloped countries I got the picture. I can't beleive that in the 90s there is still so much urban problems in this country, there's no need for it. The inner cities problems have been ignored for too long. In order to accomplish any type of long-term change, I beleive all people need to work together—like Hackworth said, we can even get the military involved. But I'd take a different approach. Education is absolutely crucial to making any type of improvement. Education provides the skills and the choices to make changes. I don't quite know how to interpret Hackworth's idea of rebuilding the inner-city with inner-city labor—at first glance I see him as saying, "Let them do what no one else wants to do." But I suppose he's just trying to kill two birds with one stone—build a sense of community along with the roads and buildings in it, so to speak, but his remark can be taken in a discriminatory manner. I suppose the communities in the inner cities do have to try to help themselves if they expect help in return, but seriously, how much can they accomplish without any federal help? Not much that would be long-term, in my opinion. I think we already have begun to pay the price for neglecting the inner-cities. Look at L.A. There was no reason for those riots to have taken place. The TV picture of people putting up signs that say "Black Owned" portray the fear these people are living with, and they shouldn't have to live in fear the way they do. Change will be slow, and not easy. I think the only way anything is ever going to be accomplished is if everybody agrees to work together, and if the new administration takes action against the problem, and that includes improving education, not cutting the education budget.

Notice that Dave and Jane concentrate on letting their ideas flow in their freewrites, not on making sure that their writing is unified or correct. But in each freewrite, a unity does emerge—Jane's focus on education, for example. Nor does ignoring style and mechanics prevent writers from coming up with some pretty powerful language—Dave's "smoldering coals of urban depravity," for example. Freewriting has allowed both Dave and Jane to explore their responses to the article without worrying about imposed structures or conventions. It can do the same for you.

Guided responses   Sometimes you will be asked to respond to specific questions about a selection in the form of discussion questions, quizzes, or exams. In this book, the Guided Responses section allows you to explore specific issues arising from the selection. These questions are not designed to test your comprehension of the reading; instead, they ask you to think about what the author says or implies, to evaluate how the author presents the material, and to formulate your own response to it. In responding to such questions informally, you can concentrate on the ideas you want to emphasize without worrying about the structural requirements of a more formal piece, such as an essay or a proposal. Below is an exercise designed to show you how to respond to questions about your reading, followed by the four Guided Responses questions for "This Was No Riot." The questions are followed by sample responses from Dave, Isa, and Jane.

❖ Exercise 5   Write answers to the Guided Responses questions for "This Was No Riot, It Was a Revolt." Try to be as specific as possible both in assessing the author's intent and in articulating your own ideas. Compare your response with those of other group members, as well as with those of Dave, Isa, and Jane. Pay particular attention to the support people offer for their views.

❖ Guided Responses

1. Hackworth opens with a look back on his own life as a poor child in Los Angeles, noting that he "wore the same 'relief clothes,' . . . ate the same 'welfare food' and suffered the same shame [as African-American and Hispanic children]." Why do you think he begins his essay with this story? How does the tale contribute to the credibility of his position?

2. In comparing the young rioters to guerrillas in Yugoslavia (now the Balkans), Korea, and Vietnam, Hackworth writes, "What all of these disadvantaged young people had in common was a blind dedication, a belief in the efficacy of sheer violence to achieve a kind of rough justice" (para. 3). How do you react to this comparison? Based on what you know of inner cities, why might young inner-city residents develop this dedication to a justice of violence?

3. In paragraphs 5 and 6, Hackworth notes differences between what happened in Los Angeles and similar incidents in wartorn nations. But he then observes that "things may not stay that way." What is he implying about the future of our inner cities if no action is taken? Do you agree with his interpretation? Why or why not?

4. Calling Los Angeles "a battered city we had to defend from ourselves," Hackworth expresses hope that "the two-day war we had here at home will focus us on what we are defending and what our priorities are" (para. 7). How does his language in these lines contribute to the effect of his assessment? Why do you think he chooses the language of war rather than more conventional social terms to describe what happened in Los Angeles?

❖ Responses to Question 1

I think Hackworth needs to open the way he does because it lends validity to the article. How better to understand the urbiculture than to actually have lived and experienced it? The reason for his short childhood biography may also be to bring his white roots to an equal level with the impoverished African Americans and Hispanics of urban America. He's attempting to bring credence to his position. Readers need to see Hackworth as sympathetic to the plight of the inner cities before they can seriously accept any of his proposals. The two-day insurgency in LA was predominantly a product of racial politics. I'm not sure if Hackworth is trying to seduce an African-American audience into some sort of concession here, or if he simply wishes to establish his "expertise" with regard to urbicultural matters. Either way, Hackworth does seem more believable as a product of such an environment, than just another opinionated white journalist throwing in his or her two cents. (*Dave*)

I think that Hackworth begins his essay with that particular story because he wants the reader to get the immediate impression that he is not the mere "outside" onlooker; he wants you to know that he was part of that urban-city subculture. By Hackworth coming from the same background as these urban minority youth, you immediately sense that his perspective will be different and unique. The tale has a very crucial contribution to the credibility of his position, because he went through the experience personally—and he's not Black or Hispanic. He analyzes the situation not as an issue of racial inequality, but as a problem of poverty and urban neglect. He lets the reader become aware that the growing youths' anger, frustration and bitterness is nothing new; and he also lets us know that it is getting worse.   (*Isa*)

❖ Responses to Question 2

I think that young inner-city residents develop this dedication to violent justice because they are born into a life of limited opportunities. Not only is there little opportunity to get out, but there are few incentives and economic resources that could help them get out and move on to a better way of life. There is no justification for crime and violence; but think of the years and years of systematic neglect and abuse from a society and government that refuses to acknowledge the existence of their problems—no wonder they explode! Urban areas all over the United States have these same problems. People live in the city with low quality education, a decaying and aging infrastructure and public housing, not to mention racial discrimination. It sounds like the third world to me.   (*Jane*)

I don't believe that the young rioters could be accurately compared to guerrillas. Although certain guerrilla factions may demonstrate a "blind dedication," I do not see this as the case in L.A. Without leadership and a unified cause, there can be no dedication. The word itself becomes irrelevant. What we witnessed that day was a reaction, a shout, a scream, to the rest of America, exhibiting the frustration, tension, and unrest that has been festering there for so long. In urban America, it's hard enough to exist day-to-day. How can there be dedication to anything in a struggle for mere survival? Unless there is some sort of unification of people, factions or ideals, then it's unlikely we will witness any dedication—to an ideal or to violent justice. Unless you can call people "dedicated" to crime, escape, aid, or just survival, there is no dedication here. (*Dave*)

❖ Responses to Question 3

Hackworth is implying that the "insurgency" in Los Angeles was spontaneous—a reaction that helped to detonate an explosive unrest. He mentions that "things may not stay that way," because spontaneity may turn into organization, with gang leadership playing a pivotal role. This would channel explosive energy in a negative direction. I can only see more violence resulting from this. Something like large-scale gang-led insurrection would only lengthen the process of revitalization; in fact it would stimulate further civil unrest. I certainly believe that action must be taken, but military intervention should be used as an additional resource to aid urban restoration, and not be placed in the lead role Hackworth suggests. The military would certainly be a necessary component, but they should be used as "staff" falling under the umbrella of civil, educational, and business leadership. (*Dave*)

I think Hackworth is implying that the Los Angeles riot was mostly a result of disorganized leadership, lack of battle strategy and lack of political goals. He compared the Los Angeles riot to the battles fought in other nations. Although there was no planning on the part of the riot participants, but it can change in years to come. These riot participants could in the future, unite and organize themselves—union does give power (as the old saying goes). This "power" could be used constructively, but it could also become a deadly force if used negatively and in the extreme. With the kind of program he talks about, constructive change can take place. But he forgets about the need for education—any program has to start with that. (*Jane*)

❖ Responses to Question 4

Hackworth wants society at large to realize that what happened in Los Angeles is very serious, and that it cannot be ignored any longer. By using the stronger term "war" he is being more dramatic and descriptive of what the actual situation is in poor urban areas across America. When he says that we had to defend Los Angeles from "ourselves," he makes me think of that old expression, "He's his own worst enemy." In a sense, that's what we are. It's what we've done as a society that has caused the problems in the inner cities, and he wants us to get our priorities straight. He also implies that the United States government has neglected this problem for too long, and that what we're defending is an unequal economic and justice system. (*Jane*)

Hackworth's use of war terms may be appropriate to what happened in L.A. because so many of the awful results mimicked scenes from a battle zone. There were deaths, looting, destruction, weapons, attacks, and warlike behavior. But while I can understand why he uses war terminology, I can't support his assessment of the situation as a "two-day war." It was more like a two-day *battle*. The war in our urban cities is still going on. There are casualties and damage, but no victor. Both sides lost ground. And we don't even see the battles that are still occurring every day in the urban cities. There's gang warfare, drugs, murder, and starvation. We on the "outside" just caught a glimpse of the hatred and violence that occurs every day on the "inside." (*Isa*)

Shared responses While active reading and individual responses both help readers make meaning of selections, discussing ideas with others can open up whole new worlds of meaning. (You have probably already noticed that differences in responses to Exercises 1–5 have occasionally prompted you to reassess your ideas.) As you discuss your responses with classmates, you can both gauge their reactions to *your* ideas and discover what *they* think. When you try to negotiate with one another in an attempt to formulate a group response, you're forced to evaluate all ideas presented in the group, whether trying to reach a consensus or simply trying to clarify the reasons for different responses. This activity not only reinforces your understanding of the material but also tests your convictions regarding your responses to it.

When you meet to discuss your responses, you should identify one member of the group as the recorder. He or she will take notes on the group discussion and report the group's conclusions to the class. All members of the group should read their responses in turn before a general discussion begins. This practice eliminates the possibility of getting "stuck" discussing the first response and then having to race through the remainder. As you listen to other group members read their responses, jot down notes to help you recall significant points. Your notes will remind you of a question you may want to ask another member, an observation you may want to offer on a response, or a challenge you may want to make to a position. Careful attention and note taking as each member reads should make for a fruitful discussion and a clear, meaningful report to the class.

Below is the Shared Responses question for "This Was No Riot," together with an exercise to acquaint you with the process of group discussion. Following the exercise are the three students' journal entries, excerpts from their discussion, and their report to the class.

❖ Shared Responses   In your journal outline some of the steps that might be taken to address the nation's urban problems. Consider the contributions that all segments of society—government at all levels, private industry, religious and social groups, private citizens, and inner-city residents themselves—can make. In your view, what are the chances for success of such a combined effort? As you discuss your responses in small groups, try to focus on the assumptions about government and individual responsibility that underlie people's responses.

❖ Exercise 6   Answer the Shared Responses question for "This Was No Riot, It Was a Revolt." As you discuss your journal responses with your group, have one person in the group record highlights of the conversation and prepare notes on the report to be made to the class. Compare your group's responses with those of other groups as well as with the sample student group, noting similarities and differences.

❖ Sample Journal Entries

Change has to start with the federal government. But people in the urban cities can do things on their own as well. If a plan that included government help and urban initiative went into place, things could change.

First, the government has to reform urban schools. Students from the city can be trained as teachers for free if they agree to work in the city schools for four years in return. This program is already working here at Merrimack, and it will mean that good new teachers will be coming into the schools in my city, Lawrence (which is maybe only a few steps above South Central LA). Then the government can provide money to improve the infrastructure, to make the school buildings better, and bring in training programs so that youth in the neighborhoods can learn to do the work themselves. Then the schools become better and the youth learn a skill.

Scholarships for urban youth should be available for other things as well as teaching and job training. The cities need architects, engineers, bankers, businesspeople—lots of different kinds of people. If the same kind of program asked students on scholarship to give back to the community, there would be great improvement.

But the people in the cities themselves have to do something. Voter registration drives worked well in the South in the Civil Rights days; they could work here as well. And people could start cleaning up the cities and letting drug dealers know that they can't operate in the neighborhoods. (This is something else that my city did.) If the neighborhoods and the government work together, then things can improve slowly but steadily.   (*Isa*)

The first step in solving the urban problems must be to specifically define the problems and the geographic locations of each targeted relief area. Next, each situation must be met with the same urgency and effort that would ordinarily be met with a disaster situation. Each state governor would be ultimately responsible for declaring such "zones." Long term discussion and bureaucracy must be avoided; we don't discuss the advantages and disadvantages with regard to helping a drowning child, or for that matter, how the child came to be in that predicament in the first place—*we save the child!* This same sense of urgency must be set here.

1. Federal aid for predetermined urban "plight zones."
2. State control regarding distribution of funds and political intervention.
3. Strengthen police force to ensure urban security and smooth transition.
4. Put able welfare recipients to work!
5. Revamp educational system.
    a. Institute national standards for education, schools, and teachers—states must comply while still keeping autonomy.
    b. Revamp the learning materials. It's time to realize that this country is multicultural and it's also time to see this as a unique advantage.

The success of any major project depends on two things: desire to succeed, and the will to desire. Much of the burden rests on the citizens of urban America, but they need a motivation factor. They need to see results—now, and the need to see that their country shares in the responsibility. (*Dave*)

1. Government at all levels can improve the education system of the inner-city, instead of making budget cuts. Programs can be made in schools to provide students with opportunities for jobs relating to their interests and give students something to hope for. By improving the education system and increasing the opportunity for financial aid, adults in the inner-city can also improve their education so they can get jobs they like.

2. I know this is easier said than done, but the government needs to provide jobs with mobility for these people.

3. Private industries can hire students as part of school programs. This will give them employees, provide students with opportunities, experience, and give them a sense of accomplishment.

4. Religious communities can institute programs that will attract youth. I can't help but think of "Sister Act," in which the nuns cleaned up the areas around their convent, and made the music during church services *fun*. Maybe there's a way in which kids can take their

musical interests and create songs suitable for a church. If it were fun and useful, then they wouldn't feel that there's no hope. This is a way youth can be taken seriously.

5. Private citizens and members of the urban community can rally together and put pressure on government officials to make sure changes are made. They can do surveys to see what problems need addressing and what might work to solve them.

6. I think there is also a need for non-religious social groups for youths and adults. Get people interested in Big Brother/Big Sister programs. Have kids who like to dance to rap and funk teach younger kids.

7. All members of society, regardless of where they live, need to be made aware of the problems that face the inner-city and how these problems affect them. Without this happening, there won't be support to make the needed changes.

While some of these suggestions may not do much to solve the problems, they can improve morale, give people something to make them feel useful, and keep kids off the streets for a time. I really believe that most of the changes need to be made by government, but I think members of society have to push in order for the changes to be made. Without morale and hope, no one will push for these changes to be made, and consequently, nothing can be accomplished. I think change can happen, but certainly not overnight. (*Jane*)

❖ Excerpts from Group Discussion

ISA: Dave seems like he's already an urban planner! Did you do some research on this or something?

DAVE: Oh, come on, you've gotta remember that I spent ten years as a business manager before I came back to school . . . this is exactly the kind of stuff I worked on, plans and things. But I think yours is interesting 'cause you seem to focus so much on education. How come?

ISA: Well, I guess my plan comes from my experience, too. I see the kids in the schools in Lawrence and I just know that unless we can do something about them—something *for* them—then we're sunk. It'll never change. I like what Merrimack's doing. It gives kids from Lawrence High a chance to go to college, and gives all the Lawrence kids teachers who've been there—you know, who grew up in the city—so they know what it's all about. The only thing I should have added is that you've got to have some support on campus for urban kids. I always felt like I was just dumped here. Now it's getting better, with programs to help kids adjust. . . .

JANE: I really think government has a big responsibility here. I mean, what Isa was talking about before, the Merrimack program. Well, we can't do stuff like that without government help. And the school buildings can't be fixed without government money. You just can't make budget cuts in these areas; government has to sink a lot of money into schools.

DAVE: I agree, but I also know from experience that you can talk potential problems to death while the problems just get bigger and bigger. Face it: when you want something done, you go to the people who've got the power to do it and the money to finance it. In business, it's usually management or the union. In the community, you go to government.

JANE: I see what you mean, but you can't just let government do everything. It's important for groups right there in the community to get involved.

ISA: Yes! That's why I like the idea of giving kids scholarships, but asking them to come back to the city. . . .

❖ Excerpt from Group Report

> We mostly agreed on the idea that government is where it has to start, that you need to go where the power and money is. But we also thought it was important that the community feel it's a part of what's going on. So at the same time that the government is offering scholarships and aid to building projects and such, local groups should be taking control of their communities.

WRITING INFORMAL RESPONSES

Freewrite for ten minutes on a focused topic
Write brief answers to Guided Responses questions
Complete Shared Responses assignments
  · Compose individual responses
  · Read responses in small groups
  · Discuss responses, noting similarities and differences, clarifying observations, questioning conclusions
  · Report to class on group discussion

In the previous pages you've observed Jane Estrella, David Michaud, and Isa Perez engaged in reading actively and writing criti-

cally about "This Was No Riot, This Was a Revolt." Your own responses to Exercises 1 through 6 have provided you with practice in
active reading and critical writing, preparing you to respond to the
remaining selections in this chapter. Along with the Hackworth article, these selections constitute a practice chapter, called "A Collage of
American Issues." Although shorter than the other chapters, which
have seven to nine readings each, it contains the same kinds of questions you'll find in the rest of the book. After you've completed the
readings, you'll see how Jane, Dave, and Isa responded to end-of-unit
formal writing assignments; and you'll have an opportunity to write
your own formal responses.

ON YOUR OWN:
A COLLAGE OF AMERICAN ISSUES

As we look around us, read newspapers and magazines, and watch
television news, we see a myriad of issues that, taken together, define
contemporary American life. Some issues call upon our knowledge of
history, some challenge our philosophical thinking, some involve our
ability to analyze numbers, and some invite us to make political
judgments. Almost all contemporary issues, however, force us to
weigh the different—and sometimes conflicting—needs of various
constituencies within our society. Hackworth's article, for example,
highlights the conflict between the need to maintain order in cities
and the need to recognize underlying causes of urban unrest.

Stuart Bykofsky, in "No Heart for the Homeless," argues that
tolerance of homeless people on our city's streets is an affront to him
and other citizens who find themselves continually accosted by desti-
tute men and women. Recognizing the need for society to help the
homeless, Bykofsky nevertheless asserts his right to ownership of
public places.

A seldom-discussed issue regarding abortion is explored in Jean
Seligmann's "The Medical Quandary." In this article, Seligmann examines the dilemma many doctors face as their ability to save premature infants increases and the technology to treat fetuses in the womb
advances. What happens when the fetus about to be aborted is capable of surviving outside the womb?

The treatment of young first-time offenders is the subject of Frank
Bentayou's "The New Chain Gangs." More and more states, according to Bentayou, are establishing "boot camps" designed to shock first
offenders into becoming productive citizens. But critics question the
success of these institutions when considered in light of their cost.

These readings offer a sense of the diversity and complexity of the issues we face today. None of the authors suggests that there are any easy answers; they all imply, however, that active participation by an informed citizenry can lead to solutions for at least some of our society's problems.

No Heart for the Homeless

STUART D. BYKOFSKY

STUART D. BYKOFSKY, *a native of the Bronx, New York, was educated at Brooklyn College, City University of New York, and began his career at the now-defunct* New York World-Telegram & The Sun. *He has spent thirty-five years in journalism, the last twenty-one at the* Philadelphia Daily News, *where he is currently a columnist. In this article, which originally appeared in the "My Turn" section of* Newsweek *magazine in 1986, Bykofsky takes what he acknowledges is an unpopular stand, arguing that the homeless people living on the streets of American cities "have got to go." Although he does offer some possible solutions to the homeless problem, Bykofsky nonetheless argues that his right to walk the streets unaccosted outweighs the rights of homeless people to live there.*

Before reading the selection, write in your journal about the images you associate with homelessness. Why are some people homeless? How responsible are they for their condition? What responsibility does society bear for alleviating the problem?

As you make notes on the reading, you may want to focus on the logic of Bykofsky's argument, the specific examples he offers, or the solutions he suggests.

I AM ABOUT TO BE HEARTLESS. There are people living on the streets of most American cities, turning sidewalks into dormitories. They are called the homeless, street people, vagrants, beggars, vent men, bag ladies, bums. Often they are called worse. They are America's living nightmare—tattered human bundles. They have got to go.

I don't know, exactly, when they got the *right* to live on the street. I don't know, exactly, when I *lost* the right to walk through town without being pestered by panhandlers. I do know I want them off my sidewalk. If you think I am heartless for saying that, can I send them to live on *your* sidewalk?

I am fed up with the trash they bring into my neighborhood. The pools of urine in apartment-house lobbies disgust me. I am fed up with picking my way down sidewalks blocked by plastic milk crates, stepping over human forms sprawled on steam gratings.

I also am fed up with newspaper columnists who periodically have a good cry in print over the plight of the street people—and the average citizen's callous reaction to them. I have yet to read that one of these columnists has taken a street person home for a bath and a meal. That happens only in movies like "Down and Out in Beverly Hills."

What are we, the heartless, supposed to do? In the Sermon on the Mount, Jesus urged his followers to "give to every one who begs from you." The horde of the homeless turns this plea into a joke. Walking to work this morning, I was approached eight times: "Mister, I'm hungry." "Can you help me out?" "You have any spare change?" "Got a quarter?" But what good would a quarter do? If I really mean to help, I should follow Jesus and give a dollar to everyone who asks. That would be $8 on my way to work—and $8 on the way home, because they are still there. That's $80 a week.   5

Early on, I felt pity for those in the streets, but their relentless begging has forced me to change *my* habits, my attitudes. Panhandlers have taught me to suspect anyone approaching me on the street. "Can I ask you something, sir?" a casually dressed man asks. Maybe he's a tourist needing directions. Maybe he just wants to know the time. No. He wants access to my pockets. Tired of being hit like a money-access machine, I'm now deaf to people in the street. I'm not happy about that, but there it is.

I am amazed by their persistence. Since I walk the same route every day, I pass the same street people on the same gratings, or curled in the same makeshift, cardboard shelters. Every time I leave my apartment building, I mean *every time*, I am panhandled by begging sentinels more steadfast than Gurkhas. Every time, I ignore them. I wish I could make them disappear.

At 6 feet 3 and 185 pounds, I'm not frightened when one shuffles up to me, dull-eyed, asking alms. They do frighten my elderly neighbors. It is psychological assault. Why should they have to put up with it?

Don't tell me that's the price we pay for living in a democracy. Tell me why they are allowed to make the street their home—day and night, hot and cold—when I can't park a car at the curb for an hour without paying a meter. How is that possible? I find it ironical that my tax money keeps the street—their home—paved and clean. That makes me their landlord. I want to evict them.

Vagrancy Laws

No one has reliable statistics about their numbers across America, but   10
authorities agree the homeless fall into three categories: (1) the economically distressed, who would work if they could find work; (2) the mentally ill, who can't work; (3) the alcoholic, the drug-addicted and others who won't work. Police once routinely arrested people sleeping in the streets, or the parks, or the railroad stations, as vagrants. Vagrancy laws were struck down because it shouldn't be a crime to be out of work. That seems right to me. No one should be arrested because he or she has no money. But by the same token, no one should be allowed to set up housekeeping on the sidewalk.

This is the nub of the problem. If I don't want them sleeping on the sidewalks, what is to be done?

People sleeping on the streets depress property values, decrease tourism, tarnish a city's reputation and inhibit customers from entering shops. In subtle ways, we already are paying the price for the homeless. I would rather pay higher taxes and get these people off the streets.

The unemployed are the easiest to help because they are able and willing to work. If they want a job, but society is unable to provide a job, then government should provide money for food and shelter to be delivered through welfare or a workfare program.

The mental patients, the "harmless schizophrenics," were turned loose when the courts decided no one should be locked up just because they were sick. Communities were to provide local facilities. Big surprise: they didn't. But some level of government must. The mentally incompetent who now have the "freedom" to die on cold streets must be steered to decent tax-supported homes or institutions that will care for them.

The drunk, the addicted and the just plain shiftless present an   15
entirely different problem. They say they are on the streets because they have nowhere else to go. We must take that excuse away from them. New facilities do not have to be built. Every community has factories and warehouses that have been closed down. Nearly every community has abandoned houses. These can be converted at minimal cost into a shelter that provides light, heat and plumbing. Call them tax-supported flophouses, call them almshouses, I don't care.

People can't be *forced* to live there, of course. They have their rights. But so do we. Once we have made shelter available, we have the right to say this: the streets are not for sleeping anymore.

❖ Focused Freewriting   Consider as possible focal points the perspective a homeless person might bring to Bykofsky's piece, the various causes of homelessness, or one of the topics you've identified in your journal.

❖ Guided Responses

1. Consider the scenario Bykofsky presents in his opening paragraph. Why do you suppose he chose to open with an admission of heartlessness? What is the effect of the names he uses for homeless people? Why does he call the homeless "America's living nightmare"?

2. Bykofsky describes in some detail the experience of being approached by homeless people (paras. 5–7). What impact do these encounters have on him? Are you sympathetic to his problem? Why or why not?

3. In paragraph 9 Bykofsky asks, "Tell me why [the homeless] are allowed to make the street their home . . . when I can't park a car at the curb for an hour without paying a meter." In your opinion, is he making a fair comparison? Is Bykofsky's use of the street to park a car equivalent to a homeless person's use of that same street to live on? Explain your response.

4. Bykofsky offers several suggestions for alleviating the problem of homelessness (paras. 13–15). How workable are these proposals? What kind of government and community action would it take to implement them? How might they be paid for? Do any of his proposed solutions offer real hope for change? Explain your responses.

❖ Shared Responses   In your journal, compose a response to Bykofsky. Address his attitude toward homeless people, society's responsibility for them, and possible solutions to the problem. As you discuss your responses in small groups, make note of the various attitudes toward homeless people reflected in members' responses.

The Medical Quandary

JEAN SELIGMANN

JEAN SELIGMANN, *a graduate of Bryn Mawr, has been on the editorial staff of* Newsweek *since 1971. Seligmann is now an editor and medical reporter for the weekly newsmagazine, focusing on women's issues. In this 1985 article she reports on some disturbing complexities of an issue that is frequently seen in black-and-white terms. As the age of "viability" for a fetus decreases, late abortions pose a serious moral and ethical dilemma for medical professionals.*

Before reading the selection, write in your journal about your own views on abortion. Think beyond blanket statements such as "abortion is murder" or "a woman has a right to her own body." What other issues are involved in the abortion question? Do you think society will ever come to a consensus on the question?

As you make notes on your reading, you may want to focus on Seligmann's definitions of terms, her descriptions of clinical procedures, or the doctors' observations on the emotional issues involved in abortion.

THE ULTIMATE HIPPOCRATIC DILEMMA, the nightmare that unsettles a good doctor's sleep: a pregnant patient, after much agony, has chosen an abortion and the doctor performs the procedure by injecting prostaglandins (hormonelike substances that induce labor) into her amniotic sac. But when, some hours later, the fetus is expelled from the woman's uterus, it is not the 22-week-old creature he had anticipated. It is 26 weeks old—and alive.

This is an unlikely scenario; 90 percent of abortions in the United States are performed before the 13th week of pregnancy, and only 1 percent, or about 13,000 procedures a year, take place after the 20th week (the start of gestation is calculated from the onset of the last menstrual period). But the branch of medicine known as neonatology—the special care of newborns—now routinely saves the lives of preemies who would have died a decade ago. Today, a premature delivery can lead to heroic—and sometimes successful—attempts to save mid-trimester babies. Increasingly, survival is possible for fetuses that can legally be aborted. At the same time, the growing ability to treat fetuses in *utero*—shunts to correct hydrocephalus or bladder blockage, drugs to alter metabolism—deepen the quandary. "When you do things to a child in the womb, you're acknowledging that you're dealing with a patient," says medical ethicist Thomas Murray of the University of Texas Medical School at Galveston. "It's hard to do that and then turn around and abort a child of the same developmental age."

While the numbers of late abortions are relatively small, the moral implications are substantial. As a result, physicians and hospitals are taking new and searching looks at their policies on abortion. Across the United States, many hospitals skirt the issue by simply refusing to perform most abortions after 20 weeks; some physicians have adopted an even earlier "personal cutoff" of 10 or 12 weeks. And when doctors do administer late abortions, they are much more likely to employ the techniques certain to kill the developing child before it leaves the womb—anything to forestall the possibility of a live birth in the operating room.

Dr. Sherwood Lynn, an obstetrician and gynecologist at Houston's Hermann Hospital, used to perform many more abortions that he does now. Today, he refers most requests to area clinics set up expressly for abortions. He does them himself only when a clear-cut medical problem jeopardizes the fetus or mother—for example, if the woman has been taking potent cancer drugs that could cause a fatal maternal hemorrhage during labor and would almost certainly kill the baby. Still, he says, "I don't like to do abortions. It's not a moral question—I just have a bad feeling about it. It's always a strain." One reason for the strain, says Dr. Paul Blumenthal, director of ambulatory care at Chicago's Michael Reese Hospital, is that one of the most widely used techniques for late abortions, dilatation and evacuation (D & E) requires the physician to crush and kill the fetus while it is still in the womb. It's one thing when a physician injects a drug to induce labor and walks away, says Blumenthal, "and another thing to actively take part in the procedure. The physician can't see what he's doing in the uterus. It's bloody and a little frightening."

No woman deliberately plans a late abortion, and most of those 5 who end up having them belong to well-recognized categories. Forty-four per cent of abortions done after the 21st week of gestation are performed on teen-agers, who may not realize that they are pregnant until they feel the baby kicking. Or they may deny the evidence of their own bodies. In states like Massachusetts, where a minor must have the consent of both parents for an abortion, "a young girl may be well into her second trimester before she gets the nerve to tell her momma, who may in turn hesitate to tell daddy," explains Dr. Phillip Stubblefield, chief of obstetrics and gynecology at Mount Auburn Hospital in Cambridge. Or, refusing to confess at all, a teen-ager may shop for a friendlier jurisdiction, delaying the procedure still further.

Other typical recipients of late abortions include poor women, who may find it difficult to scrape up $200 for the procedure or do not know how to find out where to go for the operation; women with histories of irregular menses, and women approaching menopause who attribute missed periods to their impending change of life.

Perhaps the most agonizing late abortions, however, are those that result from yet another product of modern technology. Amniocentesis, the withdrawal and analysis of amniotic fluid to identify possible genetic abnormalities like Down's syndrome in an unborn child, cannot be done until the 14th to 17th week of pregnancy. Moreover, the results of the test may not be ready until the 21st week or even later. Thus, most abortions performed because of amniocentesis findings necessarily take place in the gestation period's problematic zone. But Dr. John Carpenter, director of the prenatal diagnostic center at the Baylor College of Medicine in Houston, says he has no reservations about abortions under such circumstances. However, "I don't do it as a cold-blooded killer," he explains. "I have a great deal of empathy and sympathy for these families. They suffer grief and I suffer grief, too. But I have no qualms because I've seen the impact a seriously impaired child can have on a family."

Within the next five years, amniocentesis and its unsatisfactory timetable may be supplemented by a newer research tool: chorionic villus biopsy. This procedure, in which a small sample of the tissue lining the amniotic sac is removed and analyzed for abnormalities, can be done as early as eight weeks into pregnancy, with results at 12 weeks. In an abortion at that stage, of course, fetal viability is out of the question. But chorionic villus biopsy is more risky to the fetus than amniocentesis, and some researchers doubt that it will ever be safe enough for routine screening.

The most disturbing late abortions, of course, are those that result in live births. Although rare, they sometimes occur because the age of the fetus has been underestimated. The woman may not remember the date of her last menstrual period—or she may deliberately lie about it if she is determined to get an abortion despite an advanced pregnancy. Relying on a physical examination alone, explains Dr. Michael Burnhill, an obstetrician and gynecologist at the College of Medicine and Dentistry of New Jersey, a doctor can miscalculate fetal age by more than a month. For that reason, many physicians routinely perform an ultrasound scan for abortions after the 12th week of pregnancy. This visual image of the fetus enables a skilled practitioner to estimate its age with a high degree of accuracy.

But even when the age can be determined precisely, doctors don't always agree on when the fetus should be considered "viable," or indeed on exactly what viability means. In neonatal intensive-care units, doctors treat 24- to 26-week-old fetuses weighing as little as 1 pound 10 ounces, and 28-week preemies stand a good chance of surviving to lead healthy lives. But these are babies whose births are intended, and for whom major life-sustaining efforts are made during both labor and delivery. By contrast, observes Dr. Richard Stavis, director of the neonatal unit at Bryn Mawr Hospital in Bryn Mawr, Pa., "when you do an abortion, you're obviously not doing it in the interest of the baby's viability." Stavis considers that viability begins "in the range of 24 weeks," noting that the likelihood of survival before that point is close to zero. But even at 26 weeks, he explains, survival rates are low because the baby is born with immature lungs, skin so fragile it can be torn by surgical tape, and blood vessels that may be too minuscule for the introduction of needles and tubes necessary for monitoring and nutrition.

New Jersey's Burnhill, who has performed abortions at 26 weeks in cases of severe birth defects, believes it is unrealistic to speak of viability before that point, when the baby still weighs less than two pounds. "I don't think a 24-week fetus can ever have an independent existence," he observes, "though you can keep some of them alive on assisted ventilation for a while." Fetuses weighing less than 35 ounces, he notes, are often born with serious defects: learning disabilities, poor vision and impaired hearing. "Technological advances have been keeping them alive, not keeping them intact," says Burnhill, "and the heartbreak for the parents later is staggering."

In most cases of late abortion, physicians try to prevent such tragedies by using one of the two methods that nearly always result in fetal death. One is the relatively new D&E, in which the fetus is literally dismembered by a forceps within the uterus, limb by limb, and the "pieces" are withdrawn through the vagina. Although a D&E is safe for the mother, it can be devastating for the hospital staff; many doctors simply won't do advanced D&E's. Burnhill refuses to perform them later than 14 or 15 weeks into pregnancy, at least in part, he says, because "I have trouble getting nurses and anesthesiologists to work with me." (It may have been this technique that President Reagan was referring to when he asserted last winter that the fetus experiences pain during an abortion. However, while even a 10-week-old embryo will shrink from an instrument poked into the uterus, researchers argue that the neurological pathways necessary for pain perception are not well developed until very late in pregnancy and perhaps not until after birth.)

In the other method, the physician administers substances that first kill the fetus, then induce the labor that will expel it. Saline solution, for example, injected in small quantities into the amniotic sac, usually performs both functions. However, this procedure carries some risk to the woman; the saline may find its way into her bloodstream, causing hemorrhage or lung and kidney damage. Another procedure calls for introducing a small amount of urea into the sac, or injecting it directly into the fetus itself. At some medical centers, the heart drug digoxin is administered to the fetus before labor is induced, resulting in a fatal cardiac arrhythmia.

One of the safest methods for inducing labor in a late abortion is the "instillation" of prostaglandins, which cut off the fetus's oxygen supply. Still, there are occasional live births. Some states and hospitals require doctors to treat such a baby like any other "live" birth from premature labor, but this does not mean that extraordinary, "heroic" efforts are necessarily made to save its life. If we had an aborted baby below the age of viability that was technically live-born," says Stavis of Bryn Mawr, "we'd put it in an Isolette [incubator], keep it warm, give it oxygen and observe it. But we would not actively intervene to protect that baby from dying." To place tubes in a fetus that has no chance of survival, Stavis believes, is abusive. "It is subjecting the fetus to an experiment," he declares. "To me, that is cruel."

"Nobody who provides abortions wants to kill babies," adds   15 Stubblefield. "Nobody is in favor of infanticide. The question is, where do you draw the line? In my morality, an abortion prior to 24 weeks is a reasonable thing to do; after that it is not." And if a fetus should survive an abortion attempt, Stubblefield says, "if it looks as if it might have a chance—not just for an hour or two, but for survival to leave the hospital—then you give it everything you've got."

❖ Focused Freewriting Consider as possible focal points the meaning of the term *viability*, the reasons for performing late abortions, or one of the topics you've identified in your journal.

❖ Guided Responses

1. Seligmann quotes Thomas Murray, a medical ethicist, in defining the dilemma faced by many doctors: "When you do things to a child in the womb, you're acknowledging that you're dealing with a patient. . . . It's hard to do that and then turn around and abort a child of the same developmental age" (para. 2). Based on your reading of

the article, how would some doctors respond to Murray's statement? How do you respond? Given the words Murray uses, how do you think *he* feels about late abortions?

2. Seligmann offers dispassionate descriptions of some clinical procedures, notably in paragraphs 13 ("fatal cardiac arrhythmia") and 14 ("cut off the fetus's oxygen supply"). What effect does she achieve by presenting the procedures in such unemotional terms? Contrast these descriptions with her characterizations of D&E in paragraphs 4 and 12. Why do you think she uses more emotional words in these descriptions?

3. The strain felt by medical personnel involved in late abortions is discussed at some length in the article (paras. 1, 4, 12). In your opinion, what is the primary cause of that strain? Does it involve the morality of abortion in general? the ethics of aborting a potentially viable fetus? the nature of the procedure? Explain your response.

4. Of the seven experts Seligmann quotes in her article, all are male. Do you think female experts might offer significantly different observations? If so, specify what responses might be different and why. If not, explain why you think gender would not play a role in an expert's response.

❖ **Shared Responses**   In your journal explore ways in which the number of late abortions, especially among teenagers and poor women, can be reduced. Concentrate on the responsibility of government and community as well as of individuals. As you discuss your responses in small groups, try to determine how members' proposals reflect their attitudes toward abortion and toward the role government should play in people's personal lives.

The New Chain Gangs

FRANK BENTAYOU

Frank Bentayou *received a B.A. in English from the University of Southern Florida and an M.A. in journalism and mass communication from Kent State University in Ohio. Now a freelance writer, he*

*is currently manager of student media at Kent State. This examina-
tion of "boot camps," the latest phenomenon in American corrections policy, originally appeared in 1992 in* The Progressive
*magazine. Through interviews with officers, prison officials, prison
reformers, and criminologists, Bentayou suggests that the verdict
on boot camps' effectiveness is far from assured.*

*Before reading the selection, explore in your journal your own
attitude toward prisons. What should they accomplish? How much
emphasis should be placed on punishment? on rehabilitation? What
rights should prisoners have? what responsibilities?*

*As you make notes on your reading, you may want to focus on
Bentayou's descriptions of boot camp life, the arguments offered by
both advocates and critics of boot camps, or the ways in which the
author makes his own view known.*

SHIFT-CHANGE TIME at Ohio's Southeast Correctional Institution:
Guards are laughing as Sergeant J.A. Jeff Scudder, a short bull of a
man, struggles to fold up the sleeves of his black uniform. The coarse
fabric barely stretches over his upper arms, which are thick as hams.

Scudder's first job today is showing nine new prisoners how to
"make a tight rack"—straighten up their beds, he politely explains—
and stow their gear. But first he girds himself for battle. After wrestling with the sleeves, he slips a stiff-brim drill-instructor's hat onto
his head, bristling with stubble from a close cut.

"You have to teach these guys everything," he says. Calm and
neat in his starched uniform, Scudder strolls toward a group of men
wearing tattered white jumpsuits and clutching laundry bags. As he
approaches, he suddenly explodes and shoots out his hands to grab
two prisoners, jerking them toward a wall.

"All right, you pigs, maggots!" Scudder shouts. "Get over here at
attention! Now!" A few croak a hasty, "Sir, yes sir!" as they scramble
to comply, but Scudder swirls and seizes a youth by the collar.

"What's a matter with you, puke?" Scudder yells in his face, his   5
voice breaking, eyes popping from their sockets. "Haven't you
learned how to talk to a guard?"

"Sir, no sir! Yes, sir—" the man stammers.

"You disgusting maggot!" Scudder screams. "Gimme twenty
pushups." He hurls him to the floor, then whirls and snatches two
laundry bags. In a rage, he dumps them on the floor, too, and kicks
the limp garments repeatedly as the prisoners stare at him.

Scudder's dramatic transformation might amaze anybody who
hasn't spent time around an institution like this one. It was my second

day visiting Camp REAMS, so I understood that the young guard behaved as he is paid to do and that the facility he works for is not like most other prisons.

In fact, REAMS—the acronym stands for Respect, Education, Attitude, Motivation, and Success—is one of at least thirty-four boot camps launched by U.S. prison systems in the past nine years. State corrections officials and lawmakers are so impressed with them that they're planning at least ten more. Aimed at young, usually first-time offenders convicted of nonviolent crimes, they embody military-style discipline, chain-gang labor, and often the kind of brutal treatment Scudder displays. To the chagrin of earnest prison reformers, it is just those features that have made "shock incarceration" the fastest-growing trend in penology, applauded in middle America and embraced by recent Administrations.

According to specialists at the U.S. Justice Department's National   10
Institute of Justice, the new boot camps have sucked up tens of millions in state and Federal corrections dollars for construction and millions more for operations. Yet no one has shown clearly that this approach to punishment actually helps turn young lawbreakers away from crime.

In fact, the strategy of battering and demeaning young offenders to "scare them straight" may do the opposite. Some warn that it may instill dangerous resentment in volatile youths and send them a message that such violent behavior as their guards routinely practice has a place in our society. Still, savaging prisoners, working them hard, and subjecting them to strict—and arbitrary—rules seem to appeal to the same public that, in 1988, responded favorably to George Bush's Willie Horton campaign ads.

"I think this approach is what people want," says Major Ralph Coyle, the Camp's thirty-three-year-old commander. "They're tired of driving by and seeing a prisoner sitting on a $6,000 John Deere tractor mowing the lawn. I'm tired of it, too. So these guys work hard. And when they mow a lawn, it's with one of those little push-type reel mowers over there. People want to see these guys working."

At boot camps, they work. They clear brush, saw logs, build fences, bust up rocks—all by hand. They also suffer the insults and capricious abuse of tough guards whom they must treat with exaggerated respect.

At REAMS, hard labor starts a few days after inmates arrive; the authoritarian rule starts the moment they step into camp. On Wednesday, intake day, a van stops in a yard surrounded by a tall fence looped with razor wire. The ten passengers, first-time felons recommended for the program, have agreed to work here for three months, followed by time in a halfway house and then probation, in exchange for the shorter sentences.

"They've been briefed on what it's like here," Coyle tells me with   15
a smile. "But they don't really know what to expect."

The guards, like Scudder done up in black drill-instructor uniforms, hats low over their eyes, stand and wait a moment for effect. Then they rush the van. Screaming orders, they throw open the door and begin hurling prisoners out onto the gravel yard.

"Get outta there, you damn maggot!" "Move it, slime!" they shout.

A slender guard with a narrow mustache shoves a prisoner toward the fence, thrusting his chin to within an inch of the youth's cheek. "If I see that smirk on your face again," he growls, saliva flying, "I'm gonna put you through that goddamn fence," He pulls back and yells at the group, "Now we're gonna teach you some damn courtesy."

During the first two days, guards do just that. They shout conflicting orders, march the inmates, shave their heads, belittle them, scream epithets—"fat-boy," "crackhead," "geek," and "peter puffer." One drops out, begging to be sent to prison for his full eighteen-month term. Standing in a corner with his hands cuffed behind him, Julius Cheney, a twenty-five-year-old drug dealer, tells me, "I can't take it. I'm just gonna do my time." Then he cries.

"One or two or three will drop out," Coyle says, "usually in the   20
first couple of days. We're not for everybody. But I warn them about what happens to the young guys up the hill," he says, waving vaguely toward Southeast Correctional, the 1,600-inmate medium-security prison on whose ground Camp REAMS is located.

No one has proved prisoners at vast correctional warehouses like SCI are more apt to return to crime than boot-camp alumni, but the bandwagon for shock incarceration keeps rolling. In addition to the thirty-four like REAMS, juvenile systems have opened camps, and there are also camps for women. New York has five boot camps with a population of more than 1,500, and the state plans more. An Ohio guard jokes that "the job market for former Marine DIs [drill instructors] has never been better."

The media have covered shock prisons in a mostly supportive and uncritical manner. Some articles in newspapers and magazines focus on success stories of inmates who, in the course of boot camp, take control of their lives. Others emphasize how caring guards are beneath their rough facades. Jerome G. Miller, a prison reformer, laughs and says, "These places make great TV." In fact, all the positive media coverage, he says, "is one reason politicians love them so much. Of all the human services—if you can call corrections a human service—it's the one most likely to be run by sound bites."

Miller, who heads the Virginia-based National Center for Institutions and Alternatives, a nonprofit organization that develops alternative sentencing options mostly for criminal-defense teams, has been tracking boot camps since their emergence. The former sociology professor, correctional administrator, and author of *Last One Over the Wall*, a book about juvenile corrections, says, "This movement is just the latest corrections fad. I don't think it's necessary. If you treat people in prison decently, you can get good results."

Miller considers good results to be something better than the grim recidivism rate of felons in the United States, where at least 40 per cent return to criminal behavior, many ending up back behind bars. The national prison population has been growing at a rate of almost 7 per cent a year, according to the Washington-based Sentencing Project, a private research group. Whatever prisons are doing today is not wildly successful.

A visit to any large state institution shows why: Rehabilitation   25 plays virtually no role. Prisoners mostly laze around in their cells or the yard, pump iron, or socialize—if you can call it that. Inmates, particularly young ones, who seek what educational programs are available find themselves shunned, intimidated, and bullied by their more cynical peers.

Prison officials hope shock incarcerations will improve things. "We aim everything here at getting these kids to change," Coyle explains. "All of this discipline you've seen and the rough treatment, the hard labor, that's part of it. You have to get their attention to get them to change. Then they can feel positive about having gotten through something challenging."

If the hard work and discipline were all there is to the approach, it might represent just another vengeful response to crime. The rise in both numbers of prisoners—there are 1.1 million felons locked away in the United States, a total that doubled between 1980 and 1990, that tripled between 1970 and 1990—and the toughness of sentences reflect an increasingly harsh public attitude. To Ohio's and some other states' credit, many boot-camp planners also fold in a measure of rehabilitation aimed at these eighteen- to twenty-five-year-olds.

"This is the way we envisioned shock-incarceration camps from the beginning," says Ronald Powell, head of the New Hampshire prison system. "They're aimed at a high-risk population and must combine intensive rehabilitation services with the military boot-camp approach." He believes they need education programs, like the high-school equivalency classes REAMS offers, peer tutoring by inmates who have degrees, drug rehab, and what Powell calls "character-building sessions." Without such features, he predicts, "we'll see some notable failures in the coming years."

In 1983, Powell helped set up the first prison boot camp in Dodge County, Georgia. "Crime, in my mind, is more related to character disorders then to broader sociological trends some people cite," he says. "We try to get back to individual values. The hope is that we can take a young man with these disorders and produce, well, a man. With a few reservations, I think it works."

Critic Jerry Miller, on the other hand, has many reservations. "Yes,   30 if you include this expensive after-care, maybe there's a possibility the recidivism rate for shock prisons will improve, but who's to say a traditional prison wouldn't have the same effect if it had all these programs, halfway houses, and probationary terms?"

The point, Miller says, is that "we should concentrate on what we know works—provide rehab programs to inmates, provide alternative sentencing to many of them, get them into community-service projects." All this shouting and shoving only sends young run-amoks the wrong message, he believes: "You get all this sadism from the guards in this situation, and who knows what can happen?"

That's an issue Powell says he considered in New Hampshire. His fear was that guards could too zealously harass a particularly unstable prisoner and cause an incident, even a riot. Someone could get badly hurt or killed. Powell says that in New Hampshire, he has structured his program differently from, say, the camp in Ohio: "We tolerate no physical or verbal abuse of any kind." Coyle, however, thinks of harsh verbal commands and physical prodding as important elements of Camp REAMS.

Some policy-makers and scholars, in their search for answers, are applying standards to corrections that seem to work with other social problems. Much of what they've learned has strengthened the skeptics' position: Shock prisons do some of what the zealots claim—but only when they're set up and operated with tremendous care, a level of care that's hard for a corrections system to approach, let alone sustain.

By being selective about admissions, for instance, a corrections system might save some money—though boot camps can be costly. Oklahoma gave its 1991 boot-camp per-bed cost at $23,500, while beds at its regular prisons cost $17,800. The advantage was that the ninety-day program processes more inmates per bed each year.

"Unfortunately," says Doris MacKenzie, "the planning and train-   35 ing aren't always the best. A system might put offenders who otherwise would get probation or parole in a boot camp, and that would cost quite a lot more." A professor and criminologist at the University of Maryland, she has offered to help the Corrections Institute develop guidelines for operations. So far, no one can tell policy-makers what works. The lack of guidelines hasn't stopped corrections systems from buying drill-instructor hats and sharp uniforms, hiring some guards, and diving in.

"As it stands now," MacKenzie explains, "we've got county and city systems setting up boot camps. There are juvenile systems, too. Some of them don't have any idea what they're doing. What we want from a prison is to prompt some attitude change on the part of these young offenders. We frankly don't yet know if this is the way to get it."

Of the prison guards he's seen, Jerry Miller says, "The closest they've ever gotten to a real boot camp is *Gomer Pyle*. And I don't see much sign that the training is getting better."

In response to such concerns, the national Institute of Corrections also urges more research. Last fall, Susan Hunter, chief of the Prisons Division, issued a plea to scholars to submit proposals. The Justice Department will finance some of the efforts, though its apparent largess raises a flag to some. As Miller says, "You've got to remember that Justice under recent Republican Administrations has been a big supporter of boot camps. How likely do you think it is that studies they sponsor will show boot camps don't work?"

In fact, Anna Thompson, a correctional-program specialist at the NIC, says the Institute isn't really testing the underlying value of shock incarceration. It's just developing what she calls "an implementation and training guide for boot camps, sort of a cookbook on how to put them together."

Possibly prison boot camps, as they now operate around the country, may actually help some troubled kids change. But no one knows in what direction or for how long. Considering the kind of model such guards as Jeff Scudder present to the young men whom they pummel and excoriate, we may be unhappy with the outcome.

40

Back at Camp REAMS, Scudder finishes his hour-long performance playing bad cop, showing new inmates how to make a tight rack and precisely tuck away all personal belongings into a foot locker. Wiping his damp head and neck, he begins to transform himself back into the earnest and friendly young man he was when we first met.

"I feel I'm on a mission," he says. "These guys have lost control, and it's my mission to try to show them how to put some order in their lives."

Scudder has been masterful as a raging DI, and his intention seems laudable. Still, questions hang in the air: What is the shock camp's real effect on prisoners, and what will be its effect on society?

❖ Focused Freewriting   Consider as possible focal points the idea of a military model for prisoners, the reasons for the apparent popularity of boot camps with the public, or one of the topics you've identified in your journal.

❖ Guided Responses

1. The opening scene in this article presents the sudden transformation of the "polite," "calm," "neat" J. A. Jeff Scudder into a screaming drill sergeant, "his voice breaking, eyes popping from their sockets" (paras. 2–5). At the end of the article, Scudder is once again an "earnest and friendly young man" (para. 41). What do you think Bentayou hopes to achieve by highlighting Scudder's transformation? How do you respond to the respective descriptions?

2. Bentayou's language sometimes reveals his own attitude toward boot camps. In paragraph 10, for example, he writes that "the new boot camps have sucked up tens of millions in state and Federal corrections dollars." Where else in the article do you find him signaling his opinion? How would you characterize his attitude?

3. Corrections officials, prison reformers, and criminologists are all quoted in this article. Compare the various reasons these experts offer to support their views. Do you find any single view more valid than the others, or do you find that the conflicting views make it difficult for you to determine your own opinion? Explain your response.

4. Bentayou indicates that boot camps are extremely popular with the public, the media, and politicians. Based on your reading of this article and your own experience, why do you think this is so? What do boot camps offer that traditional prisons do not?

❖ Shared Responses   In your journal, outline a plan for an ideal prison: one that protects society, punishes offenders, and offers hope of rehabilitation. How does your plan compare with traditional prisons? with boot camps? As you discuss your responses in small groups, focus on the relative weight different plans place on protection, punishment, and rehabilitation.

Formal Responses

Once you've finished the readings in each chapter, you'll be asked to make connections between selections and to compose formal pieces of writing—essays, proposals, letters, creative works—on related topics. How do you make the transition from informal, relatively private writing to formal, public writing? It's not too daunting a task if you've kept your informal responses in a reader's journal. You can use these notes for Generating Ideas and Focusing Responses.

Generating ideas   As you reread your freewriting, guided responses, and shared responses, you'll discover that you've already done some of the work involved in composing a formal piece of writing. You'll find in your journal and annotations a wealth of ideas, many of them worthy of further exploration. You should pay particular attention at this point to connections between selections, that is, ideas that seem to recur in several works. For example, Dave Michaud noticed in reviewing his journal and annotations that Stuart Bykofsky and David Hackworth both relate situations in which certain segments of society are blamed for various social ills. This general topic became the starting point of Dave's essay exploring social issues. You can do the same with your informal writing.

As you reread your informal responses, look for comments, questions, and observations that relate to the issue you've identified. When generating ideas for formal written responses, examine selections, annotations, journal entries, and notes from group discussions with a *critical* eye. Being critical means assessing the relationships between ideas, evaluating the relative merits of ideas, and judging the strength of evidence supporting ideas. Reading and writing critically is not simply criticizing what you've read. It involves *analyzing* the material with respect to personal experience, conversations with other knowledgeable people, and your own reading. As you read through material in preparation for formal writing, you may change your mind about a selection or clarify your position on a topic, discover a flaw in a writer's argument or find support for it in another selection. Remember, the more critical you are as you reread material, the more confident you will be when you begin to write.

Below are the guidelines for Generating Ideas that appear at the end of each chapter, followed by a list of possible topics for the readings in this chapter. The guidelines are followed by Dave's notes.

❖ Generating Ideas   Reread all of your journals and annotations from the selections in this unit. Look for connections between selections or still unanswered questions. First, list those connections and questions as briefly as possible. Next, choose two or three to elaborate on. As you respond in more detail to the connections and questions, focus on one topic and consider how well it would serve you in an extended piece of writing. Then decide what kind of writing best suits your topic: Should you write a conventional essay, a poem, a short story, or a scene? Would your topic lend itself more to a letter to the editor or a personal letter? Might a proposal to solve a specific problem be a good choice? Possible topics:

1. the tendency to blame certain groups for society's problems
2. the relationship between violence and social problems
3. conflicting rights of different individuals or groups

Dave's notes:

** blame turns up in several articles—women/abortion, homeless, riots all articles seem to paint depressing picture of life here!

** government responsibility seems important in some articles violence begetting violence in LA, boot camps?

BLAME—Bykofsky tends to blame homeless for making him feel uneasy walking to & from work, seems to see them as the root of the problem. But they're not—there's clearly a problem, but they're only part of it. Another part is seen in LA riots—yeah, we can blame individuals for beating people up or looting, but you can't ignore the fact that it's a lot bigger than that. Maybe if we focus on solutions instead of trying to figure out who to blame we can get moving. (Yeah—remember the drowning child. Who cares how it happened? You just do something to save the kid!)

GOVERNMENT—govt determines when women can get abortions, how to punish first-time offenders, how much money goes to cities, what happens to homeless people. It controls everything! But we need it too, without it there'd be chaos. How can this stuff fit together? too loose—go with blame. Elaborate on proposal? Essay?

Notice that Dave lets his mind wander as he explores possible topics, to the point of talking to himself when he decides to "go with blame." This preliminary writing should be very informal because of its exploratory nature. Don't get bogged down in concerns about how well you're writing when your sole purpose is to generate ideas. The focus on good writing will come later.

❖ Exercise 7   Follow the Generating Ideas guidelines for the selections in this chapter, using Dave's notes as a model. Discuss your choices with others in your group. What advice can you give one another about how to proceed with your writing project?

Focusing responses   As you prepare to write a formal piece, remember that your goal is no longer to explore what you know or think but instead to communicate what you believe. (Of course, as you compose a draft and make revisions, you're still working out your ideas. But once you prepare your final draft, your purpose in writing should be clear.) Thus, you have an obligation to let your readers know your position and to arrange your material in such a way that they can follow your reasoning.

GENERATING IDEAS

- Read journal and annotations, looking for connections, questions
- Elaborate on two or three connections or questions
- Decide which topic will work best
- Choose a form to write in; decide how to integrate responses to selections

---

Making connections between two or more readings in a formal piece of writing involves *integrating* or *synthesizing* material. You will have to determine the relationship between the selections; Dave Michaud, for example, felt that Bykofsky and Hackworth both illustrate an increasing tendency among Americans to affix blame for social problems. Whatever the connection, your job is to make it clear as you develop your response, carefully choosing material from each selection for its importance to your argument. You would expect Dave's paper, then, to focus on Bykofsky's and Hackworth's treatment of blame.

Frequently, when integrating material from two or more sources into one paper, you will find yourself making *comparisons* (a process that almost invariably results in pointing out contrasts as well). It's only natural to try to determine how one selection relates to another, or how two selections relate to some external idea, such as government's impact on citizens. When comparing selections, make your *criteria*, or basis for comparison, clear. For example, you might compare Bentayou's and Hackworth's discussions of the causes of violence in society, or Seligmann's and Bykofsky's choices of perspective in discussing a controversial issue. Whether your comparison involves only a few sentences or constitutes the bulk of your paper, establishing and maintaining clear criteria for comparison is essential.

When trying to integrate your responses to two or more readings into a single paper, you will sometimes be allowed to choose the *form* in which you will present your response. Conventional essay, short story, scene, letter to the editor, or proposal are some of the possible forms you might use. Deciding which form to choose depends largely on your material and how you think your point will be made most forcefully. Articles such as Hackworth's lend themselves to proposals for action, for example, while Bykofsky's essay seems to invite a letter to the editor. (In fact, Bykofsky and *Newsweek* received hundreds of responses—many of them angry—to "No Heart for the Homeless.") Seligmann's and Bentayou's articles, on the other hand, may prompt you to write a short story or dramatized scene. Frequently, if the basis of your response relies more heavily on emotion than on reasoned judgment, a creative response can be quite effective. A story told from the point of view of a boot camp recruit, for example, might engage a reader in ways that a conventional essay on the impact of boot camps could not. Whatever form you choose, make sure that your readers understand your point. To that end your paper must be clearly *focused*.

A useful way to clarify your focus is to formulate a statement that captures the essence of your response. The following guidelines for focusing your ideas appears at the end of each chapter. Dave's focus statement on scapegoats is included here as well. (Dave's completed paper will appear later in the chapter.)

❖ Focusing Responses   Choose one of your extended responses and formulate a statement of one or two sentences that captures the essence of your response. Use this statement as a guide to organize your piece. (If you write an essay, letter, or proposal, the statement may actually appear as a thesis.) Dave's focus statement:

> The homeless accosting strangers on their way to work and East LA residents destroying what little they have in blind rage—each of these examples illustrate situations in which certain segments of society are blamed for various social ills. Rather than solving society's problems, scapegoating prevents us from addressing those problems profitably.

A statement like this can guide you as you write—you can measure each paragraph or section of your writing against your statement. If you seem to be drifting away from your point, you can remedy the situation as you write either by refocusing the paragraph or section or by reformulating the focus statement. In fact, reformulating the statement may provide you with a workable thesis statement for an essay, letter, or proposal by the time you've finished a draft.

Guided writing assignments   This book also contains more traditional Guided Writing Assignments, in which you're asked to respond to specific topics rather than to generate your own ideas for an essay. If you choose the guided assignments, much of the work of generating and focusing ideas will have been done for you. Even though the assignment provides a focus, however, you will still find it useful to formulate your own focused statement to help you organize your extended response. Below are two Guided Writing Assignments for these selections, along with an exercise designed to acquaint you with the technique of composing formal written responses. Jane Estrella's and Isa Perez's responses to the Guided Writing Assignments follow the exercise.

❖ Guided Writing Assignments

1. Hackworth and Bentayou both suggest that criminal violence may be caused in part by violence and other forms of oppression perpetrated by police, corrections officers, or other authority figures. Using arguments from both authors, write a letter to the editor of *Newsweek* in which you propose that one way to reduce criminal violence is to abandon government violence. Offer alternatives to "boot camp" prisons and "armed camp" inner cities.

2. Just as Bykofsky addresses homelessness by focusing on its effects on working people, Seligmann explores the abortion dilemma by focusing on its effects on medical personnel. Write an essay evaluating this approach, focusing on both the value of providing a different perspective from which to assess an issue and the limitations of that perspective. Use examples from each article to support your evaluation.

❖ Exercise 8

Compose a focus statement for *either* the ideas you identified in Exercise 7 *or* for one of the Guided Writing Assignments above. Then draft your extended piece of writing, using your focus statement as a guide.

❖ Sample Response to Question 1

```
To the Editor:

    Reading David Hackworth's "This Was No Riot,
It Was a Revolt" in last week's issue, I was re-
minded of an article I read recently in The Pro-
gressive, Frank Bentayou's "The New Chain Gangs."
I would suggest that these two articles indicate
that using government violence to reduce criminal
violence is not only ineffective but also unneces-
```

sary. In fact, the "boot camp" theory of criminal justice reflects the same mentality that uses force only to quell urban unrest.

I agree with Jerome Miller, cited in Bentayou's article. He believes that violence is unnecessary in reforming criminals. These youths are placed in correctional facilities for nonviolent crimes; there is no reason they should be treated with violence during the course of their sentences. Allow me to offer a parallel to disciplining children: It has been demonstrated in study after study that using violence and punitive measures does more harm than good in children; what children learn from violent punishment is that violence is acceptable, a part of life. How can we expect these same measures to have positive effects on prisoners, a population that may already be prone to violence?

Bentayou states that using violent measures "may instill dangerous resentment in violent youths and send them a message that such violent behavior . . . has a place in our society." What more striking example of this can we ask than the Los Angeles riots? People are subjected to violence at the hands of law enforcement, and they react with violence. In that article, Major Ralph Coyle states that the discipline and violence used on criminals makes them "feel positive about having gotten through something challenging." Oh, yes, we saw it in L.A.: violence certainly made them feel positive—positive that they wanted revenge!

While I disagree vehemently with Coyle, I do advocate the use of discipline, hard work, and education for all inmates, regardless of age or educational background. Discipline, however, is not synonymous with violence. Make them work hard. But also educate them in areas that relate to their lives. Maybe this won't be the answer, but no one really knows if violence is the answer, either. If we don't also try nonviolent measures to deliver our messages, then we will

face violent reactions--as we learned in Los Angeles last year. As a police officer in Hackworth's
article says, "Our cities are not a powder keg
waiting to explode, but they're like a slow fuse
burning all the time. . . . L.A.'s flame just got
higher." It may not take too long before such an
incendiary device leads to an explosion in our
boot camps as well.

Sincerely,

Jane Estrella

❖ Sample Response to Question 2

Examining Social Issues: How Detached
Is Too Detached?

Isa Perez

Abortion. We usually read about it from the
mother's point of view in pro-choice literature
or from the fetus's point of view in prolife literature. But what of the medical personnel who
deal with abortion every day? How do they feel
about the issue?

Homelessness. We usually read about it from
the victims' point of view in liberal literature
and the taxpayers' point of view in conservative
literature. But what of the people who pass by
homeless persons every day? How do they feel
about the issue?

Exploring issues from different perspectives
can help us come to terms with those issues by
eliminating the usual stock responses. The extreme views we often hear keep us running in circles: Each side is as intransigent and
closed-minded as the other, and nobody gets anywhere. We have to understand not only how complex

social issues are but also how far-reaching their
effects are. However, looking at homelessness and
abortion from these more detached perspectives
can be risky: We might lose sight of those most
involved as we broaden our view to include others
only marginally related to the issue.

In "The Medical Quandary," Jean Seligmann
writes of how a process called "D & E, in which
the fetus is literally dismembered by a forceps
within the uterus, limb by limb, and the 'pieces'
are withdrawn through the vagina . . . can be
devastating for the hospital staff" (37). This
view of late abortion from the perspective of
the medical personnel forces us to recognize that
the issue is not simply a battle between the
rights of the mother and the fetus. It also involves the emotional well-being of dedicated
people torn between their duty to the patient
(the mother) and their unease over the results
of their work.

Similarly, Stuart Bykofsky's "No Heart for
the Homeless" lets readers feel what it's like to
be "pestered by panhandlers" every day, twice a
day (31). Bykofsky argues that regardless of
whose fault homelessness is, he still should have
the right to walk his streets without being accosted. After all, he argues, homeless people begging for money "do frighten my elderly neighbors.
It is psychological assault" (31). When we try to
determine how to deal with homelessness, perhaps
we should be reminded of those who, although no
more responsible for the problem than anyone
else, encounter it every day.

But what happens when we look at issues
through too broad a lens? Do we risk losing sight
of the real victims--women, fetuses, homeless people? Of course we must admit that social problems
are not simple black-and-white issues. But if we
spend too much time looking at them from too many
different perspectives, we forget to deal with
the overall picture. Maybe what we have to do is
put on blinders and just <u>do</u> something.

FOCUSING RESPONSES

· Formulate a statement to capture the essence of your response
· Check each paragraph or section to determine its relevance to focus statement
· Refocus paragraphs, sections, or focus statement as needed

REVISING AND MAKING USE
OF PEER RESPONSES

As you revise the draft of your essay, letter, proposal, or creative piece, pay close attention to your *purpose*. The focus statement should say clearly and concisely what you intend to accomplish in your extended piece; when you've finished a first draft, therefore, it's a good idea to measure each section of your paper against that statement. If a good part of what you've written strays from the focus, you'll probably want to revise the focus statement rather than the entire piece. If, on the other hand, an isolated section or two strays, you should revise those sections.

Sometimes, when you've been working for a long time on a piece of writing, it's hard to see it objectively; you tend to see what you *meant* to write rather than what you've actually written. For this reason it's often helpful to see how an objective reader responds to your paper. *Peer review* offers students the opportunity to help one another through the revision process. Ordinarily, a peer review session involves reading your paper aloud to a small group whose members then respond to it. They can do this either by talking to you about your paper or by writing a response to which you can refer as you revise. The most important thing to remember when reviewing one another's papers is that everyone is there to *help*, not to disparage or discourage. The most important thing to remember once you've received responses to your draft is that it is *your* draft. *You* will decide how to use the responses; *you* will decide which advice to follow; *you* will decide what final revisions to make.

Your instructor may provide you with guidelines for responding to one another's writing, or you may use the following general guidelines:

GUIDELINES FOR PEER RESPONSE
- How would you phrase a focus statement for this paper?
- How does each section or paragraph relate to the focus statement?
- What's the best thing about the paper? Explain.
- How might the paper be improved? Explain.

These guidelines are necessarily general; they're designed to apply to many types of writing. As you become more accustomed to reviewing each other's work, however, you'll find yourself responding more and more specifically. Below is Dave Michaud's draft, along with Jane Estrella's comments. Following the responses is Dave's final paper.

The Futility of Culpability: Urban America Gets Caught in the Middle

David. J. Michaud

Powerful stuff, but focus? Is it going to be a global paper or deal with local issues? Not sure what focus is—

The notion of irresolvable blame has permitted the justification of strife and conflict throughout world history. It is the stuff of jihads and crusades, and all measure of unnecessary destruction. We've seen it on a national scale in Northern Ireland and Israel. We can observe it on a world scale in the Amazon jungle or the Antarctic ozone hole. It is when we see this notion of blame on a social scale, that I become perplexed. To appreciate this, we must first understand the power of blame. It's quite simple, really. Blame is the ultimate stalemate. It is a great wall between factions. It is a huge cog in the mechanics of resolution. With relentless blame comes endless discord. Two of the most disturbing urbiculture??

social ills in this country, urbiculture and homelessness, are currently
trapped in the cross-fire of such culpability. These are curable ills. The
responsibility of <u>who</u> caused <u>what</u> is
a moral debate that could take dec-
ades and more to resolve. Some factions, during the quincentennial
"celebration" of the discovery of the
Americas, made the assertion that Columbus's venture was actually the
root of many of today's social dilem-
mas. This search for blame has gone
too far. It's time to diagnose the
specifics and implement a remedy. If
blame must be placed, then blame the

Wow! forceful!

primordial ooze and get on with the
matter at hand.

Urban America suffers from the
maladies of racial segregation,
crime, homelessness and destruction.
This is nothing new. So much effort
has been made to find out who's responsible, that little action has resulted. There are too many people who
are determined to place blame. Reverend Jesse Jackson says on television
that the youth involved in the Los Angeles riots were not born like that
but instead made this way by society,
which had discarded them. David Hackworth, in his article "This Was Not a
Riot, It Was a Revolt," says that the
two-day insurgency was a product of
both black unrest and black opportun-
ism. Not surprising is the fact that

clearly focused here
quotes keep us fixed
on X blaming Y
blaming Z etc.

our nation's leaders are just as busy
pointing an accusatory finger as anyone else. Many elected officials
blame the conservative administrations of the past twelve years for
the current state of urbicultural affairs. Perhaps all three assessments
are correct, perhaps they are wrong.

I get your point
here the first time—
do you need to
keep repeating it?

It is irrelevant. If society is ultimately "to blame," then we are all
equally responsible, for we are all
part of society. All of the social

ills, as well as all of the social
successes, are a product, one way
or another, of society. The success
of a nation is not based on the
problems it faces, but is measured
by how those problems are resolved.

   The time to act is now. There are
at least two possible outcomes to
further inaction. First, the nation
could experience an urbicultural up-
heaval which would dwarf the L.A.
riots by comparison. Yet, equally
disturbing is the threat of total
apathy. Like the hospital staff in
an emergency room, we might grow
numb to the strife that surrounds
us. Stuart D. Bykofsky, columnist
for the <u>Philadelphia Daily News</u>,
heartlessly rejects both responsibility and concern for the homeless:
"Early on, I felt pity for those in
the streets, but their relentless
begging has forced me to change <u>my</u>
habits, my attitudes. . . . I'm now
deaf to people in the street" (31).

   Responsibility must first begin by
simply recognizing and acknowledging
the existence of urban plight, and by
taking a <u>pro</u>active stance, not a <u>re</u>-
active one. Responsibility must also
come from the inner city. Eddie Williams urges blacks to begin by helping themselves. A concerted effort is
necessary. We have to share <u>ownership</u>
of urban problems. One way to secure
the bonds of public unification is
education. We need to educate the
children who are trapped in the smoldering refuse of urban depravity,
but we also need to educate those
who are free and comfortable enough
to look in from the "outside." This
process of scapegoating must end. A
partnership bound by education can
cement the first building blocks necessary to forge a new America--a unified people each able to absorb the
others' culture and ethnicity.

Bykof. quote good.
But you haven't
been talking about
homelessness. Are
you trying to fit it in
here?

Who's he? But
doesn't education
include figuring out
causes too? And
what about
Hackworth's idea?
Can't you combine
approaches?

Dave—You use language so powerfully! I still wish I had your gift with words. But you seem to lose sight of the homelessness issue that you mention in the beginning. The one reference seems more like an example (like the emergency room) than a real focal point. Maybe you need to add more about homelessness or rephrase the statement about it. And you seem to abandon Hackworth at the end too. You used him effectively earlier in the paper. Good luck!

Dave's final draft:

The Futility of Culpability:
Urban America Gets Caught in the Middle

David. J. Michaud

The notion of irresolvable blame has permitted the justification of strife and conflict throughout world history. It is the stuff of jihads and crusades, and all measure of unnecessary destruction. We see its power every day, and if we're to solve any of our problems, global or local, we have to recognize that blame is the ultimate stalemate. It is a great wall between factions, a huge cog in the mechanics of resolution. With relentless blame comes endless discord. One of the most disturbing social ills in this country, urbiculture (problems characteristic to the inner city) is currently trapped in the cross-fire of such culpability. This is a curable ill. The responsibility of who caused what is a moral debate that could take decades and more to resolve. The search for blame has gone too far. It's time to diagnose the specifics and implement a remedy. If blame must be placed, then blame the primordial ooze and get on with the matter at hand.

Urban America suffers from the maladies of racial segregation, crime, homelessness and destruction. This is nothing new. So much effort has been made to find out who's responsible, that little action has resulted. There are too many people who are determined to place blame. Rever-

end Jesse Jackson says on television that the
youth involved in the Los Angeles riots were not
born violent but were made that way by a society
which had discarded them. Not surprising is that
our nation's leaders are just as busy pointing an
accusatory finger as anyone else. Many elected officials blame the conservative administrations of
the past twelve years for the current state of affairs in the nation's cities. Perhaps all three
of these assessments are correct; perhaps they
are wrong. If society is ultimately "to blame,"
then we are all equally responsible. We are all
"society." The success of a nation is not based
on the problems it faces, but is measured by how
those problems are resolved.

The time to act is now. There are at least
two possible outcomes to further inaction. First,
the nation could experience an urbicultural up-
heaval which would dwarf the L. A. riots by comparison. Yet, equally disturbing is the threat of
total apathy. Like the hospital staff in an emergency room, we might grow numb to the strife that
surrounds us. Stuart D. Bykofsky, columnist for
the Philadelphia Daily News, heartlessly rejects
both responsibility and concern for the homeless:
"Early on, I felt pity for those in the streets,
but their relentless begging has forced me to
change my habits, my attitudes. . . . I'm now
deaf to people in the street" (31). If his reaction typifies middle-class city dwellers, then we
are indeed in dire circumstances. Deaf to people
in the street, blind to people in the inner-city--
what comes next? Refusing to hear and see will
not prevent our cities from exploding.

Responsibility must first begin by simply
recognizing and acknowledging the existence of urban plight, and by taking a proactive stance, not
a reactive one. Responsibility must also come
from the inner city. Eddie N. Williams, president
of the joint Center for Political and Economic
Studies, urges blacks to begin by helping themselves. A concerted effort is necessary. We have
to share ownership of urban problems. Hackworth

suggests taking a direct militaristic route in
solving our urban problems. Certainly his implica-
tion that the "insurgency" in Los Angeles was
spontaneous--a reaction that helped to detonate
an explosive unrest--underscores the need for action. But military intervention should be used as
an additional resource to aid urban restoration,
and not be placed in the lead role Hackworth suggests. The military would certainly be a necessary component in any program, but they should be
used as "staff" falling under the umbrella of
civil, educational, and business leadership.

One way to secure the bonds of public unification is education. We need to educate the children who are trapped in the smoldering refuse of
urban depravity, but we also need to educate
those who are free and comfortable enough to look
in from the "outside." Of course we need to analyze the causes of social ills--but affixing
blame is not the same as isolating causes. This
process of scapegoating must end. A partnership
bound by education can cement the first building
blocks necessary to forge a new America--a unified people each able to absorb the others' culture and ethnicity.

❖ Exercise 9   Using the guidelines above, break into small groups
and respond to one another's drafts. Remember as you write your
responses that your goal is to help the writer find ways to improve the
paper, not to correct the writer's problems. Revise your draft after
evaluating the responses you receive.

Guided research assignments   If your reading sparks an interest in a
particular topic, or raises questions in your mind that remain unanswered, you may naturally wish to do further research. How you
conduct research depends on the nature of your topic; you may read
reference books, critical works, scholarly journals, newspapers or
magazines; you may also interview experts, scholars, policymakers,
or people otherwise involved with an issue.

The results of your research will be as varied as the methods used
to conduct it. Research results can be published in the form of recommendations, reports, historical analyses, and even creative works.
Sometimes, however, the research can be an end in itself: your ques-

tions are answered, or you've simply become better informed about an issue. What's important is that once you've been exposed to various perspectives, you often want to find out more. Research offers you the opportunity to do that. Each chapter in this book contains possible research topics for those who wish to explore an issue further. Below are some suggestions for research into the issues covered in this chapter:

❖ Research Topics   As you consider how to expand your reading beyond the selections in this chapter, identify in your journals and notes questions that remain unanswered or topics you'd like to explore further. Or you may consider the following:

1. The current abortion debate has its roots in similar debates over women's reproductive rights from before the turn of the century. Read historical accounts of the legal and moral battles waged over the dissemination of birth control information, the distribution of birth control devices, and the availability of abortion. Try to identify the roles played by religious leaders, medical professionals, social reformers, women's rights advocates, and politicians. What are the similarities and differences between today's battles and those fought in earlier eras? What can we learn from those early battles?

2. Poverty and crime have always been closely connected. While some believe poverty to be a leading cause of crime, others argue that the poor are in some ways responsible for their own condition. Interview people involved in the study of poverty and crime—social scientists, criminologists, prison reformers, leaders of social welfare agencies—as well as people affected by poverty and/or crime. Try to distinguish between their different perspectives on the relationship between poverty and crime. What sort of picture emerges from your interviews? Are the different perspectives hopelessly at odds with one another, or might they be combined to create a program to alleviate crime and poverty? Do you find yourself leaning toward any single perspective?

The chapters that follow address a variety of topics. Some will seem familiar—the idea of a home, for example, or the distinctions between generations. Others, such as living outside the mainstream or coping with violence, will touch only a few of you directly. Regardless of how relevant these issues are to your lives, however, active reading and critical writing will make you more aware of the diversity of the culture in which you live. And that greater awareness will make you not only a better student but also a more informed member of the larger community.

Chapter 2

Cultural Identities

Wʜᴀᴛ ɪs Aᴍᴇʀɪᴄᴀɴ ᴄᴜʟᴛᴜʀᴇ? Is there such a thing as one all-encompassing system of values, behaviors, beliefs, and ways of living that characterizes everyone in this country? The selections in this chapter suggest not. Rather, they illustrate the rich variety of cultures that together constitute the American way of life.

In the past several years a battle of sorts has been waged between those who argue that the individual cultures of different American groups should be celebrated and those who fear that such a multicultural emphasis would dilute our common culture. Traditional monoculturalists are concerned that focusing on what distinguishes us from one another can only serve to fragment society, while multiculturalists contend that an appreciation for those distinctive cultural features will result in a common respect for all cultures. The selections that follow offer a glimpse of how various Americans view themselves and their relationship to the dominant culture.

The influence of television on the dominant culture is the subject of Michael Ventura's "Report from El Dorado." Arguing that Americans actually believe that television images are reality, Ventura offers a rather disturbing view of our popular culture.

Ben Hamper describes the reality from which many Americans use television as an escape in "Growing Up in Greaseball Mecca."

Hamper characterizes working-class life in Flint, Michigan, as full of false hopes, alienation, and drudgery.

Lorene Cary's "June 1989" is a tribute to her "kids," young African-American students who seek to maintain pride in their own cultural identity within a bastion of white, upper-class culture. The fears and triumphs of these students resonate for Cary, who has come to terms with her own experiences at St. Paul's School through her writing.

In "The Children of Affluence," Robert Coles emphasizes the sense of entitlement most wealthy children feel. Regardless of the everyday fears and joys of childhood, these children go through life thoroughly convinced that "everything will work out fine."

In "What's in a Name?" Itabari Njeri examines the importance not only of individual names but of racial and ethnic labels as well. Reactions to her African name, along with the labels Africans use to refer to African Americans, convince her that names hold great significance.

The question of what precisely constitutes racial identity is the subject of David Mura's "Secrets and Anger," an article focusing on the author's mixed-race daughter. Mura's experiences as an Asian American have convinced him that race will play a key role in his daughter's development.

Mickey Roberts writes of white misapprehensions about Native Americans in "It's All in How You Say It." The narrator in the story marvels at the ignorance of those who cannot distinguish between genuine and imitation Indian culture.

Bigotry and ignorance abound in Elinor Langer's "The Chameleon," a study of white supremacist David Duke. Precisely because he is so palatable to middle America, argues Langer, Duke is perhaps more dangerous than stereotypical bigots.

Finally, a woman looks back with understanding and sympathy on the tormentors of her adolescence in Inés Hernandez's "Para Teresa." Recalling a girls' room confrontation with the school's tough girls, the narrator finally recognizes that both she and Teresa, each in her own way, demanded respect.

The cultural identities represented in this chapter are testimony to the rich variety of racial, ethnic, and social groups that constitute American society. While many of the works emphasize the problems inherent in a multicultural society, most still reflect the pride with which Americans view their different backgrounds. We may talk about a melting pot, but these selections indicate that most Americans wish to retain at least some of the cultural characteristics that distinguish them.

Report from El Dorado

MICHAEL VENTURA

MICHAEL VENTURA *has written extensively on popular culture. At present a columnist for* LA Weekly, *his most recent book is* We've Had a Hundred Years of Psychotherapy—and the World's Getting Worse, *published in 1992. In this article from* Shadow Dancing in the USA *(1985), Ventura explores the powerful hold that television and photographic images have over most Americans. Claiming that we tend to believe that image is in fact reality, Ventura argues that we have yet to define ourselves as a culture in the media age.*

Before reading the selection, write in your journal about your own television viewing habits. What kinds of programs do you watch? How are your tastes influenced by television? How close are the images on the screen to your reality?

As you make notes on your reading, you may want to focus on the historical information Ventura provides, the various distinctions he makes between reality and images, or the reasons he offers for Americans' obsession with television.

To GO FROM A JOB you don't like to watching a screen on which others live more intensely than you . . . is American life, by and large.

This is our political ground. This is our artistic ground. This is what we've done with our immense resources. We have to stop calling it "entertainment" or "news" or "sports" and start calling it what it is: our most immediate environment.

This is a very, very different America from the America that built the industrial capacity to win the Second World War and to surge forward on the multiple momentums of that victory for thirty years. That was an America that worked at mostly menial tasks during the day (now we work at mostly clerical tasks) and had to look at each other at night.

65

I'm not suggesting a nostalgia for that time. It was repressive and bigoted to an extent that is largely forgotten today, to cite only two of its uglier aspects. But in that environment America meant *America:* the people and the land. The land was far bigger than what we'd done with the land.

This is no longer true. Now the environment of America is media.   5
Not the land itself, but the image of the land. The focus is not on the people so much as it is on the interplay between people and screens. What we've done with the land is far more important now than the land—we're not even dealing with the land anymore, we're dealing with our manipulation and pollution of it.

And what we've done with the very concept of "image" is taking on far more importance for many of us than the actual sights and sounds of our lives.

For instance: Ronald Reagan stands on a cliff in Normandy to commemorate the day U.S. Army Rangers scaled those cliffs in the World War II invasion. Today's Rangers reenact the event while some of the original Rangers, in their sixties now, look on. Except that it is the wrong cliff. The cliff that was actually scaled is a bit further down the beach, but it's not as photogenic as this cliff, so this cliff has been chosen for everybody to emote over. Some of the old Rangers tell reporters that the historical cliff is over yonder, but the old Rangers are swept up (as well they might be) in the ceremonies, and nobody objects enough. This dislocation, this choice, this stance that the real cliff is not important, today's photograph is more important, is a media event. It insults the real event, and overpowers it. Multiplied thousands of times over thousands of outlets of every form and size, ensconced in textbooks as well as screenplays, in sales presentations as well as legislative packages, in religious revivals as well as per-formance-art pieces, this is the process that has displaced what used to be called "culture."

"I'm not even sure it's a culture anymore. It's like this careening hunger splattering out in all directions."

Jeff Nightbyrd was trying to define "culture" in the wee hours at the Four Queens in Las Vegas. It was a conversation that had been going on since we'd become friends working on the *Austin Sun* in 1974, trying to get our bearings now that the sixties were *really* over. He'd spent that tripletime decade as an SDS organizer and editor of *Rat*, and I'd hit Austin after a few years of road-roving, commune-hopping, and intensive (often depressive) self-exploration—getting by, as the song said, with a little help from my friends, as a lot of us did then. This particular weekend Nightbyrd had come to Vegas from Austin for a computer convention, and I had taken off from my duties at the *L.A. Weekly* for some lessons in craps (at which Jeff is quite good) and to further our rap. The slot machines clattered around us in unison, almost comfortingly, the way the sound of a large shaky air-conditioner can be comforting in a cheap hotel room when you're trying to remember to forget. We were, after all, trying to fathom an old love: America.

There are worse places to indulge in this obsession than Las   10
Vegas. It is the most American, the most audacious, of cities. Consuming unthinkable amounts of energy in the midst of an unlivable desert (Death Valley is not far away), its decor is based on various cheap-to-luxurious versions of a 1930s Busby Berkeley musical. Indeed, no studio backlot could ever be more of a set, teeming with extras, people who come from all over America, and all over the world, to see the topless, tasteless shows, the Johnny Carson guests on parade doing their utterly predictable routines, the dealers and crap-table croupiers who combine total boredom with ruthless efficiency and milk us dry—yet at least these tourists are risking something they genuinely value: money. It's a quiz show turned into a way of life, where you can get a good Italian dinner at dawn. Even the half-lit hour of the wolf doesn't faze Las Vegas. How could it, when the town has survived the flash of atom bombs tested just over the horizon?

The history books will tell you that, ironically enough, the town was founded by Mormons in 1855. Even their purity of vision couldn't bear the intensity of this desert, and they abandoned the place after just two years. But they had left a human imprint, and a decade later the U.S. Army built a fort here. The settlement hung on, and the railroad came through in 1905. During the Second World War the Mafia started to build the city as we know it now. Religious zealots, the Army, and the Mafia—quite a triad of founding fathers.

Yet one could go back even further, some 400 years, when the first Europeans discovered the deserts of the American West—Spaniards who, as they slowly began to believe that there might be no end to these expansive wilds, became more and more certain that somewhere, somewhere to the north, lay El Dorado—a city of gold. Immeasurable wealth would be theirs, they believed, and eternal youth. What would they have thought if they had suddenly come upon modern Las Vegas, lying as it does in the midst of this bleached nowhere, glowing at night with a brilliance that would have frightened them? We have built our desert city to their measure—for they were gaudy and greedy, devout and vicious, jovial and frenzied, like this town. They had just wasted the entire Aztec civilization because their fantasies were so strong they couldn't see the ancient cultural marvels before their eyes. The Aztecs, awed and terrified, believed they were being murdered by gods; and in the midst of such strangeness, the Spaniards took on godlike powers even in their own eyes. As many Europeans would in America, they took liberties here they would never have taken within sight of their home cathedrals. Their hungers dominated them, and in their own eyes the New World seemed as inexhaustible as their appetites. So when Nightbyrd described our present culture as "a careening hunger splattering out in all directions," he was also, if unintentionally, speaking about our past. Fittingly, we were sitting in the midst of a city that had been fantasized by those seekers of El Dorado 400 years ago. In that sense, America had Las Vegas a century before it had Plymouth Rock. And our sensibility has been caught between the fantasies of the conquistadors and the obsessions of the Puritans ever since.

Yes, a fitting place to try to think about American culture.

"There are memories of culture," Nightbyrd was saying, "but the things that have given people strength have dissolved. And because they're dissolved, people are into distractions. And distractions aren't culture."

Are there even memories? The media have taken over our memories. That day Nightbyrd had been driving through the small towns that dot this desert, towns for which Vegas is only a dull glow to the southwest. In a bar in one of those towns, "like that little bar in *The Right Stuff*," he'd seen pictures of cowboys on the wall. "Except that they weren't cowboys. They were movie stars. Guys who grew up in Glendale [John Wayne] and Santa Monica [Robert Redford]." Surely this desert had its own heroes once, in the old gold-mining towns where a few people still hang on, towns like Goldfield and Tonopah. Remembering those actual heroes would be "culture." Needing pictures of movie stars for want of the real thing is only a nostalgia for culture.

Nostalgia is not memory. Memory is specific. One has a relationship to a memory, and it may be a difficult relationship, because a memory always makes a demand upon the present. But nostalgia is vague, a sentimental wash that obscures memory and acts as a narcotic to dull the importance of the present.

Media as we know it now thrives on nostalgia and is hostile to memory. In a television bio-pic, Helen Keller is impersonated by Mare Winningham. But the face of Helen Keller was marked by her enormous powers of concentration, while the face of Mare Winningham is merely cameo-pretty. A memory has been stolen. It takes a beauty in you to see the beauty in Helen Keller's face, while to cast the face of a Mare Winningham in the role is to suggest, powerfully, that one can come back from the depths unscathed. No small delusion is being sold here. Yet this is a minor instance in a worldwide, twenty-four-hour-a-day onslaught.

15

An onslaught that gathers momentum every twenty-four hours. Remember that what drew us to Las Vegas was a computer fair. One of these new computers does interesting things with photographs. You can put a photograph into the computer digitally. This means the photograph is in there without a negative or print, each element of the image stored separately. In the computer, you can change any element of the photograph you wish, replacing it or combining it with elements from other photographs. In other words, you can take composites of different photographs and put them into a new photograph of your own composition. Combine this with computer drawing, and you can touch up shadows that don't match. When it comes out of the computer the finished product bears no evidence of tampering with any negative. The possibilities for history books and news stories are infinite. Whole new histories can now be written. Events which never happened can be fully documented.

The neo-Nazis who are trying to convince people that the Holocaust never happened will be able to show the readers of their newsletter an Auschwitz of well-fed, happy people being watched over by kindly S.S. men while tending gardens. And they will be able to make the accusation that photographs of the *real* Auschwitz were created in a computer by manipulative Jews. The Soviet Union can rewrite Czechoslovakia and Afghanistan, the United States can rewrite Vietnam, and atomic weapons proponents can prove that the average resident of Hiroshima was unharmed by the blast. On a less sinister, but equally disruptive, level, the writers of business prospectuses and real-estate brochures can have a field day.

Needless to say, when any photograph can be processed this way   20
then all photographs become suspect. It not only becomes easier to lie, it becomes far harder to tell the truth.

But why should this seem shocking when under the names of "entertainment" and "advertising" we've been filming history, and every facet of daily life, in just this way for nearly a century now? It shouldn't surprise us that the ethics of our entertainment have taken over, and that we are viewing reality itself as a form of entertainment. And, as entertainment, reality can be rewritten, transformed, played with, in any fashion.

These considerations place us squarely at the center of our world—and we have no choice, it's the only world there is anymore. *Electronic media has done for everyday reality what Einstein did for physics:* everything is shifting. Even the shifts are shifting. And a fact is not so crucial anymore, not so crucial as the process that turns a fact into an image. For we live now with images as much as facts, and the images seem to impart more life than facts *precisely because they are so capable of transmutation, of transcendence, able to transcend their sources and their uses.* And all the while the images goad us on, so that we become partly images ourselves, imitating the properties of images as we surround ourselves with images.

This is most blatant in our idea of "a vacation"—an idea only about 100 years old. To "vacation" is to enter an image. Las Vegas is only the most shrill embodiment of this phenomenon. People come here not so much to gamble (individual losses are comparatively light), nor for the glittery entertainment, but to step into an image, a daydream, a filmlike world where "everything" is promised. No matter that the Vegas definition of "everything" is severely limited, what thrills tourists is the sense of being surrounded in "real life" by the same images that they see on TV. But the same is true of the Grand Canyon, or Yellowstone National Park, or Yosemite, or Death Valley, or virtually any of our "natural" attractions. What with all their roads, telephones, bars, cable-TV motels, the visitors are carefully protected from having to *experience* the place. They view its image, they camp out in its image, ski down or climb up its image, take deep breaths of its image, let its image give them a tan. Or, when they tour the cities, they ride the quaint trolley cars of the city's image, they visit the Latin Quarter of its image, they walk across the Brooklyn Bridge of its image—our recreation is a *re*-creation of America into one big Disneyland.

And this is only one way we have stripped the very face of America of any content, any reality, concentrating only on its power as image. We also elect images, groom ourselves as images, make an image of our home, our car, and now, with aerobics, of our very bodies. For in the aerobics craze the flesh becomes a garment, susceptible to fashion. So it becomes less *our* flesh, though the exercise may make it more serviceable. It becomes "my" body, like "my" car, "my" house. What, within us, is saying "my"? What is transforming body into image? We shy away from asking. In this sense it can be said that after the age of about twenty-five we no longer *have* bodies anymore—we have possessions that are either more or less young, which we are constantly trying to transform and through which we try to breathe.

It's not that all this transformation of realities into un- or non- or   25
supra-realities is "bad," but that it's unconscious, compulsive, reductive. We rarely make things more than they were; we simplify them into less. Though surely the process *could*—at least theoretically—go both ways. Or so India's meditators and Zen's monks say. But that would be to *increase* meaning, and we seem bent on the elimination of meaning. We're Reagan's Rangers, climbing a cliff that *is* a real cliff, except it's not the cliff we say it is, so that the meaning of both cliffs—not to mention of our act of climbing—is reduced.

As I look out onto a glowing city that is more than 400 years old but was built only during the last forty years, as I watch it shine in blinking neon in a desert that has seen the flash of atom bombs, it becomes more and more plain to me that America is at war with meaning. America is form opposed to content. Not just form *instead* of content. Form opposed. Often violently. There are few things resented so much among us as the suggestion that what we do *means*. It *means* something to watch so much TV. It *means* something to be obsessed with sports. It *means* something to vacation by indulging in images. It means something, and therefore it has consequences. Other cultures have argued over their meanings. We tend to deny that there is any such thing, insisting instead that what you see is what you get and that's *it*. All we're doing is having a good *time*, all we're doing is making a buck, all we're doing is enjoying the spectacle, we insist. So that when we export American culture what we are really exporting is an attitude toward content. Media is the American war on content with all the stops out, with meaning in utter rout, frightened nuances dropping their weapons as they run.

"Media is the history that forgives," my friend Dave Johnson told me on a drive through that same desert a few months later. We love to take a weekend every now and again and just *drive*. Maybe it started with reading *On the Road* when we were kids, or watching a great old TV show called *Route 66* about two guys who drove from town to town working at odd jobs and having adventures with intense women who, when asked who they were, might say (as one did), "Suppose I said I was the Queen of Spain?" Or maybe it was all those rock 'n' roll songs about "the road"—the road, where we can blast our tape-decks as loud as we want, and watch the world go by without having to touch it, a trip through the greatest hologram there is, feeling like neither boys nor men but both and something more, embodiments of some ageless, restless principle of movement rooted deep in our prehistory. All of which is to say that we're just as stuck with the compulsion to enter the image as anybody, and that we love the luxuries of fossil fuel just as much as any other red-blooded, thick-headed Americans.

Those drives are our favorite time to talk, and, again, America is our oldest flame. We never tire of speaking of her, nor of our other old girlfriends. For miles and miles of desert I thought of what Dave had said.

"Media is the history that forgives." A lovely way to put it, and quite un-Western. We Westerners tend to think in sets of opposites: good/bad, right/wrong, me/you, past/present. These sets are often either antagonistic (East/West, commie/capitalist, Christian/heathen) or they set up a duality that instantly calls out to be bridged (man/woman). But Dave's comment sidesteps the dualities and suggests something more complex: a lyrical impulse is alive somewhere in all this media obfuscation. It is the impulse to redeem the past—in his word, to *forgive* history—by presenting it as we would have most liked it to be.

It is one thing to accuse the media of lying. They are, and they know it, and they know we know, and we know they know that we know, and nothing changes. It is another to recognize the rampant lying shallowness of our media as a massive united longing for . . . innocence? For a sheltered childlike state in which we need not know about our world or our past. We are so desperate for this that we are willing to accept ignorance as a substitute for innocence. For there can be no doubt anymore that this society *knowingly* accepts its ignorance as innocence—we have seen so much in the last twenty years that now we know what we *don't* see. Whenever a TV show or a movie or a news broadcast leaves out crucial realities for the sake of sentimentality, we pretty much understand the nature of what's been left out and why.

But American media *forgives* the emptiness and injustice of our daily life by presenting our daily life as innocent. Society, in turn, forgives American media for lying because if we accept the lie as truth then we needn't *do* anything, we needn't change.

I like Dave's line of thought because it suggests a motive—literally, a motive force—for these rivers of glop that stream from the screens and loudspeakers of our era. Because, contrary to popular belief, profit is *not* the motive. That seems a rash statement to make in the vicinity of Las Vegas, but the profit motive merely begs the question: *why* is it profitable? Profit, in media, is simply a way of measuring attention. Why does what we call "media" attract so much attention?

The answer is that it is otherwise too crippling for individuals to bear the strain of accepting the unbalanced, unrewarding, uninspiring existence that is advertised as "normal daily life" for most people who have to earn a living every day.

Do those words seem too strong? Consider: to go to a job you don't value in itself but for its paycheck, while your kids go to a school that is less and less able to educate them; a large percentage of your pay is taken by the government for defenses that don't defend, welfare that doesn't aid, and the upkeep of a government that is impermeable to the influence of a single individual; while you are caught in a value system that judges you by what you own, in a society where it is taken for granted now that children can't communicate with their parents, that old people have to be shut away in homes, and that no neighborhood is *really* safe; while the highest medical costs in the world don't prevent us from having one of the worst health records in the West (for instance, New York has a far higher infant mortality rate than Hong Kong), and the air, water, and supermarket food are filled with God-knows-what; and to have, at the end of a busy yet uneventful life, little to show for enduring all this but a comfortable home if you've "done well" enough; yet to *know* all along that you're living in the freest, most powerful country in the world, though you haven't had time to exercise much freedom and don't personally have any power—this is to be living a life of slow attrition and maddening contradictions.

Add to this a social style that values cheerfulness more than any other attribute, and then it is not so strange or shocking that the average American family watches six to eight hours of network television a day. It is a cheap and sanctioned way to partake of this world without having actually to live in it.

Certainly they don't watch so much TV because they're bored— there's far too much tension in their lives to call them bored, and, in fact, many of the products advertised on their favorite programs feature drugs to calm them down. Nor is it because they're stupid—a people managing the most technically intricate daily life in history can hardly be written off as stupid; nor because they can't entertain themselves—they are not so different from the hundreds of generations of their forebears who entertained themselves very well as a matter of course. No, they are glued to the TV because one of the most fundamental messages of television is: "It's all right."

Every sitcom and drama says: "It's all right." Those people on the tube go through the same—if highly stylized—frustrations, and are exposed to the same dangers as we are, yet they reappear magically every week (every day on the soap operas) ready for more, always hopeful, always cheery, never questioning the fundamental premise that this is the way a great culture behaves and that all the harassments are the temporary inconveniences of a beneficent society. It's going to get even *better*, but even now *it's all right*. The commercials, the Hollywood movies, the universal demand in every television drama or comedy that no character's hope can ever be exhausted, combine in a deafening chorus of: *It's all right*.

As a screenwriter I have been in many a film production meeting, and not once have I heard any producer or studio executive say, "We have to lie to the public." What I have heard, over and over, is, "They have to leave the theater feeling good." This, of course, easily (though not always) translates into lying—into simplifying emotions and

35

events so that "it's all right." You may measure how deeply our people know "it" is *not* all right, not at all, by how much money they are willing to pay to be ceaselessly told that it is. The more they feel it's not, the more they need to be told it is—hence Mr. Reagan's popularity.

Works that don't say "It's all right" don't get much media attention or make much money.

The culture itself is in the infantile position of needing to be   40
assured, every day, all day, that this way of life is good for you. Even the most disturbing news is dispensed in the most reassuring package. As world news has gotten more and more disturbing, the trend in broadcast journalism has been to get more and more flimflam, to take it less seriously, to keep up the front of "It's really quite all right." This creates an enormous tension between the medium and its messages, because everybody knows that what's on the news is *not* all right. That is why such big money is paid to a newscaster with a calm, authoritative air who, by his presence alone, seems to resolve the contradictions of his medium. Walter Cronkite was the most popular newscaster in broadcast history because his very presence implied: "As long as I'm on the air, you can be sure that, no matter what I'm telling you, *it's still all right.*"

Which is to say that the media has found it profitable to do the mothering of the mass psyche. But it's a weak mother. It cannot nurture. All it can do is say it's all right, tuck us in, and hope for the best.

Today most serious, creative people exhaust themselves in a sideline commentary on this state of affairs, a commentary that usually gets sucked up into the media and spewed back out in a format that says "It's all right. What this guy's saying is quite all right, what this woman's singing is all right, all right." This is what "gaining recognition" virtually always means now in America: your work gets turned inside out so that its meaning becomes "It's all right."

Of course, most of what exists *to make media of,* to make images of, is more and more disorder. Media keeps saying, "It's all right" while being fixated upon the violent, the chaotic, and the terrifying. So the production of media becomes more and more schizoid, with two messages simultaneously being broadcast: "It's all right. We're dying. It's all right. We're all dying." The other crucial message—"We're dying"—runs right alongside *It's all right.*

Murder is the crux of much media "drama." But it's murder presented harmlessly, with trivial causes cited. Rare is the attempt, in all our thousands of murder dramas, to delve below the surface. We take for granted now, almost as an immutable principle of dramatic unity, that significant numbers of us want to kill significant numbers of the rest of us. And what are all the murders in our media but a way of saying "We are being killed, we are killing, we are dying"? Only a people dying and in the midst of death would need to see so much of it in such sanitized form *in order to make death harmless*. This is the way we choose to share our death.

Delete the word "entertainment" and say instead, North Americans devote an enormous amount of time to the ritual of sharing death. If this were recognized as a ritual, and if the deaths were shared with a respect for the realities and the mysteries of death, this might be a very useful thing to do. But there is no respect for death in our death-dependent media, there is only the compulsion to display death. As for the consumers, they consume these deaths like sugar pills. Their ritual goes on far beneath any level on which they'd be prepared to admit the word "ritual." So we engage in a ritual we pretend isn't happening, hovering around deaths that we say aren't real.

It is no coincidence that this practice has thrived while the Pentagon uses the money of these death watchers to create weapons for death on a scale that is beyond the powers of human imagination—the very same human imagination that is stunting itself by watching ersatz deaths, as though intentionally crippling its capacity to envision the encroaching dangers. It is possible that the Pentagon's process could not go on without the dulling effects of this "entertainment."

When we're not watching our screens, we're listening to music. And, of course, North Americans listen to love songs at every possible opportunity, through every possible orifice of media. People under the strain of such dislocating unrealities need to hear "I love you, I love you," as often as they can. "I love you" or "I used to love you" or "I ought to love you" or "I need to love you" or "I want to love you." It is the fashion of pop-music critics to discount the words for the style, forgetting that most of the world's cultures have had songs about *everything*, songs about work, about the sky, about death, about the gods, about getting up in the morning, about animals, about children, about eating, about dreams—about everything, along with love. These were songs that everybody knew and sang. For a short time in the late sixties we moved toward such songs again, but that was a brief digression; since the First World War the music that most North Americans listen to has been a music of love lyrics that rarely go beyond adolescent yearnings. Either the song is steeped in the yearnings themselves, or it is saturated with a longing for the days when one could, shamelessly, feel like an adolescent. The beat has

45

changed radically from decade to decade, but with brief exceptions that beat has carried the same pathetic load. (The beat, thankfully, has given us other gifts.)

It can't be over-emphasized that these are entertainments of a people whose basic imperative is the need not to think about their environment. The depth of their need may be measured by the hysterical popularity of this entertainment; it is also the measure of how little good it does them.

Media is not experience. In its most common form, media substitutes a fantasy of experience or (in the case of news) an abbreviation of experience for the living fact. But in our culture the absorption of media has become a substitute for experience. We absorb media, we don't live it—there is a vast psychological difference, and it is a difference that is rarely brought up.

For example, in the 1940s, when one's environment was still one's   50 *environment*, an experience to be lived instead of a media-saturation to be absorbed, teenagers like Elvis Presley and Jerry Lee Lewis didn't learn their music primarily from the radio. Beginning when they were small boys they sneaked over to the black juke joints of Louisiana and Mississippi and Tennessee, where they weren't supposed to go, and they listened and learned. When Lewis and Presley began recording, even though they were barely twenty they had tremendous authority because they had experience—a raw experience of crossing foreign boundaries, of streets and sounds and peoples, of the night-to-night learning of ways that could not be taught at home.

This is very different from young musicians now who learn from a product, not a living ground. Their music doesn't get to them till it's been sifted through elaborate corporate networks of production and distribution. It doesn't smack of the raw world that exists before "product" can even be thought of.

The young know this, of course. They sense the difference intensely, and often react to it violently. So white kids from suburban media culture invented slam dancing (jumping up and down and slamming into each other) while black kids from the South Bronx, who have to deal with realities far more urgent than media, were elaborating the astounding graces of break dancing.

Slam dancing was a dead end. Break dancing, coming from a living ground, goes out through media but becomes ultimately transformed into another living ground—the kids in the elementary school down the street in Santa Monica break dance. Which is to say, a grace has been added to their lives. A possibility of grace. With the vitality that comes from having originated from a living ground. The media here is taking its proper role as a channel, not as a world in itself. It's possible that these kids are being affected more in their bodies and their daily lives by the South Bronx subculture than by high-gloss films like *Gremlins* or *Indiana Jones and the Temple of Doom*. Even through all this static, life can speak to life.

Of course, break dancing inevitably gets hyped, and hence devalued, by the entertainment industry, the way Elvis Presley ended up singing "Viva Las Vegas" as that town's most glamorous headliner. He went from being the numinous son of a living ground to being the charismatic product of a media empire—the paradigm of media's power to transform the transformers. The town veritably glows in the dark with the strength of media's mystique.

We do not yet know what life *is* in a media environment. We have 55 not yet evolved a contemporary culture that can supply the definition—or rather, supply the constellation of concepts in which that definition would live and grow. These seem such simple statements, but they are at the crux of the American dilemma now. An important aspect of this dilemma is that we've barely begun a body of thought and art which is focused on what is really *alive* in the ground of a media-saturated daily life. For culture always proceeds from two poles: one is the people of the land and the street; the other is the thinker. You see this most starkly in revolutions: the ground swell on the one hand, the thinker (the Jefferson, for instance) on the other. Or religiously, the ground swell of belief that is articulated by a Michelangelo or a Dante. The two poles can exist without each other but they cannot be effective without each other.

Unless a body of thought connects with a living ground, there is no possibility that this era will discover itself within its cacophony and create, one day, a post-A.D. culture. It is ours to attempt the thought and seek the ground—for all of us exist between those poles. We are not only dying. We are living. And we are struggling to share our lives, which is all, finally, that "culture" means.

❖ Focused Freewriting   Consider as possible focal points the shifting realities in the age of media, the effects of television on people's sense of well-being, or one of the topics you've identified in your journal.

❖ Guided Responses

1. Why do you think Ventura chooses Las Vegas as the focal point of his discussion in the first half of the essay? How does the history of Las Vegas contribute to his theories about television? What role does the desert play in his argument? What does Las Vegas mean to most Americans?

2. In paragraph 16 Ventura makes a distinction between nostalgia and memory, calling memory "specific" and nostalgia "vague." Based on your reading of the selection, how do you interpret this distinction? How do the media exploit our nostalgic desires?

3. When Dave Johnson says, "Media is the history that forgives," Ventura thinks about the statement through "miles and miles of desert" (paras. 27–28). How does Ventura interpret the statement? How do you respond to his interpretation, particularly his dismissal of profit as *"not* the motive" for media producers (para. 32)?

4. Ventura calls our media culture "schizoid, with two messages simultaneously being broadcast: 'It's all right. We're dying. It's all right. We're all dying'" (para. 43). On what basis does he make this judgment? Given your own exposure to media, how would you respond to his conclusions about their message?

❖ Shared Responses   In your journal, analyze some of the television shows you currently watch, including news and "reality-based" programs. What kind of message do these programs send? What are the similarities and differences between the types of programs? How do they reflect and affect our culture? As you discuss your responses in small groups, try to try to reach a consensus on the impact of television on our culture. If you can't agree on a single response, highlight the primary differences between responses.

Growing Up in
Greaseball Mecca

BEN HAMPER

BEN HAMPER *assumed the pseudonym "Rivethead" when he began writing a column for an alternative newspaper, the* Flint Voice. *He worked on the assembly line at General Motors for over ten years, during which time he earned national acclaim as a writer. In this selection, taken from his memoir* Rivethead: Tales from the Assembly Line *(1991), Hamper paints a dismal picture of life in working-class America. His humor serves only to underscore the bleak existence of the "shoprats" and their families, for whom reality means wavering between mindless jobs and the unemployment line.*

Before reading the selection, describe in your journal your early family life. What hopes did you have for a successful future? How supportive were your family and your school in preparing you for adult life?

As you make notes on your reading, you may want to focus on Hamper's characterizations of the people around him, his humor, or the images of hopelessness that abound in the selection.

FLINT, MICHIGAN. THE VEHICLE CITY. GREASEBALL MECCA. The birthplace of thud-rockers Grand Funk Railroad, game show geek Bob Eubanks and a hobby shop called General Motors. A town where every infant twirls a set of channel locks in place of a rattle. A town whose collective bowling average is four times higher than the IQ of its inhabitants. A town that genuflects in front of used-car lots and scratches its butt with the jagged peaks of the automotive sales chart. A town where having a car up on blocks anywhere on your property bestows upon you a privileged sense of royalty. Beer Belly Valhalla. Cog Butcher of the world. Gravy on your french fries.

Flint, Michigan. Detroit as seen backwards through a telescope. The callus on the palm of the state shaped like a welder's mitt. A town where 66.5 percent of the working citizenship are in some way, shape or form linked to the shit-encrusted underbelly of a French buggy racer named Chevrolet and a floppy-eared Scotchman named Buick. A town where 23.5 percent of the population pimp everything from Elvis on velvet to horse tranquilizers to Halo Burgers to NRA bumper stickers. A town where the remaining 10 percent sit back and watch it all go by—sellin' their blood, rollin' convenience stores, puffin' no-brand cigarettes while cursin' their wives and kids and neighbors and the flies sneakin' through the screens and the piss-warm quarts of Red White & Blue and the Skylark parked out back with the busted tranny.

"Just like half the other morons . . . " my old man had warned. He was certainly more wise than most of my friends' fathers. They questioned nothing. They accepted their birthrights and strode sheep-like into the vast head-fuck of the factories. My old man was at least honest with himself. He realized a ball vise when he saw one. It didn't matter that he was a five-star drunk with the cumulative ambition of an eggplant. The old man held on to a chunk of his soul, concealing it from the fangs of lamebrain labor, accomplishing a small piece of everything while doing absolutely nothing. In Flint, Michigan, that was an achievement in itself.

My old man was determined to make sure that I, Bernard Egan Hamper III, his pipsqueak namesake, the eldest of his five sons, wouldn't follow the feed line into General Motors. When I was at St. Luke's, he tore at my ass relentlessly. When it came time for high school, he often threatened to ship me off to a military academy. My mom furiously opposed this solution. Her suggestion was that I enter the seminary. Fortunately, both of these horrid plots were laid to ruin due to lack of funds.

I entered St. Michael's High School with a more determined out-   5
look on things. I was pretty sure that I didn't want any part of General Motors and I didn't profess any great yearning to become a world-class drunkard. Beyond that, I knew very little. Mike and I still clung loosely to our private visions of becoming hotshot radio personalities. We had an ever-escalating fondness for the female breast and in order to collect heavily on the mammo-meter we had to achieve some kind of cool notoriety. We figured just about any radio hack worth his beans was bound to be holdin' fort with big-busted Donovan mamas and bra-free Beatle booty.

Spurred on by parental badgering and fueled with the heady octane of boobs galore, I pulled off an amazing stunt my freshman year at St. Mike's. I wound up making the honor roll! Apparently, my leftover cronies from St. Luke's found this development hard to grasp, for on the list saluting the honor students that hung on the bulletin board in the school lobby someone had scrawled the words "How?" and "Why?" next to my name. I didn't have a ready answer. What could I say? "I owe it all to the persistence of my drunken pa and a hormonal yen for watermelon teats?"

Before my sophomore year, they closed down St. Michael's. Shit, I thought, right when I was gatherin' a groove. The diocese decided that the small parish high schools were a thing of the past. In other words, resorting to the norms of Catholicism, they had found a more lucrative method of bleeding coin out of the flock.

Ground was broken on the northern border of Flint and construction began on this enormous structure that would consolidate all of the area's Catholic high schools. Say good night to St. Mike, St. Matt, St. Agnes, St. John, St. Mary and to those southside swine, Holy Redeemer. What was wrong with them Redeemers, anyway? Couldn't they find a saint to lift a name from? Seein' as how they annually mopped ass on the football field, possibly St. Joseph of Namath would have been appropriate.

The braintrust at the diocese ran into the same predicament when they settled on the name for the new high school we were all about to attend. They called it Luke Powers High. Hmmm, Luke Powers. I must have skipped right past that guy during Bible Study. Surely, there had to be more saints out there without earthly monuments celebrating their good deeds. Luke Powers? It sounded like a cowpoke from an old episode of *The Big Valley* or the name of some pockmarked pump jockey down at the corner Sunoco.

During the tenth grade of Powers, I was able to bluff my way onto   10
the honor roll once more. It wasn't so much attributable to any sense of goal-setting on my part, I just had nothing else to do but hit the books as I baby-sat my younger brothers and sisters night in and night out. My mother was now working the second shift at McLaren Hospital. My father was quickly becoming an endangered species at home. That left me in charge of six kids to cook for, delegate chores for, clean crappy diapers for, officiate rumbles for and to safely stow in bed and bunk. When all grew peaceful, I would flip open the books.

Powers was significantly different from the small parish schools I had attended at St. Luke's and St. Mike's. My classmates weren't middle-class kids. These were not the sons and daughters of the assembly line. Most of the new blood at Powers hailed from wealthy families. Some of them weren't even Catholic. Their parents just deposited them here as a means of avoiding the turbulence of schoolin' down with white trash and blackies and hoodlums and druggies and things that go bump near the water fountain. None of them possessed any shoprat heritage nor were any likely to spend a lifetime affixing trunk lids to the ass ends of Buicks.

Things were definitely on the upswing my sophomore year at Powers. My honor roll status delighted my mother and seemed to soothe my father's doubts regarding my factory-bent tendencies. I was even beginning to think I might defy my shoprat heritage after all. I became interested in poetry and spent long hours up in my bedroom concocting silly little love poems that combined all the worst elements of Rod McKuen and my hippie mentor, Richard Brautigan. I actually penned my own large collection of poems called "Intestines of a Balloon." Ouch.

I did discover that the poetry, as awkward and schmaltzy as it was, drew great favor from the girls of my sophomore class. Suddenly I was no longer just another wiseacre with a pesky libido and murky future. My lovelorn poetics won them over. I grabbed an honorable mention for one of my poems in a contest that ran in the *Detroit News*. Presto, I was like some hippie-dippie Alan Alda twangin' heartstrings in the sap-happy Love Generation. Someone to be trusted. An alternative to the sex-starved jockos and wily potheads and the piranha greasers in their clunky Dingo boots. Everyone had an angle and since I didn't have any money or any terrific athletic prowess and I didn't dance very well, I relied on the muse of the poet to garner whatever female appreciation I could drum up.

We had an English teacher named Miss Kane who took a particular shine to my budding enshrinement as the poet laureate of Powers High. She often mimeographed my poems and passed them around her Creative Writing class. She'd read some of my poems in front of the class and the girls all smiled brightly in my direction. I smiled back, thankful for their innocence and terrible judgment of talent. Meanwhile, the guys all slouched down in their desks, half pissed that they hadn't stumbled onto such an ingenious scam.

By my junior year in high school, strange new vices had risen 15 from out of the murk to pull me under. I exchanged my textbooks for Mothers of Invention albums. I grew my hair down to my ass and attended classes on an infrequent basis. I exchanged my loner personage to join up with a small band of brooding hooligans. I spent most of my time swallowing or inhaling every type of illegal substance they would pass me. Needless to say, my two-year run on the honor roll dissolved in one glorious heap of incompletes and lazy failures.

I was feeling more and more pressure trying to hold the family together while my mother worked. The occasional run-ins with my old man were tense. He'd rip into my ass about the length of my hair, my hoodlum pals, my grades, my wardrobe, anything he could find. I would stand there in silent rage. All I could really dwell on was kicking his drunken ass. My fists would ball up and then recoil.

In the end, I was just too chickenshit to try the old man. I turned to the bonds I had made with my new friends. We ate acid at every opportunity. I sat in the back of the classroom throughout my junior year stoned to the gills on orange barrel mescaline or windowpane acid. Sometimes I laughed so hard at the proceedings taking place around me that the teacher would ask me if I had a problem. Outside of the fact that I hardly knew my name and everything around me had this incredible purple glow, there was no problem at all. Acid replaced lots of things. Most importantly, it took down reality.

By the time my senior year rolled around, things were beginning to get jumbled. My father had mysteriously slid away one autumn night and the only information any of us had was that he was shacking up with some bar floozie somewhere in southern Florida. He'd taken off without so much as an adios or a fresh change of skivvies. This desertion again thrust me into the role of surrogate dad while my mother toiled long hours on the hospital night shift.

My devotion to school matters became a complete joke. I rarely attended class, preferring to hang out at a friend's dreary apartment with a bunch of fellow lunks who were most certainly headed for jail, the morgue or General Motors. Our scholastic majors ranged from chemical abuse to hashish peddling. My long-standing reign as love poem ambassador dissolved into a mire of radical blatherings. Quaaludes became the new curse on campus and I gobbled my fair share, often falling asleep in various stairwells and auditorium catwalks.

Having arrived this far on the academic route, it was time for all students to start funneling a vision career-wise. They had guidance counselors who summoned you into their offices attempting to find what kind of mold fit you best. Doctor? Attorney? Accountant? Shoprat? No, no, no—they never mentioned shoprat. Nor did they mention serial killer, pimp, poet, ambulance driver or disc jockey. *20*

I went to the guidance counselor's office and stared at the floor. He rummaged through a thick file cabinet bursting with worthless, lunatic occupational data while I sat there and daydreamed about Darlene Ranzik's breasts. The lime green halter was the best. You got a good sideview of the complete works. They were as round as cantaloupes and easily twice the size. Some lucky fucker was gonna tie his nuts around a wedding band and be nursin' on those miracles for the rest of his life. It wouldn't be me. I didn't have a game plan in order.

The guidance counselor pulled file after file. Time dragged on and on and I sensed that he was growing increasingly edgy with my indifference to latching on to a viable vocational goal. I felt sorta sorry for him. There just wasn't anything in there for me. This seemed to upset him far more than it did me.

I began writing love poems again. For the first time, I had a specific reason why. Her name was Joanie, a hippie maiden with beautiful red hair. We had attended Catholic school together ever since St. Luke's though we had never really spoken. We were attracted to each other, but shy. The arrival of drugs seemed to knock that barrier down. Before long, we were inseparable—skipping classes, making love in my station wagon, dropping LSD at football games, trompin' off to every rotten rock 'n' roll concert within the Saginaw valley.

I enjoyed spending time at Joanie's house. It was like a replica of what I wished mine could be. Her father was a wonderful man—always fair, always friendly, always available. Not an easy trick considering Joanie's folks had eleven kids. You would think *her* father would be the ragin' alcoholic nomad. Not so. They all got along just fine and it seemed I would concoct any excuse just to visit there.

By the middle of my senior year things at home were at least 25 beginning to settle into a tolerable routine. With the old man gone there were no more early morning tantrums. No more stolen paperboy loot. No more idiot IOU's wadded up in sock drawers where our allowance money used to hide. No more intimidation and lies and confusion and guilt and surrenders to snockered lunacy. Joanie would come by and together we would cook dinner for the troop. We'd play with my brothers and sisters and once they were put in bed, we'd lie down and make love in the middle of the living room floor. It all seemed to be healing over. Even my stinkin' love poems were improving vastly.

Nothing lasts forever. One Friday night in March, while we were all huddled around wrestling and watching *The Brady Bunch,* my old man reappeared. He had been AWOL for a total of six months. And, as always, he acted like he had merely stepped out to buy a loaf of bread or get a haircut. He was wearing this ugly Hawaiian shirt and reeked of alcohol. "Hi, son," he said. I didn't respond. Within ten minutes, he was snorin' like a bulldozer on the sofa.

The old man was back and as full of shit as ever. The flooze down in Florida had tired of his mooching and sent him packing northward. Everything returned to its horrible norm. What little faith I had in anything soon evaporated. I retreated deep into my own little universe of chemicals and inhalants. The higher I got, the less it hurt. This arrangement didn't preclude me from making a major ass out of myself on a regular basis.

There was the time I flipped out in Journalism class. My job was to provide headlines for all the articles that went into the school newspaper. My fellow classmates started clamoring around me for witty scrawls to peg above their precious columns. I was totally gone. I politely told everyone to fuck off and ran outside to my car. I started it up, drove ten feet and hopped back out. It felt as though I was driving on the rims. I circled the car several times, kicking each tire. They appeared just fine. I got back in the car and goosed it. Unfortunately, during my little stoned escapade to check the tires out, I hadn't noticed that the entire Powers High marching band had paraded out to the parking lot. Some kid with a tuba went rollin' across my hood. The band instructor started screaming. I sped away shivering badly and breathin' funny.

Then there was the time I got caught rolling a mammoth joint on a desk in the school library. Miss Kane, the same teacher who thought so highly of my weepy poems, marched me right to the principal's office. The evidence was presented, a small confab was held and I was immediately expelled. My mother came up to the school to plead for my reinstatement. The principal refused. It killed me to see my mother reduced to begging. I got the principal off to the side and started talking deal. I told him if he would allow me back in school, I would become his own private narc. The idea caught his fancy. Of course what he didn't know was that I was lyin' through my teeth. We shook hands and I was reinstated. As the months went by, I became a very unpopular guy with the principal. Each time he shook me down for information, I turned dumber than a tree stump. He'd been scammed. I rolled my joints in the john from then on.

By graduation time, my old man had once again taken flight to Florida to shack up with who-knows-who. Good riddance, the family concurred. My mother finally had had her fill of the bastard and started divorce proceedings. It was only after the old man had left that my mother discovered she was going to be giving birth to the eighth addition to our clan. A child that my father would never return to see.

There must have been something in the frosty Michigan air that winter that fueled the reproduction cycle. The Catholic-as-rabbit theory was suddenly twirling amuck. Joanie called me over to her place one evening to inform me that she too was bloomin' with child. Joanie's due date was only a couple of weeks from my mother's.

Since Joanie already had accumulated enough credits to graduate, the school let her have her diploma early. She was just beginning to show and there was no way in hell they were gonna allow her to waltz the hallways in her preggy state. The nuns would have spewed pea soup and banged to their knees.

Joanie stayed home while I finished up my senior year. One day I was summoned to the counselor's office. Terrific, I thought, maybe the guy had found a job for me in that fat file cabinet of his. With a baby due, I had a feeling I might need one.

This was not the case. The counselor instructed me to have a seat and as I sat down I could gather that the news was not good. He told me that he had been poring over my transcript and found that I was several credits short of the required number necessary to graduate. All those days skipping class and chucking textbooks had finally caught up to me. The counselor said he would have to see what would need to be done and talk it over with the principal. He said he would let me know in a couple of days.

The counselor never did call me back to his office. All I can   35
assume is that when my name was mentioned, the principal must have told him to rig the paperwork so everything fell into place. He had seen enough of my act. There was no way he was going to flunk me and have me back for another fun-filled year. Here's your fuckin' diploma, get scarce and may the Lord be with you always!

After graduation, I hurriedly planned for the unknown. First up came marriage. Since we'd both been reared as God-fearin' Catholics, the inevitable solution to this teen pregnancy mishap was immediate matrimony. Abortion and adoption were sordid eight-letter words that existed only in made-for-TV movies starring Kay Lenz or Susan Dey. We tied the knot at Sacred Heart Church. My best man was some guy we found cleanin' the pews.

My uncle got me a job painting apartments for a large rental complex. After our marriage, Joanie and I moved into one of the apartments. In August, Joanie had our child, a beautiful little girl with bright red hair we named Sonya. We were poor but happy in our sudden little universe. Back at home, my brother Bob filled my role as teen nanny. Bob was much stronger than I. It worked well.

I enjoyed painting apartments. There were no human beings to contend with and everyone at the complex just left me alone. The closest thing I had to a boss was this senile old man who was the maintenance manager. Once upon a time, he had been a big-league attorney for Ford Motors. Then he had a nervous breakdown and began plowing the bottle. His son-in-law owned the company and the old man I were just another pair of his uninspired lackeys.

After months of practice, I got a routine down to where I could blaze my way through a unit in the morning, be finished by lunch and spend the rest of the afternoon reading paperbacks and listening to the oldies station on my latex-splattered transistor radio. I could have easily painted two units per day but, with the way these pricks were payin' me, I felt it only justified to give them the lowest accountable output for their lousy three bucks an hour. Besides, where several of the other maintenance workers were receiving their apartments rent-free, I was being charged the full shot just like any other tenant. What it boiled down to was that I would have to turn over half of my earnings right back to the company just to keep a roof over my family's head. They weren't gettin' anything extra out of me.

I met another guy who worked at the apartments who was in the   40
identical situation I was. His name was Glen and he was also newly married with a new baby and was living it dime-to-dime like Joanie

and I were. They lived in the apartment building next to ours and we all became accomplished at dodging the rut of constant poverty.

Glen and I received our paychecks on Mondays and we'd skim seven or eight bucks off the top of our measly pay and buy a week's worth of this piss-water beer called Columbia. The local grocer sold this crap for a dollar a six-pack, a real bargain for fun-starved minimum wagers like Glen and myself. Almost every night we held court at Glen and Barb's, swigging down this awful-tastin' beer while Barb cued up scratchy Abba singles and wonderful Lou Christie albums salvaged from the junk bins of the nearby Goodwill. We laughed and danced and got very intoxicated.

After the wives dropped off, Glen and I stayed up late talking. He was hell-bent on landing a job at General Motors and stressed all the benefits of working for the hometown team. I sucked on my lousy Columbia and shook my head.

"Have you ever noticed the looks on the faces of those bastards when they get home from work?" I asked Glen. "Fuck the money, I don't need that monster gaze."

"Well, what the hell are you gonna do when you grow up?" Glen laughed.

"I don't know," I said. And I truly didn't.　　45

"And you ride me for wantin' to get into the shop! Shit, you need another beer."

It was out of our hands anyway. There was a recession going on and the gates to Greaseball Mecca were temporarily padlocked. Job seekers were forced to follow the detour signs to McDonald's or Arby's or Maplebrook Village Apartments, at least until the Arabs let go of our balls and the market began to chug again.

I, for one, could wait.

❖ **Focused Freewriting**　Consider as possible focal points the impact of Hamper's family life on his behavior, his portrayal of the church and school, or one of the topics you've identified in your journal.

❖ **Guided Responses**

1. When the girls in his class respond positively to his poetry, the young Ben is "thankful for their innocence and terrible judgment of talent" (para. 14). What does this comment tell you about the boy's self image? Whom does he seem to hold responsible for his behavior? Refer to specific passages in the selection that support your interpretation.

2. Hamper's account is riddled with profanity and vulgar language. Find one passage with a good deal of such language and rewrite it in more commonly acceptable prose. How does your revision change the impact of the passage? Why do you think Hamper resorts to such language? What would he have lost—or gained—by eliminating its use?

3. Hamper says of his drug use in paragraph 17, "Acid replaced lots of things. Most importantly, it took down reality." Do you read this as an attempt to justify drug abuse? Does Hamper's description of his behavior suggest self-justification? Explain your responses.

4. When he's painting apartments, Hamper develops a routine whereby he finishes painting in the morning and reads for the remainder of the day. His rationale is based on the fact that he considers his compensation inadequate: " . . . I felt it only justified to give them the lowest accountable output for their lousy three bucks an hour. . . . They weren't gettin' anything extra out of me" (para. 39). Based on the young Ben's experiences with authority in general, how justified does his attitude seem to be? How would his boss view it? Whose position would you support, and why?

❖ Shared Responses   In your journal, comment on the contrast between Hamper's account and the standard concept of the American dream (with hard work, anyone can reach the top). How realistic is this dream to people in his situation? How responsible are people for their own success? To what extent do other forces influence success? In your group, highlight the differences between the perceptions of students from various backgrounds.

June 1989

LORENE CARY

LORENE CARY *received her M.A. from the University of Pennsylvania in 1978, after which she studied in England and worked for* Time *and* TV Guide. *She has both taught and served on the Board of Trustees of St. Paul's, her alma mater.* Black Ice *(1991), the memoir from which this selection is taken, recounts the story of her stay at St. Paul's, an exclusive—and, until the early 1970s, white male—boarding school. In this prologue to the book, Cary looks at St. Paul's from the perspective of a successful trustee, observing that things haven't changed a great deal in the fifteen years since she graduated.*

Before reading the selection, write in your journal about your own sense of belonging to a community. Think of a time when you felt like an outsider in a community that you should have felt part of. What made you feel left out? How did that feeling affect your behavior?

As you make notes on your reading, you may want to focus on Cary's comparisons between her own experience and that of later students, the pride she takes in her students' accomplishments, or her own confusion about how she fit into St. Paul's.

I COULD SEE THEM FROM THE DAIS: families and friends sitting on the risers, young students spilling out onto the grass, black-robed faculty members standing in front of their seats—all watching for the first graduates to begin their march down the grassy aisle between the folding chairs on the green. Someone let out a whoop as they appeared, the girls in their white dresses and the boys in their jackets and ties.

Fifteen years before I had walked down the same aisle as a graduate, and nine years later as a teacher. Now I was ending my term as a trustee.

I watched the black and Hispanic students, "my kids," come to the podium to receive their diplomas and awards from the Rector.

One young man named Harlem winked at me as he passed. His shoulders still rocked a little, just a little, like the shoulders of black men in cities, and he held himself up on the balls of his feet like the ballet dancer he had become while at St. Paul's School. I remembered him as a Fourth Former, his head cocked to one side, asking, "I'd like to know: would you send *your* daughter to St. Paul's?"

The other students had laughed in that way that teenagers do when an adult is forced to reveal herself. But we also laughed together as black people alone, safe for the moment within the group, the collective tensions and harmonic humor of it, relieved for an hour or so from our headlong rush toward individual achievement.

"My daughter will have to decide that for herself," I said. "Don't   5
you roll your eyes. I mean it. My parents did not make me come here. I was bound and determined. They *let* me, and it was not an easy thing to do.

"It won't be the same for my daughter. Neither my parents nor I really knew what we were getting into. Once you've made the journey, you can't pretend it didn't happen, that everything's like it was before except now you play lacrosse."

I had pretended, myself, many of us had. I had acknowledged my academic debt to the boarding school I'd attended on scholarship for two years. But I would not admit how profoundly St. Paul's had shaken me, or how damaged and fraudulent and traitorous I felt when I graduated. In fact, I pretended for so long that by the time I was twenty-six years old, I was able to convince myself that going back to school to teach would be the career equivalent of summering with distant, rich relatives.

Instead, I found my own adolescence, in all its hormonal excess, waiting for me at St. Paul's: old rage and fear, ambition, self-consciousness, love, curiosity, energy, hate, envy, compulsion, fatigue. I saw my adolescence in my students, and I felt it burbling inside me, grown powerful by long silence. I lost control of it one night when a black boy came to me nearly weeping because a group of white friends had told a racist joke in his presence. He hated himself, he said, because he hadn't known how to react. "It was like I couldn't move. I couldn't *do* anything," he said.

I too had known that terrible paralysis, and when the boy left, I wept with remembering. I could no longer forget, not with Westminster chimes ringing out the quarter hours, the piney mist that rolled off the pond in the morning, and the squeaking boards under our feet as we crossed Upper Common Room to the dining hall. I remembered the self-loathing, made worse by a poised bravado, as close as my own skin, that I wore over it. I remembered duty and obligation—to my family, to the memory of dead relatives, to my people. And I remembered confusion: was it true that these teachers expected less of me than of my white peers? Or had I mistaken kindness for conde-scension? Were we black kids a social experiment? If we failed (or succeeded too well) would they call us off? Were we imported to help round out the white kids' education? Did it make any difference if we were?

In the aftermath of Black Is Beautiful, I began to feel black and 10 blue, big and black, black and ugly. Had they done that to me? Had somebody else? Had I let them? Could I stop the feelings? Or hide them?

I knew that I was to emerge from St. Paul's School changed, but I did not know how, and I did not trust my white teachers and guardi-ans to guide me. What would this education do to me? And what was I to do with it?

A couple years after I taught at St. Paul's, I was asked to serve as a trustee. During my term, I visited the school for board meetings, and I talked with the students. I could feel their attention one fall evening when I told them to try to think of St. Paul's as their school, too, not as a white place where they were trespassing. The next fall a boy told me: "I *had* been thinking of it as their school. It was like I had forgotten that this is my life."

Two years later that boy's formmates elected him class president. At his graduation, Eric smiled broadly at me as he walked to the podium to receive the President's Medal. So did a girl, an excellent and feisty writer, who was awarded the Rector's Medal. I wondered if they knew, or if they would learn, that just as St. Paul's was theirs, because they had attended the school and contributed to it, so, too, was American life and culture theirs, because they were black people in America.

Sitting on the dais, I recalled how wary I'd been of John Walker, the first black teacher at St. Paul's, its first black trustee, and the first black Bishop of the Washington, D.C. diocese of the Episcopal Church. I remembered watching him walk with other board members and trying to deduce from his gait and the way he inclined his head whether the small man with the tiny eyes was traitor or advocate.

He was still on the board during my tenure, a quiet-spoken man 15 who affected people deeply by his presence. John Walker spoke wisely and from experience, but more than that, he emanated both judgment and compassion. I saw him affect my colleagues. I felt him. He filled me with hope for my own racial and spiritual healing, and courage to look back. (John Walker died in September, 1989.)

I began writing about St. Paul's School when I stopped thinking of my prep-school experience as an aberration from the common run of black life in America. The isolation I'd felt was an illusion, and it can take time and, as they say at St. Paul's, "the love and labor of many," to get free of illusions. The narratives that helped me, that kept me company, along with the living, breathing people in my life, were those that talked honestly about growing up black in America. They burst into my silence, and in my head, they shouted and chattered and whispered and sang together. I am writing this book to become part of that unruly conversation, and to bring my experience back to the community of minds that made it possible.

"You must really love the school to be on the board." The students wanted to know each time I visited. Each time I answered yes.

"Did you like it when you were here?"

I made a sour face. They looked relieved.

❖ Focused Freewriting   Consider as possible focal points the responsibility of the African-American students to make St. Paul's their own, the problems of identity faced by the students, the similarities between the students' experiences and Cary's own, or one of the topics you've identified in your journal.

❖ Guided Responses

1. As she ponders her experience at St. Paul's, Cary poses a number of rapid-fire, essentially unanswered questions (paras. 9–11). Why do you think she chooses this technique? What is the impact of the questions on you? How would the essay be affected if she hadn't used questions?

2. Describing her return to St. Paul's to teach, Cary says, "I found my own adolescence, in all its hormonal excess, waiting for me" (para. 8). What does this statement tell us about her development in the nine years since she'd graduated? Would she have come to the same realizations highlighted in the essay if she had never returned to St. Paul's? Explain your response.

3. What is the purpose, in your view, of the John Walker story (paras. 14–15)? How does this story illustrate the points Cary makes about her own and her students' experiences at St. Paul's?

4. What is the "conversation" to which Cary refers in paragraph 16? How did the "narratives . . . that talked honestly about growing up black in America" help her? How will her narrative help others?

❖ Shared Responses   In your journal explore some of the issues that arise when students of color enter a predominantly white school: What can be done to help these students think of the school "not as a white place where they [are] trespassing" (para. 12)? What can the students themselves do to eliminate this feeling? As you discuss your responses in small groups, try to synthesize them into an outline for a program to assist minority students in predominantly white schools.

The Children of Affluence

ROBERT COLES

ROBERT COLES, *child psychiatrist, educator, and author of numerous books, was educated at Harvard and Columbia universities. Most of his publications focus on children; among the most notable are* The Spiritual Life of Children *(1990),* Uprooted Children: The Early Lives of Migrant Farmers *(1970), and* Children of Crisis: A Study of Courage and Fear *(1967). In this selection Coles investigates a world little known to most Americans. First published in* The Atlantic *the essay analyzes the various forces operating in the lives of wealthy children—and what the author discovers is sometimes surprising.*

Before reading the selection, list in your journal the characteristics you assume to be typical of affluent children. What are their values? Are they spoiled? How do they look upon their wealth? upon those less wealthy? When you read the selection, compare your assumptions with Coles's findings.

As you make notes on your reading, you may want to focus on the children's choices, their confidence, and their self-images.

Comfortable, Comfortable Places

DRAMATIC AND SECLUDED; old, historic, and architecturally interesting; large and with good grounds; private and palatial; beautifully restored; big, interesting, high up, and with an uninterrupted view; so the real-estate descriptions go. In the cities, it is a town house or luxury apartment on Nob Hill, Beacon Hill, the Near North Side, the Garden District. Outside the major cities, the house is in a town, township, village, station, even crossing, anything to make it clear that one does not live simply "in the suburbs," that one is outside or away, *well* outside or *well* away, as it is so often put. The houses vary: imitation English castles; French provincial; nineteenth-century American; contemporary one-levels in the tradition of Gropius or Neutra. Sometimes the setting is formal, sometimes it is a farm—ani-

mals, rail fences, pastureland, a barn, maybe a shed or two, a flower
garden, and more recently, a few rows of vegetables. Sometimes there
is a swimming pool, a tennis court, a greenhouse. Sometimes the
house stands on a hill, affords a view for miles around. Sometimes
trees stand close guard; and beyond them, thick brush and more trees,
a jumble of them: no view, but complete privacy. Sometimes there is a
paved road leading from a street up to the house's entrance. Sometimes the road is a dusty path, or a trail—the casual countrified scene,
prized and jealously guarded.

The trees matter; so do the grass and the shrubbery. These are not
houses in a row, with patches of new grass, fledgling trees, and a bush
or two. These are homes surrounded by spacious lawns and announced by tall, sturdy trees. Hedges are common, carefully arranged. And often there is a brook running through the land.

In Texas or in New Mexico, the architecture of the houses changes,
as do to a degree the flora and fauna. Now the homes are ranches, big
sprawling ones, many rooms in many wings. Acres and acres of land
are given over to horse trails, gardens, large swimming pools, even
airplane strips for private planes. In New Mexico the large adobe
houses boast nearby cacti, corrals, and so often, stunning views:
across a valley, over toward mountains miles and miles away.

In such settings are a small group of America's children raised.
I have for years visited the homes of boys and girls whose parents
are well-to-do indeed, and sometimes quite wealthy. They are parents whose decisions have affected, in one way or another, the
working-class and poor families I have worked with—growers,
mine owners, other prominent businessmen, lawyers, and bankers,
or real estate operators. I have wanted to know how their children
grew up, how their children see themselves—and see their much
more humble age-mates, with whom they share American citizenship,
if nothing else. Put differently, I have wanted to know how the ex-
tremes of class, poverty and wealth variously affect the psychological
and moral development of a particular nation's and particular century's children.

"Comfortable, comfortable places" was the way one girl de-   5
scribed her three homes: an enormous duplex apartment in Chicago,
a ski lodge in Aspen, and a lovely old New England clapboard home
by the ocean toward the end of Cape Cod. She was not bragging; she
knew a pleasurable, cozy, even luxurious life when she saw one (*had*
one), and was at ease describing its many, consistent comforts. She
happened to be sitting on a large sofa as she offered her observation.
She touched a nearby pillow, also rather large, then moved it a bit
closer to herself. In a rather uncharacteristic burst of proprietary as-

sertiveness, the girl said: "I'd like to keep this pillow for my own house, when I'm grown up."

Children like her have a lot to look after and, sometimes, feel attached to. At the same time, they may often be overwhelmed with toys, gadgets, presents. These are children who have to contend with, as well as to enjoy, enormous couches, pillows virtually as big as chairs, rugs that were meant to be in the palaces of the Middle East, dining room tables bigger than the rooms many American children share with brothers or sisters. Always they are aware of the importance and fragility of objects: a vase, a dish, a tray, a painting or lithograph or pencil sketch, a lamp. How much of that world can the child even comprehend? Sometimes, in a brave attempt to bring everything under control, a young child will enumerate (for the benefit of a teacher or a friend) all that is his or hers, the background against which a life is carried on.

Finally, the child may grow weary, abandon the spoken catalogue and think of one part of his or her life that means *everything:* a snake that can reliably be seen in a certain stretch of mixed grass and shrubbery along the driveway; a pair of pheasants who come every morning to the lawn and appear remarkably relaxed as they find food; a dog or a cat or a pony or a pet bird; a friend who lives near a summer home, or the son or daughter of a Caribbean cook or maid; a visit to an amusement park—a visit which, for the child, meant more than dozens of toys, some virtually untouched since they arrived; or a country remembered above all others—Ireland or England, France or Switzerland.

These are children who learn to live with *choices:* more clothes, a wider range of food, a greater number of games, toys, hobbies, than other boys and girls may ever be able to imagine for themselves. They learn also to assume instruction—not only at school, but at home—for tennis, swimming, dancing, horseback riding. And they learn, often enough, to feel competent at those sports, in control of themselves while playing them, and not least, able to move smoothly from one to the other rather than driven to excel. It is as if the various outdoor sports are like suits of clothing, to be put on, enjoyed, then casually slipped off.

Something else many of these children learn: the newspapers, the radio, the television offer news not merely about "others" but about neighbors, friends, acquaintances of one's parents—or about issues one's parents take seriously, talk about, sometimes get quite involved in. These are children who have discovered that the "news" may well be affected, if not crucially molded, by their parents as individuals or as members of a particular segment of society. Similarly, parental authority wielded in the world is matched by parental authority exerted at home. Servants are called in, are given instructions or, indeed, even replaced summarily. In a way those servants—by whatever name or names they get called—are for these American children a microcosm of the larger world, as they will experience it. They are the people who provide convenience and comfort. They are the people who, by and large, aim to please. Not all of them "live in"; there are cleaning women, delivery people, caretakers, town inspectors, plumbers and carpenters and electricians, carriers of telegrams, of flowers, of special delivery letters. Far more than their parents, the children observe the coming and going, the back-door bustle, the front-door activity of the "staff."

It is a complicated world, a world that others watch with envy 10 and with curiosity, with awe, anger, bitterness, resentment. It is a world, rather often, of action, of talk believed by the talkers to have meaning and importance, of schedules or timetables. It is a world in motion—yet, at times, one utterly still: a child in a garden, surrounded by the silence acres of lawn or woods can provide. It is a world of excitement and achievement. It is an intensely private world that can suddenly become vulnerable to the notice of others. It is, obviously, a world of money and power—a twentieth-century American version of both. It is also a world in which children grow up, come to terms with their ample surroundings, take to them gladly, deal with them anxiously, and show themselves boys and girls who have their own special circumstances to master—a particular way of life to understand and become a part of.

Entitled

It won't do to talk of *the* affluent in America. It won't do to say that in our upper-middle-class suburbs, or among our wealthy, one observes clear-cut, consistent psychological or cultural characteristics. Even in relatively homogeneous places there are substantial differences in homelife, in values taught, hobbies encouraged, beliefs advocated or sometimes virtually instilled.

But it is the obligation of a psychological observer like me, who wants to know how children make sense of a certain kind of life, to document as faithfully as possible the way a common heritage of money and power affects the assumptions of particular boys and girls. Each child, of course, is also influenced by certain social, racial, cultural, or religious traditions, or thoroughly idiosyncratic ones—a given family's tastes, sentiments, ideals. And yet the sheer fact of class affiliation has enormous power over a child's inner life.

I started my work with affluent children by seeing troubled boys and girls; they were the ones I saw as a child psychiatrist *before* I began my years of "field work" in the South, then Appalachia, then the North, then the West. There are only a few hundred child psychiatrists in the United States, and rather often their time is claimed by those who have money. After a while, if one is not careful, the well-off and the rich come to be seen exclusively through a clinician's eye: homes full of bitterness, deceit, snobbishness, neuroses, psychoses; homes with young children in mental pain, and with older children, adolescents and young adults, who use drugs, drink, run away, rebel constantly and disruptively, become truants, delinquents, addicts, alcoholics, become compulsively promiscuous, go crazy, go wild, go to ruin.

We blame the alcoholism, insanity, meanness, apathy, drug usage, despondency, and, not least, cruelty to children we see or are told exists in the ghetto or among the rural poor upon various "socioeconomic factors." All of those signs of psychological deterioration can be found among quite privileged families, too—and so we remind ourselves, perhaps, that wealth corrupts.

No—it is not that simple. Wealth does not corrupt nor does it 15 ennoble. But wealth does govern the minds of privileged children, gives them a peculiar kind of identity which they never lose, whether they grow up to be stockbrokers or communards, and whether they lead healthy or unstable lives. There is, I think, a message that virtually all quite well-off American families transmit to their children—an emotional expression of those familiar, classbound prerogatives, money and power. I use the word "entitlement" to describe that message.

The word was given to me by the rather rich parents of a child I began to talk with almost two decades ago, in 1959. I have watched those parents become grandparents, and have seen what they described as "the responsibilities of entitlement" handed down to a new generation. When the father, a lawyer and stockbroker from a prominent and quietly influential family, referred to the "entitlement" his children were growing up to know, he had in mind a social rather than a psychological phenomenon: the various juries or committees that select the Mardi Gras participants in New Orleans's annual parade and celebration. He knew that his daughter was "entitled" to be invited.

He wanted, however, to go beyond that social fact. He talked about what he had received from his parents and what he would give to his children, "automatically, without any thought," and what they too would pass on. The father was careful to distinguish between the social entitlement and "something else," a "something else" he couldn't quite define but knew he had to try to evoke if he was to be psychologically candid: "Our children have a good life ahead of them; and I think they know it now. I think they did when they were three or four, too. It's *entitlement,* that's what I call it. My wife didn't know what I was talking about when I first used the word. She thought it had something to do with our ancestry. Maybe it does. I don't mean to be snide. I just think our children grow up taking a lot for granted, and it can be good that they do, and it can be bad. It's like anything else; it all depends. I mean, you can have spoiled brats for children, or you can have kids who want to share what they have. I don't mean give away all their money. I mean be responsible, and try to live up to their ideals, and not just sit around wondering which island in the Caribbean to visit this year, and where to go next summer to get away from the heat and humidity here in New Orleans."

At the time he said no more and at the time I wasn't especially interested in pursuing the subject. But as months became years, I came back to that word "entitlement." There is, as it happens, a psychiatric term that closely connects with it. "Narcissistic entitlement" is the phrase, when referring to a particular kind of "disturbed" child. The term could be used in place of the more conventional, blunter ones: a smug, self-satisfied child; or a child who thinks he owns the world, or will one day. It is an affliction that strikes particularly the wealthy child.

I recall a boy of eight I was once treating in Boston; my supervisor, a child psychoanalyst who had worked with a similar child for three years and anticipated, alas, another year or two at least of thrice-weekly office visits, being naively hopeful, and a touch simple-minded, when I remarked upon the curiosity of the boy, his evident willingness to ask me questions about all sorts of persons, places, things—and so his capacity for engagement with the world around him. Yes, she pointed out, there was indeed a measure of that, but it was best that *we* ask questions about the nature of *his* questions. As we did, the replies all reverted to him, to quite specific experiences he had gone through, and wanted to talk about. And he had actually told me that he never asked a question out of intellectual interest—rather, in his words, "because I like to know what might happen next to me."

It is hard to describe the fearfulness and sadness such a child   20
struggles with. The analyst-supervisor was convinced that there was a "special narcissism," as she called it, that a certain kind of parent offers a child.

This boy's mother was a self-dramatizing, manipulative woman who had married into a prominent family and was in her own way determined to avenge a nagging sense of social inferiority she could not get out of her system, even though her own family was supposedly "proper," relatively speaking. At times her behavior became irrational, if not psychotic. She was wrapped up in herself—when she wasn't making trouble for others in a sly, devious way. Her gift to her son, her husband's namesake, was a self-centeredness that matched her own. He became difficult at school, obstinately preoccupied with his own daydreams, and eventually, all too cut off emotionally. The father's inheritance enabled both mother and son to ignore social and economic realities that others simply had to contend with.

"Narcissism is something we all struggle with," my supervisor observed, "but some people have it more than others, and some children come from homes that have so much that all the money and possessions, all the rugs and furniture and toys and vacations and savings accounts and insurance policies, come crashing on the child's head. There is a shift from narcissism to narcissistic entitlement."

At some point a family's psychology and psychopathology engage with its social and economic life: if narcissism is something a migrant child or a ghetto child has to contend with, then it will take on one flavor (narcissistic despair, for instance), whereas for a child of wealth, narcissistic entitlement is the likely possibility. The child has much, but wants and expects more, all assumed to be his or hers by right—at once a psychological and material inheritance that the world will provide. One's parents will oblige, will be intermediaries, will go back and forth—bringing from stores or banks or wherever those various offerings that serve to gratify the mind's sense of its own importance, its own *due*.

This syndrome is one that wealthy parents recognize instinctively, often wordlessly, and fear. When their children are four, five, and six, parents able to offer them virtually anything sometimes begin to pull back, in concern if not in outright horror. Not only has a son become increasingly demanding or petulant; even when he is quiet he seems to be sitting on a throne of sorts—expecting things to happen, wondering with annoyance why they don't, reassuring himself and others that they will or, if they don't, shrugging his shoulders and waiting for the next splendid moment.

It was just such an impasse—not dramatic, but quite definite and worrisome—that prompted the New Orleans father quoted earlier to use the word "entitlement." He had himself been born to wealth, as will be the case for generations of his family to come, unless the American economic system changes drastically in the future. But he was worried about what a lot of money can do to a personality. When his young daughter, during a Mardi Gras season, kept *assuming* she would one day receive this honor and that honor—indeed, become Mardi Gras queen—he realized that his notion of "entitlement" was not quite hers, Noblesse oblige requires a gesture toward others.

25

He was not the only parent to express such a concern to me in the course of my work. In homes where mothers and fathers profess no explicit reformist persuasions, they nevertheless worry about what happens to children who grow up surrounded by just about everything they want, virtually on demand. "When they're like that, they've gone from spoiled to spoiled rotten—and beyond, to some state I don't know how to describe."

Obviously, it is possible for parents to have a lot of money yet avoid bringing up their children in such a way that they feel like members of a royal family. But even parents determined not to spoil their children often recognize what might be called the existential (as opposed to strictly psychological) aspects of their situation. A father may begin rather early on lecturing his children about the meaning of money; a mother may do her share by saying no, even when yes is so easy to say. Such a child, by the age of five or six, has very definite notions of what is possible, even if it is not always permitted. That child, in conversation, and without embarrassment or the kind of reticence and secretiveness that come later, may reveal a substantial knowledge of economic affairs. A six-year-old girl I spoke to knew that she would, at twenty-one, inherit half a million dollars. She also knew that her father "only" gave her twenty-five cents a week, whereas some friends of hers received as much as a dollar. She was vexed; she asked her parents why they were so "strict." One friend had even used the word "stingy" for the parents. The father, in a matter-of-fact way, pointed out to the daughter that she did, after all, get "anything she really wants." Why, then, the need for an extravagant allowance? The girl was won over. But admonitions don't always modify the quite realistic appraisal children make of what they are heir to; and they don't diminish their sense of entitlement—a state of mind that pervades their view of the world.

In an Appalachian home, for instance, a boy of seven made the following comment in 1963, after a mine his father owned had suffered an explosion, killing two men and injuring seriously nine others: "I heard my mother saying she felt sorry for the families of the miners. I feel sorry for them, too. I hope the men who got hurt get better. I'm sure they will. My father has called in doctors from Lexington. He wants the best doctors in all Kentucky for those miners. Daddy says it was the miners' fault; they get careless, and the next thing you know, there's an explosion. It's too bad. I guess there are a lot of kids who are praying hard for their fathers. I wish God was nice to everyone. He's been very good to us. My daddy says it's been hard work, running the mine, and another one he has. It's just as hard to run a mine as it is to go down and dig the coal! I'm glad my father is the owner, though. I wouldn't want him to get killed or hurt bad down there, way underground. Daddy has given us a good life. We have a lot of fun coming up, he says, in the next few years. We're going on some trips. Daddy deserves his vacations. He says he's happy because he can keep us happy, and he does."

Abundance is this boy's destiny, he has every reason to believe, abundance and limitless possibility. He may even land on the stars. Certainly he has traveled widely in this country. He associates the seasons with travel. In winter, for instance, there is a trip south, to one or another Caribbean island. He worries, on these trips, about his two dogs, and the other animals—the guinea pigs, hamsters, rabbits, chickens. There is always someone in the house, a maid, a handyman. Still, it is sad to say goodbye. Now if the family owned a plane, the animals could come along on those trips!

The boy doesn't really believe that his father will ever own a Lear jet; yet at moments he can imagine himself wrong. And he can construct a fantasy: "I had this dream. In it I was walking through the woods with Daddy, and all of a sudden there was an open field, and I looked, and I saw a hawk, and it was circling and circling. I like going hunting with Daddy, and I thought we were hunting. But when I looked at him, he didn't have his gun. Then he pointed at the hawk, and it was coming down. It landed ahead of us, and it was real strange—because the hawk turned into an airplane! I couldn't believe it. We went toward the plane, and Daddy said we could get a ride anytime we wanted, because it was ours; he'd just bought it. That's when I woke up, I think."

Four years after the boy dreamed that his father owned a plane, the father got one. The boom of the 1970s in the coal fields made his father even richer. The boy was, of course, eager to go on flying trips; eager, also, to learn to fly. The family owned a horse farm by then, near Lexington, Kentucky, and when the boy and his sister were not flying, they were riding. The girl learned to jump well, the boy to ride quite fast. At thirteen he dreamed (by day) of becoming an astronaut, or of becoming the manager of his father's horse farm, or of going to the Air Force Academy and afterwards becoming a "supersonic pilot."

He would never become a commercial pilot, however; and his reasons were interesting. "I've gone on a lot of commercial flights, and there are a lot of people on board, and the pilot has to be nice to everyone, and he makes all these announcements about the seat belts, and stuff like that. My dad's pilot was in the Air Force, and then he flew commercial. He was glad to get out, though. He says you have to be like a waiter; you have to answer complaints from the customers, and apologize to them, just because the ride gets bumpy. It's best to work for yourself, or work for another person, if you trust him and like him. If you go commercial, like our pilot says, you're a servant."

Many of the children I have worked with are similarly disposed; they do not like large groups of people in public places—in fact, have been taught the distinct value not only of privacy but of the quiet that goes with being relatively alone. Some of the children are afraid of those crowds, can't imagine how it would be possible to survive them. Of course, what is strange, unknown, or portrayed as unattractive, uncomfortable, or just to be avoided as a nuisance can for a given child become a source of curiosity, like an event to be experienced at all costs. An eight-year-old girl who lived on a farm well outside Boston wanted desperately to go to the city and see Santa Claus—not because she believed in him, but because she wanted to see "those crowds" she had seen on television. She got her wish, was excited at first, then became quite disappointed, and ultimately uncomfortable. She didn't like being jostled, shoved, and ignored when she protested.

A week after the girl had gone through her Boston "adventure" (as she had called the trip *before* she embarked upon it), each student in her third-grade class was asked to draw a picture in some way connected to the Christmas season, and the girl obliged eagerly. She drew Santa Claus standing beside a pile of packages, presents for the many children who stood near him. They blended into one another— a mob scene. Watching them but removed from them was one child, bigger and on a higher level—suspended in space, it seemed, and partially surrounded by a thin but visible line. The girl wrote on the bottom of the drawing, "I saw Santa Claus." She made it quite clear what she had intended to portray. "He was standing there, handing out these gifts. They were all the same, I think, and they were plastic squirt guns for the boys and little dolls for the girls. I felt sorry for the kids. I asked my mother why kids wanted to push each other, just to get that junk. My mother said a lot of people just don't know any better. I was going to force my way up to Santa Claus and tell him to stop being so dumb! My mother said he was probably a drunk, trying to make a few dollars so he could spend it in a bar that evening! I don't want to be in a store like that again. We went up to a balcony and watched, and then we got out of the place and came home. I told my mother that I didn't care if I ever went to Boston again. I have two friends, and they've never been in Boston, and they don't want to go there, except to ride through on the way to the airport."

She sounded at that moment more aloof, condescending, and snobbish than she ordinarily is. She spends her time with two or three girls who live on nearby estates. Those girls don't see each other regularly, and each of them is quite able to be alone—in fact, rather

35

anxious for those times of solitude. Sometimes a day or two goes by with no formal arrangement to play. They meet in school, and that seems to be enough. Each girl has obligations—a horse to groom, a stall to work on. They are quite "self-sufficient," a word they have heard used repeatedly by their parents. Even within one's own social circle there is no point surrendering to excessive gregariousness!

Once up on her own horse, she is (by her own description) in her "own world." She has heard her mother use that expression. The mother is not boasting, or dismissing others who live in other worlds. The mother is describing, as does the child, a state of progressive withdrawal from people, and the familiar routines or objects of the environment, in favor of a mixture of reverie and disciplined activity. And when the girl, for one reason or another, is unable to ride, she misses not only the sport but the state of mind that goes with it.

Her mother is more explicit about what happens: she tells her daughter, at times, that she wants to "leave everything" and go riding. She tells her daughter that when she is on the horse, cantering across the field or trotting down a trail, she has a "feeling" that is "better than being on a plane." She finds that she can put everyone and everything into "perspective." Nothing seems impossible, burdensome, difficult. There are no distractions, petty or boring details to attend to. One is not only away from it all but above it all. And one is closer to one's "self." The mother talks about the "self," and the child does, too. "It is strange," the girl comments, "because you forget yourself riding or skiing, but you also remember yourself the way you don't when you're just sitting around watching television or reading or playing in your room."

None of the other American children I have worked with have placed such a continuous and strong emphasis on the "self"—its display, its possibilities, its cultivation and development, even the repeated use of the word *self*. A ten-year-old boy who lived in Westchester County made this very clear. I met him originally because his parents were lawyers, and active in the civil rights movement. His father, a patrician Yankee, very much endorsed the students who went south in the early 1960s, and worked on behalf of integrated schools up north. The boy, however, attended private schools—a source of anguish to both father and son, who do not lend themselves to a description that suggests hypocrisy.

The boy knew that he, also, *would* be (as opposed to *wanted* to be) a lawyer. He was quick to perceive and acknowledge his situation, and as he did so, he brought his "self" right into the discussion: "I don't want to tell other kids what to do. I told my father I should be going to the public schools myself. Then I could say anything. Then I could ask why we don't have black kids with us in school. But you have to try to do what's best for your own life, even if you can't speak up for the black people. When I'm grown up I'll be like my father; I'll help the black people all I can. It's this way: first you build *yourself* up. You learn all you can. Later, you can *give of yourself*. That's what Dad says: you can't help others until you've learned to help *yourself*. It's not that you're being selfish, if you're going to a private school and your parents have a lot of money. We had a maid here, and she wasn't right in the head. She lost her temper and told Daddy that he's a phony, and he's out for himself and no one else, and the same goes for my sister and me. Then she quit. Daddy tried to get her to talk with us, but she wouldn't. She said that's all we ever do—talk, talk. I told Daddy she was contradicting herself, because she told me a few weeks ago that I'm always doing something, and I should sit down and talk with her. But I don't know what to say to her! I think she got angry with me, because I was putting on my skis, for cross-country skiing, and she said I had too much, that was my problem. I asked her where the regular skis were, and she said she wouldn't tell me, even if she knew! It's too bad, what happened to her.

"I feel sorry for her, though. Like my sister said, it's not fun to be   40 a maid. The poor woman doesn't look very good. She weighs too much. She's only forty, my mother thinks, but she looks as if she's sixty, and is sick. She should take better care of herself. Now she's thrown away this job, and she told my mother last year that it was the best one she'd ever had, so she's her own worst enemy. I wonder what she'll think when she looks at herself in the mirror."

This boy was no budding egotist. If anything, he was less self-centered at ten than many other children of his community and others like it. He was willing to think about those less fortunate than himself—the maid, and black people in general. True, he would often repeat uncritically his father's words, or a version of them. But he was trying to respond to his father's wishes and beliefs as well as his words. It was impossible for him, no matter how compassionate his nature, to conceive of life as others live it—the maid and, yes, millions of children his age, who don't look in the mirror very often, and may not even own one; who don't worry about how one looks, and what is said, and how one sounds, and how one smells.

Sometimes minor details of a life tell more than larger attitudes spoken and duly recorded by outside observers. The boy has learned that there are people in the ghetto who don't use his parents' kind of judgment, or have the same personal habits or concerns. The boy's sister has a similar knowledge. At twelve she could be quite pointed: "We've had a couple of maids, and they don't know why I use my mother's vaseline lotion on my arms and hands—and in winter on my face, too. They say I've got a wonderful complexion; but I don't think they know how to look real carefully at my skin—or their own, either. Maybe they don't have the time. But I see them taking a 'break,' and what do they do? They put on a TV prize show in the morning or a 'story' in the afternoon. I don't know how they can stand looking at that stuff! I've got a lot of chores. We're not spoiled here! I have to clean out the stalls and brush the horses carefully before we go riding. I have to pick up my room. My mother told me when I was real little, before I was even old enough to go to school, that she wasn't going to have me sitting and looking at television while the maid was straightening out my room. The same goes for outside the house; we have a gardener, but he's not allowed to come into the barn and help us with the animals.

"We had one maid, and she said we spent more time with the animals than she does with her children. I felt sad when she told me that. She has no understanding of what an animal needs. She was the one who was always telling me I was beautiful, and so I didn't need any lotion on my skin. I wanted to give her the lotion. She needs it. Her skin is in terrible shape. It's so dried and cracked. My mother says you can be poor and still know how to take care of yourself."

A child has learned to distinguish between her own inclinations or preferences and those of another person—a whole category of people. This girl was, at the time, not quite an adolescent; for years, however, she had been prepared for that time, and for adulthood as well—prepared by parents who wanted her to know more than how to use skin lotions, or choose "tasteful" lipstick, or shun anything but "natural" fingernail polish, or learn how to care for her hair, and wash it, and pay attention to the scalp as well. Those parents wanted her to give an enormous amount of attention to *herself*—to her thoughts, which she had been taught were worthy of being spoken, and to her body, which was going to be, one day, "attractive."

When she was six or seven she asked a lot of questions about herself. Her questions occur to all children, rich or poor. They are the banal inquiries we never quite stop asking ourselves, and don't answer all that satisfactorily, try as we do: Who am I, why am I here, whence do I come, and where am I going?—the continuing preoccupations of philosophers and novelists, but also asked (and answered allegorically) by painters such as Paul Gauguin. Children seem to prefer his approach to that of the writer. They sometimes don't pay attention to the words they themselves have elicited through their questions. After all-too-verbal family meals they may retire to a desk or table and draw pictures meant to suggest what life is and will be about. When the girl mentioned above wonders who she is, or has questions about her future, she picks up crayons and draws herself with care and affection—on a horse, in a garden, high in a tower, surveying the countryside.

In doing so, she draws upon her concrete, day-to-day experiences. She also uses those experiences in order to suggest something larger about her particular life. Especially noteworthy is the care she and others like her take with themselves as they draw. So often poor children treat themselves cursorily; they quickly sketch a rather unflattering self-portrait. Sometimes they are unwilling to complete what they have begun—as if they are unsure of life itself. A migrant child once told me in a matter-of-fact way that he had no expectation of living beyond twenty. He was simply a child who knew the score. The children of doctors and lawyers and business executives have learned the score, too. The girl mentioned above spends a half-hour drawing herself, moves her eyes toward a mirror every once in a while to check on how she actually does look, and is eventually quite proud of what she has drawn. She regards herself—though she has learned to be affectingly modest—as a rather attractive person. No wonder she once posed herself, in a picture, beside a giant sunflower. She was in no way overshadowed by the flower; if anything, it adorned her own luminous presence.

When that girl became ill with chicken pox the anguish of her mental state was noticeable and instructive. She wanted to scratch the many lesions on her face and arms, but was told by her parents that she must not. She heeded their advice. In the beginning she did scratch one pustule on her upper right arm. Her mother became quite upset. Before the mother could say a word, the child spoke up, acknowledged her awareness of the implications of her deed for the future.

"I wish I hadn't scratched that one place. I wish I could get some cream or ointment that would get rid of the scar. My mother said the doctor should look at it, and maybe he will suggest something. She says I'm lucky, it's such a small scar. But it gives me nightmares! I woke up the other night and my parents were in my room. I guess I'd been crying or shouting. In the morning, I'd forgotten everything, but my mother said I'd half-awakened, and I'd told them that a cat had been chasing me, and scratched me, and I was afraid there'd be a scar."

On another occasion, this girl chatted about her possessions. "When I leave this room and stay at a friend's, or when we go up skiing or down to our summer house, I get a funny feeling. I really miss my dolls, and my bureau—the shells and dishes my parents have brought me when they come back from trips. I have all kinds of shells, from all the Caribbean beaches. I have dishes and ashtrays from a lot of countries. I have posters; I love French posters. I hope I learn to speak French fluently. It's a beautiful language. It's strange, leaving your room and sleeping in a place that hasn't got much of anything that belongs to you, that's yours, that's *you*."

That last progression deserves respectful attention as a rather 50 forceful, intelligent, and exact analysis of the complicated psychology of class-connected "narcissistic entitlement." She and others like her grow up surrounded by possessions, animate as well as inanimate. They have learned to live with them, to look after them and to depend upon them. They have also learned to give of themselves to those "objects." When they leave for a winter or summer vacation they try to take some of their most treasured belongings with them, but often still experience a sense of emptiness or a feeling of being alone, isolated, bereft. Child psychiatrists use the expression "transitional object" to refer to a child's blanket or teddy bear or doll, taken to bed, carried around, held tight at times: at the age of four, five, six, a beacon of hope and reassurance amid the darker moments of growing up.

Few children are unable to find those "transitional objects." I have seen the poorest of American children, living the most uprooted of lives—boys and girls whose parents are migrant farm workers—cling to a dirty old rag, a stick, a rock, the cheapest of plastic toys, often obtained secondhand, maybe from someone's garbage pail. With the children of working-class parents, or of so-called "middle-income" families, there is obviously no such sad desperation. On the other hand, many of those children share rooms with brothers and sisters, and by no means assume that they are to be recipients of an apparently endless succession of gifts, vacations, pleasant surprises. In the homes of the well-to-do, in contrast, the children almost invariably have their own rooms, and the quantitative difference in material acquisitions becomes a qualitative psychological difference of sorts: an enhanced expectation of what life has to offer, and with that, a strong inclination to build a sanctuary out of one's room, one's property, one's day-to-day environment. The girl is subtle but sharp and exact when she distinguishes between what belongs to her (a piece of property) and what has become hers—an existential psychological transformation of sorts. The next step is, of course, an ironic act of personal surrender: the object and the person merge somewhat—from "that's yours" to "that's *you*."

All children struggle when very young—starting at a little under a year, in fact—to distinguish between themselves and their mothers (and fathers). They begin to realize, at two and three, that it is *they* who exist—individuals who crawl and walk and make noises and talk; individuals, that is, who have lives increasingly apart from those of their parents. As they separate they have left, needless to say, themselves. Maybe it is then, at two or three, that a person first knows loneliness, feels somewhat lost or bereft—apart from everyone and everything. Certainly, thereafter, for most children, there are re-attachments to the mother, new attachments to other persons—and to things. At the same time, the child turns inward upon occasion, makes an effort to find comfort and even pleasure in newfound solitariness. Freud, at one point, referred to "the purified pleasure ego," by which he meant a child's delight in the various excitements or satisfactions he or she can manage to find. I recall a four-year-old boy in one home I visited, not far from that of the girl just quoted above, who slid up and down a wonderfully solid circular staircase, shouting *Me, me, me;* he was in love with the dizzying speed, with the feeling of control and power he had—with himself.

Later on, at five and six, such a child becomes quite conscious of rights and wrongs, of what ought to be done if parents or teachers are to be pleased, not to mention one's own developing conscience. Psychoanalysts talk of the "idealized parent image"—that part of a child's mind that holds up examples, makes one or another kind of emphasis, insists upon directions, involvements, affiliations, activities, initiatives. The child absorbs from significant persons various notions of what matters, and how he or she should, in general, be trying to live—and tries to go along, make the necessary steps to become this or that kind of young person. The "you" girl I mentioned has, gradually and consistently, been taught tennis and swimming by coaches, cooking by a maid, riding by her mother. She has also learned how to draw and paint, play the piano, "do" ballet. She has gone abroad often, has mastered foreign words. She has become acquainted with forms of etiquette, with new protocols. She knows when to defer, when to speak up. She knows how to recognize various songs, symphonies, operatic pieces. She knows how to walk the corridors of museums, recognize the work of certain artists. And, too, she has acquired some of the psychological judgment good hostesses have: who is like whom, who belongs near whom at the table, who will be a "disaster" with whom. She used that word sometimes, when eleven or twelve, and in so doing revealed more than a "prepubescent" affinity for a way of talking, or a superficial cleverness about people. In fact, she was indicating something significant about her sense of *herself,* her invulnerability to real disaster, her ability to luxuriate in social nuance.

For the children whose words appear here, and for others, there is every reason to be mindful of bright prospects in their lives, and accordingly, to feel entitlement. Not that entitlement, it must be constantly emphasized, is incompatible with misgivings, disappointments, despair. A child can feel—being realistic—entitled to a certain kind of life, and yet have reasons to be confused or hurt. Even schizophrenics experience the distinctions, the possibilities or hindrances, that have to do with class and caste, race and place of residence. The girl whose words I called upon above had her own thoughts, one day, about these theoretical issues of mental life—after she had heard, at the age of twelve, that her father was sick and required surgery: "I hope he'll be all right. It's serious, my mother told me. I can tell it is; Daddy hasn't been smiling much. He's been worried. He has the best doctor in the country; he's the best surgeon. I met him, and he was very nice. He gave my brother and me a book he'd written, about the seashore and the clams and oysters and lobsters you find in the water and the sand. He owns a lot of land by the ocean, and he's a marine biologist, my father says, besides being a surgeon. And he's an artist, too. I wouldn't mind being a doctor myself, but I don't know if I'd want to operate on anyone. The surgeon offered to show my brother and me how he operates; we could watch him—but not when he works on Daddy. My brother said yes, but I said no. I'd rather not be there, if anything goes wrong; then, when Daddy is being operated on, I'd worry even more.

"We'll be all right. My mother says everything will turn out good. Daddy may not be home for a couple of weeks, but we can go and see him all the time. We can eat with him in his room. It'll be like going out to a restaurant. He'll have television and his own phone. We can talk with him anytime we want. He says he'll get a lot of reading done. He'll have a nice view from his room, and he'll get all the rest he'll need. Then, when he gets home, we're going away. Daddy says we'll be in Barbados for two weeks. He's promised to take us out of school. We'll get all our homework, and we won't fall back at all. My mother says it may turn out to be a blessing in disguise that Daddy got sick; he'll get a lot of rest, and he'll be much stronger. I hope so."

She was not about to acknowledge, even to herself, how worried she sensed her mother to be, despite all the assurances and reassurances, the contingency plans and arrangements. But she (and her mother) had resources that very much influenced the course of an anxious period of waiting. The dreaded outcome of the father's illness, a malignancy, did not materialize. All the money in the world could not have converted cancerous cells into normal ones. But during those days that preceded surgery, the girl and her brother felt more hope than dread, and had quite real, concrete—rather than illusory—sources of support for that hope. And during the father's convalescence the children did not hear their mother and father lamenting bills, expressing dozens of worries about, say, the loss of a

55

job, and complaints, say, about the "conditions" in the hospital. On the contrary, a moment of danger, a time of sickness and weakness, became for everyone concerned an occasion for pleasure, relaxation, new initiatives and accomplishments. The girl and her brother ended up becoming scuba divers in the warm Caribbean water; ended up going on motorcycle rides such as they had never had before; ended up knowing, more exactly than ever, how well-off their parents were, they as children were, and a future generation of the family's children might well also turn out to be. "It all came out for the best," the girl said weeks after her father was pronounced able to return to his work as a business executive. In a sense the words are a slogan of sorts constantly kept in mind by her and others: life works out mostly "for the best"—and one has a right to conclude that because one has had ample confirming evidence.

It is important that a child's sense of entitlement be distinguished not only from the psychiatric dangers of narcissism but from the less pathological and not all that uncommon phenomenon known as being "spoiled." It is a matter of degree; "spoiled" children are self-centered all right, petulant and demanding—but not as grandiose or, alas, saddled with illusions (or delusions) as the children clinicians have in mind when using the phrase "narcissistic entitlement." The rich or quite well-to-do are all too commonly charged with producing spoiled children. Yet one sees spoiled children everywhere, among the very poor as well as the inordinately rich.

   In one of the first wealthy families I came to know there was a girl who was described by both parents as "spoiled." At the time, I fear, I was ready to pronounce every child in New Orleans's Garden District spoiled. Were they not all living comfortable, indeed luxurious, lives, as compared to the lives of the black or working-class white children I was getting to know in other sections of that city?

   Nevertheless, I soon began to realize that it wouldn't do to characterize without qualification one set of children as spoiled, by virtue of their social and economic background, as against another set of children who were obviously less fortunate in many respects. One meets, among the rich, restrained, disciplined, and by no means indulged children; sometimes, even, boys and girls who have learned to be remarkably self-critical, even ascetic—anything but "spoiled" in the conventional sense of the word. True, one can find a touch and more of arrogance, or at least sustained self-assurance, in those apparently spartan boys and girls who seem quite anxious to deny themselves all sorts of presumably accessible privileges if not luxuries. But one also finds in these children a consistent willingness to place serious and not always pleasant burdens on themselves—to the point where they often struck me, when I came to their homes fresh from visits with much poorer age-mates, as remarkably *less* spoiled: not so much whining or crying; fewer demands for candy or other sweets; even, sometimes, a relative indifference to toys, however near at hand and expensive they may have been; a disregard of television—so often demanded by the children I was seeing.

A New Orleans black woman said to me in 1961: "I don't know how to figure out these rich white kids. They're something! I used to think, before I took a job with this family, that the only difference between a rich kid and a poor kid is that the rich kid knows he has a lot of money and he grows up and becomes spoiled rotten. That's what my mother told me; she took care of a white girl, and the girl was an only child, and her father owned a department store in McComb, Mississippi, and that girl thought she was God's special creature. My mother used to come home and tell us about the 'little princess'; but she turned out to be no good. She was so pampered, she couldn't do a thing for herself. All she knew how to do was order people around.

"It's different with these two children. I've never seen such a boy and such a girl. They think they're the best ones who ever lived—like that girl in McComb—but they don't behave like her. They're never asking me to do much of anything. They even ask if *they* can help *me*! They tell me that they want to know how to do everything. The girl says she wants to learn how to run the washing machine and the dishwasher. She says she wants to learn all my secret recipes. She says she'd like to give the best parties in the Garden District when she grows up, and she'd like to be able to give them without anyone's help. She says I could serve the food, but she would like to make it. The boy says he's going to be a lawyer and a banker, so he wants to know how much everything costs. He doesn't want to waste anything. He'll see me throw something away, and he wants to know why. I wish my own kids were like him!

"But these children here are special, and don't they know it! That's what being rich is: you know you're different from most people. These two kids act as if they're going to be tops in everything, and they're pleased as can be with themselves, because there is nothing they can't do, and there's nothing they can't get, and there's nothing they can't win, and they're always showing off what they can do, and then before you can tell them how good they are, they're telling the same thing to themselves. It's confusing! They're not spoiled one bit, but oh, they have a high opinion of themselves!"

Actually, children like the ones she speaks of don't allow themselves quite the unqualified confidence she describes, though she certainly has correctly conveyed the appearance they give. Boys and

60

girls may seem without anxiety or self-doubt; they have been brought up, as the maid suggests, to feel important, superior, destined for a satisfying, rewarding life—and at, say, eight or nine they already appear to know all that. Yet there are moments of hesitation, if not apprehension. An eleven-year-old boy from a prominent and quite brilliant Massachusetts family (three generations of first-rate lawyers) told his teachers, in an autobiographical composition about the vicissitudes of "entitlement": "I don't always do everything right. I'd like to be able to say I don't make any mistakes, but I do, and when I do, I feel bad. My father and mother say that if you train yourself, you can be right *almost* 100 percent of the time. Even they make mistakes, though. I like to be first in sports. I like to beat my brothers at skiing. But I don't always go down the slopes as fast as I could and I sometimes fall down. Last year I broke my leg. When I get a bad cold, I feel disappointed in myself. I don't think it's right to be easy on yourself. If you are, then you slip back, and you don't get a lot of the rewards in life. If you really work for the rewards, you'll get them."

A platitude—the kind of assurance his teachers, as a matter of fact, have rather often given him. In the fourth grade, for instance, the teacher had this written on the blackboard (and kept it there for weeks): "Those who want something badly enough get it, provided they are willing to wait and work." The boy considers that assertion neither banal nor unrealistic. He has been brought up to believe that such is and will be (for him) the case. He knows that others are not so lucky, but he hasn't really met those "others," and they don't cross his mind at all. What does occur to him sometimes is the need for constant exertion, lest he fail to "measure up." One "measures up" when one tries hard and succeeds. If one slackens or stumbles, one ought to be firm with oneself—but not in any self-pitying or self-excusing or self-paralyzing way. The emphasis is on a quick and efficient moment of scrutiny followed by "a fast pick-up."

Such counsel is not as callous as it may sound—or, ironically, as it may well have been intended to sound. The child who hears it gets, briefly, upset; but unless he or she stops heeding what has been said, quite often "a fast pick-up" does indeed take place—an effort to redeem what has been missed or lost, or only somewhat accomplished. Again, it is a matter of feeling entitled. A child who has been told repeatedly that all he or she needs to do is try hard does not feel inclined to allow himself or herself long stretches of time for skeptical self-examination. The point is to feel *entitled*—then act upon that feeling. The boy whose composition was just quoted from used the word "entitled" in another essay he wrote, this one meant to be a description of his younger (age five) brother. The writing was not, however, without an autobiographical strain to it: "I was watching my brother from my bedroom window. He was climbing up the fence we built for our corral. He got to the top, and then he just stood there and waved and shouted. No one was there. He was talking to himself. He was very happy. Then he would fall. He would be upset for a few seconds, but he would climb right back up again. Then he would be even happier! He was entitled to be happy. It is his fence, and he has learned to climb it, and stay up, and balance himself."

No Questions

If wealth offers children a lot materially, it may do so at a cost. When one is surrounded by possessions, and given everything one wants— never mind needs—and more, there is little time for some of the more reflective moments children have, often born of frustrations and denials experienced. Many of the poor or working-class children I know have become sensitive, even introspective, and, yes, spiritually awakened, not out of any inherent superiority of mind or soul, but because they have lived rough, harassed lives, and have, quite naturally, wondered *why*. But why question the basis of a hugely munificent world?

Still, I think of a New Orleans girl I knew who, in her own fashion, once tried to come to terms with what she several times referred to as her "one and only chance," by which she meant nothing less than her life. She will never be a latter-day Marx or Kierkegaard—that one knows. She is today well on her way to being a member of upper-crust, conservative New Orleans society, preoccupied with dinner parties, flowers, dances, and clothes, not to mention a suitable suitor.

Yet, when she was eight she had a habit that puzzled, worried her parents, for the short time that it lasted—a few months in a girl's long years of childhood. She would, as her mother put it, "sit and stare." In fact, the girl liked looking out the window of her parents' mansion. Across the street was one of those striking New Orleans cemeteries— the graves, the elaborate and various tombs, all above ground. The tombs cast shadows, and in the early evening or morning the girl would notice them. She wondered about who "those people" were, the departed. She wondered what kind of lives they lived, what they could tell her about those lives. She was struggling for detachment, perspective, and humor about the world she was part of. She was, in her own way, meditating about life's meaning.

But, alas, she told her parents. They were quizzical the first time; annoyed the second; admonitory the third; worried the fourth; and ready to consult a doctor the fifth. They did call a doctor; he urged intelligent restraint, and his advice proved correct. Not that there was, actually, restraint. The girl was implicitly and sometimes directly told to get on with it—life. She was, her parents decided, "a little too introverted." She had best be made "busy." They knew the enemy—inwardness. They knew the point of life: the headlong rush; the ferris wheel at the age of six, the assembly dance at the age of sixteen; the full calendar; the school choir, everyone beautifully, expensively, similarly dressed; the clock that keeps moving; the night dream that is promptly forgotten; the sigh before retiring that registers satisfaction and congratulation—no wasted time. No wasted time. No time heavy on one's hands. No time to spare. No time left. In no time, no time at all.

The girl felt the push. But it took her a while to emerge from the 70 peculiar phase her parents were convinced she must be going through. As her mother put it, "She still has a funny time up in her room, looking at that cemetery. She tells us she talks with the people in the tombs! I was horrified." She smiled. "I thought at first she was teasing me. I guess she's all right. She's just growing up. All children do a few crazy things, before they get sensible." She was right; just about all children do have their strange, wondrous, luminous, brooding, magical, redemptive moments.

The girl said, "I don't think there's anyone there, across the street, inside the cemetery. I just like to look at the place. I used to walk in there with my grandmother. I was little, and she was still alive. She told me she had lived a nice long life, and she had been happy, and she was ready to leave us, whenever God decided she had been with us long enough. She would be glad to go. One day we found her asleep, and it was late in the morning for her—nine o'clock. She was dead. My mother said there was no need to call the doctor, but we had to. I never saw her. I wanted to go in the room, but they wouldn't let me.

"The maid said they should let me in. The maid almost convinced my mother. I heard them arguing. I never heard the maid speak back to my mother like that. But my mother won. The maid came out crying. She wasn't upset because of my grandmother. The tears were for me. The maid wanted me to say goodbye to someone, but I never could. They didn't bury my grandmother in that cemetery across the street. I'd hoped they would. She and I had always been close—'real tight,' she said. If they had buried her across the street, we'd still be 'real tight.' But there isn't any room left, my mother says. I don't think that's exactly right. The maid says it's exactly wrong! The maid says she's done some listening, and she knows what's true—that my mother didn't want someone in the family buried there so near to us.

"Some of the time, when I look across the street, I might be wishing my grandmother was buried there. A lot of the time I just wonder who someone was—someone who's inside one of the little buildings. And I wonder if a long time from now there will be a girl like me, and she will be sitting, maybe, right in my room, and she will be looking at the cemetery, and I'll be there, and she'll be wondering about me! If I want, I can be buried there. The maid told me so. I guess I have a lot of time to make up my mind. It's funny, looking at a cemetery. It's funny playing there. We play there, some of us. It makes people nervous when we do; but they let us. You wonder if there are ghosts. I know there aren't, but I wonder. You hear a sound, and you think someone might be talking to you. Even with the window closed, and you're inside the house, you'll hear a noise, and you wonder. It'll be the dog, in the next room, shaking himself. But you wonder."

She stopped all that wondering within a few months. She had gone through her worrisome time, had "recovered." So the mother had it: "Thank God, she's better. She's recovered from her interest in cemeteries." An "interest"? Or was it, perhaps, a brief spell of release, of openness?

As for that child's maid, she was, as the girl's mother often said, and as the girl would grow up to say herself, "not always in control, the way she should be." Nevertheless, the maid surely deserves a little space to speak on behalf of herself, and maybe of a lot of other maids.

"I look at these folks, and my heart goes out to them. They feel sorry for me. I know they do. I hear them talking. But I feel sorry for *them.* Mind you, I feel sorry for myself, too. I'm not fooling myself. It's no good being Mr. Charlie's maid. It's no good working in the white man's kitchen and cleaning up after him, and getting his few dollars, his pat on the back—and because of the pat you're supposed to act like you've seen God's face, at last you have, and He's smiling down on you. But who is Mr. Charlie? My momma told me who he is; he's a sad one, that's who he is. They're all right, these people here. I've worked for them for fifteen years. I'll stay with them, most likely, until they carry me out, and that'll be the end of things. My momma told me: Remember that you're put here only for a few seconds of God's time, and He's testing you. He doesn't want answers, though. He wants you to know how to ask the right questions. When you show Him what you know, He'll smile on you. God's smile, that's the sunshine. God's worries, that's the night. We have to face the night. We have to face the end of things.

"These people here, they've got all that money, and all this big house, and another one out in the country, and still they won't let that little girl just be herself. She's eight or nine, and she's got an independent spirit in her, but they're determined to get rid of it, and they will, let me tell you, and soon. The girl asks me a lot of questions. That's good. She looks out on that cemetery and she starts to wondering about things. That's good. She wonders about life, and what it's about, and what the end of things will be. That's good. But she's stopping, now. That's what they want: no looking, no staring, no peeking at life. No questions; they don't want questions. They go to a church a couple of times a year, Christmas and Easter, and no one asks them any questions there. No one asks them questions anyplace they go. The people who are gone, who live across the street there in the cemetery, inside those tombs—they know what's important, they've discovered what's important, they've reached their destination. I'm poor, but at least I know that I should ask myself every day, Where's your destination, and are you going there, or are you getting side-tracked? A lot of days I wish I was them; I wish I was rich like them. Then I ask myself, Would you be any different? I don't know the answer. I mean, it's like the minister keeps saying to us in church, that 'all is vanity.' And he'll remind us that 'there's no profit under the sun.' I wonder if there is any. I wonder a lot if there's any profit under the sun. I read the Bible and I wonder. I'll ask myself one day, and I'll ask the next day, and I'll just decide not to be too sure; just keep on asking."

❖ Focused Freewriting   Consider as possible focal points the importance of personal possessions to affluent children, the demands they place upon themselves, their view of the world outside their domain, or one of the topics you've identified in your journal.

❖ Guided Responses

1. The affluent children Coles writes about have parents "whose decisions have affected, in one way or another, . . . working-class and poor families" (para. 4); they know "that the 'news' may well be affected, if not crucially molded, by their parents" (para. 9). In your view, how would this knowledge affect a child's development? How does this information help you understand the characteristics Coles describes throughout the essay?

2. From your reading of Coles's essay, how would you define his concept of "entitlement"? How does the story of the Appalachian mine owner's son (paras. 28–32) illustrate this definition? How is feeling entitled different from being spoiled?

3. In paragraphs 45 and 46 Coles describes the self-portraits drawn by wealthy and poor children, the wealthy children drawing "with care and affection," the poor children drawing "cursorily." What do these different ways of portraying themselves reveal about the children? In what ways are both wealthy and poor children alike in their drawing methods?

4. How does the final story of the New Orleans girl gazing out at the cemetery sum up the essay? What questions and ideas is the girl grappling with? Why do her parents react as they do? Why does Coles allow the maid to end the essay with her view of the situation?

❖ Shared Responses   In your journal write a brief analysis of how your socioeconomic status has affected you. Consider such questions as the relative comforts of your home, your family's status in the community, your parents' long-term financial security, your association with others better or worse off than you are, and any other factors you consider relevant. As you discuss your responses in small groups, note the similarities and differences in the assessments made by each member.

What's in a Name?

ITABARI NJERI

ITABARI NJERI, *who graduated from the Boston University School of Journalism and the Columbia University School of Journalism, is a writer for the* Los Angeles Times. *Her first collection,* Every Good-bye Ain't Gone, *was published in 1990. In this selection, originally published in slightly different form in the* Times *and reprinted in her collection, Njeri discusses the significance of names, particularly to African Americans. For a people whose given names so often reflect the bondage in which their ancestors were held, names are indeed important. And people's reactions to Njeri's name indicate that names mean far more than we may think they do.*

Before reading the selection, discuss in your journal what your name means to you. Think about how names may reflect ethnic or racial background, the significance of nicknames, and the meaning of particular given names within a family. If you've ever changed your name or nickname, discuss that as well.

As you make notes on your reading, you may want to focus on the various reactions to Njeri's name—by African Americans, whites, Africans, sympathetic people, condescending people, hostile people.

THE DECADE WAS ABOUT TO END when I started my first newspaper job. The seventies might have been the disco generation for some, but it was a continuation of the Black Power, post–civil rights era for me. Of course in some parts of America it was still the pre–civil rights era. And that was the part of America I wanted to explore. As a good reporter I needed a sense of the whole country, not just the provincial Northeast Corridor in which I was raised.

I headed for Greenville ("Pearl of the Piedmont"), South Carolina.

"*Wheeere,*" some people snarled, their nostrils twitching, their mouths twisted so their top lips went slightly to the right, the bottom ones way down and to the left, "did you get *that* name from?"

Itabiddy, Etabeedy. Etabeeree. Eat a berry. Mata Hari. Theda Bara.
And one secretary in the office of the Greenville Urban League told
her employer: "It's Ms. Idi Amin."

Then, and now, there are a whole bunch of people who greet me   5
with: "Hi, Ita." They think "Bari" is my last name. Even when they
don't, they still want to call me "Ita." When I tell them my first name
is Itabari, they say, "Well, what do people call you for short?"

"They don't call me anything for short," I say. "The name is
Itabari."

Sophisticated white people, upon hearing my name, approach me
as would a cultural anthropologist finding a piece of exotica right in
his own living room. This happens a lot, still, at cocktail parties.

"Oh, what an unusual and beautiful name. Where are you from?"

"Brooklyn," I say. I can see the disappointment in their eyes. Just
another home-grown Negro.

Then there are other white people who, having heard my decid-   10
edly northeastern accent, will simply say, "What a lovely name," and
smile knowingly, indicating that they saw Roots and understand.

Then there are others, black and white, who for different reasons
take me through this number:

"What's your *real* name?"

"Itabari Njeri is my real, legal name," I explain.

"Okay, what's your *original* name?" they ask, often with eyes
rolling, exasperation in their voices.

After Malcolm X, Muhammad Ali, Kareem Abdul-Jabbar, Ntozake   15
Shange, and Kunta Kinte, who, I ask, should be exasperated by this
question-and-answer game?

Nevertheless, I explain, "Because of slavery, black people in the
Western world don't usually know their original names. What you
really want to know is what my slave name was."

Now this is where things get tense. Four hundred years of bitter
history, culture, and politics between blacks and whites in America is
evoked by this one term, "slave name."

Some white people wince when they hear the phrase, pained and
embarrassed by this reminder of their ancestors' inhumanity. Further,
they quickly scrutinize me and conclude that mine was a post–Emancipation Proclamation birth. "You were never a slave."

I used to be reluctant to tell people my slave name unless I sur-
mised that they wouldn't impose their cultural values on me and
refuse to use my African name. I don't care anymore. When I changed
my name, I changed my life, and I've been Itabari for more years now
than I was Jill. Nonetheless, people will say: "Well, that's your *real*
name, you were born in America and that's what I am going to call

you." My mother tried a variation of this on me when I legalized my traditional African name. I respectfully made it clear to her that I would not tolerate it. Her behavior, and subsequently her attitude, changed.

But many black folks remain just as skeptical of my name as my   20
mother was.

"You're one of those black people who changed their name, huh," they are likely to begin. "Well, I still got the old slave master's Irish name," said one man named O'Hare at a party. This man's defensive tone was a reaction to what I call the "blacker than thou" syndrome perpetrated by many black nationalists in the sixties and seventies. Those who reclaimed their African names made blacks who didn't do the same thing feel like Uncle Toms.

These so-called Uncle Toms couldn't figure out why they should use an African name when they didn't know a thing about Africa. Besides, many of them were proud of their names, no matter how they had come by them. And it should be noted that after the Emancipation Proclamation in 1863, four million black people changed their names, adopting surnames such as Freeman, Freedman, and Liberty. They eagerly gave up names that slave masters had imposed upon them as a way of identifying their human chattel.

Besides names that indicated their newly won freedom, blacks chose common English names such as Jones, Scott, and Johnson. English was their language. America was their home, and they wanted names that would allow them to assimilate as easily as possible.

Of course, many of our European surnames belong to us by birthright. We are the legal as well as "illegitimate" heirs to the names Jefferson, Franklin, Washington, et al., and in my own family, Lord.

Still, I consider most of these names to be by-products of slavery,   25
if not actual slave names. Had we not been enslaved, we would not have been cut off from our culture, lost our indigenous languages, and been compelled to use European names.

The loss of our African culture is a tragic fact of history, and the conflict it poses is a profound one that has divided blacks many times since Emancipation: do we accept the loss and assimilate totally or do we try to reclaim our culture and synthesize it with our present reality?

A new generation of black people in America is reexamining the issues raised by the cultural nationalists and Pan-Africanists of the sixties and seventies: what are the cultural images that appropriately convey the "new" black aesthetic in literature and art?

The young Afro-American novelist Trey Ellis has asserted that the "New Black Aesthetic shamelessly borrows and reassembles across both race and class lines." It is not afraid to embrace the full implications of our hundreds of years in the New World. We are a new people who need not be tied to externally imposed or self-inflicted cultural parochialism. Had I understood that as a teenager, I might still be singing today.

Even the fundamental issue of identity and nomenclature, raised by Baraka and others twenty years ago, is back on the agenda: are we to call ourselves blacks or African-Americans?

In reality, it's an old debate. "Only with the founding of the 30
American Colonization Society in 1816 did blacks recoil from using the term African in referring to themselves and their institutions," the noted historian and author Sterling Stuckey pointed out in an interview with me. They feared that using the term "African" would fuel white efforts to send them back to Africa. But they felt no white person had the right to send them back when they had slaved to build America.

Many black institutions retained their African identification, most notably the African Methodist Episcopal Church. Changes in black self-identification in America have come in cycles, usually reflecting the larger dynamics of domestic and international politics.

The period after World War II, said Stuckey, "culminating in the Cold War years of Roy Wilkins's leadership of the NAACP," was a time of "frenzied integrationism." And there was "no respectable black leader on the scene evincing any sort of interest in Africa—neither the NAACP or the Urban League."

This, he said, "was an example of historical discontinuity, the likes of which we, as a people, had not seen before." Prior to that, for more than a century and a half, black leaders were Pan-Africanists, including Frederick Douglass. "He recognized," said Stuckey, "that Africa was important and that somehow one had to redeem the motherland in order to be genuinely respected in the New World."

The Reverend Jesse Jackson has, of course, placed on the national agenda the importance of blacks in America restoring their cultural, historical, and political links with Africa.

But what does it really mean to be called an African-American? 35

"Black" can be viewed as a more encompassing term, referring to all people of African descent. "Afro-American" and "African-American" refer to a specific ethnic group. I use the terms interchangeably, depending on the context and the point I want to emphasize.

But I wonder: as the twenty-first century breathes down our necks—prodding us to wake up to the expanding mélange of ethnic groups immigrating in record numbers to the United States, inevitably intermarrying, and to realize the eventual reshaping of the nation's political imperatives in a newly multicultural society—will the term "African-American" be as much of a racial and cultural obfuscation as the term "black"? In other words, will we be the only people, in a society moving toward cultural pluralism, viewed to have no history and no culture? Will we just be a color with a new name: African-American?

Or will the term be—as I think it should—an ethnic label describing people with a shared culture who descended from Africans, were transformed in (as well as transformed) America, and are genetically intertwined with myriad other groups in the United States?

Such a definition reflects the historical reality and distances us from the fallacious, unscientific concept of separate races when there is only one: *Homo sapiens.*

But to comprehend what should be an obvious definition requires   40
knowledge and a willingness to accept history.

When James Baldwin wrote *Nobody Knows My Name,* the title was a metaphor—at the deepest level of the collective African-American psyche—for the blighting of black history and culture before the nadir of slavery and since.

The eradication or distortion of our place in world history and culture is most obvious in the popular media. Liz Taylor—and, for an earlier generation, Claudette Colbert—still represent what Cleopatra—a woman of color in a multiethnic society, dominated at various times by blacks—looks like.

And in American homes, thanks to reruns and cable, a new generation of black kids grow up believing that a simpleton shouting "Dy-no-mite!" is a genuine reflection of Afro-American culture, rather than a white Hollywood writer's stereotype.

More recently, *Coming to America,* starring Eddie Murphy as an African prince seeking a bride in the United States, depicted traditional African dancers in what amounted to a Las Vegas stage show, totally distorting the nature and beauty of real African dance. But with every burlesque-style pelvic thrust on the screen, I saw blacks in the audience burst into applause. They think that's African culture, too.

And what do Africans know of us, since blacks don't control the   45
organs of communication that disseminate information about us?

"No!" screamed the mother of a Kenyan man when he announced his engagement to an African-American woman who was a friend of mine. The mother said marry a European, marry a white American. But please, not one of those low-down, ignorant, drug-dealing, murderous black people she had seen in American movies. Ultimately, the mother prevailed.

In Tanzania, the travel agent looked at me indignantly. "Njeri, that's Kikuyu. What are you doing with an African name?" he demanded.

I'd been in Dar es Salaam about a month and had learned that Africans assess in a glance the ethnic origins of the people they meet.

Without a greeting, strangers on the street in Tanzania's capital would comment, "Oh, you're an Afro-American or West Indian."

"Both."   50

"I knew it," they'd respond, sometimes politely, sometimes not.

Or, people I got to know while in Africa would mention, "I know another half-caste like you." Then they would call in the "mixed-race" person and say, "Please meet Itabari Njeri." The darker-complected African, presumably of unmixed ancestry, would then smile and stare at us like we were animals in the zoo.

Of course, this "half-caste" (which I suppose is a term preferable to "mulatto," which I hate, and which every person who understands its derogatory meaning—"mule"—should never use) was usually the product of a mixed marriage, not generations of ethnic intermingling. And it was clear from most "half-castes" I met that they did not like being compared to so mongrelized and stigmatized a group as Afro-Americans.

I had minored in African studies in college, worked for years with Africans in the United States, and had no romantic illusions as to how I would be received in the motherland. I wasn't going back to find my roots. The only thing that shocked me in Tanzania was being called, with great disdain, a "white woman" by an African waiter. Even if the rest of the world didn't follow the practice, I then assumed everyone understood that any known or perceptible degree of African ancestry made one "black" in America by law and social custom.

But I was pleasantly surprised by the telephone call I received two   55
minutes after I walked into my Dar es Salaam hotel room. It was the hotel operator. "Sister, welcome to Tanzania. . . . Please tell everyone in Harlem hello for us." The year was 1978, and people in Tanzania were wearing half-foot-high platform shoes and dancing to James Brown wherever I went.

Shortly before I left, I stood on a hill surrounded by a field of endless flowers in Arusha, near the border of Tanzania and Kenya. A toothless woman with a wide smile, a staff in her hand, and two young girls at her side, came toward me on a winding path. I spoke to her in fractured Swahili and she to me in broken English.

"I know you," she said smiling. "Wa-Negro." "Wa" is a prefix in Bantu languages meaning people. "You are from the lost tribe," she told me. "Welcome," she said, touching me, then walked down a hill that lay in the shadow of Mount Kilimanjaro.

I never told her my name, but when I told other Africans, they'd say: "*Emmmm* Itabari. Too long. How about I just call you Ita."

❖ Focused Freewriting   Consider as possible focal points the history of African-American names, Njeri's frustration with people who won't accept her name, or one of the topics you've identified in your journal.

❖ Guided Responses

1. In paragraph 4, Njeri presents a list of butchered versions of her name: "Itabiddy, Etabeedy, Etabeeree. Eat a berry. Mata Hari. Theda Bara. . . . Ms. Idi Amin." What is the effect of this list? How does the humor in some of the names reinforce Njeri's point? How would you react if your name were continually mauled in this way?

2. Njeri characterizes some African-American activists from the sixties and seventies as "blacker than thou" (para. 21). Given her explanation of the syndrome, would you consider Njeri "blacker than thou"? Why, or why not?

3. Since Njeri uses the terms "black" and "African-American" interchangeably, is she undermining her central point about the significance of names? Why, or why not? How do you think she would respond to that charge?

4. The final anecdote in Njeri's essay echoes one of her opening anecdotes, as a new acquaintance shortens her name to "Ita." What do you think is the significance of this ending? In what way is the African woman's response different from the similar American response—or are they the same? Explain your answer.

❖ Shared Responses   In your journal write a scenario in which you are introduced to someone with a traditional African name (or in which someone new reacts to your uncommon name). How would you respond? How would you explain your response? How do you think the other person would react? As you discuss your responses in small groups, compare and contrast the different scenarios, noting the reasons members offer for their responses.

❖

Secrets and Anger

DAVID MURA

DAVID MURA, *who holds a Master of Fine Arts degree from Vermont College, has published both poetry and nonfiction. His books include* Turning Japanese *(1991),* After We Lost Our Way (Poems) *(1989), and* A Male Grief: Notes on Pornography and Addiction *(1987). In this article, originally published in* Mother Jones *(1992), Mura ponders the difficulties his daughter will face because of her Japanese-American heritage. Trying to envision what her life will be like, says Mura, has caused him to reassess his own views on racial identity.*

Before reading the article, write in your journal about your own understanding of racism. Do you think the term means the same thing to whites as it does to people of color? How do guilt, anger, and victimization figure into the experience of racism?

As you make notes on your reading, you may want to focus on the continual interplay in the article between personal revelations and political statements.

ON THE DAY OUR DAUGHTER WAS BORN, as my wife, Susie, and I waited for the doctor to do a cesarean section, we talked about names. Standing at the window, I looked out and said, "Samantha, the day you were born was a gray and blustery day." We decided on Samantha Lyn, after my sisters, Susan Lynn and Lynda. I felt to give the baby a Japanese name might mark her as too different, especially since we live in St. Paul, where Asian Americans are a small minority. I had insisted that her last name be hyphenated, Sencer-Mura. My wife had argued that such a name was unwieldy. "What happens when Samantha Sencer-Mura marries Bob Rodriguez-Stein?" she asked. "That's her generation's problem," I said, laughing.

I sometimes wish now we'd given her a Japanese middle name, as Susie had wanted. Perhaps it's because I sense that the world Samantha's inheriting won't be dominated by the melting-pot model, that multiculturalism is not a project but a reality, that in the next century

125

there will no longer be a white majority in this country. Or perhaps I simply feel guilty about having given in to the dominant culture once again.

I am working on a poem about my daughter, about trying to take in her presence, her life, about trying to link her with my sense of the past—my father and mother, the internment camps, my grandparents. I picture myself serving her sukiyaki, a dish I shunned as a child, and her shouting for more rice, brandishing her *hashi* (a word for chopsticks, which I never used as a child and only began to use after my trip to Japan). As I describe Samantha running through the garden, scattering petals, squashing tomatoes, I suddenly think of how someone someday will call her a "gook," that I know this with more certainty than I know she'll find happiness in love.

I speak to my wife about moving out to the West Coast or to Hawaii, where there would be more Asian Americans. In Hawaii, more than a third of the children are *happa* (mixed race); Samantha would be the norm, not the minority. I need to spend more time living in an Asian-American community: I can't tell its stories if I'm not a part of it. As I talk about moving one evening, Susie starts to feel uneasy. "I'm afraid you'll cross this bridge and take Sam with you, and leave me here," she says.

"But I've lived all my life on your side of the bridge. At most   5 social gatherings, I'm the only person of color in the room. What's wrong with living awhile on my side of the bridge? What keeps you from crossing?"

Susie, a pediatric oncologist, works with families of all colors. Still, having a hybrid daughter is changing her experience. Often when she's in the grocery with Sam, someone will come up to her and say: "Oh, she's such a beautiful little girl. Where did you get her?" This has happened so often Susie swears she's going to teach Sam to say: "Fuck you. My genes came all the way over on the *Mayflower,* thank you."

These incidents mark ways Susie has experienced something negative over race that I have not. No one asks me where Sam came from: they assume I'm her father. For Susie, the encounters are a challenge to her position as Samantha's biological mother, the negation of an arduous pregnancy and the physical work of birth and motherhood. For me, they stir an old wound. The people who mistake Sam for an adopted child can't picture a white woman married to an Asian man.

Six ways of viewing identity: Identity is a social and historical construction. Identity is formed by political and economic and cultural exigencies. Identity is a fiction. Identity is a choice. Identity may appear unitary but is always fragmentary. Identity is deciding to acknowledge or not acknowledge political and economic and cultural exigencies.

When I address the question of raising my daughter, I address the question of her identity, which means I address the question of my identity, her mother's, our parents', and so on. But this multiplication of the self takes place along many lines. Who knows where it stops? At my grandparents? At the woman in the grocery store? At you, the imagined reader of this piece?

In the matrix of race and color in our society, there is the binary   10
opposition of black and white. And then there are the various Others, determined by race or culture or gender or sexual preference—Native Americans, Hispanic Americans, Asian Americans, Japanese Americans, women, men, heterosexuals, homosexuals. None of these definitions stands alone; together they form an intricate, mazelike weave that's impossible to disentangle.

I wrote my memoir, *Turning Japanese*, to explore the cultural amnesia of Japanese Americans, particularly those of the third generation, like myself, who speak little or no Japanese. When I give readings, people often ask if I'm going to raise Samantha with a greater awareness of Japanese culture than I received as a child. The obvious answer is yes. I also acknowledge that the prospects of teaching her about Japanese culture feel to me rather daunting, and I now have more sympathy for my nisei parents, whom I used to criticize for forgetting the past.

And yet, near the end of my stay in Japan, I decided that I was not Japanese, that I was never going to be Japanese, and that I was not even going to be an expert on Japanese culture. My identity was as a Japanese American. That meant claiming the particularities of Japanese-American history; it meant coming to terms with how the dominant culture had formed me; it meant realizing my identity would always be partially occluded. Finally, it meant that the issues of race were central to me, that I would see myself as a person of color.

Can I teach these things to my daughter? My Japanese-American identity comes from my own experience. But I am still trying to understand that experience and still struggling to find language to talk about the issues of race. My failures are caused by more than a lack of knowledge; there's the powerful wish not to know. How, for instance, can I talk to my daughter about sexuality and race? My own life is so filled with shame and regret, so filled with experiences I would rather not discuss, that it seems much easier to opt for silence. It's simpler to pretend multiculturalism means teaching her *kanji* and how to conjugate Japanese verbs.

I know that every day Samantha will be exposed to images telling her that Asian bodies are marginalized, that the women are exotic or sensual or submissive, that the men are houseboys or Chinatown punks, kung fu warriors or Japanese businessmen—robotlike and powerful or robotlike and comic. I know that she will face constant pressure to forget that she is part Japanese American, to assume a basically white middle-class identity. When she reaches adolescence, there will be strong messages for her to dissociate herself from other people of color, perhaps from the children of recent Asian immigrants. She may find herself wanting to assume a privilege and status that come from not calling attention to her identity or from playing into the stereotype that makes Asian women seem so desirable to certain white men. And I know I will have no power over these forces.

Should I tell her of how, when I look at her mother, I know my desire for her cannot be separated from the way the culture has inculcated me with standards of white beauty? Should I tell her of my own desire for a "hallucinatory whiteness," of how in my twenties such a desire fueled a rampant promiscuity and addiction to pornography, to the "beautiful" bodies of white women? It's all too much to expect Samantha to take in. It should not even be written down. It should be kept hidden, unspoken. These forces should not exist. 15

Samantha's presence has made me more willing to speak out on issues of race, to challenge the status quo. I suppose I want her to inherit a different world than the one I grew up in.

One day last year, I was talking with two white friends about the landmark controversy over the Broadway production of *Miss Saigon*. Like many Asian Americans, I agreed with the protest by Actor's Equity against the producer's casting. I felt disturbed that again a white actor, the British Jonathan Pryce, was playing a Eurasian and that no Asian-American actor had been given a chance to audition for that role. Beyond that, I was upset by the Madame Butterfly plot of *Miss Saigon*, where an Asian woman pines for her white male lover.

Both my friends—Paula, a painter, and Mark, a writer—consider themselves liberals; Mark was active in the antiwar movement during the sixties. He was part of my wedding and, at the time, perhaps my closest male friend. But neither agreed with me about *Miss Saigon*. They argued that art represented freedom of the imagination, that it meant trying to get inside other people's skin. Isn't color-blind casting what we're striving for? they said.

"Why is it everyone gets so upset when a white actor may be denied a role?" I asked. "What about every time an Asian-American actor tries out for a part that says 'lawyer' or 'doctor' and is turned down?"

But reverse discrimination isn't the answer, they replied.   20

I don't recall exactly what happened after this. I think the argument trailed off into some safer topic, as such arguments often do. But afterward, I felt angrier and angrier and, at the same time, more despairing. I realized that for me the fact that Warner Oland, a Swede, played Charlie Chan was humiliating. It did not show me that art was a democracy of the imagination. But for Paula and Mark, my sense of shame was secondary to their belief in "freedom" in the arts.

When I talked to my wife about my anger and despair, she felt uncomfortable. These were her friends, too. She said I'd argued before with them about the role of politics in art. Mark had always looked ruefully at his political involvement in the sixties, when he felt he had gone overboard with his zealous self-righteousness. "He's threatened by your increasing political involvement," Susie said. She felt I should take our disagreement as just another incident in a long friendly dialogue.

But when I talked with a black friend, Garth, who's a writer, he replied: "Yeah, I was surprised too at the reaction of some of my white artist friends to *Miss Saigon*. It really told me where they were. It marked a dividing line."

For a while, I avoided talking about my feelings when Paula and Mark came by. Susie urged me to talk to them, to work it out. "You're trying to get me to have sympathy with how difficult this is for them or for you, how this creates tensions between you and them," I said. "But I have to have this conversation about *Miss Saigon* with every white friend I have. Each of you only has to have it with me." My wife said that I was taking my anger out on her—which, in part, I was.

Finally, in a series of telephone calls, I told Paula and Mark I not   25
only felt that their views about *Miss Saigon* were wrong but that they were racially based. In the emotionally charged conversations, I don't think I used the word "racist," but I know my friends objected to my lumping them together with other whites. Paula said I was stereotyping them, that she wasn't like other whites. She told me of her friendships with a few blacks when she lived back East, of the history of her mother's involvement in supporting civil rights. "It's not like I don't know what discrimination is," she said. "Women get discriminated against, so do artists." Her tone moved back and forth between self-righteousness and resentment to distress and tears about losing our friendship.

Mark talked of his shame about being a WASP. "Do you know that I don't have a single male friend who is a WASP?" he said. I decided not to point out that, within the context of color, the difference between a WASP male and, say, an Irish Catholic, isn't much of a difference. And I also didn't remark that he had no friends of color, other than myself. I suppose I felt such remarks would hurt him too much. I also didn't feel it was safe to say them.

A few months later, I had calmer talks with Mark, but they always ended with this distance between us. I needed some acknowledgment from him that, when we began talking about race, I knew more about it than he did, that our arguing about race was not the same as our arguing about free verse versus formal verse. That my experience gave me insights he didn't have.

"Of course, that's true," he said. "I know you've had different experiences." But for him, we had to meet on an equal basis, where his views on race were considered at the start as just as valid as mine. Otherwise, he felt he was compromising himself, giving away his soul. He likened it to the way he gave away his self in his alcoholic family, where he denied his own feelings. He would be making himself a "victim" again.

At one point, I suggested we do some sessions with a therapist who was counseling him and whom I had also gone to. "No," said Mark. "I can't do that now. I need him on my side."

I can still see us sitting there on my front steps, on a warm   30
early-spring day. I looked at this man with whom I'd shared my writing and my most intimate secrets, with whom I'd shared the process of undergoing therapy and recovery, and I realized we were now no longer intimates. I felt that I had embarked on a journey to discover myself as a person of color, to discover the rage and pain that had formed my Japanese-American identity, and that he would deny me this journey. He saw me as someone who would make him a victim, whose feelings on race were charged with arrogance and self-righteousness. And yet, on some level, I know he saw that my journey was good for me. I felt I was asking him to come on that journey with me.

Inevitably I wonder if my daughter will understand my perspective as a person of color. Will she identify with white friends, and be fearful and suspicious of my anger and frustration? Or will she be working from some viewpoint I can't quite conceive, some line that marks her as a person of color and white and neither, all at the same time, as some new being whose experiences I will have to listen to and learn from? How can I prepare her for that new identity?

Will it be fair or accurate or helpful for me to tell her, "Unless the world is radically different, on some level, you will still have to choose: Are you a person of color or not?"

It took me many months to figure out what had gone down with Paula and Mark. Part of me wanted to let things go, but part of me knew that someday I'd have to talk to Samantha about race. If I avoided what was difficult in my own life, what would I be able to say to her? My black friend Alexs and I talked about how whites desperately want to do "the victim limbo," as he called it. Offered by many as a token of solidarity—"I'm just the same as you"—it's really a way of depoliticizing the racial question; it ignores the differences in power in this country that result from race.

When white people engage in conversation about racism, the first thing they often do, as Paula did with me, is the victim limbo: "I'm a woman, I know what prejudice is, I've experienced it." "I'm Jewish/working class/Italian in a WASP neighborhood, I know what prejudice is." The purpose of this is to show the person of color that he or she doesn't really experience anything the white person hasn't experienced, that the white person is a victim too. But Alexs and I both knew that the positions of a person of color and a white person in American society are not the same. "Whites don't want to give up their privilege and psychic comforts," said Alexs. "That's really why they're so angry. They have to choose whether they're going to give up power or fight for it."

Thinking this through, though, does not assuage the pain and　35 bitterness I feel about losing white friendships over race, or the distance I have seen open up between me and my white friends. Nor does it help me explain to my daughter why we no longer see Paula or Mark. The compensation has been the numerous friendships that I've begun to have with people of color. My daughter will grow up in a household where the people who visit will be from a wider spectrum than were those Japanese Americans and whites who visited my parents' house in the suburbs of Chicago.

Not that teaching her about her Asian-American self has become any easier. My wife has been more conscious than I've been about telling Sam that she's Japanese. After playing with blond Shannon, the girl from next door, Sam said: "She's not Japanese, Mom. We're Japanese." "No," said Susie. "Daddy's Japanese, and you're part Japanese, but I'm not Japanese." Sam refused to believe this: "No, you're Japanese." After a few minutes, Susie finally sorted out the confusion. Sam thought being Japanese meant you had black hair.

For many liberal whites, what seems most important in any discussion of race is the need for hope, the need to find some link with people of color. They do not see how much that need serves as a tool of denial, how their claims of solidarity not only ignore real differences but also blot out the reality of people of color. How can we move forward, they ask, with all this rage you seem to feel? How can you stereotype me or group me in this category of whiteness?

I tell them they are still unwilling to examine what being white has meant to their existence. They think their rage at being classified as a white person is the same rage that people of color feel when they are being stereotyped. It is not. When whites feel anger about race, almost always they are feeling a threat to their comfort or power.

In the end, whites must exchange a hope based on naiveté and ignorance for one based on knowledge. For this naive hope denies connections, complexities. It is the drug of amnesia. It says there is no thread from one moment to the next, no cause and effect. It denies consequence and responsibility.

For my wife, this journey has been a difficult one. The arguments   40
we have over race mirror our other arguments; at the same time, they exist in another realm, where I am a person of color and Susie is white. "I realize that in a way I've been passing too," she said a few months ago. "There's this comfort I've got to give up, this ease." At her clinic, she challenges the mainly white children's books in the waiting room, or a colleague's unconscious assumptions about Hmong families. More and more, she finds herself at gatherings where she as a white person is in the minority.

Breaking through denial, seeing how much needs to be changed, does not have to blunt the capacity for hope. For both of us, our daughter is proof of that capacity. And if I know that someday someone will call Samantha a gook, I know today she's a happy child. The love her mother and I share, the love we bear for her, cannot spare her from pain over race, and yet it can make her stronger. Sam will go further than we will, she will know more. She will be like nothing I can imagine, as I am like nothing my parents imagined.

Today my daughter told me she will grow up and work with her mother at the hospital. I'll be a grandpa and stay home and write poems and be with her children. Neither race nor ethnicity enters into her vision of the future. And yet they are already there, with our hopes, gathering shape.

❖ Focused Freewriting   Consider as possible focal points the idea of merging two ethnic identities (as in Japanese American), the discrimination that has embittered many Americans of color, the prospects for better race relations in Samantha's generation, or one of the topics you've identified in your journal.

❖ Guided Responses

1. The full title of Mura's article is "What should I tell Samantha, my biracial daughter, about *secrets and anger?* How is she going to

The names of the friends in this story have been changed.

choose an identity?" Given this title, what do you think Mura means by "secrets and anger"? What might he want to tell his daughter, and why is it so difficult to do so?

2. When Mura suggests a move to an Asian-American community, his wife expresses uneasiness: "I'm afraid you'll cross this bridge and take Sam with you, and leave me here" (para. 4). How does this scene illustrate the tensions and fears in a mixed-race marriage? Do you think Susie's fears are ungrounded? Why, or why not?

3. In an anecdote about his daughter's comment on the girl next door Mura recalls, "Sam thought being Japanese meant you had black hair" (para. 36). What does this anecdote say about children and racial identity? Why do you think Mura includes it here?

4. Mura uses the *Miss Saigon* controversy to illustrate his point that whites and people of color understand racism in fundamentally different ways. To what extent do you agree with him that white liberal hope is "a tool of denial" (para. 37) and "a drug of amnesia" (para. 39)? Explain your response.

❖ Shared Responses　In your journal respond to Mura's statement that within a generation, "the world . . . won't be dominated by the melting-pot model, that multiculturalism is not a project but a reality, that in the next century there will no longer be a white majority in this country" (para. 2). If he's right, how will you be affected? What will this reality mean to society? As you discuss your responses in small groups, focus on the effect of individuals' backgrounds on their responses.

It's All in How You Say It

MICKEY ROBERTS

MICKEY ROBERTS *(Selequia), a member of the Nooksack tribe, spear-headed the movement for federal recognition of the tribe in the 1970s. A graduate of Western Washington University, Roberts is currently pursuing a master's degree in history. She has published a number of short stories on Indian life, as well as* A History of the Nooksack Tribe of the State of Washington. *In this tale, originally published in Craig Lesley's* Talking Leaves: Contemporary Native American Short Stories *(1991), Roberts relates the story of a woman's coming to terms with white ignorance of Indian culture. A particularly insensitive remark made to her as an adult causes the narrator to remember her father's patient understanding of "the outside world."*

Before reading the article, write in your journal about your education regarding Native American culture. How did your elementary school textbooks characterize Indians, if they were mentioned at all? How are Indians characterized in the media?

As you make notes on your reading, you may want to focus on the contrasts Roberts presents between the Native American and white worlds, her use of simple storyteller's language, or her attention to detail.

EVER SINCE I WAS A SMALL GIRL in school, I've been aware of what the school textbooks say about Indians. I am an Indian and, naturally, am interested in what the school teaches about natives of this land.

One day in the grammar school I attended, I read that a delicacy of American Indian people was dried fish, which, according to the textbook, tasted "like an old shoe, or was like chewing on dried leather." To this day I can remember my utter dismay at reading these words. We called this wind-dried fish "sleet-schus," and to us, it was our favorite delicacy and, indeed, did not taste like shoe leather. It took many hours of long and hard work to cure the fish in just this particular fashion. Early fur traders and other non-Indians must have agreed, for they often used this food for subsistence as they traveled around isolated areas.

I brought the textbook home to show it to my father, leader of my tribe at that time. My father was the youngest son of one of the last chiefs of the Nooksack Indian Tribe of Whatcom County in the state of Washington. On this particular day, he told me in his wise and humble manner that the outside world did not always understand Indian people, and that I should not let it hinder me from learning the good parts of education.

Since those early years I have learned we were much better off with our own delicacies, which did not rot our teeth and bring about the various dietary problems that plague Indian people in modern times. I was about eight years old when this incident happened and it did much to sharpen my desire to pinpoint terminology in books used to describe American Indian people, books which are, most often, not very complimentary.

At a later time in my life, I had brought a group of Indian people 5 to the county fairgrounds to put up a booth to sell Indian-made arts and crafts. My group was excited about the prospect of making some money selling genuine Indian artifacts. We thanked the man who showed us our booth and told him it was nice of him to remember the people of the Indian community. The man expanded a little and remarked that he liked Indian people. "In fact," he went on to state, "we are bringing some professional Indians to do the show!"

As we stood there in shock, listening to this uninformed outsider, I looked at my dear Indian companion, an eighty-year-old woman who could well remember the great chiefs of the tribe who once owned all the land of this county before the white man came bringing "civilization," which included diseases and pollution. My friend said not a word, but took the hurt as Indian people have done for many years, realizing outsiders are very often tactless and unthinking.

Of course, we all knew that the "professional Indians" were not Indians at all, but dressed in leather and dancing their own dances. And, anyway, how does one become a "professional Indian"?

I remembered my father's words of so long ago and said to my friend as my father had said to me, "They just don't understand Indian people."

❖ Focused Freewriting   Consider as possible focal points the effect of insensitive portrayals on young Native American children, reasons behind the current interest in "genuine" Indian art and performance, or one of the topics you've identified in your journal.

❖ Guided Responses

1. What is the significance of Roberts's title? How does it relate to the two stories that make up the narrative?

2. The narrator is careful to identify her father as the "leader of my tribe" and "the youngest son of one of the last chiefs of the Nooksack Indian Tribe of Whatcom County in the state of Washington" (para. 3). Why is it important that the reader know her father's status? How would the impact of his words be affected if he weren't described in this way?

3. The narrator makes several disparaging comments about white civilization, noting, for example, that non-Indian delicacies "rot our teeth and bring about . . . various dietary problems" (para. 4). Using this and other comments, characterize the narrator's attitude toward whites. How does this attitude compare with that of her father or her aging companion? How would you account for any differences between her view and that of the older people?

4. Why is the narrator offended by the notion of "professional Indians"? What are the implications of hiring non-Indians to perform "Indian" dances?

❖ Shared Responses   In your journal elaborate on the narrator's final words to her companion. How might you explain the insensitivity of the fair organizers to a woman "who could well remember the great chiefs of the tribe"? (para. 6) What advice would you give her on how to respond to such tactlessness? In your group discussion, differentiate between responses emphasizing confrontation and those advocating more passive resistance.

—— ❖ ——

The Chameleon

ELINOR LANGER

ELINOR LANGER, *who attended Swarthmore College and the adult
degree program at Goddard College, was active in the radical movement during the 1960s. Her biography of Josephine Herbst, subtitled* The Story She Could Never Tell, *was nominated for a
National Book Critics Circle Award. This selection, excerpted from
a 1990 special report on the American neo-Nazi movement in* The
Nation, *analyzes the popularity of David Duke. Unlike other white
supremacist leaders, Duke has an image that is traditionally all-
American, and his acceptance in mainstream politics, according to
Langer, is a frightening omen.*

*Before reading the selection, write in your journal what you
know about white supremacist groups and neo-Nazis. Do you think
they pose a real threat to society? What do you think has precipitated
their current resurgence?*

*As you make notes on your reading, you may want to focus on
the variety of sources Langer quotes in painting her portrait of
Duke. Consider not only their general reliability but also their
motives for speaking out.*

IF TOM METZGER[1] HAS POSITIONED HIMSELF as far outside the system as
it is possible to be without going to jail, the opposite is true of David
Duke, who not only wants in but wants all the way in, preferably as
far as the White House. Duke is a self-assured, conventionally handsome 40-year-old Oklahoma-born Southerner who has been evading
questions on national television since he emerged as leader of the
Knights of the Ku Klux Klan in the mid-1970s—often, as a matter of
fact, the same questions. If the typical appearance by Metzger on *Race
and Reason* features the bogus exploration by host and guest of some
of the higher intricacies of their common ground, the typical Duke

---

[1] Leader of the California-based White Aryan Nation (WAR).

television appearance is a perfunctory stand-off in which the host is more interested in conveying his righteousness than in the answers, and the guest is more interested in conveying his mailing address than in the questions.

Something of the mindlessness of these stalemates is suggested by a Duke appearance last fall on *ABC News Primetime Live* with Sam Donaldson, in which to every question provided Donaldson by his researchers the answer was invariably a polite denial.

> Donaldson: "You believe in the Nazi creed, in the Nazi views?"
> Duke: "Sir, I certainly don't. . . .
> Donaldson: "If . . . you don't believe in [them], why do   5
> you tell people now that you admire Joseph Mengele?"
> Duke: "I don't say that I admire him at all."
>
>   . . .
>
> Donaldson: "You think that blacks are genetically inferior
> to whites?"
> Duke: "No sir. . . . "
> Donaldson: "You don't? Well, then, why did you write in
> your National Association for the Advancement of White Peo-
> ple newsletter in 1986, and I quote, 'Negroes are lower on the
> evolutionary scale than Caucasians'?"
> Duke: "I don't think I said that, sir."   10
> Donaldson: "You wrote it. You didn't say it, I suppose."
> And so on.
> "You said," Donaldson continued, " 'Jewish people have
> put the interest of race over the interest of the American
> people,' " citing remarks Duke made at a Klan rally near
> Clearwater, Florida.
> "I've been quoted tens of thousands of times by tens of
> thousands of publications—"
> "Did you say it? Do you deny it?"   15
> "Not in the way—I do think—"
> "Did you say it?"
> "Would you let me finish?"
> "Did you say it?"
> "Sir, I don't think I said that. . . . "   20

Duke eventually admitted to a different statement and changed the subject, though probably not before winning viewer support for his better manners.

How Donaldson could sleep that night when he had utterly failed to establish that his guest was not an ordinary racist politician leading a backlash in a period of black progress but a racial thinker whose deepest ideological roots go back to the Nazi era is little short of a wonder of nature, but then how Oprah, Donahue or Geraldo can sleep when they have consistently provided the neo-Nazis with propaganda opportunities possibly unrivaled since *Triumph of the Will* is a wonder too. For in the words of Jason Berry, a New Orleans investigative journalist who is one of the few to get to the heart of the matter of David Duke, "Duke is building a political base, grounded in Nazi master-race theory, under the noses of acquiescent Louisiana Republicans"—and few people understand what is happening.

The difference between the apparent Duke who regularly triumphs over superficial television hosts and the real Duke is less a matter of particular statements than of his system of thought. He has been so beguiling to so many interviewers over the years that the two words most frequently used to describe him have probably been "Robert Redford," but a more telling comparison would be Dorian Gray, for he has one of those ageless faces upon which neither time nor experience seems to register; and, at least on film, he looks almost the same now as he did in his 20s. His ideas, too, are changeless, expressed in set phrases and sentences labeled by various reporters as "tapes," "mantras" and "songs." A perfect exemplar of what Richard Hofstadter, in *The Paranoid Style in American Politics,* calls a demi-intellectual, he has been a passionate student of "racial science" since a precocious encounter with Carleton Putnam's *Race and Reason* at age 13. For many years he operated a Klan bookstore in the New Orleans suburb of Metairie that offered such staples of the racial movement as *Hitler's Last Testament* and innumerable works on race and culture, like Francis Parker Yockey's *Imperium,* which have the status of classics within the movement but are little known outside it. He sold the books through a mail-order catalogue, and, up to about a year ago, through his legislative office as well.

His ideas appear to have come right from his bookshelves. "I came to believe that race was the most important thing to civilization in building a society and a nation. In fact, I came to believe the most important thing in the world was people—the quality of people. I came to feel our race was being overcome by the nonwhite world," he told writer Patsy Sims, who interviewed him for her book, *The Klan,* in 1976. He says the identical thing today. The implications he draws from this conviction were perhaps best spelled out in a lament called "America at the Crossroads," which he published in his National Association for the Advancement of White People newsletter in 1983. "Immigration," he wrote,

> along with nonwhite birthrates will make white people a minority totally vulnerable to the political, social, and economic will of blacks, Mexicans, Puerto Ricans, and Orientals. A social upheaval is now beginning to occur that will be the funeral dirge of the America we love. I shudder to contemplate

the future under nonwhite occupation; rapes, murders, rob-
beries multiplied a hundred fold, illiteracy such as in Haiti,
medicine such as in Mexico, and tyranny such as in Togoland.
Am I an alarmist? Is my vision unreal? All one has to do is
look around this globe and see the Third World reality. Are
whites holding every one of the nonwhite countries down, or
are we in fact pumping billions of dollars into them along
with every technological aid that the West can produce? And
now the West itself is gradually being enveloped by nonwhite
immigration. The exploding numbers of nonwhites are slowly
wrapping formerly white nations in a dark human cocoon.
Shall a butterfly emerge, or the beast that has haunted the
ruins of every great white civilization that submitted to invasion by immigration and racial miscegenation?

Are blacks less intelligent than whites in terms of I.Q.? "Sure,"   25
Duke told *Hustler* magazine in 1982. "The average white and black
have markedly different IQ's; maybe 15 to 20 points separate the two.
I've also heard the argument that blacks are much more intelligent
than the lowest whites. But there are gorillas in this country with IQs
of 90, higher than many people. That does not make gorillas and
people the same." Is integration acceptable? "We're totally opposed to
[it]. We think integration has only caused hatred and violence between the races. We think the races should be separated—whether in
this country or even outside the country is something time will tell."
Did the Holocaust take place? "Jews gain certain advantages by promoting the Holocaust idea. It inspires tremendous financial aid for
Israel. It makes organized Jewry almost immune from criticism.
Whether the Holocaust is real or not, the Jews clearly have a motive
for fostering the idea that it occurred." Whatever the subject, his
opinions refer back to racist intellectual sources ranging from Lothrop
Stoddard's *The Rising Tide of Color* and *Racial Realities of Europe,* both
published in the 1920s, to *The Talmud Unmasked,* by Father Prainatis,
all of which he has sold. And he has even added to the literature
himself with a pamphlet called *Who Runs the Media?*—"an excellent
booklet," the catalogue description says, "documenting Zionist control of America's mass media, how the control was achieved, and the
ramifications of this alien domination," one of his favorite themes.

His program is as consistent as his principles. A subject of constant interest has been "racial betterment." Well over a decade ago, he
advocated such eugenic interventions as tax incentives for people
with high I.Q.s to have more children, and he still advocates such
programs. His equally longstanding criticism of welfare—that it encourages those with the lowest I.Q.s to have the most children—is also
more eugenic than economic. "It's against evolution," he says. "You

must understand," he has warned, "that the white people are becoming a second-class citizens' group in our own country. . . . We're losing our rights all the way across the board. White people face massive discrimination in employment opportunities, in scholarship opportunities, in promotions in industry, in college entrance examinations." On the surface, such a statement could be the platform of an illiberal but still legitimate white politician willing to trade this or swap that for a curb on the minority assistance programs that have been offered as a result of the civil rights movement, but in Duke's case its racialist roots give it a hidden meaning.

The emotional forces behind Duke's ideological fixations are beyond journalistic reach, but it is hard to resist the speculation that the need to outdo a conservative father, who spent over a decade away from home while Duke was growing up, may have played a part. The family moved a lot when he was a boy before settling in New Orleans in the early 1960s, possibly also creating a need for internal order to counter the external chaos; there is not enough biographical evidence to say. His political constancy appears to coexist with an often remarked inconstancy, not least of the heart. One has to wonder what his black nanny, Pinkie, who used to eat at the table with his family, would say if she could see him now. His womanizing was well known in and out of the racial movement long before his divorce in the early 1980s; he has a history of troubled relations with colleagues; and in other personal matters, too, he appears to have difficulty maintaining a fixed course. Widely reported to be highly obsessed with his health—he lifts weights and chews vitamin pills and health foods—he is also concerned about his image, and, according to Metzger at least, has already had a face lift. Besides articles published under his own name, he has published pseudonymously in fields ranging from the martial arts to the environment, including a sex manual that tells women how to please men. Whatever his successes in public encounters and with crowds, in private relations he seems to leave a sense of uneasiness behind.

That slipperiness does not affect his constituents, one of whom, asked recently before television cameras why she idolized Duke, replied simply, "Because he hates niggers," but it bothers some within the racial movement, who often wonder whether they can trust him or not. Metzger, who says, "I don't go out of my way to attack David Duke because he contains the seeds of his own destruction," calls him a chameleon. "Snake oil," says Rick Cooper, the Portland neo-Nazi. "He can wriggle out of any question." His newest colleagues appear to share this view. A fellow Louisiana legislator said recently on national television, "David Duke will look into your eyes and lie and expect you to believe it. He has a warped sense of what reality is," evidently without fear of contradiction. Whether these attributes are liabilities or assets for an ambitious politician can be argued, but with his smooth exterior concealing so many anomalies of character, it is hard to believe there is no portrait of him somewhere, rotting away.

The Candidate's Résumé

Whatever Duke's personality, he has always been on the move. An activist as well as a reader, he seems to have spent the years following his Putnam epiphany searching for the correct organizational form to express his convictions: the Klan in high school; the White Youth Alliance, which he formed when he was at Louisiana State University and which became affiliated with various Rockwell[2]-related splinter groups in college; and after graduation the Klan again, the base from which he made his initial national impact. Duke's leadership, first of the Louisiana Knights of the Ku Klux Klan and then of its national office, was important for several reasons, not least his recruitment of some powerful men, including Metzger in California, Louis Beam in Texas, Bill Wilkinson in Louisiana and Don Black in Alabama, many of whom remain central to the racial movement today. Duke also modernized the organization, welcoming women and Catholics for the first time, dressing in suits rather than robes and calling himself "National Director" instead of "Imperial Wizard." Under his auspices, the Klan conducted a military organizing drive that made itself felt at Camp Pendleton in California, at Fort Hood in Texas and in the Navy, and experienced something of a general revival as well.

In 1980, in part because of a struggle with Wilkinson, who was   30 running the Knights of the Ku Klux Klan's Louisiana branch, Duke left to form the National Association for the Advancement of White People, which he described then, as he does now, as a "civil rights lobby for white people" and which he has used in his march into mainstream politics. That effort began in 1975, when he won about a third of the votes during an unsuccessful statewide run for the Louisiana Senate in the campaign assisted by Metzger. He ran again with similar results in 1979 but clearly did not lose the taste, and in the late 1980s he began a new electoral phase. In 1988 he ran for President in the Democratic primaries in a number of states and, when that effort collapsed, as the presidential candidate of the Populist Party, a campaign backed primarily by the party's organizational alter ego, the Liberty Lobby. In February 1989 he was elected to the Louisiana leg-

---

[2] George Lincoln Rockwell, leader of the American Nazi party.

islature from Metairie as a Republican and, although he lost a bid for the party's official nomination, he is now running in Louisiana's open primary as a maverick Republican for the U.S. Senate seat held by Democrat J. Bennett Johnston.

What is important about Duke's political biography, however, is that although it is usually represented as a succession it is actually more of an accretion. On the course from his adolescent Klan membership to his present Republicanism, Duke has touched all the important bases of the racial movement in the United States and abandoned none. His relationships with former associates such as Metzger and Beam might not be what they once were, but they are not known to be broken either, and Duke's political entourage is full of familiar faces. When he announced his Democratic presidential bid in Atlanta in 1988, there cheering him on was Don Black, the Alabama Klan leader, who is best known for his role in a neo-Nazi/Klan attempt to overthrow the government of the island of Dominica in return for land for paramilitary training camps. Black was technically Duke's successor in the national Knights of the K.K.K. and is married to Duke's former wife. Also at the announcement were Daniel Carver, then the Imperial Wizard of a different Klan organization, the Invisible Empire, and such old-line racists as Ed Fields, founder of the National States Rights Party and editor of its paper, *The Thunderbolt*, with which Duke had some connection as long ago as college.

In addition to Black, whose political life began as a Rockwell follower, Duke is also actively associated with two other men whose Nazi ties go directly back to the time of George Lincoln Rockwell: James Warner, head of an anti-Semitic church, newsletter and book publishing operation known as the New Christian Crusade Church in Metairie, Louisiana, who began as an information officer for the National Socialist White People's Party, the successor to Rockwell's American Nazi Party, and Ralph Forbes, head of a similar operation in Arkansas called the Sword of Christ Good News Ministry, who started out as the so-called commander of the American Nazi Party's western division. Warner, a longtime partner of Duke in the book business, resumed a ruptured relationship with him to assist in his legislative campaign and in January 1990 served as an elected Duke delegate to the Louisiana Republican convention. Forbes, who recently made an unexpectedly strong bid for the G.O.P. nomination for lieutenant governor of Arkansas, is publisher of a newspaper called *The Truth*, whose inaugural edition (January 1989) announced in banner type, "Good News America: There Is a White Christmas in Your Future"; sold Rockwelliana as well as many other items of neo-Nazi memorabilia, such as "Musik of the Afrika Corps"; included several pages of "satire" calling Michael Dukakis "Michael Dukikiz," presenting Willie Horton as I.R.S. commissioner and Rabbi Meir Kahane as chief justice; and featuring a mock pledge of allegiance to ZOG, presumably to illustrate the fate America so narrowly escaped. . . . Forbes was the director of Duke's 1988 presidential campaign. So dense and long-lived are Duke's Nazi associations, in fact, that you would think the only way he could escape them would be through reincarnation. Like the fictional General Guzman in Lawrence Thornton's novel *Imagining Argentina,* Duke "sees history from the time of the Romans to the rise of Hitler as a dark age in which men and women of many nations became philosophically perverted, denying the necessity of a single-minded vision, of the purity he believes Hitler saw and embraced as fiercely as a wild-eyed prophet . . . on a windy mountaintop." Like Guzman, too, he "has met secretly in heavily guarded houses deep in the jungle, or in cafes in tiny villages where he has looked across the table at Mengele and lesser exponents of that dream which he feels more than ever was defiled by the faint of heart, the women in man's spirit," communing with his mentors—if only, in Duke's case, in his dreams.

How much Duke's present admirers understand of his vision is open to question. His campaign literature avoids obvious racialist formulations while bluntly attacking the "illegitimate welfare rate," minority set-asides, illegal immigration and affirmative action in language designed to appeal to the "middle-class, productive" American. The Louisiana Coalition Against Racism and Nazism, which follows Duke closely, believes he has been successful in detaching his past from his present, following a "dual strategy" by which "in public he promotes moderate conservatism, keyed to racial issues," while "within his activist circle, he continues a second campaign, a shadow campaign, [embodying his] long-term design, his dream of a genetically engineered super race, born into existence by a legion of white supremacists."

As unlikely as it seems that any American politician with even a hint of such a vision could get very far, the fact is that Duke is doing well. For his legislative campaign from tiny Metairie, more than $130,000 came in from supporters around the country, and his Senate race has raised more than $700,000 so far. He has a mailing list of about 30,000 donors. A poll commissioned by three-term Senator Johnston shows Duke with a 98 percent name recognition factor compared with Johnston's own 88 percent. General polls show Duke running with about 25 percent of the public's support, well ahead of the official Republican candidate, State Senator Ben Bagert, though far behind the 60 percent of Democratic incumbent Johnston. Since 26 percent of Louisiana's voters are black, Duke would need 70 percent of the white vote in order to get to Washington.

Throughout his career, Duke has consistently done better than people have expected. His staff points out that two days before he won his legislative seat polls showed him running behind, and concludes that people are reluctant to tell poll takers their true opinions—a view shared by reporters, who are seeing large crowds on the campaign trail. A similar phenomenon may be occurring at the legislature, where the House, against all predictions, passed a Duke-sponsored antiaffirmative action bill at the end of May, a development that left opponents so nonplused that one of them, searching for explanations other than that people agreed with the bill's contents, cited the full moon. According to recent reports, Duke is also finding himself increasingly more welcome in the New Orleans social and political establishment. With each step forward, the possibility of the Republican Party mobilizing against Duke decreases. Like other ideological politicians, he may sell out as he moves up—but then again, he may not. The only thing that can be said for certain is that as long as David Duke is in elective office—any office—the gap between the racial movement and conventional politics will get narrower.

❖ **Focused Freewriting** Consider as possible focal points the threat posed by neo-Nazi groups, the significance of Duke's mainstream popularity, or one of the topics you've identified in your journal.

❖ **Guided Responses**

1. Early on in her portrait, Langer chastises television news reporters and talk-show hosts for providing neo-Nazis with "propaganda opportunities" (para. 22). Why do you think Langer sees these shows simply as propaganda? On what grounds—besides profit—would producers of programs such as *PrimeTime Live, Oprah, Donahue,* and *Geraldo* justify the shows? Do you think there is any value in airing neo-Nazi views? Explain your response.

2. Langer takes up much of the first half of this selection with quotations from Duke himself, often with little commentary to accompany them. Why do you think Langer chooses to make so few comments of her own? What is the effect of these quotations and in what way might their impact be different had Langer chosen simply to paraphrase Duke?

3. Langer contends that Duke's racist politics "appear to have come right from his bookshelves" (para. 24), calling him a "demi-intellectual" (para. 23). Based on your reading of the article, why do you think it's important for Duke to base his politics on apparently intel-

lectual theories? How does this approach set him apart from the stereotypical racist? Why does it make his theories more dangerous?

4. In the section titled "The Candidate's Résumé," Langer enumerates Duke's many associations with extreme racists, neo-Nazis, and Klan officers. What is the purpose of a résumé? What do you think Langer hopes to accomplish by using this title? Do you think she succeeds? Why, or why not?

❖ Shared Responses   In your journal explore the possible reasons for David Duke's popularity outside extreme racist circles. What does his success say about our society's values? How does it illustrate our problems? How can we address these problems? As you discuss your responses in small groups, try to reach a consensus about the causes of Duke's popularity. If you can't develop a common response, highlight the primary differences between individual responses.

Para Teresa[1]

INÉS HERNANDEZ

Inés Hernandez *is Nimipu (Nez Percé Indian) and Chicana. She has taught English and Chicano studies at the University of Texas, Austin, and is currently assistant professor of Native American studies at the University of California at Davis. This poem, from the collection* Con Razón, Corazon: Poetry *(1977), tells of an encounter between schoolgirls who have different ways of exhibiting cultural pride. The understanding that the narrator has achieved through the years prompts her to acknowledge her old enemy as a sister.*

Before reading the selection, write in your journal about how you perceive the struggle to maintain pride in one's particular ethnic or racial heritage while living in a sometimes hostile dominant culture. When is rebellion a good thing? When is it better to achieve within the dominant culture? Is it possible for people of color to strike a balance between the two cultures?

As you make notes on your reading, you may want to focus on the concrete images used to illustrate the two different methods of defiance.

A tí-Teresa
Te dedico las palabras estás
que explotan de mi corazón[2]

That day during lunch hour
at Alamo which-had-to-be-its-name
Elementary
my dear raza
That day in the bathroom

[1] For Teresa.
[2] To you, Teresa, I dedicate these words that explode from my heart.

147

Door guarded
Myself cornered
I was accused by you, Teresa
Tú y las demas de tus amigas
Pachucas todas
Eran Uds. cinco.[3]

Me gritaban que porque me creía tan
          grande[4]
What was I trying to do, you growled
Show you up?
Make the teachers like me, pet me,
Tell me what a credit to my people I
          was?
I was playing right into their hands,
          you challenged
And you would have none of it.
I was to stop.

I was to be like you
I was to play your game of deadly
          defiance
Arrógance, refusal to submit.
The game in which the winner takes
          nothing
Asks for nothing
Never lets his weaknesses show.

But I didn't understand.   5
My fear salted with confusion
Charged me to explain to you
I did nothing *for the teachers*.
I studied for my parents and for my
          grandparents
Who cut out honor roll lists
Whenever their nietos'[5] names appeared
For my shy mother who mastered her
          terror
to demand her place in mother's clubs
For my carpenter-father who helped
          me patiently with my math.

[3] You and the rest of your friends, all Pachucas, there were five of you.
[4] You were screaming at me, asking me why I thought I was so great.
[5] Grandchildren's.

For my abuelos que me regalaron lápices
      en la Navidad[6]
And for myself.

Porque reconocí en aquel entonces
una verdad tremenda
que me hizo a mi un rebelde
Aunque tú no te habías dado cuenta.[7]
We were not inferior
You and I, y las demás de tus amigas
Y los demás de nuestra gente[8]
I knew it the way I know I was alive
We were good, honorable, brave
Genuine, loyal, strong

And smart.
Mine was a deadly game of defiance,
      also.
My contest was to prove
beyond any doubt
that we were not only equal but superior
      to them.
That was why I studied.
If I could do it, we all could.

You let me go then,
Your friends unblocked the way
I who-did-not-know-how-to-fight
was not made to engage with you-who-
      grew-up-fighting
Tu y yo, Teresa[9]
We went in different directions
Pero fuimos juntas.[10]

In sixth grade we did not understand
Uds. with the teased, dyed-black-but-
      reddening hair,
Full petticoats, red lipsticks
and sweaters with the sleeves

---

[6] Grandparents who gave me gifts of pencils at Christmas.
[7] Because I recognized a great truth then that made me a rebel, even though you hadn't noticed it.
[8] And the rest of your friends / And the rest of our people.
[9] You and I.
[10] But we went together.

pushed up
Y yo conformándome con lo que deseaba
        mi mamá[11]
Certainly never allowed to dye, to tease,
        to paint myself
I did not accept your way of anger,
Your judgements
You did not accept mine

But now in 1975, when I am twenty-eight   10
Teresa
I remember you.
Y sabes—
Te comprendo,
Es más, te respeto.
Y, si me pérmites,
Te nombro—"hermana."[12]

❖ Focused Freewriting   Consider as possible focal points the difference in understanding between the narrator as child and as adult,
the timeless adolescent conflict between "rebels" and "conformists"
of all races, or one of the topics you've identified in your journal.

❖ Guided Responses

1. Why do you think Hernandez shifts between Spanish and English in the poem? How might her intended audience have influenced
this decision? Recopy the poem all in one language. How does the
impact change?

2. How does Teresa perceive the narrator's behavior? What does
the narrator mean when she explains the "verdad tremenda" (great
truth; stanza 6), and how does that justify, in her own mind, her quest
for good grades?

3. Why do you think Teresa and her friends let the narrator go?
Does Teresa come to an understanding of their sisterhood earlier than
the narrator? Explain your response with references to the poem.

4. How do you think Teresa would respond to this poem if she
were to read it in 1975? Would she reach the same conclusions as the
narrator? Would she consent to being called "hermana" (sister)? Explain your response.

---

[11] And I conforming to my mother's wishers.
[12] And do you know what, I understand you. What's more, I respect you. And, if
you permit me, I call you my sister.

❖ Shared Responses   In your journal explore the importance to an ethnic group of maintaining its native language. What are the advantages and disadvantages for the group? for the dominant society? As you discuss your responses in small groups, distinguish between responses based primarily on personal experience and those based primarily on beliefs or social theories.

❖ Generating Ideas   Reread all of your journals and annotations from the selections in this unit. Look for connections between selections or still unanswered questions. First, list those connections and questions as briefly as possible. Next, choose two or three to elaborate on. As you respond in more detail to the connections and questions, focus on one topic and consider how well it would serve you in an extended piece of writing. Then decide what kind of writing best suits your topic: Should you write a conventional essay, a poem, a short story, or a scene? Would your topic lend itself more to a letter to the editor or a personal letter? Might a proposal to solve a specific problem be a good choice? Possible topics:

1. the power of the dominant culture over subcultures
2. the importance of socioeconomic status in defining culture
3. the significance of names and language
4. the pitfalls of cultural elitism
5. clashes between and within cultures

❖ Focusing Responses   Choose one of your extended responses and formulate a statement of one or two sentences that captures its essence. Use this statement as a guide to organize your piece. (If you write an essay, letter, or proposal, the statement may actually appear as a thesis.)

❖ Guided Writing Assignments

1. Many of the writers in this chapter (Cary, Coles, Roberts, Hamper, and Mura) explore the impact of cultural issues on children. If children are to live harmoniously in a multicultural society, these issues must be resolved. Drawing from several of these selections, write a proposal for an elementary school program that introduces students to different cultures and fosters tolerance and understanding. Be sure to consider socioeconomic as well as racial and ethnic issues.

2. Using different approaches, Ventura and Mura each discuss the importance of mass media in transmitting cultural values. Using your own experience of television and movies, write a letter to the editor of a major newspaper criticizing the media's role in undermining cultural harmony. Consider such issues as the portrayal of people of color; the predominance of beautiful, wealthy families on television;

the presentation of violence and its consequences; the treatment of various social concerns; or other issues you find relevant.

3. Hamper and Coles present contrasting views of white America, usually considered the dominant culture. One might argue from these selections that it is primarily socioeconomic status, not color, that determines the dominant culture. Mura, Njeri, and Cary, however, would seem to argue the opposite: that even privileged members of minority groups suffer at the hands of the white, dominant culture. Choose one of these positions and, using evidence from the selections, construct an argument to support your view.

4. David Duke's ideas are obviously at odds with those of most of the other authors in this chapter. Using material from the selections as well as your own imagination, construct a conversation between David Duke and one of the people of color represented here. Allow the characters to cite intellectual sources to support their arguments as well as personal experience.

❖ Research Topics   As you consider how to expand your reading beyond the selections in this chapter, identify in your journals and notes questions that remain unanswered or topics you'd like to explore further. Or you may consider the following:

1. Research the history of the Ku Klux Klan in the United States. Consider the organization's beginnings, the sources of its membership and support, its relationship with other white supremacist groups, and the reasons for its resurgence in the past decade. Explore also how civil rights groups have fought it, how the media have covered it, and its prospects for the near future.

2. David Mura refers at length to the controversy over the casting of a white man to play the lead role in *Miss Saigon.* Using that incident as a starting point, research issues of race and ethnicity in movies, television, and/or theater. You may wish to concentrate on the difficulties faced by actors of color, the portrayal of various ethnic and racial groups on stage and screen, or the history of one group in the performing arts. After doing your research, you may want to come back to Mura's anecdote and decide whether or not you agree with his position.

—— Chapter 3 ——

A Sense of Home

I F YOU WERE TO ASK several members of your class to explain what the terms *home, family,* and *community* mean to them, you'd probably end up with as many different definitions as people interviewed. The variety of racial, ethnic, religious, socioeconomic, and other cultural factors that enter into such definitions defies attempts by politicians and religious leaders to impose a generic concept of home, family, or community on the public. During the 1992 presidential campaign the impossibility of defining such terms became apparent as both Democrats and Republicans sought to embrace "family values."

For many people, the term *family* conjures up the image of a working father, a homemaker mother, and two or three well-groomed, polite children living in a neat house in the suburbs. The reality of family is often quite different, however: Many families are headed by a single parent; many include grandparents and other relatives; still others include live-in partners who are not married. In addition, recent census data indicates that the number of Americans who live alone is steadily increasing—how do these people fit into a definition of family?

And what do today's families call home? While Americans still may envision that neat house in the suburbs, in fact we call a number of different locales and dwellings home. Urban centers house millions of people; rural areas, while sparsely populated, remain home for a significant number of Americans; institutions of various sorts—schools, hospitals, prisons—are home to more people. And, sadly, an increasing number of Americans have no one place to call home.

This chapter presents a number of different communities, each of which offers its own definition of home:

In Lev Raphael's "Okemos, Michigan," a homosexual couple establishes a satisfying family life in suburban America, despite their apprehensions about fitting into a traditional community.

A young girl's first foray away from the security of her family is the subject of Lorene Cary's "Welcome to St. Paul's." As Libby enters an exclusive boarding school, she realizes that this will be her home for much of the next two years.

In "Cupcake Land," Richard Rhodes uses humor to temper his dismay at the increasing blandness of Kansas City, his hometown. His nostalgic reveries recall a livelier, more diverse community than he sees now.

Joseph L. White's dismay is presented more seriously, as he criticizes white social scientists' attempts to define "Black Family Life" using a "deficit-deficiency" model. White argues that if they developed a model based on African-American families, the relative health of African-American family life would be acknowledged.

Children's loss of family and community life when mothers are incarcerated is the subject of Virginia A. Huie's "Mom's in Prison: Where Are the Kids?" How can children have a sense of home and family when they are forcibly separated from their mothers?

Other types of adversity are highlighted in "The Remarkable Journey of Willie Edward Gary," Wil Haygood's portrait of one man's debt to the impoverished community that supported him in his quest for an education.

Solutions to the problem of homelessness are offered in Steven VanderStaay's "Ask a Homeless Person. . . ." Scorning programs developed by social service agencies, the homeless people who speak out in this selection have built their own communities.

Finally, in "Harvest Home," David Bradley emphasizes the importance of ritual and tradition in maintaining strong family ties. Legendary figures join forces with ordinary family members to maintain a vibrant tradition.

As you read the vastly different stories told in this chapter, you should begin to appreciate the infinite variety of communities in this country, as well as the intrinsic value to the individual of a sense of home.

Okemos, Michigan

LEV RAPHAEL

LEV RAPHAEL, *a native of New York City, received an M.F.A. in creative writing at the University of Massachusetts, Amherst and a Ph.D. in American studies from Michigan State University, where he taught until 1988. In addition to being a prize-winning author of over thirty short stories, he has also written a literary study,* Edith Wharton's Prisoners of Shame, *and co-authored (with Gershen Kaufman) two self-help books. His collection* Dancing on Tisha B'Av *won a 1990 Lambda Literary Award. In this essay, originally published in John Preston's* Hometowns: Gay Men Write About Where They Belong *(1991), Raphael explores a quintessential image of American tradition—turning a house into a home—through the eyes of a gay man. His account of how home ownership contributes to a sense of belonging and of family calls into question the characterization of homosexuality as an "alternative lifestyle."*

Before reading the selection, write in your journal about the images you associate with home. How important are the surroundings? the dwelling itself? the people with whom you live?

As you make notes on your reading, you may want to focus on the contrasts between city life and suburban life, the conflicts between Raphael's need for privacy and his gay pride, and his burgeoning sense of family.

WE WERE JUST LOOKING—that's all I had agreed to.

Five years ago, I had reluctantly said I would "look," after Gersh, my life partner, had called while I was at a conference in San Francisco. He told me that we should buy a house in Okemos (where we had separate apartments) instead of trying to rent one, because there weren't many rentals available in Okemos just then. I felt both sick and stunned at the idea of owning a house, let alone our actually living together, and the day after he called, I came down with the flu.

I had grown up in Washington Heights, that hilly and park-filled upper Manhattan neighborhood as remote to many New Yorkers as

Riverdale or even Albany, though it's now infamous for the cocaine sales and murders scarring its Depression-era buildings and shaded boulevards. Back then, I thought of houses as completely alien, out in the suburbs, something to visit or drive by. And I pictured them as negatively as Birkin did in *Women in Love:* " 'The world all in couples, each in its own little house, watching its own little interests, and stewing in its own little privacy—it's the most repulsive thing on earth.' "

But Indian Hills, the Okemos subdivision in which we saw our third house one sunny May morning, was not at all repulsive. It is an oak-lined neighborhood of about two hundred houses, a few miles from Michigan State University in East Lansing, with curving streets; old blue spruce, maples, scotch pines, towering arbor vitae, weeping willows, and magnolias; overgrown yew hedges and shrubs; lots of nearly an acre; and thirty- or forty-year-old houses set well back from the road. There are some large homes, but this is not the wealthiest part of a prosperous and stoutly Republican suburb studded with Michigan State faculty members, but dominated by Lansing-area professionals whose wives wear mink and drive Cutlass Cierras, Jaguars, and the occasional Porsche. The houses in Indian Hills are not at all pretentious, like the newer, Tudoresque ones in nearby subdivisions that dwarf their tiny lots with only a scrap of yard.

Indian Hills is even more appealing given that a few minutes   5
away you could be in any featureless part of the homogenized Midwest, swamped by malls and minimalls, wholesale outlets, fast-food and video encampments, and grim acres of parking lots. Best of all, the day we saw our house, we drove off East Lansing's and Okemos' main street, Grand River Avenue, to cross a narrow bridge into the subdivision. The road curved around a golf course, which was studded with groups of shirtless hunky young men as picturesque as baby lambs on an English lord's estate. "Beautiful," I murmured. And it all was, though the four-bedroom house we stopped at looked like a simple ranch-style house from outside. It was fronted at the street by a ginkgo tree—which I recognized from its fan-shaped leaves because one had grown in the park near my elementary school in Inwood. Finding the ginkgo and having crossed the bridge made me feel I had entered some childhood fantasy.

Up near the house was an enormous flowering tree in full bloom, whose wide-spreading boughs started from just a few feet above the ground; the blossoms were pink, edged with white. I discovered it was a hawthorn, the first one I had ever had named for me, and so, like a child learning the word for *table*, I felt suddenly possessed of mysterious but useful information.

Years before this morning, in New York, I had gone apartment hunting with my best friend Kris, and we unexpectedly and angrily fled from one with a sumptuous view of the Hudson because the apartment made us feel very anxious. "This is an *awful* place," my friend said, confused by the intensity of her feeling. "Something *terrible* happened there!" It *did* feel awful, almost possessed, but this house on Chippewa Drive felt welcoming and warm. From a brick-walled vestibule, we stepped into a large open living room-dining room (the "great room") with a stone fireplace at one end. The long wall with large windows facing the back was not parallel with the one opposite it, nor was one in the dining area—somehow these anomalies were delightful. My partner and I looked at each other, and kept looking as we moved through the house, which was bigger and deeper than it had seemed from the street, and far more beautiful. The colors throughout were royal blue, maroon, beige, and orange, and kept appearing in varying combinations in shades, curtains, custom-made rugs. Our tiny, tipsy-sounding realtor with big hair explained it was a red-ribbon house—you could move right in without having to change or prepare anything. That expression made me think of a contest capped by prizes and applause.

Each room drew us into the next. Details kept bursting on us like fireworks: the Italian tiles in the kitchen, exquisite fabric on the living-room walls, honey-colored pine in the room I knew would be my study because it faced that glorious hawthorn in the front yard. We were falling in love not just with the house, but with the idea of ourselves there, with the idea of a home. We fit in. We looked at it twice more that day, brought Gersh's two sons over to see what they thought (since they would be spending about half of their time with us), we looked at each other and said yes, and we made our offer that evening.

Gersh had wanted to live with me for years, but I had never believed it was possible—not because I doubted that gay men could live loving and happy lives together, but partly because Michigan, and more particularly the East Lansing area, had already become my home as an outwardly straight man, and I was unprepared to make the shift, to emerge, to give up my anonymity. I had come to Michigan in 1981 to do a doctorate, but really to escape my family, and more important, to escape New York. It was a city I no longer had the courage or patience to live in: dirtier, noisier, more crowded and dangerous than the city I had thought was the center of the universe when I was growing up. Two and a half years in bucolic Amherst, Massachusetts, had shown me I could flourish outside of New York.

I fell in love with Michigan when I got here, exploring MSU's lush and spreading campus, traveling around the state with its more than three thousand miles of shoreline, up to Hemingway country, to Lake Michigan, Lake Huron, the Keewenau Peninsula, crossing the Mackinac Bridge at sunset. Life seemed simpler here, less oppressive, more inviting; like Jodi Mitchell's free man in Paris, here in Michigan, "I felt unfettered and alive." Of course, being a graduate student is a strange mix in which the elements of slavery are often masked by romanticism, but even as I was finishing my degree, I knew that I would want to stay here: people were friendlier, without the walls that any city demanded for survival. And most important, I could write here. In the mid-eighties, I had finally begun to feel that I had a career as a writer, and an audience.

Gersh was also a transplanted New Yorker (we had even gone to the same high school ten years apart) and felt about Michigan as I did. But having already made his great plunge into the future through divorce, he was ready and eager for a complete life together. The most I had previously agreed to was getting an apartment in the same complex that he lived in. No one would see us, I thought. And here was the other side of living where we did: visibility. There were no crowds to lose yourself in. So this sudden about-face, the abruptness of my decision to say yes to the house, to our living together, was all the more astonishing.

When we finally moved into the house, I was paranoid about being observed every time we were out in the enormous backyard with its two sassafras trees, maples, and oaks, or trimming hedges in the front, or even walking to the front door with groceries. In New York, neighbors had seemed tamer, less threatening, even though they were sometimes just on the other side of a wall. You chatted with them in elevators or lobbies, at the mailboxes, but their scrutiny was something I rarely thought of. Here, I felt exposed and vulnerable, and it didn't help that every year when Gay Pride day came along, letters in MSU's student newspaper and the Lansing State Journal condemned homosexuality with unswerving hatred that masked itself as Christian love and salvation. My partner tried to calm my anxieties with jokes, but it turned out that I was right. We *were* being watched, though not in the way I had imagined.

As we began shaping the house to become our own, we started a series of changes that kept escalating like those series of five-year plans in the Soviet Union. After fruitless attempts to trim back the overgrown yews that were at practically every corner of the house, we started having them removed. Then we began replanting. My world expanded as we became habitués of local greenhouses and entered a community of gardeners. Each conversation I had about soil conditions, sunlight, pests, drought stress, winter kill marked how different this world was for me. I began to worry about how certain shrubs were doing, consulting books and experts, and plants became a permanent and enjoyable part of my conversation as I began to feel at home with them, and with the soil under my fingernails after an afternoon of planting.

The new and more interesting evergreens we planted at the front of the house, under the study window in a raised, stone-edged bed, got our neighbors' attention. On either side of us and across the street lived elderly men and women, and all remarked on how well we were taking care of the house, especially that we were raking the leaves in the fall and not letting them scatter onto someone else's lawn. The lawn itself was a frequent subject of conversation. The previous owners had left it alone, which meant in the summer it was seared, thin, brown, and the rest of the year not much better, but we hired a lawn-care firm and then installed an underground sprinkling system. People walking by on a nice day, from several streets over, would remark on the lovely changes in the property. They had been watching. And I realized I did the same. As we drove into or out of Indian Hills, I found myself intensely aware of changes in people's yards, new plantings, problems with a tree or shrub, remodeling. I was becoming deeply connected to this place.

We also began changes in the house itself And each alteration, however minor, had the effect of making me feel more stable, more rooted, more secure—whether it was new locks, a French door between the vestibule and the living room, and ultimately an entirely remodeled master bathroom and a new roof. All of this was as exciting as working outdoors on the trees and shrubs because I had always lived in rental apartments, which stayed quintessentially the same no matter how creatively I moved my furniture around.

The greatest change was adding a deck onto what had been a scruffy screened porch and having the porch itself enclosed and heated and made into a sun room. The large windows let in the outside but also made the house more open. I was growing less afraid of that, after we had taken out the ugly chain-link fence the previous owners kept because of their dogs. This was a profound new reality for me. In just two years we had stripped the house bare of its ugly, obscuring yews, and opened up the backyard to the unexpected: a dog wandering through, utility repairmen up on their poles, the glances of strangers in other yards.

This was *my* house. I could do what I wanted. I could be what I wanted. If we hugged or held hands on the deck, it was our business and no one else's. Owning a house and creating a home had this entirely unexpected effect: it made me gradually more proud, aggres-

15

sive, more determined to be out, to overcome the years of silence and lies. I see now that living in an apartment, or even renting a home would have continued the climate of hiding because the front door opens into transience. Here, I felt committed to living in this place, to voting for a board of supervisors that would slow the rate of growth in our township, to signing petitions about road closures or recycling, to writing letters to local officials so that my voice would be heard. I cared about the environment in this beautiful neighborhood—so quiet you could always hear the mourning doves—in ways I never could have in New York because someone else would be responsible there, surely.

If I had previously felt suspicious and even hostile toward the idea of living in a house, perhaps part of my distance was the inevitable image of children. With only a few isolated moments of longing, I had never wanted to be a father, but that's what I became when we moved in together, because Gersh shared custody with his ex-wife, who lives a few minutes away. He was determined to stay in Okemos after his divorce, so that he could be near his two boys, and so that they could easily travel to and from school from either parent's home with minimum disruption. Both boys knew me and seemed to like me, but the bonds that developed between us were as powerful as my connection to the physical in my environment. In the last four years, my sense of time has shifted radically, and I am much more attuned to the seasons, as well as to the stages of a life. I eagerly note the first crocuses of spring and feel comforted by the smell of burning leaves in the fall, just as I am aware of the boys getting taller, rifling out, leaving the whining of childhood behind for the testing of adolescence.

It was David, the eldest, who at fourteen started talking about doing things "as a family"—a term that Gersh and I were determined not to force on them. David wanted to go out to eat, all four of us, and to play board games and card games, especially ones he was good at. Many nights we played hours of hearts, and like any family, each game recalled wild jokes and terrific plays of previous games. It was clear to me that we were all building a history together.

Gradually, I was drawn into the boys' lives, and have become an acknowledged "third parent" for them. It started with my helping with their homework, especially their writing assignments, and then running errands for them or with them—to their mother's house, to the mall, into town, to a friend's, or just going for a ride. Having two adults in the house made scheduling a lot easier for Gersh, because he didn't have to be the only one the kids relied on. The "backup" has been particularly valuable when there have been family arguments, because we can then break down into teams and someone always seems to be reasonable and in control, able to act as a sounding board.

Each year has brought new levels of closeness—like David telling me things he asked me not to share with his father, or coming in after school and chatting about his day. He has told us that those chats have been the high point of each day, a chance for the two of us to get to know each other outside of the constraints of the group. Aaron, the younger son, and I have gone out by ourselves to see movies or shop, and my feelings for the boys have been a surprise. Talking to people who don't know me, I often reply to a comment about their children with, "Yes, my son does that too." The first time I mentioned this to the boys, they seemed very pleased. They can't have been too surprised, because we've all shared a great deal in the last four years. We have season tickets for the football team, and even went out to the Rose Bowl in 1988 when Michigan State was the Big Ten Champion (and we beat USC!). We have also taken short trips together, seen rock concerts and musicals at MSU's concert hall.

Having two children living with us, and feeling ourselves a family, has unexpectedly helped ground me in the reality of my own identity as a gay man. I have found myself explaining news items to the kids about gay rights, sharing my outrage over Jesse Helms and other troglodytes, letting them, in other words, know what moves and alarms me. I am a news addict, and both boys have become used to watching the evening news and talking about it, asking questions. Living with people who love me has had the effect of making my freedom at home more precious, and the public opprobrium gays and lesbians deal with every day more pernicious. Gersh and I are not shy about being affectionate with each other, nor do we keep our involvement in gay causes secret. If anything, we have been convinced that modeling a healthy, committed, and politically aware and active relationship between two men is crucial. How we live has the potential of being a message to the boys that will hopefully override the sick and destructive messages about gays that they are bombarded with by our culture and by their peers. We don't expect them to battle homophobia on their own, but at least they understand it from the inside.

The sense of security and family we have felt propelled us into an unexpected series of activities. Gersh and I are founding members of a study group of faculty and staff at Michigan State University that meets regularly with the aim of establishing a Gay and Lesbian Studies Program at the university. We are also founding members of a Lansing-area coalition of gay and lesbian groups meeting to bridge the various gaps between the two communities and develop joint political action. Both groups have met at our house on various occasions, and the kids are well-informed of their aims. Gersh has been offering a workshop at MSU's counseling center on self-esteem for gay men. We are both committed to making Lansing and Michigan more open, more accepting, and more protective of lesbians and gay men—because this is our home, and we cannot accept anything less.

When Gersh and I first met, marveling at how much we had in common, our home was the world of ideas, because we started writing articles and then a book together. Everything we have co-authored has been published, and our joint teaching and lecturing has likewise been as powerful for our students and audiences as for us—knitting us together, creating a world of shared experiences. All of that laid a foundation for living together and ultimately making Okemos prove to us what Elizabeth Bowen says in her novel, *The Death of the Heart*, that "home is where we emotionally live."

❖ Focused Freewriting   Consider as possible focal points the life of a homosexual in a predominantly straight community, the process involved in turning a house into a home, or one of the topics you've identified in your journal.

❖ Guided Responses

1. Raphael focuses early on the seemingly vast difference between big-city and small-town living. Based on this essay, why do you suppose he fears his neighbors in town as he never feared his city neighbors? What did New York offer that Okemos cannot? What is it about home ownership that helps Raphael adjust to his new surroundings?

2. Much of Raphael's narrative is taken up with the alterations he and his life partner make to the house and grounds. Why do you think he focuses attention on these changes? How do they affect his sense of belonging in the house? his sense of belonging to the neighborhood?

3. In paragraph 19 Raphael observes, "It was clear to me that we were all building a history together." Other than the fact that he and Gersh are now living in the same dwelling, how might owning the house contribute to this new sense of family? What contribution do Gersh's sons make in turning the house into a home?

4. In what ways does owning the house serve to make Raphael a more fervent activist for gay and lesbian rights? What connections to you see between his settling down in Okemos and his renewed sense of activism?

❖ Shared Responses   In your journal explore the feelings you associate with a house or apartment you've called home. What did the physical dwelling itself mean to you? What is the significance of your family situation during the time you lived in this place? Explain your responses. As you discuss your responses in small groups, comment on the ways in which dwellings and family situations affected members' concepts of home; compare one another's responses with Raphael's observations.

Welcome to St. Paul's

LORENE CARY

LORENE CARY *(biographical information on p. 89) describes in this selection from* Black Ice *her first evening at St. Paul's. She explores her feelings of entering foreign, and possibly hostile, territory through careful observation of the distinctions between those who belong at the school and those who feel like outsiders.*

Before reading the selection, write in your journal about the first time you settled into a new place away from your family—a summer camp, a school, your first apartment. What memories come to mind? Consider the excitement, the apprehension, the pleasure, and the pain of the experience.

As you make notes on your reading, you may want to focus on Cary's acute awareness of being an outsider: her observations of the landscape and the architecture, her responses to the predominantly white population, her ambivalent feelings toward her family's presence.

THE BIG, GRAY CLAPBOARD RECTORY formed a triangle at the center of school with the two red-brick chapels: the homey Old Chapel and the towering Gothic. The brick was repeated in stolid dormitory houses built before the Depression; in low, modern ones that rose in the middle to two-story diamond windows; in the art studios that perched next to a waterfall. White clapboard houses made cheerful spots of light against the grass and trees. An amber-colored system of ponds and streams watered the grounds and enforced a graceful but informal spacing between buildings. From the center greensward to the dining hall or to the meadow behind the Rectory or to the gray granite library, poised like a shrine at the edge of the reflecting pond, we had to cross bridges girded by stone and masonry arches. It was the most beautiful place I'd ever seen, and the most plentiful.

As we headed up the brick walkway toward the Rectory receiving line, I felt a public family face spreading over our countenances. Someone asked us how we'd come up. How long was the drive? Did we drive straight through? Were we tired? Would we like refreshments?

A student runner was dispatched to find my old girl. We were guided into the house by a receiving line of older white students and a few unidentified adults. A black student greeted us, too. His name was Wally Talbot, he told us, and he was president of the Sixth Form. He was a few inches taller than I. He had a smile for the adults that was quick and bright, and a wink for me.

"Did he say that he was president of the School?" my mother whispered.

"I think that's what he said," my father answered, and we all   5 turned around and looked again at the black student who was joking easily with the white students beside him.

The Rector, Mr. Oates, made us a hearty greeting as we walked toward the parlor. He was a smallish man, compact, robust. He looked straight at me and pronounced my name carefully. He looked evenly at my parents, and with respect. He knew where we had driven from, knew that my father had had to take the day off from school. I did not know whether to be flattered or disturbed that a man who'd never seen me knew so much about me and my folks.

We passed through the wide foyer of the Rectory, into an outer parlor and then a large, rectangular living room. My mother and I caught each other taking inventory: fireplaces, bay windows, bookshelves, French doors, rear patio, enclosed porch. Sunlight and birdsong drifted in from gardens. In the outer rooms, more new students arrived with their parents, and more old students greeted them.

I found myself wishing that Mike Russell were there. As Mr. Oates took a moment to exchange some man-talk with my father (they took on the look that men got when they put their hands in their pockets, tilted their heads to one side, and put aside the milder wife-and-kids smiles), I suspected that I had come to this place all on the recommendation of one professionally attentive creature who was now unpacking *his* bags at Harvard. It was the social ease and gentleness that blew so balmy around me that brought Russell to mind. It had been just that confidence that had seduced me, the poise that passed my understanding and made me think that if I were where he'd come from, I, too, would emerge young, gifted, and black for all to admire.

Instead, I stood awkward and ridiculous, cloaked in a makeshift composure so brittle that I seemed fairly to rattle inside it like seeds in a gourd. Instead of Mike Russell, the dashing Wally with his up-tilted eyes and sidelong glances implied a camaraderie I did not feel. Lanky white students made coffee-table conversation. The omniscient Rector, plain-spoken and gray-haired, welcomed us into my new "community." And from where we stood in the Rectory, the green-and-brown grounds spread out around us, pushing the world away, holding me in as if I had been caught in a slide-projector show.

How was I to know (since I could not read Wally's dashing eyes)   10 that other black students had felt the same way? Not until years later was I able to ask them outright and resurrect the strangeness of it all. Ed Shockley, who graduated in my class, can still remember standing outside the Rectory looking at the grounds and wondering whether his white classmates would jump him in the woods.

Lee Bouton, one of the first nineteen girls to arrive at St. Paul's in 1971, came to the Rectory without any family at all. As a tenth-grader, she flew from Washington, D.C., to Boston, caught a bus from Boston to Concord, and then a taxi from Concord to St. Paul's. She carried her own luggage from one transport to the next. It was January when she and the other girls arrived to begin coeducation at St. Paul's. The driver let Lee out in the snow in front of an administration building. The switchboard operator inside caged Jeremy Price to come pick up his charge.

Mr. Price "took me to the Rectory, where the welcoming tea was going on. There were parents there, and other students, and I walked through the door with Jeremy Price, feeling very intimidated. He'd taken my bag. I didn't know where my room was. I didn't know anything. And I walked in, and you know how when you walk into that [outer parlor] there's a couch facing the doorway? Well, Loretta [the other black girl] was sitting right in the middle of the couch, and she jumped up and said: 'Ooooooooooh! Here's another one!' And she came over and gave me this big hug. And right behind her was Mike Russell with this big, beautiful smile. I felt like, maybe it's going to be all right, you know?"

My family and I stood in the Rectory just a year and a half after Lee's first tea. Unlike her, I was armed with the experience of a proper, on-campus interview, and I was escorted by attractive young parents and a cuddly kid sister. Unlike Ed Shockley, I was not afraid that the white boys were going to catch me alone in the woods one night and beat me up. But for the first time, I had a whiff, as subtle as the scent of the old books that lined the wall, of my utter aloneness in this new world. I reached into myself for the head-to-the-side, hands-on-hips cockiness that had brought me here and found just enough of it to keep me going.

My dormitory was around the corner from the Rectory, over a bridge and across the road from the library. Inside, just off the common room, steps led to the open doorway of the housemaster. He, too, was on hand to greet us.

I wasn't sure about Mr. Hawley. He had a round face whose top   15
half was nearly bald and whose bottom half was covered over with a
full, tweed-colored beard. Between the top and bottom halves a pair
of glasses perched on a small nose and caught the light. He made a
funny face when he spied my sister: "And look what you brought
along! We've got a couple of those creatures running around somewhere. I'll see if they've been run over yet by some station wagon
gone berserk."

I was later to learn that all the intelligence and will, all the imagination and mischief in that face was revealed in the pale eyes behind
the glasses, but on this first meeting, I could only bring myself to
concentrate on the beard and the Kriss Kringle mouth.

Mr. Hawley, it turned out, had family in Philadelphia, so we
talked about the city, and my parents described for him just exactly
where we lived.

Like other St. Paul's buildings, the Hawleys' house had alcoves,
staircases, and a courtyard, that presented to me a facade of impenetrable, almost European, privacy. The housemaster's home was directly accessible from the dormitory, but only by going from the
vestibule into the common room, then up stairs, through a heavy
wooden door, into a hallway, and another, inner door. Once in the
living room, I could see through the windows that we were across the
street from the gray granite library, but I would not have known it had
the drapes been pulled. The architecture that I so admired from the
outside did not yield itself up to me from within as I had expected. I
now felt disconcerted, as I had in the Rectory. Mr. Hawley wanted to
know just how far one would drive along Baltimore Pike to get to
Yeadon, and I, standing in his living room, had no idea where his
kitchen might be.

Mrs. Hawley, a short, soft-spoken woman, appeared from the rear
hallway. Like her husband, she said ironic things, but more gently.
Startlingly blond children came with her, one peeking from behind
her skirt.

Mr. Hawley directed us to my room and showed my father where   20
to park by the back door so that we could unload more handily. We
carried my things up from a basement entrance. Doors whooshed
open and closed as other girls and their families came and went, and
the halls echoed with the sounds of mothers' heels.

My room faced east. In the afternoon it seemed dull and empty
and dark.

"This'll be lovely when you get it all fixed up," my mother said,
by which I assumed that it looked dull to her, too.

Fine dust had settled contentedly over the sturdy oak bureau and
cloudy mirror, over the charming, squat little oak desk and chair and

in the corners of the closet. White people, as we said, were not personally fastidious (any black woman who'd ever been a maid could tell
you that, and some did, in appalling detail, so I'd heard stories). I was
determined to give the place a good wash.

The casement windows matched those elsewhere on campus. My
father opened one, tightened the wing nut to hold the sash in place,
and stood looking out into the meadow. Then he peeked into the room
next door, which was still empty, and recalled how, at Lincoln University, the first students to arrive scavenged the best furniture in the
dormitory. "If there's any furniture you don't like, better speak now,"
he joked. "I guess you wouldn't want to do that here."

I checked the room next door, and pronounced, with laughter but   25
not conviction, that I'd gotten a fair bargain.

The room seemed crowded with all of us about. I found myself
chattering on, very gaily, about where I would put my things. What
with the windows at one end, the narrow bed against one wall, the
bureau, the desk, the radiator, the closet, the door leading into the
next room, the door leading in, and the economy of my possessions,
there were few options, realistically, for interior design.

Still, I could not stop buzzing. So long as we stood crowded
together in the room, my sister jumping on the naked mattress, my
mother wondering about smoking a cigarette, my father by the open
window clenching his jaw and rubbing the back of his neck, and me
burbling and babbling as if words were British soldiers marching in
pointless columns, bright and gay, with flags and bright brass buttons
on crimson-colored breasts, on and on and on into battle; so long as
we had nothing to do except to wait for the next thing to do; so long
as the intolerable closeness remained and the intolerable separation
loomed to be made, so long would this adrenaline rush through me,
anarchic, atavistic, compelling.

Outside the move-in continued. Convinced that I was missing yet
another ritual of initiation, I ran down the hall to check the bulletin
board. As I stood reading, an Asian boy propelled himself into the
vestibule. He introduced himself without smiling and asked me my
name. Then, addressing me by the name I gave, he asked whether or
not I lived in Simpson House.

"Listen," he said. "There's a girl upstairs. She's just moved in. Her
name is Fumiko, and she's from Japan. She can hardly speak any
English at all. She understands a lot, but she really needs someone to
go and make her feel welcome."

"Do you speak Japanese?"   30

"Of course not." (He was Chinese-American.) He appeared to be
reevaluating me. "Look, is anyone else around?"

"I don't know. I've just arrived myself."

"Well, welcome! Look, we've been helping her, but she needs a girl in her own house, and guys can't come in. Maybe you can tell some of the other girls. Really, she's only just come to the country."

Reluctantly, I agreed. I went to the room on the second floor that the boy had described, and found her. I introduced myself. We tried hard to pronounce each other's names, and we laughed at our mistakes. Fumiko was taller than I. She kept suppressing bows. We agreed to meet again later.

I returned to my family much calmer than I'd left, and I told them about my new friend. Now my mother seemed agitated. Just before we left for dinner, she began to tell me what items of clothing should go into which drawer.

"You always put underwear in the top. See, it's the shallowest one. Big, bulky things like sweaters and jeans go down at the bottom. But, now, please don't just jam your things in. I don't want you walking around here with stuff that's all jerked up."

"I know where things go."

"Listen. Skirts, your good pants, all that stuff needs to be hung up. Let's see how this is packed." My mother unzipped one of the suitcases on the bed. "You know, maybe you might want us to take this big one home. I can't see where you have room to store it."

I watched my mother lift layers of underwear delicately from their berths. Her hands, precise, familiar, called up in me a frenzy of possession. "I've got all night to unpack," I said. "Please don't. I should do that."

"I'll just help you get started. Lord, I hope you don't start putting together any of those crazy outfits you concoct at home. I know you think that stuff looks cute, but it doesn't. You didn't pack any of those fishnet stockings, I hope." Mama selected a drawer for panties and one for bras and slips. I'd brought a girdle—hers, of course—that was hidden in the next layer.

"I *really* want to do that myself."

"I'm not taking anything away from you." Her voice rose with maternal indignation.

"Let the child do it herself," my father said.

I knew that they were going to fight. It would be a silent fight, because we were, even in this room, in public, so long as we were on school grounds. I did not see how we would avoid it. We'd been cooped up together, as my parents called it, all day.

Then my mother laughed. "All right, all right. I was just getting you started," she said. "You'd think I was doing something wrong."

We left for dinner, and I closed my door.

"No locks," my father commented. "I wonder if they ever have any problems."

35

40

45

Outside old students lounged in groups, throwing Frisbees and tossing balls with lacrosse sticks. They halloed one another across the green and complimented new haircuts and tans.

Even the parents knew each other. Mothers in A-line skirts bent their heads together, and the pastel-colored sleeves of the cardigans they'd thrown over their shoulders flattened against one another like clothes on a rack. Fathers shook hands and laughed in loud voices. At first, they all looked the same to me. People whom we had passed a couple times nodded at us like old acquaintances, and we nodded back with well-prepared poise, although I had no idea whether or not I had spoken to or even seen them before.

As my eyes grew accustomed to the landscape, I noticed different   50 varieties of families. There were fancy white people in big foreign sedans, the women emitting, as I passed near them, a complex cosmetic aroma; there were plain, sturdy people whose hair and nails alike were cut in blunt, straight lines and whose feet were shod in brown leather sandals. Less exotic families emerged from chrome-and-wood station wagons; they wore baggy beige shorts. Almost no one was fat. I could only make out these few gradations, and it unhinged me to know that just a few hours before I had not noticed a one. We ascended the brick pathway to the Upper School building, where meals were served, and we remembered how perilous the walk had been in winter. "Get ready," my parents teased.

After dinner chapel bells announced the First Night Service. Everywhere around us parents were climbing into empty cars and driving away. The air had grown cool. I did not know how to say good-bye to my family. I wanted the leave-taking to be over and my part done right. I wished them gone and was ashamed at the thought. "Please stay," I begged. "Just until chapel's over."

The First Night Service took place, according to tradition, on the first day of each term since the nineteenth century, in the Old Chapel. The Old Chapel was built in the shape of a cross, with smooth rows of wooden pews in the three lower segments and high-backed seats along the walls. The pulpit stood where Christ's head would have hung if he in his gaunt passion had been nailed to this most charming symbol of suffering. Unlike the grand New Chapel this church was small and homey. It did not dwarf or intimidate us.

In the Old Chapel my mind flipped through its familiar images of pious devotion: the Jesus, blond and bland, wispy beard and wistful eyes, who had smiled at me from over my great-grandparents' bed, from the Sunday-school room at Ward A.M.E., from the illuminated cross over the pulpit, and from cardboard fans and free calendars produced by black funeral parlors; the brunet Jesus who stretched his arms out toward his disciples at the Last Supper in my laminated reproduction of Leonardo da Vinci's oil. *Take, eat.*

The Rector appeared in the pulpit, shorter than he had seemed in the Rectory, and businesslike. I heard him, despite the close intimacy of the chapel, as if he were speaking from far away. Yet even from such a distance, his words—the content of them, if only I could take them out of that solid, white voice, but I could not quite—had everything to do with me right then. He talked to us of our fears and our dreams, of our new career, of the challenges of our life together.

Then he spoke of tradition. Boys had come and gone before us, sitting in these same pews, thinking and feeling these same thoughts and feelings. They had grown into men and gone out into the world prepared, by a St. Paul's education, to do something worthwhile.

My own voices were talking back to him, and so long as he spoke, I could not control the dialogue. Part of the tradition, my eye. I was there in spite, despite, to spite it. I was there because of sit-ins and marches and riots. I was there—and this I felt with extraordinary and bitter certainty—as a sort of liberal-minded experiment. And, hey, I did not intend to fail. I remember yawning and yawning, sucking in air with my mouth closed and my face taut.

Finally, I gave up the effort to pull in his faraway voice. I let myself drift into silence. I watched the old dust settle in the red- and yellow- and blue-tinted sunlight. Above and around the stained-glass windows thick curls of paint peeled away from the walls. Below the windows gold lettering of memorial plaques shone dimly through the dust. A faded semicircle of ornate print above one window reminded us of boys who played in the streets of Jerusalem. In this close, cool chapel, I could not imagine Jerusalem, its noise or its sun. I could not imagine anything. I knew now what they wanted: "No boy shall leave here unimproved."

When the doors opened, I pressed through them into a wash of cool orange twilight. I took off my shoes and was surprised by the wet grass and the freedom to run through it. I ran across grass, asphalt, and brick, past the round post office, the art building, over the bridge. It had been selfish of me to ask them to stay. Daddy would have to drive eight hours tonight. Mom would be tired. Carole had had it. I felt a stitch in my side.

They were waiting at the car. My mother looked at me with dramatic maternity. We were back to baby names, to the familiar fury of the separation I had dreamt of. I heard my sister wail, but I could not see her past my mother. I hugged my mother and my father in the moist air. My cheeks were wet from their kisses. I hugged my sister and felt the panic in her small, perfect body. The soles of my feet throbbed from the bricks.

"Don't stay here in this place," Carole cried. "Aren't you going to   60
come home? You can't stay here!"

My parents got her into the car, and in those days before seat belts,
she flailed around in the back seat as I walked my mother to the
passenger side. I was sick with my betrayal of Carole and ashamed
that I begrudged my parents the thin shreds of devotion I dredged up
and flung their way.

I did what I needed to do. I said the things they needed to hear. I
told them that I loved them. I told them that I would miss them. It was
true, and it was enough, after all.

They drove away slowly. My mother looked back and waved. My
sister cried and cried. I watched her face and waved to it, until it was
no more than a speck, until they turned the corner and were gone.

❖ Focused Freewriting   Consider as possible focal points the implications of integration programs such as the one at St. Paul's, the
idea of assimilation into the dominant culture, a personal experience
with leaving behind a secure home, or one of the topics you've identified in your journal.

❖ Guided Responses

1. The young Lorene seems to memorize every aspect of her
physical surroundings, for example, the campus (para. 1), the Rectory
(para. 7), and the Hawleys' house (para. 18). Given her observations,
what do you think is the significance of these details to the young girl?
Why might she find herself so keenly aware of the physical characteristics of the place?

2. Lorene's family members seem awkward as they settle her into
her dormitory room (paras. 21–47), suddenly uncertain of their roles.
Explore the significance of the family's interactions in this scene—
Mrs. Cary's attempts to direct the unpacking, Mr. Cary's reminiscences about his college dormitory, and any other behavior you find
relevant.

3. While sitting through First Night Service, Lorene finds herself
unconsciously responding to the sermon: "My own voices were talking back to him, and so long as he spoke, I could not control the
dialogue" (para. 56). How would you explain her reaction to the sermon? What must the St. Paul's tradition mean to her? How can she
feel a part of it?

4. Midway through moving in, Lorene is asked to ease the anxiety of Fumiko, the newly arrived Japanese student. Why does Cary
focus attention on this scene? How does the Asian boy's request

subtly change her view of herself at St. Paul's? What effect does the brief conversation with Fumiko have on Lorene? on the reader?

❖ Shared Responses In your journal discuss your feelings in a situation in which you felt like an "other," an outsider in a closed society. How did you react to the situation? What insights did you gain from it? What value is there in experiencing the feeling of "otherness"? As you discuss your responses in small groups, emphasize the various factors that cause people to feel like outsiders.

Cupcake Land:
Requiem for the Midwest in the Key of Vanilla

RICHARD RHODES

RICHARD RHODES, *a native of Kansas City, Missouri, was educated at Yale University and served as a visiting scholar at Harvard during the 1989–90 academic year. His extensive publications include* A Hole in the World *(1990),* The Making of the Atomic Bomb *(1987),* Looking for America *(1979), and* The Inland Ground. *He has been awarded a Pulitzer Prize and a National Book Critics Circle Award for Fiction. In this essay, first published in 1987 in* Harper's *magazine, Rhodes pokes fun at the lily-white community of greater Kansas City. But his purpose appears more serious as he recalls the livelier Kansas City of his youth and as he contemplates the consequences of social isolation.*

Before reading the selection, comment in your journal on your impression of midwestern cities like Kansas City as compared with coastal cities like New York or Los Angeles. Do you think midwesterners have different priorities, different standards, different expectations? Explain your responses.

As you make notes on your reading, you may want to focus on the distinction between the Kansas City of Rhodes's youth and the present-day city, his attitude toward Kansas Citians, or his judgments about "Cupcake Land's" prejudices.

IN ONE CORNER of a decorative bridge on the Country Club Plaza, a shopping district in Kansas City, Missouri, a massive bronze sculpture attracts the attention of tourists. They are drawn to the work first of all by the colorful flags of the United States and Great Britain that fly overhead and seem to proclaim for it some undefined official status. Approaching the display, they discover that it depicts a man and a woman seated on or emerging from an undefined bronze mound. The man and the woman turn out to be Winston and Clementine Churchill—Winnie staring moodily ahead, Clemmie with folded hands observing her husband benevolently. *Married Love,* the sculpture is titled. By pushing a button on a sort of wooden jukebox behind it, one can listen to a scratchy recording of Churchill speaking to the British people in the dark days of the Second World War; "blood, toil, tears, and sweat" is sometimes discernible over the noise of traffic—Kansas Citians approaching the Plaza to shop.

Married Love originated as a small coffee-table piece by one Oscar Nemon. Nemon was an acquaintance of a Kansas City dentist, Joseph Jacobs; Jacobs saw the Churchill piece in Nemon's Oxford home several years ago. Impressed, Jacobs brought home a photograph. One of his dental patients is Kansas City business leader Miller Nichols, whose father, J. C. Nichols, built the Plaza, and whose realty company operates it today. With Miller Nichols captive in his dentist's chair one day, Jacobs confronted him with the photograph. "It's no wonder that our young people have gotten away from traditional values," the dentist says he told the realtor, "when they don't have symbolism to inspire them." Nichols liked the idea of a Churchill statue on the Plaza; it's been fashionable in Kansas City to celebrate the British wartime leader ever since Joyce Hall, the founder of Hallmark Cards, courted his friendship back in the 1950s by sponsoring a national tour of Churchill's leisure-time paintings. "Get that sculptor over here and let's talk about it," Nichols told Jacobs a few weeks later. Nemon was only too willing to scale the little sculpture up to heroic size.

Nichols, a man who pinches his inherited dollars until the eagles squeal, wasn't about to pay for the work himself. He turned fund-raising over to his wife, Jeannette, who assembled privately the nearly $500,000 that the statue and the endowment for its upkeep required. Jacobs says he suggested the title *Married Love.* What was merely kitsch at coffee-table scale thus found epic realization in bronze; the Country Club Plaza, with statuary already at hand of penguins, Indian braves, and sleeping babes, acquired the world's first Chatty Churchill.

Welcome to Cupcake Land.

I've lived in Kansas City for forty-four of my fifty years. I wasn't   5
responsible for the first eighteen, after which I lit out for the East Coast as fast as my legs would carry me. But I came back here of my own volition, to teach and then to write, and I have to own responsibility for the other twenty-six. Partly I got stuck here—wife, children, then ex-wife with custody of the children. Maybe, as an editor friend once theorized, there's something irredeemably provincial in my soul. I like the country around here, rolling hills, prosperous farms. I even

like the weather, which ranges from 20 below zero to 115 in the shade, from blizzards to tornadoes to swampy Bangkok heat, and which prepares you—good preparation for journalism—to be comfortable, even relieved, anywhere in the world.

Kansas City was a paradise once, or so it seemed to me when I was a boy in the years just after World War II. The edges of the rough cow town it once was had been sanded and polished to splinter-free nostalgia by an intelligent, benevolent, remarkably nonpartisan city government: the old arrangement of wide, sweeping boulevards and well-kept parks still functioned, the streets were safe, mass transit by electric streetcars and buses was a dream (miles and miles of clean, quiet travel for a nickel, transfers free—I could and did roam the city unescorted at the age of eight). Neighborhoods abounded: children walked to school; you knew the little girls next door and the old man down the block; ladies hung washboards over the backs of chairs on sunny afternoons and used rainwater and vinegar to wash their waist-length hair; on summer evenings roaring with locusts, lawn chairs came out and people called across front yards.

And then the suburbs arose, Cupcake Land, and sweetened Kansas City's plainspoken urban soul. We were more Elmer Gantry here once than George F. Babbitt. How many cities across the land have been similarly Cupcaked? What the hell happened to my town?

Curiously, although the cities of the East and West Coasts regularly forge ahead of the Midwest in many aspects of popular culture, in Cupcaking the Midwest has permanently held the lead. The Holy Grail of Cupcake Land is pleasantness, well-scrubbed and bland, and the Northeast Corridor is too crowded and dirty and ethnic, California too highly coveted, too expensive, and therefore too much on the make, quite to measure up. My hometown is the very heart of Cupcake Land. Not by accident has Kansas City become the best test market for new products in the United States; what we consume (to paraphrase Walt Whitman) you shall consume, for every longing belonging to us as good belongs to you.

Cupcake Land is petit point and paisley and white wicker. It's professionally catered deb parties. It's the standing ovation, a tribute audiences here accord almost every performance of classical music or ballet or theater, preferring effusion to critical appreciation and too timid to remain seated when fellow Cupcakes stand. Cupcake Land is Laura Ashley and Buick and Pierre Deux, yellow ribbons on every tree to declare Cupcake solidarity with distant hostages, memorials to Christa McAuliffe a thousand miles from Concord. When the goods at a bake sale staged to raise money for charity cost more to bake than they return in sales, I know I'm in Cupcake Land. I know I'm in

Cupcake Land when a thorough search of an expensive, well-furnished house turns up not one serious book.

Cupcakes wear Ivy League styles of clothing, sort of: button-down shirts for the men in easy-care Perma-Prest; demure skirts and one-piece bathing suits for the women. Cupcakes usually do not attend Ivy League schools, however; they attend state universities, because they believe that going to school out of state looks pretentious, isolates them from the gang, and excludes them from the network of potential business contacts they will need after graduation. Cupcakes do pledge fraternities and sororities; Cupcake Land itself is a working out in maturity of the values, such as they are, learned so painfully in the crucible of the fraternity or the sorority house.

Cupcake men drink beer in moderation at backyard barbecues; Cupcake women don't drink at all, fearing to misbehave ("I get so silly"), or drink "A glass of white wine, please." If the waiter specifies "Chablis?" they answer "That will be fine." "Chardonnay?" would elicit an identical response. Since to Cupcakes the only point of ordering a glass of wine is not to seem standoffish about drinking, the type of wine isn't an issue; and since Cupcakes in general know little about wine beyond what they've learned from television advertisements, making it an issue would appear snobbish to their friends. So of course they don't.

The suburban home and yard are the sturdy trunk and root of Cupcake Land. The ideal yard in Cupcake Land is a monoculture of bluegrass or zoysia (a hardier Southern hybrid), a carpet of brilliant green maintained unvarying through the vicissitudes of summer with herbicides, pesticides, fertilizer, mowing, trimming, and irrigation. The front yards of Cupcake Land, whatever their extent and however inviting their shaded green swards, aren't used. They're purely decorative, like the pristine curb spaces in front of Cupcake houses, where cars in urban neighborhoods would be parked. Cars in Cupcake Land belong in built-on garages with the garage doors closed. Garages for cars exemplify the Golden Rule of Cupcake Land, which is, *A place for everything and everything in its place.* In the spotless kitchens of Cupcake Land, hoods like the hoods condemned criminals wear to the gallows hide the blender and the food processor, and white-enameled tin lids painted with meadow flowers disguise the plain, functional heating coils on the electric range. In Cupcake bathrooms, a needlepoint cover, slotted on top and bottomless, slips over the Kleenex box.

Cupcakes go to church. They're comforted to find so many similarly dressed and like-minded people gathered together in one place. If the sermons are dull, the setting is peaceful. God's in his heaven; all's right with the world, except in unimaginable places like Iran.

The Empress of Cupcake Land is Nancy Reagan, whom Kansas City Cupcakes adore—always impeccable, all her deals under the table, devoted to a cause for which she has found a pleasant solution ("Just say no") that is the equivalent of Cupcake Land's pleasant solution to poverty ("Just get a job"), to AIDS and teenage sex ("Just keep your legs crossed"), and to the national debt ("Just quit spending"). Ronald Reagan is the Emperor of Cupcake Land, of course, pleasantness personified, financing the imperial expansion on plastic, resplendent in his new clothes.

I've had some luck identifying when Kansas City ceded its south side   15
to Cupcake Land (I grew up on the east side of town, now the black ghetto, where the old urban life persisted a few years longer). It began around the time I was born, not much before. The late Edward Dahlberg remembered a brawnier and more vigorous Kansas City, for example, in his 1964 autobiography, *Because I Was Flesh*. "A vast inland city," he described it, "a wild, concupiscent city." He recalled "a young, seminal town" where "the seed of its men was strong." Clearly this is not yet Cupcake Land; the period Dahlberg is evoking is the decade before the First World War, when he was a small boy. "There were more sporting houses and saloons than churches" in Kansas City then, he says. Remembering those forthcoming days he asks heatedly, "Could the strumpets from the stews of Corinth, Ephesus, or Tarsus fetch a groan or sigh more quickly than the dimpled thighs of lasses from St. Joseph or Topeka?"

But by the 1930s, on the evidence of Evan S. Connell's autobiographical 1959 novel, *Mrs. Bridge*, Cupcake Land was up and running, as if it came along one sinister Christmas complete and fully assembled, in a Pandoran box. Mrs. Bridge, a young Kansas City society matron, already shops on the Country Club Plaza, where presumably she bought her guest towels:

> She had a supply of Margab, which were the best, at least in the opinion of everyone she knew, and whenever guests were coming to the house she would put the ordinary towels in the laundry and place several of these little pastel towels in each of the bathrooms. They were quite small, not much larger than a handkerchief, and no one ever touched them. After the visitors had gone home she would carefully lift them from the rack and replace them in the box till next time. Nobody touched them because they looked too nice; guests always did as she herself did in their homes—she would dry her hands on a piece of Kleenex.

Mrs. Bridge is conversant primarily with just such matters as towels, Connell observes, as well as "the by-laws of certain committees, antique silver, Royal Doulton, Wedgwood, the price of margarine as compared to butter, or what the hemline was expected to do." She knows the bedrock rules of Cupcake Land, which would seem not to have changed much these past sixty years. "Now see here, young lady," she scolds one of her daughters, "in the morning one doesn't wear earrings that dangle."

Edward Dahlberg revisited Kansas City late in life; his cantankerous but perspicacious reaction confirms the area's Cupcaking:

> These cities, which are full of every kind of man and woman dirt, and have the most repulsive sex and movie dives, and prurient penny-arcade nudes, and pornographic postcard streets like Twelfth, have citizens, who are crazy about the word CLEAN. Clean health, clean living, clean politics! Only the corrupt can use this tabu word so easily.

Not many blacks live in Cupcake Land: white flight was a major force behind its founding, and it's nearly impossible to cross the invisible lines that toothless laws tolerate and realtors maintain. Recently I rented an apartment in an old restored building in midtown Kansas City (wonderful Nutbread Land, a slice of the spirited Kansas City I remember from childhood, trucks unloading outside grocery stores and buses going by, people of all sizes and shapes and colors walking real sidewalks, some of them talking to themselves). "Funny thing," the rental agent told me, "the people who rent here are almost always from somewhere else. Kansas Citians all want new." To find the new, however diminished—and to escape the desegregation of the public-school system that began in 1955 and is still not complete—Cupcake recruits moved en masse across the state line into Johnson County, Kansas, last year's cow pasture become this year's pseudo-Colonial or French Provincial suburb. Freight wagons used to follow the Santa Fe Trail from Kansas City out through Johnson County; developers today, putting up houses and shopping malls along that trail, seem bent on moving the city itself to Santa Fe.

Not that Kansas City Cupcakes dislike blacks, exactly. They avoid them not necessarily because they think them inferior but because they know them to be different, Cornbread rather than Cupcake, just as the blue-collar whites who live south and east of Kansas City in Pancake Land are different. In that difference Cupcakes measure a strong potential for unpleasant encounter. "What would I *say* to one?"

Connell, in *Mrs. Bridge*, reinforces this analysis, depicting discomfort rather than active hostility in black-white relations at the borders of the Country Club District. "The niggers are moving in," Mrs. Bridge's daughter announces provocatively one day:

> Mrs. Bridge slowly put down the tray of cookies. She did not know just what to say. Such situations were awkward. On the one hand, she herself would not care to live next door to a

20

houseful of Negroes; on the other hand, there was no reason
not to. She had always liked the colored people she had
known. She still thought affectionately of Beulah Mae [a laun-
dress long departed for California] and worried about her,
wondering if she was still alive. She had never known any
Negroes socially; not that she avoided it, just that there
weren't any in the neighborhood, or at the country club, or in
the Auxiliary. There just weren't any for her to meet, that was
all.

The Country Club Plaza is supposed to be a place for strolling,
window-shopping, watering at one of its several outdoor cafes. (Al-
ternatively, one may ride in a horse-drawn carriage, à la Central Park:
at the height of the season more than a dozen carriages work the
Plaza, an area only about ten city blocks in extent. They tour no park
but streets of storefronts. They do not want for customers.) A little
posse of black children biked into this pleasant setting one afternoon
in the heyday of breakdancing. They unrolled their pads of cardboard
and linoleum, cranked up their ghetto blasters on a centrally located
corner outside a men's clothing store, and got down. They were good;
spinning and double-jointing through their repertoire, they drew an
appreciative crowd. But the Nichols Company doesn't want vulgar
street entertainment within the confines of the Plaza, particularly
when the entertainers are unlicensed and black. Security guards elbowed through the crowd, spread-eagled the children against the
wall, handcuffed them (or tried to—the cuffs kept slipping off one
small boy's wrists), and dragged them away.
    In a subsequent year teenagers began to cruise and promenade
the western end of the Plaza, to see and be seen, perhaps drawn by
the McDonald's installed in a mall building there without golden
arches but with a bronze statue of a seated lad eating a bronze hamburger and reading a bronze book. The Nichols Company reacted to
the promenading as if it had been assaulted by Cuban mercenaries.
First it tried to barricade the streets. That inconvenienced paying
adults as well as conspiring teens. Next it sent in its security guards,
gun-toting men paid not much more than minimum wage and trained
initially only eight hours in their trade—lawsuits for brutality and
false arrest are still pending. Finally the Nichols Company arranged
with the Kansas City Police Department to set up a command post on
the Plaza, *et in Arcadia ego*, from which police fanned out to arrest
anyone committing even the most obscure infraction—shirt unbut-
toned, one taillight out, taking a leak in the parking-lot bushes. That
draconian measure seems to have cleared the kids away. I walked
with them one Saturday night not long before the end. They were, for
the most part, clean, wonderfully wide-eyed, and duded up—and
black. Their real offense was that they scared Cupcakes away.

To obscure its bawdy history Kansas City lays claim to an ersatz nobility. Its livestock show is the American Royal, its debutantes debut at a Jewel Ball, and the trademark of its best-known local industry, Hallmark Cards, is a crown. An exhaustive Name-the-Team contest that received more than 17,000 entries preceded the establishment in Kansas City of its baseball team; we were asked to believe that team owner Ewing Kauffman, a self-made pharmaceutical tycoon, considered those thousands of alternatives seriously before he came up with his choice, the Kansas City Royals, and with the team logo, a distinctly Hallmark-like crown.

The apotheosis of Kansas City's pretentious Anglophilia was a   25
wedding party in London last June for the twenty-one-year-old stepdaughter of the U.S. Ambassador to the Court of St. James's, Charles Price II, a good-old-boy Kansas City banker whose wife Carol is heiress to Omaha's Swanson TV-dinner fortune. Melissa Price's wedding dominated the pages of *The Kansas City Star*—a headline I particularly cherish read SIX-TIER, 500-EGG CAKE WILL BE SHOWPIECE OF RECEPTION—and nearly one hundred of Kansas City's elect flew to London for the event. "Sensible young people," the *Star's* society editor wrote of the couple thus honored, "who believe in some of life's solid dividends, such as friendships and careers." The name of the Berkeley Hotel, the editor noted in a helpful aside, is "pronounced Barkley." There was breathless speculation that Nancy Reagan might attend the wedding, her presence transmuting Cupcake to Pound Cake—the Prices are inevitably canonized in Kansas City social notes as Reagan intimates—but no such imperial benevolence was bestowed.

I've concluded that Kansas Citian Calvin Trillin, writing in the *New Yorker*, declared Arthur Bryant's Kansas City barbecue to be the best in the world to gull such pretensions. Bryant's isn't even the best barbecue in Kansas City (their sauce, which Trillin seems to have confused with Lourdes water, tastes overwhelmingly of cayenne). Bryant's is situated in the heart of Kansas City's black ghetto, a place very few Cupcakes normally, by choice, even remotely approach. Arthur Bryant is gone now, but in his day the tables were rickety, the windows dirty, the neighborhood risky, and the barbecue bad. Back in the 1950s, Bud Trillin's high-school crowd went to Bryant's for barbecue to be daring. Cupcakes traipse down to Seventeenth and Brooklyn now because they think it's sophisticated. Eating *greasy* cayenne-embittered pork in a ghetto barbecue joint identifies them, mirabile dictu, as *New Yorker* readers.

The real humorist in Trillin's family is his daughter, Greenwich Village born, who spotted the change in Kansas City from urban paradise to Cupcake Land on a visit here when she was a little girl. Two days of driving from shopping center to shopping center led her to ask her stolid father, Daddy, is this a city? Dearest daughter, of course it is, Bud informed her. Then how come, she pounced, we never *walk?*

Most Kansas City Cupcakes work for large, impersonal corporations, which partly explains their enthusiasm for conformity. They commute home from work to Cupcake Land every afternoon fearing for their jobs, and the angst such fear engenders colors all the other hours of their lives. I have heard bright and talented adults, who do not hesitate to speak up on issues of national politics, lower their voices in public places when discussing the doings of their corporations, afraid they might be overheard by someone who might pass on their usually innocuous testimony to the éminences noires of directordom. The Soviet Union can't be any worse in this regard. If you can't say something good about something, as I've been told many times out here, don't say anything at all. Cupcakes don't. They don't dare.

As political institutions, corporations aspire to nationhood, they often do command budgets larger than many of the nations of the world, and expect their employees to die for them. In dispensing raises and advancement they make it clear that they value loyalty more than achievement. Within such institutions even the most talented employees frequently come to believe that they are qualified for no other work (the Man Without a Country syndrome), that only the corporation's benevolence sustains them.

At the bottom of the cup in Cupcake Land is a deep insecurity   30 about the consequences of individual expression. Cupcakes are usually only one generation removed from the urban working class or the farm. They wear their newfound bourgeois respectability awkwardly. Like the maids and nannies of Victorian England, but with no such compelling evidence walking the streets around them, they believe that only their conformity to the narrowest standards of convention protects them from the abyss.

Their fear stales friendship and love; in personal relations Cupcake men and women give off a continual sense of disapproval and unease. They don't mean to be difficult; they're only continually fearful that your actions or theirs might reveal them to be parvenus. "Between you and I" is standard English in Kansas City, Cupcakes working too hard to get their grammar right. When such hypervigilance extends to sex it's deadly; in bed with a Cupcake (to speak in the simplified but useful jargon of transactional analysis), child encounters parent instead of child encountering child. "I don't mind. I enjoy cuddling. Let's try again next time." Cupcakes, I'm afraid, lack spice.

A year ago I moved to the Missouri countryside to find out what rural life had become in the thirty years since I left the farm. (My farm career was an adolescent interlude, six years at a boys' home and farm outside Independence, Missouri—but we bused ourselves to school in Kansas City.) The morning of the first day of my visit I met the farmer I would be following, whom I call Tom Bauer, at the outdoor feeding floor where he finishes hogs for market. One of the hogs had a prolapsed rectum, Tom explained, which he was going to try to fix.

The poor animal wasn't hard to identify. Knee-high, weighing about 100 pounds—half-grown—it was pink, with coarse white hair, and a swollen, bluish tube of tissue protruded from its body behind. Because of attacks by the other hogs the prolapse was bloody. "You cain't always fix 'em," Tom told me. "Sometimes you work them back in and they come back out. Then you've lost the animal for sure. But we're gonna try."

Tom's big sixteen-year-old son, Brett, was at hand. He slipped into the pen and skillfully caught the hog by a back leg and dragged it out into the aisle. His father pulled on a sterile plastic glove. "We got to haul it up by its hind legs and hang it over the gate," Tom directed. Brett caught the other leg and worked the animal around as if it was a wheelbarrow until its belly approached the gate, which was framed with smooth iron pipe. But the hog's legs were slippery with brown, pungent hog manure. Strapping kid though he is, a reserve guard in high-school football, Brett struggled to lift the animal into position.

I didn't think I was being tested, that first day on the farm, but on the other hand, the boy needed help. I took a deep breath—not, in those redolent surroundings, the wisest decision I ever made— stepped to Brett's side, grabbed one shit-covered leg, timed my effort with the boy's, and heaved the hog over the gate so that it hung down bent at the hip, its butt in the air. Brett and I held on then while Tom carefully worked the poor animal's rectum back into its body, the hog screaming in unavoidable pain. "Gross," Brett said. Then his dad was finished and he let the animal gently down. It didn't prolapse again— it lived, to be trucked at 250 pounds to the slaughterhouse for pork chops to grace the tables of Cupcake Land.

I adjusted to the realities of farm work quickly enough, having grown up in the trade. But I realized that first morning as I pushed through my initial cultural shock how far removed Kansas City has become from the countryside that sustains it. Cupcake Land is farther removed yet—too far, I fear, for any straightforward recovery. To make life pleasant seems a worthy enough goal in the abstract, but increasing control and decreasing surprise is finally stifling. Full-blown and pathological, it results in life-threatening sensory deprivation. Cupcake children in their pervasive and much remarked ennui show symptoms of such deprivation. Only last summer a crowd of well-provisioned Johnson County teens raged through their suburban neighborhoods smashing cars; Cupcake opinion of the rampage blamed permissive education.

Talk is general these days of a brutal recession on its way, the ugly sequela of the Reagan years. That would be a terrible betrayal of Cupcake trust. Chatty Churchills won't guard the gates to Cupcake Land then, or tea cozies hood the disaster, or cuddling comfort the bewildered, or credit cards pay the bills. If any good might come from such a consequence it would be the lifting of the burden of pretension from Cupcake backs.

Like other Cupcake outposts across the land, this plainspoken river-bluff city I know and still grudgingly love has glazed over its insecurities with pretension. Sooner or later, such artificial barriers always collapse. The Missouri River will still be around then, ready in its brown flood to sweep the stale crumbs away. People I respect who care about this place counsel patience, but it's been a damned long wait.

❖ Focused Freewriting   Consider as possible focal points Rhodes's nostalgia, the metaphors used to describe "Cupcake Land," or one of the topics you've identified in your journal.

❖ Guided Responses

1. Why does Rhodes call greater Kansas City "Cupcake Land?" What images does this appellation call to your mind? How do you respond to his other names: "Nutbread" (para. 19), "Cornbread" and "Pancake" (para. 20), and "Pound Cake" (para. 25)? How does the article's subtitle, "Requiem for the Midwest in the Key of Vanilla," color your reading of the selection?

2. Rhodes implies that segregation in Kansas City has less to do with racial prejudice than with social unease (para. 20). Based on your reading of the entire essay, do you agree with his analysis? What other sections of the essay deal with racial issues, and what conclusions do you draw from reading them?

3. After describing the repair of the pig's rectal prolapse, Rhodes observes that Kansas City's current lifestyle "results in life-threatening sensory deprivation" (para. 36). How does the farm story serve to reinforce this conclusion? Why does Rhodes think it dangerous for the city to continue its existence as "Cupcake Land"?

4. After reading the entire selection, how do you interpret the opening anecdote about the Churchill sculpture? What is the signifi-

cance of the many details that Rhodes uses in relating the story of how the sculpture came to grace the Plaza bridge?

❖ Shared Responses　In your journal write a brief description of your hometown. If possible, try to use the kind of figurative language found in Rhodes's essay. What would you name your town? How would you describe its values? Is your impression predominantly positive or negative? Why? As you discuss your responses in small groups, emphasize the positive and negative connotations of each group member's characterization of his or her town.

—— ❖ ——

Black Family Life

JOSEPH L. WHITE

JOSEPH L. WHITE, *a graduate of San Francisco State College and Michigan State University, is a professor of psychology and comparative cultures at the University of California, Irvine. His work in the civil rights movement during the 1960s led to his integral role in developing black studies programs in California schools. Throughout his career White has championed the study of black psychology from an African-American rather than a European-American frame of reference. In this selection, excerpted from* The Psychology of Blacks: An Afro-American Perspective *(1984), White argues that characterizations of African-American family life based on the "deficit-deficiency" model necessarily present a negative image. In its stead he offers a model based on the extended family, which provides a more positive perspective from which to observe black family patterns.*

Before reading the selection, describe in your journal what you consider to be a "normal" family pattern. How important is it for children to be raised in such a family? How would you characterize your own family with regard to the norm you've described?

As you make notes on your reading, you may want to focus on the contrasts in the two descriptions of black family life offered by the author. Consider such issues as gender roles, reasons for certain family configurations, and judgments made by experts analyzing families.

Introduction

THE EMERGING VIEW of Black family life is that its underlying genotype, its basic structure, consists of an extended family group made up of a number of legally related and nonlegally related adults and children who come together within a mutually supportive social, psychological, and economic network to deal conjointly with the responsibilities of living (Stack, 1974). This pattern of family life with its

188

emphasis on mutual solidarity, cooperation, and interdependence originated in Africa and has persisted despite its going through several cycles of formation, breakup, and reformulation brought about by slavery, a century of migration out of the rural South, and restrictive welfare codes (Nobles, 1978). During the periods of breakup and reformulation the extended family may take on a different surface or phenotypical appearance; however, if the Black family is observed across sufficient time and geographical space, its basic extended structure will reappear (Gutman, 1976).

The Deficit-Deficiency Model

The view of the core structure of the Black family as an extended family grouping is not shared by all observers. The traditional view of the Black family, which has evolved from the works of Frazier (1939), Elkins (1968), Moynihan (1965), and Rainwater (1970), is one of a disorganized, single-parent, subnuclear, female-dominated social system. This is essentially the deficit-deficiency model of Black family life. The deficit-deficiency model begins with the historical assumption that there was no carry-over from Africa to America of any sophisticated African-based form of family life and communal living. Viable patterns of family life either did not exist because Africans were incapable of creating them, or they were destroyed beginning with slavery and the separation of biological parents and children, forced breeding, the master's sexual exploitation of Black women, and the accumulative effects of three hundred years of economic and social discrimination. As a result of this background of servitude, deprivation, second-class citizenship, and chronic unemployment, Black adults have not been able to develop marketable skills, self-sufficiency, future orientation, and planning and decision-making competencies, instrumental behaviors thought to be necessary for sustaining a successful two-parent nuclear family while guiding the children through the socialization process.

In a society that placed a premium on decisive male leadership in the family, the Black male was portrayed as lacking the masculine sex role behaviors characterized by logical thinking, willingness to take responsibility for others, assertiveness, managerial skills, achievement orientation, and occupational mastery. The Black male in essence had been psychologically castrated and rendered ineffective by forces beyond his control. He is absent within the family circle and unable to provide leadership and command respect when he is present. After generations of being unable to achieve the ideal male role in the family and in American society, the Black male is likely to be inclined to compensate for his failure by pursuing roles such as the pimp, player, hustler, and sweet daddy, which are in conflict with the norms of the larger society. The appearance of these roles in male behavior in the Black community, rather than being interpreted as a form of social protest, reinforces the majority culture stereotypes of Black males as irresponsible, lazy, shiftless, and sociopathic.

The Black woman does not fare much better in terms of how she is portrayed in the deficit-deficiency model of Black family life. She is regarded as the head of the household, a matriarch who initially received her power because the society was unwilling to permit the Black male to assume the legal, economic, and social positions necessary to become a dominant force within the family and community life. Having achieved this power by default, the Black female is unwilling to share it. Her unwillingness to share her power persists even when the Black male is present and willing to assume responsibility in the family circle, since she is not confident of the male's ability to follow through on his commitments. Confrontation over decision making and family direction is usually not necessary because the Black male is either not present in the household on any ongoing basis or is regarded as ineffective by the female when he is present.

The impact of the matriarchial family on the sex-role development   5 of the children in relationship to the dominant social system, which has a precedent for clearly distinguishing between acceptable male and female social roles, is considered to be devastating. The Black male child has no adequate father figure to emulate in acquiring the conventional masculine instrumental behaviors typified by responsibility taking, resourcefulness, independence, occupational preparation, and cool-headed, logical decision making. To make matters worse, the mother may ventilate her anger and disappointment with the father for not being able to fulfill his role as a provider on the male child by expressing an attitude that men are no good, irresponsible, and only interested in conquering women sexually. When trying to discourage behavior that she considers undesirable, the mother is likely to compare the child to his father by telling him that he is going to turn out to be a no-count man, just like his father. The effect of an absent role model, coupled with the negative image of masculinity that is being projected, prevents the male child from acquiring the confidence he needs to resolve successfully the issues associated with his identity and psychosexual development as he evolves through adolescence and early adulthood. The final outcome of this female-dominated socialization process is the creation of still another generation of Black males who will be unable to build the internal security and social role skills necessary to become heads of households, interact productively in relationships with women, and serve as sound role models for their own children.

The Black female child, on the other hand, is constantly exposed to a cadre of women in authority and decision-making roles within the family—not only her own mother, but a community of women made up of aunties, grandmothers, cousins, and other women neighbors who occupy the same positions in their families. Presented with this abundance of feminine role models without the balancing input from adult males in fatherlike roles, the Black female child is vulnerable to developing an exaggerated notion of her own role as a future adult and parent. She has no real idea of what male–female teamwork is all about, since she has had very little, if any, exposure to decision-making models where the male is part of the process. To further complicate matters, she has also heard her mother and other adult females bad-mouth Black males for their inability to take care of business. She has been admonished to learn to take care of herself and not to become dependent on some no-count man who would be unable to fulfill his responsibilities. In short, she has been told to "keep her pants up and her dress down," lest she fall victim to a situation where she will have a flock of children with no father to assist her in the child-rearing process.

When the offspring of these matriarchial families meet in the next generation as adults, it is difficult to conceive of how they could develop a mutually satisfying relationship. The male is confused, doesn't know who he is, and lacks the emotional maturity required for the ongoing responsibilities of family living. The Black female has an exaggerated sense of her own worth, doesn't have much confidence in the male's ability to meet his obligations over a prolonged period of time, and has very little preparation for the give-and-take of male-female relationships. These kinds of sisters have been known to sell their men "woof tickets" with statements to the effect "I was working and taking care of myself when I met you, I'm working and taking care of myself now, and I'll be working and taking care of myself when I leave you." Putting two people like these, who have been reared in matriarchial families, together in a conjugal union or marriage of their own would seem to represent the beginnings of another vicious, destructive, deficit-deficiency cycle with the "web and tangle of pathology" recreating itself.

The proponents of the pathology-oriented, matriarchial family model did not consider the possibility that a single-parent Black mother could serve as an adequate role model for the children of both sexes. The notion that the mother could reflect a balance of the traditional male and female roles, with respect to mental toughness and emotional tenderness, was largely ignored because of the rigid classification of psychosexual roles in American society. In the Black community, however, the categorization of social role behaviors based on gender is not as inflexible. It is conceivable that a Black mother could project a combination of assertive and nurturant behaviors in the process of rearing children of both sexes as nonsexist adults.

With the reality of accelerating divorce rates, in recent years the single-parent family headed by a woman has become a social reality in Euro-America. This reality has been accompanied by an attempt on the part of social scientists to legitimate family structures that represent alternatives to the nuclear family while reconceptualizing the social roles of males and females with less emphasis on exclusive behaviors. The concept of androgyny has been introduced to cover the vast pool of human personality traits that can be developed by either sex (Rogers, 1978). A well-balanced person reflects a combination of both instrumental and expressive traits. The latter include feeling-oriented behaviors formerly considered feminine, such as tenderness, caring, and affection. Thus, it is conceptually possible for a white, single androgynous female parent to rear psychologically healthy, emotionally integrated children. It is interesting how the sociology of the times make available to white Americans psychological concepts designed to legitimatize changes in the family, in child-rearing patterns, and in relationships between the sexes. Yet, these same behaviors when first expressed by Afro-Americans were considered as pathological.

The Extended Family Model

The extended family, in contrast to the single-parent subnuclear family, consists of a related and quasi-related group of adults, including aunts, uncles, parents, cousins, grandparents, boyfriends, and girl friends linked together in a kinship or kinlike network. They form a cooperative interface with each other in confronting the concerns of living and rearing the children. This model of family life, which seems able to capture not only the strength, vitality, resilience, and continuity of the Black family, but also the essence of Black values, folkways, and life styles, begins with a different set of assumptions about the development and evolution of Black family life in America.

The Black extended family is seen as an outgrowth of African patterns of family and community life that survived in America. The Africans carried with them through the Mid-Atlantic passage and sale to the initial slave owners a well-developed pattern of kinship, exogamous mating, and communal values, emphasizing collective survival, mutual aid, cooperation, mutual solidarity, interdependence, and responsibility for others (Nobles, 1974; Blassingame, 1972). These values became the basis for the Black extended family in America. They were retained because they were familiar and they allowed the slaves to have some power over destiny by enabling them to develop their own styles for family interaction. A consciousness of closeness to others, belongingness, and togetherness protected the slave from being psychologically destroyed by feelings of despair and alienation and the extended family provided a vehicle to pass the heritage on to the children (Fredrickson, 1976; Gutman, 1976). Slaves in essence created their own communal family space, regardless of whether the master was paternalistic or conducted a Nazilike concentration camp.

To understand the cultural continuity, it is necessary to depart from the traditional hypothesis that slave masters and their descendants exercised total psychological and social control over the development of Black family life and community institutions. The slaves were much more than empty psychological tablets on which the master imprinted an identity. These early Blacks were able to find ways of creating psychological space and implementing African cultural forms that whites were unaware of and did not understand. Once in the New World the African recreated a sense of tribal community within the plantation milieu through a series of extended kin and kinlike family networks that carried on the cultural values of responsibility for others, mutual aid and collective survival. First- and second-generation American slaves who were separated from biological kin by continued activity at the auction block and newly arriving slaves who were sold to different plantations were incorporated into the extended family structures of existing plantations. It was not essential for the survival of African conceptions of family life that biological or legal kinship ties be maintained. When a people share a philosophy of interdependence and collective survival, persons who are not biologically or legally related can become interwoven into newly created and existing kinlike networks. Cultural patterns once established seem to endure, especially if they work. The extended family survived because it provided Afro-Americans a support system within the context of a shared frame of reference. Along with other African customs and beliefs, an African family identity was passed along to the children as the link between generations through the oral tradition.

Once the philosophy of collective survival and interdependence was set into place as the foundation for community living, the extended family evolved through a series of cycles of formation, breakup, and reformation as the slaves who were without the recourse to legal rights to protect kinship structures and conjugal unions were transferred from place to place. Much later, with the beginnings of the Industrial Revolution after the Civil War, the pattern of Black family life based on combinations of kinship and kinlike networks continued, despite the emergence of the nuclear family among Euro-Americans. The growth of the individual nuclear family in Euro-America seemed to correspond with the competitive and individualistic values of the market place. The cycles of formation, breakup, and reformation of the extended family continued as Blacks migrated farther north and west towards the cities at the turn of the century during the pre and post periods of the two world wars and into the modern age.

According to Gutman (1976), who in his extensive studies of the Black family used vital statistics of births, deaths, and conjugal unions kept in plantation ledgers, census bureau statistics, and regional and local population records, the true structure of the Black family only emerges when the Black family is observed over a period of at least two or three generations. It seems to go through four identifiable stages. The phenotypical structure may appear to be different at selected times during the transition periods, but the underlying genotype is one that involves a sense of communalism, interdependence, collective survival, and mutual aid.

The first stage, beginning in Africa or with a stable plantation   15 population, involves an extended family composed of biologically related kin who are socially connected with similar groups to form a community. In the second stage the biological kin network becomes scattered as a result of trades or later by successive migrations. During the third stage the remaining individual and newly arriving Blacks come together in a combination of new kinship and kinlike structures. During this period the extended family is being rebuilt through new conjugal unions, marriages between young people, and the arrival of some folks who were members of the original family. In the fourth stage the extended family is completely visible again.

The Black extended family, with its grandparents, biological parents, conjugal partners, aunts, uncles, cousins, older siblings, boyfriends, girlfriends and quasi-kin, is an intergenerational group. The members of this three-generation family do not necessarily reside in the same household. Individual households are part of a sociofamilial network that functions like a minicommunity. The members band together to share information, resources, and communal concern (Stack, 1974). There is no central authority, matriarchial or patriarchial. Decisions are made on an equalitarian model with input and outcomes determined by who is available at a given time, who has expertise with reference to a given problem, and one's prior experience and track record in decision making. This is likely to give some edge to the tribal elders. They are looked up to within the extended family network as resource people and advisors because they have the life experience that is highly valued in the Black community. As in the past, the family is held together over time and across geographical space by a shared experience frame and a common set of values involving interdependence, mutual aid, resilience, communalism, and collective responsibility (Nobles, 1978). These values transcend sex roles and allow both men and women to participate in and contribute to the management of economic resources, child rearing, community activism, and other issues of family life without being categorically restricted on the basis of gender. The fluid distinction between social sex roles offers both men and women in the Black family network the opportunity to emerge as decision makers, influence molders, and household managers.

It could be argued that the Black extended family exists and persists primarily because Black people face the common fate of oppressive economic and social conditions, that it exists out of necessity as a way of surviving in an oppressive class system. Politically and economically oppressed people have historically banded together for survival, whether it be in internment camps, labor unions, or women's movements. It would follow from this argument that the Black extended family would disappear as Black people moved up the socioeconomic ladder. Yet the extended family does not appear to be disappearing with rising economic fortunes. McAdoo's (1979) work with upwardly mobile middle and upper-middle class Black families suggest that not only does the extended family model persist when Blacks move up the socioeconomic ladder but the Afro-American values of mutual aid, interdependence, and interconnectedness also remain as the guiding ethos of family existence.

Being part of a close-knit extended family group is a vital part of Afro-American life. Wherever Blacks appear in numbers of two or more, whether it be on predominately white college campuses, professional baseball teams, fraternal groups, street corners, store-front churches, automobile factories, or professional conferences, they soon seem to form a quasi-family network, share information and resources, get together, git down, rap, and party. White folks don't know what to make of this. The idea of sharing, closeness, and interdependence expressed in sociofamilial groups is so deeply ingrained in the fabric of the Afro-American ethos that it is not likely to give way to the nuclear family with its stress on isolation, competition, and independence. If anything, the traditional nuclear family may be moving toward becoming more like the Afro-American extended family.

To the extent that the extended family model represents a more accurate way of categorizing the Black family and capturing its strengths, the question arises as to why generations of the Black ghetto's Euro-American occupation army represented by sociologists, their graduate students, census takers, welfare workers, law-enforcement personnel, and bill collectors could only find broken, disorganized, single-parent, female-dominated families. The answer to this question involves several complex, interrelated reasons.

First, white observers may have been guided by a constricted 20 cultural frame of reference where the only viable form of family life consisted of a two-parent family contained within the boundaries of a single household. When they didn't find this single household nuclear family operating in the Black community, their constricted model prevented them from being able to assess correctly the differences they observed. They mistakenly labeled differences as deviant, therefore pathological.

Second, Black folks themselves have been known to be deceptive about the membership of their families when being questioned by authorities representing the white establishment whom they mistrust, such as law-enforcement personnel, bill collectors, and welfare workers. Given the restrictive nature of the welfare system, it is not hard to imagine why a Black woman would not be truthful to a public assistance worker about the nature of her conjugal relationships, regardless of whether they involve a legal husband, boyfriend, sweet daddy, or transient male friend. Carol Stack (1974) contends that the welfare system as it was traditionally structured worked against the emergence of stable conjugal unions within the extended family.

Third, the very nature of white institutions works against the Black extended family as it attempts to fulfill its collective responsibilities and functions within the context of Afro-American values (Nobles, 1978). Wade Nobles, a nationally recognized expert on the Black family, tells a story about moving his nephew, a high school student, from the boy's mother's residence in Louisiana to his household in Berkeley, California. There were no major psychosocial adjustment problems associated with the nephew's making the transition from the Louisiana branch of the Nobles extended family to the Berkeley, California, branch. The problem came about when Dr. Nobles attempted to explain to the Internal Revenue Service how he came by an adolescent dependent in the space of one year with no legal papers to back him up. If Professor Nobles, who holds a Ph.D. from Stanford University, had difficulty explaining the composition of his extended family with the addition of this adolescent nephew, try to imagine what low-income Black aunties or grandmothers go through when they are trying to get aid for dependent children residing in their household who are not their biological or legal offspring, or for that matter what Black college freshmen go through trying to explain the income of their multiple extended-family parents divided by the number of dependent cousins, siblings, nieces, nephews, and fictional kin to college financial aid officers.

Finally, the true nature of the Black family may be clouded by confusing an observation of a phenotype at any given moment with the underlying or basic genotype as the Black family goes through periods of emergence and reemergence. A Black family moving through the rural to urban transition or following jobs from one urban environment to another may at any given observational point, while it is reforming by building new groupings and reestablishing old networks, appear to be a single-parent home, a nuclear family, or a partially developed extended family. All three models can coexist within the core structure and dynamics of the extended family.

The Black child growing up in the extended family is exposed to a variety of role models covering a wide age span whose social behaviors are not completely regulated by conventional sex roles. This offers the children a greater opportunity to incorporate a balanced pattern of expressive and instrumental behaviors. Since parents may not be equally effective as role models at every stage of the child's development, the presence of a range of role models allows the children a series of options at any stage of their development in terms of adults they might seek out for guidance. . . .

Conclusion

The deficit-deficiency model of Black family life in America represents   25
a case where viewing Black family life through the inappropriate lens of the nuclear family contributed significantly to the perception of pathology and deviance. The emergence of the extended family model as a way of conceptualizing the Black family allows researchers greater freedom to move in the direction of understanding the strengths and coping strategies that the Black family has used to survive through successive cycles of formation and reformation, the family's role in preserving the Black heritage, and the way the supportive family network contributes to the growth and development of its members throughout the life cycle. At the applied level it is essential that social service agencies operating in the Black community reorganize their thinking about what constitutes a family in ways that will facilitate the delivery of a more comprehensive, well-coordinated package of services designed to strengthen the extended family and its support systems, rather than contributing to the breakup of the extended family by using a restrictive system of administrative rules based on the single-parent, subnuclear family.

Through discussion groups, workshops, and community forums, Black couples need to be provided with opportunities to look at the impact of cultural values on their relationship strategies, expectations, and goals, and to examine to what extent their values are congruent with the Afro-American ethos of genuineness, mutual aid, and interdependence. Finally, the nature of family life is changing in American society. With the advent of working mothers, rising divorce rates, and changing concepts of psychosexual roles, the family is moving outside the isolated nuclear framework for support systems and resource networks to assist with the concerns of living and child rearing. In developing alternative approaches to cope with the concerns of families in the contemporary era, a great deal can be learned from the cooperative and interdependent strategies that have been successful within the Black extended family.

References

BLASSINGAME, JOHN. *The Slave Community*. New York: Oxford University Press, 1972.

ELKINS, STANLEY. *Slavery: A Problem in American Institutions and Intellectual Life*. Chicago: University of Chicago Press, 1968.

FRAZIER, E. FRANKLIN. *The Negro Family in the United States*. Chicago: University of Chicago Press, 1939.

FREDRICKSON, GEORGE. "The Gutman Report," *The New York Review*, September 30, 1976, pp. 18–22, 27.

GUTMAN, HERBERT. *The Black Family in Slavery and Freedom, 1750–1925*. New York: Vintage Books, 1976.

MCADOO, HARRIET. "Black Kinship," *Psychology Today*, May 1979, pp. 67–69, 79, 110.

MOYNIHAN, DANIEL PATRICK. *The Negro Family: The Case for National Action*. Washington, D.C.: U.S. Government Printing Office, 1965.

NOBLES, WADE. "Africanity: Its Role in Black Families," *The Black Scholar*, June 1974, pp. 10–17.

——. "Toward an Empirical and Theoretical Framework for Defining Black Families," *Journal of Marriage and Family*, November 1978, pp. 679–688.

RAINWATER, LEE. *Behind Ghetto Walls: Black Family Life in a Federal Slum*. Chicago: Aldine, 1970.

ROGERS, DOROTHY. *Adolescence: A Psychological Perspective*, 2nd Edition. Monterey, Calif.: Brooks/Cole, 1978.

STACK, CAROL. *All Our Kin: Strategies for Survival in a Black Community*. New York: Harper & Row, 1974.

❖ **Focused Freewriting** Consider as possible focal points the possible reasons that black families have developed as they have, why investigators have judged some black families to be deficient, or one of the topics you've identified in your journal.

❖ **Guided Responses**

1. How does the deficit-deficiency model explain its negative characterization of African-American males and females? Do you agree with that characterization, or do you agree with White that

social scientists should reconsider their assessment of African-American families in light of recent changes in white families (para. 9)? Explain your response.

2. Both the deficit-deficiency model and the extended family model point to slavery as a cause of the particular configuration of African-American families over the past century. Based on your reading, which interpretation of the effects of slavery do you find more convincing? Explain your response.

3. White contends that "white observers may have been guided by a constricted cultural frame of reference where the only viable form of family life consisted of a two-parent family contained within the boundaries of a single household" (para. 20). Given what you know about families today, how accurate would you say White's claim is? Do you think this claim effectively discredits the deficit-deficiency model? Why, or why not?

4. According to the story of Wade Nobles (para. 22), how might the government's definition of a home and family be considered a deficit-deficiency model? In your view, how can the government accommodate extended families such as those presented in this selection?

❖ Shared Responses   In your journal explore the phenomenon of the extended family. Consider such issues as how the extended family alters the notion of home as a single dwelling, the advantages and disadvantages of relying on an extended rather than a nuclear family, and situations in which an extended family might assume great importance. As you discuss your responses in small groups, try to synthesize individual responses into one coherent statement; if you can't come to a consensus, clarify the differences between responses.

---❖---

Mom's in Prison: Where Are the Kids?

VIRGINIA A. HUIE

VIRGINIA A. HUIE *holds an M.A. in communications from Stanford University. She is currently a Leo Beranek fellow at WCVB-TV, a Boston television station. In this article, originally published in 1992 in* The Progressive *magazine, Huie calls upon the reader to think about a problem rarely considered by the general public. The unavoidable fact that imprisoning single mothers renders their children temporary orphans complicates any debate over the need for incarceration. The possible solutions offered here address both practical and humanitarian concerns related to prison reform.*

Before reading the selection, explore in your journal your thoughts about children of women in prison. Where do you think the children go? How do you think the experience affects them? What might be done to alleviate their problems?

As you make notes on your reading, you may want to focus on the statistics that support the author's conclusions, the observations of specialists, or the descriptions of specific programs to serve children of prisoners.

ONE MORNING NINE YEARS AGO, Jennifer Anderson, a twenty-five-year-old mother of two in Ohio, gave her son Tommy a reassuring kiss and hug. "Mommy always comes back," she told him. "Don't worry."

The next time two-year-old Tommy (the names in this story have been changed) heard from his mother, she was 2,000 miles away. "Tommy, I'm going to be here for a long time," Anderson said as she tried to stop her voice from trembling. "I won't be able to come home for a long, long time."

Anderson was calling Tommy from the California Institution for Women at Frontera. After a month-long trial in Concord, California, she was convicted of shooting and killing her husband.

Tommy did not know what "killed" or "prison" meant. Nor did he have a clear understanding of how long a six-year sentence was. But he could sense that his world had turned upside down.

Tommy's plight is not unique. A growing number of children are   5 separated each year from their mothers by jail and prison bars. Approximately 80 per cent of imprisoned women are mothers of dependent children under the age of eighteen. Between 70 and 90 per cent are single parents, most of them unemployed and relying on public assistance. Prior to imprisonment, 85 per cent of these women had legal custody of their children and were the primary caregivers.

According to the Center for Children of Incarcerated Parents at Pacific Oaks College in Pasadena, the population of children of imprisoned parents has soared from 21,000 in 1978 to one million in 1990 and could reach two million by the year 2000.

These children suffer traumatic loss, guilt, fear, and a sense of failure. For the infant, maternal separation may spell a sudden end to the only secure, continuous bond she knows. A toddler feels bewildered and becomes anxious and fearful that she will be abandoned again by other caregivers. The school-age child is tormented by the fear that she is to blame; she thinks she was "bad" and that's why Mommy's in jail. The adolescent feels rejection and bitterness.

The children are the innocent victims of their parents' crimes, prisoners' advocates say, sidelined by a penal system which emphasizes punishment over rehabilitation. Since the focus of corrections systems has been on individual punishment, inmates' family ties and the special needs of their children have been treated as a marginal concern. Consequently, when a parent is "doing time" on the inside through imprisonment, the children are "doing time" on the outside. The children are, in effect, punished along with the parent—by shock of sudden migration through revolving care arrangements, and by the possible permanent loss of the parent-child bond.

"They shouldn't be punished," says Marilyn Nystrom, an instructor from Las Positas College in Livermore who teaches the TALK (Teaching and Loving Kids) program at Santa Rita County Jail. "We have a responsibility to these children. Once you arrest somebody, you're responsible for their physical well-being. That makes us responsible, in turn, for the children who are not being taken care of."

The plight of children of imprisoned parents is one of the major   10 unaddressed issues in our country. "These kids are really a forgotten population," says Ellen Barry, director of Legal Services for Prisoners with Children, a national, San Francisco-based advocacy group. "They haven't done anything wrong. . . . It's very likely that they could end up with very serious problems in the school system, possibly end up in jail themselves as juveniles."

Barry stresses the immediate need to confront the devastating and prolonged effects on children when a mother lands behind bars. "It's important to do something now to make sure these kids are not forgotten," says Barry, "and that they get the kind of attention and love they need now so that they don't feel they have to perpetuate a damaging cycle."

Given the nation's burgeoning prison population, the plight of such children is becoming more apparent, their needs more pressing. More women than ever before are entering the Federal, state, and local lockups. In the last decade, the female prison population jumped 300 per cent—from 13,482 to more than 40,000. The Bureau of Justice Statistics reports that most women are behind bars for nonviolent offenses, which include larceny, petty theft, forgery, welfare fraud, prostitution, and drug abuse. Hard economic times and stressful home lives underlie many of these women's crimes. And the nation's tough-on-crime policy and stiffer sentencing laws are ensnaring increasing numbers of women.

"If a woman has an eighth-grade education, she can't afford child care, she's got three kids, and her old man split on her, what in the world is she going to do besides sell her body at night while her kids are sleeping, or write a bad check?" says the Reverend Deborah Haffner, director of the Elizabeth Fry Center, a San Francisco-based halfway house for inmate mothers and their young children.

A majority of children of female prisoners are cared for by extended family members, usually grandparents, fathers, or other relatives. Others are placed in foster homes. In the mother's absence, children are uprooted and shuttled from one home to another, pulled out of schools, separated from siblings, taunted by peers, and left alone to cope with uncertainties of disrupted lives.

Studies of early childhood development show that individualized nurturing and continuous attachment with a primary caregiver are required to ensure the physical and emotional well-being of an infant or young child. Because incarcerated women are usually primary caregivers, the loss of a mother is particularly acute for these children. Erosion of this vital family tie seriously injures a child's ability to receive and give love, establish meaningful interpersonal relationships, form a set of values, and exercise his or her intellectual abilities.

Children who lack affection may manifest a greater tendency to develop self-destructive and delinquent behavior that imperils not only the child, but other people as well. "The children who fail to bond have a much higher risk of growing up without a conscience," warns Nystrom, who is also a marriage, family, and child therapist. These children are ideal candidates for the next generation of offenders, Nystrom says.

"I call it a hereditary stretch of incarceration," says Deputy Lin Otey of Santa Rita County Jail, "We've had whole families in jail at the same time." Otey says familial cellmates are commonplace at the jail, which currently houses 2,400 male and female inmates.

In recognition of the social costs incurred by putting prison walls between parent and child, a growing number of correctional institutions nationwide are adopting innovative programs to address the needs of families in crisis. These programs take into consideration the deleterious effects of parent-child separation of children, and the importance of consistent care during childhood. The Prison MATCH (Mothers and Their Children) program in San Bruno, California, provides a child-centered environment for contact visits between inmates and their children. Established thirteen years ago, Prison MATCH is a national model for prison children's centers throughout the country.

Across the Bay, the TALK program at Santa Rita County Jail offers a similar setting in the jail's gymnasium to facilitate bonding between mother and child. TALK, modeled after a program at the Sybil Brand Institution in Los Angeles, marked its first anniversary last May. Both Prison MATCH and TALK programs were founded on the premise that frequent contact between an inmate and her child is vital in preserving and strengthening the mother-child tie and in alleviating the child's emotional distress. The programs try to help inmate parents enhance childrearing skills through parenting classes, self-esteem workshops, and counseling services.

Since most female offenders are imprisoned for nonviolent 20 crimes, correctional halfway houses for these women and their children are often a more suitable and cost-effective alternative than incarceration. California sponsors the Community Prisoner Mother-Infant Care Program, a network of seven community-based halfway houses for low-risk female prisoners and their children. In this approach, young children live with their mothers while the mothers serve their sentences. Job training and rehabilitative services are also provided to prepare the mothers for reintegration into the community.

Community groups also provide assistance. Friends Outside, a prisoner outreach enterprise, drives children to facilities to visit their inmate parents, and takes the children on outings to the circus, fairs, and beaches. With eighteen chapters throughout California, Friends Outside also provides referrals for food, shelter, and jobs for prisoners about to be released. Grandparents' support networks, ex-offender family groups, and substance-abuse programs are also appearing across the nation as more families deal with the stress of imprisonment.

As politicians authorize plans to build more walled compounds ringed with barbed wire to warehouse the nation's mushrooming inmate population, they might consider the advice of Elizabeth Fry, a Quaker who led the prison reform movement in the early Nineteenth Century. In one of her reports to the King of France she wrote:

"When thee builds a prison thee had better build with the thought ever in thy mind that thee and thy children may occupy the cells."

❖ Focused Freewriting   Consider as possible focal points the role society plays in perpetuating criminal behavior, the dilemma inherent in incarcerating single mothers, the long-term effects of parental incarceration on the children, or one of the topics you've identified in your journal.

❖ Guided Responses

1. Huie's opening story calls up a child's worst terror: the fear of being abandoned. How does this story prepare readers to accept her conclusions about the treatment of prisoners' children? Do you think her use of the story is justified? Why, or why not?

2. It would seem that the incarceration of mothers effectively denies most of their children a sense of home. To what extent do you agree with Huie that society has a responsibility to supply stable home environments for children of prisoners? Explain your response.

3. Huie argues in paragraph 20, "Since most female offenders are imprisoned for nonviolent crimes, correctional halfway houses for these women and their children are often a more suitable and cost-effective alternative than incarceration." Given the information provided in the rest of the article, to what extent would you consider halfway houses to be cost-effective? What other purposes would they serve?

4. Some argue that the tougher the punishment, the less likely a person is to commit a crime. According to this line of thinking, the plight of prisoners' children should act as one more deterrent to female crime. How would Huie respond to this argument? How do you respond?

❖ Shared Responses In your journal outline a program that could serve the needs of prisoners' children. Consider questions such as the following: How much contact would it allow between the prisoner and the child? Where would the children live? What role would the extended family play? How would the program be funded? As you discuss your responses in small groups, try to synthesize individual responses into one coherent statement. If you can't come to a consensus, highlight the reasons for differences of opinion.

The Remarkable Journey
of Willie Edward Gary

WIL HAYGOOD

WIL HAYGOOD, *a graduate of Miami University, has worked at the* Charleston Gazette *and the* Pittsburgh Post Gazette. *A feature writer for the* Boston Globe *since 1984, he has won a National Headliners Award for feature writing; his latest book,* King of the Cats: The Life and Times of Adam Clayton Powell, Jr., *was published by Houghton Mifflin in 1993. In this article, originally published in 1992 in the* Boston Globe Magazine, *Haygood presents an African-American version of the traditional rags-to-riches story. His characterization of Indiantown emphasizes the impact a community can have on its young people, often providing them with a moral foundation that supports them in their quest for success.*

Before reading the selection, explore in your journal your feelings about the concept of the American dream. Do you believe that a dirt-poor child from a tiny backwoods town can reasonably expect to "make it big" in this society? Can a community provide its children with the strength to overcome formidable obstacles in their journeys to success? Explain your responses.

As you make notes on your reading, you may want to focus on the nature of the Indiantown community, the values held by its members, or the impression it makes on outsiders.

THEY'RE LITTLE NOWHERE TOWNS—Okeechobee and Sand Cut, Pahokee and Indiantown—snug places in the backwoods of southern Florida. Travel town to town, up and across Route 1—along the migrant road loop—and you'll see figures loping down orange groves, wading into sugarcane fields. Time just seems to peel away. Farmland has long demanded a cruel price, no mater what region of the country. Southern Sundays, however, can unfold like blankets. There's an outdoor church service under way on a streetcorner in Pahokee. The sun's up; the minister's voice is high; the chairs are aluminum. A mere dozen gathered souls looking for strength, convinced that the size of their congregation is plenty enough. Mock religion elsewhere, but not here, not in the deep, deep South.

Lake Okeechobee cuts a huge swath across this region of Florida. There's not another lake in the South with its size and sweep. Follow the lake south from Pahokee for 20 miles—past Port Mayaca, past the grave where Turner Gary lies—and you'll come upon Indiantown. It's edged by cane and bean fields, by orange groves. You can spend a few days in and around Indiantown and also sense it's edged by something else: endurance. There are a few honky-tonk joints, rows of shotgun and rooming houses, and plenty of yapping dogs. It's an old, weathered town that never screamed of opportunity. And the farther away Willie Edward Gary got, the easier it was to come back.

Willie Edward Gary is an hour or so finished with his mama's Sunday dinner here in Indiantown. He's in the middle of the road talking to L. C. Howard. L. C. Howard is 80 years old. From where the old man is, in the road, he can turn on his heels and get a full view of the Evergreen First Baptist Church. It was built in 1986. L. C. Howard oversaw the carpentry work. He came to Indiantown in 1935, from Georgia; left one Southern town for another, left one miserable place for another with a little less misery. Those were Depression days; the babies had to be fed.

In 1967, Willie Edward Gary left this little town, walked right up out of the sugar-cane fields and orange groves and went away to college. He was the first black person from Indiantown to go to college. L. C. Howard and his wife, Gertrude, helped out. Gertrude sewed his pants. L. C. just smiled. The smile was as rich as applause. L. C. was good friends with Willie Edward's daddy, Turner Gary: two unlettered Southern men, wishing everything in their own souls for the boy's success. "We did what we could for him," says L. C. Howard, smiling.

The boy actually left for college on a football dream and a prayer.   5
The scholarship from Bethune Cookman, a tiny black school in Daytona Beach, was conditional; and no need to worry the townfolk about the conditional part, which meant he had to make the team first. At Bethune Cookman he was cut before summer's end. The dream seemed yanked all at once. The road led back to Indiantown. Yet the curse of Indiantown had long been the orange groves, the bean fields, the sticky cane.

Frantic, and with something coming alive in him, Willie Edward Gary hustled up the road to Raleigh, North Carolina, to Shaw University. He knew North Carolina. The Gary family had worked in migrant camps up around Hendersonville, in the hills. He showed up at

Shaw uninvited and unexpected. He begged for a football scholarship. "Go home, boy," the black coach said to the black kid. He slept
anywhere. He begged food. He stood on the sidelines of the football
practice field, getting in the way; it seemed weird sure enough. He
toted a water bucket; coaches looked at him out of the corner of their
eyes, then rolled those same eyes in another direction. Not a soul
knew him over at the admissions office. He cried inside for a chance
to play.

One afternoon a player went down, injured. The coach looked at
Willie Edward Gary, 5 feet 8 inches tall, and told the boy to get some
pads on if he really wanted his chance. The players realized as quickly
as the coach did: The boy from Indiantown could tackle. Willie Edward Gary—in 1967, in a year in the American South when so much
that was improbable was happening—received a scholarship.

After Shaw, Willie Edward Gary went to law school. After law
school he opened a law practice in Stuart, Florida, east of Indiantown.
Years rolled on, and the lawyer became a stunning success. Recently,
when Shaw University was faced with bankruptcy—"They were two
to three weeks from boarding up the place," recalls Gary—one of the
administrators phoned Willie Edward Gary and asked for a little
help, just like Willie Edward Gary had asked for a little help 25 years
earlier. Willie Edward Gary signed over a $10 million check to Shaw
University.

Religion and football, dreams and a work ethic—they are the pistons
that surely drive much of the American psyche. And they've all
driven a part of Willie Edward Gary. But there's quite possibly another, even more powerful clue to the impossibility of it all.

One summer night in 1947, a hard-working woman of God, Mary   10
Gary, went into labor. Complications set in, and she and the midwife
were rushed to the hospital. It didn't look good, for mother or child.
The Gary's gathered close. Palms touched palms. In the end, both
mother and child pulled through, although Mary Gary's health took
a downward turn forevermore. "Went through lots with him," Mary
Gary says about the baby she gave birth to. "Like to lost me and him."

Mary Gary named the baby she gave birth to in that hospital on
that painful night Willie Edward Gary.

The Garys owned a farm, and Mary's massive hospital bills took
the farm and the land around it. Turner moved his wife and kids and
went to work. It was work in the migrant labor camps. Turner Gary
never asked the government for a damn dime; never told his kids
about any stacked deck. It was the work ethic, the blessing against the
curse.

Who knows what gentle demons drive Willie Edward Gary? Might not a birth that caused the loss of so much, of so many dreams—that spiraled a mother downward into poor health yet actually showed a family just how strong it was against the winds—might that be more than enough to drive a boy to unimaginable heights?

"What struck me, right here," says L. C. Howard, tapping his thin chest as if his heart is stretched across the surface of his breastbone, "is that the boy came *back*."

It was a good working family farm, in Eastman, Georgia, Turner and 15 Mary Gary proud of the land that surrounded them—200 acres of it—and their children raised up under morning sky. Before they purchased their own land, they had been sharecroppers. Their own farm brought economic independence; for a while the only crops they shared were their own. Then came the birth of Willie Edward, and the mounting hospital bills. One day Turner Gary had a roof over his family's head, and the next day he was loading them for an uncertain future. They wouldn't complain; they'd work.

In 1948 the Garys landed in Canal Point, Florida. There was plenty of work in the fields. Mary Turner, like other parents, would put her babies in potato sacks next to the cane fields. They'd howl; she'd pick. "You talk about hard work—110-degree temperatures, insects biting you, no shade trees in sight. I grew up in that," says Willie Gary. " 'Day care' was field care."

When they had picked enough beans, cabbage, sweet corn, and oranges in Florida, they'd move up the coast, into North Carolina, to pick potatoes. "One thing I always hated about North Carolina," Gary says, "is that North Carolina let white farmers pass a law that said migrant kids could only go to school half a day." At 11:30 the little migrant children would be given a sandwich and a carton of milk. Trucks waited with open doors in the school parking lot to drive them to the fields. "Gloria and I both grew up in that. We wanted to go to school and couldn't."

Gloria was his childhood sweetie. She saw the man in the boy before a lot of others did. She also saw the persistence. "He didn't have anything, but he had a plan, a goal," she says. "The first time we went out, he asked me if I wanted something to eat. Guys around my school didn't ask me that." But there was a period when she thought twice about him, when she tried to convince herself that she didn't like him at all.

"Why's that, baby?" Willie Gary wants to know.

"Let me tell you why. We had gone to a hootenanny," she says. 20 "After the hootenanny, he came back by the house. He wanted a kiss.

I decided to give him a kiss. He put everything he had in that kiss. Too aggressive."

They're in the kitchen of their Stuart, Florida, home. They married when she was 19 and he was 21—and they married when they believed in the righteousness of what they were doing, if no one else did. They married in a relative's front yard. They've picked beans together in wet fields. They've looked out onto one sorrowful day that followed another sorrowful day, and even with that, they've felt rich together. This was long before any appreciable amounts of money started rolling in, long before they both finished school at Shaw. They love just to see each other walk up and down the stairs. They've raised four boys.

"They had special little barracks, or they would put us all in a gym," he's saying to her about their days in migrant camps. "You remember that, babe? We'd all talk in one big room."

"Your parents would take your clothes to the field," she remembers.

"You changed wherever you could," he says.

"You never got a chance to make friends," she says. "You were   25 always moving."

"Every year after the Carolina crops," he remembers, "we'd end up back in South Florida."

There seemed to be such fear out in those orange groves. If you got caught stealing oranges—depending on the sheriff—you could be charged with a felony. Little Gloria Royal—later Gloria Gary—heard about a sheriff who caught someone with stolen oranges. As the tale went, the sheriff split the orange with a knife and told the thief he'd get as many years in prison as seeds fell from the orange. The story might be apocryphal; it might be true.

John Fleming was working for the North Carolina Baptist Church organizations in the late 1950s in and around Hendersonville, North Carolina, toting Bibles and going into the migrant camps. His mission went beyond religion, however, which is why he had problems with the Baptist organizations. "They wanted statistics," says Fleming of the church organizations. "We thought migrant conditions demanded more than statistics." Fleming, now a retired educator in Raleigh and a Gary acquaintance, found hungry children in the camps, and inadequate housing. "What really amazed me about Gary is that he came up in that environment. Those kids were really handicapped."

Elizabeth Johnson began teaching in the camps in 1954, right out of Florida A & M. "I never seen anything like it," she says. "It was really a bad situation." One of her pupils was Willie Edward Gary. What impressed her about so many of the children was how eager they seemed to learn, how they'd wrap their arms around those books as if they were holding someone's flesh. "They were very much into school," says Johnson. "There were a lot of brains riding up and down the roads on those buses."

In 1960, Turner and Mary Gary settled in Indiantown. There were 11   30
children, and it's a wonder they all squeezed into the shack that still stands out on a back-country road east of Lake Okeechobee. Turner strung a wire and hung a lantern from it so the kids could jitterbug outside in the evenings. He found work on a white man's farm. "Daddy, if you gonna farm, why can't we farm for ourselves?" Willie asked one day. "Why don't we just buy a truck, buy produce, and resell it?"

Turner couldn't figure it out, but his boy, Willie, struck a deal for a truck, began loading it with melons, began selling the melons, became a businessman in and around Indiantown. He'd drop melons off at Gloria's house and drive off without picking up the money—"trying to get in little favors with her," he admits. There was Willie Gary, going to school, going to football practice, coming home, and shifting gears on the truck and selling watermelons, then coming home again and reading his father's mail and answering it, because Turner Gary couldn't read or write.

But those who knew Turner Gary say the man was brilliant in other ways—in his kindness and his work ethic. Never raised a hand to his wife. Fed strangers when his own family was hardly getting by. There might not have been a prouder moment in his life than when his boy went off to college.

The conditional-scholarship routine was common at many of the black colleges in the South, especially for football, where practices began before school started. It was a noisy grapevine. Players showed up, just flat-out hungry for opportunity. In Indiantown, news of a conditional scholarship to Willie Gary was worthy of celebration. "Farm Boy Gets a Scholarship," said the headline in an area newspaper.

"My daddy was happy," Gary recalls. To get in shape, he ran dirt roads, ran around the cane fields, the very fields he wanted to get away from; he ran by liquor-filled men outside honky-tonks in Indiantown who rose up and threw words of support at him. He didn't quite know the currency of all that, but he knew it helped, their collective support; Gertrude Howard sewing his pants, a handout here, a handout there. "I had to fight for them," says Willie Gary. "I couldn't let them down."

He caught a bus on the side of the road, 20 miles from Indiantown,   35
which took him to Bethune Cookman. He had on high-water pants, stitched too short by a woman who cared for him dearly. Back in

Indiantown they all wished him success, blessed him with the very thought of it. But if he failed they wouldn't fall apart. Cold winds strike anywhere and at any time. They knew as much. And the cane fields—and this was the curse—weren't going anywhere. There'd be work.

The thinking across much of America was that life in the South stopped because of the emotional war taking place there during the '60s. But it didn't. In ways huge and small, life went on. On the campus of Bethune Cookman, a lot of boys were trying to impress a coach so they could play football. Every day after practice, the coach would assemble players, and he would begin calling out names of players who didn't make it. It was so public, and it seemed so brutal. But the coach had to ready a football team. "I prayed to God I wouldn't hear my name," recalls Gary.

Four weeks' worth of tryouts rolled by, and Willie Gary didn't hear his name. He snatched bucketloads of confidence from the coach's silence. The fifth and last week of practice the coach didn't call names out loud; by then the kids had at least earned the right to privacy when learning their fate. Gary was summoned to the coach's office. The coach said, "Son, you gotta go home." The boy from Indiantown heard it, but he didn't want to believe it. "I begged him, with tears in my eyes," Gary recalls. "I didn't want to let Indiantown down. I told him I'd be the trainer; I'd mop the floors. Just let me make it. He said, 'I'm sorry. You gotta go.' "

He had arrived on the Bethune campus quietly, and he left quietly. No one said an unkind word back in Indiantown. But the silence was a pain of its own kind. Willie Edward Gary had one foot back in the cane fields and knew it. His parents could do little. "They didn't have no money," he says. He asked his high school coach if he knew anyplace where he might rummage a tryout. The coach told him about Shaw University, in Raleigh. Just hearing about another place where there might be a chance was like lightning. "I threw a suitcase on the back of a wooden truck we used to sell watermelons from," he says. "Had a rope tied around the suitcase. They dropped me off on Route 1. Took a Greyhound bus to Raleigh."

Shaw is a little school on the edge of downtown Raleigh, founded in 1865 by Henry Martin Tupper, a native of Monson, Massachusetts. Seized with a missionary zeal during the Civil War, in which he fought, Tupper wanted to go to Africa. Instead, a New York Baptist organization dispatched him to the South, where he found plenty of missionary work. Over the years the college built a dental and law and medical school. All that was back in the 1920s. It was impressive enough to be called Shaw University. Those graduate programs are gone now. It's a small school. In reality, it always has been. The spirit's strong; graduates refer to themselves as "the Shaw family."

Willie Edward Gary arrived on campus and made a beeline for the   40
coach's office. "I said, 'I'm Willie Gary. Did the coach ever call you?' " The coach looked at Willie Gary, dumbfounded. "No," the coach replied. And when Willie Gary finished his appeal, the coach looked at him and told Willie Gary to go home. "We got too many players here already." When Willie Gary pleaded some more, the coach found another excuse. He told the boys there was no insurance policy to cover players not on scholarship. Willie Gary told the coach he didn't have any money, didn't have a way back to Florida, didn't have a place to sleep the night. The coach wished him well.

Willie Gary walked over to the men's dormitory, started waving hellos around. Night came on. There was a sofa in the lounge. He bunked there, couldn't bear to phone home. Someone handed him a blanket. The journey from Florida had tired him, and sleep came quick enough.

David Walker had been recruited from Cleveland to play football for Shaw. "I had been there for about a week," recalls Walker. "Had maybe 120 ballplayers come in. About a week later, I saw this little pigeon-toed guy walking across campus. It was Gary. He just showed up on campus one day. We heard this guy was going to try to play football. A lot of us sort of chuckled to ourselves. Nobody wanted to tell him to go home."

Willie Gary started hanging around the football field at practices, being stared at the way strangers are; folks wondered if he was lost. "It was the strangest thing," says Walker. "When I got there I had a room assignment, people to greet me." Walker snatched food from the cafeteria to give Gary. Other players did the same. Gary looked them in the eye and told them he had no place to go. They thought he meant home. He meant the cane fields, the orange groves: no place to go back to. "You can bunk with me," Walker found himself saying to Gary one day. Walker could hardly believe he said it. "Frankly," says Walker, "I wasn't expecting him to stay."

Every day, there was Willie Edward Gary, hustling across campus with the football players. His pants were too short. The shirts were too big. Walker came up out of the rough side of Cleveland. Looking at Gary, Walker thought he was better off than the kid from Florida, and that wasn't saying much. "I looked at this brother and said, this brother's on hard times."

Jimmy Young had been recruited from Madison, Florida. Young   45
was a good-hearted country boy, orphaned out to relatives after his father deserted the family and his mother died during childbirth. "What was so interesting about this guy," Young says about Gary,

"was he had platform shoes, to make you look taller, and a big flattop. He said, 'Man, I came down from Bethune Cookman. They wouldn't let me play. I got cut.'" Being from Florida, Young established a rapport with Gary. "He just wanted to go to school. You could tell."

The thinking among coaches was that Gary would be gone soon. If the heat wouldn't get him, the tedium would. "When players would go to practice, I'd clean up the locker room," he recalls. "Hard work was nothing to me. Worked in fields all my life." One of the coaches had walked in the locker room, saw Gary's back bent over a mop and the floor, and said, "Son, you want to make it, don't you?"

When a Shaw player went down in practice one afternoon, the head coach looked down—then over at Gary. The coach told him to go put some shoulder pads on. "Gary, you been waiting for a shot. We're gonna see what you can do."

"I thought he wasn't that good a player," Jimmy Young says. "He was a good player." Gary lined up at nose guard. Young lined up a few steps back, at linebacker. And Young was shocked at how the 5-foot-8-inch Gary could crack ballcarriers, how he just threw his whole body into them with a reckless abandon. Willie Gary started seeing coaches whispering about him, about the latest hit. It was a good feeling. It was everything.

Over at the admissions office, they were more than a little amused about him. "Willie came with no money, no scholarship, no nothing," recalls Thomas Kee, who was a campus administrator at the time and an unofficial athletic adviser. Shaw found a scholarship for Willie Edward Gary. Mary Gary's boy was now a Shaw man.

They played schools like Johnson C. Smith, North Carolina A & T,   50
Bethune Cookman. Once they arrived on the campus of Savannah State College, in Georgia. "Y'all look like a choir. Where's the football team?" a Savannah State player said to them. Shaw licked Savannah, 28-6. After the game, a Shaw player asked a couple of Savannah players, "Y'all want us to sing for you?"

They were big-shouldered country boys riding across the South. No one, to this day, says a good word about the bus, but it got them there. Often, there'd be a voice rising from some darkened corner of the bus. It was Willie Gary, singing Sam Cooke gospel songs, plucking a guitar. Not just trying to sing and trying to pluck a guitar, but doing both skillfully. "We found ourselves amazed by that," says Walker.

There was more about Gary that amazed his teammates. He seemed so eerily restless. Football and academics didn't seem to be enough. A wall clock couldn't guide his days and weeks. The boy stretched hours. It was as if he feared the world would be snatched from beneath him if it was tilled. Raised on a work ethic, he couldn't still his body.

He started a lawn-mower business in Raleigh. He recruited customers off the streets, put ads in the Raleigh papers. After football season he'd make weekend runs in a truck loaded with melons. Players didn't know what in the world to think when they'd go into town and see Gary unloading melons from his daddy's truck.

Once Jimmy Young and some others walked down to the Chicken Box, near campus. For 50 cents you could get a chicken breast laid between two slices of white bread. A week later Young was back, with some other players but not Gary. When they looked behind the counter, back toward the kitchen, there was Willie Gary, in white hat and apron—working. "We looked up one day and saw Gary down there throwing chickens," says Young, guffawing.

David Walker, the Shaw player from Ohio, traveled to Indiantown   55
one spring weekend with Gary. Walker was amazed at the town's pride in his friend. "It was like the whole town was so proud that one of their own had gone off to play football." A day after they arrived, the two boys started talking about needing money to get back to school. Turner Gary, Willie's father, pointed to the fields. One earned one's way in this life.

"My father was something else," Willie Gary says, with reverence.

Before Willie Gary left Shaw, he had blocked eight punts. It set a school record.

Turner Gary was a farmer, a father, a husband, and a listener. He kept a family together through hard years. When Willie Gary suggested to his father ways to make money—let's buy a truck, let's sell melons—Turner Gary listened.

In 1984, Turner Gary took sick and was hospitalized. Cancer had spread through his body. Family members who visited him in the hospital were careful not to bring their own worries into his room. They wanted to keep quiet the divorce of Freddie Gary, Willie's brother.

One day Turner Gary looked up from his hospital bed. Freddie   60
was at the door. Turner Gary knew his children, saw on the boy's face that something was amiss. Matter of fact, he knew about the divorce. Family secrets have a way of spreading. "Son, I'm getting ready to leave your mama," Turner Gary said. He was talking about dying. "Do you see me with my head down? Don't walk in here with your head down." There was the littlest bit of edge in his voice. "I want you to do one thing. If you have to go to sleep on the floor of your business, I want you to. Don't let your business fold. I want you to

make enough money to raise my grandkids." Turner Gary didn't say his kids; he said *grand*kids. Looking to the future; that's what breaks Freddie Gary up—that sick man, lying there, dying, and still looking forward.

They brought Turner Gary home to die. He was confined to bed under doctor's orders, but his son Willie saw his eyes wandering toward the window, outside. Willie dressed his daddy, slipped him into the wheelchair, and wheeled him out and around Indiantown. Friends waved from the corner; the air felt good. When Mary Turner found out, she was angry. This was her ailing husband. But they were his boys.

After being wheeled around Indiantown, seeing folk, seeing L. C. Howard, seeing others, he was taken back inside. He died several days later. "Me and my husband lived together for 45 years," Mary Gary is saying, sitting a spell, resting, after preparing Sunday dinner for the Gary clan. "Had 11 kids. I raised all of them to get grown. Three died, but they lived to get grown."

It's a fine house, more fine than any of the homes in Indiantown. But it's informal, too. Children and grandchildren and family friends come and go. Mary Gary would have walked across Lake Okeechobee before she would have left Indiantown. Her boy Willie had the home built. "Man, I lived for the day I could build my mama and daddy a home, and they wouldn't have to work in the hot fields," he says.

A block from Mary Gary's home sits the Evergreen First Baptist Church. Rev. J. L. Gary is the minister. J. L. is Willie's brother. The choir is made up of Gary children. Matter of fact, the entire congregation is Gary family. It's the Garys' church. Willie Edward Gary built his mama a church, too.

When Willie Gary was graduated from North Carolina Central Law 65 School in 1974, he set up offices in Stuart, Florida, 25 miles from Indiantown. He dabbled briefly in domestic law, then started taking malpractice cases. He gained some attention for going into small southern Florida towns—appearing before all-white juries—and winning huge judgments for his clients.

In Palatka, he won a $50,000 judgment for a black man who had been killed in an auto accident, the highest amount ever issued in that town in a wrongful death case. That caused some buzz. Since then, he's climbed the personal-injury ladder with amazing success.

Most of his clients are white. Blacks, he says, have been led to believe that black lawyers are ineffective. The admission pains Gary, but he doesn't spend much time crying. His success seems measured in the old fashioned work ethic. "He works hard," says Henry Hunter, a personal-injury lawyer who argued cases with Gary when he first began his law practice. "He's personable with the jury."

In 1986, Ray Vernon Nettles, 27, of Vero Beach, Florida, was riding a bicycle out on Route 1 in Port St. Lucie. Dusk was settling. Nettles was hit by a car occupied by tourists from Pennsylvania. His leg dangled like a broken tree branch. He would eventually lose it.

After conducting an investigation, the Pennsylvania couple's insurance company found out that Ray Nettles had both drinking and drug problems, had been a ne'er-do-well, had alcohol in his body on the evening he was hit. Groaning, bleeding, Nettles also had hollered something about suing.

The insurance company steeled itself for trial, its strategy pinned   70
on the hope that it could convince a jury that the insurance company shouldn't be held liable, that Nettles had recklessly ridden his bicycle too close to the oncoming car that night, that the accident was unavoidable. The Nettles family— white—called in Willie Gary. There would be no settlement. "Take a case like that," says Hunter. "takes heart, takes guts."

"You need a local boy like me on a case like that," says Gary.

When the trial got under way, the defense hired a group of experts from California—paid them $250,000—to draw charts showing that the highway was poorly lighted.

When Willie Gary did his investigation into Ray Nettles' life, he found that the young man had been trying to straighten out his life, had taken a stab at rehabilitation. Ray Nettles also worked, every day of the week.

The trial lasted two weeks. "I said, 'Mr. Juror, you ever had a relative had problems with alcohol?' "says Willie Gary, recalling his summation to the jury:

" 'You love them any less? You understand it's a sickness, a dis-   75
ease. Jurors, Ray Nettles is a good man. I'm proud to be representing this boy. You see these California people. They come over here and try to show us country folks what we see on our highways. They came in here and tried to put him down like he was a nobody. His daddy was an alcoholic. Tender age of 13, he had to work after school. He did that 'cause his father had a heart attack. But these highfalutin people from California wouldn't know nothing about that. Here is little Vernon, shouldering the burden of his sisters and brothers. Sure, he started drinking. He played the hand that was dealt him. You know the story of the prodigal son?

" 'Jurors, there's a reason for having the Betty Ford Center. She was the wife of the president. The United States of America opened its arms to Betty Ford that day that she admitted her problem and said, "Come on in."

" 'Ladies and gentlemen, are you going to open your doors for Vernon Nettles? Vernon Nettles wants to come home today. He's married. Got a good wife. Let him come home, members of the jury.' "

Ray Nettles was awarded $4 million. Willie Gary took home 40 percent of that. There's one more thing that deserves mention: Ray Nettles worked in the orange groves, picking oranges.

Willie Gary has won awards as high as $10 million. He was in his office the other day. A call came in from Massachusetts. A lady was on the other end, telling Willie Gary that her husband's twin-engine plane went down. She suspects mechanical deficiency with the structure of the aircraft. She wants Willie Gary. He heads a law firm with two dozen lawyers. It boasts an equal representation of white and black attorneys. Some are Ivy League-trained lawyers. And here's Willie Gary, from itty-bitty North Carolina Central Law School. You dip your bucket in the well of knowledge and bring up from it what you will. "I didn't go to Harvard Law, didn't go to Yale Law," he points out in speeches. He tells students that he doesn't want to be the best black lawyer in America, just the best lawyer. The Gary law offices are housed in a building in Stuart overlooking the lake. He owns the building. There's a marina outside the building. Owns that, too.

Gloria Gary heads Gary Enterprises, a family business housed in the law offices. They've got money now, but Gloria Gary still does her own cooking. They've seen the world, but there's hardly a Sunday when they don't get over to Indiantown, to sit with Mary Gary. Truth be told, the money has been a surprise. "One day you look up and your accountant tells you you're a millionaire," she says. Her husband sometimes gives money away like it grows on trees. "I told him," says Gloria, "one more pledge, and off with your head." She's half-kidding, of course. In addition to the $10 million they gave to Shaw, they give money to provide medical care for migrant workers. "He's always been generous," she says. "I get mad at him sometimes, because it seems like people take advantage of him. He's always been like that. His father was the same way." 80

Willie and Gloria Gary were recently invited to the White House for a United Negro College Fund dinner hosted by President Bush. "Here you are in the White House," says Willie Gary. "And you can only think about Sand Cut, Pahokee, Silver City, the cane fields, the orange groves." At the reception, before the guests had taken their seats, President Bush walked over to Willie Gary, president of the United Negro College Fund, and asked, "Who *is* this man Willie Gary?"

The sun has come up beautifully over the sugar-cane fields this morning. But the fields today across Florida are quiet. It's a Sunday.

Gloria and Willie Gary are rolling down the road, having just left a church service where they were guests. There were a lot of field workers at the church, people holding on, people with calluses on their hands; Gary kind of people. Gloria's got a cousin in the Pahokee hospital with cancer. The minister had put his hand on gloria Gary's forehead and uttered something about driving the cancer from her cousin's body. The guttural voice of the minister, the way the congregation had pulled up close to her, the collective praying—all touched Gloria Gary. A teaspoon's worth of tears filled her eyes.

"She was always one of those sickly children," Willie Gary says about the cousin. A minister's palm laid to the back of someone's head, hollering about the demon of cancer, vowing it will be cleansed from someone's body? This car is not the place to doubt such faith. Willie and Gloria Gary once worked in cane fields where one day looked as pitiful as the next. They're rolling by cane fields now—the cane's high and green, ready for cutting— with Sam Cooke crooning gospel from the tape deck of their Rolls-Royce, which just hums along in its own fine silence.

❖ Focused Freewriting Consider as possible focal points the source of Gary's strength through his college years, the conditions his family endured as migrant laborers, his father's influence, or one of the topics you've identified in your journal.

❖ Guided Responses

1. When the medical bills for Gary's birth forced his father to sell the farm, his family spent the next twelve years as migrant laborers. How did the migrant workers maintain a sense of community during their travels? Based on what Haygood tells us about their family life, how would you describe the values that helped them endure?

2. Gary's teammates at Shaw University considered him restless, "as if he feared the world would be snatched from beneath him if it was tilled" (para. 52). What do you think fueled this restlessness? How did the values he embraced in Indiantown serve to give his life direction while he was in college?

3. Many successful people who hail from places like Indiantown never look back, much less return; yet Willie Edward Gary has settled down close to his childhood home and returns regularly. Given what Haygood writes about the community, how would you explain Gary's choice to remain close to his home?

4. "Home" means much more than a dwelling or a town. In your own words, characterize what makes Indiantown, Florida, a home. What contributes to the sense of community in the town? What values do the inhabitants espouse?

❖ Shared Responses In your journal discuss the sense of community (or lack of it) in your hometown. Consider such topics as the extent to which you feel protected by the community, the pride the community takes in its successful young people, and its responses to members in need. As you discuss your responses in small groups, try to characterize the ideal supportive community.

❖

"Ask a Homeless Person . . ."

STEVEN VANDERSTAAY

STEVEN VANDERSTAAY, *a teacher and writer, is currently completing a Ph.D. at the University of Iowa. After spending several summers traveling the country to record the observations of homeless people, he wrote* Street Lives: An Oral History of Homeless Americans *(1992). Most of the royalties from this book go to homeless organizations. In this selection from* Street Lives, *VanderStaay provides a platform for homeless people to speak of their successes. Recognizing their alienation from one another as well as from society, the people interviewed here focus on building their own communities and offering one another support similar to that given by an extended family.*

Before reading the selection, list in your journal what kinds of assistance you think different types of homeless people need in order to get back on their feet. Who should provide these services? Who should pay for them? How should they be supervised?

As you make notes on your reading, you may want to focus on the differences in language between VanderStaay and the people he interviews, the similarities between programs, or the recurring emphasis on specific needs.

HOMELESS PEOPLE SEEK SOLUTIONS that account for their own experience. Persons homeless through loss of work see employment as their greatest need; others stress a safe and affordable home as the foundation upon which they can base other progress. Most recognize that effective drug and alcohol treatment must accompany job assistance and housing programs for people who need it.

Assumptions about such solutions vary widely among homeless people, depending—again—upon their experience. People recently homeless through accident or mishap tend to want "another chance," a little help in getting back on their feet. "I've always worked, always gotten by," one recently homeless man told me. "Now I just need that chance to show what kind of a worker I am."

221

Homeless people with little experience of middle-class success have less faith in the viability of hard work and perseverance to lift them out of destitution. As previous chapters have shown, many of these people remained poor while working hard and fell into homelessness despite their determination to do otherwise. They argue that the conditions of life, employment, and housing they face make middle-class notions of "boot-strap" success nearly impossible to achieve. Their feelings range from despair to anger, buttressing their view that only drastic measures can bring the changes they need to solve the problems they face. Disillusioned, they see homelessness as an urgent crisis of immense proportions few understand or care about. As a friend of mine puts it, "No one hears our cries."

These people cry for help beyond housing—for child care, medical attention, substance-abuse programs, and jobs. Surveys that cite high rates of personal problems among the homeless come as no surprise to homeless people themselves, many of whom freely admit personal difficulties that complicate their situations. "I need some help," "I'm still weak for it," "It was my fault I dropped out," are statements common to their stories. Those without debilitating problems see them in their family and friends, in the people who share their soup lines, and in the other homeless people they meet on the street.

But the idea that people should be punished for behavior they   5
already suffer under makes no sense to homeless people. They view so-called austerity programs, designed to make emergency housing purposefully uncomfortable, as ludicrously cruel and counterproductive—measures akin to feeding starving children sour milk as punishment for missing breakfast. And that thousands of street addicts and alcoholics want rehabilitation they cannot get, strikes them as beyond comprehension.

Most homeless people I've interviewed also want to cut defense spending, the charitable assistance we send abroad, and tax breaks for the rich. They are nearly unanimous in wanting to substantially raise the minimum wage, increase support for dependent families, veterans, and the disabled, and in their desire for housing programs that integrate poor families into middle-class neighborhoods. Most see universal health care as an essential human right. They want schools that give a ghetto child a chance, streets that permit safe passage, a war on drugs that cares for the wounded, and job assistance programs that provide jobs, not assistance.

Most homeless people also mistrust the social service system. This is not to say they disagree with the idea of such services; rather, they fault the system for its failure to deliver them. They say that government and charitable funds earmarked for the poor and homeless rarely reach them, that caseworkers become adversaries, not advocates, and that job-training programs too often provide jobs for the trainers, not the trainees. It would be more effective, they argue, to receive assistance directly—either as employment, housing, or cash—rather than through service agencies where much of it is siphoned into salaries and operating expenses. Interestingly, it was a conservative administration—Nixon's—that actually proposed such a plan, the "Family Assistance Program." Of course, the plan met stiff opposition from Democrats and Republicans alike and was soundly defeated.

But one should resist the temptation to paint the suggestions raised by homeless people in the terms of party politics. Less concerned with affixing blame than finding solutions, most homeless people have little patience for the ideological battles that characterize public discussion of the crisis. As one man explained it to me, "Don't tell me I ain't got a job, I know that. And don't tell me why I ain't got one either. Tell me where I can get one."

Consequently, the solutions that homeless people suggest not only lack the political homogeneity common to those who speak for them, they point to new ways of thinking about the problem and the nation.

This is particularly evident in the frequent references homeless   10
people make to communities. Whether speaking of family, neighbors, neighborhoods, or "the homeless," homeless people commonly speak of themselves in relation to a body of people who share their situation and who live where they do, and they frame their ideas in terms that are at once personal and community-based.

This sense of community is particularly evident in what may be the most salient characteristic of the solutions homeless people seek for themselves: the desire to help each other. I have heard versions of the following scenario, for example, from homeless men and women on both coasts, and in the North, South, and Midwest:

> I think maybe if I could get some money I'd get a house and
> put some people up. Because, well, I can't say for you or for
> anybody else, but now that I've been homeless I'd see it as
> a waste of money to spend much on an apartment. You
> know, one of these bi-level apartments, six, seven hundred
> dollars a month. I'd rather get a place where I can put some
> people up, give 'em a place to stay where they can actually
> live—not permanent, but some place where a man or a
> woman can be long enough to get themselves together and
> get back on their feet. Where they can live. Have some
> rules, you know, but a place. Give 'em a door key and kind
> of work together.

Wishful thinking? Perhaps. But homeless assistance programs that succeed—even those that attract mainstream attention—speak to the viability of such ideas. "Study after study" has shown that "the homeless are different from other people," notes one essay on programs that work for homeless people: "They are profoundly alone." Accordingly, building support networks and community alliances is a key to their success.

It should be noted that this sense of alliances is much more than a vague wish for togetherness or cooperation: it is a strategic response to perilous conditions. Like survivors of a devastating earthquake or other natural disaster, homeless people have little choice but to take shelter together. Similarly, it is a mistake to assume these communities to be racially bound. Homeless people frequently say they have much more in common with other homeless people, regardless of race, than with any larger, housed community. And many of the communities homeless people form for themselves—whether a precarious "squat" in an abandoned building, or a cooperative household—are virtual models of integration.

The programs described in the testimonies that follow reaffirm these concerns. Whether the target population is homeless youth or homeless men, the programs that homeless people themselves advocate provide stability, opportunity, and the kind of community-building that fosters self-reliance and long-term structures of peer-support.

Community-based, long-term approaches of this nature are es-   15
pecially prevalent among shelters and programs established for women. One of many such organizations is the Elizabeth Stone House, which operates a residential mental health alternative, a battered women's program, and a transitional housing program in the Boston area. Stressing a "therapeutic community" and individual goal-setting to foster self-empowerment, the Elizabeth Stone House provides a broad range of programs and assistance options through which the women it serves work to meet their own needs. Furthermore, because the organization serves a broad population and sets no financial restrictions for admission to its programs, the communities and networks it fosters are themselves rich with opportunities for mutual assistance. Women combine households, make friends, and share support and encouragement across class and racial boundaries.

Elsewhere, informal communities of poor women have led cooperative, neighborhood campaigns to rescue buildings that threatened whole communities with homelessness. Many such efforts have generated new "community households" on the model of large, extended families. In them groups of precariously housed people combine resources, skills, and housing in small networks of mutual support.

Other communities combine peer support with opportunities for homeless people to work for their own betterment on a political level. Justice House, a radical Christian community of homeless people in Roanoke, Virginia, fosters rehabilitation and personal growth among its members, while encouraging lobbying, marches, and other direct action campaigns on behalf of homeless people. In this way organizations like Justice House build solidarity among homeless people while empowering their own participants through meaningful work, and peer support.

But the communities to which homeless people refer are not merely those they have formed among themselves. While people with homes may not accept the homeless people in their streets as neighbors, the reverse is rarely true. Homeless people usually have a much more inclusive definition of community, which includes those with homes and those without.

This recognition is painful. It affirms the alienation and abandonment that homeless people feel. Similarly, reintegrating homeless people into other communities is no easy task. In many ways it is like welcoming veterans back from war: they return changed and scarred, sometimes disillusioned and bitter. Reintegration, moreover, means building housing instead of hotels, bringing jobs to poor communities, and accepting the poor as our neighbors. It means placing comparable schools in disparate neighborhoods, and considering new paradigms of cooperation, interdependence, and of the maintenance and distribution of resources.

Yet, while homelessness exposes the fragility of our lives and the vast inequalities of our society, it also points up the great resilience of people and their ability to create networks of support and connection under the most harrowing of circumstances. Solutions that work for homeless people draw strength and momentum from this resilience and ability. [20]

Finally, allowing homeless people to work together for their own betterment is self-perpetuating. Solutions that build communities give meaning to people who suffer in isolation, creating contexts in which other difficulties can be overcome.

The testimonies that follow give witness to this. Each addresses a disability—drug addiction, unemployment, or destitution—and in each case rehabilitation occurs in the context of a community. This fact points up the initial absence of community in the inception of the problem, and the responsibility of the larger, societal "community" in the breakdown of its smaller, communal units.

Similarly, the testimonies often reframe the notion of a "solution." "Some people want to get back up into the mainstream where they can get that apartment, that washer and dryer, and keep them to themselves," explains Stewart Guernsey, a Boston-area lawyer who left Harvard's divinity school to form a cooperative household and advocacy center with a group of formerly homeless people. "But others have come to see that vision of independence as part of their problem."

This perspective generates what might be called New Movement solutions—cooperative, grass-root, self-help programs that place responsibility upon homeless people while entrusting them with the tools, services, and resources they need to better themselves. Although disparate, such programs share certain features: they tend to be formed through trial and error, to depend on peer support, to be long-term, to be "tight ships" with strict, consistent rules, to be small, and to employ few "experts"—though this is not universally true. Such programs have been shown to benefit both those who seek to (re)enter the mainstream and those who fit Mr. Guernsey's latter description and seek other alternatives.

The programs described in some of the testimonies that follow are   25 not necessarily the best or most proven. But each is a program that speaks to the concerns of homeless people and one that homeless people eagerly speak for. There are not many such programs, though the "movement" is clearly growing. Those described here were chosen for the alternatives they suggest and the stories through which they are told.

However, it must be remembered that, with the proper context of support, homelessness need not have occurred for any of these people. To this end, efforts that strengthen family connections and community ties among people before they become homeless are implicitly advocated in each narrative. Homeless people, perhaps more fully than anyone else, recognize the value of a home and know that keeping one can mean the strength and support people need to maintain everything else.

Interestingly, there is evidence that the "new movement" of programs described here may become just such an effort. ACE, which began by organizing women in the so-called welfare hotels of New York City, has already changed its focus to the neighborhoods of Central Harlem, where many of the hotel residents come from. And Second Home, which initially sought to provide a refuge from the streets of Boston, has now begun a neighborhood boxing program as an alternative to the attractions of the local gangs who make those streets so violent.

It is said that some people are stronger where they've been broken. Perhaps, ultimately, this will be true of these immediate communities, and, by extension, of the larger communities of which they are a part.

SHARE
Seattle, Washington
DOUG CASTLE

In the fall of 1990 Doug Castle walked from his encampment under Seattle's I-90 freeway to a "tent city" he had heard of near the Kingdome. Helping set up tents and distribute materials donated to the city, he became swept up in the current of a movement among Seattle-area homeless people to create their own alternative to the shelter system. That alternative continues today in one of the most closely watched and controversial programs in the country— closely watched because of the strength of its model; controversial because it stands as a direct challenge to the shelter and social service system which, it claims, unnecessarily wastes millions of dollars paying social workers, sociologists, and other experts for programs the homeless are better able to run themselves. Mr. Castle is white and in his late thirties.

SHARE MEANS SEATTLE HOUSING AND RESOURCE EFFORT. There is no   30
agency that is SHARE. Any person who believes that there is a homeless crisis, and that the solution must come from the efforts of homeless people rather than the government, can be a member of SHARE. There is no president, no dues, no board of directors.

I wasn't involved until tent city. This was late November, right after Thanksgiving. All the shelters were full and it got around on the streets that that's where everybody was going, so I walked on down. There were 39 people living in 5 tents. I'm a big camping enthusiast and know a lot about tents, so I started helping out. And, you know, it was either that or go back under the I-90 bridge. So I stayed.

Less than three weeks later we had 45 tents, 148 people—we were the third largest shelter in the state of Washington, and we were doing it in a mud field with tents.

I expected the community to be up in arms about it. But where I was just shocked is that we had all this community support. The community was feeding us, bringing us blankets, bringing us clothes. . . . We passed out five thousand sleeping bags and seven thousand coats, to homeless and low-income people down there. I mean people brought donations down by the truck load.

See people liked the idea that homeless people were looking for a helping hand, not a handout. I mean we were willing to get up and do something about our own future and were not going to be dependent upon social agencies to decide that future. That was the start, the key. Everything else just followed from that.

Because of our community support the city became forced to find   35
an equitable solution and . . . well, the Metro bus barn was sitting

vacant, so we got that as a transitional building. The deal was, if we could run things for ourselves, the city would find us a permanent location.

Realistically, I don't believe the city expected us to succeed. That way once we'd failed they could come in, say "Oh this place is too whatever." You know, too many fights, too many drunks, too much neighborhood impact. Then they'd say, "Hey we tried, but the home-less people can't do it."

We surprised everybody. We got the panhandlers to go some-where else. Every other Saturday we'd average fifty big black trash bags full of trash, cleaning up the area. It wasn't even our trash, but it proved a point: we were saying, "We're solving our own problem. Now unless you can come up with a better solution, just let us do our thing."

Not that there wasn't problems. The third day we were in the bus barn we had a fight between six people, four of them men, two of them women. In the process of getting this fight broke up, I got my nose broken, I got five stitches in my eyes, a detached retina, and a concussion. Spent the night in the hospital. And like I said this was the third night the bus barn was open.

It was chaos, and everybody in the place knew it. Everybody knew we weren't going to make the month of December if we didn't do something. But that's what I think is so remarkable, what we did: we voted ourselves the toughest set of rules of any shelter anywhere. And we chose it for ourselves. No sociologist making sixty-thousand a year crammed it down our throats. And that's why it worked. And because it worked the city was forced to come through on their word. That's how we got this place, the Aloha Hotel.

Back in tent city, the bus barn, even here today, we have had   40 24-hour security—all done internally, by homeless people. Everyone works: we man our own telephones, we prepare our own meals, wash our own clothes. Only three of us are paid. Myself, I make $150 a week for the 96 hours I spend on the job, but it's worth it for me because we put people into jobs and homes. I know how important that is because I know what it means to be homeless.

Our target population are single men, 25 to 40 years old. We're not exclusionary, but that's our target population, the group that has no other place to turn. And if you divide the homeless into the 30 percent drug or alcohol addicted, 30 percent mentally ill, and 30 percent down and out for situational reasons, the last 30 percent is the one we're after: people we believe can function in society if they're given some transitional help in getting reestablished.

But if someone's action plan includes drug or alcohol rehabilitation we'll accept that. As long as it's part of their success plan we're more than cooperative. See we give you 90 days. If we give you those 90 days we want to know what you can do with it. What will be your action steps financially, employmentwise, housingwise, and your other personal goals?

You have to line out a personal success plan and you're required to show that you're working on it. You're required to save $75 a week, you're required to put in 15 hours a week of work around here, and you're required to pay $5 a week for room and board. If you can't find the work yourself, we'll find it for you. Lots of our residents find each other jobs. They find a job, come back the next day and say, "Hey, they need two more people!" But you have to save that money, and you have to follow the rules.

It takes dedication to make this work. But it works. Already we're running a 50 percent success rate. Our first 90 days isn't even up—it won't be up until this weekend. But of the original 30 we moved in with, 15 have already moved on to some form of permanent housing. Another 6 or 7 have been thrown out for rules infractions. The idea there is not to waste time on people we can't help—or who won't help themselves. 'Cause this is not a flophouse. We need flophouses, I mean people deserve a bed, but there are other places for that. But if someone's willing to work to help himself, he deserves more. That's what we're here for.

This way we can free up bed spaces in shelters and help that 30   45 percent we're shooting at. And this kind of concept can work anywhere in America because there are homeless people who want out everywhere. We've even had Canadians come down and do interviews here; they're interested in starting this kind of program there.

Our success goes back to our stringent rules, the 90 days we offer, and the people we work with. By and large, these people just want a chance, and they're willing to scratch and claw every inch. They make that inch and they go for another. You give 'em that break and they'll work for it.

It's a way of getting back in control of your life. Little things, like running our desk or being security around here, it gives you a sense that you're doing a job well done. That helps your self-worth. A lot of these people come in with a poor outlook on things and it just turns them around.

We had this woman, Crissy, who came to us pregnant. Shy, quiet, and timid. I mean all she had was a garbage bag with some clothes in it and the baby she was carrying. She had been a dispatcher for one of the cab companies. Then her husband skipped town, and that cost her where she was living. Eventually she lost everything: house, family, job, then her kids were taken away from her because she was homeless.

At the bus barn she helped run our desk. Then when we moved over here, she was on the executive committee, the screening committee, head of the desk, and probably the only person that got less sleep than me. She was here two months and when she left she was a fireball. Nothing was going to stop her. At that point she had a car, two vanloads of stuff, $700 in the bank, and an apartment.

Then this couple we had, they just moved out. He's disabled, and   50
they had been living on the street for I don't know how long. But we helped him receive Social Security, she got a job, and they saved up the money until they could get an apartment over in Freemont. It's not public housing or anything. And she was able to get a son back that she had lost. Just one big happy family.

See, it doesn't take paying somebody $60,000 a year to run a transitional house like this. A man making $60,000 a year, that has never been homeless, what does he know? There are people among the homeless who can do it. And it's more cost-effective if they do.

Most homeless people are intelligent. Many have some college education. I have two years of training in audio-engineering; I used to be the sound man and assistant manager for one of the largest nightclubs in NYC. But when people saw me living under a bridge, they just assumed that I'd always been living under that bridge.

Once you get that far down, where you're worrying about your absolute day-to-day survival . . . believe me I could take you around and let you stand in some of the food lines, let you stand in some of the clothing lines, and you will see that it will take up all of your day. You don't have time to go job hunting, you don't have time to worry about staying clean. You're worrying about putting a roof over your head that night and putting a meal in your belly. And due to the bureaucracy and red tape it takes to get those things, that's all you have time for.

See, to be an ally to a homeless person is very simple: approach him with an open mind and listen to his story. Don't listen with the idea that he's a typical Terry the Tramp—listen to him as a person.

And don't go to a bureaucrat for answers; ask a homeless person   55
what he needs, and what he can do with your help. And let us in your neighborhoods. You know, if we can put a good program together, accept us in your neighborhood.

I mean, to start, people are gonna need clean clothes, a hot shower, and a place to sleep. Now some people who are homeless—

lots of society—if you covered those needs that's all they want. But others, all that's going to do is jump start 'em enough to want more. And that's where we come in.

YouthCare: Orion Multi-Service Center
Seattle, Washington

NIKI

The Orion Multi-Service Center opened in 1983 as a collaborate effort by YouthCare, a private, nonprofit agency founded to assist the city's many runaway, homeless, and abandoned youth. Designed to offer and coordinate a broad range of services, the center's many programs include drug, job, and casework counseling, health care, meals, recreation, a drop-in center, a school, and an outreach team that's on the streets of the city every night.

YouthCare services—including family reconciliation, gang intervention, in-home counseling, and emergency and transitional housing—are available by referral through the Orion Center. A program of intensive mental health services will be added this year. Like all Orion services, its approach will be custom-tailored to the needs of the youth the center serves.

According to Phil Sullivan, development director for YouthCare, these needs include respect, individual self-help plans, and as much distance as the youth want.

As one teen put it, "I want a place that doesn't want to make me a son, 60 *but that gives me my own space and helps me to make it through." Many of the homeless and runaway teenagers in the Seattle area I've spoken to believe the Orion Center is that place. The story of Niki, who now works for Youth-Care, demonstrates the effectiveness of such an approach. Niki is white and 20 years old.*

I WAS AT HOME with my parents and I was on drugs. Heavily. I didn't want to go back to school because I needed drugs to be there, but to be there meant I couldn't be out getting drugs. I told my mom I wouldn't go and she told me I'd have to move out if I didn't. So I left.

I'd live off people who would support me, or we'd find an empty house and just stay there with sleeping bags or blankets. And then I lived off of my dealer. He gave me drugs and money and I did runs for him.

And there was one time—lots of people at the center still don't know this—but I was downtown with a "boyfriend" quote pimp and two of the outreach workers from the Orion Center came up and offered me condoms. I refused them, like to pretend I wasn't out there doing that. But I was. Only they didn't come up and say it, you know, they didn't call me anything. And though they knew what I was doing they never brought it up at the center. Even to this day.

I mean that was important, that earned my trust. They offered me something and left it at that. Never judging me or bringing it up.

Everyone at the Orion Center is like that. They give you the support you need but they don't tell you what to do with your life. And when you do something good they let you know it. They stand behind you in everything. And that's what helped me.

At home it was all negative. Don't do this, don't do that. Like I would do one good thing and they would say, "But look you're still bad over here." That brought me down because nothing I did was good. But at the Orion Center they focused on where I was improving and gave me the support to keep on going. They never brought up negative aspects of my life and that was what I needed. I mean look how far I've come with my life now.

I got started there when a friend introduced me and I began to see Tom, who's a drug counselor there. Because like my nose was bleeding real bad . . . even the dealer I was with wanted me to get off. Tom wanted to get me to this program where you go away for a month or two to get drug help, but I didn't want to be away that long. People move around quickly on the street and I didn't want to come back and not know where everyone was.

And he was cool with that, because that was what I wanted. I mean he'd been there before himself, so he knew what it was like. He was there on my side and because of that I started to quit on my own. I even started school there 'cause they have the best teachers that help you one-on-one and work with you from where you're at.

I moved out from the dealer and into an apartment with a friend who was an alcoholic and started drinking. I went from drugs to alcohol. And I was still trying to go to school—drinking, going out all night, running around, trying to get the money to pay for all that alcohol. 'Cause remember, where I was before the drugs were free.

And then I got a job working for YouthCare and they gave me . . . I mean even working there I got support. Because they knew I was still living out there and having difficulties. But I finally got sick of it because I had to get up early and go to work and that's no fun if you're out all night and hung over. I moved in with a friend's uncle, who said I could stay there to get away from the alcohol. I wanted to concentrate on the job, get on with my life because I could see the opportunity they were offering.

I stayed there until I could get into the YAIT—that's Young Adults in Transition—at the YMCA, and I stayed there for a month. You have

65

70

to have a job, open up a savings account—things like that so you can get an apartment when you leave.

I found an apartment, cheap, and stayed there and saved up some more money. And then my job went to full-time and I moved into a better place, got medical and dental insurance, and passed my GED. I took my GED book to work every day and during slow times they let me bring it out and study. And like if I had a question about something all I had to do was ask.

My plans now are to start college as soon as I get a little bit more stable, then go on to become a counselor to work with youth. I still speak to lots of the youth out on the street and they know I'm there to listen to them and that I know what it's like. And I've helped other friends, people who've followed in my footsteps and who now have apartments and jobs. I feel good about that.

It's not like everyone I talk to listens. I can think of lots of people who came into some money, like they inherited it or something, and who decided to go out and blow it. And I have other friends who tried to get off the streets but fell back down and who are now working again to get into an apartment and a job. And like . . . well, my boyfriend right now—he's a supporter for me and I'm a supporter for him. He says if it wasn't for me he'd be back in the CD [Central District] doing what he used to be doing.

See the thing the Orion Center understands and that other places don't is that when you're out on the street you do what you want when you want it. You're very responsible. You have to be to take care of yourself because out there anything can happen. It's pretty scary. This is especially true if you're female. I mean I got into some rough spots, but I was always pretty sly and able to take care of myself.

But when you enter a program or a foster home you've suddenly got all these constraints. And if you've been out on you're own you don't want that. And you learn to have a hard time trusting people because so many people have turned on you.

That's why you have to deal with youth the way the Orion Center does. It's not like going into some office to get help and they tell you to do this and that. A lot of places, they'll say "Hey are you living on the street! Well gosh, tell me about it!" The Orion Center doesn't demand that kind of information. They treat you like a friend. If you don't want advice they won't give it to you.

People on the street don't like nosy people. I think that's why lots of them open up to me. 'Cause I come out being their friend. I don't care about where they're living or what they're doing. But I know how to deal with them, based on my own experience, and that makes me a good person for them. That's why I'm getting involved in it from this end now.

Banana Kelly Community Improvement Association South Bronx, New York City

ANNE

In 1978 a handful of South Bronx residents stopped demolition of three abandoned buildings on the crescent-shaped section of Kelly Street where they lived. Working with brooms, buckets, and their bare hands, the residents began the long process of cleaning and repair that eventually transformed the buildings into a housing cooperative for twenty-one families.

Out of that self-help success emerged the Banana Kelly Community 80 *Improvement Association, a grass-root housing rehabilitation organization.*

Banana Kelly (BK) stresses a multidimensional approach that provides job training, employment, substance-abuse prevention, and education in the process of restoring and upgrading housing. In this way precariously housed people become permanently housed participants in BK's building-by-building South Bronx crusade.

Broadening their work to include homeless families, Banana Kelly set aside whole buildings for their use. When housing alone did not prove sufficient for the myriad needs of these families, BK set out to try something different. Under the guidance of the National Center for Housing Management, a Washington, D.C., consulting firm, they established a trial project that tied a work preparation and community improvement program to the leases signed by 18 previously homeless families who received apartments in a recently rehabilitated building. BK then placed staff members in the building to better foster a sense of community-based support for the families and their plans.

Results have been startling. After 20 months in the program, five of the families have found work and four have returned to school. Others volunteer at a day care and Red Cross shelter. Banana Kelly is now working to expand the program to all the buildings they manage.

Anne, whose story follows, is a resident-participant in the test program. She is an African American in her thirties.

I WAS IN THE PRINCE GEORGE. I don't know if you've heard about it, but it's   85 a New York City welfare hotel, and it's hell. The murder, the rape, the corruption . . . crack vials and garbage. Hundreds of people in that hotel and it's like that everywhere.

I couldn't exist in that environment. I had to separate myself from it—stay away as much as possible. I enrolled in college; I had my kids in school. And when the bus dropped them off I was there to take them to a youth center, keep them out of that hotel. Because if you don't you lose them, you lose yourself.

I remember I was there 16 days when my social worker gave me a check for $1,600 to give to the hotel. I said "Damn, you pay this much for me to stay in that filth and you won't let me get an apartment?" I think they want families to get in and stay in that system, 'cause there's no way they're helping them to get out of it. And the hotels will suck you in, keep you in the system even more.

I wasn't always homeless. I had an apartment for three years. But then the landlord decided to sell the building 'cause there were so many problems. The new landlord came along and wanted more money for my apartment, a lot more. I fought it. I went to court with him for six months. The judge gave me a section 8 certificate and told me to find another place. But nobody would take a section 8 certificate. I couldn't find a place anywhere. So I became homeless and they placed me in the hotel.

But I refuse to waste my brains and life. I prayed and worked every day to get out of there. To stay there would have been to give up and I couldn't. I know what I want for my life and my kids, and it wasn't that.

Other people get weak and give up. They say everybody has a   90
backbone, but it depends on you and what you got for a backbone. People give up, use drugs to hide from reality, 'cause that reality is so bad. I saw it happen. The kids stand there hungry and they use the foodstamps to shoot up. Then they come to my door and beg for bread for their children. 'Cause it will get to you. . . .

I got out because of Banana Kelly. I realized what was on the other side and they were there to help me work for it. I got my interview and I was approved for an apartment. The work-prep rider came in then. That helped a lot because I looked at it like, there are people out there who still care, who believe I can do it for myself. And that was a shock, because when you're homeless you find the people you meet don't care, and you have to stay out of their way. But with Banana Kelly it was different.

We learn how to care for our building. We meet in a tenants' association, meet together when we have a problem. And if we have a problem with a tenant we decide what to do. Banana Kelly helps us learn how to handle the problem but we handle it ourselves.

Like if a tenant is involved in drugs, we say to them, "Hey, do you want to stay here? Then treat this place like it's yours." We send warning letters. Then we see what happens and decide what to do.

We also take charge to help select the families that come into our buildings. We take charge of our problems. When we hired a super and the super didn't live up to our standards, we fired him and got another.

There was another situation where one tenant was robbed in the 95 building. I put out a memo for an emergency meeting and we got together to decide what to do. We were doing tenant patrols in the nighttime but we boosted it up to the daytime too. Those who work or go to school participate in the evening and the others help out in the day.

And we share childcare, baby-sit for each other. Me for instance, my neighbor helps out. And Banana Kelly helps out. They've got after-school programs: people meet your child to help them with their school work.

Right now I'm working as a VISTA volunteer for my work-prep. I work with Banana Kelly to help set up more programs like this. I'm in contact with new tenants, working to help screen tenants and to expand this model to other buildings. But mainly I'm in school. I enrolled in Laguardia College in Queens. Right now I go to school at night 'cause I'm working with Banana Kelly during the day.

It's what I want, not what I need. See you can't just look at what you need 'cause then you'll backtrack. You have to look for what you want, and to keep looking only at that.

That's why Banana Kelly works. They don't do it for you. But they make it so you can do it. They give you the confidence by helping you see what you can do. It's what you can do for yourself with Banana Kelly as your backbone.

❖ Focused Freewriting   Consider as possible focal points the variety of causes for homelessness, the self-images of the people interviewed, or one of the topics you've identified in your journal.

❖ Guided Responses

1. VanderStaay agrees with those who equate punishing homeless people for their condition with "feeding starving children sour milk as punishment for missing breakfast" (para. 5). How do you respond to this statement? Do you think current programs tend to "punish" homeless people? Explain your response.

2. Doug Castle's plea, "if we can put a good program together, accept us in your neighborhood" (para. 55), echoes VanderStaay's earlier statement, "Reintegration . . . means . . . accepting the poor as our neighbors" (para. 19). Based on your reading of this selection, why do you think these men see integrated neighborhoods as an

answer to homelessness? Do you think plans that involve reintegrating homeless people into middle-class communities can succeed? Why, or why not?

3. Niki continually mentions trust as one of the reasons she has stayed at the Orion Center. After reading her story, what else do you think Orion offers her that she hasn't had before? Do you think Niki will eventually achieve her goals? Explain your response.

4. What does Anne mean when she says, "See you can't just look at what you need 'cause then you'll backtrack. You have to look for what you want, and to keep looking only at that" (para. 98)? How can considering only *needs* cause people to regress? What kind of *wants* is Anne talking about? Do you agree with her analysis? Why, or why not?

❖ Shared Responses   In your journal respond to Castle's admonition, "And don't go to a bureaucrat for answers; ask a homeless person what he needs, and what he can do with your help" (para. 55). Do you think homeless people have the wherewithal to solve all their problems? Can a "sociologist making sixty-thousand a year" (para. 39) be of use, even if he or she has never experienced homelessness? Explain your responses. As you discuss your responses in groups, try to determine how both homeless people and professionals might work together to find solutions.

——— ❖ ———

Harvest Home

DAVID BRADLEY

DAVID BRADLEY *is a professor of English at Temple University. Educated at the Universities of Pennsylvania and London, he received a Guggenheim fellowship in 1989. His novel* The Chaneysville Incident *won the 1982 PEN/Faulkner prize. As he describes his family's traditions in this essay, originally published in Carolyn Anthony's* Family Portraits: Remembrances of Twenty Distinguished Writers *(1989), Bradley creates a legend of an enduring clan, individually susceptible to human frailty but collectively capable of surviving death and destruction. His focus on Harvest Home allows him to re-create the rituals associated with clan celebrations, thereby emphasizing the mythic qualities of the family.*

Before reading the selection, record in your journal some observations on traditional holiday celebrations in your home. What roles do different family members take? What rituals are followed? What memories from past holidays are elicited from each celebration?

As you make notes on your reading, you may want to focus on the roles assigned to family members, the characterization of Uncle John, or the emphasis on wandering and coming home.

THANKSGIVING 1988. In the house my father built my mother and I sit down to dine. A snowy cloth and ivory china give wintry background to browns of turkey and stuffing and gravy, mild yellow of parched corn, mellow orange of candied yams. Amidst those autumnal shades cranberry sauce flares red like flame in fallen leaves, and steam rises like scentless smoke. Head up, eyes open, I chant prefabricated grace (Father, we thank Thee for this our daily bread which we are about to partake of . . .) and long for the extemporaneous artistry of my father, now almost a decade dead. His blessings—couched in archaic diction ("Harvest Home," he called this holiday) and set in meter measured as a tolling bell—were grounded in a childhood in which daily bread was hoped for, not expected; his grace had gravity, unlike this airy ditty I now mutter.

Still, it seems there is even in this doggerel dogma (. . . May it nourish our souls and bodies . . .) an echo of his voice. Hope flutters in me, rises as I come to the end (. . . in Jesus' name and for His sake . . .), then hangs, gliding in the silence, as I pause and listen. My mother sits, head bowed, patient and unsurprised; for nine years I have paused so, just short of "amen." What I wait for she has never asked. And I have never before said.

Once there were more of us. For once we were a mighty clan, complete with house and lineage. As we are dark (and sometimes comely), outsiders might expect us to trace that lineage to Africa, but we have benign contempt for those who pin their pride to ancestries dotted by the Middle Passage or *griot*-given claims to Guinean thrones. For what is Africa (spicy groves, cinnamon trees, or ancient dusky rivers?) to a clan that knows, as we know, the precise when and where of our origin: on March 10, 1836, in Seaford, Delaware. Then and there a justice of the peace named Harry L-something (the paper is browned, the ink faded, and ornate script all but undecipherable) certified that a "Col. man by the name of Peter Bradley" was henceforth a freedman. This Peter was our progenitor.

Outsiders might wonder that we do not fix our origin in 1815, the year of Peter's birth. The reason: the slave laws—what oxymoron that!—decreed that a bondsman had right to neither property nor person. Peter could not own a family, for he did not own himself. But on March 10, Peter's master gave Peter to Peter for Peter's birthday; this not only made him, legally, his own man but entitled him to purchase a (black) woman. He could have owned her, and any children he fathered on her. But he did not. Peter wed a free woman; thus the two sons he sired were free from the moment of their birth. But Peter, by that time, was not. For after being given by his master to himself he gave himself to his Master, and became a minister of the gospel.

Such service became a clan tradition. Both Peter's sons became   5
ministers, licensed by the African Methodist Episcopal Zion Church, the first denomination organized by American blacks who chafed at the unequal opportunity offered by the Methodist Episcopal Church. One son was "M. A."—we do not know his full name, or date of birth. The other was Daniel Francis, born in 1852. Through him our line descends.

Daniel Francis became a minister at the age of nineteen. Although we know nothing of his early assignments, we are sure that they were plentiful, for Zion Methodists followed the dictate of John Wesley that ministers should never stand long in any pulpit, lest they become too powerful. And we know that the Presiding Bishop eventually sent him to Williamsport, Pennsylvania, where he met Cora Alice Brewer. Though in those rigid times, Daniel Francis, at forty-four, would have been called a confirmed bachelor and Cora Alice, at twenty-seven, old enough to be called a spinster, love blossomed into marriage in 1896. The first fruit of the union was a man-child, John, born in 1898. A daughter, Gladys, followed in 1900. More sons, David and Andrew, were born in 1905 and 1906, after the family left Williamsport for Sewickley, Pennsylvania, outside Pittsburgh.

The house came in 1911, when Daniel Francis, who had been reassigned at least five times since Williamsport, was sent to a church called Mt. Pisgah, in the town of Bedford, in the south-central part of Pennsylvania. As Mt. Pisgah had no parsonage, Daniel Francis went ahead of the family to find a place to live. On the train he met a man named Bixler, who offered to sell him an eleven-acre homestead two miles west of Bedford, near the hamlet of Wolfsburg. The price was steep (seven hundred and fifty dollars), the terms usurious (one hundred dollars down, one hundred per year plus annual interest and a widow's dower), but Daniel Francis found both price and terms acceptable, perhaps because there were no other terms at all. And so, in the spring of 1912, our clan took up residence in our first permanent home.

But Daniel Francis did not see the Wolfsburg property as just a home. In early 1915 he announced plans to create what the local weekly, the *Bedford Gazette,* called a "an attractive summer resort for those of his race who will gather here from Pittsburgh and Western Pennsylvania." His future plans called for the building of a "large tabernacle for divine services, lectures and entertainments" and in time a normal school for the education of black craftsmen modeled on Tuskegee Institute—Booker T. Washington, Daniel Francis told the *Gazette,* had promised to come to Wolfsburg to speak. Although Booker T. Washington never did appear, a camp meeting was held in August on a sylvan portion of the homestead (christened "Green Brier Grove" in printed advertisements) and the next year a loan from the Bedford County Trust Company liberated the deed from Bixler's clutches and brought Daniel Francis's dream closer to reality. But Zion Methodists, like Wesley, feared empire-building pastors; later that year the bishop kicked Daniel Francis upstairs, appointing him Presiding Elder, the spiritual and financial manager of a group of churches in Pennsylvania and eastern Ohio.

But though the promotion killed a dream, it established our clan's mark of achievement: a successful son is he who follows in his father's footsteps and goes a step further. And though it forced us once again to wander, we never forgot the homestead. Somehow we made mortgage payments. By 1921 the homestead was ours, free and clear. A year later we returned to it. It was not, however, a joyful repatriation. On October 15, 1922, Daniel Francis died of "diabetes mellitus." His first son, John, now at twenty-one our chieftain, paid one hundred dollars for a funeral and secured a permit of removal. We escorted the body of Daniel Francis back to Wolfsburg, he to be buried in Mt. Ross, the local Negro cemetery, we to live.

The homestead did not long save us from wandering. Bedford,   10 which to Daniel Francis seemed prosperous enough to support even black ambitions, soon proved capable of supporting few ambitions at all. White youths who wished to do more than sell hats to each other had to leave, if only to get higher education. Black youths, regardless of ambition, were virtually exiled; Bedford had no place for blacks skilled with pens rather than push brooms, and its small black community offered opportunity for exogamy. Some blacks made do. Bradleys do not make do.

And so we dispersed. Gladys married a man named Caldwell and settled in Cleveland, Ohio. David finished high school, won a scholarship, and went South to college. Andrew, after graduation, attached himself to the local Democratic party—a quixotic alliance, as Bedford blacks were fewer and less powerful than Bedford Democrats—and then went east to Harrisburg, the capital. John, who supported the clan until Andrew's graduation, married and settled in Sewickley, and fathered three daughters. But though we dispersed, the homestead remained—a haven in time of trouble, a gathering place for feasts, a totem signifying that, though we were wanderers, we were not Gypsies.

That is what it signified to outsiders. And so it was that in 1956, our clan's one hundred and twentieth year, the *Gazette*, by then a daily, found our clan of local interest. "The rise of the Bradley family from the enforced degradation of slavery to dignity and high achievement is not unparalleled in the history of the American Negro," wrote reporter Gene Farkas. "But it is certainly one of the more outstanding examples of hard-won Negro accomplishment in the nation and the state. In the annals of Bedford County, the story of the Bradley family is without precedent . . . for it was from these hills and valleys, from the one-room schoolhouse at Wolfsburg and the old Bedford High School . . . that the Bradley boys emerged to eminence and respect."

Cosmopolitans and outsiders would have said that it was Andrew who had risen highest; in 1954, he became State Budget Secretary and the first black to sit in the Pennsylvania Governor's Cabinet. But local interest, and perhaps a sense of our clan's traditions—he even used the phrase "the footsteps of his father"—caused Farkas to give more space to David, who in 1948 had been elected an AME Zion General Officer—a step beyond Daniel Francis's final rank of Presiding Elder.

Though his new duties called for travel, he was free to fix his base where he chose; David purchased land adjacent to the homestead and built what Farkas called "a modern stone bungalow," in which he housed both his own family and Cora Alice, who spent her days in the spartan familiarity of the homestead but at night enjoyed the sybaritic comforts of indoor plumbing and central heating.

Farkas did a good job for an outsider. Although he did not specifically mention another of David's contributions to the clan, that he alone of the third generation sired a son to carry on the name, the photographs that accompanied the story did depict the lad, David Jr., then six. And though Farkas did give short shrift to John, not mentioning the names of his wife and children (as he did with David and Andrew) and referring to his occupation with a euphemism (". . . he has worked for a private family for 25 or 30 years"), in this he only reflected the values of outsiders; men who hold advanced degrees and cabinet posts are commonly deemed more noteworthy than those who held rakes in "private" service. Farkas cannot be blamed for this affront to our dignity. How was he to know that the man so slighted was the chief among us? For the tale as Farkas told it was the tale as we told it to him. Sadly, it was the tale as we were telling it to our children. Except at Harvest Home.

Even when I was too young to comprehend a calendar I knew Harvest   15
Home was coming; I could tell by the smell of my grandmother, Cora Alice. Usually she spent her days in the old homestead crocheting, reading the *Gazette*, and listening in on the party line. But the week before Harvest Home she abandoned leisure, stoked up her big Majestic coal stove, and got busy baking: tangy gingerbread, golden pound cakes, and pies of pumpkin, sweet potato, and mince. In the evening she would come back to the house my father built perfumed with molasses and mace, and I would crawl into her lap and lick surreptitiously at the vestiges of brown sugar that clung to her upper arms. The night before the feast she would not return at all. That would be my signal; I would sneak to my window to keep watch on the homestead a hundred yards away. At last I would see a sweep of headlights. I would press my ear against the gelid glass and listen. The sounds of car doors slammed, greetings shouted, would not satisfy me—I would stand, shivering, until I heard an odd and mighty booming. Then I would know the clan was gathered.

The next afternoon would find us in the rear chamber of the homestead, arrayed around a dark Victorian table with saurian legs and dragon feet. To an outsider the order of our seating might have seemed to loosely reflect Fifties customs—most of the children placed at a separate table and all the men at the main table, while the women served. In fact, it reflected our deep reverence for name and blood. The segregated children had the blood—they were of the fifth generation—but had it through their mothers; none had the name. The women who served—including Cora Alice herself, who, although she presided over the gathering, did so from the sideboard—had the name by marriage. The only woman at table not of the blood was my Uncle Andrew's wife, Gussie, who made it clear she waited on no one. She also smoked and drank in public. (My grandmother had declared her mad; she was left alone.) My cousins—the women of our fourth generation—although they'd lost the name through marriage, had the blood and so had seats. Their husbands had seats only as a courtesy to the chief of a related clan—once a husband tried to displace his wife; Cora Alice took away his plate. The men of the third generation had both blood and name, and so had seats of honor. And I too had a seat of honor: a creaky chair, made tall with cushions, set at the table's foot. For I was David, son of David, the only male of the fourth generation, the only hope for the continuation of the name.

I, of course, did not then understand why I alone among the children had a seat at the table. But I was glad I did. For when all closed eyes and bowed heads to listen to my father bless our gathering in fervent baritone extempore, I could raise my head and look down the table, a virtual continent of sustenance—Great Lakes of gravy, Great Plains of yams, tectonic plates of turkey slices thrust upward by the bulk of the bird itself, which rose like Rushmore. But in the place of the visage of Washington or Lincoln this Rushmore was crowned by a huge dark head with massive jowls, pebbly with beard, a broad flat nose, a gently sloping forehead, grizzled brows: the visage of our clan chief, my Uncle John.

Uncle John was titanic. Below his head was a neck thick with muscle and a broad chest, powerful and deep, on which his huge hands prayerfully rested, the fingers like a logjam. When the food was duly blessed the jam burst. For Uncle John did not eat—he fed. His plate—actually a spare meat platter—was filled and refilled with turkey, potatoes, and stuffing all drenched with tureens of gravy, and garnished with enough corn on the cob to fill a field—once I counted a dozen ears lying ravished by his plate, and always I watched his trench work with apprehension, convinced that one day he would explode.

He made all the noise of an explosion. He did not talk—he roared. He roared with jokes—always corny and often in poor taste—and aphorisms—"You can live forever if you don't quit breathin'!"—and responses to conversational gambits—once Uncle Andrew twitted him about his shabby clothing. "Rags to riches! I ain't rich yet!" Uncle

John roared, off and on for the next twenty years. Mostly, though, he roared with a laugh as big as he was, so concussive it subsumed all ordinary vibrations. Halfway between a boom and a cackle, Uncle John's laugh was like a bushel of corn husks rustling in a hundred-gallon drum. It was not precisely a pleasant sound, but to me it was a Siren song—or perhaps the call of the wild.

When I was small I would leave my place as soon as I could to go 20 and stand beside him. He would be busy devouring dessert—quarters of pie, one each of pumpkin, sweet potato, mince—like Cronus consuming his children, but would catch me up in the crook of his arm and balance me effortlessly on his knee, where I would sit in greatest contentment, remarkably unoffended by his smell—sweat, smoke, and bay rum (which he used for no good reason, since he rarely shaved). When I grew too big for that I would simply stand beside him while he finished eating. Then we would go to kill his car. He didn't call it that, of course. He termed it "blowing out the pipes" and claimed that without it the car—a spavined station wagon—would never climb the mountains between Bedford and Sewickley. But to me, at six or seven, it seemed like bloody murder.

From the back of the wagon he would take a quart jar of kerosene—he called it "coal oil"—and give it to me to hold while he started the engine, raised the hood, and removed the air cleaner. Then he would take the jar and begin to pour the coal oil into the unsuspecting intake manifold. The engine would pause in shock, then sputter, bark, and bellow at the same time, while from the tail pipe issued gouts of greasy black smoke. Meanwhile Uncle John poured more coal oil into the carburetor, his expression like that of a father administering foul-tasting medicine to an ailing child. When the jar was empty he would leap behind the wheel and pump the throttle; the engine would scream and thrash madly on its mounts, while the smoke from the tail pipe would take on bile-green overtones and show tiny flicks of flame. After a while Uncle John—at some clue known to him alone—would stop pumping. The engine would rattle, almost stop. Then the kerosene would clear through the cylinders; the grateful engine would settle into a smooth, fast idle, and Uncle John would smile.

Years later I marveled at all of this, not because the car survived it, but because we did. For it took no mechanical genius to see that we had toyed with tragedy, that that abused engine could easily have exploded, covering us with burning fuel, shredding us with shrapnel, generally blowing us to Kingdom Come. And I marveled that, even had I known that then—which I of course did not—it would have made no difference. Because then—and now—those dangerous pyrotechnics seemed a fitting prerequisite for what followed. For when the smoke showed clean and white I would sit beside Uncle John as he gently slipped the throttle—helping, he said, the pistons settle down—and recounted chronicles of the clan.

Clan history was nothing new—I heard it every day. But what I heard daily were parables, intended to indoctrinate me with the values and courage that had let us rise up from slavery. At Harvest Home, Uncle John told a different story—unpretentious, earthy, human as an unlimed outhouse. Cora Alice told me about Daniel Francis, after the barn was struck by lightning, burning his hands in the steaming ashes as he searched for nails with which to rebuild. Uncle John told me about my grandfather misjudging the dosage when he wormed the mule. David told me about the Christmas Eve when he, knowing his family was too poor for presents, asked for nothing and cried himself to sleep—but woke to find a hand-carved train, three walnuts, and one incredible orange. Uncle John told me about the time my father had the back of his pants gored by a roving bull. My grandmother and father told me of the glory of my people. Uncle John told me that we were *people.* This was vital. For it was something we were forgetting.

On Harvest Home 1957 I was drummed out of my clan. My crime was lying—a peccadillo, outsiders might say, especially as all children tell lies occasionally, some frequently. But I lied almost constantly, even when there was nothing to be gained. My father said I'd rather crawl up Fib Alley than march down Truth Street; this drove him crazy. For he believed a sterling reputation was some shield against the sanctions society—both American and Bedford County—could bring to bear on a Negro male. He was proud that we were held in high repute and feared what would happen to me—to all of us—were our name to lose its luster because of my lying. He announced that he would break me of it.

But he did not realize how good a liar I'd become—so good I took 25 him in. For a while I told him many obvious lies, let him catch and punish me. Then I tapered off. Catching me less often, he assumed I was lying less. But on that morning he discovered . . . well, I don't recall exactly what he discovered; some silken web of half-truths I had been spinning out for weeks. He confronted me, hard evidence in his hands, hot fury in his face.

Corporal punishment was not his way. His cat-o'-nine-tails was a Calibanian tongue wetted with Prosperian vocabulary, his lashes sad scenarios starring the local sheriff. That morning he seemed so angry I expected J. Edgar Hoover to make a cameo appearance; I could not imagine what salt he would rub into the wounds—I doubt the usual "thou shalt never amount to anything if thou keepest this up" would suffice. But he was too angry for anything like the usual treatment; he simply looked at me coldly and in a frighteningly quiet voice said, "Bradleys don't lie."

That statement rocked me. For I knew—at least I thought I knew—that it was true. My grandmother did not lie. My father surely did not lie. In the Church he had a reputation for truthfulness—and was in some quarters hated for it. His historical writing was marred by a concern for literal truth; he wouldn't say that two and two were four unless he had a picture of both twos and did the arithmetic three times. And God knows he preached what he saw as truth, and practiced what he preached. So I believed him when he said Bradleys did not lie. But I also knew that I did lie.

On any other day the conclusion of the syllogism—that I was not a Bradley—would have disturbed me. But that day was Harvest Home. I sat in my favored place, accepting accolades and choicest bits of feast food—the heel of the bread, the drumstick of the turkey—that all thought were my due, as sole heir to the name, but I knowing in my heart I had no right to them. I could barely eat.

Later, in the car, I only half listened to Uncle John's chronicle, wondering if I could ever explain to him that I had no right to listen at all. But in the midst of my dilemma I detected a variation from an earlier telling. "Wait," I said. "That's not what you said before."

"No," he said easily. "But don't it work out better this way?"   30

"Well, yeah," I said—and it did work out it better—"but it's not the truth."

"Oh yeah," he said. "The truth. Well, truth is funny. Because you never know it all. So you end up makin' things up to fill in the blanks. Everybody does that. But some folks always makes things up that's make folks sound good, make things sound clean and pretty. Trouble is, the truth usually turns out to be whatever makes the most sense. And if you think you got the whole truth, if it don't make sense, you better make a few things up. And even if you're wrong, it makes a better story." He paused, looked at me. I can't imagine what was on my face—amazement, probably, to hear the head of my clan drumming me back into it as firmly as I'd been drummed out. "Now don't you dare ever tell your daddy I said that," he admonished. And then he sent his laughter rustling and booming around the car.

It is interesting to speculate what would have happened if the *Gazette* had done a follow-up on The Bradley Family Twelve Years Later. By 1968 Andrew had served a second term in the cabinet and served there no longer only because the Democrats had lost the Statehouse— he remained a force in the Party, and had had influence with both the Kennedy and Johnson administrations. He had also followed in at least one of Daniel Francis's footsteps, becoming a trustee of Lincoln

University, an institution originally dedicated to the education of blacks. David, meanwhile, retraced his father's footsteps even as he stepped beyond; still a General Officer, he was rumored to be a strong candidate for Bishop, the highest office in the Church, and also preached at Mt. Pisgah, which was now too small to pay its own pastor. David Jr. seemed poised to follow. A senior in high school, he had been admitted to the University of Pennsylvania and awarded several national scholarships. Occasionally he too occupied the pulpit of Mt. Pisgah. Such facts could have led a reporter to believe the Bradley family was still upward bound, might even have caused him or her to see a rising track in tragedy; though Cora Alice had died in 1960, her funeral was resplendent with dignitaries: two ministers and a Presiding Elder of the AME Zion Church, and—the Democrats were then still in power—several state cabinet secretaries and the governor himself. Had such a story been done—it wasn't—the reporter might have written that, after a hundred and thirty-two years of freedom, the Bradleys continued to rise.

To say that, though, the reporter would have had to ignore clippings from the *Gazette* itself—a 1962 story describing the destruction of the Bradley homestead by a fire, a photo of the ravished house, its windows like blackened eyes, its clapboard siding stripped away, revealing underlying logs. But to be fair, few reporters would have seen the fire as metaphor. Fewer still would have explored the implications of the fire's aftermath: that for months the house stood unrepaired; that the eventual repairs were minimal; that they were financed by a note co-signed by only David and Andrew; that money to repay the loan was to come from rental of the homestead—to whites. And none, probably, would have understood that the *Gazette's* account of Cora Alice's funeral reiterated an ancient insult. For although the second paragraph noted the careers of David and Andrew, the clan's chief was not mentioned until the final paragraph, and in passing: "She is survived by another son, John Bradley of Scwickley."

I was only nine when my grandmother died, and so recall little of the pomp and circumstance that surrounded her death. I do recall the lavish spread of ham and turkey and covered dishes brought by neighbors to assuage our grief. I recall that Uncle John ate little. And I recall that at the end of the day I stood beside him on my father's lawn while he looked sadly at the homestead. "I guess that's that," he said, and turned away.

And I do recall my grandmother's final Harvest Home. I remember overhearing my elders in council. The only items on the agenda were her failing health and her refusal to give up her days in the homestead. It was moved and seconded that Uncle Andrew take her to Harrisburg to see a specialist. During discussion the opinion was stated (loudly) that no doctor could cure the fact that my grandmother was ninety years old, but the countermotion ("Let her live the way she wants until she dies") was ruled out of order. The motion carried on a two-to-one vote. Council was adjourned, *sine die*. I remember the meal itself—the mood: heavy, the food: dry, the laughter: absent without leave. And I remember how quiet Uncle John was as he watched my father and Uncle Andrew get my grandmother settled in Uncle Andrew's Chrysler. Mostly I remember how, after my grandmother was driven away, Uncle John went to work with coal oil and a vengeance; I can still hear the sounds he tortured from the engine, the fan belt screaming, the valve lifters chattering like dry bones, the exhaust bellowing like nothing known to man.

Mostly I recall the burning of the house. For if our homestead was once a totem, was it not a totem still? Was not the burning a harbinger of greater doom? For months I would go, sometimes in the dead of night, and circle the hulk of our homestead like a satellite in orbit, pulled down and thrown up simultaneously. In daylight I would peer into the now exposed basement, full of detritus, alive with rats, in darkness sniff the scorched and rotten timber, seeking a message in the rubble and the stench. And when the house was lost to me—repaired and occupied by people my grandmother would have dismissed as poor white trash—I sought a message in the keepsakes of our clan—chipped photographs, browned bills and deeds, yellowed newspaper clippings. When I combined those mementos with my memories I found discrepancies. And when I thought about what made most sense I found a devastating truth: Bradleys did lie.

Most of our lies were common cover-ups of minor moral failures. Others drove to the heart of our history—it seemed doubtful, for example, that Booker T. Washington had ever heard of Daniel Francis. But no lie was as destructive as the one we'd told about my Uncle John.

There are many ways to say it. Then, when clichés were new to me and irony was *terra incognita,* I would have said that Uncle John was our black sheep. Now I say he was the nigger in our woodpile, proof that though Bradley blood flowed in dreamers, power brokers, and preachers, it also flowed in a hewer of wood, a drawer of water, a man content to work in service all his life. This embarrassed us, especially as he was not the least among us; he was the first. And so, while we did not deny him, we denied him his place. We allowed outsiders to see him as a minor footnote to our grand history. And then, made bold by headlines and column inches, tokens Society respects, we had forgotten the rules by which a clan exists and survives. Our junior elders—my father and Uncle Andrew—had rebelled

against our rightful leader. This, I decided, was the message of the
burned boards and beams of the house of Bradley. Our house had
fallen because we had fallen away.

I did not want to fall away. For the years between the burning and   40
my graduation were hard, lonely, desperate years. I needed my people. I needed my clan. I needed my chief. And though I despaired that
we had fallen too far from our ways, I hoped that we had not.

I hoped hardest when those years were ending, when to the world
outside I seemed poised to take my clan to greater heights. I feared
those heights. And so, on the night of my commencement, as my class
assembled for its final march, I stood quietly despairing. They chattered about parties and graduation gifts. I wanted only one gift: the
presence of my chief. I doubted I would get it. I had sent him an
invitation, but Uncle John was almost seventy and Sewickley was
more than a hundred mountainous miles away. To make it worse, a
violent thunderstorm was raging. Only a fool would make the trip.

But as we marched up to the auditorium door I saw him standing
outside the hall, his threadbare coat and tattered sweater soaked with
rain, his eyes searching for me in the line of robed seniors. "Who's
that?" one of my classmates whispered. "My Uncle John," I said. In
that moment he saw me. And even in the auditorium they heard, over
the pounding of the processional, his booming, rustling laugh.

On Wednesday, September 26, 1979, the *Gazette* recounted the tale of
Bradley clan much as it had in 1956 as part of the page-one obituary
of the Reverend David H. Bradley. The burial at Mt. Ross Cemetery
would be private, but, later, friends would be received at the Louis
Geisel Funeral Home. Memorial services set for the next day, the
Gazette anticipated, would be appropriately impressive; two AME
Zion bishops—mentioned by name—were scheduled to appear.
Among the surviving family was listed "John, of Sewickley."

Uncle John was too ill to attend the burial or memorial service, but
I prevailed upon the husband of some cousin I did not recall to drive
him to the wake, even though his legs were too weak to carry him
inside. And so I saw him for the last time when I sat beside him in the
car.

He seemed small, shrunken. He joked, but feebly, and when I   45
teased him about the new clothes he was wearing he said, "Rags to
riches! Guess I'm gettin' there," but with no force behind it. And he
did not even try to laugh. That depressed me, to be honest, more than
my father's death, for it told me that my uncle's death would not be
long in coming. The death of a father causes grief; the death of a chief
causes fear. I was especially fearful. For when he died the chieftain-
ship would descend to me. I was not ready. I was not worthy. And so

I sat beside him and cast about for something that would conjure up his laughter.

Inside, I told him, there were two wakes, in adjacent rooms. In our room there was no casket—we'd buried my father that morning. But in the other, in a grand, flower-bedecked coffin lined with crinoline, a rail-thin ancient white lady was laid out. Bedford being a small town, many visitors paid respects in both rooms. Seeing this, the undertaker, to make things more convenient, had opened the doors between the rooms. This caused no problem—until some of my father's ministerial colleagues arrived. Although ignorant of the specific arrangements, they knew just what to do on such sad occasions. Gliding as if on casters, they went to my mother and murmured comfort, then came to give me that two-fisted handshake of condolence before moving on to their next target: the deceased. When they saw no casket they did not panic—they said more comforting words while shaking their heads in sadness, their eyes covertly scanning. Eventually they locked onto the casket in the other room and launched themselves in that direction.

"I should have let them go," I told Uncle John. "But I just couldn't. So I said, 'Gentlemen, please don't go over there. Because if you do you're going to think he suffered a lot more than he did.' " I laughed, hoping that he would laugh too. But his reaction was but a polite chuckle. "Damn," I said. "I should have let them go."

He looked at me and smiled. "Well, don't let it bother you, son. Next time you tell it, you will." And then he did laugh. Not long, but long enough. Not loud, but loud enough.

He died nine months later. I did not attend the funeral. It would have been too quiet. Oh, there would have been sound aplenty—slow hymns, generous lies, even laughter—of a sort. But it would not have been his laughter, a laugh that could shake the earth. And hearing other laughter would have made me know that he and his laugh were gone.

I will never be made to know that, I've decided. I have the right   50
to that decision, for I am clan chief now. I do not have all the wisdom that a chief needs, but I have come to understand some things. I understand that the hypocrisy and hubris that brought our house to ruin were inevitable dangers. For any fool could see that black people in America could not rise on wings of doves. To even think of rising we should have quills of iron, rachises of steel. Of course, we do not have such mighty wings. And so we stiffen our pinfeathers with myths, flap madly, and sometimes gain a certain height.

This my clan did. We told ourselves good stories, said we were destined for the skies and launched forth. It worked. We rose. But as we rose we learned that flight is a risky and temporary thing, that there are powerful downdrafts in American air. Our solution was simple: don't look down. That worked too. But it brought us to another danger; we lost contact with the ground.

We were not wrong to dream of rising. Nor were we wrong to keep our eyes fixed ever upward—we did not make the air so treacherous. We were wrong because we ceased to listen for the echoes from below. This, I have decided, we will do no longer. We will rise no further until we do. And so I pause and listen, each year at Harvest Home, as now I pause and listen, while the steam rises from the cooling feast food and hangs accusing in the air. My mother grows impatient; I hear her chair creak with shifting weight. And it comes to me that I could lie about this. Could say I heard laughter booming, or heard, at least, an ancient echo. But truth makes a better story. And so I say, "Amen."

❖ **Focused Freewriting**   Consider as possible focal points the difference between the family as portrayed in the newspaper article and the private family, the emphasis on upward mobility, the family stories, or one of the topics you've identified in your journal.

❖ **Guided Responses**

1. Bradley's childhood memories of Harvest Home include a variety of sensory experiences: the smells of cooking, the sight of the table, and the sound of Uncle John's laughter, among others (paras. 15–22). How do these images serve to establish the impression that his is in fact a "mighty clan"? Why does the perception of a child seem more appropriate than that of an adult in creating this impression?

2. When the homestead burns, Bradley is certain that the event is "a harbinger of greater doom." Obviously, the dwelling itself holds great significance for the author; it is "a totem" (para. 37). Precisely what does the homestead represent to Bradley? How does its burning reveal to him what that "greater doom" is?

3. What does Bradley mean when he concludes, "we lost contact with the ground"; "we ceased to listen for the echoes from below" (paras. 51–52). How does he feel that the clan has failed itself?

4. Bradley's essay ends as it begins, with his pause between the end of the blessing and the final "Amen." What is he listening for? What is the significance of his decision not to lie about what he hears? To whom would he be lying? Do you take this ending as positive? Why, or why not?

❖ Shared Responses   In your journal speculate on why the notion of the great clan is so important to someone like Bradley. Consider such questions as how membership in the clan provides him with an identity, how it helps him work out moral and philosophical problems, and how it offers him a history as well as a home. As you discuss your responses in small groups, focus on the influence of group members' own family backgrounds on their responses.

❖ **Generating Ideas** Reread all of your journals and annotations from the selections in this unit. Look for connections between selections or still unanswered questions. First, list those connections and questions as briefly as possible. Next, choose two or three to elaborate on. As you respond in more detail to the connections and questions, focus on one topic and consider how well it would serve you in an extended piece of writing. Then decide what kind of writing best suits your topic: Should you write a conventional essay, a poem, a short story, or a scene? Would your topic lend itself more to a letter to the editor or a personal letter? Might a proposal to solve a specific problem be a good choice? Possible topics:

1. the importance of a specific place to call home
2. the support of a community
3. looking back at one's hometown
4. various definitions of *family*
5. society's responsibility for fostering a sense of home

❖ **Focusing Responses** Choose one of your extended responses and formulate a statement of one or two sentences that captures its essence. Use this statement as a guide to organize your piece. (If you write an essay, letter, or proposal, the statement may actually appear as a thesis.)

❖ **Guided Writing Assignments**

1. White writes of two different models used to describe African-American families. Haygood, Bradley, and Cary provide illustrations of the home life of three such families. Write an essay in which you use these examples to compose your own definition of African-American family life. Pay particular attention to such issues as socioeconomic status, sex roles, and family traditions and values. In what respects are these families similar to and different from the models found in White's essay? How do they compare with your own?

2. Haygood tells the story of a family that prevails over severely adverse conditions, Huie recounts tales of families destroyed by similar conditions, and VanderStaay provides examples of homeless people helping themselves. Write a letter to the editor of a major newspaper emphasizing the need for community support for those encountering adversity. Consider questions such as the following: How does a sense of community contribute to the stability of a family? What responsibility does society at large have to support families? To what extent is the presence of a traditional nuclear family (i.e., mother,

father, and children) necessary to success? How can unrelated people constitute a family?

3. Both Raphael and Cary explore the feeling of "otherness" that must be overcome in order to consider a place home. Using these two selections for reference, write a story or a scene about the notion of integrating oneself into a community. Focus on such issues as transforming a dwelling into a home, relating to others in the community, and maintaining solidarity with one's own culture within the larger culture.

4. While many of the features that distinguish the Midwest from the East are found in both Kansas City and Okemos, Rhodes and Raphael offer profoundly different perspectives on their respective towns. Write an essay comparing and contrasting Raphael's Okemos and Rhodes's Kansas City. Focus on such issues as the community's response to those who are different, the relative stability of home life in each community, the relationship between the community and the world beyond, and anything else you consider relevant. Based on your reading of these selections, explain why you would feel more comfortable in one community or the other.

❖ **Research Topics**   As you consider how to expand your reading beyond the selections in this chapter, identify in your journals and notes questions that remain unanswered or topics you'd like to explore further. Or you may consider the following:

1. One of the most prevalent "buzzwords" of the past decade has been the term "family values." Explore various characterizations of this term by looking at how social scientists, religious leaders, political activists, and public officials use it. Try to determine how these various groups define the term, what factors they think contribute to and detract from strong family values, the impact family values have on society at large, the relationship between government and family values, and who they think holds primary responsibility for protecting family values.

2. Since the rise of the suburbs after World War II, the idea of a hometown has become less a reality and more a nostalgic reverie. Read several accounts of the changing demographics of American society since 1945, paying particular attention to how these changes affected families (both extended and nuclear). According to these accounts, how genuine is the nostalgic image of the hometown of years gone by? How has the increasing suburbanization of society been detrimental to families? How has it strengthened them? How do suburbanites develop a sense of community? What support systems have arisen as substitutes for the extended family?

Chapter 4

From Generation to Generation

YOUTH AND AGE HAVE BEEN THE SUBJECT of human inquiry for centuries: Medical researchers study the physiological process of growth and aging; social scientists study the psychological, political, social, and economic effects of growing older; creative writers portray the processes of growing up and growing old in poetry, fiction, drama, and song. That different generations have different values is self-evident; the development of those values and their influence on generational behavior, on the other hand, are subjects worthy of exploration. How do different generations view their respective worlds? How do young people cope with growing independence? How do the elderly adjust to loss and change?

What it means to be young, middle aged, or elderly depends also on social and cultural factors: Growing up and growing old are entirely different experiences now than they were in the days of the extended family, the self-contained community, and the prevailing belief in America's economic, technological and moral superiority. Furthermore, images of youth and age differ among ethnic groups who have settled in this country, often causing conflict between immigrant parents and their Americanized children. Socioeconomic status also influences the various elements of the aging process. The readings that follow present various experiences of different generations, many of them flavored by cultural and social factors.

In "Two Kinds," Amy Tan tells the story of a young Chinese-American girl's rebellion against her mother's quest to produce a child prodigy. The collision between parent and child is exacerbated by the conflict between Chinese and American values.

A different kind of rebellion is the subject of Lorene Cary's "First Time," a story about her initial experience with marijuana. One of the unexpected consequences of her experiment is a heightened awareness of her isolation at her exclusive preparatory school.

Adrian Nicole LeBlanc explores a deadly serious problem facing youth in "You Wanna Die with Me?" As an epidemic of teen suicides plagues a working-class town, parents try to reach children who see little reason for living.

David Leavitt, in "The New Lost Generation," claims that his generation, having come of age in the seventies, has no clear identity and little in common with those who grew up either in the 1960s or in the 1980s. Like the teenagers in LeBlanc's article, Leavitt's generation feels itself drifting through a meaningless existence.

Susan Nunes explores memories that link one generation with another in "A Moving Day," a story in which the narrator helps her aging parents move out of their family home. Images from the past, particularly the internment of Japanese Americans during World War II, hover over the family as they pack away their belongings.

In "Thirty-ninth Anniversary" Cathy Stern expresses wonder at the swift passage of time and contemplates a future that is now upon her. Reflecting on the slow deterioration of her home, Stern comes to terms with the idea of her and her husband's growing old.

Reflective in a different way, Mary Catherine Bateson's "Emergent Visions" calls into question our culture's belief in the straight, forward path toward a single career, blaming this myth for the sense of failure many adults feel when their lives change direction.

Finally, the need for elderly people to maintain a sense of control over their lives is the subject of Patsy Neal's "My Grandmother, the Bag Lady." As she watches her grandmother hoard the few possessions she has left, Neal begins to understand the significance of the old woman's losses.

Taken together, these selections provide a multigenerational collage of contemporary American life. As you read them, you will find familiar images in some selections, while others will offer you a glimpse of life through the eyes of another generation or culture.

❖

Two Kinds

AMY TAN

AMY TAN, *a native of Oakland, California, received a master's degree in linguistics from San Jose State University. Her best-selling novel* The Joy Luck Club, *from which this selection is taken, was a finalist for the National Book Award and the National Book Critics Circle Award in 1989. In addition to writing essays for such magazines as* Life *and* The Threepenny Review *and fiction for* The Atlantic *and* Lear's, *Tan has also published another critically acclaimed novel,* The Kitchen God's Wife *(1991), and a children's book,* The Moon Lady *(1992), based on a chapter in* The Joy Luck Club. *In this story about Jing-Mei Woo and her mother, Tan explores not only the generational conflict between mothers and daughters but also the clash of two cultures, one demanding unquestioning respect for parents and the other encouraging independence on the part of the younger generation.*

Before reading the selection, write in your journal about a time when you first willfully began to resist the wishes of your parents. Looking back, why did you feel you had to rebel? How do you interpret your rebellion from the perspective of an adult?

As you make notes on your reading, you may want to focus on the conflict between cultures, the disparity between reality and dreams, and the tug-of-war between mother and daughter.

My MOTHER BELIEVED you could be anything you wanted to be in America. You could open a restaurant. You could work for the government and get good retirement. You could buy a house with almost no money down. You could become rich. You could become instantly famous.

"Of course, you can be prodigy, too," my mother told me when I was nine. "You can be best anything. What does Auntie Lindo know? Her daughter, she is only best tricky."

America was where all my mother's hopes lay. She had come to San Francisco in 1949 after losing everything in China: her mother and father, her family home, her first husband, and two daughters, twin baby girls. But she never looked back with regret. Things could get better in so many ways.

We didn't immediately pick the right kind of prodigy. At first my mother thought I could be a Chinese Shirley Temple. We'd watch Shirley's old movies on TV as though they were training films. My mother would poke my arm and say, "*Ni kan*. You watch." And I would see Shirley tapping her feet, or singing a sailor song, or pursing her lips into a very round O while saying "Oh, my goodness."

"*Ni kan*," my mother said, as Shirley's eyes flooded with tears.   5
"You already know how. Don't need talent for crying!"

Soon after my mother got this idea about Shirley Temple, she took me to the beauty training school in the Mission District and put me in the hands of a student who could barely hold the scissors without shaking. Instead of getting big fat curls, I emerged with an uneven mass of crinkly black fuzz. My mother dragged me off to the bathroom and tried to wet down my hair.

"You look like Negro Chinese," she lamented, as if I had done this on purpose.

The instructor of the beauty training school had to lop off these soggy clumps to make my hair even again. "Peter Pan is very popular these days," the instructor assured my mother. I now had hair the length of a boy's, with curly bangs that hung at a slant two inches above my eyebrows. I liked the haircut, and it made me actually look forward to my future fame.

In fact, in the beginning I was just as excited as my mother, maybe even more so. I pictured this prodigy part of me as many different images, and I tried each one on for size. I was a dainty ballerina girl standing by the curtain, waiting to hear the music that would send me floating on my tiptoes. I was like the Christ child lifted out of the straw manger, crying with holy indignity. I was Cinderella stepping from her pumpkin carriage with sparkly cartoon music filling the air.

In all of my imaginings I was filled with a sense that I would soon   10
become perfect. My mother and father would adore me. I would be beyond reproach. I would never feel the need to sulk, or to clamor for anything.

But sometimes the prodigy in me became impatient. "If you don't hurry up and get me out of here, I'm disappearing for good," it warned. "And then you'll always be nothing."

Every night after dinner my mother and I would sit at the Formica-topped kitchen table. She would present new tests, taking her examples from stories of amazing children that she read in *Ripley's Believe It or Not* or *Good Housekeeping, Reader's Digest,* or any of a dozen other magazines she kept in a pile in our bathroom. My mother got these magazines from people whose houses she cleaned. And since she cleaned many houses each week, we had a great assortment. She would look through them all, searching for stories about remarkable children.

The first night she brought out a story about a three-year-old boy who knew the capitals of all the states and even of most of the European countries. A teacher was quoted as saying that the little boy could also pronounce the names of the foreign cities correctly. "What's the capital of Finland?" my mother asked me, looking at the story.

All I knew was the capital of California, because Sacramento was the name of the street we lived on in Chinatown. "Nairobi!" I guessed, saying the most foreign word I could think of. She checked to see if that might be one way to pronounce *Helsinki* before showing me the answer.

The tests got harder—multiplying numbers in my head, finding   15
the queen of hearts in a deck of cards, trying to stand on my head without using my hands, predicting the daily temperatures in Los Angeles, New York, and London. One night I had to look at a page from the Bible for three minutes and then report everything I could remember. "Now Jehoshaphat had riches and honor in abundance and . . . that's all I remember, Ma," I said.

And after seeing, once again, my mother's disappointed face, something inside me began to die. I hated the tests, the raised hopes and failed expectations. Before going to bed that night I looked in the mirror above the bathroom sink, and when I saw only my face staring back—and understood that it would always be this ordinary face—I began to cry. Such a sad, ugly girl! I made high-pitched noises like a crazed animal, trying to scratch out the face in the mirror.

And then I saw what seemed to be the prodigy side of me—a face I had never seen before. I looked at my reflection, blinking so that I could see more clearly. The girl staring back at me was angry, powerful. She and I were the same. I had new thoughts, willful thoughts—or, rather, thoughts filled with lots of won'ts. I won't let her change me, I promised myself. I won't be what I'm not.

So now when my mother presented her tests, I performed listlessly, my head propped on one arm. I pretended to be bored. And I was. I got so bored that I started counting the bellows of the foghorns out on the bay while my mother drilled me in other areas. The sound was comforting and reminded me of the cow jumping over the moon. And the next day I played a game with myself, seeing if my mother would give up on me before eight bellows. After a while I usually

counted only one bellow, maybe two at most. At last she was beginning to give up hope.

Two or three months went by without any mention of my being a
prodigy. And then one day my mother was watching the *Ed Sullivan
Show* on TV. The TV was old and the sound kept shorting out. Every
time my mother got halfway up from the sofa to adjust the set, the
sound would come back on and Sullivan would be talking. As soon as
she sat down, Sullivan would go silent again. She got up—the TV
broke into loud piano music. She sat down—silence. Up and down,
back and forth, quiet and loud. It was like a stiff, embraceless dance
between her and the TV set. Finally, she stood by the set with her hand
on the sound dial.

She seemed entranced by the music, a frenzied little piano piece   20
with a mesmerizing quality, which alternated between quick, playful
passages and teasing, lilting ones.

"*Ni kan*," my mother said, calling me over with hurried hand
gestures. "Look here."

I could see why my mother was fascinated by the music. It was
being pounded out by a little Chinese girl, about nine years old, with
a Peter Pan haircut. The girl had the sauciness of a Shirley Temple. She
was proudly modest, like a proper Chinese child. And she also did a
fancy sweep of a curtsy, so that the fluffy skirt of her white dress
cascaded to the floor like the petals of a large carnation.

In spite of these warning signs, I wasn't worried. Our family had
no piano and we couldn't afford to buy one, let alone reams of sheet
music and piano lessons. So I could be generous in my comments
when my mother bad-mouthed the little girl on TV.

"Play note right, but doesn't sound good!" my mother complained. "No singing sound."

"What are you picking on her for?" I said carelessly. "She's pretty   25
good. Maybe she's not the best, but she's trying hard." I knew almost
immediately that I would be sorry I had said that.

"Just like you," she said. "Not the best. Because you not trying."
She gave a little huff as she let go of the sound dial and sat down on
the sofa.

The little Chinese girl sat down also, to play an encore of "Anitra's
Tanz," by Grieg. I remember the song, because later on I had to learn
how to play it.

Three days after watching the *Ed Sullivan Show* my mother told me
what my schedule would be for piano lessons and piano practice. She
had talked to Mr. Chong, who lived on the first floor of our apartment
building. Mr. Chong was a retired piano teacher, and my mother had

traded house-cleaning services for weekly lessons and a piano for me to practice on every day, two hours a day, from four until six.

When my mother told me this, I felt as though I had been sent to hell. I whined, and then kicked my foot a little when I couldn't stand it anymore.

"Why don't you like me the way I am?" I cried. "I'm *not* a genius! 30 I can't play the piano. And even if I could, I wouldn't go on TV if you paid me a million dollars!"

My mother slapped me. "Who ask you to be genius?" she shouted. "Only ask you be your best. For you sake. You think I want you to be genius? Hnnh! What for! Who ask you!"

"So ungrateful," I heard her mutter in Chinese. "If she had as much talent as she has temper, she'd be famous now."

Mr. Chong, whom I secretly nicknamed Old Chong, was very strange, always tapping his fingers to the silent music of an invisible orchestra. He looked ancient in my eyes. He had lost most of the hair on the top of his head, and he wore thick glasses and had eyes that always looked tired. But he must have been younger than I thought, since he lived with his mother and was not yet married.

I met Old Lady Chong once, and that was enough. She had a peculiar smell, like a baby that had done something in its pants, and her fingers felt like a dead person's, like an old peach I once found in the back of the refrigerator; its skin just slid off the flesh when I picked it up.

I soon found out why Old Chong had retired from teaching piano. 35 He was deaf. "Like Beethoven!" he shouted to me. "We're both listening only in our head!" And he would start to conduct his frantic silent sonatas.

Our lessons went like this. He would open the book and point to different things, explaining their purpose: "Key! Treble! Bass! No sharps or flats! So this is C major! Listen now and play after me!"

And then he would play the C scale a few times, a simple chord, and then, as if inspired by an old unreachable itch, he would gradually add more notes and running trills and a pounding bass until the music was really something quite grand.

I would play after him, the simple scale, the simple chord, and then just play some nonsense that sounded like a cat running up and down on top of garbage cans. Old Chong would smile and applaud and say, "Very good! But now you must learn to keep time!"

So that's how I discovered that Old Chong's eyes were too slow to keep up with the wrong notes I was playing. He went through the motions in half time. To help me keep rhythm, he stood behind me and pushed down on my right shoulder for every beat. He balanced pennies on top of my wrists so that I would keep them still as I slowly played scales and arpeggios. He had me curve my hand around an apple and keep that shape when playing chords. He marched stiffly to show me how to make each finger dance up and down, staccato, like an obedient little soldier.

He taught me all these things, and that was how I also learned I   40
could be lazy and get away with mistakes, lots of mistakes. If I hit the wrong notes because I hadn't practiced enough, I never corrected myself. I just kept playing in rhythm. And Old Chong kept conducting his own private reverie.

So maybe I never really gave myself a fair chance. I did pick up the basics pretty quickly, and I might have become a good pianist at that young age. But I was so determined not to try, not to be anybody different, and I learned to play only the most ear-splitting preludes, the most discordant hymns.

Over the next year I practiced like this, dutifully in my own way. And then one day I heard my mother and her friend Lindo Jong both talking in a loud, bragging tone of voice so that others could hear. It was after church, and I was leaning against a brick wall, wearing a dress with stiff white petticoats. Auntie Lindo's daughter, Waverly, who was my age, was standing farther down the wall, about five feet away. We had grown up together and shared all the closeness of two sisters, squabbling over crayons and dolls. In other words, for the most part, we hated each other. I thought she was snotty. Waverly Jong had gained a certain amount of fame as "Chinatown's Littlest Chinese Chess Champion."

"She bring home too many trophy," Auntie Lindo lamented that Sunday. "All day she play chess. All day I have no time do nothing but dust off her winnings." She threw a scolding look at Waverly, who pretended not to see her.

"You lucky you don't have this problem," Auntie Lindo said with a sigh to my mother.

And my mother squared her shoulders and bragged: "Our prob-   45
lem worser than yours. If we ask Jing-mei wash dish, she hear nothing but music. It's like you can't stop this natural talent."

And right then I was determined to put a stop to her foolish pride.

A few weeks later Old Chong and my mother conspired to have me play in a talent show that was to be held in the church hall. By then my parents had saved up enough to buy me a secondhand piano, a black Wurlitzer spinet with a scarred bench. It was the showpiece of our living room.

For the talent show I was to play a piece called "Pleading Child," from Schumann's *Scenes From Childhood*. It was a simple, moody piece that sounded more difficult than it was. I was supposed to memorize the whole thing. But I dawdled over it, playing a few bars and then cheating, looking up to see what notes followed. I never really listened to what I was playing. I daydreamed about being somewhere else, about being someone else.

The part I liked to practice best was the fancy curtsy: right foot out, touch the rose on the carpet with a pointed foot, sweep to the side, bend left leg, look up, and smile.

My parents invited all the couples from their social club to witness 50 my debut. Auntie Lindo and Uncle Tin were there. Waverly and her two older brothers had also come. The first two rows were filled with children either younger or older than I was. The littlest ones got to go first. They recited simple nursery rhymes, squawked out tunes on miniature violins, and twirled hula hoops in pink ballet tutus, and when they bowed or curtsied, the audience would sigh in unison, "*Awww,*" and then clap enthusiastically.

When my turn came, I was very confident. I remember my childish excitement. It was as if I knew, without a doubt, that the prodigy side of me really did exist. I had no fear whatsoever, no nervousness. I remember thinking, This is it! This is it! I looked out over the audience, at my mother's blank face, my father's yawn, Auntie Lindo's stiff-lipped smile, Waverly's sulky expression. I had on a white dress, layered with sheets of lace, and a pink bow in my Peter Pan haircut. As I sat down, I envisioned people jumping to their feet and Ed Sullivan rushing up to introduce me to everyone on TV.

And I started to play. Everything was so beautiful. I was so caught up in how lovely I looked that I wasn't worried about how I would sound. So I was surprised when I hit the first wrong note. And then I hit another, and another. A chill started at the top of my head and began to trickle down. Yet I couldn't stop playing, as though my hands were bewitched. I kept thinking my fingers would adjust themselves back, like a train switching to the right track. I played this strange jumble through to the end, the sour notes staying with me all the way.

When I stood up, I discovered my legs were shaking. Maybe I had just been nervous, and the audience, like Old Chong, had seen me go through the right motions and had not heard anything wrong at all. I swept my right foot out, went down on my knee, looked up, and smiled. The room was quiet, except for Old Chong, who was beaming and shouting, "Bravo! Bravo! Well done!" But then I saw my mother's face, her stricken face. The audience clapped weakly, and as I walked back to my chair, with my whole face quivering as I tried not to cry, I heard a little boy whisper loudly to his mother, "That was awful," and the mother whispered, "Well, she certainly tried."

And now I realized how many people were in the audience—the whole world, it seemed. I was aware of eyes burning into my back. I felt the shame of my mother and father as they sat stiffly through the rest of the show.

We could have escaped during intermission. Pride and some   55 strange sense of honor must have anchored my parents to their chairs. And so we watched it all: The eighteen-year-old boy with a fake moustache who did a magic show and juggled flaming hoops while riding a unicycle. The breasted girl with white makeup who sang an aria from *Madame Butterfly* and got an honorable mention. And the eleven-year-old boy who won first prize playing a tricky violin song that sounded like a busy bee.

After the show the Hsus, the Jongs, and the St. Clairs, from the Joy Luck Club, came up to my mother and father.

"Lots of talented kids," Auntie Lindo said vaguely, smiling broadly.

"That was somethin' else," my father said, and I wondered if he was referring to me in a humorous way, or whether he even remembered what I had done.

Waverly looked at me and shrugged her shoulders. "You aren't a genius like me," she said matter-of-factly. And if I hadn't felt so bad, I would have pulled her braids and punched her stomach.

But my mother's expression was what devastated me: a quiet,   60 blank look that said she had lost everything. I felt the same way, and everybody seemed now to be coming up, like gawkers at the scene of an accident, to see what parts were actually missing.

When we got on the bus to go home, my father was humming the busy-bee tune and my mother was silent. I kept thinking she wanted to wait until we got home before shouting at me. But when my father unlocked the door to our apartment, my mother walked in and went straight to the back, into the bedroom. No accusations. No blame. And in a way, I felt disappointed. I had been waiting for her to start shouting, so that I could shout back and cry and blame her for all my misery.

I had assumed that my talent-show fiasco meant that I would never have to play the piano again. But two days later, after school, my mother came out of the kitchen and saw me watching TV.

"Four clock," she reminded me, as if it were any other day. I was stunned, as though she were asking me to go through the talent-show torture again. I planted myself more squarely in front of the TV.

"Turn off TV," she called from the kitchen five minutes later.

I didn't budge. And then I decided. I didn't have to do what my   65 mother said anymore. I wasn't her slave. This wasn't China. I had listened to her before, and look what happened. She was the stupid one.

She came out of the kitchen and stood in the arched entryway of the living room. "Four clock," she said once again, louder.

"I'm not going to play anymore," I said nonchalantly. "Why should I? I'm not a genius."

She stood in front of the TV. I saw that her chest was heaving up and down in an angry way.

"No!" I said, and I now felt stronger, as if my true self had finally emerged. So this was what had been inside me all along.

"No! I won't!" I screamed.   70

She snapped off the TV, yanked me by the arm and pulled me off the floor. She was frighteningly strong, half pulling, half carrying me toward the piano as I kicked the throw rugs under my feet. She lifted me up and onto the hard bench. I was sobbing by now, looking at her bitterly. Her chest was heaving even more and her mouth was open, smiling crazily as if she were pleased that I was crying.

"You want me to be someone that I'm not!" I sobbed. "I'll never be the kind of daughter you want me to be!"

"Only two kinds of daughters," she shouted in Chinese. "Those who are obedient and those who follow their own mind! Only one kind of daughter can live in this house. Obedient daughter!"

"Then I wish I weren't your daughter. I wish you weren't my mother," I shouted. As I said these things I got scared. It felt like worms and toads and slimy things crawling out of my chest, but it also felt good, that this awful side of me had surfaced, at last.

"Too late change this," my mother said shrilly.   75

And I could sense her anger rising to its breaking point. I wanted to see it spill over. And that's when I remembered the babies she had lost in China, the ones we never talked about. "Then I wish I'd never been born!" I shouted. "I wish I were dead! Like them."

It was as if I had said magic words. Alakazam!—her face went blank, her mouth closed, her arms went slack, and she backed out of the room, stunned, as if she were blowing away like a small brown leaf, thin, brittle, lifeless.

It was not the only disappointment my mother felt in me. In the years that followed, I failed her many times, each time asserting my will, my right to fall short of expectations. I didn't get straight *As*. I didn't become class president. I didn't get into Stanford. I dropped out of college.

Unlike my mother, I did not believe I could be anything I wanted to be. I could only be me.

And for all those years we never talked about the disaster at the   80
recital or my terrible declarations afterward at the piano bench. Neither of us talked about it again, as if it were a betrayal that was now
unspeakable. So I never found a way to ask her why she had hoped
for something so large that failure was inevitable.

And even worse, I never asked her about what frightened me the
most: Why had she given up hope? For after our struggle at the piano,
she never mentioned my playing again. The lessons stopped. The lid
to the piano was closed, shutting out the dust, my misery, and her
dreams.

So she surprised me. A few years ago she offered to give me the
piano, for my thirtieth birthday. I had not played in all those years. I
saw the offer as a sign of forgiveness, a tremendous burden removed.

"Are you sure?" I asked shyly. "I mean, won't you and Dad miss
it?"

"No, this your piano," she said firmly. "Always your piano. You
only one can play."

"Well, I probably can't play anymore," I said. "It's been years."   85

"You pick up fast," my mother said, as if she knew this was
certain. "You have natural talent. You could be genius if you want to."

"No, I couldn't."

"You just not trying," my mother said. And she was neither angry
nor sad. She said it as if announcing a fact that could never be dis-
proved. "Take it," she said.

But I didn't at first. It was enough that she had offered it to me.
And after that, every time I saw it in my parents' living room, standing in front of the bay window, it made me feel proud, as if it were a
shiny trophy that I had won back.

Last week I sent a tuner over to my parents' apartment and had the   90
piano reconditioned, for purely sentimental reasons. My mother had
died a few months before, and I had been getting things in order for
my father, a little bit at a time. I put the jewelry in special silk pouches.
The sweaters she had knitted in yellow, pink, bright orange—all the
colors I hated—I put in mothproof boxes. I found some old Chinese
silk dresses, the kind with little slits up the sides. I rubbed the old silk
against my skin, and then wrapped them in tissue and decided to take
them home with me.

After I had the piano tuned, I opened the lid and touched the
keys. It sounded even richer than I remembered. Really, it was a very
good piano. Inside the bench were the same exercise notes with hand-
written scales, the same secondhand music books with their covers
held together with yellow tape.

I opened up the Schumann book to the dark little piece I had played at the recital. It was on the left-hand page, "Pleading Child." It looked more difficult than I remembered. I played a few bars, surprised at how easily the notes came back to me.

And for the first time, or so it seemed, I noticed the piece on the right-hand side. It was called "Perfectly Contented." I tried to play this one as well. It had a lighter melody but with the same flowing rhythm and turned out to be quite easy. "Pleading Child" was shorter but slower; "Perfectly Contented" was longer but faster. And after I had played them both a few times, I realized they were two halves of the same song.

❖ Focused Freewriting   Consider as possible focal points Jing-mei's insecurity about her own ability, her mother's need to produce a child prodigy, a personal experience with parent-child conflict, or one of the topics you've identified in your journal.

❖ Guided Responses

1. After failing to memorize the Bible page, Jing-mei cries at her reflection in the mirror, calling herself "sad" and "ugly" before recognizing "the prodigy," which was "angry, powerful" (paras. 16–17). What has she recognized in the mirror image of herself? How does her recognition reflect the normal development of a child? Having read the entire story, do you think this marks a positive turning point in Jing-mei's life? Explain your response.

2. Jing-mei's hysterical reminder to her mother of the lost babies doesn't result in an angry outburst; instead, her mother's "face [goes] blank" as she "[backs] out of the room, stunned" (paras. 76–77). Since Tan doesn't tell us what happened next, speculate on how Jing-mei reacts to her mother's response. What do you think the young girl learns from this episode? How well do you think it reflects a child's desire to inflict pain on a parent? Explain your response.

3. When her mother offers Jing-mei the piano for her thirtieth birthday, she once again tells her daughter, "You just not trying." From then on, Jing-mei claims, the piano "made me feel proud, as if it were a shiny trophy I had won back" (paras. 88–89). How does this conversation with her mother raise the piano to trophy status? Why does Jing-mei say that she's won the trophy *back*? What is the significance of this incident for the relationship between mother and daughter?

4. When Jing-mei discovers the Schumann piece at the end of the story, she suddenly realizes that "Pleading Child" and "Perfectly Con-

tented" are "two halves of the same song." How does this discovery help her understand the battles with her mother? What does she learn about her own behavior? Do you think her realization brings her peace of mind? Why, or why not?

❖ Shared Responses   In your journal explore the need most children have to rebel against their parents. Why might rebellion be considered healthy behavior? unhealthy? How can it become dangerous? How can both parents and children prevent rebellion from driving a permanent wedge between them? As you discuss your responses in small groups, try to explain how family background and culture influence individual students' responses.

First Time

LORENE CARY

LORENE CARY *(biographical information on p. 89) recounts in this selection from* Black Ice *the story of her first experience with marijuana, exploring her and her fellow students' anxiety about final exams, adolescent fears of appearing foolish, and the overriding sense of otherness felt by African-American students in a white, privileged world.*

Before reading the selection, recall in your journal a dangerous but exciting incident in your life, a time when you knew you had broken a rule. What impact did the incident have on you? What fears and memories did the experience provoke? How do you look upon the incident now?

As you make notes on your reading, you may want to focus on the conflicting emotions Libby feels: her childhood memories, her excitement at the new experience, her fear of being caught, her insecurity, or her need for acceptance.

ON THE NIGHT BEFORE MY ENGLISH EXAM, a boy who lived on Philadelphia's Main Line approached me as I walked down the drafty cloister from the dining room. Doug Ballard and I had had a couple of conversations about where he lived, and how to get there from my house, as if, I thought ironically, I were in danger of being invited.

"Lib," he called from a few steps behind me. "So, are you ready for English tomorrow?"

"I don't know." I slowed my pace to wait for him in case he had a good story to tell. We watched for teachers to crack around exam time, and in winter, what with the cold, dark weather, and the pace of work and sports, one of the new ones was bound to lose it. Doug had the mischievous look of someone with naughty info.

"What's up with you?"

Doug jogged a few steps to catch up with me. We were even with 5
the side door that opened onto the back path toward the Chapel and the woods.

"Listen," he said in a confidential voice. "Some kids are going out a little later to party. You really ought to come."

I began shaking my head.

"Wait a minute," he said. "It's just a few people. *Very* discreet. The worst thing before exams is to get all tensed up. Hey, you look tense. I just thought I'd ask."

It worried me that I looked tense. I had thought I was on the verge of enlightenment, but perhaps not. Perhaps this highstrung fatigue was exhaustion. I had exulted in my appearance that morning, thinking it my badge of courage. "I have read the word of the Lord our God until my eyes burned like the very fires of hell. . . . " The fact was, I just looked bad, ragglely, as they said in Philly.

I looked at Doug. He looked great. He and his crowd would   10
sashay into the examination refreshed, their minds clear to write about all the ideas I was hanging onto by the hair of my chinny-chin-chin. *They'd do fine and I would miss out on my HH!*

"Sure," I said coolly.

"Really?" Doug seemed surprised. Immediately, I had second thoughts. Maybe he'd had a bet with someone. "Nah, Libby'll never party with you." Maybe I had just provided the evening s entertainment.

"Aw, cool," he added in the nick of time. "That's great." He seemed sincere.

"I don't have anything to give you for this," I said. Was I incurring financial obligations? I wondered. Would I be required at some time to pay back?

"Oh, please." Doug made a dismissive movement with his head,   15
as if I had tried to hand him a dollar for driving me to the supermarket in a Porsche.

Off we went, out the side door of the cloister, along the gritty, ice-packed path, down the wooden snow steps, across the bridges over the pond, and around the hockey rink into the woods.

Half a dozen students assembled in a tiny clearing and got down to business at once. Until the little pipe came round to me, I watched my new pals. They seemed not to mind. They were watching me, too. I decided to take a hit.

"No, you're wasting it all," someone told me.

"Take it like this—" Doug took the pipe from me carefully, so as to avoid burning his fingers on the hot bowl of the pipe or dropping it in the snow. He sucked in a mouthful of smoke, and then, instead of breathing out, inhaled again a few times, short, tiny breaths, as if to force the stuff deeper into his lungs. "Try it."

The figures around me (I could barely see their faces) were becom-   20
ing impatient. Smoke that trailed off into the air could be going into

one of them. I took a puff. The wad of weed crackled in the bowl. Heat from one inhalation traveled up the stem to burn my lips.

"Whoa!" someone said. "It's steaming now!"

"Great, give it here."

I handed the thing away and sucked in as Doug had done. Tears sprang to my eyes. Furry smoke curled at the back of my nose and throat. Should I choke it down?

"Suck," Doug whispered.

I drew it in until the burning went beyond my throat and into my   25
lungs. I felt as if it would drown me to inhale again. I let out my breath in tiny bits, afraid that the burning would come back up.

"How's that feel?" someone asked me.

"Does it feel great?"

"I feel dizzy," I said. Actually, I felt stupid. I couldn't regain the rhythm of my own breathing.

The pipe appeared again, I had cleared up by now. If I could only get this thing right, I thought. Again it burned. "Hot lips," I croaked.

They laughed hysterically and lifted the pipe out of my fingers. I   30
didn't feel like laughing.

Doug asked me for a cigarette. The get-high folkways had it that smoking a cigarette would extend the high. I passed cigarettes all around, thinking in that way to attenuate my debt for my two gulps of weed, and still hoping that the lovely feeling would kick in.

I did have a delayed response to drugs, after all. It had taken a double dose of anesthetic to get me under for my tonsil operation when I was a kid. As I stood with my feet in the snow like the Grinch on Christmas morning, I remembered the hospital in South Philadelphia when I was seven. I remembered dozing lightly and waking up in the hallway outside a big, noisy room with white lights. That was the operating room, I had thought. A tall black man was standing over me, ready to roll my bed into the room. He was wearing a green cap, gathered around the bottom and puffed out over his head like a Victorian night cap. People in the white room were laughing and talking together casually. I had never heard doctors speak like that. "Hey, wait a minute," the man yelled to the doctors and nurses. "This child is still awake."

"She is?"

"Are you awake?" he asked me.

I nodded yes. I had been trying to go to sleep like a good girl. I   35
had lain "still as death"—one of my old relatives (I wondered who) had always used that phrase, and that's what I had tried to do. I had been able to doze, ever so gently, but not sleep. I couldn't get my thumb into my mouth. What had they done to my arm? I couldn't sleep without sucking my thumb. Then the man with the green gown

and cap smiled at me and rubbed my cheek with his forefinger. It felt good to be rubbed. I was glad that he was not as angry as he had seemed when I'd opened my eyes. Then they gave me another needle. "You'll be asleep in a minute, sweetheart. Don't worry."

When I awoke, my throat hurt. It burned. I was alone in a gray room. Not alone, there were other crib beds with other sleeping children. I could look out a big window and see the hallway. A nurse walked by. I tried to call her to ask where my mother was, but she walked fast and did not look my way. I tried to put my thumb in my mouth, but I could not. The doctors had a cast on my arm. I looked at my hand. It was no more than a foot away from my face. I could not get it any closer. I began to cry. My throat felt as if it would tear open with each sob.

I snapped out of my reverie when I felt the hot pipe being pressed into my hand again.

"No, thanks," I said. "I'm afraid that that stuff just doesn't work with me."

"Doesn't work, eh? You look pretty wasted to me."

"Could be that it affects your body differently," one of the girls   40
theorized dreamily. "Do you have other allergies? Food allergies? Respiratory?"

"Oh, yeah. I'm allergic to everything."

"Maybe that's it."

"Or maybe it's just that it's your first time."

"Lib! Is this your first time getting high?"

"Or not getting high."   45

They giggled a great deal.

"Well, if it's not doing any good, don't waste it. Pass it here."

"You are *so* greedy."

"Who's greedy? I haven't had any more than you have."

"One potato, two potato, three potato, four—"   50

"*Shhhhh.*"

We all went silent. "What?"

"I think I saw a match."

"Oh, God," I moaned.

"Shhhhh."   55

Even people who didn't party knew what a match in the woods meant: Sr. Ordoñez. He was thought to go walking in the woods to bust people. He carried his little package of imported cigarettes with him, they said, and you could avoid him if you watched for his match.

"What're we going to do?"

"Run!"

"Are you kidding? And attract his attention for sure?"

"I know. We'll hide."   60

I looked around desperately. The woods were bare.

"We'll be munchkins!" one of the girls said in a muffled shriek.

"Right!"

"Quick!"

"Down!" 65

"Under the snow!"

The girls were first. They lay on the snow and scooched around in it like huskies settling in for sleep. Then they scooped snow on top of themselves. Little mountains of snow piled up.

"I can't breathe!"

Giggles and puffs of steamy breath floated up from the mounds like spirits out of fresh graves.

I lay in the snow, too. I did not own a parka with a hood, nor was 70 I wearing a hat. The snow nuzzled into my collar and melted down my neck. I felt it smash against the back of my Afro and work toward my scalp.

"I gotta go," I said. No one responded. I got up and shook myself. I do not remember whether anyone noticed my leaving or spoke to me. I only knew that I had to get out of the snow. It felt like a trap, like I'd be trapped for good. I had to get back to my house, back to my warm bed with my red-and-white afghan and the alarm clock ticking beside me.

I came to a creek that burbled under its icy coating. To cross it, I had to traverse two logs laid lengthwise over the place where the creek dropped a foot to empty into the pond. I was not sure that I could negotiate the crossing, but I could not summon the resources to look for another. I stepped onto the logs. The crust of snow slipped off one log to reveal a thicker crust of ice. My foot plunged over the edge of the log toward the creek. I saw sharp rocks in the creek bed, and felt my calf scratch against the log.

"You could die here," I said to myself. "See those rocks? You could slip over and hit your head and die."

I sniveled with shame. I slipped and crawled and clawed my way over and ran when I got to the woods on the other side.

Again, the voice inside chided me. "Running now? Couldn't run back in the fall, when the sun was shining, and the ground was flat and the grass was green. Uh-unh. No. It was so hard to run, wasn't it? Bet you'll run now."

I'd sign up for Señor's class next year, that's what I'd do. So what 75 if I was scared of him? Better to be scared of him in class than running away from him in the woods.

Back in the house, the lights in the hallway blazed at me. For some reason, I wanted to see Janie, but she wasn't there. I couldn't think what to do next, so I walked along the third floor and back, and then down to the second floor and back. I ran into Mandy Butler, and I noticed, with some resentment, how attractive and petite she was, how at ease with other boys and girls.

"I'm looking for Janie," I said.

"Janie? I think she may be down in Mr. Hawley's," Mandy said.

"Oh."

"His door was open, and I heard voices. I bet he's having a feed, 80 or snacks or something."

"Oh. Maybe I'll go down." I did not feel capable of sitting with a ginger ale on Mr. Hawley's rug and impersonating myself.

Mandy peered at me. "Libby, are you OK?"

"I don't feel so hot. I just wanted to see Janie." Why was I repeating myself?

"Libby!" She got up close to me. "Libby, you are high!" Mandy Butler whooped. "That's a riot! *You* are high. You *are*, aren't you?" Tiny bubbles of spittle collected at the corners of her mouth.

"I guess so. *Please* stop shouting."   85

"Oh, my God! This is a *scream!*"

I turned to go down the steps.

"Don't go to Hawley's." She grabbed my elbow. "What are you doing? Use the back staircase. I can't believe this."

When I got to my room, Pam Hudson popped her head in from next door. "Where have you been? I thought you were going to come back and study for English. I've been here grinding away waiting for company. Were you at the library or—"

Pam's voice, husky and full of good-natured scolding, filled me   90 with blubbery remorse.

"I'm sorry," I said.

"Libby, what's wrong?"

"I'm sorry. You were here waiting for me, and I said I'd be back to study English, and I should have been studying English." When the tears came, they burned my eyes, and I wondered why.

"Aw, don't get upset. Listen, don't *cry* about it." Pam could be big and maternal when she needed to be, what with that deep voice and those square white fingers and folksong-gray eyes. She came and sat next to me on the bed and put her arms around me. Pam always smelled as if she'd slept in her clothes, and I breathed in the scent of her, familiar and comforting as a steeping bag. "Hey, look at me.

"Libby? Libby! *You are high.*"   95

"Oh, Christ, shut up, Pam." You could talk to Pam like that sometimes.

"Aw, Lib, now you're going to have a crying jag." She said it with true compassion even though she was laughing.

"Jag" sounded like a bad word. I'd heard it before, and I knew what it meant. "I've got to wash my face," I said, "and then we'll study for English."

She looked at me and laughed outright. "Go the hell to bed," she said.

"I have to brush my teeth first."   100

"The hell with your teeth. It takes years to grow a cavity."

Pam threw my clothes into a heap. I lay down and allowed her to tuck me in. "Take it," she said, as I tried to straighten my own bed-clothes. "Just shut up for once and take it." She rubbed me a little and turned out the light.

"Pam," I asked, feeling my stomach churning, "would you wind my clock and set it for six?"

"What, are you crazy?"

"No, really, please. I've *got* to get up early."   105

"OK," she said in a singsong. "But don't blame me if you end up losing another clock." I'd ruined two clocks that year by chucking them across the room in my sleep. When I was sure Pam was gone, I listened to the ticking. It was like the loud tick-tock in my great-grand-father's room. I thought how I would have disgraced him, disgraced my whole family, if I'd been caught, suspended, expelled. The other kids would apply to Andover or Exeter, no doubt, but I'd be back home, on my behind. When the alarm rang, I awoke to find my thumb in my mouth.

❖ Focused Freewriting   Consider as possible focal points Libby's awareness of being different, the ritual nature of the party, a personal experience with breaking the rules, or one of the topics you've identified in your journal.

❖ Guided Responses

1. When Doug asks her to join the party, Libby worries about his motives: "Maybe he'd had a bet with someone. . . . Maybe I had just provided the evening's entertainment" (para. 12). How does this comment illustrate normal teenage insecurity? Based on your reading of the story, what other reasons do you think might account for Libby's insecurity? Do you think she's oversensitive? Why, or why not?

2. Cary opens her story with a description of her state of mind as she prepares for final exams, and in paragraph 9 observes, "I had exulted in my appearance that morning, thinking it my badge of courage. 'I have read the word of the Lord our God until my eyes burned like the very fires of hell. . . .'" Why does she place such

importance on the appropriate preparation? What is the significance of her religious references? How would you characterize the significance of final exams in Libby's life?

3. As she feels the smoke burning her throat and lungs, Libby recalls her tonsillectomy from years before (paras. 32–37). Why, other than the physical sensation of a raw throat and the reference to drugs, would this incident come to the surface? What emotions does Libby the teenager share with Libby the child? How does the ending of the story reinforce the impact of the tonsillectomy flashback?

4. Why does Cary present the escape from Señor Ordoñez (paras. 70–75) in such a dramatic fashion? Why does Libby chide herself as she attempts to cross the creek? Of what significance is her decision to take Señor's class the following year?

❖ Shared Responses   In your journal, comment on the diversity (or lack of it) at your school. How does your racial/ethnic/religious/class identity shape your perception of the place? What makes your environment comfortable or uncomfortable for people from various backgrounds? Explain your responses. As you discuss your responses in small groups, highlight the differences in the perceptions of students from various backgrounds.

———— ❖ ————

"You Wanna Die with Me?"

ADRIAN NICOLE LEBLANC

ADRIAN NICOLE LEBLANC *received a master's degree in philosophy from Oxford University. A former fiction editor for* Seventeen *magazine, LeBlanc is currently working on a fellowship in legal writing at Yale University. In this 1986 article from* The New England Monthly, *LeBlanc reports on her return to the high school from which she graduated in 1982, a school plagued by a rash of teen suicides. Highlighting the sense of apathy among students in her story, she paints a frightening picture of a generation so alienated that death can seem preferable to familiar existence.*

Before reading the selection, comment in your journal on your familiarity with the issue of teen suicide. Do you see it as an isolated or a universal problem? What kind of guidance regarding suicide did your high school, church, or other social organization offer to teens in your area? What information from other classes might shed some light on this issue?

As you make notes on your reading, you may want to focus on the nature of Leominster as a community, the reasons that some students turn to suicide, the response of the community, or the details of the students' lives.

A LANKY GIRL DESCENDS from a yellow school bus. She walks the path leading to her white, clean home surrounded by green fields and mountains. Her older sister washes the car. The girls begin to argue and the younger girl slaps her sister across the face. In her bedroom, the young girl sits and cries. She takes off her baseball hat, pulling her ponytail through the opening above the adjustable band. She picks up a framed picture of her parents. She remembers the time her mother said she didn't love her. She takes her father's rifle out of a closet. As the camera pulls away from the bedroom window, the gun cracks.

The projector clicks off. From the darkened high school auditorium come claps and whistles. Several students mockingly sob and console one another. Others wriggle, their laughter careless, inattentive. Many bite their fingernails and stare indifferently ahead, caught in the numb monotone of a second-period assembly.

"Will those of you who haven't made airplanes out of the HELP cards please put them in your pockets?" asks today's Samaritan, stepping forward. A HELP plane sails past her. Students laugh. The assistant principal beckons for help from the teachers lining the perimeter of the gym. They arch their backs, coming off the wall slowly, and ease around the rough room. "Hey, *you!*" a teacher yells, pointing to a boy in the bleachers. *"NOW!"* The boy smirks and bounces down the rows. The teacher pushes him toward the exit.

Imagine you are a student here, at Leominster High. It's the fourth time this year you've had to listen to people talking about depression and death. The white-haired ladies speaking soothingly onstage— representatives of the Samaritans, a suicide-prevention group sent in from Framingham to help you—have already given you their pamphlets. You remain unresponsive to their pleas.

"This is a tough scene, and it's tough to cope," says the Samaritan   5 onstage now, her passé language causing you to roll your eyes. Your neighbor picks lint off his jeans; another stretches and yawns. "Oh, Christ," a student behind you mutters, "here we go again." There's hissing. One girl writes a note to her friend. "You must be mad that you live in Leominster," the Samaritan continues, "because it's only known for one thing these days. Suicide."

Leominster is a largely working-class city of thirty-four thousand, forty miles west of Boston, with a strong French Canadian and Italian heritage. Its usual claim to notoriety is the group of factories that produced the first plastics in the nation. Lately it has had a more somber reputation. Between February 1984 and March 1986, ten Leominster teenagers died sudden, violent deaths, and eight of those committed suicide. This morning's assembly aims to avoid number nine.

"It's always a mistake to kill yourself," says the Samaritan. One boy sleeps through the presentation. A group of "trade rats" from the vocational high school jumps down from the bleachers en masse. The Samaritan tries to continue. "There's *got* to be *someone* you can talk to," she says.

"Listen to her," says the assistant principal, his voice rising.

"Listen to each other," says the Samaritan, her face strained and weary. Shoving and hustling one another, students pour down from their seats.

"Pay attention to the signals, keep your eyes open," the Samaritan   10 yells. "Listen!"

"Talk to someone!" screams the assistant principal, lost among a crowd of heads and denim. "And go to your fourth-period class!"

About five weeks before her death, fifteen-year-old Melissa Poirier was beaten up twice in one day. That morning in school she had been jumped in the bathroom. Melissa and the two girls who attacked her were suspended, so Melissa went home. Soon after, one of her assailants went to her house, offering a truce. She asked Melissa to join her and the third girl so they could talk and work out the differences they were having over a boy. Melissa accompanied the girl to Pheasant Run, a derelict ski trail behind the high school where kids often drink and get stoned. The third girl waited beyond the trail. When Melissa arrived, the two girls assaulted her again. One held her down while the other pounded, and then the two traded positions. Half an hour later, Melissa managed to escape to a nearby garage, where she crouched behind a car for over an hour. She then made her way back home, carefully, through the woods.

Melissa was an extremely pretty young girl with thick, long hair, a button nose, shining eyes, and a neat, budding figure. When her classmates finished with her that day, her nose was fractured and both of her eyes were black. The blood vessels on her forehead had broken from repeated blows. Her face was swollen and her ribs were bruised.

"Melissa was tiny, five feet tall, and wicked cute," says one close girlfriend. "The girls never liked her because the guys did. Mel was hassled all the time."

The fight left Melissa despondent. Her mother, who noticed that   15
she was afraid to go outside, encouraged her to see a therapist, but after three sessions, Melissa refused to return.

Andrea Paquette had been Melissa's best friend since fourth grade. The girls had started to grow apart (Andrea became involved with student government, and Melissa with drugs), but the two kept up their morning ritual of a walk before homeroom.

"She cried every day when the bell rang," says Andrea. "She never wanted to go in. Melissa hated school more than anything."

On the average morning at Leominster High, what Melissa Poirier wanted to avoid goes something like this: you might come in on time, drop your books off (if you took any home) but keep your coat on (to look as if you'd just entered the building, without books). You'd head straight for the girls' bathroom. You'd inhale the smoke and shiver; the bathroom is always cold. Graffiti covers the chipped gray paint on the windows and the doorless stalls: "Just beca use Im no slut doesnt mean I should become a fuckin nun Im no slob like most girls in this fuckin school!" You'd have fifteen minutes to get ready before the heads, the local drug population, took over the washroom. You'd comb your hair and watch your friends comb theirs and lean on a radiator half-covered with hardened wads of gum. You'd try to find your reflection between the black letters of the spray-painted SUCK on a mirror fogged with hair spray. You'd talk and look and tuck in your shirt. You'd put on a little more makeup, comb back your feathered hair one more time, then leave.

In the main corridor, dented light-brown lockers line the cinder-block hallways. Gray paint covers the old graffiti, and new graffiti covers the gray—"Helter Skelter, AC/DC, Led Zeppelin, DIE!" Boys, lined up by now outside the bathroom, shuffle and laugh, arms folded across their chests. Most wear denim jackets and high-tops or leather jackets and work boots. All collars are up.

The boys would tease you those early mornings, especially if   20 they'd been smoking or drinking. You would try to get by untouched but very noticed. Some students kept bottles in their lockers and drank in the locker-room shower stalls. Some had gone to McDonald's for breakfast and had dumped out half their Cokes and refilled the cups with booze, usually vodka. Some students didn't drink, of course, but certainly no one thought it strange if someone skipped classes, went to an empty house with a friend, and drank away the afternoon. So you'd lean against the lockers with friends, eyeing everyone but the person you were talking to, trying to see who was out by who was in school that day, and wait for the tardy bell. And then, maybe, you'd go to homeroom. Otherwise, you'd leave.

"And that's if you were one of the good kids," Melissa Poirier's mother says, a year after her daughter's death. "You just try and imagine what it was like to be one of the kids on the other side of the fence, one of the ones inside those detention halls, getting suspended, getting yelled at and punched at and hauled out two times a week. One of the kids called stupid by your teachers and, when you did go to class, one of those who was asked, 'Why did you bother to come?' "

Psychologists say the most dangerous time for a suicidal person is after emerging from depression or crisis. In fact, after planning a suicide, adolescents often look and feel better because a decision has been made, the burden lifted.

"It's like looking through a tunnel," says Susan Warner-Roy, who founded SPACE (Suicide Prevention Awareness Community Education) in 1980. Warner-Roy's own husband, Neil, hanged himself four years ago. "The darkness in the tunnel is the depression, and at the end of the tunnel is the light, the end of pain. To the suicidal kid, the light at the end of the tunnel is death." A couple of days before her death, Melissa's mood began to pick up. For the first time in months, Melissa seemed happy, upbeat.

"I thought to myself, 'Melissa's finally happy,' " says her friend, Andrea. "Her problems are finally over." But despite Melissa's abrupt mood swing, the suicidal symptoms were still apparent: Melissa gave Andrea some brand-new clothes she hadn't worn yet. Melissa wouldn't make plans with Andrea for that afternoon. Melissa had written this poem to Andrea just one week before:

> Andrea Happy Andrea,
>   Joyful Andrea,
>   I Love Andrea,
>   I shall miss her,
> She will hurt but will heal,
>   Andrea is strong
>   Andrea is brave
> Andrea has helped a great deal
>   She will pull through
> She always knew this would
>   be the way
>   The end of the day!
>   My end.

So Melissa Poirier may have been in an especially dangerous 25 frame of mind when she and another friend, Melody Maillet, left Leominster High School early on November 1, 1984. Pushing out the bright yellow doors of a side entrance, Melissa and Melody turned left on Exchange Street and walked the potholed road scattered with Coke cans and trash. The girls probably strolled downtown, past the variety stores and barbershops and tenements, past the pale houses of the plain Leominster streets. They walked past Monument Square, newly renovated and green. They may have walked by the Vietnamese and Cambodian apartments near Red's Variety and the Elbow Lounge. The girls then returned to Melissa's home with a bottle of cheap champagne they'd bought along the way, put on a Pink Floyd album, and began to drink.

The Wall, a series of songs depicting the progressive alienation of a rock star on the downswing, ranked high on the girls' list of revered albums. Each song, metaphorically "another brick in the wall," denotes the social forces propelling the rocker's snowballing anomie—parents, school, his wife—and the failure of the star's struggle to be understood. "Comfortably Numb," Melissa's favorite Pink Floyd song, expresses the rocker's peaking detachment. Melissa doodled the lyrics in her notebooks and in letters to friends:

> Hello,/Is there anybody in there . . . I hear you're feeling down . . . Can you show me where it hurts/ . . . I can't explain you would not understand/This is not how I am/I have become comfortably numb . . . ,/The child is grown/The dream is gone/And I have become/Comfortably numb.

The final song of the album Melissa quotes verbatim, in one of the five suicide notes the girls left behind:

"Life sucks and then you DIE!" *Goodbye cruel world I'm leaving you now and thiers nothin you can Say To make me change my mind!* YES SA! I Love to Die I'd be happier I know it! So Please Let me Go. No hard feelings. Don't Be Sad ReJoyce Its my new beginning! It Didn't hurt I'm free and happy.

Melissa Poirier's mother, Mariette, came home for lunch on that November day and found her daughter and Melody on the floor of the upstairs bedroom, with the Poirier family's 12-gauge shotgun beside them. The medical examiner found high levels of alcohol in the blood of both girls. Exactly how Melissa and Melody committed double suicide remains unconfirmed. Friends believe that Melissa bent forward and leaned on the gun, which was pointed at her stomach, and that Melody climbed on her back. Mariette Poirier says she believes each girl shot herself.

Winnifred Maillet, Melody's mother, suspects foul play. (Susan Warner-Roy's husband, Neil, whose own suicide preceded Melody's by four years, was Winnifred's brother. And Winnifred's son, Bobby, had drowned in 1980.) Since Melody's death more than two years ago, Winnifred has worked to prove that the handwriting in Melody's own suicide note was not her daughter's. The graphology has become an obsessive project. When Winnifred says her daughter was not suicidal, there is an urgent determination in her voice: "We never saw her without the pretty smiling eyes. Always smiling like the dickens. She was always happy."

"She went out. She was happy," says Melody's father, Albert, who works in quality control for Digital Equipment Corporation. "She didn't have any problems at all. She had a few problems at school, and was always upset about being put on suspension once in a while, for maybe being tardy or not coming to school, but nothing out of the ordinary."

But Melody's friends feel certain that she was suicidal. One girl-   30
friend says Melody had been asking people to commit suicide with her for a while, sometimes seriously, sometimes as a joke: "You wanna die with me?" Melody would say. "Melissa was the first one to say yes," says the friend. The two girls were known as partying buddies who shared a mutual love for acid rock.

"They dropped acid before an' shit, but they were really getting into it toward the end," says a close girlfriend of Melissa's. "We were losin' them."

Although adamant about Melody's emotional stability, Winnifred Maillet spoke of Melody's devotion to a print still hanging in her daughter's old bedroom among a collection of her things—Van Halen posters, a purple metallic electric guitar, and a black leather jacket she had bought. It shows a young girl who looks startlingly like Melody, a five-foot-eight Canadian beauty with jet black hair, olive skin, and huge, emerald eyes. The girl in the picture is tall and dark, but her eyes are detached, expressionless, complacent, while Melody's were warm. The girl's head is encircled by a lavender halo and she holds lavender feathers and a fan. The girl's skin is death-white.

"She loved the purple halo, said it was her purple haze," Melody's mother explains. Winnifred has since surrounded Melody's grave—a small pillar with Melody's picture in a crystal ball on top, leaning on a porcelain unicorn—with purple flowers. Acid rocker Jimi Hendrix popularized Purple Haze in his song about that form of LSD. And Melody referred to the purple haze, and to four of her classmates who died before her, in one of her suicide notes:

> Good Bye 'I did cuz I had to' I have to live among the Purple Haze! Tell Cecilia I love her very much! Im took advantage of you without realizing it! But now I will be happy with Jeff Mike David + Scott. 'Mom and Dad I love you' even though I've never tobl you, Im sorry It has to be this way I don't want to hurt anyone I love the Rest of the family very much. . . .

Leominster is not alone. Teenage suicides nationwide have more than doubled since 1960. It's the second most common cause of death among youngsters between the ages of fifteen and twenty-four, and the number two killer among college students. One adolescent commits suicide every two hours. Cluster suicides, as in Leominster, have also continued to climb since the first documented case in Berkeley, California, in 1966. In Plano, Texas, seven occurred in one year. Three teenagers ended their lives in five days in Omaha, Nebraska. In New York's Putnam and Westchester counties, there were five in one month.

But why has Leominster joined this select and tragic group? For one thing, it has a very low residential turnover rate. Many kids in town will go to work in the factories after graduating from high school. It's impossible to know how youngsters interpret these circumstances, of course. But whatever Leominster's particular source of pain, its teenage suicide rate right now is ten times the national average. 35

Jeffrey Bernier was Leominster's first. On February 22, 1984, Jeff and his friends gathered in the Bernier family's second-story tenement, in the heart of Leominster's French Hill, which was built in the mid-nineteenth century to house Canadian laborers. School had let out early. Jeffrey took a .357 Colt revolver from his father's gun collection and began playing Russian roulette. Ignoring pleas from his friends to stop, Jeffrey placed the muzzle to his throat and pulled the trigger. The bullet passed through his skull and lodged in the ceiling. Jeffrey was fourteen. A teacher described him as a normal boy and an average student who "liked machine shop very much." Jeffrey's father said he had warned his son never to point a gun, at anyone.

Two weeks later, on March 7, 1984, Michael J. Bresnahan, also a freshman at the Trade High School's auto body shop, cut classes with a group of friends. They went to the apartment of Matt Fallon, who wasn't home. There, Alan Arsenault picked up a .30-caliber rifle and shot Michael in the chest. A close friend said they were all very stoned, that it was an accident. Bresnahan's mother described her son as "a good little boy" who was looking forward to his sixteenth birthday and a job that awaited him at a local gas station. "It's a waste of life," she said.

Two months later, on May 11, 1984, the first double suicide struck Leominster. Trade school seniors Scott Nichols and David Dombrowick drove into the concrete loading dock of the RVJ trucking company at what police called "a very high rate of speed." A friend who had been with Scott and David earlier said that they had been driving around, planning their graduation parties (only a few weeks away) and getting high. They had shared seven joints between them in under an hour.

Scott Nichols had been depressed for a long time and had talked about killing himself for over a year. He had recently lost his job, and his girlfriend had split with him. His friends said he also had problems at home.

"After it happened," says Todd Holman, a 1984 graduate who   40
knew both boys from the trade school, "Scott seemed like the person it would have happened to." Both Scott and David had reputations as "serious partiers." Says Holman, "Better life to them just meant better drugs—better mescaline, better pot." But like many of the people who knew him, Holman believes David Dombrowick never intended to kill himself. "People don't like to do things alone in life," Holman says. "Adults don't want to live alone. Kids don't like to be alone, either. Scott just didn't want to die by himself."

The Poirier-Maillet suicides followed, bringing the total number of deaths to six. The year after the girls' double suicide was particularly difficult for the high school, says Assistant Principal Peter S. Michaels. Some students made bizarre claims that they were approached by six men in hooded black capes, carrying swords, with the number six scrawled on their foreheads in blood. For weeks after the supposed visit of the hooded men, students unscrewed number nines from the building and turned them upside down. Some students removed numbers from the classroom doors, exempting six. Others drew sixes on their notebooks and papers. They wrote notes to their dead friends on what is sometimes referred to as The Wall, a long cinder-block corridor in the basement of the main school: "Why did you guys leave us?" "We miss you!" "Melissa and Melody live on!"

Nine months passed before Leominster witnessed its seventh teenage death, suicide number five. (Jeffrey Bernier's death in the game of Russian roulette was officially ruled an accident, while Alan Arsenault, who shot Michael Bresnahan, has been convicted of manslaughter.) On August 14, 1985, Randy Cleremont and three friends sat on the railroad tracks behind Nashua Street, drinking. A train approached and they moved. Randy jumped back onto the tracks as the train sped nearer. Thrown twenty-nine feet, he struck a utility pole and slid down a dirt embankment. His friends said he was not drunk. They said he had heard their screams. They said that Randy saw the train, and that he did not want to move.

Two months later, on October 23, 1985, John P. Finn, fifteen, and a friend who remains unidentified walked out of their third-period trade class. Leaving the school by a side entrance, they turned right and traced the battered picket fence circling the wide arch of road leading downtown. They took a left at the first variety store they came upon, passed the recently closed Carter Junior High School, and soon arrived at the home of a friend named Billy Lovetro. John Finn started to tease his friend with a .38-caliber revolver. Feeling uncomfortable, the boy went out on the porch. He heard a shot and told a neighbor to call an ambulance immediately, then ran to school to get help. Finn was Leominster's eighth death in twenty months, suicide number six.

John Finn had been living with the Lovetro family because he had been having problems at home. The local newspaper mentioned John's lingering trademark—"an incredible smile."

On December 31, 1985, Billy Lovetro followed his best friend's lead—he drove into a concrete wall. Earlier, Billy is said to have taken a girlfriend to the spot on Adams Street where the wall stood and had told her, "This is where I'm going to do it." Leominster's superintendent of schools told a reporter, "I just don't know what to do anymore."   45

The school had handled the first death like any other—a moment of silence in the morning, a planned yearbook dedication, the morning announcement about calling hours. With the second, officials mandated the same procedure and prayed it would be the last. When Melody and Melissa died, the school established a Sudden Death Protocol. The steps, according to guidance counselor Patricia Pothier, were simple: "Don't call school off. Don't lower the flag. Play it low key without being callous. No glamour."

Dr. Pamela Cantor of Newton, Massachusetts, is former president of the American Association of Suicidology. Cantor says there is a contagion effect in these situations. "They must not treat the kid as a hero," she says. "The school must explain the event not as an act of intelligence or coherence but as a tragedy that was the result of stupidity." Calling school off, dedicating the yearbook—such actions, Cantor believes, only heighten the effect of making the dead kid popular. "If you take a kid who is very troubled, with no stature or identity in school," she says, "he sees how the suicides are the center of attention. Other kids might get carried away in the emotion of it all. Their fragility in their depression allows them to see suicide as a model."

In the high school corridors, at hangouts around town, and on the street, the suicides are clearly on the minds of Leominster's teenagers. And they want to talk about it. "Subconsciously, in everyone's mind now, suicide is an option," says Diana DeSantis, a 1986 graduate of Leominster High who was vice-president of her class for four years. "You're upset. You say, 'I'm depressed.' You tell your mother, and it doesn't help. You tell your teacher, maybe, and it doesn't help. So you tell a friend, maybe even a professional—the same. Suicide might be next on the list. It's just higher up on your list of options in Leominster than anywhere else."

"How can you ever get used to it?" asks Matt Mazzaferro, another 1986 graduate, now attending Brandeis. "We were shocked every time. Each one was a whole different person." Mazzaferro modifies the assertion that his peers were looking for glamour. "They were just looking not to be another face in the crowd," he said. "That was their way to make noise." Often, the methods of their deaths are more accurately remembered than any aspect of their lives: people ask, "Was that the one who . . . ?"

"It was my birthday when that last freshman killed himself," says   50
a junior. "At first I was kinda pissed off, you know, 'cause I wanted to have a wicked great day, but afta homeroom it didn't really matter, I didn't give a shit, really. 'Cause it wasn't like it was new or anything, like the first ones. It didn't wreck my day or nothing."

"After the first few the atmosphere was real gloomy around here," says one secretary at the high school. "But by the third or fourth they got numb to it. It isn't such a big deal to them anymore." As one counselor puts it, "The kids are all suicided out." A student says, "I mean, afta *seven*, what difference does one or two make? Christ, you sit in homeroom and they say we haveta have this moment of silence, and you're like, 'Fuck, not again,' but it doesn't *surprise* you. I mean, it's not like some shock or somethin' when you hear it all the time."

Leominster has tried and is still trying. Parents have started support groups; the community has sponsored lectures. The Leominster Youth Committee was formed to look at the problems facing the kids—and then, on March 26, 1986, freshman George Henderson came home from track practice and shot himself in the head, the first suicide in three months.

Henderson's suicide vitiated the by-then usual explanations. The kids who killed themselves had been tough kids—some fought, most drank, most did drugs. They had reputations. Academically, some had special needs. Many of them had problems at home. Diana DeSantis says that, with the exception of George Henderson, all the students who had killed themselves had "the attitude": "They would be the kind of kids who would say, 'Life sucks. Adults suck. The high school sucks. Everything sucks. I just want to party.' "

But George Henderson didn't seem like the other nine at all. He never cut school. He didn't drink or smoke. He was on the honor roll. He was only fourteen and, according to a neighbor, came from a family that "did everything together," from mountain climbing to canoeing. His death seemed to be the one that bothered Leominster's adults most, because George was the first one they really could not understand.

"I don't know why people are so afraid to say it," says one sopho-   55
more. "He was the first kid who they didn't think was a real loser."

But the students of Leominster High weren't puzzled by George's suicide. To his peers, he wasn't a model boy—he was a freshman brain who had failed a Spanish quiz, maybe a nice kid, but a nerd, a wimp. His peer category may have been different from that of the students who died before him—he wasn't a burnout, or a head—but in a school that perceives jocks as the in crowd and druggies as cool, George had lost both ways. Being a brain was his marker among the crowd, and faltering grades may have threatened his identity at a time when peer acceptance was acute. "I wouldn't have gotten all upset about getting a warning card or nothing," says a sophomore. "But I can kind of understand how something like that could have really depressed *him*."

"With someone like that you can understand," says a freshman. "School was wicked important and stuff to him."

According to guidance counselors at Leominster High, the deaths have sparked dialogue. They say the students are more willing to talk about their problems, are more alert and more sensitive. "It's brought us closer," says one senior. "All the hugging and crying has made us tighter." But among the students, opinion diverges: " 'How are you, are you feeling suicidal today?' " asks a junior sweetly, mocking a counselor. " 'I haven't seen you in two years and even though you're flunking all your classes you are doing just fine. Things will be just fine, now, won't they? *Won't* they?' "

Some students harbor anger. They resent the reputation their city has acquired and feel betrayed by the friends who have left them. "Suicide is the ultimate act in selfishness," says a sophomore. "Why bother crying about a selfish brat?" One counselor shares her favorite explanation: "It's the ultimate temper tantrum," she says. "Kids who can't have their lives the way they want them don't want life at all."

Outside the community, too, the response can be just as cold.   60 Leominster and nearby Fitchburg have one of the oldest high school football rivalries in the nation, and school spirit runs deep. Leominster won the game last year, but Fitchburg got its licks in. KILL LEOMINSTER, read the inscription on the Fitchburg rooters' T-shirts, BEFORE THEY KILL THEMSELVES.

The dominating ambience of bewilderment and exhaustion makes Leominster's grief difficult to detect. Many adults refuse to discuss the tragedies at all. One student wrote a letter to the editor of the local newspaper after the death of John Finn, asking the community to confront the dangers rather than run away: "I've never felt such a sense of deep loss, pain or fear as during these three years at Leominster High," the letter read. "It's sad to think that some day our children are going to ask us what high school is like. What will we say? I spent most of my high school years mourning the loss of my friends. . . . Somebody must do something. We need help."

Donald Fredd, an English teacher, was so concerned about the section he teaches on existentialism that he has recently modified the course. "Camus and Sartre[1] believe the choice to live is the most profound decision one can make, and you're telling kids that these great thinkers believed the choice must be made every day. That you must get up in the morning and decide whether you're going to go through with it or end it right then and there. That it's up to the individual *alone* to decide. In the context of these tragedies I've become slightly paranoid. How will the students take it? How seriously?

[1] Albert Camus (1913–1960), French philosopher, dramatist, and novelist, won the Nobel Prize in 1957; Jean Paul Sartre (1905–1980), the French existentialist philosopher, won the Nobel Prize for literature in 1964.

How literally? What about the real bright ones? What about the ones who are down?"

Teachers, friends, and parents have substantial cause to worry about overlooking the symptoms. The teenagers who took their lives left plenty of clues first, as 80 percent of all suicides do. But "the problem is," says Patricia Pothier, the guidance counselor, "how do you tell the difference between symptoms of suicidal feelings and the normal business of being a teenager in the eighties?" Although preventive and educational measures are being taken, few Leominster residents feel their little city has witnessed its last teenage suicide; those most actively involved in the aftermath still anticipate the next one. "I think it'll slow down," says one graduate who enrolled at the University of Massachusetts this fall. "Maybe at the rate of just one or two a year."

On the morning of a recent Samaritan assembly, a pair of sophomores held a homeroom period of their own in the woods, smoking. But then they reentered the building to hear what the Samaritans had to say. "They just said the usual stuff about suicide like they did last time," says a girl named Celeste in the corridor afterward. "It was dumb," her friend Carol adds.

It is time to go. The two girls start walking down the corridor. 65 Carol turns her head when they are halfway down the hall.

"*You* can leave this school anytime you want," she yells. Then she begins to spin. "An-y-ti-me!" she yells, her voice waving louder and softer with her turns. She spins faster, sending her pocketbook flying, then jerks to a halt. The strap wraps tightly around her thin, young waist.

❖ Focused Freewriting   Consider as possible focal points the chosen methods of suicide, the attitude of the surviving students, a personal experience related to suicide, your attitude toward the Leominster students, or one of the topics you've identified in your journal.

❖ Guided Responses

1. The scene that opens LeBlanc's article is disturbing: after witnessing a film clip depicting a teenager's suicide, students laugh, make fun of the film, or look bored. Why do you suppose the students react this way? What might be the connection between their response to the film and their personal experience? Why do you think LeBlanc opens with this scene?

2. LeBlanc pays particular attention to details of the school day (e.g., paras. 18–20) and the town of Leominster (e.g., para. 25). What

purpose do these details serve? How do the details help readers understand what motivates students to commit suicide? How do they help readers identify with the town and its inhabitants?

3. Much of the lives of Leominster teens seems to revolve around drugs and alcohol. What do you think is the relationship between substance abuse and suicide? Does the substance abuse contribute to the suicide rate, or is it more a symptom of existing problems? Explain your response.

4. Parents, counselors, teachers, and teenagers all respond to the suicides in various ways. What seems to motivate these different responses? Which response(s) do you find more understandable than the others? more appropriate? Why?

❖ Shared Responses In your journal, write a brief response to the student who said, "I mean, afta *seven* [suicides], what difference does one or two make?" (para. 51). How might you convince him that each suicide does make a difference? How would you help him think about issues beyond the individual suicides? As you discuss your responses in small groups, try to integrate individual responses into one coherent statement. If the views presented are too far apart to be synthesized, explain the differences in the responses.

❖

The New Lost Generation

DAVID LEAVITT

DAVID LEAVITT *is the author of* The Lost Language of Cranes, *a novel that was dramatized by the Public Broadcasting Service in 1992. Among his other publications are* A Place I've Never Been *(1990) and* Family Dancing *(1984); his fiction and essays have also been published in* Esquire *magazine, where this essay originally appeared in 1985. In this selection, Leavitt attempts to characterize his generation, using the term Gertrude Stein coined to refer to young expatriate artists in Paris during the 1920s. Focusing on the social revolutionaries of the 1960s and the materialists of the 1980s, Leavitt concludes that his generation has no real identity of its own.*

Before reading the selection, answer the following questions in your journal: How would you characterize the young adults of the 1980s? What kinds of values did they seem to have? Do you see the generation of the 1990s as different in any way? If so, how? What insights from other courses can help you understand this essay?

As you make notes on your reading, you may want to focus on the characteristics of the "new lost generation": its selfishness, its pessimism, its isolation, or its bitterness.

My GENERATION has always resisted definition. The younger siblings of the Sixties, we watched riots from a distance, sneaked peeks at the *Zap Comix* lying around our older siblings bedrooms, grew our hair long, and in prepubescent droves campaigned door to door for McGovern. When I was ten I played the guitar and wanted to be like Joni Mitchell. A friend of my sister's, a fellow who must have fancied himself a Bill Graham in the making, arranged for me to sing my own compositions in a series of little concerts given in the communal dining hall of Columbae House. By the time I was old enough to take part in any real way, disillusion had set in, people had given up, cocaine was the drug of choice. Tail end. We have always been the tail end—of the Sixties, of the baby boom. We hit our stride in an age of burned-out, restless, ironic disillusion. With all our much-touted

291

youthful energy boiling inside us, where were we supposed to go? What were we supposed to do?

Now the Rainbows and the Moon Units of the world (conceived at love-ins, "birthed" in birthing rooms) are hitting their teens. They are computer-literate. They own their own Apple Macintoshes. They watch MTV on VCRs. Those with an artistic inclination rent video cameras, make their own films, and proclaim that written language will soon degenerate until it serves as a vehicle for nostalgia, eclipsed by the shot—videotape and its new alphabet of images.

My generation is somewhere in between. Born too late and too early, we are partially what came before us and partially what followed. But we can make certain claims. We are the first generation, for instance, that is younger than television. We knew the Vietnam War as something about as real as the *Mannix* episodes it seemed to interrupt so often. We learned stealth by figuring out how to get around our parents' efforts to ration the number of hours we watched each day. And we are the first generation whose members usually cannot remember their first plane trip. And the first in recent history that has never seen its friends missing in action or lost in combat or living and working in Canada.

It should have been perfect, the perfect time and place. As our parents always reminded us, we had so much they had not even been able to imagine as children. So little harm came to us. And yet, on those bright afternoons of my childhood, when I sat indoors, watching sunlight reflect off the face of *Speed Racer* on the television, I was already aware that rips were being made in the fabric of perfection. When my parents shouted at each other, their voices sounded like fabric ripping. My friends sat in the cafeteria of our middle school reading brightly colored books with titles like *The Kids' Book of Divorce*. On television the Brady Bunch and the Partridge Family continued on their merry ways. Sometimes I closed my eyes and tried to will myself through the television's scrim of glass and into their world. It was, in its own way, as appealing and as inaccessible as the world of the folk dancers, of my brothers and sisters, who went to college and were free of the big house with its burden of memories. But I knew that if I broke through the television, I wouldn't instantly emerge in that magical community of Sherman Oaks, with its homecoming dances, ice-cream floats, and wise maids. Instead I'd find circuits and wires, the complicated brainworks of the famous "tube."

In the real world, real parents were splitting up, moving out, 5 questioning and in some cases rejecting the commandment to marry and have a family, commandments that had been the foundation of their parents' lives. In my family it was happening against our wishes. In a community where the divorce rate had reached a record high, and every family seemed to have at least one child in prison, or in a hospital, or dead of an overdose, my parents had never even separated. Still, there were sharp words, often, and a sense of desperate effort and hard, unrewarded labor through it all. We felt it in the politics of playing records, of who did the dishes, and who really cared around here, and who had slaved for whom for how long. Sometimes it seemed to me that we walked around the house opened up and bleeding, yet talking, laughing, smiling, like actors in a horror movie who, during a break in the shooting, simply forget to remove the prop knives from their backs or mop up the imitation blood. In this case the blood was real, though we pretended it wasn't.

I watched. During *Star Trek* my mother brought me dinner on a tray. Sometimes, after watching for hours and hours, I would have to get very close to the screen in order to focus, even though I knew it was bad for my eyes. Sometimes I'd see how close I could get, let the lenses of my eyes touch the hot lens of the television, soak in the pure light.

When my brother and sister were my age, they had already seen much more of the world than I will probably ever see. They'd gone to India, Guatemala, Cuba, Hong Kong. They'd worked in prisons, and organized striking farm workers, and driven across the country half a dozen times each. They'd read Kerouac, Castaneda, *Zen and the Art of Motorcycle Maintenance.* And when, as a child, I'd ask them about their lives, they'd tell me about the movement. Movement. It seemed an appropriate word, since they moved all the time, driven by exploratory wanderlust into the vast American wilderness. I possess no similar desire whatsoever, and neither, I think, do most members of my generation. Rather than move, we burrow. We are interested in stability, neatness, entrenchment. We want to stay in one place and stay in one piece, establish careers, establish credit. We want good apartments, fulfilling jobs, nice boy/girl friends. We want American Express Gold Cards. Whereas my brother and sister, at the same age, if asked, would probably have said that their goals were to expand their minds, see the world, and encourage revolutionary change.

I've never thought of myself as naive; I've never imagined that I might lead a sheltered life. I am, after all, "sophisticated," have been to Europe, understand dirty jokes and the intricacies of sexually transmitted diseases. This is my milieu, the world I live in, and I have almost never stepped beyond its comfortable borders. A safety net surrounds my sophisticated life, and the question is, of course, how did it get there? Did I build it myself? Was it left for me? Sometimes I feel as if I live in a room with mirrored walls, imagining that the tiny space I occupy is in fact endless, and constitutes a real world. I remember when I first moved to New York, and I was looking for work, I dropped my résumé off with the manager of the Oscar Wilde Memorial Bookshop—a political gay book store—and he asked me to tell him about my "movement experience." For a few seconds I blanked out. I thought he was talking about a dance.

Last year I went with three friends to see the film *Liquid Sky*, which was enjoying a cult following in lower Manhattan. The film portrays a culture of young people who live in lower Manhattan, dress in outlandish costumes, and spend most of their nights in wildly decorated clubs—a culture of young people very much like the young people in the theater that night watching the film. Margaret, the heroine, explains that she has moved beyond the suburban dream of having a husband, and also moved beyond the middle-urban dream of having an agent (and hence a career), and has now recognized the pointlessness of striving for anything. Her new dream lover is an alien creature that thrives on the chemicals released in the brain during orgasm and that will ultimately devour Margaret in the course of a final, quite literally cosmic climax. Perhaps the moment in the film that stuck most to my ribs is the one in which Margaret's ex-lover and exacting teacher, a man in his late forties, accuses her of dressing like a whore. She retaliates with a childish sneer that his jeans (throwbacks to his own heyday) are just as much a costume as her push-up bras and red leather skirts. Of her peers, she says something like, "At least we don't pretend we aren't wearing costumes."

At least we don't pretend we aren't wearing costumes? Well, yes, I   10
guess they don't, I thought. For Margaret, to pretend one isn't wearing a costume is contemptible. She rejects the idea that the way one dresses might represent a claim made about the world today, or project an idea for the world tomorrow. Hell, there probably won't be a world tomorrow. Clothes have to do with what we aren't, not what we are. Screw art, let's dance.

And yet Margaret lets something slip when she makes this claim. She implicates herself by referring to her friends, her cronies, as "we." The "we" in *Liquid Sky* is disloyal, backstabbing, bitchy, and violent. But it is still a "we"; it is a group, defined by its belief in its own newness, its own green youthfulness; it is a generation. In performance spaces, bars that double as art galleries, clubs with names like 8B.C. or Save the Robots, on the darkest and most dangerous streets of New York, a culture is being born out of the claim that there is no culture—that it's all mere dress-up, mere fakery, mere whooping-it-up-before-the-plague. This culture is downtown. It basks in the limelight of the present moment. It avoids tall buildings. Poverty is its kin, its company, and sometimes its reality, but it draws the curious rich like flies. Then real estate possibilities emerge out of nowhere: tenements turn into town houses, yet another chic colorful neighborhood for the new rich emerges. Sometimes I wonder whether my generation's lunatic fringe of trendsetters keep moving into more and more dangerous parts because the gentrified keep pushing them out of the neighborhoods they've pioneered, or because they're attracted to the hopeless edge of the city, where the future means finding food and drugs to get you through tomorrow. That is about as far as you can get from long-term investments. And the irony is, of course, that where they have gone, the rich young future-mongers of the generation ahead have followed, attracted by the scent of potential development. Farther east, and farther down, their worlds keep moving. It is sometimes decadent, destructive, dangerous. It is sometimes gloriously, extraordinarily fun.

I've seen that world. Good yuppie that I am, I've even dipped my toe in its freezing waters on select Saturday nights and Sunday mornings when an urge to dance came over me like an itch. When I was an undergraduate I was friends with a couple of women who became lovers and took to walking around the campus with dog collars around their necks connected by a link chain. And I remember going with them once to have tea at the home of one of their mothers—a big brownstone in the East Sixties, on the same block where Nixon used to live. They marched defiantly through the foyer, their very entrance a calculated affront, me following meekly, while the mother strove not to notice the white-blond tint of her daughter's hair, or the double nose ring (she had pierced the nostril herself in the bathroom), and offered to take my jacket. "So how is school going, honey?" the mother said. In the course of tea she made a valiant effort to call her daughter "Max," as Max currently insisted. (Her real name was Elizabeth.) And a year later, in New York, I walked home from a party one night with an NYU student and her friend, a boy dressed like Boy George—eyeliner, dreadlocks, lipstick. And they were going to steal the boy's sister's food stamps so they could get something to eat. They said this matter-of-factly. And when I expressed amazement that the girl's affluent parents didn't send her enough money to buy food, she said equally matter-of-factly, "Oh, they send me plenty of money, but I use it all up on booze and drugs." Without a trace of self-consciousness she said it; but with more than a trace of self-pity.

It was Saturday night and we were going to a party. It was always Saturday night and we were always going to a party. Someone was stoned. Someone was drunk, lying snoring on the big sofa in the library. Someone was wearing Salada tea-bag fortunes as earrings. In their rooms, the boys were experimenting with eye makeup. In their rooms, the girls were experimenting with mushrooms. It was Saturday night and we were going to a dress party (everyone had to wear a dress), to a gender-transcendence party, to a party supporting the women's center, supporting the Marxist Literary Group, supporting the Coalition Against Apartheid. My friends were not active in these organizations; we expressed our support by giving the parties. For days beforehand we'd trade twelve-inch singles, mix them on our stereos, compete to produce the greatest dance tape ever, the one that would bring the dancers to the floor in an orgiastic heap.

The favorite songs that year, I think, were "Dancing With Myself," by Billy Idol, and "I Wanna Be Sedated," by the Ramones. But "Rock Lobster" seemed to turn up on every tape, as did "We Got the Beat" and "I Love a Man in a Uniform."

A photographer friend of mine used to come to all the parties that year, throw her camera out into the pulsating dark as arbitrarily as Richard Misrach, who was known for blindly aiming his camera out into the dark Hawaiian jungle. It became a kind of joke, Jennie's presence at every party. You could count on seeing yourself a few days later, stoned or drunk or vomiting, or making out with someone you didn't recognize on a sofa you couldn't remember. In the photographs bodies were frozen in the midst of flight, heads shook in beady haloes of light and sweat, clothes flew and were suspended, forever revealing small patches of white skin. There was a quality of ecstasy. But when I see those pictures these days, I think *I was mad.*

I don't remember ever feeling as much joy as I did that year, when, on any Saturday night, on a crowded dance floor I'd hear my favorite song begin. It was as if my body itself had become an instrument, pulled and plucked and wrenched by the music, thrown beyond itself. This was no love-in of the Sixties, no drug-hazed ritual of communion. We were dancing with ourselves. Someone joked that each of us could have had on his own individual Walkman.

The mornings after such evenings always began around two in the afternoon. Exhausted and hung over, we would go back to the big rooms where the parties had taken place to confront the hundreds of empty beer cans and cigarette stubs, the little clots of lost sweaters stuffed into corners, forgotten, never to be retrieved. Sunlight streamed in. While the guests slept in late, and Jennie toiled in her darkroom, frenzied with creation, the partygivers took out their mops.

Like our older brothers and sisters, my generation belongs to gyms. We find Nautilus equipment consoling. Nothing gets in your way when you're bench pressing, or swimming, or running, not even the interfering subconscious that tended to muck up all those Seventies efforts at psychological self-improvement. Muscles appear as a manifestation of pure will.

In contrast to our older brothers and sisters, however, the fact that we believe in health does not necessarily mean that we believe in the future. The same bright young person who strives for physical immortality also takes for granted the imminence of his destruction. At Brown University, students voted last October on a referendum to stock poison tablets in the school infirmary, so that in the event of a nuclear catastrophe, they could commit suicide rather than die of fallout. As if nuclear disaster, rather than being a distant threat, were a harsh reality, an immediacy, something to prepare for. I am reminded of Grace Paley's description of an eighteen-year old in her story "Friends." "His friends have a book that says a person should, if properly nutritioned, live forever . . . He also believes that the human race, its brains and good looks, will end in his time."

Brains and good looks. Last year I went dancing at Area for the   20
first time, arguably the choicest dance club in New York. (A friend of mine who is more of an expert than I in these matters insists that the club called Save the Robots is choicer, since it is frequented by the people who work at the Area and does not open until after Area has closed.) At this point Area was dressed in its nuclear holocaust garb. On our way in, we passed tableaux vivants of people in Karen Silkwood suits, peeling lurid green candy off sheets on a conveyor belt. Women danced inside fantastic, menacing pseudo-reactors. Signs reading DANGER-RADIOACTIVE MATERIAL glowed above the dance floor. Later, at the bar, I was introduced to an artist who had been asked to create a work of art in support of the nuclear freeze, and was thinking of carving a mushroom cloud out of a block of ice. It was hard for me to keep from wondering about the famed holocaust anxiety of my postnuclear generation. The world after the bomb, it seemed to me, had become a cliché, incorporated into our dialogue and our culture with an alarming thoughtlessness. Do most of us dream, like Eddie Albert as the President in the movie *Dreamscape,* of a parched postholocaust landscape, peopled by weird half-human monsters and scared children wailing, "It hurts! It hurts!" I doubt it. I think we purport to worry about the world ending much more than we actually do.

Because the terror of knowing the world could end at any moment haunts them so vividly, older people seem to believe that it must be ten times worse for the young. The realization that nuclear disaster is not only possible, but possibly imminent, writes the noted essayist Lewis Thomas, "is bad enough for the people in my generation. We can put up with it, I suppose, since we must. We are moving along anyway . . . What I cannot imagine, what I cannot put up with . . . is what it would be like to be young. How do the young stand it? How can they keep their sanity?"

Well, I want to say, we do. Indeed, I think we are more sane and less hysterical about the issue of nuclear holocaust than are the generations ahead of us. We do not go crazy, because for us the thought of a world with no future—so terrifying to Dr. Thomas—is completely familiar; is taken for granted; is nothing new.

I have tried time and again to explain this to people who are older than I. I tell them that no matter how hard I try—and I have closed my eyes tightly, concentrated, tried to will my mind to do it—I simply cannot muster an image of myself fifty, or twenty, or even ten years in the future. I go blank. I have no idea where or what or even if I'll be. Whereas my parents, when they were young, assumed vast and lengthy futures for themselves, a series of houses, each larger than the one before, and finally the "golden years" of retirement, knitting by fires, bungalows in Florida. I think we have inserted into our minds the commercialized image of the mushroom cloud and the world in flames in order to justify a blind spot in us—an inability to think beyond the moment, or conceive of any future at all, which makes us immune to the true horror felt by older people. This blind spot has more to do with our attitude toward the nuclear family than with nuclear disaster—with the fact that our parents, as they now reach the golden years they once looked forward to, are finding themselves trapped in unhappy marriages or divorced, are too bitter to ever consider loving again, or are desperate to find a new mate with whom they can share those last happy years that they were promised, that they worked so hard for, that they were so unfairly cheated out of.

And we—well, we aren't going to make the same mistakes they did. Alone at least, we're safe—from pain, from dependency, from sexually transmitted disease. Those who belong to no one but themselves can never be abandoned.

It is 1983. I have just graduated from college and, like most of my friends, lead the sort of life that makes a good biographical note in the back of a literary magazine—"living and working in Manhattan." Most mornings, I have to get up at 7:30 A.M.—unnaturally early for someone like me, who finds it hard to fall asleep before 3:00. I don't eat breakfast, I shower in three minutes, timed. From inside my apartment, where it is warm, I head out into the cold, begin the long trek to the subway. My station is famous for its poor design. If I have a token, I must run down one staircase and up another to get to the train. Sometimes the train doors close on my nose. Other times I'm lucky. I squeeze in, find a space to stand. The train begins to move,

25

and there are newspapers in my eyes, painted fingernails, noses, the smell of toothpaste and coffee everywhere around me. People are nodding, falling asleep on their feet. For six months now, this subway ride in the morning and afternoon has been the closest I have come physically to another human being.

I arrive at my office. For the length of the morning, I work, taking frequent breaks. I visit the cookie lady in publicity. I visit the water cooler. I gossip with friends on the phone, thinking about lunch.

I used to think there was something gloriously romantic about the nine-to-five life. I used to imagine there could be no greater thrill than being part of the crush riding the escalator down from the Pan Am building into Grand Central at 5:00. The big station ceiling, with its map of stars, would unfold above you, the escalator would slip down under your feet—you, so small, so anonymous in all that hugeness and strangeness. Yet you'd know you were different. Light on your feet at rush hour, you'd dodge and cut through the throng, find your way fast to the shuttle. Like the north-or-south-going Zax in Doctor Seuss, you'd have one direction, and no choice but to move in it.

Ha, as the old woman who has worked forty years in accounting says to everyone. *Ha-ha.*

It's 5:30. Outside the sun has set. Inside other people are still typing, still frenzied. Everyone works harder than you, no matter how hard you work. Everyone makes more than you do, no matter how much you make. You slip out silently, guilty to be leaving only a half hour late, wondering why you're not as ambitious as they are, why you don't have it in you to make it.

But when you get outside, the wind is cold on your face, the streets are full of people herding toward the subway. You put on your Walkman. You think that tonight you might like to go dancing. Then the Pointer Sisters come on, and you realize that, like John Travolta tripping down the streets of Brooklyn in *Saturday Night Fever,* you already are.

30

A few years after I stopped going, the Saturday night folk dancing ritual at Stanford ceased. Lack of interest, I suppose. The women wrapped in gypsy fabric and the boys with dirty feet were getting cleaned up and prepping for their GMATs. Today they are baby-boomers. They are responsible, says a *People* magazine ad, for "the surge in microchips, chocolate chips, and a host of special services to help Boomers run their two-career households." They work, live, love in offices. They have "drive."

My generation, in the meantime, still trots outside their circle, eager to learn the steps. In every outward way we are perfect emulators. We go to work in corporations right out of college. We look good in suits. But we also have haircuts that are as acceptable at East Village early-hours clubs as they are at Morgan Stanley. And (of course) at least we don't pretend we're not wearing costumes.

There are advantages to growing up, as we did, on the cusp of two violently dislocated ages; advantages to becoming conscious just as one decade is burning out, and another is rising, phoenixlike, from the ashes of its dissolution—or disillusion. If the Sixties was an age of naive hope, then the Eighties is an age of ironic hopelessness—its perfect counterpart, its skeptical progeny. We are the children of that skepticism. We go through all the motions. But if we tried then to learn the steps from our brothers and sisters because we believed in what they were doing, we follow in their footsteps now for almost the opposite reason—to prove that we can sell out just as well as they can, and know it too.

I remember, as a child, listening to my mother talk about fashions. "Once you've seen stiletto heels come and go three times, you'll realize how little any of it means," she said. I don't think I knew yet what a stiletto heel was, but I understood already and perfectly how little any of it meant. It came to me very early, that ironic and distanced view on things, and it's stayed.

The voice of my generation is the voice of David Letterman, 35 whose late-night humor—upbeat, deadpan, more than a little contemptuous—we imitate because, above all else, we are determined to make sure everyone knows that what we say might not be what we mean. Consider these words from Brett Duval Fromson, in an op-ed piece for *The New York Times:* "Yuppies, if we do anything at all, respect those who deliver the goods. How else are we going to afford our Ferragamo pumps, Brooks Brothers suits, country houses, European cars, and California chardonnays?" The balance of the irony is perfect—between self-mockery and straight-faced seriousness, between criticism and comfy self-approval. "If we do anything at all," Fromson writes, leaving open the possibility that we don't. Certainly, he acknowledges, during the recession we "didn't give much thought to those who wouldn't make it." And now I am thinking about a headline I read recently in *The Village Voice,* above one of a series of articles analyzing Reagan's victory last November. It read DON'T TRUST ANYONE UNDER THIRTY.

Mine is a generation perfectly willing to admit its contemptible qualities. But our self-contempt is self-congratulatory. The buzz in the background, every minute of our lives, is that detached, ironic voice telling us: At least you're not faking it, as they did, at least you're not pretending as they did. It's okay to be selfish as long as you're upfront about it. Go ahead. "Exercise your right to exercise." Other people are dying to defend other people's right to speak, to vote, and to live, but at least you don't pretend you're not wearing a costume.

What is behind this bitterness, this skepticism? A need, I think, for settledness, for security, for home. Our parents imagined they could satisfy this urge by marrying and raising children; our older brothers and sisters through community and revolution. We have seen how far those alternatives go. We trust ourselves, and money. Period.

Fifteen years ago you weren't supposed to trust anyone over thirty. For people in my generation, the goal seems to be to get to thirty as fast as possible, and stay there. Starting out, we are eager, above all else, to be finished. If we truly are a generation without character, as is claimed, it is because we have seen what has happened to generations with character. If we are without passion or affect, it is because we have decided that passion and affect are simply not worth the trouble. If we stand crouched in the shadows of a history in which we refuse to take part, it is because that's exactly where we've chosen to stand.

Characterlessness takes work. It is defiance and defense all at once.

During my freshman year in college I remember going to see Mary   40
Tyler Moore as a woman paralyzed from the neck down in *Whose Life Is It Anyway?* At intermission I ran into a friend from school who was practically in tears. "You don't know what it's like for me to see her like that," he said. "Mary's a metaphor for my youth. And looking at her on that stage, well, I can't help but feel that it's my youth lying paralyzed up there." Later, a woman I know told me in all earnestness, "When I'm in a difficult situation, a real bind, I honestly think to myself, 'What would Mary have done?'I really do." I know people who significantly altered the shape of their lives so that they could stay up every weeknight for a 2:30 to 4:00 A.M. Mary tripleheader on Channel 4 in New York. Even John Sex, the East Village's reigning club maven, is famous for his early-morning rendition, at the Pyramid club, of the Mary theme.

Remember those words? "Who can take the world on with her smile? Who can take a nothing day and suddenly make it all seem worthwhile?" And of course, at the end of the opening credits, there is the famous epiphany, the throw of the hat. "You're gonna make it after all," sings Sonny Curtis, who faded quickly into obscurity, but whose dulcet voice will live forever in reruns, and in our hearts. She throws the red cap into the air; the frame freezes, leaving Mary's hat perpetually aloft, and Mary perpetually in the bloom of youthful anticipation. The great irony of that shot, underscoring the show's tender, melancholy tone, is that as the seasons wore on, and new images of a shorter-haired Mary were spliced into the opening credit sequence, it always remained the same. So that even in the last, saddest season with Mary pushing forty and wanting a raise and still not married, we are still given a glimpse of Mary as she used to be, young Mary, full of youthful exuberance, and that image of Mary and her hat and her hope gently plays against the truth of what her life has given her. The fact is that Mary's life stinks. She is underpaid in a second-rate job at a third-rate television station. Her best friends, Rhoda and Phyllis, have both left her to fail in spin-offs in other cities, and she doesn't even have a boyfriend. That's Mary's life, and even the clever tactic of changing the last line of the theme song from "You're gonna make it after all" to "Look's like you've made it after all" fails to convince us that it's anything but rotten.

But Mary presses on, and the great epic film, which all episodes of the Mary show comprise, ends as it began—with Mary not getting married. The camaraderie of the newsroom has provided her less with a bond of strength than with a buffer against sorrow. Mary and her friends share one another's loneliness, but they don't cure it. The station closes down, the lights go out, and still young Mary throws her hat.

I see Marys often these days; the other day I saw one going into a deli on Third Avenue in the Eighties, just after work. She's younger, a bit fatter, better paid, so she wears silk blouses with ruffles and bows. And because she lives in New York, she's a bit more desperate, the pain is a little closer to the surface. It's 9:00, and she's just gotten off from work. She buys herself dinner—chicken hot dogs, Diet Coke, Haagen-Dazs,—and heads home to the tiny apartment, with a bathtub in the kitchen, for which she pays far too much. And I can't help but think that, even as a child, when the going-ons in that Minneapolis newsroom were the high point of her week, she knew she was going to end up here. Remember the episodes where Mary and Lou quit in order to protest how little money they make? Mary is forced to borrow from Ted. Nothing upsets her more than the realization that, for the first time in her life, she's in debt. She never asked for more than a room to live in, after all, and someplace to go each day, and perhaps a little extra money for a new dress now and then.

Here in New York, all the prime-time shows of my childhood have found their way, like memories or dreams, to the darkest part of the night. First there's *Star Trek* and the familiar faces of the *Enterprise* crew. Tonight they are confronted with an android that has become human because it has felt the first pangs of love. Once again, no woman can win Kirk, because he's already married to the most beautiful woman of them all—his ship. At 1:00 *The Twilight Zone* comes on, another lost astronaut wanders a blank landscape, the world before or after man. At 1:30, only an hour before Mary begins, I watch the *Independent News*. I am, by this time, on the floor, and close to sleep. The newscaster's voice clucks amicably, telling us that Mary Tyler Moore has checked herself into the Betty Ford Center. She has bravely admitted to having a problem, and she is battling it.

I leap up. I stare at the screen. The image has already passed, the   45
newscaster moved on to another story. And I think, how sad that Mary's life has come to this. And yet, how good that she is bravely admitting to having a problem, and battling it. And I wonder if Mary Tyler Moore sat and looked at herself in the mirror before she made the decision; sat and looked at herself in the mirror and asked herself, "What would Mary do?"

Mary would do the right thing. And that is a comfort to me, this dark night, as I drag myself from the living room floor and click the television into silence. We have learned a few things from Mary. We have learned, on a day-to-day basis, how to do the right thing. We have learned to be kind and patient with one another, to give comfort. We have learned how to be good and generous friends.

It is late. The apartment is close and quiet. Tonight I am alone, but this weekend I will be with my friends. Like the folks in Mary's newsroom or the crew of the *Enterprise* bridge, we are a gang. We go dancing, and afterward, to an all-night deli for babkas and French toast, our clothes permeated with the smell of cigarettes. We walk five abreast, arm-in-arm, so that other people must veer into the street to avoid hitting us. When we decide the time has come to head back uptown, we pile into a cab, sometimes five or six of us, and sit on each other's laps and legs, and feel happy that we have friends, because it means we can take cabs for less than the price of the subway. It is nearly dawn, and a few sour-looking prostitutes are still marching the sidewalks of the West Side Highway in the cold. In a moment when we're not looking a sun will appear, small and new and fiery, as if someone had thrown it into the air.

❖ Focused Freewriting   Consider as possible focal points the influence on young people of television and movies, the idea of wearing costumes, a disillusioning experience you have had, your attitude toward this generation, or one of the topics you've identified in your journal.

❖ Guided Responses

1. Threaded throughout the essay is an extended analysis of *The Mary Tyler Moore Show*, presented in part to explain the loneliness, the

despair, of Leavitt's generation. Based on your knowledge of this program, how accurate do you find his analysis? Do you agree or disagree with his assessment of Mary's life? Explain. What other interpretations of the show are possible?

2. In paragraphs 12 and 13 Leavitt describes the particular decadence of his youth, mentioning his lesbian-lover friends, the wealthy young woman stealing food stamps, and the bizarre parties on Saturday nights. Each of these images suggests rebellion. How does this rebellion differ from that of the youth of the 1960s? From your own generation? Against what is each group rebelling?

3. In paragraph 37 Leavitt comments that his parents sought security by raising families, while his older siblings sought it "through community and revolution." Members of his generation, on the other hand, put their trust in "ourselves, and money. Period." Based on what Leavitt tells readers in the rest of the essay, how do you account for his generation's lack of faith in family or community? Do you think he's right? Why, or why not?

4. According to Leavitt, one of the primary reasons members of his generation are so disillusioned is that they have lived under the specter of nuclear annihilation all their lives. Considering the portrait he paints of himself and his peers, does this explanation seem adequate? Why, or why not? What other reasons might you offer for his generation's "lost" status?

❖ Shared Responses   In your journal write a brief analysis of a television series that seems to epitomize your generation. How do the characters represent your concerns? What issues relevant to your lives does the series raise? As you discuss your responses in small groups, compare and contrast the different shows members of the group chose, focusing on the similarities and differences in their analyses.

A Moving Day

SUSAN NUNES

Susan Nunes *is the author of a collection of short fiction,* A Small Obligation and Other Stories of Hilo, *and several children's books, including* Coyote Dreams *and the forthcoming* The Last Dragon. *Born in Hawaii to a Japanese mother and Portuguese father, she moved recently to Berkeley, where she is working on her first full-length novel. In this story, originally published in* Home to Stay: Asian American Women's Fiction *(1990), edited by Sylvia Watanabe and Carol Bruchac, Nunes intersperses childhood memories with commentary on the internment of Japanese Americans during World War II and observations on the importance of tangible objects. A sense of loss hovers over the story as the narrator explores the ways in which different family members recall and relinquish the past.*

Before reading the selection, write in your journal about a home in which you spent much of your childhood. What images present themselves? How do different members of the family recall the home? What artifacts (furniture, books, knickknacks) evoke what kind of memories?

As you make notes on your reading, you may want to focus on the contrasts in the story: between parents and children, between American and Japanese culture, between the mother's and the father's reactions to the move.

Across the street, the bulldozer roars to life. Distracted, my mother looks up from the pile of linen that she has been sorting. She is seventy, tiny and fragile, the flesh burned off her shrinking frame. Her hair is grey now—she has never dyed it—and she wears it cut no-nonsense short with the nape shaved. She still has a beautiful neck, in another life, perfect for kimono. She has taken a liking to jeans, cotton smocks, baggy sweaters, and running shoes. When I was a child she wouldn't leave the house without nylons.

Her hands, large-jointed with arthritis, return with a vengeance to the pile of linen. I have always been wary of her energy. Now she is making two stacks, the larger one for us, the smaller for her to keep. There is a finality in the way she places things in the larger pile, as if to say that's it. For her, it's all over, all over but this last accounting. She does not look forward to what is coming. Strangers. Schedules. The regulated activities of those considered too old to regulate themselves. But at least, at the *very* least, she'll not be a burden. She sorts through the possessions of a lifetime, she and her three daughters. It's time she passed most of this on. Dreams are lumber. She can't *wait* to be rid of them.

My two sisters and I present a contrast. There is nothing purposeful or systematic about the way we move. In fact, we don't know where we're going. We know there is a message in all this activity, but we don't know what it is. Still, we search for it in the odd carton, between layers of tissue paper and silk. We open drawers, peer into the recess of cupboards, rummage through the depths of closets. We lift, untuck, unwrap, and set aside. The message is there, we know. But what is it? Perhaps if we knew, then we wouldn't have to puzzle out our mother's righteous determination to shed the past.

There is a photograph of my mother taken on the porch of my grandparents' house when she was in her twenties. She is wearing a floral print dress with a square, lace-edged collar and a graceful skirt that shows off her slim body. Her shoulder length hair has been permed. It is dark and thick and worn parted on the side to fall over her right cheek. She is very fair; "one pound powder," her friends called her. She is smiling almost reluctantly, as if she meant to appear serious but the photographer has said something amusing. One arm rests lightly on the railing, the other, which is at her side, holds a handkerchief. They were her special pleasure, handkerchiefs of hand-embroidered linen as fine as ricepaper. Most were gifts (she used to say that when she was a girl, people gave one another little things—a handkerchief, a pincushion, pencils, hair ribbons), and she washed and starched them by hand, ironed them, taking care with the rolled hems, and stored them in a silk bag from Japan.

There is something expectant in her stance, is if she were wait-   5
ing for something to happen. She says, your father took this photograph in 1940, before we were married. She lowers her voice confidentially and adds, now he cannot remember taking it. My father sits on the balcony, an open book on his lap, peacefully smoking his pipe. The bulldozer tears into the foundations of the Kitamura house.

What about this? My youngest sister has found a fishing boat carved of tortoise shell.

Hold it in your hand and look at it. Every plank on the hull is visible. Run your fingers along the sides, you can feel the joints. The two masts, about six inches high, are from the darkest part of the shell. I broke one of the sails many years ago. The remaining one is quite remarkable, so thin that the light comes through it in places. It is ribbed to give the effect of cloth pushed gently by the wind.

My mother reaches for a sheet of tissue paper and takes the boat from my sister. She says, it was a gift from Mr. Oizumi. He bought it from an artisan in Kamakura.

Stories cling to the thing, haunt it like unrestful spirits. They are part of the object. They have been there since we were children. In 1932, Mr. Oizumi visits Japan. He crosses the Pacific by steamer, and when he arrives he is hosted by relatives eager to hear of his good fortune. But Mr. Oizumi soon tires of their questions. He wants to see what has become of the country. It will be arranged, he is told. Mr. Oizumi is a meticulous man. Maps are his passion. A trail of neat X's marks the steps of his journey. On his map of China, he notes each military outpost in Manchuria and appends a brief description of what he sees. Notes invade the margins, march over the blank spaces. The characters are written in a beautiful hand, precise, disciplined, orderly. Eventually, their trail leads to the back of the map. After Pearl Harbor, however, Mr. Oizumi is forced to burn his entire collection. The U.S. Army has decreed that enemy aliens caught with seditious material will be arrested. He does it secretly in the shed behind his home, his wife standing guard. They scatter the ashes in the garden among the pumpkin vines.

My grandfather's library does not escape the flames either. After the Army requisitions the Japanese school for wartime headquarters, they give my mother's parents twenty-four hours to vacate the premises, including the boarding house where they lived with about twenty students from the plantation camps outside Hilo. There is no time to save the books. Her father decides to nail wooden planks over the shelves that line the classrooms. After the Army moves in, they rip open the planks, confiscate the books, and store them in the basement of the post office. Later, the authorities burn everything. Histories, children's stories, primers, biographies, language texts, everything, even a set of Encyclopaedia Brittanica. My grandfather is shipped to Oahu and imprisoned on Sand Island. A few months later, he is released after three prominent Caucasians vouch for his character. It is a humiliation he doesn't speak of, ever.

All of this was part of the boat. After I broke the sail, she gathered the pieces and said, I'm not sure we can fix this. It was not a toy. Why can't you leave my things alone?

For years the broken boat sat on our bookshelf, a reminder of the brutality of the next generation.

Now she wants to give everything away. We have to beg her to keep things. Dishes form Japan, lacquerware, photographs, embroidery, letters. She says, I have no room. You take them, here, *take* them. Take them or I'll get rid of them.

They're piled around her, they fill storage chests, they fall out of open drawers and cupboards. She wants only to keep a few things—her books, some photographs, three carved wooden figures from Korea that belonged to her father, a few of her mother's dishes, perhaps one futon.

My sister holds a porcelain teapot by its bamboo handle. Four   15
white cranes edged in black and gold fly around it. She asks, Mama, can't you hang on to this? If you keep it, I can borrow it later.

My mother shakes her head. She is adamant. And what would I do with it? I don't want any of this. Really.

My sister turns to me. She sighs. The situation is hopeless. You take it, she says. It'll only get broken at my place. The kids.

It had begun slowly, this shedding of the past, a plate here, a dish there, a handkerchief, a doily, a teacup, a few photographs, one of Grandfather's block prints. Nothing big. But then the odd gesture became a pattern; it got so we never left the house empty-handed. At first we were amused. After all, when we were children she had to fend us off her things. Threaten. We were always *at* them. She had made each one so ripe with memories that we found them impossible to resist. We snuck them outside, showed them to our friends, told and retold the stories. They bear the scars of all this handling, even her most personal possessions. A chip here, a crack there. Casualties. Like the music box her brother brought home from Italy after the war. It played a Brahms lullaby. First we broke the spring, then we lost the winding key, and for years it sat mutely on her dresser.

She would say again and again, it's impossible to keep anything nice with you children. And we'd retreat, wounded, for a while. The problem with children is they can wipe out your history. It's a miracle that anything survives this onslaught.

There's a photograph of my mother standing on the pier in Honolulu   20
in 1932, the year she left Hawaii to attend the University of California. She's loaded to the ears with leis. She's wearing a fedora pulled

smartly to the side. She's not smiling. Of my mother's two years there, my grandmother recalled that she received good grades and never wore kimono again. My second cousin, with whom my mother stayed when she first arrived, said she was surprisingly sophisticated—she liked hats. My mother said that she was homesick. Her favorite class was biology and she entertained thoughts of becoming a scientist. Her father, however, wanted her to become a teacher, and his wishes prevailed, even though he would not have forced them upon her. She was a dutiful daughter.

During her second year, she lived near campus with a mathematics professor and his wife. In exchange for room and board she cleaned house, ironed, and helped prepare meals. One of the things that survives from this period is a black composition book entitled, *Recipes of California.* As a child, I read it like a book of mysteries for clues to a life both alien and familiar. Some entries she had copied by hand; others she cut out of magazines and pasted on the page, sometimes with a picture or drawing. The margins contained her cryptic comments: "Saturday bridge club," "From Mary G. Do not give away," underlined, "chopped suet by hand, wretched task, bed at 2 a.m., exhausted." I remember looking up "artichoke" in the dictionary and asking Mr. Okinaga, the vegetable vendor, if he had any edible thistles. I never ate one until I was twenty.

That book holds part of the answer to why our family rituals didn't fit the norm of either our relatives or the larger community in which we grew up. At home, we ate in fear of the glass of spilled milk, the stray elbow on the table, the boarding house reach. At my grandparents', we slurped our chasuke. We wore tailored dresses, white cotton pinafores, and Buster Brown shoes with white socks; however, what we longed for were the lacy dresses in the National Dollar Store that the Puerto Rican girls wore to church on Sunday. For six years, I marched to Japanese language school after my regular classes; however, we only spoke English at home. We talked too loudly and all at once, which mortified my mother, but she was always complaining about Japanese indirectness. I know that she smarted under a system in which the older son is the center of the familial universe, but at thirteen I had a fit of jealous rage over her fawning attention to our only male cousin.

My sister has found a photograph of my mother, a round faced and serious twelve or thirteen, dressed in kimono and seated, on her knees, on the tatami floor. She is playing the koto. According to my mother, girls were expected to learn this difficult stringed instrument because it was thought to teach discipline. Of course, everything Japanese was a lesson in discipline—flower arranging, calligraphy, judo, brush painting, embroidery, everything. One summer my sister and I had to take ikebana, the art of flower arrangement, at Grandfather's school. The course was taught by Mrs. Oshima, a diminutive, softspoken, terrifying woman, and my supplies were provided by my grandmother, whose tastes ran to the oversized. I remember little of that class and its principles. What I remember most clearly is having to walk home carrying one of our creations, which, more often than not, towered above our heads.

How do we choose among what we experience, what we are taught, what we run into by chance, or what is forced upon us? What is the principle of selection? My sisters and I are not bound by any of our mother's obligations, nor do we follow the rituals that seemed so important. My sister once asked, do you realize that when she's gone that's *it?* She was talking about how to make sushi, but it was a profound question nonetheless.

I remember, after we moved to Honolulu and my mother stopped   25
teaching and began working long hours in administration, she was less vigilant about the many little things that once consumed her attention. While we didn't slide into savagery, we economized in more ways than one. She would often say, there's simply no time anymore to do things right.

I didn't understand then why she looked so sad, but somehow I knew the comment applied to us.

So how do I put her wish, whatever it was, into perspective? It is hidden in layers of silk, sheathed in the folds of an old kimono that no one knows how to wear any more. I don't understand why we carry out this fruitless search. Whatever it is we are looking for, we're not going to find it. My sister tries to lift a box filled with record albums, old seventy-eights, gives up, and sets it down again. My mother says, there are people who collect these things. Imagine.

Right, just imagine.

I think about my mother bathing me and singing, "The snow is snowing, the wind is blowing, but I will weather the storm." And I think of her story of a country boy carried by the Tengu on a fantastic flight over the cities of Japan, but who chooses in the end to return to the unchanging world of his village. So much for questions which have no answers, why we look among objects for meanings which have somehow escaped us in the growing up and growing old.

However, my mother is a determined woman. She will take noth-   30
ing with her if she can help it. It is all ours. And on the balcony my father knocks the ashes of his pipe into a porcelain ashtray, and the bulldozer is finally silent.

❖ Focused Freewriting Consider as possible focal points the influence of parents on their children's choices, the idea of assimilation into the dominant culture, a personal experience with leaving a home behind, or one of the topics you've identified in your journal.

❖ Guided Responses

1. When the narrator looks at the miniature boat (para. 6), a flood of memories washes over her. Not all of the stories she recalls are related specifically to the boat, and yet she says, "All of this was a part of the boat" (para. 11). What is it about the boat that causes her to recall all of the stories? How does the condition of the boat reflect her point?

2. In paragraphs 4 and 5 the narrator describes a photograph of her mother taken in 1940, and in paragraph 20 she describes one taken in 1932. What kind of memories do these two photos evoke? How is the memory of each different? Why does the narrator spend so much time describing the photos?

3. Permeating the entire story is the humiliation of Japanese Americans at the hands of the United States government during World War II. Why does the task of moving call up these memories? How do the young people, represented by the narrator and her sister, respond to stories of internment? How do those who endured the relocation camps deal with the memories?

4. According to the narrator, "The problem with children is they can wipe out your history" (para. 19). This pronouncement is at odds with traditionally romanticized views of children, and yet there is conviction in the narrator's voice. How does the story support her view? What forces other than children conspire to "wipe out your history"? Based on the story, do you think that any of these forces prevail? Explain your answer.

❖ Shared Responses In your journal write about ethnic, cultural, or religious traditions that you have carried on, as well as one or two that have died out. Why do you think some traditions survive while others do not? Do you think individuals exercise much choice over continuing traditions, or do other forces dictate what survives? Explain your responses. As you discuss your responses in small groups, try to formulate some general statements about the importance of traditions.

Thirty-ninth Anniversary

CATHY STERN

CATHY STERN *earned an M.A. in English and creative writing from the University of Houston. Although her desire to be a poet emerged in a writing class in 1950, she began composing in earnest only in the late 1970s, after her children had grown. Since then she has won the Houston Discovery Prize for Poetry and has had poems publish-ed in numerous magazines, including* The New Yorker, *the* Georgia Review, *and* The New Republic. *In this poem, originally published in Sondra Zeidenstein's* A Wider Giving: Women Writing After a Long Silence *(1988) and reprinted in* Shenandoah, *Stern uses images of an aging house to convey both the comforts and fears associated with growing older with a life partner. As she lies in bed listening to her husband breathing, she wonders how time could have flown past so quickly without her noticing it.*

Before reading the poem, describe in your journal your concept of the future. How did you perceive your future when you were younger? To what extent do you think of your future as having arrived? What age do you consider to be "old"?

As you make notes on your reading, you may want to focus on the narrator's sense of changes having occurred without being noticed.

Another small, blue tile fell from the wall
this morning near the edge of the tub, one more

small thing to fix, the house ungluing after
years of holding on. Outside another squirrel

runs up the leaning pine again, another fall   5
is here, the wood fence losing out to weather.

We've hardly seen it happening—layer,
and crust, and crack—and I've scarcely questioned all

the years I've slept secure with you. But now
sometimes, afraid, I wake up and lean over   10

in the middle of the night to listen for your breath,
holding mine like a pain, remembering how

we always thought the future was in the future,
and now it's now, its wingbeats overhead.

❖ Focused Freewriting   Consider as possible focal points the idea
of physical aging, of things falling apart, of changing relationships, or
one of the topics you've identified in your journal.

❖ Guided Responses

1. Why is the fallen tile so important? How does the image of the
house "ungluing" relate to the narrator's sense of aging?

2. What is the significance of the squirrel? the season? How are
the two related to one another and to the narrator's central concern?

3. The narrator refers to her husband only briefly, contrasting the
"secure" sleep of earlier years with her new fears. Why does she focus
on sleeping and night? How do these images illustrate her feelings
differently than, say, a scene at the kitchen table?

4. How is the title appropriate? Why do we celebrate anniversa-
ries? What positive and negative connotations does the notion of a
thirty-ninth anniversary hold?

❖ Shared Responses   In your journal explore your feelings about
the changes that come with aging. How does the fear of being alone
relate to aging? In what ways does aging free us? restrict us? In what
way is an older person's concept of the future different from that of a
younger person? Explain your responses. As you discuss your responses in small groups, focus on why members view aging the way
they do.

❖

Emergent Visions

MARY CATHERINE BATESON

MARY CATHERINE BATESON *is the daughter of world-famous anthropologists Gregory Bateson and Margaret Mead. Herself an anthropologist and linguist with a Ph.D. from Harvard University, she is a professor at George Mason University. Her memoir of her parents,* With a Daughter's Eye, *won wide critical and popular acclaim. In this selection from her book* Composing a Life (1990), *Bateson questions the popular notion of a successful life as one which has moved steadily toward a clear goal. She suggests that in tumultuous times such as these, a fitting metaphor for individual growth should not be the knight in quest of the Holy Grail but rather the knight errant, who wanders the world seeking various challenges.*

Before reading the selection, write in your journal about your own career aspirations. When you were a child, how did you respond to the question, "What do you want to be when you grow up?" How have your ambitions changed? What relationship does your college education have to your career plans? to your life plans?

As you make notes on your reading, you may want to focus on the uncertainty that seems to permeate the selection. Consider the similarities and differences among the various groups Bateson presents.

I BELIEVE THAT OUR AESTHETIC SENSE, whether in works of art or in lives, has overfocused on the stubborn struggle toward a single goal rather than on the fluid, the protean, the improvisatory. We see achievement as purposeful and monolithic, like the sculpting of a massive tree trunk that has first to be brought from the forest and then shaped by long labor to assert the artist's vision, rather than something crafted from odds and ends, like a patchwork quilt, and lovingly used to warm different nights and bodies. Composing a life has a metaphorical relation to many different arts, including architecture and dance and cooking. In the visual arts, a variety of disparate elements may be arranged to form a simultaneous whole, just as we combine our simultaneous commitments. In the temporal arts, like music, a sequential diversity may be brought into harmony over time. In still other arts, such as homemaking or gardening, choreography or administration, complexity is woven in both space and time.

When the choices and rhythms of lives change, as they have in our time, the study of lives becomes an increasing preoccupation. This is especially true now for women. The biography sections of bookstores continue to expand as scholars chronicle the few famous women and discover others whose achievements have not yet been noted and honored. Others try to understand the texture of the hidden and unrecorded lives of women in our own and other cultures. The women's history movement has many different elements, some of them parallel to the black history movement: the need to make the invisible visible, the desire to provide role models and empower aspirations, the possibility that by setting a number of life histories side by side, we will be enabled to recognize common patterns of creativity that have not been acknowledged or fostered. The process starts with the insistence that there have been great achievements by women and people of color. Inevitably, it moves on to a rethinking of the concept of achievement.

Women today read and write biographies to gain perspective on their own lives. Each reading provokes a dialogue of comparison and recognition, a process of memory and articulation that makes one's own experience available as a lens of empathy. We gain even more from comparing notes and trying to understand the choices of our friends. When one has matured surrounded by implicit disparagement, the undiscovered self is an unexpected resource. Self-knowledge is empowering.

Nevertheless, there is a pattern deeply rooted in myth and folklore that recurs in biography and may create inappropriate expectations and blur our ability to see the actual shape of lives. Much biography of exceptional people is built around the image of a quest, a journey through a timeless landscape toward an end that is specific, even though it is not fully known. The pursuit of a quest is a pilgrim's progress in which it is essential to resist the transitory contentment of attractive way stations and side roads, in which obstacles are overcome because the goal is visible on the horizon, onward and upward. The end is already apparent in the beginning. The model of an ordinary successful life that is held up for young people is one of early decision and commitment, often to an educational preparation that launches a single rising trajectory. Ambition, we imply, should be focused, and young people worry about whether they are defining their goals and making the right decisions early enough to get on track. You go to medical school and this determines later alternatives, whether you choose prosperity in the suburbs or the more dramatic and exceptional life of discovery and dedication. Graduation is supposed to be followed by the first real job, representing a step on an ascending ladder. We don't expect long answers when we ask children what they want to be when they grow up, any more than we expect a list of names in response to questions about marriage. In fact, assumptions about careers are not unlike those about marriage; the real success stories are supposed to be permanent and monogamous.

These assumptions have not been valid for many of history's most   5 creative people, and they are increasingly inappropriate today. The landscape through which we move is in constant flux. Children cannot even know the names of the jobs and careers that will be open to them; they must build their fantasies around temporary surrogates. Goals too clearly defined can become blinkers. Just as it is less and less possible to replicate the career of a parent, so it will become less and less possible to go on doing the same thing through a lifetime. In the same way, we will have to change our sense of the transitory and learn to see success in marriages that flourish for a time and then end. Increasingly, we will recognize the value in lifetimes of continual redefinition, following the Biblical injunction, "Whatsoever thy hand findeth to do, do it with thy might" (Ecclesiastes 9:10).

Many of society's casualties are men and women who assumed they had chosen a path in life and found that it disappeared in the underbrush. These are easiest to recognize in areas where continuity used to be greatest.

In the American Midwest, farmers have been losing their farms and finding themselves without path or purpose. Working on land that often has been in the family for several generations, they have interpreted their lives in terms of continuity even as the economics and the technological nature of farming have been steadily changing. The story of the foreclosed farmer is comparable to that of the displaced homemaker who assumed that marriage defined both her work and her security. She has been no more an idle dependent than the farmer, but she too defined herself in terms of a niche that proved evanescent.

Others do not become visible casualties, because they are protected by contracts or union rules from facing the challenges of change. What they lose, and what the society loses through them, is the possibility of learning and development.

In the academic world, the tenure system still supplies a high degree of security and campuses still project serene images of continuity. Young teachers who choose or are forced to leave often feel that their lives are ending, like foreclosed farmers and displaced homemakers. But watching men and women who have left as they reconstruct and redirect their lives, I have become convinced that for many of them this discontinuity has been a move from stagnation to new challenge and growth, just as divorce often represents progress rather than failure.

All too often, men and women are like battered wives or abused 10 children. We hold on to the continuity we have, however profoundly it is flawed. If change were less frightening, if the risks did not seem so great, far more could be lived. One of the striking facts of most lives is the recurrence of threads of continuity, the re-echoing of earlier themes, even across deep rifts of change, but when you watch people damaged by their dependence on continuity, you wonder about the nature of commitment, about the need for a new and more fluid way to imagine the future.

The twentieth century has been called the century of the refugee because of the vast numbers of people uprooted by war and politics from their homes and accustomed lives. At the time of the Iranian revolution, my husband and I had lived in Iran for seven years. We had to adjust to the loss of our property there, including our books and papers, the loss of jobs, and the destruction of the institutions we had devoted those years to building. But seven years is minor compared to the dislocations that others faced. Some adjusted quickly, finding ways to affirm themselves and their skills in a new environment, bridging discontinuity. Others are still adrift; burdened by the broken assumptions of continuity.

Another set of discontinuities is created by the shifting business and industrial environment. Towns that have depended on a single industry for generations suddenly find half their people unemployed, with no way to learn new skills or find new homes. In this era of hostile takeovers and leveraged buyouts, continuity at the executive level is suddenly interrupted, businesses are restructured, and career managers find themselves facing "outplacement." Even monks and nuns must learn new skills as neighborhoods change around their monasteries; religious orders today must plan on turnover and constantly revised vocations. The fine old idea of a path and a commitment turns out to be illusory for many people, not only for geographical and political refugees but for cultural refugees displaced by the discontinuities of custom and economy. Even those who continue to wear the same professional label survive only because they have altered what they do. Being effective as a banker or a restaurateur or a general means that one has relearned one's craft more than once.

It is time now to explore the creative potential of interrupted and conflicted lives, where energies are not narrowly focused or permanently pointed toward a single ambition. These are not lives without commitment, but rather lives in which commitments are continually refocused and redefined. We must invest time and passion in specific goals and yet at the same time acknowledge that these are mutable. The circumstances of women's lives now and in the past provide examples for new ways of thinking about the lives of both men and women. What are the possible transfers of learning when life is a collage of different tasks? How does creativity flourish on distraction? What insights arise from the experience of multiplicity and ambiguity? And at what point does desperate improvisation become significant achievement? These are important questions in a world in which we are all increasingly strangers and sojourners. The knight errant, who finds his challenges along the way, may be a better model for our times than the knight who is questing for the Grail.

❖ Focused Freewriting Consider as possible focal points the American ideal of success, the effects of a changing economy on individual lives, the differences in expectations between men and women, or one of the topics you've identified in your journal.

❖ Guided Responses

1. Bateson claims that women "read and write biographies to gain perspective on their own lives" (para. 3). How can biography help us envision our own lives? In what ways can biographies establish guidelines for defining ourselves? Do you think the primary importance of a biography is to tell the story of the individual subject or to make a statement about humanity in general? Explain your answer.

2. When Bateson speaks in paragraph 1 of the difference between the patchwork quilt and the wood sculpture, she is attempting to highlight differences in the way we perceive our lives. How does the quilt differ from the sculpture in its creation, design, and use? How are these differences analogous to the various paths of human achievement?

3. In what ways are "men and women like battered wives or abused children" (para. 10)? What is it that keeps the victim from escaping the persecutor? What persecutes ordinary men and women, and why can't they escape? Do you think this metaphor offers hope? Why, or why not?

4. In paragraph 12 Bateson refers to "cultural refugees" who are "displaced by the discontinuities of custom and economy." How would you define "cultural refugee"? What characteristics do cultural refugees share with geographical or political refugees? How are they

different? Why do you think Bateson focuses on the image of the refugee?

❖ Shared Responses   In your journal comment on the contemporary notion of education as leading toward a single career path. Where do you think this notion originated? How well does it suit society? you? Do you think times have changed sufficiently to mandate a rethinking of this linear model of achievement? Explain your responses. As you discuss your responses in small groups, comment on how members' personal experiences have influenced their responses.

❖

My Grandmother, the Bag Lady

PATSY NEAL

PATSY NEAL, *in addition to her literary credits, is also a three-time all-American basketball player. A member of several world-touring American teams, Neal was inducted into the AAU Women's Basketball Hall of Fame in 1993. Along with numerous articles on sports, Neal has written poetry and textbooks. At present she is the wellness coordinator at Memorial Mission Medical Center in Asheville, North Carolina. In this essay, which first appeared in 1985 in* Newsweek, *Neal examines the shrinking world of her elderly grandmother. By pausing to understand the older woman's idiosyncrasies, Neal comes to appreciate her grandmother's dignity and sympathize with her struggle to maintain a sense of self.*

Before reading the selection, write in your journal about elderly people you know. How does their behavior differ from that of younger people? What elements of their behavior do you find difficult to understand? What elements seem clearly understandable? As you make notes on your reading, you may want to focus on the contrast between the family's perception of the grandmother's needs and her own perceptions.

A<small>LMOST ALL OF US</small> have seen pictures of old, homeless ladies, moving about the streets of big cities with everything they own stuffed into a bag or a paper sack.

My grandmother is 89 years old, and a few weeks ago I realized with a jolt that she, too, had become one of them. Before I go any further, I had best explain that I did not see my grandmother's picture on TV. I discovered her plight during a face-to-face visit at my mother's house—in a beautiful, comfortable, safe, middle-class environment with good china on the table and turkey and chicken on the stove.

320

My grandmother's condition saddened me beyond words, for an 89-year-old should not have to carry around everything she owns in a bag. It's enough to be 89, without the added burden of packing the last fragments of your existence into a space big enough to accommodate only the minutest of treasures.

Becoming a bag lady was not something that happened to her overnight. My grandmother has been in a nursing home these last several years; at first going back to her own home for short visits, then less frequently as she became older and less mobile.

No matter how short these visits were, her greatest pleasure came 5
from walking slowly around her home, touching every item lovingly and spending hours browsing through drawers and closets. Then, I did not understand her need to search out all her belongings.

As she spent longer days and months at the nursing home, I could not help noticing other things. She began to hide her possessions under the mattress, in her closet, under the cushion of her chair, in every conceivable, reachable space. And she began to think that people were "stealing" from her.

Unsteady

When a walker became necessary, my mother took the time to make a bag that could be attached to it, so that my grandmother could carry things around while keeping her hands on the walker. I had not paid much attention to this bag until we went to the nursing home to take her home with us for our traditional Christmas Eve sharing of gifts.

As we left, my grandmother took her long, unsteady walk down the hallway, balancing herself with her walker, laboriously moving it ahead, one step at a time, until finally we were at the car outside. Once she was safely seated, I picked up her walker to put it in the back. I could barely lift it. Then I noticed that the bag attached to it was bulging. Something clicked, but it still wasn't complete enough to grasp.

At home in my mother's house, I was asked to get some photographs from my grandmother's purse. Lifting her pocketbook, I was surprised again at the weight and bulk. I watched as my mother pulled out an alarm clock, a flashlight, a small radio, thread, needles, pieces of sewing, a book and other items that seemed to have no reason for being in a pocketbook.

I looked at my grandmother, sitting bent over in her chair, rum- 10
maging through the bag on the walker, slowly pulling out one item and then another, and lovingly putting it back. I looked down at her purse with all its disconnected contents and remembered her visits to her home, rummaging through drawers and through closets.

"Oh, Lord," I thought with sudden insight. "That walker and that purse are her home now."

I began to understand that over the years my grandmother's space for living had diminished like melting butter—from endless fields and miles of freedom as a child and young mother to, with age, the constrictions of a house, then a small room in a nursing home and finally to the tightly clutched handbag and the bag on her walker.

When the family sent her to a nursing home, it was the toughest decision it had ever had to make. We all thought she would be secure there; we would no longer have to worry about whether she had taken her medicine, or left her stove on, or was alone at night.

But we hadn't fully understood her needs. Security for my grandmother was not in the warm room at the nursing home, with 24-hour attendants to keep her safe and well fed, nor in the family who visited and took her to visit in their homes. In her mind her security was tied to those things she could call her own—and over the years those possessions had dwindled away like sand dropping through an hourglass: first her car, sold when her eyes became bad and she couldn't drive; then some furnishings she didn't really need. Later it was the dogs she had trouble taking care of. And finally it would be her home when it became evident that she could never leave the nursing home again. But as her space and mobility dwindled, so did her control over her life.

Dignity

I looked at my grandmother again, sitting so alone before me, hair   15
totally gray, limbs and joints swollen by arthritis, at the hearing aid that could no longer help her hear, and the glasses too thick but so inadequate in helping her to see . . . and yet there was such dignity about her. A dignity I could not understand.

The next day, after my grandmother had been taken back to the nursing home and my mother was picking up in her room, she found a small scrap of paper my grandmother had scribbled these words on:

"It is 1:30 tonight and I had to get up and go to the bathroom. I cannot go back to sleep. But I looked in on Margaret and she is sleeping *so* good, and Patsy is sleeping too."

With that note, I finally understood, and my 89-year-old bag-lady grandmother changed from an almost helpless invalid to a courageous, caring individual still very much in control of her environment.

What intense loneliness she must have felt as she scribbled that small note on that small piece of paper with the small bag on her walker and her small purse next to her. Yet she chose to experience it alone rather than wake either of us from much-needed sleep. Out of her own great need, she chose to meet our needs.

As I held that tiny note, and cried inside, I wondered if she   20 dreamed of younger years and more treasured possessions and a bigger world when she went back to sleep that night. I certainly hoped so.

❖ Focused Freewriting Consider as possible focal points the sense of loss that many old people feel, Neal's struggle to understand her grandmother, or one of the topics you've identified in your journal.

❖ Guided Responses

1. How do you react initially to Neal's statement that her grandmother has become a "bag lady" (para. 2)? How do you react when you realize her real meaning? Given the understanding Neal comes to in the essay, do you think this sensational opener is justified? Why, or why not?

2. Neal relates in paragraph 6 that her grandmother fears that people in the nursing home are " 'stealing' from her." While Neal's use of quotation marks implies that thefts are not a problem in the home, the impression of theft nevertheless remains. In what ways are people stealing from her grandmother? What is being stolen? Who is stealing?

3. Neal insists that her grandmother has an incredible dignity about her (para. 15). How does that dignity manifest itself? How does Neal's description of the woman's infirmities underscore that dignity?

4. The note left after her grandmother's visit (para. 17) helps Neal understand the woman's struggle. What does the note reveal about her grandmother? How does it help explain the dignity Neal sees in the woman?

❖ Shared Responses In your journal comment on the common practice today of caring for elderly people in nursing homes. How does life in a nursing home serve the needs of old people? How does it create anxiety in them? How much can contemporary families be expected to do in caring for their elderly relatives? Explain your responses. As you discuss your responses in small groups, distinguish between responses based primarily on personal experience and those based primarily on beliefs or social theories.

❖ Generating Ideas   Reread all of your journals and annotations from the selections in this unit. Look for connections between selections or still unanswered questions. First, list those connections and questions as briefly as possible. Next, choose two or three to elaborate on. As you respond in more detail to the connections and questions, focus on one topic and consider how well it would serve you in an extended piece of writing. Then decide what kind of writing best suits your topic: Should you write a conventional essay, a poem, a short story, or a scene? Would your topic lend itself more to a letter to the editor or a personal letter? Might a proposal to solve a specific problem be a good choice? Possible topics:

1. the disillusionment of young people
2. relationships between adults and children (including teenagers)
3. looking back on one's life
4. the significance of home to younger and older people
5. a sense of purpose in life (or lack of it)

❖ Focusing Responses   Choose one of your extended responses and formulate a statement of one or two sentences that captures its essence. Use this statement as a guide to organize your piece. (If you write an essay, letter, or proposal, the statement may actually appear as a thesis.)

❖ Guided Writing Assignments

1. LeBlanc, Cary, and Leavitt all write about substance abuse by young people; yet the reasons for the behavior seem different in each selection. Write a proposal to address the various causes of substance abuse as proposed by these writers, paying particular attention to such issues as the socioeconomic status of the people involved, their motives for drug and/or alcohol use, and their sense of purpose in life. Try to draw conclusions about the basic similarities and differences in the various reasons given to explain substance abuse, and base your proposal on these conclusions.

2. Bateson discusses the problems of people whose lives are disrupted because their sense of purpose has been so singular, while Leavitt recounts the disillusionment of people whose lives seem to lack a sense of purpose. In an essay compare these two generations, focusing on such issues as the different perspectives of youth and age, the impact of the larger culture on individual decisions, and the expectations that younger and older people have for themselves.

3. Both Nunes and Stern offer images of people looking back on their lives. Write a letter to your grandparents, your parents, or your children in which you discuss the notion of reassessing one's life. Focus on such issues as the importance of a home, the feeling of having taken too much for granted, and the sense of coming face to face with the future.

4. Each in her own way, both Tan's Jing-mei Woo and Neal's grandmother are rebelling against roles their families have imposed on them. Using these two selections as examples, explore in an essay or a story the similarities and differences between extreme youth and old age. Consider such issues as the need to be forceful in asserting a sense of self, the desire to cling to possessions, and the pain that results as different people's needs come into conflict.

❖ Research Topics   As you consider how to expand your reading beyond the selections in this chapter, identify in your journals and notes questions that remain unanswered or topics you'd like to explore further. Or you may consider the following:

1. Examine the issue of substance abuse among young people for the last three decades. What substances did young people choose in the 1960s, the 1970s, and the 1980s? What seemed to be the causes of the abuse? If the abusers considered themselves rebels, what were they rebelling against? How did authorities and specialists deal with the problem? What conclusions do you draw regarding the issue now that you have a more historical perspective?

2. Recent years have seen a steady rise in the publication of women's biographies, as well as books and articles based on women's stories. Read several accounts explaining the importance of women's stories, and then choose a figure whose biography seems to bear out these accounts. What seems to be unique about women's stories as opposed, say, to men's or to more general stories applicable to both men and women? Why is it important for women to tell their own stories? How might the influx of women's biographies change the way we as a society view success and achievement?

Chapter 5

Educational Opportunities

O NE OF THE CORNERSTONES of contemporary American democracy is the
right to education. Ideally, every child in the United States is given an
equal opportunity to pursue success through twelve years of state-
supported schooling. But how equal are the opportunities for education offered our children?

In 1954, the Supreme Court ruled that segregated schools by definition denied African-American children an equal right to education.
Since that time other battles have been fought to give an equal education to physically challenged students, to mentally and emotionally
challenged students, and to students whose first language is not English. Certainly more children than ever before are going to school, but
the quality of their education still varies according to where they live,
how much money their parents make, what language they speak, and
what race or ethnic group they belong to.

Access to education and funds to support it are not the only issues
that affect equal educational opportunities, however. Other crucial
factors include the role of parents in educating their children, the
teaching methods employed in schools, and the learning abilities of
the children themselves.

The selections that follow explore the notion of equal educational
opportunities. While some highlight success stories, many conclude
that the goal of equal education has yet to be achieved.

Jonathan Kozol's "Public Education in New York" exposes shocking disparities between wealthy, primarily white schools and poor, primarily African-American and Hispanic schools in one New York City school district. Kozol finds it difficult to uncover any reason other than racial discrimination to explain the inequities.

What can happen to students offered a second-rate education is the subject of Mike Rose's "'I Just Wanna Be Average,'" a memoir of the author's years in the vocational track in high school. Rose concludes that tracking students virtually ensures that their career paths will never stray from the original track.

Shirley Lauro's play *Open Admissions* illustrates the need for more than just access to education. The clash between a harried white teacher and a frustrated African-American student emphasizes the problems that arise when admirable programs suffer from lack of support.

The cultural adjustment of Native American students in higher education is the subject of William G. Tierney's "Native Voices in Academe." Tierney offers suggestions for institutions serving Indian students; he also provides a forum in which Native-American students and educators can offer their own observations.

Alfie Kohn's "Home Schooling" examines an option more and more parents are taking advantage of, as they find public and private schools inadequate for any number of reasons. While home schooling has its critics and Kohn recognizes its limitations, the cases he presents are success stories.

That sometimes even the best intentions can go awry is revealed in Michael Dorris's "Adam Goes to School." The time and energy Dorris and his son's teachers put into Adam's education may make them feel that they have helped the boy, but in the end Dorris must admit that his son has made little progress.

Neil Miller, in "Gay Teachers, Gay Students," explores an issue seldom discussed in secondary schools. Through interviews with a number of homosexual teachers and students in Boston area high schools, Miller concludes that while awareness of this issue is increasing, gay high school teachers and students remain, by and large, in the closet.

Finally, Lee Little Soldier, in "Cooperative Learning and the Native American Student," writes about a success story in the education of students normally considered disadvantaged. The principles of cooperative learning, Little Soldier claims, are well suited to the cultural values of Native Americans.

The selections in this chapter provide a rather sweeping view of American education, from kindergarten through college. The variety of experiences recounted here indicates that there is no such thing as a single, clearly defined American system of education. Rather, it seems that a number of factors—race, socioeconomic status, sexual orientation, location, parental involvement, and individual handicaps—influence both the nature and the quality of education in this country.

❖

Public Education
in New York

JONATHAN KOZOL

JONATHAN KOZOL, *who has written extensively on educational is-*
sues, was an elementary school teacher in the Boston area during the
1960s and consultant to the United States Office of Education from
1965 to 1966. Among his works are Death at an Early Age *(1967),*
Free Schools *(1972), and* The Night Is Dark and I Am Far from
Home *(1975). In this selection, taken from his most recent book,*
aptly named Savage Inequalities: Children in America's
Schools *(1991), Kozol contrasts a modern, attractive, well-staffed,*
and well-equipped school in an affluent neighborhood with a win-
dowless, overcrowded, understaffed, and poorly equipped ghetto
school nearby. His observations speak for themselves.

> *Before reading the selection, write in your journal about your*
> *own experiences in elementary school. Was the building attractive,*
> *well maintained, and adequately equipped? Were the teachers en-*
> *gaging? What was the racial and ethnic makeup of the student*
> *body? How much have those years influenced your current educa-*
> *tional and career plans?*

> *As you make notes on your reading, you may want to focus on*
> *Kozol's use of statistics, his physical descriptions, or his frequent*
> *questions.*

IN ORDER TO FIND PUBLIC SCHOOL 261 in District 10, a visitor is told to
look for a mortician's office. The funeral home, which faces Jerome
Avenue in the North Bronx, is easy to identify by its green awning.
The school is next door, in a former roller-skating rink. No sign identifies the building as a school. A metal awning frame without an
awning supports a flagpole, but there is no flag.

In the street in front of the school there is an elevated public
transit line. Heavy traffic fills the street. The existence of the school is
virtually concealed within this crowded city block.

330

In a vestibule between the outer and inner glass doors of the school there is a sign with these words: "All children are capable of learning."

Beyond the inner doors a guard is seated. The lobby is long and narrow. The ceiling is low. There are no windows. All the teachers that I see at first are middle-aged white women. The principal, who is also a white woman, tells me that the school's "capacity" is 900 but that there are 1,300 children here. The size of classes for fifth and sixth grade children in New York, she says, is "capped" at 32, but she says that class size in the school goes "up to 34." (I later see classes, however, as large as 37.) Classes for younger children, she goes on, are "capped at 25," but a school can go above this limit if it puts an extra adult in the room. Lack of space, she says, prevents the school from operating a prekindergarten program.

I ask the principal where her children go to school. They are 5 enrolled in private school, she says.

"Lunchtime is a challenge for us," she explains. "Limited space obliges us to do it in three shifts, 450 children at a time."

Textbooks are scarce and children have to share their social studies books. The principal says there is one full-time pupil counselor and another who is here two days a week: a ratio of 930 children to one counselor. The carpets are patched and sometimes taped together to conceal an open space. "I could use some new rugs," she observes.

To make up for the building's lack of windows and the crowded feeling that results, the staff puts plants and fish tanks in the corridors. Some of the plants are flourishing. Two boys, released from class, are in a corridor beside a tank, their noses pressed against the glass. A school of pinkish fish inside the tank are darting back and forth. Farther down the corridor a small Hispanic girl is watering the plants.

Two first grade classes share a single room without a window, divided only by a blackboard. Four kindergartens and a sixth grade class of Spanish-speaking children have been packed into a single room in which, again, there is no window. A second grade bilingual class of 37 children has its own room but again there is no window.

By eleven o'clock, the lunchroom is already packed with appetite 10 and life. The kids line up to get their meals, then eat them in ten minutes. After that, with no place they can go to play, they sit and wait until it's time to line up and go back to class.

On the second floor I visit four classes taking place within another undivided space. The room has a low ceiling. File cabinets and movable blackboards give a small degree of isolation to each class. Again, there are no windows.

The library is a tiny, windowless and claustrophobic room. I count approximately 700 books. Seeing no reference books, I ask a teacher if encyclopedias and other reference books are kept in class-rooms.

"We don't have encyclopedias in classrooms," she replies. "That is for the suburbs."

The school, I am told, has 26 computers for its 1,300 children. There is one small gym and children get one period, and sometimes two, each week. Recess, however, is not possible because there is no playground. "Head Start," the principal says, "scarcely exists in District 10. We have no space."

The school, I am told, is 90 percent black and Hispanic; the other   15
10 percent are Asian, white or Middle Eastern.

In a sixth grade social studies class the walls are bare of words or decorations. There seems to be no ventilation system, or, if one exists, it isn't working.

The class discusses the Nile River and the Fertile Crescent.

The teacher, in a droning voice: "How is it useful that these civilizations developed close to rivers?"

A child, in a good loud voice: "What kind of question is that?"

In my notes I find these words: "An uncomfortable feeling—being   20
in a building with no windows. There are metal ducts across the room. Do they give air? I feel asphyxiated. . . ."

On the top floor of the school, a sixth grade of 30 children shares a room with 29 bilingual second graders. Because of the high class size there is an assistant with each teacher. This means that 59 children and four grown-ups—63 in all—must share a room that, in a suburban school, would hold no more than 20 children and one teacher. There are, at least, some outside windows in this room—it is the only room with windows in the school—and the room has a high ceiling. It is a relief to see some daylight.

I return to see the kindergarten classes on the ground floor and feel stifled once again by lack of air and the low ceiling. Nearly 120 children and adults are doing what they can to make the best of things: 80 children in four kindergarten classes, 30 children in the sixth grade class, and about eight grown-ups who are aides and teachers. The kindergarten children sitting on the worn rug, which is patched with tape, look up at me and turn their heads to follow me as I walk past them.

As I leave the school, a sixth grade teacher stops to talk. I ask her, "Is there air conditioning in warmer weather?"

Teachers, while inside the building, are reluctant to give answers to this kind of question. Outside, on the sidewalk, she is less constrained: "I had an awful room last year. In the winter it was 56 degrees. In the summer it was up to 90. It was sweltering."

I ask her, "Do the children ever comment on the building?"   25

"They don't say," she answers, "but they know."

I ask her if they see it as a racial message.

"All these children see TV," she says. "They know what suburban schools are like. Then they look around them at their school. This was a roller-rink, you know. . . . They don't comment on it but you see it in their eyes. They understand."

On the following morning I visit P.S. 79, another elementary school in the same district. "We work under difficult circumstances," says the principal, James Carter, who is black. "The school was built to hold one thousand students. We have 1,550. We are badly overcrowded. We need smaller classes but, to do this, we would need more space. I can't add five teachers. I would have no place to put them."

Some experts, I observe, believe that class size isn't a real issue.   30 He dismisses this abruptly. "It doesn't take a genius to discover that you learn more in a smaller class. I have to bus some 60 kindergarten children elsewhere, since I have no space for them. When they return next year, where do I put them?

"I can't set up a computer lab. I have no room. I had to put a class into the library. I have no librarian. There are two gymnasiums upstairs but they cannot be used for sports. We hold more classes there. It's unfair to measure us against the suburbs. They have 17 to 20 children in a class. Average class size in this school is 30.

"The school is 29 percent black, 70 percent Hispanic. Few of these kids get Head Start. There is no space in the district. Of 200 kindergarten children, 50 maybe get some kind of preschool."

I ask him how much difference preschool makes.

"Those who get it do appreciably better. I can't overestimate its impact but, as I have said, we have no space."

The school tracks children by ability, he says. "There are five to   35 seven levels in each grade. The highest level is equivalent to 'gifted' but it's not a full-scale gifted program. We don't have the funds. We have no science room. The science teachers carry their equipment with them."

We sit and talk within the nurse's room. The window is broken. There are two holes in the ceiling. About a quarter of the ceiling has been patched and covered with a plastic garbage bag.

"Ideal class size for these kids would be 15 to 20. Will these children ever get what white kids in the suburbs take for granted? I don't think so. If you ask me why, I'd have to speak of race and social class. I don't think the powers that be in New York City understand, or want to understand, that if they do not give these children a sufficient education to lead healthy and productive lives, we will be their victims later on. We'll pay the price someday—in violence, in economic costs. I despair of making this appeal in any terms but these. You cannot issue an appeal to conscience in New York today. The fair-play argument won't be accepted. So you speak of violence and hope that it will scare the city into action."

While we talk, three children who look six or seven years old come to the door and ask to see the nurse, who isn't in the school today. One of the children, a Puerto Rican girl, looks haggard. "I have a pain in my tooth," she says. The principal says, "The nurse is out. Why don't you call your mother?" The child says, "My mother doesn't have a phone." The principal sighs. "Then go back to your class." When she leaves, the principal is angry. "It's amazing to me that these children ever make it with the obstacles they face. Many *do* care and they *do* try, but there's a feeling of despair. The parents of these children want the same things for their children that the parents in the suburbs want. Drugs are not the cause of this. They are the symptom. Nonetheless, they're used by people in the suburbs and rich people in Manhattan as another reason to keep children of poor people at a distance."

I ask him, "Will white children and black children ever go to school together in New York?"

"I don't see it," he replies. "I just don't think it's going to happen.   40 It's a dream. I simply do not see white folks in Riverdale agreeing to cross-bus with kids like these. A few, maybe. Very few. I don't think I'll live to see it happen."

I ask him whether race is the decisive factor. Many experts, I observe, believe that wealth is more important in determining these inequalities.

"This," he says—and sweeps his hand around him at the room, the garbage bag, the ceiling—"would not happen to white children."

In a kindergarten class the children sit cross-legged on a carpet in a space between two walls of books. Their 26 faces are turned up to watch their teacher, an elderly black woman. A little boy who sits beside me is involved in trying to tie bows in his shoelaces. The children sing a song: "Lift Every Voice." On the wall are these hand-written words: "Beautiful, also, are the souls of my people."

In a very small room on the fourth floor, 52 people in two classes do their best to teach and learn. Both are first grade classes. One, I am informed, is "low ability." The other is bilingual.

"The room is barely large enough for one class," says the principal.   45

The room is 25 by 50 feet. There are 26 first graders and two adults on the left, 22 others and two adults on the right. On the wall there is the picture of a small white child, circled by a Valentine, and a Gainsborough painting of a child in a formal dress.

"We are handicapped by scarcity," one of the teachers says. "One fifth of these children may be at grade level by the year's end."

A boy who may be seven years old climbs on my lap without an invitation and removes my glasses. He studies my face and runs his fingers through my hair. "You have nice hair," he says. I ask him where he lives and he replies, "Times Square Hotel," which is a homeless shelter in Manhattan.

I ask him how he gets here.

"With my father. On the train," he says.   50

"How long does it take?"

"It takes an hour and a half."

I ask him when he leaves his home.

"My mother wakes me up at five o'clock."

"When do you leave?"   55

"Six-thirty."

I ask him how he gets back to Times Square.

"My father comes to get me after school."

From my notes: "He rides the train three hours every day in order to attend this segregated school. It would be a shorter ride to Riverdale. There are rapid shuttle-vans that make that trip in only 20 minutes. Why not let him go to school right in Manhattan, for that matter?"

At three o'clock the nurse arrives to do her recordkeeping. She   60
tells me she is here three days a week. "The public hospital we use for an emergency is called North Central. It's not a hospital that I will use if I am given any choice. Clinics in the private hospitals are far more likely to be staffed by an experienced physician."

She hesitates a bit as I take out my pen, but then goes on: "I'll give you an example. A little girl I saw last week in school was trembling and shaking and could not control the motions of her arms. I was concerned and called her home. Her mother came right up to school and took her to North Central. The intern concluded that the child was upset by 'family matters'—nothing more—that there was nothing wrong with her. The mother was offended by the diagnosis. She did not appreciate his words or his assumptions. The truth is, there was nothing wrong at home. She brought the child back to school. I thought that she was ill. I told her mother, 'Go to Montefiore.' It's a private hospital, and well respected. She took my advice, thank God. It turned out that the child had a neurological disorder. She is now in treatment.

"This is the kind of thing our children face. Am I saying that the city underserves this population? You can draw your own conclusions."

Out on the street, it takes a full half hour to flag down a cab. Taxi drivers in New York are sometimes disconcertingly direct in what they say. When they are contemptuous of poor black people, their contempt is unadorned. When they're sympathetic and compassionate, their observations often go right to the heart of things. "Oh . . . they neglect these children," says the driver. "They leave them in the streets and slums to live and die." We stop at a light. Outside the window of the taxi, aimless men are standing in a semicircle while another man is working on his car. Old four-story buildings with their windows boarded, cracked or missing are on every side.

I ask the driver where he's from. He says Afghanistan. Turning in his seat, he gestures at the street and shrugs. "If you don't, as an American, begin to give these kids the kind of education that you give the kids of Donald Trump, you're asking for disaster."

Two months later, on a day in May, I visit an elementary school in 65 Riverdale. The dogwoods and magnolias on the lawn in front of P.S. 24 are in full blossom on the day I visit. There is a well-tended park across the street, another larger park three blocks away. To the left of the school is a playground for small children, with an innovative jungle gym, a slide and several climbing toys. Behind the school there are two playing fields for older kids. The grass around the school is neatly trimmed.

The neighborhood around the school, by no means the richest part of Riverdale, is nonetheless expensive and quite beautiful. Residences in the area—some of which are large, free-standing houses, others condominiums in solid red-brick buildings—sell for prices in the region of $400,000; but some of the larger Tudor houses on the winding and tree-shaded streets close to the school can cost up to $1 million. The excellence of P.S. 24, according to the principal, adds to the value of these homes. Advertisements in the *New York Times* will frequently inform prospective buyers that a house is "in the neighborhood of P.S. 24."

The school serves 825 children in the kindergarten through sixth grade. This is approximately half the student population crowded into P.S. 79, where 1,550 children fill a space intended for 1,000, and a great deal smaller than the 1,300 children packed into the former skating rink; but the principal of P.S. 24, a capable and energetic man named David Rothstein, still regards it as excessive for an elementary school.

The school is integrated in the strict sense that the middle- and upper-middle-class white children here do occupy a building that contains some Asian and Hispanic and black children; but there is little integration in the classrooms since the vast majority of the Hispanic and black children are assigned to "special" classes on the basis of evaluations that have classified them "EMR"—"educable mentally retarded"—or else, in the worst of cases, "TMR"—"trainable mentally retarded."

I ask the principal if any of his students qualify for free-lunch programs. "About 130 do," he says. "Perhaps another 35 receive their lunches at reduced price. Most of these kids are in the special classes. They do not come from this neighborhood."

The very few nonwhite children that one sees in mainstream classes tend to be Japanese or else of other Asian origins. Riverdale, I learn, has been the residence of choice for many years to members of the diplomatic corps. 70

The school therefore contains effectively two separate schools: one of about 130 children, most of whom are poor, Hispanic, black, assigned to one of the 12 special classes; the other of some 700 mainstream students, almost all of whom are white or Asian.

There is a third track also—this one for the students who are labeled "talented" or "gifted." This is termed a "pull-out" program since the children who are so identified remain in mainstream classrooms but are taken out for certain periods each week to be provided with intensive and, in my opinion, excellent instruction in some areas of reasoning and logic often known as "higher-order skills" in the contemporary jargon of the public schools. Children identified as "gifted" are admitted to this program in first grade and, in most cases, will remain there for six years. Even here, however, there are two tracks of the gifted. The regular gifted classes are provided with only one semester of this specialized instruction yearly. Those very few children, on the other hand, who are identified as showing the most promise are assigned, beginning in the third grade, to a program that receives a full-year regimen.

In one such class, containing ten intensely verbal and impressive fourth grade children, nine are white and one is Asian. The "special" class I enter first, by way of contrast, has twelve children of whom only one is white and none is Asian. These racial breakdowns prove to be predictive of the schoolwide pattern.

In a classroom for the gifted on the first floor of the school, I ask a child what the class is doing. "Logic and syllogisms," she replies. The room is fitted with a planetarium. The principal says that all the elementary schools in District 10 were given the same planetariums ten years ago but that certain schools, because of overcrowding, have been forced to give them up. At P.S. 261, according to my notes, there was a domelike space that had been built to hold a planetarium, but the planetarium had been removed to free up space for the small library collection. P.S. 24, in contrast, has a spacious library that holds almost 8,000 books. The windows are decorated with attractive, brightly colored curtains and look out on flowering trees. The principal says that it's inadequate, but it appears spectacular to me after the cubicle that holds a meager 700 books within the former skating rink.

The district can't afford librarians, the principal says, but P.S. 24, 75 unlike the poorer schools of District 10, can draw on educated parent volunteers who staff the room in shifts three days a week. A parent organization also raises independent funds to buy materials, including books, and will soon be running a fund-raiser to enhance the library's collection.

In a large and sunny first grade classroom that I enter next, I see 23 children, all of whom are white or Asian. In another first grade, there are 22 white children and two others who are Japanese. There is a computer in each class. Every classroom also has a modern fitted sink.

In a second grade class of 22 children, there are two black children and three Asian children. Again, there is a sink and a computer. A sixth grade social studies class has only one black child. The children have an in-class research area that holds some up-to-date resources. A set of encyclopedias (World Book, 1985) is in a rack beside a window. The children are doing a Spanish language lesson when I enter. Foreign languages begin in sixth grade at the school, but Spanish is offered also to the kindergarten children. As in every room at P.S. 24, the window shades are clean and new, the floor is neatly tiled in gray and green, and there is not a single light bulb missing.

Walking next into a special class, I see twelve children. One is white. Eleven are black. There are no Asian children. The room is half the size of mainstream classrooms. "Because of overcrowding," says the principal, "we have had to split these rooms in half." There is no computer and no sink.

I enter another special class. Of seven children, five are black, one is Hispanic, one is white. A little black boy with a large head sits in the far corner and is gazing at the ceiling.

"Placement of these kids," the principal explains, "can usually be 80 traced to neurological damage."

In my notes: "How could so many of these children be brain-damaged?"

Next door to the special class is a woodworking shop. "This shop is only for the special classes," says the principal. The children learn to punch in time cards at the door, he says, in order to prepare them for employment.

The fourth grade gifted class, in which I spend the last part of the day, is humming with excitement. "I start with these children in the first grade," says the teacher. "We pull them out of mainstream classes

on the basis of their test results and other factors such as the opinion
of their teachers. Out of this group, beginning in third grade, I pull out
the ones who show the most potential, and they enter classes such as
this one."

The curriculum they follow, she explains, "emphasizes critical
thinking, reasoning and logic." The planetarium, for instance, is employed not simply for the study of the universe as it exists. "Children
also are designing their own galaxies," the teacher says.

A little girl sitting around a table with her classmates speaks with   85
perfect poise: "My name is Susan. We are in the fourth grade gifted
program."

I ask them what they're doing and a child says, "My name is
Laurie and we're doing problem-solving."

A rather tall, good-natured boy who is half-standing at the table
tells me that his name is David. "One thing that we do," he says, "is
logical thinking. Some problems, we find, have more than one good
answer. We need to learn not simply to be logical in our own thinking
but to show respect for someone else's logic even when an answer
may be technically incorrect."

When I ask him to explain this, he goes on, "A person who gives
an answer that is not 'correct' may nonetheless have done some interesting thinking that we should examine. 'Wrong' answers may be
more useful to examine than correct ones."

I ask the children if reasoning and logic are innate or if they're
things that you can learn.

"You know some things to start with when you enter school,"   90
Susan says. "But we also learn some things that other children don't."

I ask her to explain this.

"We know certain things that other kids don't know because
we're *taught* them."

She has braces on her teeth. Her long brown hair falls almost to
her waist. Her loose white T-shirt has the word TRI-LOGIC on the front.
She tells me that Tri-Logic is her father's firm.

Laurie elaborates on the same point: "Some things you know.
Some kinds of logic are inside of you to start with. There are other
things that someone needs to teach you."

David expands on what the other two have said: "Everyone can   95
think and speak in logical ways unless they have a mental problem.
What this program does is bring us to a higher form of logic."

The class is writing a new "Bill of Rights." The children already
know the U.S. Bill of Rights and they explain its first four items to me
with precision. What they are examining today, they tell me, is the
very *concept* of a "right." Then they will create their own compendium
of rights according to their own analysis and definition. Along one

wall of the classroom, opposite the planetarium, are seven Apple II computers on which children have developed rather subtle color animations that express the themes—of greed and domination, for example—that they also have described in writing.

"This is an upwardly mobile group," the teacher later says. "They have exposure to whatever New York City has available. Their parents may take them to the theater, to museums. . . ."

In my notes: "Six girls, four boys. Nine white, one Chinese. I am glad they have this class. But what about the others? Aren't there ten black children in the school who could enjoy this also?"

The teacher gives me a newspaper written, edited and computer-printed by her sixth grade gifted class. The children, she tells me, are provided with a link to kids in Europe for transmission of news stories.

A science story by one student asks if scientists have ever falsified   100
their research. "Gergor Mendel," the sixth grader writes, "the Austrian monk who founded the science of genetics, published papers on his work with peas that some experts say were statistically too good to be true. Isaac Newton, who formulated the law of gravitation, relied on unseemly mathematical sleight of hand in his calculations. . . . Galileo Galilei, founder of modern scientific method, wrote about experiments that were so difficult to duplicate that colleagues doubted he had done them."

Another item in the paper, also by a sixth grade student, is less esoteric: "The Don Cossacks dance company, from Russia, is visiting the United States. The last time it toured America was 1976. . . . The Don Cossacks will be in New York City for two weeks at the Neil Simon Theater. Don't miss it!"

The tone is breezy—and so confident! That phrase—"Don't miss it!"—speaks a volume about life in Riverdale.

"What makes a good school?" asks the principal when we are talking later on. "The building and teachers are part of it, of course. But is isn't just the building and the teachers. Our kids come from good families and the neighborhood is good. In a three-block area we have a public library, a park, a junior high. . . . Our typical sixth grader reads at eighth grade level." In a quieter voice he says, "I see how hard my colleagues work in schools like P.S. 79. You have children in those neighborhoods who live in virtual hell. They enter school five years behind. What do they get?" Then, as he spreads his hands out on his desk, he says: "I have to ask myself why there should be an elementary school in District 10 with fifteen hundred children. Why should there be an elementary school within a skating rink? Why should the Board of Ed allow this? This is not the way that things should be."

❖ Focused Freewriting   Consider as possible focal points the contrasts between the school buildings, one of the observations made by the teachers or principals, or one of the topics you've identified in your journal.

❖ Guided Responses

1. In his first paragraph, Kozol states, "No sign identifies the building as a school. A metal awning frame without an awning supports a flagpole, but there is no flag." How does this litany of missing things set the tone for the selection? What do these details say about the district's attitude toward the school?

2. The principal of P.S. 79 warns that if those in power "do not give these children a sufficient education to lead healthy and productive lives, we will be their victims later on. We'll pay the price someday—in violence, in economic costs" (para. 37). Later, his warning is echoed by a cab driver: "If you don't . . . begin to give these kids the kind of education that you give the kids of Donald Trump, you're asking for disaster" (para. 64). What connection do you see between poor education and crime? Why do you think so little attention is paid to inner-city schools?

3. P.S. 24, according to Kozol, "contains effectively two separate schools: one of about 130 children, most of whom are poor, Hispanic, black, assigned to . . . special classes; the other of some 700 mainstream students, almost all of whom are white or Asian" (para. 71). Based on your reading of the selection, how can this division be explained? Is it legitimate educational tracking? overt racism? something else? What does the situation say about American society?

4. Kozol allows several of the P.S. 24 students to speak at length about their education yet quotes very little from the P.S. 261 and 79 students. Why do you suppose he makes this distinction? What do the quotations from children of all three schools reveal about their experience of school? How would the impact of Kozol's work be affected if the quotations were eliminated?

❖ Shared Responses   In your journal explain to the students of P.S. 261 and 79 why they do not have facilities equivalent to those of P.S. 24. Be as honest as you can: If you believe that the discrepancy is justified, or that such inequities are inevitable in a free society, then explain your reasoning. If, on the other hand, you believe that the situation is unjust, explain why you think so. As you discuss your responses in small groups, try to determine how members' own experiences affect their responses.

"I Just Wanna Be Average"

MIKE ROSE

MIKE ROSE, *who grew up in poverty in Los Angeles, is now the associate director of the UCLA writing programs. Along with poetry and academic essays, he has published several books, including* Writer's Block: The Cognitive Dimension *(1984) and* Perspectives on Literacy *(1989). Rose wrote* Lives on the Boundary *(1989), from which this selection is taken, to challenge "educators, policymakers, and parents to re-examine their assumptions about the capacities of students and the way they're taught and tested." The selection illustrates the dangers of "tracking" students.*

Before reading the selection, evaluate in your journal the academic policies of your high school. Did the school use tracks? Were students encouraged, challenged to achieve? How well did the school serve your needs?

As you make notes on your reading, you may want to focus on Rose's descriptions of individual students and teachers, his metaphors, or the transitions between his personal experience and his general observations.

IT TOOK TWO BUSES to get to Our Lady of Mercy. The first started deep in South Los Angeles and caught me at midpoint. The second drifted through neighborhoods with trees, parks, big lawns, and lots of flowers. The rides were long but were livened up by a group of South L.A. veterans whose parents also thought that Hope had set up shop in the west end of the county. There was Christy Beggars, who, at sixteen, was dealing and was, according to rumor, a pimp as well. There were Bill Cobb and Johnny Gonzales, grease-pencil artists extraordinaire, who left Nembutal-enhanced swirls of "Cobb" and "Johnny" on the corrugated walls of the bus. And then there was Tyrrell Wilson. Tyrrell was the coolest kid I knew. He ran the dozens like a metric halfback, laid down a rap that outrhymed and outpointed Cobb, whose rap was good but not great—the curse of a moderately soulful kid trapped in white skin. But it was Cobb who

342

would sneak a radio onto the bus, and thus underwrote his patter with Little Richard, Fats Domino, Chuck Berry, the Coasters, and Ernie K. Doe's mother-in-law, an awful woman who was "sent from down below." And so it was that Christy and Cobb and Johnny G. and Tyrrell and I and assorted others picked up along the way passed our days in the back of the bus, a funny mix brought together by geography and parental desire.

Entrance to school brings with it forms and releases and assessments. Mercy relied on a series of tests, mostly the Stanford-Binet, for placement, and somehow the results of my tests got confused with those of another student named Rose. The other Rose apparently didn't do very well, for I was placed in the vocational track, a euphemism for the bottom level. Neither I nor my parents realized what this meant. We had no sense that Business Math, Typing, and English-Level D were dead ends. The current spate of reports on the schools criticizes parents for not involving themselves in the education of their children. But how would someone like Tommy Rose, with his two years of Italian schooling, know what to ask? And what sort of pressure could an exhausted waitress apply? The error went undetected, and I remained in the vocational track for two years. What a place.

My homeroom was supervised by Brother Dill, a troubled and unstable man who also taught freshman English. When his class drifted away from him, which was often, his voice would rise in paranoid accusations, and occasionally he would lose control and shake or smack us. I hadn't been there two months when one of his brisk, face-turning slaps had my glasses sliding down the aisle. Physical education was also pretty harsh. Our teacher was a stubby ex-lineman who had played old-time pro ball in the Midwest. He routinely had us grabbing our ankles to receive his stinging paddle across our butts. He did that, he said, to make men of us. "Rose," he bellowed on our first encounter; me standing geeky in line in my baggy shorts. " 'Rose'? What the hell kind of name is that?"

"Italian, sir," I squeaked.

"Italian! Ho. Rose, do you know the sound a bag of shit makes   5
when it hits the wall?"

"No, sir."

"Wop!"

Sophomore English was taught by Mr. Mitropetros. He was a large, bejeweled man who managed the parking lot at the Shrine Auditorium. He would crow and preen and list for us the stars he'd brushed against. We'd ask questions and glance knowingly and snicker, and all that fueled the poor guy to brag some more. Parking cars was his night job. He had little training in English, so his lesson plan for his day work had us reading the district's required text, *Julius Caesar,* aloud for the semester. We'd finish the play way before the twenty weeks was up, so he'd have us switch parts again and again and start again: Dave Snyder, the fastest guy at Mercy, muscling through Caesar to the breathless squeals of Calpurnia, as interpreted by Steve Fusco, a surfer who owned the school's most envied paneled wagon. Week ten and Dave and Steve would take on new roles, as would we all, and render a water-logged Cassius and a Brutus that are beyond my powers of description.

Spanish I—taken in the second year—fell into the hands of a new recruit. Mr. Montez was a tiny man, slight, five foot six at the most, soft-spoken and delicate. Spanish was a particularly rowdy class, and Mr. Montez was as prepared for it as a doily maker at a hammer throw. He would tap his pencil to a room in which Steve Fusco was propelling spitballs from his heavy lips, in which Mike Dweetz was taunting Billy Hawk, a half-Indian, half-Spanish, reed-thin, quietly explosive boy. The vocational track at Our Lady of Mercy mixed kids traveling in from South L.A. with South Bay surfers and a few Slavs and Chicanos from the harbors of San Pedro. This was a dangerous miscellany: surfers and hodads and South-Central blacks all ablaze to the metronomic tapping of Hector Montez's pencil.

One day Billy lost it. Out of the corner of my eye I saw him strike 10
out with his right arm and catch Dweetz across the neck. Quick as a spasm, Dweetz was out of his seat, scattering desks, cracking Billy on the side of the head, right behind the eye. Snyder and Fusco and others broke it up, but the room felt hot and close and naked. Mr. Montez's tenuous authority was finally ripped to shreds, and I think everyone felt a little strange about that. The charade was over, and when it came down to it, I don't think any of the kids really wanted it to end this way. They had pushed and pushed and bullied their way into a freedom that both scared and embarrassed them.

Students will float to the mark you set. I and the others in the vocational classes were bobbing in pretty shallow water. Vocational education has aimed at increasing the economic opportunities of students who do not do well in our schools. Some serious programs succeed in doing that, and through exceptional teachers—like Mr. Gross in *Horace's Compromise*—students learn to develop hypotheses and troubleshoot, reason through a problem, and communicate effectively—the true job skills. The vocational track, however, is most often a place for those who are just not making it, a dumping ground for the disaffected. There were a few teachers who worked hard at education; young Brother Slattery, for example, combined a stern voice with weekly quizzes to try to pass along to us a skeletal outline of world history. But mostly the teachers had no idea of how to engage the imaginations of us kids who were scuttling along at the bottom of the pond.

And the teachers would have needed some inventiveness, for none of us was groomed for the classroom. It wasn't just that I didn't know things—didn't know how to simplify algebraic fractions, couldn't identify different kinds of clauses, bungled Spanish translations—but that I had developed various faulty and inadequate ways of doing algebra and making sense of Spanish. Worse yet, the years of defensive tuning out in elementary school had given me a way to escape quickly while seeming at least half alert. During my time in Voc. Ed., I developed further into a mediocre student and a somnambulant problem solver, and that affected the subjects I did have the wherewithal to handle: I detested Shakespeare; I got bored with history. My attention flitted here and there. I fooled around in class and read my books indifferently—the intellectual equivalent of playing with your food. I did what I had to do to get by, and I did it with half a mind.

But I did learn things about people and eventually came into my own socially. I liked the guys in Voc. Ed. Growing up where I did, I understood and admired physical prowess, and there was an abundance of muscle here. There was Dave Snyder, a sprinter and halfback of true quality. Dave's ability and his quick wit gave him a natural appeal, and he was welcome in any clique, though he always kept a little independent. He enjoyed acting the fool and could care less about studies, but he possessed a certain maturity and never caused the faculty much trouble. It was a testament to his independence that he included me among his friends—I eventually went out for track, but I was no jock. Owing to the Latin alphabet and a dearth of Rs and Ss, Snyder sat behind Rose, and we started exchanging one-liners and became friends.

There was Ted Richard, a much-touted Little League pitcher. He was chunky and had a baby face and came to Our Lady of Mercy as a seasoned street fighter. Ted was quick to laugh and he had a loud, jolly laugh, but when he got angry he'd smile a little smile, the kind that simply raises the corner of the mouth a quarter of an inch. For those who knew, it was an eerie signal. Those who didn't found themselves in big trouble, for Ted was very quick. He loved to carry on what we would come to call philosophical discussions: What is courage? Does God exist? He also loved words, enjoyed picking up big ones like *salubrious* and *equivocal* and using them in our conversations—laughing at himself as the word hit a chuckhole rolling off his tongue. Ted didn't do all that well in school—baseball and parties and testing the courage he'd speculated about took up his time. His textbooks were

Argosy and *Field and Stream*, whatever newspapers he'd find on the bus stop—from the *Daily Worker* to pornography—conversations with uncles or hobos or businessmen he'd meet in a coffee shop, *The Old Man and the Sea*. With hindsight, I can see that Ted was developing into one of those rough-hewn intellectuals whose sources are a mix of the learned and the apocryphal, whose discussions are both assured and sad.

And then there was Ken Harvey. Ken was good-looking in a puffy 15 way and had a full and oily ducktail and was a car enthusiast . . . a hodad. One day in religion class, he said the sentence that turned out to be one of the most memorable of the hundreds of thousands I heard in those Voc. Ed. years. We were talking about the parable of the talents, about achievement, working hard, doing the best you can do, blah-blah-blah, when the teacher called on the restive Ken Harvey for an opinion. Ken thought about it, but just for a second, and said (with studied, minimal affect), "I just wanna be average." That woke me up. Average?! Who wants to be average? Then the athletes chimed in with the clichés that make you want to laryngectomize them, and the exchange became a platitudinous melee. At the time, I thought Ken's assertion was stupid, and I wrote him off. But his sentence has stayed with me all these years, and I think I am finally coming to understand. it.

Ken Harvey was gasping for air. School can be a tremendously disorienting place. No matter how bad the school, you're going to encounter notions that don't fit with the assumptions and beliefs that you grew up with—maybe you'll hear these dissonant notions from teachers, maybe from the other students, and maybe you'll read them. You'll also be thrown in with all kinds of kids from all kinds of backgrounds, and that can be unsettling—this is especially true in places of rich ethnic and linguistic mix, like the L.A. basin. You'll see a handful of students far excel you in courses that sound exotic and that are only in the curriculum of the elite: French, physics, trigonometry. And all this is happening while you're trying to shape an identity; your body is changing, and your emotions are running wild. If you're a working-class kid in the vocational track, the options you'll have to deal with this will be constrained in certain ways: You're defined by your school as "slow"; you're placed in a curriculum that isn't designed to liberate you but to occupy you, or, if you're lucky, train you, though the training is for work the society does not esteem; other students are picking up the cues from your school and your curriculum and interacting with you in particular ways. If you're a kid like Ted Richard, you turn your back on all this and let your mind roam where it may. But youngsters like Ted are rare. What Ken and so many others do is protect themselves from such suffocating madness by taking on with a vengeance the identity implied in the vocational track. Reject the confusion and frustration by openly defining yourself as the Common Joe. Champion the average. Rely on your own good sense. Fuck this bullshit. Bullshit, of course, is everything you—and the others—fear is beyond you: books, essays, tests, academic scrambling, complexity, scientific reasoning, philosophical inquiry.

The tragedy is that you have to twist the knife in your own gray matter to make this defense work. You'll have to shut down, have to reject intellectual stimuli or diffuse them with sarcasm, have to cultivate stupidity, have to convert boredom from a malady into a way of confronting the world. Keep your vocabulary simple, act stoned when you're not or act more stoned than you are, flaunt ignorance, materialize your dreams. It is a powerful and effective defense—it neutralizes the insult and the frustration of being a vocational kid and, when perfected, it drives teachers up the wall, a delightful secondary effect. But like all strong magic, it exacts a price.

My own deliverance from the Voc. Ed. world began with sophomore biology. Every student, college prep to vocational, had to take biology, and unlike the other courses, the same person taught all sections. When teaching the vocational group, Brother Clint probably slowed down a bit or omitted a little of the fundamental biochemistry, but he used the same book and more or less the same syllabus across the board. If one class got tough, he could get tougher. He was young and powerful and very handsome, and looks and physical strength were high currency. No one gave him any trouble.

I was pretty bad at the dissecting table, but the lectures and the textbook were interesting: plastic overlays that, with each turned page, peeled away skin, then veins and muscle, then organs, down to the very bones that Brother Clint, pointer in hand, would tap out on our hanging skeleton. Dave Snyder was in big trouble, for the study of life—versus the living of it—was sticking in his craw. We worked out a code for our multiple-choice exams. He'd poke me in the back: once for the answer under A, twice for B, and so on; and when he'd hit the right one, I'd look up to the ceiling as though I were lost in thought. Poke: cytoplasm. Poke, poke: methane. Poke, poke, poke: William Harvey. Poke, poke, poke, poke: islets of Langerhans. This didn't work out perfectly, but Dave passed the course, and I mastered the dreamy look of a guy on a record jacket. And something else happened. Brother Clint puzzled over this Voc. Ed. kid who was racking up 98s and 99s on his tests. He checked the school's records and discovered the error. He recommended that I begin my junior year in the College Prep program. According to all I've read since, such a shift, as one report put it, is virtually impossible. Kids at that level rarely cross tracks. The telling thing is how chancy both my placement into and exit from Voc. Ed. was; neither I nor my parents had anything to do with it. I lived in one world during spring semester, and when I came back to school in the fall, I was living in another.

Switching to College Prep was a mixed blessing. I was an erratic   20 student. I was undisciplined. And I hadn't caught onto the rules of the game: Why work hard in a class that didn't grab my fancy? I was also hopelessly behind in math. Chemistry was hard; toying with my chemistry set years before hadn't prepared me for the chemist's equations. Fortunately, the priest who taught both chemistry and second-year algebra was also the school's athletic director. Membership on the track team covered me; I knew I wouldn't get lower than a C. U.S. history was taught pretty well, and I did okay. But civics was taken over by a football coach who had trouble reading the textbook aloud—and reading aloud was the centerpiece of his pedagogy. College Prep at Mercy was certainly an improvement over the vocational program—at least it carried some status—but the social science curriculum was weak, and the mathematics and physical sciences were simply beyond me. I had a miserable quantitative background and ended up copying some assignments and finessing the rest as best I could. Let me try to explain how it feels to see again and again material you should once have learned but didn't.

You are given a problem. It requires you to simplify algebraic fractions or to multiply expressions containing square roots. You know this is pretty basic material because you've seen it for years. Once a teacher took some time with you, and you learned how to carry out these operations. Simple versions, anyway. But that was a year or two or more in the past, and these are more complex versions, and now you're not sure. And this, you keep telling yourself, is ninth- or even eighth-grade stuff.

Next it's a word problem. This is also old hat. The basic elements are as familiar as story characters: trains speeding so many miles per hour or shadows of buildings angling so many degrees. Maybe you know enough, have sat through enough explanations, to be able to begin setting up the problem: "If one train is going this fast . . ." or "This shadow is really one line of a triangle. . . ." Then: "Let's see . . ." "How did Jones do this?" "Hmmmm." "No." "No, that won't work." Your attention wavers. You wonder about other things: a football game, a dance, that cute new checker at the market. You try to focus on the problem again. You scribble on paper for a while, but the tension wins out and your attention flits elsewhere. You crumple the paper and begin daydreaming to ease the frustration.

The particulars will vary, but in essence this is what a number of students go through, especially those in so-called remedial classes.

They open their textbooks and see once again the familiar and impenetrable formulas and diagrams and terms that have stumped them for years. There is no excitement here. No excitement. Regardless of what the teacher says, this is not a new challenge. There is, rather, embarrassment and frustration and, not surprisingly, some anger in being reminded once again of long-standing inadequacies. No wonder so many students finally attribute their difficulties to something inborn, organic: "That part of my brain just doesn't work." Given the troubling histories many of these students have, it's miraculous that any of them can lift the shroud of hopelessness sufficiently to make deliverance from these classes possible.

Through this entire period, my father's health was deteriorating with cruel momentum. His arteriosclerosis progressed to the point where a simple nick on his shin wouldn't heal. Eventually it ulcerated and widened. Lou Minton would come by daily to change the dressing. We tried renting an oscillating bed—which we placed in the front room—to force blood through the constricted arteries in my father's legs. The bed hummed through the night, moving in place to ward off the inevitable. The ulcer continued to spread, and the doctors finally had to amputate. My grandfather had lost his leg in a stockyard accident. Now my father too was crippled. His convalescence was slow but steady, and the doctors placed him in the Santa Monica Rehabilitation Center, a sun-bleached building that opened out onto the warm spray of the Pacific. The place gave him some strength and some color and some training in walking with an artificial leg. He did pretty well for a year or so until he slipped and broke his hip. He was confined to a wheelchair after that, and the confinement contributed to the diminishing of his body and spirit.

I am holding a picture of him. He is sitting in his wheelchair and 25 smiling at the camera. The smile appears forced, unsteady, seems to quaver, though it is frozen in silver nitrate. He is in his mid-sixties and looks eighty. Late in my junior year, he had a stroke and never came out of the resulting coma. After that, I would see him only in dreams, and to this day that is how I join him. Sometimes the dreams are sad and grisly and primal: my father lying in a bed soaked with his suppuration, holding me, rocking me. But sometimes the dreams bring him back to me healthy: him talking to me on an empty street, or buying some pictures to decorate our old house, or transformed somehow into someone strong and adept with tools and the physical.

Jack MacFarland couldn't have come into my life at a better time. My father was dead, and I had logged up too many years of scholastic indifference. Mr. MacFarland had a master's degree from Columbia and decided, at twenty-six, to find a little school and teach his heart out. He never took any credentialing courses, couldn't bear to, he said, so he had to find employment in a private system. He ended up at Our Lady of Mercy teaching five sections of senior English. He was a beatnik who was born too late. His teeth were stained, he tucked his sorry tie in between the third and fourth buttons of his shirt, and his pants were chronically wrinkled. At first, we couldn't believe this guy, thought he slept in his car. But within no time, he had us so startled with work that we didn't much worry about where he slept or if he slept at all. We wrote three or four essays a month. We read a book every two to three weeks, starting with the *Iliad* and ending up with Hemingway. He gave us a quiz on the reading every other day. He brought a prep school curriculum to Mercy High.

MacFarland's lectures were crafted, and as he delivered them he would pace the room jiggling a piece of chalk in his cupped hand, using it to scribble on the board the names of all the writers and philosophers and plays and novels he was weaving into his discussion. He asked questions often, raised everything from Zeno's paradox to the repeated last line of Frost's "Stopping by Woods on a Snowy Evening." He slowly and carefully built up our knowledge of Western intellectual history—with facts, with connections, with speculations. We learned about Greek philosophy, about Dante, the Elizabethan world view, the Age of Reason, existentialism. He analyzed poems with us, had us reading sections from John Ciardi's *How Does a Poem Mean?*, making a potentially difficult book accessible with his own explanations. We gave oral reports on poems Ciardi didn't cover. We imitated the styles of Conrad, Hemingway, and *Time* magazine. We wrote and talked, wrote and talked. The man immersed us in language.

Even MacFarland's barbs were literary. If Jim Fitzsimmons, hung over and irritable, tried to smart-ass him, he'd rejoin with a flourish that would spark the indomitable Skip Madison—who'd lost his front teeth in a hapless tackle—to flick his tongue through the gap and opine, "good chop," drawing out the single "o" in stinging indictment. Jack MacFarland, this tobacco-stained intellectual, brandished linguistic weapons of a kind I hadn't encountered before. Here was this *egghead*, for God's sake, keeping some pretty difficult people in line. And from what I heard, Mike Dweetz and Steve Fusco and all the notorious Voc. Ed. crowd settled down as well when MacFarland took the podium. Though a lot of guys groused in the schoolyard, it just seemed that giving trouble to this particular teacher was a silly thing to do. Tomfoolery, not to mention assault, had no place in the world he was trying to create for us, and instinctively everyone knew that. If nothing else, we all recognized MacFarland's considerable intelligence and respected the hours he put into his work. It came to this:

The troublemaker would look foolish rather than daring. Even Jim Fitzsimmons was reading *On the Road* and turning his incipient alcoholism to literary ends.

There were some lives that were already beyond Jack MacFarland's ministrations, but mine was not. I started reading again as I hadn't since elementary school. I would go into our gloomy little bedroom or sit at the dinner table while, on the television, Danny McShane was paralyzing Mr. Moto with the atomic drop, and work slowly back through *Heart of Darkness,* trying to catch the words in Conrad's sentences. I certainly was not MacFarland's best student; most of the other guys in College Prep, even my fellow slackers, had better backgrounds than I did. But I worked very hard, for MacFarland had hooked me. He tapped my old interest in reading and creating stories. He gave me a way to feel special by using my mind. And he provided a role model that wasn't shaped on physical prowess alone, and something inside me that I wasn't quite aware of responded to that. Jack MacFarland established a literacy club, to borrow a phrase of Frank Smith's, and invited me—invited all of us—to join.

There's been a good deal of research and speculation suggesting   30 that the acknowledgment of school performance with extrinsic rewards—smiling faces, stars, numbers, grades—diminishes the intrinsic satisfaction children experience by engaging in reading or writing or problem solving. While it's certainly true that we've created an educational system that encourages our best and brightest to become cynical grade collectors and, in general, have developed an obsession with evaluation and assessment, I must tell you that venal though it may have been, I loved getting good grades from MacFarland. I now know how subjective grades can be, but then they came tucked in the back of essays like bits of scientific data, some sort of spectroscopic readout that said, objectively and publicly, that I had made something of value. I suppose I'd been mediocre for too long and enjoyed a public redefinition. And I suppose the workings of my mind, such as they were, had been private for too long. My linguistic play moved into the world, like the intergalactic stories I told years before on Frank's berry-splattered truck bed, these papers with their circled, red B-pluses and A-minuses linked my mind to something outside it. I carried them around like a club emblem.

One day in the December of my senior year, Mr. MacFarland asked me where I was going to go to college. I hadn't thought much about it. Many of the students I teach today spent their last year in high school with a physics text in one hand and the Stanford catalog in the other, but I wasn't even aware of what "entrance requirements" were. My folks would say that they wanted me to go to college and be a doctor, but I don't know how seriously I ever took that; it seemed a sweet thing to say, a bit of supportive family chatter, like telling a gangly daughter she's graceful. The reality of higher education wasn't in my scheme of things: No one in the family had gone to college; only two of my uncles had completed high school. I figured I'd get a night job and go to the local junior college because I knew that Snyder and Company were going there to play ball. But I hadn't even prepared for that. When I finally said, "I don't know," MacFarland looked down at me—I was seated in his office—and said, "Listen, you can write."

My grades stank. I had A's in biology and a handful of B's in a few English and social science classes. All the rest were C's—or worse. MacFarland said I would do well in his class and laid down the law about doing well in the others. Still, the record for my first three years wouldn't have been acceptable to any four-year school. To nobody's surprise, I was turned down flat by USC and UCLA. But Jack MacFarland was on the case. He had received his bachelor's degree from Loyola University, so he made calls to old professors and talked to somebody in admissions and wrote me a strong letter. Loyola finally accepted me as a probationary student. I would be on trial for the first year, and if I did okay, I would be granted regular status. MacFarland also intervened to get me a loan, for I could never have afforded a private college without it. Four more years of religion classes and four more years of boys at one school, girls at another. But at least I was going to college. Amazing.

In my last semester of high school, I elected a special English course fashioned by Mr. MacFarland, and it was through this elective that there arose at Mercy a fledgling literati. Art Mitz, the editor of the school newspaper and a very smart guy, was the kingpin. He was joined by me and by Mark Dever, a quiet boy who wrote beautifully and who would die before he was forty. MacFarland occasionally invited us to his apartment, and those visits became the high point of our apprenticeship: We'd clamp on our training wheels and drive to his salon.

He lived in a cramped and cluttered place near the airport, tucked away in the kind of building that architectural critic Reyner Banham calls a *dingbat*. Books were all over: stacked, piled, tossed, and crated, underlined and dog eared, well worn and new. Cigarette ashes crusted with coffee in saucers or spilled over the sides of motel ashtrays. The little bedroom had, along two of its walls, bricks and boards loaded with notes, magazines, and oversized books. The kitchen joined the living room, and there was a stack of German newspapers under the sink. I had never seen anything like it: a great flophouse of language furnished by City Lights and Café le Metro. I read every title. I flipped through paperbacks and scanned jackets and memorized names: Gogol, *Finnegan's Wake*, Djuna Barnes, Jackson Pollock, *A Coney Island of the Mind*, F. 0. Matthiessen's *American Renaissance*, all sorts of Freud, *Troubled Sleep*, Man Ray, *The Education of Henry Adams*, Richard Wright, *Film as Art*, William Butler Yeats, Marguerite Duras, *Redburn*, *A Season in Hell*, *Kapital*. On the cover of Alain-Fournier's *The Wanderer* was an Edward Gorey drawing of a young man on a road winding into dark trees. By the hotplate sat a strange Kafka novel called *Amerika*, in which an adolescent hero crosses the Atlantic to find the Nature Theater of Oklahoma. Art and Mark would be talking about a movie or the school newspaper, and I would be consuming my English teacher's library. It was heady stuff. I felt like a Pop Warner athlete on steroids.

Art, Mark, and I would buy stogies and triangulate from MacFarland's apartment to the Cinema, which now shows X-rated films but was then L.A.'s premiere art theater, and then to the musty Cherokee Bookstore in Hollywood to hobnob with beatnik homosexuals—smoking, drinking bourbon and coffee, and trying out awkward phrases we'd gleaned from our mentor's bookshelves. I was happy and precocious and a little scared as well, for Hollywood Boulevard was thick with a kind of decadence that was foreign to the South Side. After the Cherokee, we would head back to the security of MacFarland's apartment, slaphappy with hipness.

Let me be the first to admit that there was a good deal of adolescent passion in this embrace of the avant-garde: self-absorption, sexually charged pedantry, an elevation of the odd and abandoned. Still it was a time during which I absorbed an awful lot of information: long lists of titles, images from expressionist paintings, new wave shibboleths, snippets of philosophy, and names that read like Steve Fusco's misspellings—Goethe, Nietzsche, Kierkegaard. Now this is hardly the stuff of deep understanding. But it was an introduction, a phrase book, a Baedeker to a vocabulary of ideas, and it felt good at the time to know all these words. With hindsight I realize how layered and important that knowledge was.

It enabled me to do things in the world. I could browse bohemian bookstores in far-off, mysterious Hollywood; I could go to the Cinema and see events through the lenses of European directors; and, most of all, I could share an evening, talk that talk, with Jack MacFarland, the man I most admired at the time. Knowledge was becoming a bonding agent. Within a year or two, the persona of the disaffected hipster would prove too cynical, too alienated to last. But for a time it was new and exciting: It provided a critical perspective on society, and it allowed me to act as though I were living beyond the limiting boundaries of South Vermont.

35

❖ **Focused Freewriting** Consider as possible focal points the defense mechanisms students use to "get through" school, the responsibility of teachers to engage students, the idea of a teacher acting as mentor, or one of the topics you've identified in your journal.

❖ **Guided Responses**

1. Rose calls the vocational track the "dumping ground for the disaffected" (para. 11), "a curriculum that isn't designed to liberate you but to occupy you" (para 16). Based on your reading of the selection and your own experience, how accurate do you consider his assessment? Explain your response. What alternatives to a vocational track might be offered to students?

2. Rose pauses in his account of the school to relate the death of his father, bringing the reader into the present as he describes his dreams of the man (paras. 24–25). Why do you suppose he tells this story? Without it, how would the impact of the remaining paragraphs be affected?

3. Rose writes of Brother Clint, the first teacher to recognize his talents, "He was young and powerful and very handsome, and looks and physical strength were high currency" (para. 18). Jack MacFarland, the other mentor, is described quite differently: "His teeth were stained, he tucked his sorry tie in between the third and fourth buttons of his shirt, and his pants were chronically wrinkled" (para. 26). And yet MacFarland's influence is profound. Why do you think Rose concentrates on physical descriptions? What, in your view, accounts for the change in young Mike's perception?

4. Explain in your own words the realization Mike comes to as he immerses himself in MacFarland's collection of books (paras. 34–37). What immediate impact do the books have on his life? How do they help him redefine himself?

❖ **Shared Responses** In your journal, describe a teacher who had a profound impact on your life. Did the teacher's subject matter have anything to do with his or her influence? How relevant was the teacher's personality? What did he or she do to engage you? In what way did your encounter with this teacher change your life? As you discuss your responses in small groups, try to come up with a list of common characteristics of highly influential teachers.

Open Admissions

SHIRLEY LAURO

SHIRLEY LAURO, *a graduate of Northwestern University and the University of Wisconsin, is a teacher, novelist, and playwright. Her play* A Piece of My Heart *was produced in 1989 by the Manhattan Theater Club;* Open Admissions *won the Dramatists' Guild Hull-Warriner Award in 1982 and was produced on television by CBS. In this play, originally published in 1983 in* Off-Off Broadway Festival Plays, *Lauro explores the frustrations not only of under-prepared students seeking higher education but also of well-meaning though ineffectual teachers. The interplay between Calvin and Alice points up the deficiencies in a system that ostensibly offers disadvantaged students the opportunity of a college education.*

Before reading the selection, write in your journal about your identity as a college student. Do you feel entitled to an education, or do you feel more like an impostor? Is the college atmosphere familiar to you? Do you think your instructors recognize your abilities and deficiencies? What do you expect to accomplish with a college education?

As you make notes on your reading, you may want to focus on the repetition of certain words and phrases, or on how the stage directions support the action.

The Characters

PROFESSOR ALICE MILLER: Professor of Speech Communications. Started out to be a Shakespearean scholar. Has been teaching Speech at a city college in New York for 12 years. She is overloaded with work and exhausted. Late thirties. Wears skirt, blouse, sweater, coat, gloves. Carries briefcases.

CALVIN JEFFERSON: 18, a Freshman in Open Admissions Program at the College. Black, powerfully built, handsome, big. At first glance a

355

streetperson, but belied by his intensity. Wears jacket, jeans, cap, sneakers. Has been at the College 3 months, hoping it will work out.

The Place

A cubicle Speech Office at a city college in New York.

The Time

The Present. Late fall. 6 o'clock in the evening.

The play begins on a very high level of tension and intensity and builds from there. The level of intensity is set by CALVIN *who enters the play with a desperate urgency, as though he had arrived at the Emergency Room of a Hospital, needing immediate help for a serious problem. He also enters in a state of rage and frustration but is containing these feelings at first. The high level of tension is set by both* ALICE *and* CALVIN *and occurs from the moment* CALVIN *enters.* ALICE *wants to leave. She does not want the scene to take place. The audience's experience from the start should be as if they had suddenly tuned in on the critical round of a boxing match.*

CALVIN's *speech is "Street Speech" jargon. Run-on sentences and misspellings in the text are for the purpose of helping the actor with the pronunciations and rhythms of the language.*

The Speech office of Professor Alice Miller in a city college in New York. A small cubicle with partitions giving ¾ of the way up. Windowless, airless, with a cold antiseptic quality and a strong sense of impersonalness and transience. The cubicle has the contradictory feelings of claustrophobia and alienation at the same time. It is a space used by many teachers during every day of the week.

On the glass-windowed door it says:

SPEECH COMMUNICATIONS DEPT.

Prof. Alice Miller, B.A., M.A., Ph.D.

There are other names beneath that.

In the cubicle there is a desk with nothing on it except a phone, a chair with a rain coat on it, a swivel chair and a portable black board on which has been tacked a diagram of the "Speech Mechanism." Room is bare except for these things.

At Rise: Cubicle is in darkness. Muted light filters through glass window on door from hallways. Eerie feeling. A shadow appears outside door. Someone enters, snapping on light.

It is ALICE. *She carries a loose stack of essays, a book sack loaded with books and a grade book, one Shakespeare book, two speech books, and a portable cassette recorder. She closes the door, crosses to the desk, puts the keys in her purse, puts purse and booksack down and dials "O."*

ALICE: Outside please (*Waits for this, then dials a number.*) Debbie? Mommy, honey . . . A "93"? Terrific! Listen, I just got through. I had to keep the class late to finish . . . So, I can't stop home for dinner. I'm going right to the meeting . . . no, I'll be safe . . . don't worry. But you go put the double lock on, ok? And eat the cold meatloaf. (*She puts essays in book sack.*) See you later. Love you too. (*She kisses the receiver.*) Bye.

(*She hangs up, puts on coat, picks up purse and book sack, crosses to door and snaps off light. Then opens door to go.* CALVIN *looms in doorway.*)

ALICE: OOHH! You scared me!
CALVIN: Yes ma'am, I can see I scared you okay. I'm sorry.
ALICE: Calvin Washington? 10:30 section?
CALVIN: Calvin Jefferson. 9:30 section.
ALICE: Oh, right. Of course. Well, I was just leaving. Something   5
you wanted?
CALVIN: Yes, Professor Miller. I came to talk to you about my grades. My grade on that Shakespeare project especially.
ALICE: Oh. Yes. Well. What did you get, Calvin? A "B" wasn't it? Something like that?
CALVIN: Umhmm. Thass right. Somethin like that . . .
ALICE: Yes. Well, look, I don't have office hours today at all. It's very dark already. I just stopped to make a call. But if you'd like to make an appointment for a conference, I'm not booked yet next month. Up 'till then, I'm just jammed.
CALVIN: Thass two weeks! I need to talk to you right now!   10
ALICE: Well what exactly is it about? I mean the grade is self-explanatory—"Good"—"B" work. And I gave you criticism in class the day of the project, didn't I? So what's the problem?
CALVIN: I wanna sit down and talk about *why* I got that grade! And all my grades in point of fact.
ALICE: But I don't have office hours today. It's very late and I have another commitment. Maybe tomorrow—(*She tries to leave.*)
CALVIN: (*voice rising*) I have to talk to you *now!*
ALICE: Look, tomorrow there's a Faculty Meeting. I can meet you   15
here afterwards . . . around 12:30. Providing Professor Roth's not scheduled to use the desk.
CALVIN: I got a job tomorrow! Can't you talk to me right now?
ALICE: But what's it about? I don't see the emergen—

CALVIN: (*voice rising loudly*) I jiss *tole* you what it's about! My project and my *grades* is what it's about!

ALICE: (*glancing down the hall, not wanting a commotion overheard*) All right! Just stop shouting out here, will you? (*She snaps on light and crosses to desk.*) Come on in. I'll give you a few minutes now.

(*He comes in.*)

ALICE: (*She puts purse and book sack down and sits at desk.*) Okay.　20 Now then. What?

CALVIN: (*Closes door and crosses UC. Silent for a moment, looking at her. Then:*) How come all I ever git from you is "B"?

ALICE: (*stunned*) What?

CALVIN: This is the third project I did for you. An all I ever git is "B."

ALICE: Are you joking? This is what you wanted to talk about? "B" is an excellent grade!

CALVIN: No it's not! "A" is "excellent." "B" is "good."　25

ALICE: You don't think you deserved an "A" on those projects, do you?

CALVIN: No. But I got to know how to improve myself somehow, so maybe sometime I can try for a "A." I wouldn't even mind on one of those projects if I got a "C." Thass average—if you know what I mean? Or a "D." But all I ever git from you is "B." It don't matter what I do in that Speech Communications Class, seems like. I come in the beginnin a it three months ago? On the Open Admissions? Shoot, I didn't know which end was up. I stood up there and give this speech you assigned on "My Hobby." You remember that?

ALICE: (*Reads note on desk.*) About basketball?

CALVIN: Huh-uh. That was Franklin Perkins give that speech. Sits in the back row?

ALICE: (*Tosses note in wastebasket.*) Oh. Yes. Right. Franklin.　30

CALVIN: Umhmm. I give some dumb speech about "The Hobby a Makin Wooden Trays."

ALICE: Oh, yes. Right. I remember that.

CALVIN: Except I didn't have no hobby makin wooden trays, man. I made one in high school one time, thass all.

ALICE: (*Leafs through pages of speech books.*) Oh, well, that didn't matter. It was the speech that counted.

CALVIN: Umhmm? Well, that was the sorriest speech anybody　35 ever head in their lives! I was scared to death and couldn't put one word in front a the other any way I tried. Supposed to be 5 minuets. Lasted 2! And you give me a "B"!

ALICE: (*Rises, crosses to DR table and puts speech books down.*) Well, it was your first time up in class, and you showed a lot of enthusiasm and effort. I remember that speech.

CALVIN: Everybody's firss time up in class, ain't it?

ALICE: Yes. Of course.

CALVIN: (*Crosses DR to* ALICE.) That girl sits nex to me, that Judy Horowitz—firss time she was up in class too. She give that speech about "How to Play the Guitar"? And man, she brought in charts and taught us to read chords and played a piece herself an had memorized the whole speech by heart. An you give *her* a "B."

ALICE: (*Crosses to desk, picks up book sack and puts it on desk.*) Well,   40
Judy's organization on her outline was a little shaky as I recall.

CALVIN: (*Crosses end of desk.*) I didn't even turn no outline in.

ALICE: (*Picks up purse and puts it on desk.*) You didn't?

CALVIN: (*Leans in.*) Huh-uh. Didn't you notice?

ALICE: Of course! It's—just—well, it's been sometime—(*She quickly takes the grade book from book sack and looks up his name.*) Let me see, oh, yes. Right. Here, I see. You didn't hand it in . . .

CALVIN: Thass right, I didn'.   45

ALICE: You better do that before the end of the term.

CALVIN: I can't. Because I don't know which way to do no outline!

ALICE: (*Looks up name in grade book and marks it with red pencil.*) Oh. Well . . . that's all right. Don't worry about it, okay? (*She puts grade book away.*) Just work on improving yourself in other ways.

CALVIN: What other ways? Only things you ever say about anything I ever done in there is how I have got to get rid of my "Substandard Urban Speech!"

ALICE: (*Picks up 2 files from desk and crosses to UCR file cabinet.*)   50
Well, yes, you do! You see, that's your real problem, Calvin! "Substandard Speech." It undercuts your "Positive Communicator's Image!" Remember how I gave a lecture about that? About how all of you here have Substandard Urban Speech because this is a Sub—an *Urban* College. (*She puts on gloves.*) Remember? But that's perfectly okay! It's okay! Just like I used to have Substandard Midwestern Speech when I was a student. Remember my explaining about that? How I used to say "crik" for "creek," and "kin" for "can" and "tin" for "ten"? (*She crosses in back of desk and chuckles at herself.*) Oh, and my breathiness! (*She picks up purse.*) That was just my biggest problem of all: Breathiness. I just about worked myself to death up at Northwestern U. getting it right straight out of my speech. Now, that's what you have to do too, Calvin. (*She picks up book sack and keys.*) Nothing to be ashamed of—but get it right straight out! (*She is ready to leave. She pats* CALVIN *on the shoulder and crosses UC.*)

CALVIN: (*Pause. Looks at her.*) Thass how come I keep on gittin "B"?

ALICE: "That's."

CALVIN: (*Steps in to* ALICE.) Huh?

ALICE: "That's." Not "Thass." Can't you hear the difference? "That's" one of the words in the Substandard Black Urban Pattern. No final "T's." Undermining your Positive Image . . . labeling you. It's "Street Speech." Harlemese. Don't you remember? I called everyone's attention to your particular syndrome in class the minute you started talking?

(*He looks at her, not speaking.*)

ALICE: It's "last," not "lass;" "first," not "firss." That's your   55
friend, that good old "Final T!" Hear *it* when I talk?

CALVIN: Sometimes. When you say *it*, hit*t*in *it* like tha*t!*

ALICE: Well, you should be going over the exercises on it in the speech book all the time, and recording yourself on your tape recorder. (*She pats book sack.*)

CALVIN: I don't got no tape recorder.

ALICE: Well, borrow one! (*She turns away.*)

CALVIN: (*Crosses in back of* ALICE *to her right.*) On that Shakespeare   60
scene I jiss did? Thass why I got a "B"? Because of the "Final T's?"

ALICE: (*Backs DS a step.*) Well, you haven't improved your syndrome, have you?

CALVIN: How come you keep on answerin me by axin me somethin else?

ALICE: And that's the other one.

CALVIN: What "other one"?

ALICE: Other most prevalent deviation. You said: "ax-ing" me   65
somethin else.

CALVIN: Thass right. How come you keep axin me somethin else?

ALICE: "Asking me," Calvin, "asking me!"

CALVIN: I jiss did!

ALICE: No, no. Look. that's classic Substandard Black! Text book case. (*She puts purse and book sack down and crosses to diagram on blackboard.*) See, the jaw and teeth are in two different positions for the two sounds, and they make two completely different words! (*She writes "ass-king," and "ax-ing" on the blackboard, pronouncing them in an exaggerated way for him to see.*) "ass-king" and "ax-ing." I am "ass-king" you the question. But, the woodcutter is "ax-ing" down the tree. Can't you hear the difference? (*She picks up his speech book from desk.*) Here.

(CALVIN *follows her to desk.*)

ALICE: Go over to page 105. It's called a "Sharp S" problem with 70
a medial position "sk" substitution. See? "skin, screw, scream"—those
are "sk" sounds in the Primary Position. "Asking, risking, frisking,—
that's medial position. And "flask, task, mask"—that's final position.
Now you should be working on those, Calvin. Reading those exercises over and over again. I mean the way you did the Othello scene
was just ludicrous! "Good gentlemen, I *ax* thee—" (*She crosses to the
board and points to "ax-ing." She chuckles.*) That meant Othello was
chopping the gentlemen down!

CALVIN: How come I had to do the Othello scene anyhow? Didn
git any choice. An Franklin Perkins an Sam Brown an Lester Washington they had to too.

ALICE: What do you mean?

CALVIN: An Claudette Jackson an Doreen Simpson an Melba Jones
got themselves assigned to Cleopatra on the Nile?

ALICE: Everyone was assigned!

CALVIN: Uh-huh. But everybody else had a choice, you know 75
what I mean? That Judy Horowitz, she said you told her she could
pick outa five, six different characters. And that boy did his yesterday? That Nick Rizoli? Did the Gravedigger? He said he got three,
four to choose off of too.

ALICE: (*Crosses to* CALVIN.) Well some of the students were "right"
for several characters. And you know, Calvin, how we talked in class
about Stanislavsky and the importance of "identifying" and "feeling"
the part?

CALVIN: Well how Doreen Simpson "identify" herself some Queen
sittin on a barge? How I supposed to "identify" some Othello? I don't!

ALICE: (*Crosses to blackboard, picks up fallen chalk.*) Oh, Calvin,
don't be silly.

CALVIN: (*Crosses center.*) Well, I don'! I'm not no kind a jealous
husband. I haven' got no wife. I don' even got no girlfriend, hardly!
And thass what it's all about ain't it? So what's it I'm supposed to
"identify" with anyhow?

ALICE: (*Turns to* CALVIN.) Oh, Calvin, what are you arguing 80
about? You did a good job!

CALVIN: "B" job, right?

ALICE: Yes.

CALVIN: (*Crosses to* ALICE.) Well, what's that "B" standin for?
Cause I'll tell you somethin you wanna know the truth: I stood up
there didn' hardly know the sense a anythin I read, couldn't hardly
even read it at all. Only you didn't notice. Wasn't even listenin, sittin
there back a the room jiss thumbin through your book.

(ALICE *crosses to desk.*)

CALVIN: So you know what I done? Skip one whole paragraph, tess you out—you jiss kep thumbin through your book! An then you give me a "B"! (*He has followed* ALICE *to desk.*)

ALICE: (*Puts papers in box and throws out old coffee cup.*) Well that   85
just shows how well you did the part!

CALVIN: You wanna give me somethin I could "identify" with, how come you ain' let me do that other dude in the play . . .

ALICE: Iago?

CALVIN: Yeah. What is it they calls him? Othello's . . .

ALICE: Subordinate.

CALVIN: Go right along there with my speech syndrome, wouldn'   90
it now? See, Iago has to work for the Man. I identifies with him! He gits jealous man. Know what I mean? Or that Gravedigger. Shovelin dirt for his day's work! How come you wouldn't let me do him? Thass the question I wanna ax you!

ALICE: (*Turns to* CALVIN.) "Ask me," Calvin, "Ask me!"

CALVIN: (*Steps SR.*) "Ax you?" Okay, man. (*Turns to* ALICE.) Miss Shakespeare, Speech Communications 1! (*Crosses US of* ALICE.) Know what I'll "ax" you right here in this room, this day, at this here desk right now? I'll "ax" you how come I have been in this here college 3 months on this here Open Admissions an I don't know nothin more than when I came in here? You know what I mean? This supposed to be some big break for me. This here is where all them smart Jewish boys has gone from the Bronx Science and went an become some Big Time doctors at Bellvue. An some Big Time Judges in the Family Court an like that there. And now it's supposed to be my turn.

(ALICE *looks away and* CALVIN *crosses R of* ALICE.)

CALVIN: You know what I mean? (*He crosses UR.*) An my sister Jonelle took me out of foster care where I been in 6 homes and 5 schools to give me my chance. (*He crosses DR.*) Livin with her an she workin 3 shifts in some "Ladies Restroom" give me my opportunity. An she say she gonna buss her ass git me this education I don't end up on the streets! (*Crosses on a diagonal to* ALICE.) Cause I have got *brains!*

(ALICE *sits in student chair.* CALVIN *crosses in back, to her left.*)

CALVIN: You understand what I am Communicatin to you? My high school has tole me I got brains an can make somethin outta my life if I gits me the chance! And now this here's supposed to be my chance! High school says you folks gonna bring me up to date on my education and git me even. Only nothin is happenin to me in my head except I am getting more and more confused about what I knows and what I don't know! (*He sits in swivel chair.*) So what I wanna "ax" you is: How come you don't sit down with me and teach me which way to git my ideas down instead of givin me a "B."

(ALICE *rises and crosses UR.*)

CALVIN: I don't even turn no outline in? Jiss give me a "B." (*He* 95 *rises and crosses R of* ALICE.) An Lester a "B"! An Melba a "B"! An Sam a "B"! What's that "B" standin for anyhow? Cause it surely ain't standin for no piece of work!

ALICE: Calvin don't blame me!

(*CALVIN crosses DR.*)

ALICE: I'm trying! God knows I'm trying! The times are rough for everyone. I'm a Shakespearean scholar, and they have me teaching beginning Speech. I was supposed to have 12 graduate students a class, 9 classes a week and they gave me 35 Freshmen a class, 20 classes a week. I hear 157 speeches a week! You know what that's like? And I go home late on the subway scared to death! In Graduate School they told me I'd have a first rate career. Then I started here and they said: "Hang on! Things will improve!" But they only got worse . . . and worse! Now I've been here for 12 years and I haven't written one word in my field! I haven't read 5 research books! I'm exhausted . . . and I'm finished! We all have to bend. I'm just hanging on now . . . supporting my little girl . . . earning a living . . . and that's all . . . (*She crosses to desk.*)

CALVIN: (*Faces* ALICE.) What I'm supposed to do, feel sorry for you? Least you can *earn* a livin! Clean office, private phone, name on the door with all them B.A.'s, M.A.'s, Ph.D.'s.

ALICE: You can have those too. (*She crosses DR to* CALVIN.) Look, last year we got 10 black students into Ivy League Graduate Programs. And they were no better than you. They were just *perceived* (*Points to blackboard.*) as better. Now that's the whole key for you . . . to be perceived as better! So you can get good recommendations and do well on interviews. You're good looking and ambitious and you have a fine native intelligence. You can make it, Calvin. All we have to do is work on improving your Positive Communicator's Image . . . by getting rid of that Street Speech. Don't you see?

CALVIN: See what? What you axin *me* to see? 100

ALICE: "*Asking*" me to see, Calvin. "*Asking*" me to see!

CALVIN: (*Starts out of control at this, enraged, crosses UC and bangs on file cabinet.*) Ooooeee! Ooooeee! You wanna *see*? You wanna *see*? Ooooeee!

ALICE: Calvin stop it! STOP IT!

CALVIN: "Calvin stop it"? "Stop it"? (*Picks up school books from desk.*) There any black professors here?

ALICE: (*Crosses UR.*) No! They got cut . . . the budget's low . . .   105
they got . . .

CALVIN: (*interrupting*) Cut? They got CUT? (*Crosses to* ALICE *and backs her to the DS edge of desk.*) Gonna *cut you,* lady! Gonna cut you, throw you out the fuckin window, throw the fuckin books out the fuckin window, burn it all mother fuckin down. FUCKIN DOWN!!!

ALICE: Calvin! Stop it! STOP IT! YOU HEAR ME?

CALVIN: (*Turns away, center stage.*) I CAN'T!! *YOU* HEAR *ME?* I CAN'T! *YOU* HEAR *ME?* I CAN'T! YOU GOTTA GIVE ME MY EDU-CATION! GOTTA TEACH ME! GIVE ME SOMETHING NOW! GIVE ME NOW! NOW! NOW! NOW! NOW! NOW!

(CALVIN *tears up text book. He starts to pick up torn pages and drops them. He bursts into a wailing, bellowing cry in his anguish and despair, doubled over in pain and grief. It is a while before his sobs subside. Finally,* ALICE *speaks.*)

ALICE: Calvin . . . from the bottom of my heart . . . I want to help you . . .

CALVIN: (*barely able to speak*) By changin my words? Thass nothin   110
. . . nothin! I got to know them big ideas . . . and which way to git em down . . .

ALICE: But how can I teach you that? You can't write a paragraph, Calvin . . . or a sentence . . . you can't spell past 4th grade . . . the essay you wrote showed that . . .

CALVIN: (*rises*) What essay?

ALICE: (*Crosses to UL files, gets essay and hands it to* CALVIN.) The autobiographical one . . . you did it the first day . . .

CALVIN: You said that was for *your* reference . . . didn't count . . .

ALICE: Here . . .   115

CALVIN: (*Opens it up. Stunned.*) "F"? Why didn't you tell me I failed?

ALICE: (*Crosses to desk, puts essay down.*) For what?

CALVIN: (*Still stunned.*) So you could teach me how to write.

ALICE: (*Crosses DL.*) In 16 weeks?

CALVIN: (*Still can't believe this.*) You my teacher!   120

ALICE: That would take years! And speech is my job. You need a tutor.

CALVIN: I'm your job. They outa tutors!

ALICE: (*Turns to him.*) I can't do it, Calvin. And that's the real truth. I'm one person, in one job. And I can't. Do you understand? And even if I could, it wouldn't matter. All that matters is the budget

... and the curriculum ... and the grades ... and how you look ... and how you talk!

CALVIN: (*Pause. Absorbing his.*) Then I'm finished, man.

(*There is a long pause. Finally:*)

ALICE: (*Gets essay from desk, refiles it and returns to desk.*) No,   125
you're not. If you'll bend and take what I can give you, things will
work out for you ... Trust me ... Let me help you Calvin ... Please ... I
can teach you speech ...

CALVIN: (*Crosses to UC file cabinet. Long pause.*) Okay ... all right,
man ... (*Crosses to student chair and sits.*)

ALICE: (*Crosses to desk, takes off rain coat and sits in swivel chair.*)
Now, then, we'll go through the exercise once then you do it at home
... please, repeat after me, slowly ... "asking" ... "asking" ... "asking" ...

CALVIN: (*long pause*) Ax-ing ...

ALICE: Ass-king ...

CALVIN: (*During the following, he now turns from* ALICE, *faces front,*   130
and gazes out beyond the audience; on his fourth word, lights begin to fade
to black:) Ax-ing ... Aks-ing ... ass-king ... asking ... asking ...
asking ...

Blackout

❖ Focused Freewriting Consider as possible focal points the
closed-in atmosphere of Alice's office, the gulf between Alice and
Calvin, the mounting tension in the play, or one of the topics you've
identified in your journal.

❖ Guided Responses

1. The opening stage directions describe Alice's office as "Windowless, airless, with a cold antiseptic quality and a strong sense of
impersonalness and transience." How does this atmosphere contribute to the tension in the play? What insights does it give the reader
into Alice's behavior? How does it help to explain Calvin's frustration?

2. Why has Alice given Calvin Bs from the beginning of the term?
How do you respond to her explanations of the grade? Why is Calvin
unsatisfied with these grades? What do they represent to him?

3. When Alice is trying to explain to Calvin the problems of
"Substandard Speech," she uses herself as an example: "Just like I
used to have Substandard Midwestern Speech when I was a student.
Remember my explaining about that?" (para. 50) Why do you think

Alice dwells on her experience at Northwestern? How relevant is her experience to Calvin? What does the passage tell us about the relationship between the two?

4. The final fadeout occurs as Calvin practices pronouncing the word *asking* correctly. What is the significance of this ending? Why do you think Lauro chose this word for Calvin to repeat? Do you think the play's conclusion is positive? Why, or why not?

❖ Shared Responses   In your journal write a proposal designed to help students like Calvin achieve success in college. Focus not only on academic assistance but on financial and social aid as well. Comment also on the support that faculty members need when faced with underprepared students. As you discuss your responses in small groups, try to come to a consensus about the key features of such a support program. If you can't reach agreement, then highlight the primary differences in members' responses.

Native Voices
in Academe

WILLIAM G. TIERNEY

WILLIAM G. TIERNEY *is associate professor and senior research associate at the Center for the Study of Higher Education at Pennsylvania State University. In the course of this study, Tierney traveled to colleges across the country to interview Native American educators and students. His report, originally published in 1991 in* Change *magazine, places the responsibility for acculturation on institutions as well as on students, arguing that in addition to asking students to adapt to the mainstream culture, educators must also learn about their students' cultures. The various Native Americans with whom he speaks echo his findings.*

Before reading the selection, discuss in your journal what adjustments you had to make when coming to college. Does the institution represent a culture hitherto unfamiliar to you? If so, explain the differences between that culture and your own. If not, focus on more general adjustments to college life.

As you make notes on your reading, you may want to focus on the many examples Tierney uses to support his conclusions, his reliance on firsthand accounts, or the personal experiences of the people interviewed.

I RECENTLY COMPLETED a two-year ethnographic study for the Ford Foundation about the problems Native American students face when they go to college. Some problems parallel what countless other students face when they go to college, such as a lack of academic preparation or a feeling of loneliness at being away from home for the first time. Other problems are unique to Indian students: native beliefs about science that might conflict with what is taught in a biology class, or the feeling that one must return home for specific ceremonies even if it means a class must be missed or an exam skipped. Family obligations are paramount for most Indian students.

367

Regardless of the challenges that American Indian students encounter, each issue is enveloped in the often-conflicting cultures of the students and their institutions. The solutions to the problems need to be addressed as such. By arguing that the way we deal with Indian students must be approached as a cultural dilemma, I am not suggesting that we retum to the old-fashioned perspectives of a culture of poverty or cultural deficit models developed in the 1960s—to the contrary.

Far too often when we think of tribal peoples, false pictures arise. The Indian is a romantic figure in America's past, and their portraits sometimes evoke sentimentality. Those pictures freeze Indians in an era that does not accurately portray them today. Other pictures raise the specter of alcoholism or poverty so that one feels pity and sadness. Pictures such as these make it appear as if Native Americans are helpless and need the aid of white society.

A grain of truth exists in any portrait. For example, one cannot help but feel moved by native author James Welch's remarkable novel, *Fool's Crow,* about Native American society in Montana in the 19th century. Moreover, poverty and alcoholism are indeed contemporary problems. Some of the worst poverty in the United States exists on Indian reservations, where unemployment sometimes approaches 80 percent. But the problem with these pictures is that they are frightfully incomplete. As one student said to me:

> I was in an English class, and the TV show *20/20* had just showed a very slanted show about Indians in a city. Lots of alcohol and drug abuse. The students in the class kept saying Indians had better clean up our act, that we didn't treat people right, and the teacher just allowed it. It made me mad. I told the students that they didn't understand. We know alcohol is a problem, but if they lived in a place where there were no jobs and racism was always putting you down, then they'd have similar problems. My dad is an alcohol and drug abuse counselor, and I know the problems. I told the teacher that she had better educate herself before she lets conversations like that take place. I know she was really surprised that an Indian would speak up like that. I get along with Anglos ok, but it's at times like that where they'll backstab us.

In a few short words, this student summarized a variety of issues.   5
The mass media's misrepresentation of minority people in general and Native Americans in particular provides misinformation that leads to comments by individuals such as those in the student's class. And such comments make people angry. The student knew about the problems Indians face; she didn't need a television show to tell her.

Indeed, the teacher missed a unique opportunity by not calling on the student to speak to the class instead of a television reporter.

Over the past year, Dr. Clara Sue Kidwell, Dr. Bobby Wright, and I have interviewed Indian students and educators for this issue of *Change*. We wanted them to talk about the educational experiences of American Indians and offer a more complete portrayal than we normally see of Indian students, educators, and their families. The individuals come from throughout native America—Flathead, Sioux, Arikara, Chippewa, and Blackfeet. Their academic careers are as varied as the many tribes that exist in America.

One person we interviewed has gotten a Ph.D. and is now a tribal college president. Another is a single mother of three and a returning adult student to Montana State University; she hopes to become a veterinarian. A third student attends a tribal college and wants to get her teaching certificate, while a fourth has just gotten a doctorate from UC–Berkeley and has written her dissertation on American Indian women and leadership. A fifth individual has just graduated from college and intends to pursue a master's degree.

Each has a lively and pointed story to tell that stands in stark contrast to the normal portraits drawn of Native Americans and their education. What we hear about from each of these individuals are the struggles, obstacles, or encouragement that they encountered in school. In particular, the sense of obligation they all feel to their families and tribes is stunning. Education for these people does not fit the "me" decade of the 1980s at all; in this light, perhaps everyone has much to learn about how we might think of education.

Certain themes emerged from the stories that also fit my own two-year analysis of Native American college-going patterns. In the profiles that accompany this article, the unique stories of five individuals are presented more fully. In what follows I touch on three general themes.

Student Lives, Cultural Lives

Over the last 20 years we have grown more accustomed to different typologies of students—full-time and part-time, tradational-aged and adult, men and women, for example. With American Indian students we must extend these typologies even further to ask if the student comes from a reservation or from the city; does "traditional" indicate whether or not he or she participates in ceremonies; does the individual speak a native language; or has the individual gone to all-Indian schools? Each of these characteristics influences the way an Indian student approaches college life.

By and large, only a small segment of the population of a mainstream campus has any feeling for the pressures and struggles that an Indian student faces. Faculty often overlook the quiet Indian student in the classroom who may not get good grades, but who also does not cause any trouble. It is commonplace to realize that faculty are trained in their discipline and may not know much about the culture of their institution or the surrounding environment. A lack of understanding in the backgrounds and culture of Indian students is one of the key problems related to Indian student retention. One faculty member related to me how, when she was hired for her position, she was told that she would have many Indian students in her classroom and that most of them had gone to boarding schools. She remembered:

> I thought that was just great because where I come from, back East, boarding schools are for the elites. Exeter, that kind of school. Well, I got here and I found something else. I had never seen an Indian until I got here. I had a lot of learning to do, and I did it on my own.

Another instructor on a different campus also noted how unprepared she felt to teach Native Americans. "I'm a white woman from Detroit," she said, "and I first thought: this is crazy; what am I doing?" Eventually, she took numerous trips on her own volition to the reservation to learn more about tribal life. A student applauded the instructor's efforts but pointed out that the teacher was the exception to the rule: "It's beyond my comprehension why people don't want to learn about the population they're teaching. These people have forgotten about Indians." Another student agreed, adding: "It's a big problem. Even though most students are Anglos, this place has a lot of Native Americans and nobody knows about them except the few who reach out."

"Some faculty put us down," observed one female student. "And they don't realize they're doing it." " 'You're doing so well for a Native American,' they'll say," explained her friend. Another student continued, "I don't want to be treated special. I don't think that they should think that because we're Indian we should get special treatment, but usually we're just anonymous." And still, some faculty are supportive and helpful. One student provided a snapshot of a faculty member who helped:

> I was here once before, and I got terrible grades and left. When I came back I got more terrible grades on my first exams. My math teacher took me aside after he handed out the exam and asked me to see him. I had planned to go, but I didn't. The next class, he walked with me after class and we

spoke. He offered me tips on how to study. After every exam we went over my mistakes. I got so I liked it.

The lesson to be learned here is relatively straightforward. Any student who enters academe must learn about the cultural mores of the institution. If they are to survive, they need to learn how to adapt. Many of these lessons may have nothing to do with traditional areas of knowledge, such as whether the student's writing and math skills are sufficient. Although all students must learn about the institution's culture, the difference is greatest for minority groups such as Native Americans, who will find that culture distinctly different.

Most of our efforts have been geared toward helping the student 15 become more fully integrated into the mainstream. Academic support centers, summer school classes, and orientation programs all have tried to stem the alienation that many minority students face on mainstream campuses. But the students' comments made above, and the attached student profiles, point out a different posture that institutions should take.

Instead of helping the student become integrated into the mainstream, we need to help our organizational participants—faculty, in particular—become oriented to their students. To Indian students, integration often implies assimilation which, in turn, means the loss of their culture. Indian people have no desire to lose their culture. Indeed, they want to maintain and strengthen it. Although academic support centers, orientation programs, and the like are all well-intentioned, we need to reverse the logic if we are truly to aid ethnic minorities.

Rather than force the student to adapt to the organization, we need to develop ways in which the organization might adapt to the student. We need to socialize faculty to the learning styles and lives of those they educate, and faculty need to be encouraged and rewarded for learning more about their students. For Indian students, this might mean that a closer involvement takes place between faculty and what occurs in tribal communities—whether in urban areas such as Minneapolis and Denver, or on reservations such as the Flathead or the White River Apache. We need to be more sensitive as to how we arrange teaching, learning, and the life of the university so that we may benefit from what native peoples have to offer, and, in turn, they may benefit from the fruits of a college education.

Bridges

Recently, we have focused many of our efforts on building bridges between two- and four-year institutions. Many states and institutions have developed transfer policies that have led to an easier flow for community college students. Again, such bridges are essential for American Indian students; as with most ethnic minorities, over 50 percent of Indian college students attend two-year institutions.

However, bridges are of no use if no one travels over them. I am suggesting a problem exists that needs to be more forcefully addressed. Community colleges, like all institutions, have manifold functions and roles. As with all of American higher education, no general rule pertains to every two-year college. However, we must be more clear about what we desire from specific institutions.

At one university I visited, individuals expected students who did   20
not meet their admissions criteria to first go to the community college. "We're really not set up to aid in remediation," commented a faculty member. "We're working out an articulation agreement with the local community college," added another. The assumption was that the community college was better able to deal with student remediation; once the students overcame academic deficiencies, they could then transfer to the university. Yet, when I visited the community college, it was clear that they viewed their function more as a vocational effort than one of transfer. "We serve our clientele," argued the president. His definition of service to the clientele could be judged by the percentage of students who got jobs when they finished their coursework. The community college, by the way, was extremely effective in providing jobs for its students.

The point here is not that anyone is consciously perpetuating injustices or "cooling out" students, to use a phrase from another era. However, obvious misperceptions exist about institutional roles. One group of individuals hurt by these misperceptions is comprised of Indian students who desire a four-year degree. Simply stated, if the culture of a two-year institution is geared toward vocational certificates, then that is what students will work toward. Yet, if the university tells students that, before they will be able to compete at the university, they should attend the community college, that advice is not sufficient.

Tribal colleges offer one solution. Students may learn the basic skills needed for college work, and the smaller size of the institutions provides opportunities for aiding students in fulfilling whatever educational goal they desire—a vocational course, or coursework to meet the university's requirements. Specific problems also reside with tribal colleges, however. The institutions are seriously underfunded. Congress has yet to allocate what the institutions have been appropriated. Further, mainstream universities know little, if anything, about the makeup of tribal institutions, so few bridges have been built.

Although we need to develop institutions that have clearer identities we must not implicitly exclude people on the basis of race. A community college that is set up for vocational training, or a public university that emphasizes academic learning, or a private college that encourages scientific inquiry need to address more straightforwardly how their institutions might more fully incorporate Native Americans rather than assume that students who do not meet specific criteria should look elsewhere.

Staying Power

I have visited one institution where there have been over 15 different studies about Native Americans during the last 30 years. Although the language of the first report reflects the time in which it was written, the recommendations are not much different from many of the suggestions made today: hire more Indian faculty, develop an American Indian studies center, create better student services, and offer earlier intervention programs. Many task forces and study groups have been created, yet we have not done enough in terms of implementing the recommendations.

Organizations have notoriously poor memories. A new president   25
comes into office and undertakes a study with a different group of people about "the Indian problem." The recommendations invariably have costs attached to them that the institution does not have, and we then move on to study another problem. My point is not that we should be cynical about commissions or study groups; rather, we need to create strategic plans with longer time horizons than those of a year or two. Overall organizational strategies need to be developed. Far too often, one part of an institution develops a program in isolation from the rest of the university, resulting in the absence of any sense of coordination. Further, someone often gets a good idea and finds funds to implement the idea. Yet, criteria for whether specific goals have been reached are absent. The funding runs out, and the university lets the program die. The cycle begins again when someone gets another good idea and locates a funding source. Universities need to come to terms with which programs help Indian students and which programs do not. In an era of fiscal short-falls, we must have specific criteria with which to base financial decisions.

Native American recruitment and retention is not an issue that will evaporate or be solved overnight. This is a generational issue, and we need to think about it in this manner. How well equipped are we to deal not only with our Indian students today, but also with Native American students who are now in the first grade? I am suggesting that we need to reorient the way we approach this issue and others.

Let me summarize: First, instead of looking to see how we can change the student to fit the college environment, we must reorient the environment to make the student welcome. Second, we need to make concern for cultural diversity a central issue at all institutions, regardless of institutional mission. Third, we must recognize that if we are to enact the first two points, time and staying power, along with coordination and a clear sense of specific goals, are fundamental to the enterprise.

Finally, these points arise out of American Indian students' and educators' voices and concerns about education. If we are to change our environments and focus on cultural diversity, a first step in that direction is to listen to native voices and learn from them.

Profiles

DR. JUDY ANTELL

Tribe: Chippewa
Major: Sociology/Native American Studies
School: Mankato State University/UC–Berkeley

KIDWELL: What was your main motivation to go to college?

ANTELL: I got to college on a fluke. I wasn't prepared either by 30
coursework, social setting, or family setting to go to college, let alone
graduate school. I went to a small high school in Minnesota not far
from White Earth. A representative from the Bureau of Indian Affairs
came to the counseling office and told me there were funds for me to
go to college—that as an enrollee of the White Earth Reservation I was
entitled to go to college.

Before that I was planning to be a receptionist, because that was the only thing I knew women could do. I knew women could answer the phone and take messages and sit at a desk, so I thought, hey, that is what I will do. My parents didn't know anything about college, so I picked one. The reason I picked it was because it was far from home, and pretty large, and was good in social sciences, and that was Mankato State University. I went there for four years, and everything was really orderly and tidy on my transcript. I went to all the classes right when they told me to do it. Everything just fell into place one by one. And I never took an incomplete or failed to finish a course. I was real steady as a student, but not real imaginative. All I knew was to go by the rules, and so I did.

KIDWELL: What kinds of activities were you involved in outside the classroom?

ANTELL: I was politicized to a degree by becoming one of the charter members of the first Indian organization on Mankato State's campus in the 1960s. I became involved in Indian things, and more classes started to appeal to me if they had something to do with minorities, and not just Native Americans. Then, I never thought of graduate school. I got a degree in sociology, and the frustration with sociology was that there wasn't a category in sociology called race relations or ethnic studies.

KIDWELL: Graduate school takes a lot of independence and initiative. After playing by the rules all through your undergraduate career, how did you make the transition to the independence necessary to go to graduate school?

ANTELL: During my senior year of college, one of the faculty, the chair of the sociology department at the time and one of my teachers, came to me one day and asked me if I would consider staying. They really thought I was an excellent student and wanted to recruit me to stay there as one of their graduate students. That was the first time I was offered a job. I mean, there was such a thing as graduate school for me! This was all a surprise. It was the first time that I thought, you mean, my God, somebody actually wants me? It sounds funny, but it is true to this day, and I have talked about it with other Indian graduate students. We expect to see a letter in the mailbox saying that we are not supposed to be here, and they are going to take it all back. I think Indian people our age go through our lives thinking, "this can't really be happening to me. It's not true. I'm not that smart. I'm not that intelligent. I shouldn't be here." So I was amazed when they asked me to go to graduate school there, and it was at that point that I thought, gee, maybe I could go to graduate school other places too.

KIDWELL: So you eventually got a master's degree and then worked for a time. Why did you decide to get a Ph.D.?

ANTELL: Going to graduate school this last time took probably the most initiative because I gave up a well-paying job and my whole living situation, including friends and a lot of things that went along with that move. It was a real culture shock. Here I was at 35 years old, and I didn't have any friends here, I didn't have any financial resources, I didn't have the big job title that I used to have. I had nothing.

KIDWELL: What helped you to succeed?

ANTELL: I think the Native American studies faculty was the thing that helped me through the most. I don't think anyone else ever came to help me, to talk to me. I really love our program. I think it is a good place. I feel like we get along well and share things, share feelings, or

35

books—we share everything—and I feel really, really good about it. So that is where I am coming from. [The program] is what kept me here.

KIDWELL: You wrote your dissertation on American Indian women 40 in positions of political leadership. How did you choose that topic?

ANTELL: I have always been interested in women, and in the past I was a TA for women's studies and created and taught a course in the Sociology Department called "Women in American Society." I was interested in women's studies and Native American studies.

The person who proposed the topic was a faculty member. I said that I wanted to talk to him, and he said, "well, what are you doing as a graduate student?" I was thinking of doing something on Native American women and motherhood, and I didn't know exactly what I wanted to do. He was very straightforward, and he said something to the effect that, "oh, motherhood, we have so much on motherhood. What we need is somebody to do some analysis and writing about women as political activists. It hasn't been done yet." He said Indian women are running the Indian country, and to write about that. "Forget this motherhood stuff. Put women on a different plane." I took it seriously.

KIDWELL: What directions will your future scholarship take?

ANTELL: I would like to figure out how Indian people do politics. What is it we are really trying to do? We talk a lot about self-determination. That seems to be the phrase of the '70s and '80s, and now into the '90s. A lot of government studies are supporting this idea. The Supreme Court is going in totally different directions, and undermining our sovereignty. Is there some kind of common goal that we as Indian people are working toward? How do things get to be that way?

KIDWELL: One final question. What will you tell your son Daniel 45 about going to college?

ANTELL: By virtue of his growing up with my friends and his friends, it is going to be routine for him—not like it was for me. Times change!

DR. ELGIN BADWOUND

Tribe: Sioux
Title: President
School: Ogalala Lakota College, South Dakota

TIERNEY: Tell me about how you got involved in working for tribal colleges.

BADWOUND: I got out of the army in 1972 after being in Vietnam for 14 months. When I went home to the reservation, I was ready to do something, to help my people, and a friend told me that they had just started a tribal college. He asked me if I wanted to tutor adults to help them get their GED. I went to work and discovered I really enjoyed working at the college. Initially, it was like a normal job, but after a while I saw that the potential for the college was very great in terms of educating the people. I kept working there and eventually became president. A few years ago, I left the presidency to get a doctorate. I've completed my degree and now they hired me again as president. So, for 20 years I've been very closely involved with higher education.

TIERNEY: What's the potential for the college?

BADWOUND: It provides a community-based, culturally relevant 50 postsecondary education for the Sioux people. Local education was previously unavailable to us, and when we sent students to a large university, they never completed their degree. The students experienced culture shock. In a larger respect, I see the tribal college as promoting tribal self-determination and providing trained human resources to build tribal leadership.

TIERNEY: What do you mean by tribal self-determination?

BADWOUND: Historically, Indian nations were independent until the Europeans took our lands. The federal government negotiated treaties with different Indian tribes in the 19th century, but the tribes have always considered themselves sovereign nations. The reality is that the federal government administers tribal affairs through federal policies that are often detrimental and paternalistic. The way I see it, the goal of Indian nations has always been to govern their own affairs, to take control of their lives.

TIERNEY: How does a tribal college do that?

BADWOUND: We do two things. We need to teach skills so that students can deal with mainstream society and get jobs. But we also offer knowledge about tribal history and culture. We teach classes in culturally appropriate ways that will be very different from large lecture classes at a university. In effect, we teach students to deal with the two worlds.

TIERNEY: What do you mean when you say there are "two 55 worlds"?

BADWOUND: Indian people think differently from whites. In Western society, competition is important, the individual is important. You achieve status by acquiring money, power, position. You have a new house, a two-car garage, and so forth. In the tribal world, the extended family is the basis of the social structure. It is a non-materialistic definition of the world. One achieves status not by accumulating material wealth, but by how the individual works to advance the interest and well-being of all members of society. In fact, if you have money or status you are expected to give so that others can gain. So, what I am talking about is the ability for students to understand the white world and prosper in it, but also to maintain their ties to Indian ways. For example, I have just gotten a doctorate, but I can't flaunt my degree, saying "I'm better than all of you." I am equal with everybody. We don't deal with people hierarchically. People may recognize that I have a particular knowledge, but how I get measured is not in terms of material wealth. The question is what I do with this knowledge that will promote the interest of the tribal society. And for me, that's working for the tribal college.

TIERNEY: What are the challenges that confront tribal colleges in the 21st century?

BADWOUND: The greatest obstacle to tribal colleges is funding. Unlike mainstream postsecondary institutions that have access to state appropriations and so forth, we must rely on the Tribally Controlled College Assistance Act from Congress. During the Reagan years they cut our funding in half. We now receive $1,900/FTE; when the act was written in 1978, the bill called for $4,000/FTE. So we don't have a stable base of funding. Another problem is that most other institutions can draw on tuition as a primary source of funds. On my reservation we have extreme poverty and unemployment at around 80 percent. So it's a Catch-22. To charge tuition would mean that those who need an education couldn't get it, but without the tuition we must rely on the federal government to live up to its treaty obligations.

TIERNEY: Given all these problems and challenges, I'm curious why you went back to the reservation. You have a doctorate from a good institution and could probably be offered numerous jobs anywhere in the United States. Why did you return to South Dakota?

BADWOUND: My parents were very strong, traditional people. 60 They spoke the Sioux language, they participated in tribal ceremonies, they believed in sharing. I feel compelled to go back and contribute to helping our tribe achieve self-determination. This is a kind of calling; it's kind of my destiny. A lot of people are depending on me. It's pretty hard to turn your back on your own people. I believe what I've learned will help my children, and my children's children. So I look forward to the struggles that lie ahead.

TRACY CLAIRMONT

Tribe: Flathead
Major: Social Welfare
School: University of California, Berkeley

KIDWELL: What was your main motivation to go to college?

CLAIRMONT: My parents, definitely. My mom just graduated from high school, but my dad got a degree from a four-year business school. My parents own a business, and my dad's the director of Kicking

Horse Job Corps in Montana. They are really big on education. They did have the means to send me to college, so I was gone. But I wanted to. I had all these big dreams. I was going to get out of Montana and go to the big city and probably never come back. Once I got here, I was away from my family, and now the only thing I want to do is go back.

KIDWELL: What are your plans now that you have just graduated from Berkeley?

CLAIRMONT: I am going to get a master's degree in social welfare. My emphasis will be on child welfare, and I would like to work on different reservations. I know there is a tremendous shortage of Native American social workers to work with Native American people. Most of them are non-Indian on the reservations.

KIDWELL: What helped you the most to succeed at Berkeley? 65

CLAIRMONT: The first year I was here I didn't do well. It was a tremendous transition because I come from this town of 1,600 people. I was related to half of them and I knew the other half. And then I came here. I had never been in a big city for any length of time. I had traveled, but I had never been in a big city. It came time for my parents to leave, and they said, OK, we're leaving, and I was really scared. I didn't even know how to sign up for classes. I had never been taught any of this stuff. My mom and I were trying to figure it out, and I just started writing down classes. I didn't have any idea what to take. I just figured that maybe after I take these classes I'll learn something so I will know what to take next time. I didn't know anything about college. It was totally foreign. The first year I didn't do well at all. I was going by what friends in the dorms told me. I had a really good roommate. She had been in a "summer bridge program," so she knew what she was doing and helped me a lot. She told me the basics, but I didn't understand how to study. I didn't know anything.

I kept going. There wasn't anything else I could do. After the first year I started getting into classes more and realizing that there were some classes I would really enjoy. I started getting into the Native American Studies Department. I started making friends with a lot of the professors and wasn't intimidated by them, even though they were smart! I started to make friends with them and people in the department, and once that started happening, everything went really well after that. My grades were really good the rest of the three years that I was here. Seriously, I think the Native American Studies Department pretty much saved me.

KIDWELL: Where do you see yourself being in 10 years?

CLAIRMONT: I figure I will go into graduate school and specialize in child welfare and, just like I did here, develop a feel for what I really want to do. If I go into something like studying fetal alcohol syndrome, I would like to go into program development. I have a million ideas. That's why I have to go to graduate school and figure out a focus. There are so many things I want to do. There is a tremendous amount of teenage pregnancy on our reservation—not just Indian girls, but everybody. Some sort of support program for girls who are pregnant, or an intervention program, are desperately needed. I see so many things that need to be done and that are being done in cities that would be really good on the reservation to help things out.

KIDWELL: How have you dealt with the social life at Berkeley?   70

CLAIRMONT: I thought it was weird that nobody knows each other at all. Back home I never had to tell anybody I was Indian. That was one thing that drove me nuts being here in the city because I don't look obviously Native American. I look like my mom, and she's non-Indian. When I came down here I kept having to explain myself, explain that I'm Native American and I come from the Flathead Reservation. I kept having to answer questions like, "do you have plumbing on the reservation?"—and they were serious!

KIDWELL: What kind of advice would you give Indian students about going on with their education and getting a college degree?

CLAIRMONT: I think it is a good thing. I wouldn't push anybody to go very far away, though. I wouldn't say that if you want to go to college, you should go to the best one possible. I would try to prepare them for it, just talk to them, tell them what is going to happen, tell them what it is like, just give them an idea of what is going to happen when they go to college. I didn't even know you didn't go to class eight hours a day! Just tell them so they are not scared to do it.

My dad and my mom never actually told me to go to college, but I started to realize that was what they had been telling me in these different kinds of ways: "Go ahead, go get your education, but we want you to come back, and we want you to put it to good use."

Not everybody could go away and do what I did, so I can bring it   75 back and help them, and it's not like a personal benefit. It has to be for everybody. It is a responsibility for improving the lives of everybody. So, I would definitely impress upon young people the responsibility that they have in getting an education, and they should bring it back and try to help the people who didn't have the opportunities they did. Help the tribe.

LZETTA LATTERGRASS

> *Tribe: Arikara*
> *Major: Education*
> *School: Turtle Mountain Community College*

TIERNEY: Tell me about why you chose Turtle Mountain.

LATTERGRASS: Actually, I went to Mary College in Bismarck, North Dakota, before I came here, but I found it very, very difficult. It wasn't that it was difficult academically. At the time, I was a single parent with three children under eight years old. I knew that I wanted a college degree, and to get one I left the reservation. Although there are a lot of Indian people in Bismarck, I felt sort of isolated. And with my kids, I had my hands full! I liked Mary College, but I always felt left out. Most of the students are traditional-aged white college kids, and here I was an Indian with children. I really had nothing in common with them, so after a year I left. One good thing was that I met the man I married in Bismarck. I moved to Turtle Mountain because my husband is from here; I'm from the Fort Berthold Indian Reservation. I worked for a while in a job, and Bob and I had two more children. But it was always in the back of my mind to get a college education. Turtle Mountain made good economic sense; it's affordable. To get a good job and to help Indian people you've got to have a college degree. So, I've been here a year and will graduate in June.

TIERNEY: What's it like?

LATTERGRASS: It's great! I know what I want to do, what kind of degree I want, and Turtle Mountain is helping in every way they can. I've learned first-hand that I'm good with children; I find it rewarding.

I'm taking courses in education and the basics, the general educa-   80
tion courses. They are demanding classes, but I can handle them. Last year I made the president's list. Classes are not as large as at a university, and most everybody's Indian. It's a very different kind of college. There are a lot of older people, and the younger ones aren't as nervous as I was at Mary. We all work together in class—it's not competitive. We get grades and there are tests, but they are always working with you until you get it right. The teachers are very helpful. You know everybody and feel right at home. You don't have to explain yourself, and there's no stereotypes.

TIERNEY: What kinds of stereotypes?

LATTERGRASS: Most people don't understand Indians. They'll look at us and define us in one way or another. "Oh, you're Indian," they'll say, "you must be good at art." Or they'll tell me that I shouldn't try hard classes. The worst is when people think they're being positive and they say something like, "you do good work for an Indian." I do good work, period!. This semester I'm taking economics and biology, and they're tough classes. I'm challenged here, but it's in a positive way.

TIERNEY: It sounds like Turtle Mountain is a lively place.

LATTERGRASS: Exactly, I don't have the time, but I make time for the college. They sent a bunch of us to New York City in the summer to speak on behalf of tribal college students. I'm also going to a meeting of the National Indian Education Association so I can learn what else is going on. I'm a student representative to the board of the American

Indian Higher Education Consortium. All of these things enable me to speak out on behalf of students—Indian students. And at the college, you feel like it's your own. If you don't think something is right, you can talk with the president. It's not like a big university where students are supposed to sit and be quiet.

TIERNEY: What advice would you give other students? 85

LATTERGRASS: Get involved. Don't believe people when they say you can't do it, or they want to fit you into a particular hole. Expect the best of yourself. And work on study skills.

TIERNEY: How about teachers? What would you tell faculty who don't know anything about Indian students and have them in their classes?

LATTERGRASS: I'd tell them to try to get to know Indian people. Make an extra effort. Indian students might appear shy; I know I was shy when I first left the reservation. But now I speak up. People say I won't keep quiet! And I won't anymore; there's too much to do. Teachers need to visit reservations and learn our ways. I never understand why teachers think they need to know *what* they teach, but they don't need to know *who* they teach. They need both. Indian people have a lot to offer, and if teachers are willing to reach out, I bet they'll learn something.

TIERNEY: When you finish here what's next?

LATTERGRASS: We're going to UND next year. I want my bache- 90
lor's. It might take me a little bit longer because of the kids, but I won't give up. I want to teach history or English. I want to teach so that I can tell Indian students something about our own people so that they learn our history, and so that white students will understand us better.

ROBERTA STANDISH

Tribe: Blackfeet
Major: Animal Science-Veterinary Medicine
School: Montana State University

WRIGHT: Who influenced you to go to college?

STANDISH: My high school counselor. I got married when I was a junior, so I never finished high school. I took my GED when I was 17 and immediately started at Montana. It was the only way I felt I could escape from being a maid in a motel—forever. I always wanted to be a doctor. I knew I didn't have the educational background, but if I tried, I could do it. But I dropped out. I'm just returning after 12 years, after my kids got older.

WRIGHT: What are you studying? Why?

STANDISH: Animal science. I intend to go on to Vet School. Why? I was always interested in cows and horses. My grandfather has a ranch. The way I look at it, humans need cows—if I can make bigger and better cows, I'll help humans!

WRIGHT: What's a normal day for you?   95

STANDISH: Getting up at 6 a.m.; getting my children ready for school; a little reading; driving nine miles to campus. I usually carry no less than 15 credits per quarter. I go to classes, then I try to juggle my household and personal business (family responsibilities) in the time that's left.

My school day usually ends at 3:00 p.m., and I go to work till 6:00 p.m. I get home about 6:30—and get the kids ready for bed. I study from 9:00 p.m. to midnight. In between, I try to participate in other activities, like the Animal Science Club.

WRIGHT: Who do you socialize with?

STANDISH: My sister and my children. I try to take an hour a day to visit with friends.

I do a lot with the Indian Club—try to help out and get to the   100
meetings. I go to the Indian Drumming Group every Wednesday night; that's something I can take my kids to.

WRIGHT: What will you do after graduation?

STANDISH: I have a friend who's two years ahead of me. He's in the Vet School and knows about the regional veterinary schools. I still get scared. It's a daily struggle to get along in the white world, but he's paving the way and encouraging me. I'll go to Vet School in Washington or Oregon.

WRIGHT: What advice would you give an Indian student coming to study here?

STANDISH: I would advise them to get a personal advisor. I went to other schools and was just a number. The best thing I did was get an advisor. Indian students get so discouraged because they're afraid. They don't have anyone to show them the ropes. Usually, their financial aid is messed up and they just go home. I've never had proper funding. I would advise students not to give up—to get involved. If I didn't follow that advice, I'd be gone a long time ago.

WRIGHT: If you could give advice to your teachers, what would   105
you say?

STANDISH: I would say they need to understand Indian students. I had to go to an instructor one time about a Crow student who was afraid and sat in the back of the class. I told the instructor, and he took him aside and gave him one-on-one attention. Instructors need to take a personal look at that one Indian student; they need to take time to know that person in order to understand.

WRIGHT: What factors have helped you succeed here?

STANDISH: The personal interest taken by my advisors and instructors.

Actually, I got into a research project for 3 credits, and then I heard about the Minority Biomedical Research Support Program (MBRS). Without the MBRS program, I'd never be able to go on with my research. This program is the number-one factor to involve Indians in research.

My best friend is my sister, and she's helping keep me in school,   110
too.

❖ Focused Freewriting   Consider as possible focal points traditional depictions of Native Americans, one of the personal stories highlighted, or one of the topics you've identified in your journal.

❖ Guided Responses

1. One of the most "stunning" revelations of Tierney's study is "the sense of obligation [Native American students] all feel to their families and tribes . . ." (para. 8). How do the interviews with students and educators bear out this observation? Why do you think this characteristic is so prevalent among Indian students?

2. Tierney identifies miscommunication between universities and community colleges as one problem that plagues Native American students seeking higher education. If community colleges are indeed successful as vocational schools, how can the problem of preparing students for university admission be solved? How can universities and colleges work together to provide a transition for needy students?

3. Dr. Elgin Badwound views the mission of the tribal college as "promoting tribal self-determination and providing trained human resources to build tribal leadership" (para. 50). How do the experiences of the others interviewed support this statement? How does this statement reflect Tierney's conclusions?

4. In her interview Izetta Lattergrass chastises faculty members who "think they need to know *what* they teach, but they don't need to know *who* they teach" (para. 88). What evidence from Tierney's report and from the other people interviewed illustrates this statement? Do you think Lattergrass's comment applies to most college teachers you've encountered? Explain your response.

❖ Shared Responses   In your journal identify a nonmainstream student population that could be better served by your institution.

Using Tierney's conclusions as a general guide, outline several strategies that might help these students adjust to college. As you discuss your responses in small groups, try to identify strategies that would apply to many groups and single out those that would affect only specific groups.

—— ❖ ——

Home Schooling

ALFIE KOHN

ALFIE KOHN holds a B.A. from Brown University and an M.A. from the University of Chicago. A contributor to The Nation, Psychology Today, *and the* Georgia Review, *his book* No Contest: The Case Against Competition *was published in 1986. He is currently a visiting lecturer at Tufts University and a member of the summer faculty at Phillips Academy, Andover. In this 1988 article from* The Atlantic, *Kohn investigates a little-known practice in American education. Using examples of parents who educate their children at home for various reasons, Kohn explores both the reaction of the educational establishment to the practice and the rationale offered by organizations formed to support home schooling.*

Before reading the selection, write in your journal what you think of home schooling. What are its advantages and disadvantages? Do you think children can get a better education at home than at school? Explain your reasoning. Why do you think parents would want to teach their children at home?

As you make notes on your reading, you may want to focus on Kohn's shifting emphasis between individual cases and general observations and statistics.

PERHAPS NO SINGLE college acceptance has ever been the source of such widespread jubilation as that of Grant Colfax, in the spring of 1983. When this teenager from rural California was offered a place in Harvard's incoming freshman class (he was also admitted to Yale), several hundred thousand interested observers regarded the event as a vindication. The reason was that Grant's learning to that point had taken place almost exclusively at home. As though setting out to replicate the childhoods of historical heroes, he studied English and science by the light of a kerosene lantern—when he wasn't feeding animals, building sheds, or chopping wood on the family's fifty-acre farm.

Grant's admission to an Ivy League school—he was graduated, in biology, from Harvard last year with high honors and a Fulbright scholarship to study livestock in New Zealand—made an irresistible human-interest story for the network news and at least one weekly tabloid. But it was also a milestone for the home-school movement, whose proponents and visibility continue to increase.

Those who choose to educate their own children fall, roughly speaking, into two camps, each with its own ideology, newsletter, and nearly legendary standard-bearer. Holt Associates, founded by the late education critic John Holt, in Boston, is heir to the alternative-school movement. Those who receive the bi-monthly *Growing Without Schooling*, which still features reminiscences about Holt and scraps of prose by him, are likely to be skeptical of institutions. The group's libertarian inclinations are tempered by a mostly secular New Age progressivism. The newsletter is sprinkled with references to the likes of Ivan Illich and Paul Goodman.

What Holt is to the Growers, Ray Moore is to the fundamentalist-Christian home-schoolers, who find public education unfit by virtue of its godlessness. Where Holt talks of trusting children to learn without adult interference, Moore emphasizes the importance of family values, which he believes are endangered by a socialistic state. Moore's Hewitt Research Foundation and curriculum supply center, in Washougal, Washington, puts out *The Parent Educator and Family Report*, which, like its secular New England counterpart, is filled with letters from readers. Its tone is decidedly different, though. "Are all public schools bad?" Moore asks rhetorically in one recent issue. "Hardly. Some are headed and staffed by consecrated Christians."

Partly because some home-schoolers try to lie low to avoid facing truancy charges, and partly because the movement is by its nature decentralized, no one can say with any certainty how many parents are now teaching their own children. When Holt was alive (he died in 1985), he put the number in the low five figures but admitted that this represented a tactical decision: he chose to underestimate the movement's significance so as not to scare the educational establishment into reaction. Moore, if anything, errs on the side of hyperbole, insisting that at least a million children are being educated at home, including the handicapped and those who are part of migrant families.

A more reasonable guess comes from Patricia Lines, a policy analyst for the U.S. Department of Education and an acknowledged expert on the subject. In a 1985–1986 survey she counted about 50,000 subscribers to various curriculum services that provide home-schoolers with teaching materials. If one assumes that this represents something like a quarter of all those learning at home—which comports with the results of a poll taken by the Home School Legal Defense

Association, in Great Falls, Virginia, and if one also assumes that Lines missed some suppliers and that more parents have taken their children out of conventional public or private schools since her survey, then the result is a current estimate of between 200,000 and 300,000. That number could be off the mark, but no one has been able to devise a more precise method for arriving at any other.

The estimation process is complicated by a high turnover rate. A private survey conducted in Washington state found that two thirds of all home-schooled children had been in that situation for two years or less, while a Florida survey found that only 30 percent of the students learning at home had done so during the previous year. Theoretically, such figures could simply reflect a new surge of popularity for home schooling, but the evidence available, most of it anecdotal, suggests that an interest in the practice is often short-lived. "The national average is that home-schoolers last one year," says James Prichard, who produces lesson plans for Accelerated Christian Education, a Texas firm. "They find out it's not what the parents thought it was or the parents must go back to work or something."

Bearing the sole responsibility for educating one's children—answering their questions, monitoring their progress, boning up on a range of subjects, finding appropriate texts, planning the lessons every day—can be daunting. For a working parent, it is obviously impractical; for anyone, it is likely to be more difficult than it appears. For every home-schooled child there are approximately twenty in private schools and 160 in public schools. Moreover, hardly anyone imagines that the practice will ever constitute a real threat to the jobs of professional educators.

The difficulties notwithstanding, an apparently growing number of parents keep at it. A handful of private and state-sponsored studies done in recent years offer some information about who home-schoolers are. They are far more numerous in the West and South than elsewhere. The typical home-school family is middle-class and white, and at least one of the parents has some college education. In something like nine out of ten such households the mother does most of the teaching. Boys and girls are equally likely to be taught at home.

Parents choose to keep their children out of conventional schools   10
for a variety of reasons. Some just don't want to give up their children for the better part of the day. Often the parents have what the libertarian author Stephen Arons calls "an unarticulated feeling that the child belong[s] at home and not in an institution." Some parents conclude that their children, whose actual contact with a public-school teacher may amount to only a few minutes a day, are unlikely to receive an adequate education in the public schools. (Thus, when pressed by school superintendents as to whether they are really teaching their

own children six hours a day, they will reply, with Holt: "Who's teaching them six hours a day in the classroom?")

Though many home-schoolers are disenchanted with what conventional classroom teaching offers, the members of the two camps disagree about the source of the problem. Holtians are likely to complain about rigid, autocratic, standardized procedures and a lack of opportunity for questioning and hands-on learning. Ray Moore, in contrast, speaks of parents who are "sick and tired of the teaching of evolution in the school as a cut-and-dried fact," along with other evidence of so-called secular humanism. These parents want more structure, not less, and they are therefore more likely to use curriculum services than are the readers of *Growing Without Schooling*. Of the 50,000 parents using such services, according to Lines, all but about 8,000 have chosen providers that are explicitly Christian. The workbooks supplied by Accelerated Christian Education are based exclusively on memorizing facts and taking fill-in-the-blank tests. Religious themes are woven through all subjects: eighth-grade math students, for example, are asked to construct a bar graph of the number of Scripture verses a hypothetical person memorizes each month.

That the preponderance of home-schoolers are motivated by religious concerns is suggested by the relative size of the Holt and Moore mailing lists: approximately 5,000 and 30,000, respectively. The group that has been established to defend home-schoolers in court, the Home School Legal Defense Association, is a Christian organization. Its founder, Michael Farris, also represents creationists and other fundamentalists on different educational issues. Both Farris and the National Association of State Boards of Education estimate that religion—usually Christianity—is the prime incentive for 90 percent of home-schoolers. Others, including Moore and Lines, think this figure is high, but few surveys have addressed the question directly.

The parents who are home-schoolers can be found anywhere along a continuum of educational philosophies, stretching from a free-form, non-directive approach to a regimented, almost institutional style of teaching.

Grant Colfax and his younger brothers Drew and Reed emerged from the nondirective end of the spectrum. "We didn't try in any way to mimic the public schools—it was more or less what the boys were interested in," Micki Colfax, fifty, explained in her Boonville, California, kitchen one morning while she eviscerated a chicken. The Colfaxes used no set curriculum, no tests, no deadlines. History and mathematics might be put on hold for six months while the boys studied science. But the word *study* seems inappropriate for describing much of what happened on the Colfax farm. Things needed to be done, the children had to do them, and learning simply happened along the way. After the family had lived for years without telephone service, Grant and his brothers cleared a path through the forest and installed a phone line themselves. The family wanted a guesthouse, so Drew and Reed, aged sixteen and fourteen at the time, figured out how to build one from the ground up. These projects, of course, offered intensive lessons in mathematics, engineering, and other applied sciences, and regular studies were suspended while they were under way. Micki Colfax estimates that the boys spent an average of two or three hours a day doing something that resembled formal schooling—a period that increased threefold on rainy days.

This estimate, however, does not include countless hours of inde-   15
pendent reading. Micki and her husband, David, rarely watch television, but they do read books. Their sons regularly supplemented the sizable family collection with full armloads from the local library. The Colfaxes subscribe to twenty magazines, and reading matter is piled up in the bathroom, the kitchen, and the bedrooms. Micki and David finally had to ban reading at dinner in favor of discussions about current events and literature. Despite—of perhaps because of—the absence of formal reading lists and exams, Grant had read all of Dickens by the time he was thirteen, and Drew had read all of Twain by that age. "The parents' job is largely one of pointing them in the right direction and being available when they have questions," David Colfax says. The Colfaxes have summarized their experiences and outlined their teaching methods in a book titled *Homeschooling for Excellence,* available from Mountain House Press, in Philo, California.

Carol Prudhon, who is teaching her six-year-old son and eight-year-old daughter in their Evansville, Wisconsin, home, sees her role differently. Her children's day begins promptly at 8:30 with the Pledge of Allegiance. They practice the violin, study reading and math for thirty minutes each, and stop briefly for a snack. Then come spelling, phonics, creative writing, science, and penmanship. The afternoon is for reading aloud, social studies, and special projects. The children also help around the house: baking bread, sorting laundry, and gardening. Each fall Prudhon sketches the year's curriculum; every Sunday night she writes her lesson plans for the next week. "Some people say I'm too regimented, but I'm getting great results," she says. "Some people drop everything when there's a bird on the windowsill and make birds their science lesson for the day. I think that's ridiculous."

Prudhon subscribes to Ray Moore's service and estimates that it accounts for 90 percent of her curriculum. She takes her children to weekly meetings with fifteen other local Christian home-schooling families for such enrichments as art, music, and storytelling. All but a few of these families base their teaching on one or another curriculum service, and the religious subtexts of those materials are typically supplemented by homegrown Bible lessons.

For Peter Bergson and Susan Shilcock, who are home-schooling their four children in Bryn Mawr, Pennsylvania, learning is a function of neither construction projects nor prescribed texts. "Our children's lives involve massive amounts of what the outside world would call play," says Bergson, who makes his living as an educational consultant. "We challenge the distinction between work and play." Instead of just playing house, his children have set up an elaborate community of dolls, which involves publishing a newspaper (*The Dolltown Daily News*) and running a mail system for them. This, of course, entails work on writing and spelling skills. Interaction with the outside world is not neglected, however. At age seven, one daughter opened up her own bakery, shopping for ingredients, printing advertisements, and earning very real money—kept in her own checking account—for her muffins and cookies.

That the children have supplied the initiative and the ideas for most of their activities is no coincidence. "Home schooling provides more of an opportunity to continue the natural learning process that's in evidence in all children," Bergson says. In the classroom "you change the learning process from self-directed to other-directed, from the child asking questions to the teacher asking questions. You shut down areas of potential interest."

As the Colfaxes do, Bergson and his wife keep hundreds of books   20
around to be opened at will. At an early age and without any parental pressure, Amanda, now eleven, became a prolific reader. She was "going through them so quickly I assumed she was just skimming them," Bergson says. But a few questions quickly demonstrated her remarkable retention. Formal testing is eschewed by Bergson and by most home-schoolers, because, they say, it is unnecessary. As Carol Prudhon puts it, "By working with them every day, I know what they know."

In the case of Grant and Drew Colfax, Harvard University was apparently satisfied with what they knew, and what they were capable of learning. The fact that Grant and Drew, who is now in his sophomore year at Harvard, are outspokenly irreligious has not prevented Ray Moore and other Christians from trading on their successes. "We're often being used as examples by people whose philosophy we reject and abhor—fundamentalist, holy-roller types," Grant says, "As a biology major, I studied the very stuff they're taking their kids out of school to avoid."

Grant's acceptance by Harvard and Yale, and Drew's by those schools and also Princeton, Amherst, and Haverford, is obviously welcome news for home-schoolers of all stripes. Interviews and board scores naturally assume more significance in the absence of a grade-point average (Grant's and Drew's SAT scores were quite good, both in the mid-1300's), but most admissions officers "will work with anything when a student presents credentials, and no student would be discounted" because he was home-schooled, according to R. Russell Shunk, the president of the National Association of College Admission Counselors.

As for broader indicators of the success of home schooling, controlled studies on achievement are in short supply. Susannah Sheffer, the editor of *Growing Without Schooling*, grins when she is asked for data. "See, home-schoolers hate that. They tend not to believe that learning can be measured—especially by standardized tests." She and other proponents offer anecdotal accounts of children who failed and failed in the classroom but flourished when taught at the kitchen table.

The few hard numbers that do exist—virtually all of them collected in the past few years—are uniformly positive. Studies conducted by the Departments of Education in Alaska, Washington, and Tennessee indicate that the average home-schooled student outperforms his or her traditionally schooled counterpart across the board. Brian D. Ray, a doctoral candidate at Oregon State University, has been collecting all the research on the subject he can get his hands on for an academic quarterly newsletter he edits called *Home School Researcher*. His data corroborate the state studies, showing that the great majority of home-schooled students score above average on achievement tests. "I've seen no evidence that they tend to be weak in any areas," Ray says. This conclusion is echoed by Lines and others.

In Woodinville, Washington, a high school guidance counselor 25 and amateur researcher named Jon Wartes undertook his own study. He sorted through the Stanford Achievement scores of all home-schooled students in the western part of the state who had taken the test in 1986, and compared those scores with national norms. With the single exception of first graders' performance in math, where home-schooled children scored in the forty-ninth percentile, those who were taught by their parents were above the 50 percent mark at every grade level and in every subject. In reading the median score of home-schooled children was at the sixty-seventh percentile, in listening-comprehension skills at the seventy-sixth. "One could speculate that home-schoolers as a group are very nurturing, caring parents," Wartes says. "Perhaps [their children] spent a lot of time being read to on their parents' laps."

Critics of home schooling are concerned about more than academic achievement, however. They fear for the social development of children deprived of the company of their peers. David Johnson, a social psychologist who teaches at the University of Minnesota, has found that children in competitive classrooms have lower self-esteem than those who learn cooperatively but that those who learn individually are in the worst shape of all. "Any kid who's isolated is in real danger," Johnson says. He pronounces home schooling a "bad idea," because it takes children away from their peer group. "If [parents] knew the data, they wouldn't do it."

To this criticism home-schooling proponents have two standard responses. First, they insist that the reality of a child's social life at school is, if anything, a good argument *for* home schooling. The conservative Christians talk about the importance of being socialized by family members rather than by undesirables in the school yard. Holt, in his book *Teach Your Own,* offers a different version of the same argument: "In all but a very few of the schools I have taught in, visited, or know anything about, the social life of the children is mean-spirited, competitive, exclusive, status-seeking, snobbish. . . ."

Second, the home-schoolers reply that their children are not social isolates; they interact regularly with other children in extracurricular and recreational activities. In the Washington survey two thirds of home-schoolers said they usually or always scheduled time during the day for their children to play with others. About the same proportion told Jon Wartes that their children spent at least twenty hours a month with other children. The only research on non-achievement variables, conducted by John Wesley Taylor V in 1986, found that half of a random sample of 224 home-schooled children scored at or above the ninety-first percentile on the Piers-Harris Children's Self-Concept Scale, a psychological test that measures self-esteem, while only 10 percent were below the national average.

Upon arriving at Harvard, neither of the Colfax brothers found the social scene any more intimidating than did their fellow freshmen—which is to say, it was a challenge to almost everyone in their classes. In fact, Drew says, being home schooled, "you don't know how nervous you *should* be." When he heard about what others had experienced in high school, he was anything but envious. "All the games people had to play, the mind-trips the teachers played, the whole social scene at high school, sounds really pathetic. I feel very lucky that I avoided all that." Four-H Club meetings aside, Drew acknowledges that he had little day-to-day interaction with kids his own age as he was growing up, "but it wasn't like we were lonely or deprived." As for encounters with the opposite sex, his older brother says, "There was one romantic interlude before I got here, then I made up for lost time, and that's all I'm going to say."

In place of straightforward nationwide guidelines, parents who seek   30
permission to teach their children at home face a bewildering array of
state laws, district standards, and contradictory court decisions.
Home schooling is not absolutely illegal anywhere in the country, and
many states have enacted legislation over the past few years that has
made the practice easier to pursue legally. In Missouri a parent who
files a notice of intent essentially cannot be refused permission. In
North Dakota, Iowa, and Michigan, in contrast, only certified teachers
can be home-schoolers. Other states require children to pass standardized achievement tests or receive instruction comparable to that in
public schools. In some states home schooling is permissible if one
goes through the formality of declaring one's home to be a private
school.

Considerable disparities are likely to be found in home-schooling
requirements even within a given state. One school district may offer
resources and assistance to home-schoolers, while a neighboring district goes to court to keep a child in school. What's more, a single area
may give mixed signals. Although Iowa's law is among the most
restrictive in the nation, Des Moines has instituted an innovative
home-instruction program in which visiting teachers oversee the education provided by parents.

While judges in at least five states over the past few years cited
the vagueness of home-schooling laws as grounds for striking them
down, litigation on the issue has, if anything, compounded the confusion. Home-schooling advocates like to cite the 1972 Supreme Court
decision *Wisconsin* v. *Yoder*, which allowed a religious exception to
compulsory schooling after eighth grade for the Amish, but the high
court has never ruled on home schooling per se. Most school districts
that threaten to sue parents over the issue end up resolving the case
out of court, though the record is mixed for those cases that do go
before a judge. "The lawyers on both sides can find precedent to
support the arguments they're going to make," says Cheryl Karstaedt,
an assistant attorney general in Colorado who has researched the
subject. "It depends on the circumstances of the particular case and—
though I dislike saying it—the personalities involved." The same
seems to be true for those home-schoolers who, rather than wait to be
dragged into court for violating truancy laws, have taken the initiative
to sue. As plaintiffs, home-schoolers argue that approval requirements violate their civil rights, that equal protection under the law is
violated when regulations are not applied uniformly, and that religious freedom supersedes compulsory-attendance laws.

Taken together, several recent, well-publicized cases illustrate the
judicial inconsistency that both sides face. In March of last year Mas-

sachusetts's highest court fashioned a compromise: a Christian couple had the right to teach their own children, but the school district had the right to review their curriculum. Virginia courts, meanwhile, were finding against home-schoolers in two cases, ruling in one of them that untrained parents could not legally treat their home as a private school. However, a Texas judge handed the movement a whopping victory last year in *Leeper, et al.* v. *Arlington Independent School District,* which made it almost impossible for a school district to refuse permission to home-schoolers or even to make permission conditional on test scores.

Michael Farris, whose five-year-old Home School Legal Defense Association has 7,000 member families, who pay $100 a year for protection and advice, is worried now about a rather different case he lost. Last August a federal appeals court ruled in *Mozert* v. *Hawkins County Public Schools* that a group of fundamentalist Christians in Tennessee could not keep their children out of particular classes just because they found godless influences in the textbooks. Farris expects to hear this ruling cited soon by school districts in home-schooling cases. If the First Amendment's protection of the free exercise of religion "doesn't allow you to opt out of instruction that violates your religious beliefs," he predicts prosecutors will argue, "it doesn't matter whether it's part of the day or all of the day." If you can't reject a textbook, in other words, how can you reject formal schooling altogether?

Despite the courtroom battles in which home-schoolers and their advocates often find themselves, they face no organized national opposition. Responses from the educational establishment range from indifference to low-key wariness. The idea itself is unobjectionable, educators frequently argue, but not all parents can be trusted to teach their children adequately. The right of parents to yank their kids out of school must be weighed against the state's obligation to make sure that those children are really learning something.

"We're not saying a parent doesn't have the right to keep a child at home, but a child has to be able to meet certain academic requirements," says Mary Fulrell, the president of the National Education Association. In 1984 the NEA approved a policy statement that acknowledged the reality of home schooling but recommended that home-schoolers demonstrate their competence as teacher, request permission every year, submit to extensive monitoring by local school administrators, comply with attendance laws having to do with the amount of time children should spend in school, have their children tested regularly, and so on. Having made its position known, the NEA has seen no need to take further action or to campaign against home-schooling laws.

The National Association of Elementary School Principals came out flatly against home schooling in its platform for the current school year. "The kind of arguments we're hearing are the same kind we were hearing when we were integrating schools: rights under the First and Fourteenth amendments," says Sam Sava, the group's executive director. "The problem is that many home-schoolers don't want to ask *anyone's* permission. They think it's their right under the Constitution." But the organization is not mobilizing to act on its policy statement, which fills two dozen lines in the forty-three-page platform.

If anyone is directly challenging the right of parents to teach their children, it is not teachers and principals but school boards. August Steinhilber, the general counsel to the National School Boards Association, calls home schooling a "small issue" and denies that any of his constituents is afraid it will grow to the point that public-school funding could be jeopardized. Why, then, are parents being prosecuted? "We have a responsibility to make sure [children] are being properly educated," he says.

Virginia Roach, a project director at the National Association of State Boards of Education, take a conciliatory position. "The school boards don't want to be in court or in the papers any more than the parents want to be," she says. They "look for ways to work together instead of [pursuing] an automatically adversarial relationship," but because a few parents on the fringes do not adequately educate their children, NASBE doesn't think that standardized testing or review of curriculum is unreasonable. Officially NASBE is committed only to clarifying home-schooling laws so as to eliminate confusion about what is permitted and what is required.

Home-schoolers themselves are divided on how much regulation 40 is reasonable. Farris, who considers home-schoolers to be competing with public-school systems, says that requiring approval from school boards is "like saying to Avis you can rent a car if you get Hertz's approval." As for permitting children to continue in home schooling only if their performance on achievement tests meets some arbitrary standard, Farris says fine—providing the same standard is applied to children in public schools. In his book *Compelling Belief: The Culture of American Schooling,* Stephen Arons argues that the legal restrictions have less to do with concern that home-schooled children will suffer than with educators' defensiveness about the tacit message of home schooling. "When a family seeks approval of a authority, it is implicitly challenging the professionalization of education," he writes. "Many educators seem to regard their occupational survival as dependent upon their insistence that they, and only they, can adequately define, create, and judge quality education."

But some home-schoolers are not terribly interested in affirming their inherent right to educate their children as they see fit. They simply want to get on with the process, and are happy to check in with the authorities if this means they will be able to teach their own.

❖ Focused Freewriting   Consider as possible focal points one or more of the reasons offered for home schooling, the different methods used by various home-schoolers, or one of the topics you've identified in your journal.

❖ Guided Responses

1. Kohn divides the home-schooling movement into two camps: libertarians who find conventional schooling too constraining and religious fundamentalists who object to the secularization of education. Of the reasons offered by each camp to support its position, which do you think are more convincing and why? Do you think either camp's reasoning provides sufficient justification for keeping children out of school? Why, or why not?

2. Home-schooler Peter Bergson says that in conventional schools, "you change the learning process from self-directed to other-directed, from the child asking questions to the teacher asking questions. You shut down areas of potential interest" (para. 19). Based on your experience of formal education, do you agree with this view, either in part or in full? Explain your response. What evidence do you see in this article that home schooling does or does not encourage "self-directed" learning?

3. In paragraph 30, Kohn states that "parents who seek permission to teach their children at home face a bewildering array of state laws, district standards, and contradictory court decisions" and goes on to provide examples. Why do you think he focuses on these confusing and contradictory rulings? Based on your reading of the article, what do you think these examples say about official responses to home schooling?

4. Although Kohn begins with the story of Grant Colfax's admission to Harvard, he mentions only one other such success, that of Grant's brother Drew. After reading the arguments for and against home schooling in this article, do you think many other home-schooled children could gain admission to prestigious colleges? Why, or why not? Do you think that college acceptance should be a measure of the success of home schooling? Why, or why not?

❖ Shared Responses   In your journal, write a response to social psychologists such as David Johnson, who "fear for the social development of children deprived of the company of their peers" (para. 26). Were your social experiences at school primarily positive or negative? How well do you think those experiences prepared you for adult life? Do you think your experiences were typical? As you discuss your responses in small groups, note the extent to which personal experience is reflected in each member's response.

Adam Goes to School

MICHAEL DORRIS

MICHAEL DORRIS, *a founding member of the Dartmouth College Native American studies program, published his novel* A Yellow Raft in Blue Water *in 1987. In 1992 he co-authored the novel* The Crown of Columbus *with his wife, writer Louise Erdrich. His 1989 book* The Broken Cord, *winner of the National Book Critics Circle Award for nonfiction and the Heartland Prize, is Dorris's personal account of the struggles of a family dealing with fetal alcohol syndrome. His adopted son Adam, who has the condition, suffers from a host of physical and mental disabilities. This selection relates the story of Adam's early years of schooling.*

Before reading the selection, write in your journal about your own parents' response to your performance in school. Did they pressure you to do well? Were they proud of your accomplishments? How did they react when you did not succeed despite your effort?

As you make notes on your reading, you may want to focus on Dorris's use of specific examples, his characterization of Adam's teachers, or his self awareness.

WHEN I THINK BACK ON THAT TIME, this is the scene that is conjured: at the sound of Adam's tread on the road Skahota barks eagerly, I take a sheet of steaming cookies out of the oven, and Sava pushes a chair to the table for Madeline. We always had cats living in our barn, usually named according to a prevailing theme—the most friendly were Sierra Madre, Sierra Leone, Sierra Blanca, and Sierra Nevada— and in this vision they stretch and prepare to join the party.

It is impossible that our lives were really so well ordered, so under control. On my old calendars I see the notation of many doctor visits, medical appointments in Boston. I constantly read books about learning theory and tried innovative experimental programs, searching for an approach that would be effective for Adam. My first inclination, a sort of 1960s flower child theory, was to be nonintrusive and natural, to let Adam find his own appropriate level, to allow him to be "free." I was inspired by a cartoon I had hung on the refrigerator. It showed a classroom in which all the students faced forward in perfect rows of desks—except for one American Indian student who sat on the floor and looked the other way. The exasperated (insensitive) teacher berated, "Why can't you be like other people?" Well, I was not going to be *that* guy! Beneath the caption I had written: "Don't worry if Adam: 1) wets his pants; 2) disrupts a group; 3) does sloppy activities; 4) refuses to do activities; 5) does nervous hand movements, etc.; 6) is grumpy; 7) hits; 8) takes a long time." I doubt if my good intentions lasted very long.

On the "positive reenforcement" front, I mimeographed a checklist of Adam's daily home and school activities, each of which, when executed, gained him a "star." A minimal accumulation of stars at the end of the day produced a "certificate" and a designated number of certificates could be spent, like money, for toys, fast food, or anything else he desired. The sheets, titled "Adam's Day," included such categories as "Sat Still at Breakfast," "Stayed Dry in the Morning," "Was Cheerful at _____," and "Got Undressed by Self."

The concept of saving, however, was lost on Adam, and still is. He is a living embodiment of the Roman poet Horace's adage *"Carpe diem"* ("Seize the day"). Tomorrow, as a concept, is no competition for *now,* and after a month or so of mixed results the lists were put aside. Denial of privilege was no more effective. There was nothing Adam wanted enough that the threat of its loss would alter his spontaneous behavior. If I said, "Adam, if you don't stay dry, you'll have to wear a diaper to school," he would, without embarrassment, wear a diaper. If I threatened to banish him to his room unless he sat still during an activity, he would accept the consequence without complaint—and *I* would feel like a rotten bully. Not that there weren't bursts of progress, whole weeks of operation on a new plateau in some area or another.

With total concentration, occasional hysteria, and insistent instruction, I could coerce, encourage, or manipulate Adam into modifying unacceptable behavior. But the moment I stopped pushing, ceased to monitor, he reverted to old habits. Nothing seemed "automatic" with him. There was no branching curiosity, no internal motivation to be more grown up, no quick building on previous experience, no secure gain. Regardless of how much energy I, or his teachers, expended, Adam, for the first hundred or so repetitions, always eventually wound up back at Go. His maturation was a pitched battle between our exhortation and his indifference, yet outwardly he remained serene, forgiving of adult frustration, content with and impervious to whatever new method we might employ.

5

Sweet disposition was Adam's talent, and it was so striking that it often obscured his lack of progress. In recent years I've wondered how I could have closed my eyes for so long to the fact that Adam had enduring disabilities—three years after his adoption I wrote a psychologist that I was "convinced that there is nothing permanently wrong with Adam. I'm sure you hear that from every parent with whom you work, but I think I've been open in making a judgment. . . . While it is obvious that he is developmentally young for his chronological age in certain areas, his improvements have been dramatic, erratic, and far more rapid than I would have predicted." I concluded my five single-spaced pages by noting: "I guess if I could wish one thing for him it would be for him to be more vulnerable—for disapproval and approval to matter more than they do—for him to get his kicks out of other people more. He has this insulation, and a good thing he did, of course, in his past, but it's time for it to come down a bit, and I need to know how to help him to trust. He is a sweet, loving, affectionate, and gentle boy—as nice a person as I've ever met."

A succession of teachers reacted the same way, as evidenced by the observations they sent home at the end of every school year. "Adam is a delightful boy and a real pleasure to have in my class," commented his third-grade teacher. "Adam is a very loving child. I enjoy working with him," said his fourth-grade instructor. "He's doing *so well* this year! It's hard to believe it's the same youngster," wrote the school principal at the beginning of the fifth grade. All these good men and women were determinedly optimistic. They praised Adam's "progress" in things like map making and social studies, his fondness for reading books, his great interest in art, the leaps he was making in friendships and self-control. They proclaimed his mastery of basic arithmetic ("He understands the process of addition and subtraction and has computed problems with the use of counters and the number line. . . . He has demonstrated good ability and understanding with regard to our unit on geometry"), vocabulary, telling time.

I saved these encomia in a scrapbook as an antidote to discouragement. They testified to what I wanted to believe, and I quoted them to psychologists and doctors and new homeroom teachers as proofs. It is only now, in retrospect, that I see them for what they were—collective delusion, wishful thinking. At no time in his life could Adam, by any stretch of the imagination, read a map or comprehend the principles of geometry. In eight years at the Cornish School he never once received so much as a telephone call or an invitation from a "friend." He never stayed in his seat for more than a few minutes unless he was supervised.

When Adam was young, people fell in love with him and with the idea of him. He was a living movie-of-the-week hero, an underdog who deserved a happy ending. On top of that, he had good manners, an appealing face, me to broker and block for him. He was the only full-blood Indian most people at his school had ever met. His learning problems at first appeared so marginal, so near to a solution. With just the smallest nudge they would pass over the line into the normal range. Every good teacher, every counselor, every summer camp director Adam encountered in grade school and high school viewed him as a winnable challenge and approached his education with initial gusto and determination. He teetered in his ability so close to the edge of "okay" that it seemed impossible that, with the proper impetus, he would not succeed. I understood this conviction perfectly and succumbed to it for fifteen years. I sometimes had the fantasy that if I could penetrate the fog that surrounded Adam's awareness and quickly explain what was what, he would be fine. He was just slightly out of focus.

The fact was, improvement was hard to come by and even harder   10
to sustain once it had appeared. Reviewing those end-of-the-year teacher reports, it is now clear that in grade after grade Adam was working at the same level on exactly the same tasks. Every year he started fresh, showed promise up to a point, then couldn't take the next step. His learning curve resembled more than anything else one of those carnival strong-man games in which a platform is struck with a weighted mallet and a ball rises up a pole toward a bell. In my son's case, sometimes the bell rang, but then the ball always fell back to earth. He was the little engine that couldn't make it over the mountain, and, in frustration and disappointment, without ever actually saying so, all but a dedicated few eventually stopped thinking that his trip was worth their effort.

But what a few those were. It may sound odd to say it, but Adam has been in his life incredibly fortunate in some areas, and special education teachers are one of them. Olivia Alexion arrived at the Cornish Elementary School when Adam was in the second grade and led him through the maze of the next seven years with unflagging affection and devotion. She was very young, barely out of college, but possessed a patience and long view that perfectly equipped her for the job. Ms. Alexion was a realist who acted as though she had a short memory—that is, she had the ability to forget setbacks and to maintain steady optimism even when, year after year, she was required to repeat identical lessons for Adam. She and I formed a kind of conspiracy, an allegiance that sometimes demanded daily communication so that his victories at home or at school could be consolidated, built upon. We were the day and night shifts of the same factory, and Adam was on our assembly line, inching forward at a slow pace, but forward all the same. She wrote hundreds of notes about his activities, recorded each incremental step, celebrated each tentative advance, railed against each slippage. She believed as fiercely as I that Adam had unrealized resources. She was the antithesis of detached.

What was in it for her, I privately wondered now and then. Was it ego? Was it the will not to be defeated? She worked long hours for little pay and spent many evenings researching in the library to develop new techniques. At first I hesitated to sing her praises too loudly to other parents with children in special education—I didn't want to give away how much attention she was devoting to Adam—but it turned out that we all felt the same way about her. She concentrated on each of her students as if he or she were the only child in the world, and because of her each of them surpassed what had been regarded as maximum potential.

When Adam was halfway through the fourth grade, Ms. Alexion decided to schedule a WISC-R IQ test for him on a Saturday morning in January. She believed he had previously tested "low," and that in an ideal examination environment his scores would show significant improvement. She and I would sit in the room while Adam was questioned and this, she was sure, would alleviate his feelings of anxiety as well as mute his tendency to become easily distracted in any new situation.

The results, however, fell into the same range: a verbal IQ of 63–77; a performance IQ of 63–81; and a full-scale IQ of 64–76. As always, there was a wide scatter pattern. Adam scored best on picture completion and object assembly and lowest on block design, coding, and similarities. In other words, tasks that had to do with abstract reasoning were the most difficult for him.

This wasn't what I wanted to hear, so I all but dismissed the   15
results in a long, rationalizing letter to Ms. Alexion. I noted that the WISC was "in significant part culture biased" in favor of "mainstream America"—as if Adam, the son of a Dartmouth professor, living in Cornish, New Hampshire, came from some exotic society. While allowing that, at age ten, such "terms as 'alike/different,' 'older/younger' " were confusing to Adam, I brought all my anthropological mumbo jumbo into play in denying the accuracy of his scores: "The sequential arrangement of pictures to form a story that 'makes sense' depends for its validity on a shared understanding of proper organization. The idea of 'ordering' a story, rather than trying to make sense out of the existing order presented, reflects a Western sense of 'controlling' the world rather than the idea of dealing with the world 'as is.' " I was really cooking.

"The test stresses some types of performance over others," I protested. "The oft-repeated direction 'work as quickly as possible' has little meaning for a child raised to emphasize process rather than strict efficiency." Was that how I raised Adam? And yet, how persuasive I sounded to myself. I could explain anything where Adam was concerned. In my defense of him, his liabilities were nothing more than pointers to the fact that, as an Indian, he conceived the world in different, preferable, terms. To read the sheaf of my letters during those years one would gather I believed that Adam was lucky not to be able to tell time, to tell a nickel from a quarter from a penny, or to consistently discriminate between large and small. The world, American Culture, individual assessors had the problems—Adam was just as he should be.

I must have been a formidable force for Adam's teachers to deal with as I tried to intellectually or culturally coerce them into sharing my views. I talked more than I listened, demanded reports of "progress," and vigorously protested any opinions that seemed to limit Adam's chances. To judge him lacking in innate ability, I darkly hinted, implied poor teaching, racism, or a defeatist attitude. My justification for pressure was rooted in my wish that Adam be all right, but it stemmed also from pride, from my arrogance, my terror.

I look back now at Adam's Cornish report cards, at all those *Satisfactory*'s and C's in math and science and history that I had insisted appear, all those passing marks, when in truth he didn't grasp for more than a minute any of the material. To what extent was Adam's steady progress from one grade to another due to my bluster? How far did Ms. Alexion lead him by the hand? To what degree did his teachers, for liberal or self-image reasons of their own, need to believe that he should be granted the benefit of the doubt? Yet the further on paper Adam got ahead, the further he fell behind.

❖ Focused Freewriting   Consider as possible focal points the various methods Dorris uses to motivate Adam, the pain he feels when his son doesn't succeed, his self-analysis, or one of the topics you've identified in your journal.

❖ Guided Responses

1. Dorris opens the selection with an idyllic reverie: he is baking cookies, the pets gather around the table with the younger children, and Adam returns from school to the warmth of a happy family. Why do you think Dorris begins with this scene? What does it tell us about his feelings for his family? about his acceptance of the reality of Adam's condition?

2. When Dorris describes the various methods he used to help Adam progress, he always acknowledges their failure. Yet Adam "remained serene, forgiving of adult frustration, content with and imper-

vious to whatever new method we might employ" (para. 5). What motivates Dorris and Adam's teachers to persevere? For whom are they carrying out their program? What would be the consequences— for themselves as well as for Adam—if they acknowledged defeat?

3. Describing the reports from Adam's elementary school teachers, Dorris writes of them, "They testified to what I wanted to believe, and I quoted them to psychologists and doctors and new homeroom teachers as proofs. It is only now, in retrospect, that I see them for what they were—collective delusion, wishful thinking" (para. 8). Why would teachers take part in this "collective delusion"? Given what Dorris tells us about Adam and himself, what do you think motivated the teachers? Did the reports serve any useful purpose? Explain your response.

4. Dorris claims that his response to negative reports of Adam's ability stemmed from his own "pride," "arrogance," and "terror" (para. 17). Based on your reading of the selection, explain how Dorris can be considered proud and/or arrogant. What is the cause of his terror?

❖ Shared Responses In your journal compose a dialogue between Dorris and yourself as one of Adam's teachers. How would you try to convince his father that the boy should not be expected to achieve as other children do? How would you respond to the justifications Dorris uses? As you discuss your responses in small groups, try to combine responses, using the most convincing, compassionate, and reasonable responses from individual members.

Gay Teachers, Gay Students

NEIL MILLER

NEIL MILLER, *a freelance writer, is the author of* Out in the World: Gay and Lesbian Life from Buenos Aires to Bangkok *(1992). An earlier book,* In Search of Gay America, *won the 1990 American Library Association Prize for lesbian and gay nonfiction and a Lambda Literary Award. This 1992 article, originally published in the* Boston Globe Magazine, *effectively brings gay life on high school campuses "out of the closet." While much of the gay activism occurs at exclusive boarding schools, Miller finds that some suburban high schools are now also grappling with the twin issues of how to counsel gay students and how to acknowledge gay teachers.*

Before reading the article, write in your journal about how your high school dealt with homosexuality. How did students treat classmates they suspected or knew were gay? How did the administration handle intimidation of gay students? How did teachers approach the issue?

As you make notes on your reading, you may want to focus on the distinctions Miller makes between students and teachers, his examples of successful gay/straight alliances, or his use of quotations from gay students and teachers.

IT IS A WARM SPRING NIGHT, and the young man with the ponytail is going to a gay dance—his first—and he is delighted and nervous. For most of his time at school, the Phillips Exeter senior couldn't imagine "coming out" in a dorm populated by varsity football and lacrosse players. But last year, he joined the New Hampshire boarding school's gay/straight alliance, established to educate the campus on homosexual issues. At gay/straight alliance meetings, you don't have to state your sexual orientation; you can just come to terms with yourself at your own pace in a supportive atmosphere. Today, on the way to the dance, the young man says, "I guess I'm gay," astonished at his own forthrightness. A few months earlier, he didn't feel comfortable uttering the words.

The dance is part of a weekend "retreat" of prep school gay/straight alliances taking place at America's oldest and richest private school, Phillips Andover. With its ancient elms and tradition-bound quadrangles, the alma mater of George Bush seems an unlikely spot for the unfolding of the latest chapter of the sexual revolution. In fact, Andover has been a pioneer in such matters; 4½ years ago, it approved the formation of the first gay/straight alliance at an East Coast prep school.

Downstairs at Graham House, where the gathering is being held, some 40 or so students are quizzing undergraduates from Tufts and the Massachusetts Institute of Technology about what it's like to be gay and in college. Upstairs, their faculty advisers are comparing notes: At Choate, everything is "warm and fuzzy—homosexuality is a feel-good issue," a teacher reports; at Andover, where the gay/straight alliance has been around for much longer, being a member isn't as "cool" as it once was; at one posh New England boarding school, the headmaster is said to have refused to permit the formation of a gay/straight alliance.

Following dinner at the Commons, there is a performance of the musical *In Trousers*, the first of the *Falsettos* trilogy, about a gay married man and his relationships. Directed by the student president of Andover's gay/straight alliance, the musical serves as campus-wide entertainment on a Saturday night and receives an enthusiastic response. Then comes the dance, in the social hall of a nearby Unitarian church. It's the first gay and lesbian dance for most of the students, and the enterprise has a slightly awkward air. The students dance in groups, still reluctant to pair off with someone of the same sex.

"I can't wait till I go off to college next year," says the senior with   5
the ponytail. "Someplace where being gay is kind of, well, normal."

High schools are one area in which little has changed: Gay and lesbian teachers overwhelmingly remain in the closet, fearful of the personal and professional consequences of coming out. Gay teen-agers are isolated, facing rejection both at home and at school. A 1989 study by the US Department of Health and Human Services found that gay and lesbian adolescents make up almost a third of all teen-age suicides. The situation is particularly acute in public schools. There, antigay comments are common currency long after ethnic and racial slurs have been deemed unacceptable; cautious administrators and school boards often discourage open discussion that might create a more accepting atmosphere.

One teacher in a white-collar Boston suburb described attitudes prevailing at her school this way: "We counsel gay students not to come out. They'd get killed. At our school, male students get harassed just for being in drama or chorus."

Today, students and teachers around New England are trying to change those attitudes, with much of the momentum coming from elite boarding and day schools. A year and a half ago, among private schools, only Andover and Concord Academy had campus gay/straight alliances. Since then, such organizations have sprung up at Exeter, Milton Academy, Choate Rosemary Hall, Northfield Mount Hermon, Buckingham Browne & Nichols, The Winsor School, The Putney School, and Brewster Academy. A gay/straight alliance was established at Newton South High School last spring. Cambridge Rindge and Latin has a similar organization, called Project Ten East. Few students in these groups identify themselves as gay or lesbian; in a world of teen-age macho and peer pressure, coming out is still a bold step, even in ostensibly tolerant surroundings.

Concord Academy and Milton Academy now have three openly gay teachers; Andover boasts two, and Cambridge Rindge and Latin and Newton South one each. An organization called GLISTEN—Gay and Lesbian Independent School Teacher Network—was created in December 1991 to serve as a vehicle for raising the issue in the prep school world. A GLISTEN conference held at Milton Academy this past April was attended by almost 300 people, and the keynote speaker was Milton headmaster Edward P. Fredie. Milton seniors spend two to three weeks learning about the gay movement as part of a civil rights course; a unit on gay and lesbian history, designed by Arthur Lipkin, a research associate at the Harvard Graduate School of Education, was given a test run at Cambridge Rindge and Latin last year. In an effort to promote a more diverse faculty, Concord Academy advertises job openings in gay newspapers.

Most of the teachers crusading for a more accepting attitude to- 10 ward homosexuality in secondary schools are young; many came out while in college and refuse to go back into the closet. "Part of what is happening is due to the new militancy within the gay movement and a refusal to be intimidated," says Kevin Jennings, an openly gay history teacher at Concord Academy and founder and cochairman of GLISTEN. "In addition, the AIDS crisis has forced educators to see the consequences of refusing to deal with sexuality. It has forced them to listen."

Progress does not necessarily come easily. Prep schools worry about what effect the presence of gay teachers and gay-friendly groups will have on admissions and endowments. Incidents such as the recent L. Lane Bateman case, in which the head of the Exeter drama department was convicted of possession and distribution of pornography, exacerbate such concerns. (Bateman was closeted and not involved with the school's gay/straight alliance.)

When a lesbian physical education teacher at a Boston-area day school announced she wanted to come out, she was told she could not do so, and she resigned. At the St. Paul's School, in Concord, New Hampshire, "We want to move carefully," says vice president John Buxton, concerned that too much attention to the issue could be divisive. Even at supportive Milton Academy, the gay/straight alliance was left off a list of student organizations in the catalog, an omission that officials ascribe to an oversight.

While some parents applaud the new openness, others are uneasy. "You hear both sides," says Clinton J. Kendrick, a New York investment manager who has two children at Andover. "There are some parents who say it's wonderful. There are others who say it makes them very nervous and it's not acceptable."

Kendrick, who also serves on the Andover school's board of trustees, believes that the presence of a gay/straight alliance on campus could prove confusing to students unsure about their sexual orientation. But the overriding issue, in his view, is that of individual rights. "I am trying to emerge from the '50s," he says. "I believe very strongly that people have civil rights. The important thing is to have effective teachers, straight or gay."

When hundreds of Cambridge Rindge and Latin students and teach- 15
ers marked National Coming Out Day in October last year by wearing pink triangles (the symbol gays were forced to wear in Nazi death camps), Rev. Earl W. Jackson, a staunch opponent of gay rights, came to the school to protest. In his view, the only reason a gay teacher would want to be open with his students is "to push the agenda for homosexuality."

Rev. Jackson, who is the pastor of the New Cornerstone Exodus Church, in Mattapan, advocates the firing of openly gay teachers and believes that gay/straight alliance-type organizations have no place in public schools. "We are not going to let anyone stand up and say, 'I'm a lesbian,' " he says. "In fact, we don't want anyone to stand up and say, 'I'm a heterosexual,' either. I don't see the point."

Openly gay and lesbian faculty offer a variety of responses as to why it is important for teachers to come out in school: to provide role models to both gay and straight students, to fight prejudice, to be honest with their students. At boarding schools, relationships between teachers and pupils extend beyond classroom hours, to the playing field, dining room, and dormitory. For a teacher to keep such a crucial part of his or her private life hidden becomes difficult—and demoralizing. As Concord Academy's Jennings puts it, "I came out because I had to. I couldn't stay in teaching if I didn't. It was too damaging to my self-esteem. The constant energy I was putting into hiding was draining my ability to interract with students. And it was also making me feel I was a bad person."

Some administrators are sympathetic. "In an ideal world, I really don't believe that one's sexuality is a matter of anyone's concern," says Milton Academy headmaster Fredie. "But until we deal with the range of homophobia, then it becomes absolutely necessary for students and teachers who are ready to take that courageous step [to come out of the closet]." Fredie believes that chapel, where ethical issues are traditionally discussed, is an appropriate forum for teachers to discuss their sexual orientation.

Andover headmaster Donald W. McNemar contends that the school must make sure that all students have someone to look up to. "Some of our students are going to lead a gay or lesbian life," he says. "We would want them to have some role models in the faculty, as well."

The role-model issue, combined with the alarming rate of suicide 20 among gay teen-agers, is a compelling impetus for many homosexual teachers to make their sexuality known. Some are determined to spare another generation the same experience they themselves had as high school students. Concord Academy's Jennings describes how, wracked by guilt after his first teen-age homosexual experience, he washed down 140 aspirins with a glass of gin. Milton Academy's Todd Fry, an openly gay English teacher, also planned to kill himself while he was in high school. "Obviously, every teen-ager who is gay isn't suicidal, but a lot of kids feel so alone and so isolated," says Fry. "In speaking at various schools, I can certainly pluck those kids out of the audience. They are the ones who come up to speak to me afterward. I could give you the names of four suicidal kids right now in western Massachusetts I happen to know."

Despite this sense of urgency, most openly gay and lesbian teachers maintain they don't want their reputation as educators to rest with a single issue. Milton Academy's Fry, for instance, has gained high marks for his stewardship of a series of Youth Outreach weekends during which 150 students from private schools work at Boston-area homeless shelters. In a November 1989 letter to the school newspaper, in which he revealed his homosexuality, Fry wrote, "Please bear in mind that most of the time I am not thinking about gay and lesbian issues. When you see me talking with someone, we're probably talking about something else." At Andover, meanwhile, the school's openly lesbian assistant athletic director, Kathy Henderson, says, "The way I want to be remembered is as a great coach."

At the Andover athletic office, Lisa Hamilton, the captain of the girls' lacrosse team, is talking about homosexuality at Andover and, in particular, about coach Henderson. "When everyone first gets here, they are really amazed," says Hamilton. "Most of the kids haven't been comfortable with homosexuality. They come from Greenwich, Connecticut, or from snotty parts of New York. They are really surprised that no one here has a problem with it. By their last two years—I guess it has something to do with maturity— they realize it isn't a big deal."

When Hamilton first tried out for lacrosse, other students asked her, "Do you know?" about coach Henderson. "They really didn't take it beyond that," she says. "But there was some weird feeling that people thought they had to tell me. It wasn't that they wanted to sit there and make fun of her."

In a school where most of her female classmates look as if they stepped out of the J. Crew catalog, Hamilton is determined to dress in her own style. "I'm not your usual little preppy girl. You get a lot of hassle for not shaving your legs or not dressing and wearing your hair like everyone else. What Kathy told me was to "be yourself,' " Hamilton says. "That really meant a lot to me. A lot of teachers at this school would say, 'Do your best,' but they wouldn't necessarily encourage you to be an individual. From Kathy I got a different message."

When Kathy Henderson came to Andover eight years ago, at age   25
28, she was still struggling with her homosexuality. On her first day on the job, someone walked into her office and saw her picture of the University of New Hampshire women's lacrosse team on the wall and said, "Any dykes in that picture? I hate dykes." Henderson stayed in the closet for two years. From the moment she arrived, though, she was constantly hearing about Andover's commitment to diversity, honesty, and integrity. She felt that by concealing an important part of herself she wasn't living up to the values the school espoused. Finally, she stood up at a faculty meeting and announced she was a lesbian. "I tell my classes," she says. "I don't really talk to my team unless they want to talk about it. When we are out there, we only have an hour-and-a-half practice, and we practice."

Since coming out of the closet, Henderson has felt much more welcome at Andover. Last spring, she co-taught an English class, with the proviso that she be allowed to teach Fannie Flagg's novel *Fried Green Tomatoes at the Whistle Stop Cafe*. In the book, she explains, the relationship between the two central female characters is more explicitly lesbian than in the film adaptation. "The kids loved it," she says. "They got to look at sex roles in a new way. And it was a change from Faulkner!"

Henderson is one of four faculty advisers, two homosexual and two heterosexual, of Andover's gay/straight alliance. The organization was started by a lesbian student who came out in a letter to the school newspaper, *The Phillipian*. Today, headmaster McNemar praises the "real courage" exhibited by that founding student. The gay/straight alliance, he says, "is important as a statement in a community that all students, regardless of race, class, and sexual orientation, are respected and are part of the place."

Still, gay/straight alliance advisers estimate that there are nearly 20 gay faculty members at the school, but only two are out of the closet. Last year, four students were openly gay or lesbian in a student body of more than 1,200. Posters advertising gay/straight alliance events are routinely torn down. Much of the campus is "scared to death" of the issue, according to Steven Sultan, who headed the group until he graduated in June.

Controversy erupted last year over a longstanding school policy that permits only legally married couples to reside in nondormitory campus housing. The gay/straight alliance proposed extending the privilege to partners of gay and lesbian faculty, but the school balked. Trustees say they have no objections to single, openly gay teachers living in dormitories. But they are unwilling to liberalize the rules to put gay and lesbian relationships on the same footing as that of married, heterosexual ones.

The school's reluctance to implement policy changes has been   30 disillusioning. As Kathy Henderson puts it, "When you first start your gay/straight alliance and get initial approval, it is similar to when you first come out and find that the majority of people in your life still love you and care about you. That's wonderful. But over time, you begin to look for an existence as equally fulfilling as that of heterosexuals. That is when it gets tougher. And that is where we are right now."

The complaints of gay faculty and students at Andover may appear trivial compared with the situation prevailing in the public schools. At Newton North High School, for example, in one of Boston's most liberal suburbs, there are no openly gay students or faculty, no alliance, just brochures in the library entitled, "I Think I Might Be Gay . . ." and "I Think I Might Be Lesbian . . ."

The only time one closeted senior at Newton North heard anything positive about homosexuality was in his honors English class, when the teacher noted that Walt Whitman was gay. "At North, the word 'faggot' is a totally common thing," the student says. "We've already had a racial incident this year. If they don't accept black people, they are never going to accept gay people."

Midway through his senior year, this student became depressed. He talked with his mother, who suggested he go to the Boston Alliance for Gay and Lesbian Youth, which meets twice weekly in the basement of a Beacon Hill church. "I've made a lot of friends through BAGLY," he says. "If I hadn't found BAGLY, if I had been going on like I was, I would have really been in bad shape." He says that had there been an openly gay teacher at North, he might have confided in him.

One closeted teacher at the school believes that it is important for gay teachers to be open about their homosexuality but is convinced such candor would have severely negative consequences. "People wouldn't and couldn't be held accountable," the teacher fears. "I'm afraid they would smash my car. This isn't *Blackboard Jungle*. But it is a school with a mixed population and strong feelings."

Last year, however, at neighboring Newton South High School, 35 Matt Flynn came out of the closet at the beginning of his senior year. A Vietnamese who was adopted as an infant by a Newton couple, Flynn is personable and popular. He is also a star gymnast. When he told his friends he was gay, they were shocked at first but were eventually "cool and accepting." His straight friends now give him advice about his love life. Coming out was a "boulder being lifted off my back," Flynn says. "But you have to be strong. You know that bad things will be said, and you have to anticipate the worst."

After he came out, Flynn helped lead a petition drive to persuade the Newton School Committee to approve the distribution of condoms at both high schools. Seven hundred signatures were garnered from students at South and North, and a third of the faculty and some 30 parents were persuaded to support the drive. In the end, the School Committee approved the proposal by a 7–1 vote.

His activism and openness about his sexuality won Flynn a good deal of respect in Newton. Linda Shapiro, director of counseling at Newton North, says, "Just seeing him is a help to all the kids at Newton South. He does them a favor." At South's graduation ceremonies, the valedictorian praised Flynn for helping the entire class to grow.

A week after Flynn told his friends about his sexuality, Bob Parlin came out to his history classes at Newton South, making him only one of a handful of teachers in the public schools around Boston to declare their homosexuality. (Parlin, who has been teaching at South for more than five years, is the lover of Concord Academy teacher Kevin Jennings.) "The kids were fantastic," Parlin recalls. "They came up and hugged me afterwards." An exception was one student who began to withdraw from class discussions and stopped doing his homework.

After a couple of weeks, though, the student began to participate in class again as if nothing had happened.

As a result of Parlin's announcement, things have changed significantly at Newton South. A series of educational programs on homosexuality has taken place, including skits performed in freshman homerooms by members of the drama club. Last spring, at Parlin's prodding, Newton South established a gay/straight alliance. Ten to 12 students attended the first meetings. Except for Matt Flynn, all identify themselves as heterosexual.

At Newton North, the administration has tried to be supportive,   40
but without an openly gay teacher like Parlin to push the issue, that support has not amounted to much. Principal James Marini concedes that the school hasn't been as active on the subject as Newton South. "Whenever opportunities arise for us to affirm the respect and dignity for all races, ethnic groups, gender issues, and sexual preference issues, we do so," he says.

The principal's comments aside, at Newton North's senior prom this past spring, the gay student interviewed for this article showed up with a female friend as his date. At South's prom, Matt Flynn went with his boyfriend. Bob Parlin brought Kevin Jennings. At one point during the evening, both male couples were slow-dancing across the floor, in the midst of a crowd of heterosexual couples. No one seemed to pay any attention. "That," says Parlin, "is progress."

❖ Focused Freewriting   Consider as possible focal points the identity problems faced by gay teenagers, the appropriate role for school administration to take in dealing with gay issues, the question of whether gay teachers should come out, or one of the topics you've identified in your journal.

❖ Guided Responses

1. Miller chooses to open his article with the image of a high school senior, "delighted and nervous," on his way to a dance. Given the topic of this selection, why do you think the author made this choice? How would the effect have been different had he opened with paragraph 6 ("High schools are one area in which little has changed . . .")?

2. In paragraph 6, Miller writes that in public high schools "anti-gay comments are common currency long after ethnic and racial slurs have been deemed unacceptable." Others quoted in the article make the same connection between gay issues and race or ethnicity issues. On what basis is this connection made? In your view, do gay and lesbian rights qualify as civil rights issues? Explain your response.

3. When the father of two Andover students says, "The important thing is to have effective teachers, straight or gay" (para. 14), he voices a slightly different opinion from the headmaster, who believes that openly gay teachers are necessary so that gay students "have some role models in the faculty" (para. 19). Others contend that openly gay teachers can "fight prejudice" and "be honest with their students" (para. 17). Having read Miller's article, how important do you think it is for gay teachers to come out? What are the implications for gay students? straight students? the teachers themselves?

4. Miller notes that the openness of many elite preparatory schools is not matched by public high schools. To what do you attribute this disparity? Why would it be more difficult to approach gay and lesbian issues in a public school?

❖ Shared Responses   In your journal write a response to a closeted gay student from your old high school seeking your advice. What would you say to the student? Would you advise him or her to come out? Why, or why not? As you discuss your responses in small groups, focus on the effect of individuals' attitudes toward gay life on their responses.

❖

Cooperative Learning and the Native American Student

LEE LITTLE SOLDIER

LEE LITTLE SOLDIER, *a professor of education at Texas Tech University, has published widely in educational anthropology and Native American issues. In this 1989 article from the* Phi Delta Kappan, *Little Soldier emphasizes the need for educators to become more aware of the cultural needs of Indian students. Cooperative learning, she concludes, reinforces many Native-American values and can therefore provide an ideal educational program for Indian children.*

Before reading the article, write in your journal about the way you were taught in elementary school. How was the classroom set up? Was most of your time spent listening to your teacher, or did you engage in group work? How competitive was your school experience? How well do you think your early education has served you?

As you make notes on your reading, you may want to focus on the value systems Native-American students bring to school, the causes for their generally low self-image, or the support Little Soldier offers for her view.

DESPITE SIGNIFICANT ADVANCES in the education of Native American students over the past two decades, serious problems persist. The dropout rate remains alarmingly high, enrollment in higher education is low, and teen pregnancy, suicide, and substance abuse continue at disproportionately high rates.

The Indian Education Act of 1972 has proved to be an important force for change. The act, which provides federal funds for programs in schools serving Native Americans, also sparked systematic efforts to build a solid research base that could give direction to the much-

416

needed changes. However, the need for active research continues as schools seek better ways to teach Native American students.

Attempts to upgrade the quality of education for Native Americans while remaining sensitive to cultural issues have led to some notable improvements. The numbers of Native American teachers, supervisors, and administrators have increased, and the training of teachers and other school personnel now focuses on developing their sensitivity to the special needs of students from diverse backgrounds. Although some families still harbor feelings of alienation—if not hostility—toward schools and schooling, Native American parents are now more involved in the schooling of their children than ever before. Moreover, modifications in the curriculum have closed the gap between school experiences and the daily lives of Native American students and have increased the holding power of the schools.

It is a truism that education must have personal meaning for students. Thus educators must begin where the students are, with material that is relevant to their culture. Yet if education is to provide students with an array of life choices, then mastery of basic skills is also essential. Bridging the gap between the Indian and non-Indian worlds is crucial to the success of schooling for Native Americans.

While the topic of *what* to teach for cultural relevance—the curriculum and materials—is clearly important, I wish to discuss the equally important topic of *how* to teach Native Americans in ways that are compatible with their culture. For Native American students raised in traditional cultures, a school learning environment that is insensitive to behavioral differences caused by cultural patterning can undermine all the good that a teacher may be trying to achieve. We must use what is known about traditional Native American family life and child-rearing practices to build a smoother transition from home to school and to create a school environment that is more compatible with that of the home. Educational objectives may remain the same, but the means of achieving them must match the learning styles and social and communication patterns of the students.

Despite vast differences among Native American tribes, certain core values characterize these diverse cultures. For example, Native Americans respect and value the dignity of the individual, and children are afforded the same respect as adults. Although outsiders may view Native American parents as too permissive, nonetheless they teach their children to seek the wisdom and counsel of their elders. At the same time, traditional Indian families encourage children to develop independence, to make wise decisions, and to abide by them. Thus the locus of control of Indian children is internal, rather than external, and they are not accustomed to viewing adults as authorities who impose their will on others. Native American students entering school for the first time may respond with confusion and passivity to an authoritarian teacher who places many external controls on them.

Other core values of Native Americans include cooperation and sharing. The idea of personal property may be foreign. Because traditionally they come from extended families, Native American children tend to be group-centered rather that self-centered. They are accustomed to sharing whatever they have with many family members, a habit that can unnerve non-Indian teachers who emphasize labeling possessions and taking care of one's *own* belongings. If such teachers do not understand the notion of common ownership, they can easily mislabel certain behaviors as "stealing."

Moreover, Native American students may enter school far more advanced that their non-Indian counterparts in such social behaviors as getting along with others, working in groups, taking turns, and sharing. Too often these strengths are not recognized or rewarded in school.

Harmony is another core value of Native Americans—harmony with self, with others, and with nature. Paleo-Indians could not have survived had they not used their environment productively. Even today, Native Americans generally take no more that they can use and live in balance with their surroundings.

The perception of time by Native Americans traditionally differs   10
from that of the European world. Native Americans view time as a continuum with no real beginning or end. There is an emphasis on living in the present and not worrying a great deal about the future; the future will take care of itself. Native Americans are generally patient; they are not clock watchers. Obviously, strict adherence to rigid schedules may not be comfortable for students whose lives outside of school are far less regimented.

One major stumbling block to the school success of Native American students has been their low self-esteem and lack of pride in being "Indian." Stereotypes concerning Native Americans are still unknowingly perpetuated by teachers who were exposed to these same stereotypes when they were students. American society has generally failed to recognize the important contributions of Native Americans, past and present. Indeed, some teachers know nothing about Native Americans who have succeeded and who have become leaders in the mainstream of society.

Racism and prejudice continue in many states with large populations of Native Americans, particularly in areas near reservations. Since we acquire our self-concept by interacting with others, it is understandable that young Native American children who begin to interact with non-Indians may pick up negative cues and come to feel that there is something wrong with being Indian.

The media have done little to help. Indian children are still exposed to old westerns. When asked whether they want to be a cowboy or an Indian, young Indian children frequently opt for cowboy, because cowboys always win.

The problem facing educators is to build a warm, supportive learning environment for Native American students without compromising educational goals and without investing a lot of money—which most school districts don't have. The answer to this problem may lie at least partly in an old concept that is receiving renewed emphasis: cooperative learning.

Inexpensive and easy to implement, cooperative learning shifts the burden for achievement from the teacher alone to *all* individuals in the classroom. Instead of a single teacher and 26 students, 27 teachers work together toward mutually established goals. At any grade level, stronger students can tutor weaker students—sometimes more effectively than adults. Most students know who's the best—whether at reading or playing ball. Rather than hide these differences behind cute labels for reading groups or grade-level codes on textbooks, why not use the strengths of the students to help their peers?

To make cooperative learning work, we must rid ourselves of the notion that students who help other students are somehow "cheating." We in American education are so programmed to view learning as an individual—indeed, a competitive—activity that we tend to overlook the value of group methods for reaching individual goals. Certainly, individual effort has its value, and group effort is not always appropriate. but opportunities abound for cooperation that enhances individual achievement.

Cooperative learning is based on principles of team sports, and Indian students have a heritage of playing team sports and are avid team competitors. When teachers label Native American students as noncompetitive, they often base their conclusion on pitting one student against another in an academic setting. Such individual competition creates a dilemma for the Native American student whose culture traditionally teaches helping rather than competing with others.

A teacher using cooperative learning will set up teams composed of four or five students of mixed ability. If the class is socially or socioeconomically heterogeneous, students from different backgrounds will have opportunities to work together, to appreciate their differences, and consequently to feel better about themselves. Cooperative learning teams work toward a common goal. Team members

15

discuss problems, make decisions, and quiz and encourage one another. The teacher serves as resource, guide, evaluator, catalyst—a teaching role that is compatible with the attitudes of Native American students, who look to their elders for wisdom and counsel.

Assessment in a cooperative setting differs, too. Teams are evaluated and rewarded on the basis of progress toward the shared goal. Imagine the esprit de corps that develops because the achievement of each student is critical to the success of the whole group. Although there may be some competition between groups, such competition need not be a part of cooperative learning.

Students who work in cooperative settings tend to feel better about themselves because they are more successful and because they feel better liked.[1] (If Indian and non-Indian students are teamed, the enhancement of feelings between the two groups is a bonus.) Certainly our schools have not done much to improve the self-esteem of Indian students. In light of statistics that indicate that Native Americans fall farther behind in achievement with each year in school, we should be willing to try cooperative learning as a potential answer to the problems of school failure and lack of self acceptance among Native Indians.

Cooperative learning could also help students learn to accept one another. As students begin to feel that they are respected and have greater control over their lives in school, they tend to develop a better attitude toward school and to show more concern for others.

A meta-analysis of 122 individual studies and a significant body of other research have shown cooperative learning to be more effective than traditional learning techniques in a number of ways.[2] Cooperative learning was found to be particularly useful in raising academic achievement and promoting inter-racial friendships in urban classrooms.[3] Follow-up studies of cooperative learning should be conducted with Native American students—in both homogeneous and racially mixed classrooms. The evidence suggests a good fit between Native American students and cooperative learning, but more research is needed.

Research on cooperation in the classroom is not new, but the development and dissemination of specific cooperative learning

20

[1] Carol Ascher, "Cooperative Learning in the Urban Classroom," *Intercultural Development Research Association Newsletter,* February 1987, pp. 5–6, 8.
[2] David Johnson et al., "Effects of Cooperative, Competitive, and Individualistic Goal Structures on Achievement: A Meta-Analysis," *Psychological Bulletin,* vol. 89, 1981, pp. 47–62.
[3] Robert Slavin, "Cooperative Learning: Applying Contact theory in Desegregated Schools," *Journal of Social Issues,* vol. 41, 1985, pp. 45–62.

methods began only in the 1970's.[4] To date, materials supporting six cooperative learning techniques have been published. Three of these techniques have been developed and evaluated by the Center for Social Organization of Schools at Johns Hopkins University.[5]

However, the techniques of cooperative learning cannot be mastered by reading about them. They have to be tried, tested, and modified to fit the needs of each classroom situation. Both teachers and students may need time to get used to somewhat higher levels of noise in the classroom, to increased student movement, to greater student autonomy, and to less reliance on the teacher as an authority figure and a font of knowledge. Both teachers and students will have to learn to feel at ease with new patterns of control and classroom communication and with a teacher/student relationship based on cooperation, trust, and autonomy.

The potential benefits of cooperative learning for Native American students are clear. Cooperative learning appears to improve student achievement, and it also matches such traditional Indian values and behaviors as respect for the individual, development of an internal locus of control, cooperation, sharing, and harmony. Cooperative learning can improve the attitudes of students toward themselves, toward others, and toward school, as well as increasing cross-racial sharing, understanding and acceptance.   25

If Native Americans are to have a wider array of choices in their adult lives, our schools must be more responsive to the major problems in Indian education and more willing to experiment to find solutions. It all begins with the willingness of individual teachers to seek better ways to meet the needs of Native American students without compromising the quality of their education.

❖ Focused Freewriting   Consider as possible focal points images of Indians in the media, differences between Native American and mainstream American cultures, or one of the topics you've identified in your journal.

---

[4] Ascher, op. cit.

[5] Slavin, op. cit. See also David Johnson and Roger Johnson, *Learning Together and Alone* (Englewood Cliffs, N.J.: Prentice-Hall, 1975); Shlomo Sharan and Yael Sharan, *Small Group Teaching* (Englewood Cliffs, N.J.: Educational Technology Publications, 1976); Robert Slavin and Eileen Oickle, "Effects of Cooperative Learning Teams on Student Achievement and Race Interrelations," *Sociology of Education,* vol. 54, 1981, pp. 174–80; and Robert Slavin, "Students, Teams, and Achievement Divisions," *Journal of Research and Development in Education,* vol. 12, 1978, pp. 39–49.

❖ Guided Responses

1. Little Soldier notes that some Native American parents "still harbor feelings of alienation—if not hostility—toward schools and schooling" (para. 3). Based on your reading of the article, why do you think parents would feel this way? Do you think these feelings are justified? Why, or why not?

2. In paragraph 5, Little Soldier warns that "a school learning environment that is insensitive to behavioral differences caused by cultural patterning can undermine all the good that a teacher may be trying to achieve." In what ways are schools sometimes insensitive to cultural differences? How can this problem be remedied?

3. In paragraphs 6 through 10, Little Soldier lists a number of cultural values shared by most Indian tribes. Choose two of those values, and explore in detail how they might conflict with the values emphasized in traditional American classrooms.

4. Some critics refer to cooperative learning as "the blind leading the blind." How would Little Soldier respond to this criticism? Do you agree with her assessment of the value of cooperative learning (for all students, not just Native Americans)? Why, or why not?

❖ Shared Responses   In your journal comment on Little Soldier's assertion that *how* teachers educate children is as important as *what* they teach. Are teaching methods as important as the material taught? Explain your response, using examples from your own experience. As you discuss your responses in small groups, focus on the effect of individuals' experiences on their responses.

❖ **Generating Ideas**   Reread all of your journals and annotations from the selections in this unit. Look for connections between selections or still unanswered questions. First, list those questions and connections as briefly as possible. Next, choose two or three to elaborate on. As you respond in more detail to the connections and questions, focus on one topic and consider how well it would serve you in an extended piece of writing. Then decide what kind of writing best suits your topic: Should you write a conventional essay, a poem, a short story, or a scene? Would your topic lend itself more to a letter to the editor or a personal letter? Might a proposal to solve a specific problem be a good choice? Possible topics:

1. the influence of parents and other role models in education
2. making realistic expectations of students
3. support for minority and underprivileged students in public schools
4. the pitfalls of cultural separatism
5. racial and ethnic issues on college campuses

❖ **Focusing Responses**   Choose one of your extended responses and formulate a statement of one or two sentences that captures its essence. Use this statement as a guide to organize your piece. (If you write an essay, letter, or proposal, the statement may actually appear as a thesis.)

❖ **Guided Writing Assignments**

1.   Write a letter to an official of the state or federal Department of Education suggesting how to deal with cultural differences. You might argue that the purpose of education is to assimilate students into the mainstream culture, that education should validate the student's own culture, or that it should provide a bridge between cultures. Make reference to Little Soldier and Tierney (and perhaps Lauro) in your letter.

2.   Rose, Kozol, and Lauro all contend that our educational system fails to serve some of its neediest students. Outline a proposal that these three authors might jointly prepare to remedy inequalities in elementary, secondary, and postsecondary education. Consider not only academic issues but social and cultural issues as well. Refer to specific details in the three selections to support points in the proposal.

3. Miller's and Tierney's articles both emphasize the need for students to have educational role models that reflect their own cultural identities. Referring to both articles as well as to your own experience, write an essay arguing for or against the idea that such specific role models are necessary. Consider such issues as the influence of teachers on a student's life, the school's responsibility to individual students and to the group, possible conflicts between parents and teachers as role models, and any other issues you consider relevant.

4. Dorris and Kohn both focus on the significant role parents play in their children's education. Compose a conversation between Dorris and one of the parents cited in Kohn's article in which the two discuss the benefits and drawbacks of parental involvement. What advice do you think Dorris might offer the other parent? How would that parent respond to his story?

❖ Research Topics   As you consider how to expand your reading beyond the selections in this chapter, identify in your journals and notes questions that remain unanswered or topics you'd like to explore further. Or you may consider the following:

1. Research the recent history of racial tensions on college campuses. As you explore the issue, try to determine which races and ethnic groups are targeted most often. What causes of the problem are identified in various accounts? How do different schools address the problem? What solutions can you suggest? Based on your research, what do you think the future holds for race relations on campus?

2. Kozol and Rose, and to a lesser extent Little Soldier, suggest that public education in the United States does not offer equal opportunity to all students. Examine the public school system in your local area to determine how well it lives up to the notion of equal opportunity. Consider evidence such as curriculum plans, special education, extracurricular programs, parent organizations, racial and ethnic mix of students and teachers, physical facilities, and budgets. Interview students, parents, teachers, and school officials to assess their views of the system. In your conclusion, try to explain why the system does or does not provide equal opportunity for all students.

Chapter 6

Finding Meaning in Work

I N THE LAND OF OPPORTUNITY, everyone should find fulfillment in his or her job. Work should suit the abilities and the inclinations of the worker, and compensation should support a comfortable standard of living. Of course, not all jobs meet the standards of the ideal occupation. For every fulfilling job there seems to be more than one tedious, stressful, or unsavory job; for every satisfied worker there seems to be more than one alienated, frustrated, or burned-out worker.

In addition, the value society places on different kinds of work often has little to do with the nature of the work itself. Some helping professions offer low salary and esteem, while professions geared toward exploiting hardships are highly rewarded and enjoy significant prestige. Still other occupations gain recognition through the efforts of one or two charismatic leaders. It would seem that there are as many different work stories as there are workers. Some of those stories are told in the following selections, where work is seen as alternately dignified, underrated, ennobling, and numbing. The nature of the job itself doesn't seem to matter much—some of the most exalted jobs have their unsatisfactory moments, while some of the humblest offer tremendous rewards.

In "The Indian Basket," Mickey Roberts's narrator recalls the pride that her grandmother put into her baskets traded for old clothes. The narrator's thoughts return to the old woman as she contemplates, years later, paying $250 for a basket made by an unknown hand.

Ben Hamper returns in "At War with the Minute Hand," recounting the strategies assembly-line workers use to counteract the numbing monotony of their jobs. The real enemy of the worker, according to Hamper, is not the boss but the clock.

Erik Larson's "Forever Young" tells the story of the growth of Ben & Jerry's Homemade Inc. Begun as a small ice cream parlor in Burlington, Vermont, the company has grown steadily, causing its founders to worry about its continuing commitment to social change.

Jonathan Langston Gwaltney allows the subject of his account, "Maude DeVictor," to speak for herself. DeVictor, the woman credited with uncovering the connection between Agent Orange and a host of diseases, defied attempts to silence and even fire her for simply doing her job.

In Ana Castillo's "Napa, California," migrant farm workers regain their pride as they envision joining labor activist César Chávez. The dignity they lose as they pick the grapes is regained as they rally behind their leader.

A fulfilling job in the confines of a prison is the subject of David Arnold's "A Free Press Flourishes Behind Bars." Arnold tells the story of the Stillwater federal penitentiary's newspaper, the *Mirror*, and its editor, lifer Robert Taliaferro.

Finally, Lars Eighner's "On Dumpster Diving" presents an analysis of an activity few of us would consider an occupation. Regardless, Eighner's description of what he calls scavenging reads much like a training manual for any labor-intensive job.

The selections in this chapter explore the notion of work from a number of different perspectives. They differentiate jobs undertaken to fulfill ambitions from those forced upon an unwilling laborer, jobs that raise the worker to new heights of achievement from those that lead the worker in neverending circles, and jobs that earn the praise and respect of outsiders from those that label the worker worthless or degenerate. Taken together, the selections provide an enlightening, if sometimes disturbing, look at what work means in the American marketplace.

— ❖ —

The Indian Basket

MICKEY ROBERTS

MICKEY ROBERTS *(biographical information on p. 134) speaks in this
selection from* Talking Leaves, *through a narrator who reminisces
on a cold winter's day about her basket-selling journeys with her
mother and grandmother. The true value of the baskets was clear to
her people; today their value is measured in dollars.*

*Before reading the selection, describe in your journal the pride
you took in creating something of your own. Even if you write about
a childhood craft, try to recall the feelings associated with producing
a finished product.*

*As you make notes on your reading, you may want to focus on
the details—of place, of climate, of objects—Roberts uses.*

THE YEAR WAS 1988, a bitterly cold morning in early winter. I
held the small Indian basket, beautiful and artistic in the distinctive
Native American tradition. It was clearly no copy of an Indian basket—it was the real thing and I did not have to be told that it was
authentic.

The basket was laid out on a table at a garage sale and the ticket
said it was for sale for $250. I inquired of the owner as to who had
made the basket and was told it was made by "The Thompson River
Tribe." The owner went on to say the basket was well worth the
money, for the Indians no longer made these works of art. I did not
satisfy an urge to ask if tribes made baskets, for, being fair to the man,
he could not have known the name of the Indian artist when it had
never been asked for in the first place!

As I stood holding the basket, I remembered a bitterly cold day in
the year 1939. It was the beginning of the winter season. We walked
the streets of Bellingham—my mother, my great-grandmother, and
me. We were selling Indian baskets. I was a very small girl and I kept
saying I wanted to go home but my mother kept saying, " . . . just one
more house."

We all carried baskets—large ones, small ones, round ones, square ones. Some of them were rectangular, with perfectly fitted covers, which were designed to be used as picnic baskets. How many hours of hard labor these baskets represented for my grandmother who could speak only in her native tongue! My grandmother had worked hard all her life and she had raised many children and had also raised my mother, who was her granddaughter. Somehow she had survived the changes that life had forced upon her with the changing life in a different culture.

At each house my mother would ask the occupant to look at the   5
Indian baskets and suggest a price of a few articles of used clothing. If the woman of the house decided to look at the baskets and bring out some clothing she didn't want, the bargaining would begin. As in the case of our tribe's treaty, two generations earlier, the main decision would be at the discretion of the newcomer, and many hours of labor would go for a few shirts or dresses.

These days the price of Indian baskets is very high, and they are mostly owned by non-Indians. These treasures, obtained at less than bargain basement prices, are now being sold at premium prices, if they are obtainable at all. They are collector's items, but the name of the person who labored to make them is rarely known.

As we peddled our treasures in those early years, we probably appeared to be a pitiful people. We were, however, living in as dignified a manner as possible while selling a part of our culture for a few articles of used clothing.

We really hadn't much left to give.

❖ Focused Freewriting   Consider as possible focal points the meaning of the baskets to the narrator and her family, the significance of the basket at the yard sale, or one of the topics you've identified in your journal.

❖ Guided Responses

1. Roberts begins her story, "The year was 1988, a bitterly cold morning in early winter," and later has her narrator recall "a bitterly cold day in the year 1939" (para. 3). Why do you think she repeats the original image so precisely? How does the repetition emphasize the point of the story?

2. Why do you think the narrator chooses to tell us that her grandmother "could speak only in her native tongue" (para. 4)? What does the woman's language have to do with her basket-weaving skills?

3. What does the narrator mean when she says, "We were . . . selling a part of our culture for a few articles of used clothing" (para. 7)? Why does she use the term "our culture" rather than "our handiwork," or simply "our baskets"?

4. Comment on the way Roberts presents this story—the simple language, the apparent digressions, the unconventionally slim plot. Why do you think she relates the story this way? How would the impact of the story change if it were told in a more conventional manner?

❖ Shared Responses   In your journal speculate on why Indian baskets command such a high price today. Do you think the reason has to do with a recognition of their artistic value, their rarity, or their social significance? Who do you think profits most from the sales? As you discuss your responses in small groups, try to reach some general conclusions about the social and monetary value of Indian handiwork.

—— ❖ ——

At War with the Minute Hand

BEN HAMPER

BEN HAMPER *(biographical information on p. 79) uses this selection from* Rivethead *to introduce the reader to some of the "shoprats" he worked with on the assembly line, highlighting the strategies they used to get them through the shift.*

Before reading the selection, discuss in your journal a job or regular household responsibility that you hated. What was it about the task that made it so unpalatable? What did you do to get yourself through it?

As you make notes on your reading, you may want to focus on Hamper's characterizations, his metaphors, or his dark humor.

I MET ALL KINDS OF BIZARRE INDIVIDUALS during my first year at GM Truck & Bus, characters who would prove to be constants throughout my factory tenure. Dementia and derangement were rampant traits. Most of these guys were not unlike myself—urped forth from the birthrights of their kin, drowsy with destiny, uninspired, keen for drink, unamused with the arms race or God or the Middle East, underpaid and overpaid, desperate, goofy, bored and trapped. It was the rare one who would come out and fib in the middle of a card game about how he didn't really belong here. We belonged. There were really no other options—just tricky lies and self-soothing bullshit about "how my *real* talent lies in carpentry" or "within five years I'm opening a bait shop in Tawas." We weren't going anywhere. That pay stub was like a concrete pair of loafers. Sit down, shut up and ante.

Our linemate Dan-O was an irreplaceable native up in our neck of the Jungle. He was the master of diversions. His relentless pranks kept us entertained and loose. More importantly, he had a terrific knack for keepin' our minds off that wretched clock.

Each night Dan-O would have a new trick. I recall the time he took a long cardboard tube used to hold brazing rods, painted it all psyche-delic, and passed it off to the unsuspecting as a porno kaleidoscope. He told all the guys that if they held it directly into the overhead lights

430

and looked through the hole, they would get a gorgeous glimpse of *Hustler*'s Miss August. There was never any shortage of volunteers.

There was never any Miss August either. The victim grabbed the peep tube, tilted it straight up to the lights, only to get doused with a generous flow of water right in the eyeball. Dan-O also made sure to line the peephole with black paint. Not only did the victim wind up drenched, he'd also slink away sportin' a shiner the size of a tennis ball.

Another Dan-O favorite was his "crucified wallet" trick. He would nail down an old wallet into the woodblock floor in the aisle- 5 way, flip the wallet closed to conceal the nail, and insert the torn corner off a $20 bill. Invariably, some guy would stroll by and notice the apparent gold mine. As we pretended to look the other way, the victim casually glanced around and, feeling unnoticed, swooped down for the wallet only to wind up tumbling on his face or develop- ing an instant hernia. The Jungle would explode in laughter as the victim retreated sheepishly.

The most entertaining of Dan-O's pranks, from a spectator's view, was the "charging tarantula" trap. Dan-O would take fishing line, attach it to a very realistic-looking rubber tarantula, and rig the fish line so that at the flick of his wrist the tarantula would come scamper- ing out from beneath a stock crate near the aisleway. For bait, Dan-O would crumple up a dollar bill and place it in the aisle. The innocent pedestrian would come along, start to reach for the dollar, and . . . SHIT GOD ALMIGHTY . . . the bug-eyed terror you would see in the faces of these victims was enough to send you howling to your knees. After the victim had fled, Dan-O would leisurely reset the trap and we'd await the next pigeon. Man, the time just flew.

The absolute craziest co-worker I met during my first year was my relief man, Jack. He was a doper, the pied piper of dumbdom, always banged to the gills on some queer mix of speed, mescaline, hash or cocaine. As my relief man, his duties were to come around twice per night and spell me for my break period. I would often hang around as Jack ran through my job. Though there was something plainly dangerous about, him, it could never be denied that Jack was always a great source for laughter. His rantings were legend.

Jack also presented me with one of my first confrontations with an enigma that had been bothering me since I had hired in. He was so resolute in his hatred toward General Motors that it completely baf- fled me as to why he hung around. He had this persecution complex that ate at him like a bellyful of red ants. I didn't really understand it. I was still relatively raw, but I assumed a deal was a deal. GM paid us a tidy income and we did the shitwork. No one was holding a gun to anyone's head. I didn't harbor any hatred toward GM. My war was with that suffocating minute hand. With Jack, General Motors was the taproot for all that was miserable and repellent in his life. To hear him tell it, GM was out to bury him. He was obsessed with vengeance and anarchy.

For instance, one night Jack arrived to send me on break. Before doing so, he raced around the corner to buy a pack of smokes. A moment later, he reappeared screechin' his lungs out. Apparently, the cigarette machine had eaten his money. An unfortunate break? Not the way Jack saw it. This was just another GM conspiracy designed to crank up the animosity level. The war was on. Jack reached into my workbench and grabbed my sledgehammer. I had a very uneasy feeling about the look on his face.

Moments after Jack charged off with my sledgehammer, I heard   10
the sound of glass being shattered. The pounding continued. He was obviously destroying the vending machine. GM had absolutely nothing to do with these machines. They were serviced by private vendors. Still Jack bashed away at the machine as if he were poundin' the very last breath out of Roger Smith[1] himself.

Finally, Jack returned. He had about two dozen packs of cigarettes bunched to his chest. Blood trickled from his fore-arms. His smile was one demented line stretching from ear to ear. The war had been won. From that day on, Jack always referred to my sledgehammer as the Better Business Bureau. He was convinced that he had delivered a furious blow against the infernal GM empire. All he really did was deprive the department of access to cigarettes for the next several months.

Whenever I asked Jack why he just didn't quit and move on to something that was less aggravating, he would jump all over me. "Goddamnit, that's *precisely* what they're banking on. That I'll weaken and bow to their endless tyranny. NO WAY! They'll have to drag me out of here."

Besides the crazies, there was also the occasional violent type. We had one guy up in the Jungle, a black dude named Franklin, who kept our department on constant edge. He was forever picking fights with co-workers. It wasn't any kind of racial thing, Franklin had it in for everyone. When something set him off, he just went to whalin' on people.

One night, he got Henry, our Quality man. Henry had refused to give Franklin an extra pair of work gloves. Franklin became enraged. Later in the shift, he snuck up on Henry and smashed him over the

---

[1] Then chairman of General Motors. [ed.]

head with a door latch. Henry received a dozen stitches in the back of his skull and Franklin got thirty days on the street.

Franklin worked as a utility man, floating daily from job to job depending on where he was needed. At the beginning of every shift you could hear him throwin' his customary shitfit about what job the foreman had assigned him to cover. It didn't matter what type of job it was, easy or difficult. He'd scream and holler and demand to see his union rep.

I felt a certain amount of pity for our boss. No matter how he tried to soothe the situation, it only made it worse. For example, I firmly believe that if our foreman were to have come up to Franklin one sunny afternoon and told him his only duty for the shift would be to fornicate with Miss America on some sandy beach with a dozen bottles of chilled Dom Perignon at hand, he would have thrown himself into a blind rage and accused the boss of denying him the right to sweat it out all night on the door hang job.

Franklin didn't pull any of his crap with the veterans or guys who outbulked him. He preyed mainly on the timid, the brittle and the rookies. The rookies were at a severe disadvantage. Without having served the first ninety days of their probation period, there was no way they could risk swinging at anybody. To do so would mean instant termination. GM didn't have time to sort out who was to blame in these skirmishes. You could get sucker-punched while saying a rosary and still receive the same punishment as your attacker. It was professional suicide for any rookie to fight back. Franklin exploited this situation and made a career out of intimidating rookies.

Besides his violent streak, there was something else about Franklin that had me very intrigued. He was forever writing stuff down on little notepads, scraps of cardboard, napkins—anything he could find. Several co-workers I talked to joked that he was probably just scrawling down ransom notes or bomb threats. One thing was for certain. Franklin wouldn't allow a soul to see what he was writing. If you came anywhere near him while he was jotting, he'd quickly cram the paper away.

My curiosity was gettin the best of me. Jerome Franklin. Bully. Terrorist. Cutthroat. Man of letters? I had to find out what was behind his mysterious sideline. One evening, while Franklin was covering Roy's old job across the line from me, I went over to the picnic bench and began thumbing through the sports section. In between jobs, Franklin was furiously hammering out something on a piece of paper towel. I decided to make my move.

"Shit, Franks, you rewritin' the Bible over here?"

"Just some bullshit to pass the time," he muttered.

15

20

"Mind if I took a look?" A big pause. A brutal pause. A pause with a vanity plate that read U EAT ME. Finally, Franklin gave me a nervous grin. "Go ahead," he said. "But I don't want one word of this shit bein' spread through the department or it's your ass."

I laid out the paper towel on the picnic bench. The printing was barely legible. Grease spots and sealer smudges covered the page. I began reading and was quickly amazed. Franklin was writing *poetry* of all things. The poetry was not only a surprise, the damn shit was red-hot. He had some great lines in there, plenty of imagery and anger and this passionate raw beauty that welded together in a furious glide. The guy wasn't writing as much as he was attacking the beast. The poetry leapt at your spine and shook you down.

"Jesus, Franks, this stuff really kicks ass."

Franklin shrugged and dumped another load of pencil rods into   25
his bin. He said nothing. He was obviously uncomfortable about being exposed as someone who could actually accomplish something more than pounding skulls and bustin' out teeth.

I read on. Who'd have ever believed it? The resident high priest of mayhem was a poet of enormous talent. No whiny art-fag lip service here. No candy-ass dime-a-rhyme. Franklin got in and got out. No excess baggage, no gristle. It was all red meat and arteries burstin' wide open and gray matter boiling in flame. He had the goods, the bads and plenty of the uglies. I put down the paper towel and was about to say something. Franklin cut me off.

"Not a word. Let's just fuckin' drop it."

In the nights to come I hounded Franklin to let me check out his writings, but he always blew me off. I knew better than to press the matter too far and run the risk of having my face flattened, so I just gave up. It was sad that he couldn't funnel his hostility into something more worthwhile than brawling with co-workers and behaving like the campus bully.

Franklin never did change his stance. Within a couple of months, GM had him by the balls. His constant fighting combined with his atrocious attendance record had finally dug him a hole so deep that even the union couldn't bail him out. He was fired and they had to bring up three guards to haul him away.

There's probably no tellin' what he's whalin' on today, nine years   30
removed from the Jungle. Apartment walls. Cell bars. The skulls of the bewildered. Possibly, there's a typewriter mixed in there somewhere. I hope so. I would hate to think that all of that rattlesnake scrawl died along with the job. What a waste.

After a few weeks I managed to develop a good rapport with another black dude, Robert, the mig-welder who worked right down from me. Having been sequestered in Catholic schools my entire

youth and adolescence, I didn't have much of an opportunity to meet many black folk until I hired on with GM. You just didn't find too many bro's hangin' around the communion rail hummin' verses of "Holy, Holy, Holy" while awaiting their tongue's worth of Mr. Christ. Just your basic bunch of white hypocrites sheenin' their souls for another week's worth of fetch and wretch.

While Robert was from Alabama, our stories were much the same. His forefathers, like mine, had drifted into this moron dragnet lookin' for steady work and a pocketful of beer change.

And like my father and me, Robert liked to drink. Once he'd had a few, he'd start in with hilarious stories of his childhood in the backwoods. He talked about the perverse sexual practices of his cousins and their clumsy endeavors with farm critters, the white trash hookers who'd lay it all out on a haymow while charging the bystanders a buck a pop to watch it go down. It was all very funny and that prick minute hand would buzz by in circles.

We'd often end up discussing our fates as proud American truck builders. We both shared the contention that neither one of us should've ever been forced to attend even one miserable day's worth of formal education. What good was schooling to someone who was just gonna turn screws and shoot sparks the rest of his life? Robert suggested that this time could have been better spent gettin' high and chasin' females. I would heartily agree, insisting that *anything*—masturbating, bowling, fishing, blowing up banks—would've been better than the crap all those nuns had crammed down my throat.

If Robert tended to be a pissed-off sulk at times, he had every right to be. He'd been divorced a couple of times and the Friend of the Court was slicin' him to pieces. They took the child support right out of his check and, on Thursday nights, while everybody would be gettin' all giddy over the big numbers starin' back at them from their pay stubs, Robert would be slouched over his workbench tryin' his damndest to formulate a budget from the remains of his week's earnings.

It was a shame that guys like Robert had to drag their asses through the Jungle nine hours a night, inhaling fire and growing deaf from the din, only to wind up taking home a paycheck that was more in line with what your average zithead from Taco Bell was making. But, like so many shoprats, Robert had mortgaged his soul to the bitch goddesses of whiskey and women, and he paid for it every Thursday night.

Robert introduced me to an old guy known only as Louie who worked at the end of our line in the repair station. Louie had a great little racket goin' for himself. He peddled half pints of Canadian Club and Black Velvet up and down the line in the Cab Shop area. He

charged three bucks a bottle, almost double the store rate, but who was gonna argue. The booze was in the door, you didn't have to wait for it, and Louie delivered right to your bench.

When ordering from Louie, all one had to do was slip the word down the line through a network of fellow workers. You passed on your selection and detailed your location by using the numbers stenciled onto the big iron pillar nearest your job. It was like conjuring up a genie. You'd lay out your money on top of your bench and Louie would come stragglin' down the aisle just like Mr. Green Jeans with the booze stashed somewhere in his floppy coveralls. What a wonderful little microcosm of American capitalism Louie had goin' for himself. Just goes to show that there's an endless array of clever ventures one can concoct to assure that one's grandkids are able to afford the sissy college of their choice. All by ourselves, Robert and I probably paid off a couple semesters.

Shoprat alcohol consumption was always a hot debate with those who just didn't understand the way things worked inside a General Motors plant. While not everyone boozed on a daily basis, alcohol was a central part of many of our lives. It was a crutch not unlike the twenty cups of coffee millions of other Americans depend on to whisk them through their workday. We drank our fair share of coffee, but the factory environment seemed to lend itself toward something that was a great deal more potent and rejuvenating.

I frequently found myself defending this custom with nonfactory   40
acquaintances. They conveniently put the blame for everything square in the laps of those who drank on the job: "NO WONDER the Japanese are moppin' up the market floor with your asses! NO WONDER my new vehicle farts like a moose full of chickpeas! NO WONDER the rear end of my Chevy Suburban rattles like a Hari Krishna in a cement mixer! NO WONDER they want to phase out all you juicers and replace you with robotics!"

The criticisms came from all sources—friends, neighbors, retirees, relatives, the local media. It was a popular bandwagon full of self-righteous dickheads and know-nothings. The yappin' hypocrisy that never ceased to amuse: "IT'S THOSE OVERPAID, SPINELESS FACTORY HACKS AND THEIR DEMONIC CRAVING FOR FIRE-WATER! THEY REPRESENT TOTAL HUMILIATION TO THE GREAT AMERICAN WORK ETHIC! THOSE INGRATES CAN'T BE SATISFIED WITH THEIR GARGANTUAN PAYCHECKS OR THE FACT THAT THEY POSSESS MORE MEDICAL COVERAGE THAN EVEL KNIEVEL COULD PISS AWAY IN A MILLION UNSUCCESS-FUL BUS HURDLES! TO TOP IT OFF, THEY'RE ALL CODDLED AND PROTECTED BY A UNION THAT WOULD PROBABLY EMBRACE

RICHARD SPECK[2] AS JUST A MISUNDERSTOOD DRIFTER WITH A HARMLESS YEN FOR VODKA AND ROPE TRICKS!"

Oftentimes, the *Flint Journal*, the unofficial GM gazette, would devote large portions of their editorial page to the miserable whines of these blowhards. "I worked in the plant for thirty-six years and never once needed to rely on alcohol . . . " "I think that it is an outrage that my neighbor, a GM employee, spends half of his shift sitting in a bar . . . " "The autoworker of today is weak and corrupt and . . . " Blah, blah, blah.

It's one thing to be harangued by those who have gone before— the forebears, the sit-down strikers, the providers of the torch, my very own grandfather—but to be put through the verbal shredder by townsfolk who've never even *seen* the innards of an auto factory, well, that was a different matter. Their pious deductions always made me squirm.

The total farce of it all is that given our jobs, these same moany denizens would be lined up right next to us at the barstools and beer coolers if they could somehow weasel in the gate. They'd lose that sacred work ethic baloney and clasp on to Louie's coveralls faster than you can say "the mercury reads 118 in the Paint Department tonight." Keep in mind, the grass is always greener on the other side until it's your turn to jump the fence and chop the shit down.

There is simply no need for apologies. Hell, when you get right down to it, General Motors management doesn't even pay much heed to the drinking habits of its own work force. They realize it would be a massive and futile effort on their part to attempt to stymie a widespread tradition. And moreover, they really don't give a good goddamn who's tippin' and who isn't just as long as the parts keep flowing by in their assigned locations. Start sending down inferior product and then drinking would become an issue.

Drinking right on the line wasn't something everyone cared for. But plenty did, and the most popular time to go snagging for gusto was the lunch break. As soon as that lunch horn blew, half of the plant put it in gear, sprinting out the door in packs of three or four, each pointed squarely for one of those chilly coolers up at one of the nearby beer emporiums. Talk about havoc. It was like some nightly cross between the start of the Indy 500 and chute-surfin' out of the fuselage of a burning jet. Engines racing. Tires squealing. Pedestrians somersaulting over car hoods.

45

[2] Convicted of murdering eight student nurses in Chicago during the 1960s. [ed.]

I half expected one night to find Marlon Perkins propped in a jeep near the gate narrating this frantic migration: "Notice, friends, the fleet mobility of our subjects. The wide eyes and gaping mouths are timeless clues that another pilgrimage to the watering hole is well under way."

A half hour is all most workers had. Make no mistake, this small opportunity to bust open the monotony of shop grind helped many guys avoid cracking up, cracking skulls, missing work or mutating into supervisional bullies. A jumbo of beer certainly wasn't gonna save anyone's life, but the odds were it would certainly enhance it. John DeLorean himself proved that factory critters can't triumph above the ordinary on black coffee and Twinkies alone. Hell no. On a clear day you *can* see General Motors and, if you squint a little harder, you can also see a frosty quart of Budweiser just as plain as the cocaine attaché case at the end of the motel bed.

It was during these early years that my old friend Denny and I spent our lunch breaks together. With a double-up arrangement not much different from mine, Denny was able to tag along as we indulged in every shoprat's dream scam: the Double Lunch. With our jobs securely covered by co-workers, we could slide out and overlap the two lunch periods designated for the two separate truck lines. Instead of a half hour for lunch, we now had a sprawling hour and twelve minutes to get lost. It was wonderful what you could avoid accomplishing with that extra forty-two minutes off.

One particular double lunch from that period has always stood   50
out. The plant was really roasting that night with the kind of corraled heat that often rendered the overhead fans useless and forced a horde of dehydrated reeking shoprats to line up at the drinking fountain and gulp down salt tablets.

On that night, Denny came to my job with an invitation to slug down a few at lunch. Though nothing in the world sounded better than cold beer, I knew we would have to be careful. The beer was always a godsend goin' down, but you had to watch out for the fatigue factor it brought on when the heat was high. If you overdid it you ran the risk of drowsing out during the second half of the shift. By night's end you'd be totally gassed and ornery enough to punch out your own grandmother.

But the offer was just too appealing. "I like beer," I said. "Beer tastes good."

At the convenience store we stood in line behind three attractive young ladies. They were purchasing diet pop and wine coolers. I remember thinking that they must be part of some very special breed, a sorority of angels who simply forbade themselves to perspire. They giggled and fussed with their perfect hair—all the while glaring at us with their terrible animal eyes.

We smiled back at them. It was all so hopeless. We couldn't help our appearance. We didn't normally smell this way. It was the $12.82 an hour and the benefits package and the opportunity to swill a cold one in between breaks in the madness that doomed us to trudge into convenience stores lookin' like Spam patties in wet suits. Our grandfathers had taken this route. Our fathers were right behind them. Now it was our turn to be thirsty, rank and every bit as unlucky.

We took our quarts of Mickey's Malt Liquor and headed for the 55 back of the employees' lot. It was always wise to park in a section far, far removed from the roving eye of the surveillance cameras. Otherwise, the guards might scope you down as you tipped that cold chalice to your lips and decide to wheel out and give you some shit. This rarely happened, but it was a nuisance all the same. There would be ID requests. There would be boring lectures. Sometimes there might even be a slow shuffle down to the Labor Relations office.

Denny and I drank, mostly in silence, while a Lesley Gore Greatest Hits tape poured out of the dash of my Camaro. We were beginning to feel human, the beer workin' its magic, the edge dissolving, the shoprat's humble version of the multiple martini lunch. We sat there staring off into the smokestacks with the weight of the world gradually sliding through the floorboard. The guards and the bossmen were absolute madmen. How could anything that felt so good be a punishable offense? Our screws were all in place. Our welds were shining brightly. It was all working out. What could be the problem?

We both loved Lesley Gore and, on this most humid of nights, Les was really lettin' us have it: "California Nights," "I Don't Wanna Be a Loser," "That's the Way Boys Are"—her complete arsenal. We slurped faster and faster on our malt liquor jumbos. At that precise moment, there was very little doubt that we had everyone in the galaxy squarely beaten.

We were on a roll. We raced back to the convenience store, this time purchasing two forty-ouncers of Mickey's Malt. We hit on the beer and sang along with Lesley and laughed at our great fortune. We looked like trash, we smelled like death, we had no idea who was winning the wars or the rat race or the relentless struggle to get on top. It was all so very meaningless. Someone would be declared the victor and the rest of the world would roll over and begin to plot tomorrow's lousy comeback.

"I've gotta admit," Denny laughed, "it doesn't get much better than this. The whole world is on fire and here we are parked in the shadow of this mausoleum drinkin' the coldest beer on the planet.

With Lesley Fucking Gore! No one else on the face of this earth is doing this! NO ONE!"

"I wonder what Lesley Gore is doin' right this minute," I mused.   60
"I wonder what Al Kaline and Roger Smith and Sister Edward Irene are up to—right NOW! Right this very second. I feel sorry for their asses!" We laughed until our sides ached.

Nine fifty-four returned to the assembly line. Denny and I hustled back in to relieve our partners. In the nights to come we were never really able to recapture whatever it was that led to that precious double lunch we spent with Lesley Gore. After a while, we simply quit tryin'. Perhaps we were just crazy from the heat. It was known to happen. Whatever the cause, we always remembered the night we had you and you and the rest of the world thoroughly dicked for seventy-two minutes.

❖ Focused Freewriting Consider as possible focal points the sense of futility that permeates the selection, the anger so many of the workers feel, the rationalization of drinking on the job, or one of the topics you've identified in your journal.

❖ Guided Responses

1. In paragraphs 3 through 6, Hamper describes a series of practical jokes his linemate Dan-O plays. After the initial humor wears off, how do you respond to these pranks? What do you think they say about the men on the line? How does the nature of the men's work influence them to resort to such tricks? How does the opening paragraph help you to understand this behavior?

2. Hamper is shocked when he discovers Franklin's talent for poetry. The material is obviously powerful, but Hamper's description doesn't sound at all like traditional descriptions of good poetry. What do you think motivates Franklin's poetic impulses? Why do you think he continues to write? Why does he insist that his poetry remain a secret?

3. Hamper describes Louie's illicit liquor business as "a wonderful little microcosm of American capitalism" (para. 38). How seriously do you take this description? How does the business reflect the good and bad sides of American capitalism?

4. What is the purpose of the final scenes, in which Hamper and Denny drink and listen to Lesley Gore? Why are they never able to recapture the feeling of that night? When Hamper says, "At that precise moment, there was very little doubt that we had everyone in the galaxy squarely beaten" (para. 57), is he being ironic? Explain your response.

❖ **Shared Responses** In your journal write a response to Hamper's statement that nobody on the assembly line "should've ever been forced to attend even one miserable day's worth of formal education" (para. 34). Why would this statement make sense to Hamper? How would educators or employers react to it? As you discuss your responses in small groups, try to determine how members' own experiences of such work influence their responses.

Forever Young

ERIK LARSON

ERIK LARSON, *who received a Ph.D. from the University of Iowa, has been an English professor at the City University of New York since 1971. His articles have appeared in numerous publications, among them* Harper's, The Nation, The New Republic, Prairie Schooner, *and* North American Review. *This article, written for* Inc. *magazine, chronicles the growth of Ben & Jerry's Homemade Inc. during the 1980s. Founders Ben Cohen and Jerry Greenfield had never intended to oversee a corporate giant, and the phenomenal success of their product has upset the "family" feel of the company.*

Before reading the article, explore in your journal your feelings about corporate responsibility. What, aside from profit, should be the priorities of corporations? Do they owe anything to their local communities? to society as a whole? Explain your responses.

As you make notes on your reading, you may want to focus on Larson's use of statistics and figures, his characterizations of individuals within the company, or his use of anecdotes.

BEN COHEN IS CONFIDENT THAT HE, for one, is weird enough to carry on the funky good works of Ben & Jerry's Homemade Inc., the company he cofounded. There is evidence to support this. A year ago, for example, Ben stripped down and swathed himself sumo style, then marched out into the shipping-and-receiving bay at Ben & Jerry's headquarters in Waterbury, Vt. Rick Brown, the company's director of sales, came out dressed the same way. They squared off amid the cheers and blood-lust stomp of nearly all the company's employees, and did what any pair of normal American executives would do, what Lee Iacocca no doubt would do if he had to settle a debate of this magnitude. Ben and Rick puffed out their pale and prodigious stomachs and bounced each other, a couple of human bumper cars trying to determine once and for all who had the baddest belly in the Ben & Jerry's empire.

But these days Ben is worried. What started out as a simple ice-cream parlor has now, almost in spite of itself, become a growth company, doubling in size each year through 1986, adding scores of new employees, reaching $31.8 million in sales last year. The company got to this point by breaking rules and taking chances, and by a lot of good luck. Its puckish marketing maneuvers and dense ice cream won it goodwill and sales; the sheer energy of its young, dedicated work force kept the company from stumbling, albeit sometimes just barely.

Once, Ben could be confident that everyone else at the company was just as weird as he, that everyone got off on the funk and adventure, and most important, that everyone bought into his philosophy of corporate responsibility—that Ben & Jerry's existed for one reason, to act as a force for social change. But lately, the company has gotten so businesslike, so corporate. Its explosive growth has stressed and eroded the Ben & Jerry's culture, diminished the fun, brought strangers into the happy family. There are controls, departments, memos. Product introductions take so much more effort than they used to, require so many approvals. And now Ben finds he faces resistance from within to some of his favorite ideas and policies—even the company's five-to-one salary ratio, which limits the top salary to five times that of the lowest-paid employee. You can almost see the spore of change. Some of Ben & Jerry's managers actually wear ties from time to time; the top marketing man, Allan Kaufman, roves the halls dressed like Indiana Jones, in bush hat and jacket.

All this comes as Ben is trying to pull back from day-to-day management and as competition rises for dominance of the superpremium ice-cream market. Last year, wholesale factory shipments totaled $500 million, according to Find/SVP, a market-research firm. Ben & Jerry's, ranked third by Find/SVP, now faces the likes of Pillsbury, which owns Häagen-Dazs; Kraft, owner of Frusen Gladje; and Steve's Homemade Ice Cream, run by Richard Smith, an aggressive, streetwise marketeer.

Ben's office shudders—this is no metaphor. His office takes up the 5 hind end of a leased trailer, and it shakes when the wind gusts. Ben is wearing gray denim with a band of red showing at the neck. He's got an unruly beard and scraggly smoke-tipped hair, which wisps off his balding scalp. He looks like a chubby Central American guerrilla— Daniel Ortega Cohen. But Ben is a capitalist guerrilla; that rim of Marxist red is the neckline of a Ben & Jerry's cow T-shirt. His company is 10 years old this year. "Now, we're at the stage of young adulthood," Ben says. "I'm kinda interested in kicking the kid out of the house, and the kid pretty much wants to split."

But does the kid still possess all the right values? Is the kid "weird" enough, a term that Ben and Jerry use as shorthand to describe the things that make the company unique? Can funk survive the big bad world of business? "I know so many liberal, nonconforming parents who end up having conservative kids," Ben says. He quickly qualifies this—he doesn't really believe that's the case here. He just wants to be sure, and to feel secure that his company will continue stretching the boundaries of what a socially responsible business can be.

The events of the past year, however, have not brought him this security. A kind of cultural revolution has taken place at Ben & Jerry's. It began last February at the Hulbert Outdoor Center, in Fairlee, Vt., when 18 senior managers climbed ropes together, fell from ladders into one anothers' arms, trudged bound and blindfolded across a frozen field, and bared their souls in a tearful night of confession and self-critique.

The revolution at Ben & Jerry's is more than a simple internal struggle to come to terms with growth, change, and success. The company is an experiment. It is founded on principles alien to mainstream business. If Ben & Jerry's ever becomes just like any other corporation—Ben's great dread—the experiment will have failed. Ben, says chief operating officer Fred Lager, "is looking to show other people that you can run a business differently from the way most businesses are run, that you can share your prosperity with your employees, rewrite the book on executive salaries, rewrite the book in terms of how a company interacts with the community—and you can *still* play the game according to the rules of Wall Street. You can still raise money, still go to the banks, still have shareholders who are getting a good return on their investment."

For Ben, the company is the message. But this message has at times been contradictory.

There is a saying at Ben & Jerry's that Ben is Ben. This is invoked,   10 in-house, as a kind of verbal elixir, a spiritual hit of Anacin, to cope with some new change of course, some new idea, some new contradiction between what Ben says the company will do and what it actually does. The greatest contradiction involves growth, and it has marked the company's history ever since May 5, 1978, the day Ben Cohen and Jerry Greenfield opened an ice-cream parlor in a renovated Burlington, Vt., gas station. All along, Ben has questioned and feared growth, disputing the maxim that a business either grows or it dies. From time to time he calls on the company to stop growing and look inward. But all along Ben & Jerry's grew—quickly. And Ben, with his maverick marketing ideas, has often been the cause.

He and Jerry, best friends since seventh grade, had no intention of doing more than starting an ice-cream parlor. Once the business got going, they planned to sell it and move on. Their ice cream, rich and packed with tasty shrapnel, sold well from the first day. Something always seemed to force them to grow, some new cost, some unexpected threat—the need, for example, to increase sales just to cover the repair bills of an ancient ice-cream truck, whose breakdowns were consuming all the company's cash flow.

Ben and Jerry, uneasy with the cash-based morality of corporations, nonetheless found themselves and their company becoming far more businesslike. In 1982, they even hired a bona fide businessman, an M.B.A., no less—Fred Lager, known universally as "Chico." He had owned and operated and then sold a successful Burlington nightclub. As chief operating officer, he is now the company's fiscal soul, Ben's foil. Any measure to improve profits or control costs is known in-house as being "Fredlike." Employees who come up with money-saving ideas win the Fred-of-the-Month award, a Fred's Famous T-shirt—the Fredlike thing to do is nominate yourself for the award. Under Chico's direction, the company slashed costs, boosted production, and started making some real money.

For the founders, this was a moral and fiscal plateau. Success played to Jerry's qualms about business. Granted, ice cream is not napalm. But becoming a businessman—a successful businessman—was too much for his Aquarian psyche. He retired late in 1982 and moved to Arizona; he had no intention of coming back. (He returned in 1985.) Ben, saddened, alone, sharing Jerry's fears, put the company on the block. "I had this horrible feeling come over me that I had become a businessman," Ben says. "Worse, that now I was just some kind of mindless cog in the overall economy, taking in money with one hand and paying it out with the other, adding nothing."

He did not sell, however. Another Vermont entrepreneur persuaded Ben to keep the company and find a way to run it that would ease his conscience. Ben decided he would make the company a force for social change and began to consider Ben & Jerry's as being held in trust for the community. This, moreover, gave him a way—the only way, he believes—to justify further growth. The more the company grew, he reasoned, the more good works it could pursue. But to grow, it would need to build a new factory with greater capacity. To pay for the plant, Ben took the company public but offered the first shares only in Vermont, to Vermonters, thereby making the community the real, not just metaphoric, owner. He deliberately set the minimum-buy price low. "We wanted to make it available to all economic classes," says Ben. "We were seeking somewhat to redistribute wealth."

Now, Ben & Jerry's had stockholders to worry about—not just 15 stockholders, but neighbors, friends. To be socially responsible meant the company *had* to grow.

The bigger the company got, the more heat it drew from competitors, in particular Richard Smith, of Steve's Homemade, who threatened a preemptive national blitz with look-alike ice cream. Instead of pursuing controlled growth—Ben's plan had been to enter one major market a year—he responded to the threat by entering eight new major markets over a nine-month period, including Atlanta and Los Angeles. For a man who questions growth, Ben has come a long way. This year, the company's sales may surpass $45 million, up more than 40%, with profits sure to top last year's $1.4 million.

Ben could *say* stop, but he could not do it.

What he could control, or at least shape, was Ben & Jerry's mission. Throughout the company's growth, a culture evolved that emphasized fun, charity, and goodwill toward fellow workers up and down the line. In September 1985, the company founded The Ben & Jerry's Foundation Inc., which receives 7.5% of the company's pretax income and spends it on a broad array of causes. Jeff Furman, vice-president and a director, came up with the five-to-one salary ratio. The company hires the handicapped, provides free therapy sessions—including anonymous drug and alcohol counseling—to any employee who needs it, and takes workers on all-company outings to baseball and hockey games in Montreal. There is a changing table for babies in the men's room as well as in the women's room.

The best way to sample life at Ben & Jerry's is to sit in on one of the company's staff meetings, held once a month in the receiving bay of the Waterbury plant. Production stops so every employee can attend.

Coffee. Cider doughnuts, freshly made. It's 8 a.m. on a Friday. 20 Some 150 managers and line workers jam the bay, all sitting in folding chairs, knee to lumbar region, like passengers on a cut-rate flight to Shanghai. There are four neckties, three skirts; Allan Kaufman comes dressed to explore the Temple of Doom. Otherwise, the dress is basic woodchuck. Levis. Timberland boots. Nikes. Ben is absent, but Jerry is here, in weary slacks, a cow T-shirt, and a crumpled red flannel shirt, tails out, one button fastened.

The routine stuff comes first. Jerry reports on Ben's effort to open an ice-cream parlor in Moscow, with profits used solely to support East-West exchange programs. He updates the progress on another of Ben's ideas, the plan to refurbish and maintain a New York City subway station for one year, and explains how the idea is currently bogged down in bureaucracy and transit authority/union debate. The company, expecting the deal to fall through, ran an ad in *The New York*

Times asking the public for other marketing ideas. One suggestion, now read out loud, calls for the company to produce large, collapsible cardboard boxes emblazoned with the Ben & Jerry's logo and cows—and distribute these to the homeless in New York as places to sleep.

Next, Jerry talks about Joy. This is not something he takes lightly, Ever since his return to Ben & Jerry's, his role has been to serve as the embodiment of Ben & Jerry's spiritual soul; his is a clear blue space on the organizational chart. He proposes a "Joy Committee," charged with putting more joy into the workday. No one giggles.

"There was an incredible amount of discussion about this at the department-head meeting," he tells the crowd. "There were a lot of varied opinions, ranging from some people who felt it was too much fun at work already . . . "

He times this like a comedian. A wall of laughter cuts him off.

"That was a minority opinion, by the way." 25

But this question of joy at work has lately become a serious issue. Jerry gets serious.

"There was pretty much an agreement that things at work are tough, and that with all the tasks we have to perform, and the stress people are under, it would be a good idea to try to infuse a little more joy." He asks if anyone's interested. Hands go up; the crowd applauds.

Chico now rises and announces the birthday of an employee. Someone shouts that Chico should sing a Frank Sinatra version of "Happy Birthday." The Sinatra part is a joke, because Chico is known to be tone-deaf and can barely sing any version of "Happy Birthday," let alone Sinatra's. Chico seems unwilling at first, but the applause is insistent. There are hoots, whistles. Slowly he rises, puts out one hand, palm up, the international symbol of crooners everywhere, and begins to sing. Everybody joins in, in a warm and slow and sweet rendition.

These meetings are fun. Joyful. This is not the spooky, overheated joy conjured up by get-rich preachers at tent revivals. These people like being here, they like one another.

For all the fun, however, the Ben & Jerry's Way has its stressful 30 side—a pervasive sense of crisis that has always lingered within the company. No one has ever been entirely sure where Ben & Jerry's was headed, or where it ought to head. Every now and then Ben would talk about slowing growth, maybe stopping growth altogether—$50 million once seemed a good number, and the company aimed at that. In lieu of planning, Ben & Jerry's relied on a small cadre of energetic, motivated staff, universalists who could drop everything when the alarm bells rang.

And the bells ring often at Ben & Jerry's. Milly Badger, controller since she joined the company in 1985, says she tells new hires to come to work in running shoes and be prepared to sprint from one task to another. "We don't have adequate staff to do the job," she says. "If you have any knowledge of anything, and people know it, they're going to come to you."

When the company was small, this was kind of fun. Everyone knew everyone else; employees were like family. But growth brought malaise. Departments began duplicating work. Communications broke down. Employees, for example, found out about the company's new Springfield, Vt., plant from newspaper accounts. And Badger recalls a meeting in which Jim Rowe, director of retail operations, announced his department's plans to add 50 new stores. She was shocked. That kind of expansion would require heavy support from her department, yet she knew nothing about it. Production was likewise in the dark. "I said, 'We can't do that,' " Badger recalls. "He said, 'Well, it's done.' " And just who were all these new workers and managers roaming the halls? Says Wendy Yoder, a shift supervisor and five-year employee: "It's hard to feel you're part of a big family if you don't know the brothers and sisters."

Within the context of ordinary corporate life, these sins are hardly lethal. But at Ben & Jerry's, they constituted violations of an unwritten agreement: give the company 110%, and you should get it right back—maybe not in cash, but certainly in joy. The forces that once held Ben & Jerry's together and made it lean and nimble had fallen out of alignment.

Says Ben, "Everybody was trying to do the right thing, everybody was putting out an incredible amount of effort." But even tasks as routine as preparing for a trade show became complicated. Product introductions were handled as if they were the first the company had ever made. "We didn't have good systems or standard operating systems. So every time we had to do something that was pretty much a repetitive process, it would get started from the beginning—instead of just pulling out the procedure and following it." Ben holds out his hands, flutters them. "I had this image of these molecules jiggling, going back and forth like this, instead of going in a straight line. Eventually we'd get the job done, but it took a whole lot more energy."

Consider, for example, the crisis that took place in spring of 1987, one crisis too many for some of the Ben & Jerry faithful—the crisis, says plant manager Jim Miller, that "woke the sleeping giant."

The company, in keeping with Ben's quest to be first, wanted to become the first ice-cream maker to produce pints with tamper-evident seals, and ordered a new machine supposedly capable of doing the job. It bought another machine, too, this one to automate the process of filling pints, previously done by hand. The idea was to get both machines up and running before summer. What could possibly go wrong?

The machines came late, and when they did arrive, they proved cantankerous, difficult to master. Each alone was new technology. Together, they were confounding. Demand was up, the summer was approaching, but instead of making more ice cream, the plant was producing less. The company abandoned the tamper-evident seal machine and scrambled to get the other one working. "We realized how painfully clear it had all been and how foolish we were for trying to do two things at once," Chico says.

The awareness came a bit late.

One Friday, Chico walked to the loading dock to see how things were going. To his horror, he discovered the company would be short that coming week by well over 300 pallets of ice cream. He sounded the alarm. He called for all hands to man the production line. He, Ben, Jerry, and nearly everyone else did a stint, wiping containers, emptying the garbage. Jerry, as Undersecretary of Joy, hired a masseuse to give workers massages during their breaks. Some staffers cooked dinner for the crew. The company ordered in pizza. This was war.

There was a positive side to the struggle. Some employees felt it rekindled the spirit of the old days. "The drawback," Chico says, "was that once again we were running around like chickens with our heads cut off, scrambling, trying to put out a fire. People came through, people always come through. But I think every time you go through something like that you lose a little credibility, and it becomes a little harder to go to them the next time and say, well, guess what? Another fire."

The culture, the Ben & Jerry's Way, is clearly under pressure. Most symbolic is the debate over salary and the five-to-one ratio. Right now, based on that ratio, the highest possible salary is $84,240. Jeff Furman says the ratio helps screen employees—new hires come already knowing they won't get rich and, presumably, having already accepted the company's broader mission. Ben feels the ratio helps the company more fully recognize the role of the workers who actually make the ice cream. If managers want more money, fine, but first raise the lowest salaries. He believes many companies pay their executives far too much money.

There is broad agreement at Ben & Jerry's with the underlying concept. But the ratio rankles some managers. Chico doesn't like it. He says it makes recruiting difficult. Allan Kaufman, for example, declined three job offers from the company, until his own financial condition improved enough to allow him to accept the salary Ben offered. Of the first salary offered—$50,000—Kaufman says: "It was a

40

joke." Rick Brown, director of sales, figures he's making 60% to 70% of what he could make elsewhere.

Jim Rowe, director of retail operations, flat-out rejects the ratio. "I, for one—I'm materialistic. I realize other people aren't that way. I'm also a career person. I'm an expert at what I do. I've trained for years and years and years. I don't think the five-to-one ratio recognizes that." Meanwhile, some of the people to whom Rowe has sold franchises are making well over $100,000 a year.

Rowe questions, too, the need for everyone to be weird. "I don't claim to be that way," he says. "I claim to have a talent in a different area that's also needed by this company."

This is the kind of thing that worries Ben Cohen. He worries that his managers see the company's existing social programs—The Ben & Jerry's Foundation, for example—as fulfilling its mission and that no new programs are needed; that they've grown fearful of undertaking risky projects; that they see any project that does not optimize profits as being unworthy of pursuit. "Some people feel the company's first goal is to make as much money as possible, and then spend it in a socially responsible way," Ben says. He does not agree. "I see those values as influencing the way the company does business in all facets, and influencing how it makes all its decisions." 45

In the old days, Ben kept himself informed and in touch through the monthly staff meetings. Employees would break into small groups, mull over a specific problem, then return with solutions. This was genuine two-way communication. But over time the meetings had changed—"degenerated," Ben says. They became one-way affairs with him talking at the crowd. Last September, after the production crunch, Ben brought back the old format to ask a simple question: what are the most pressing problems confronting us?

David Barash, director of human resources and corporate communications, spent a night helping Ben categorize the responses. He recalls: "It was like having this eight-ton dumptruck back up and dump its load over you."

Whereas once employees had been privy to every decision management made, now they felt left out. No one knew what anyone else was doing. And where, by the way, was Ben & Jerry's headed? The employees, says Barash, were asking, "What are we? What do we want to be? Where do we want to go?" They complained about getting mixed signals regarding growth, the great Benlike debate. If anything, growth was accelerating.

By some accounts, Ben was stunned. Ben, however, says "elation" better describes his reaction: "I felt that we were on the track. The first step in making anything better is to identify the problems. That's what we had done. And we were about to start working on those problems."

Hulbert Outdoor Center, Fairlee, Vt. One by one, each of 18 Ben & 50 Jerry's managers, including Chico Lager, climbs a ladder, then falls backward into the arms of fellow employees. This teaches trust. They break into two groups, blindfold themselves, are roped together, and set off across a field, trying to locate three big rubber tubes. This teaches teamwork. They all spend a night doing mind maps—tracing their heads onto a large piece of paper, then dividing the silhouette into four parts, asking four questions: What do you want said about you when you leave Ben & Jerry's? What are the three things you hold most dear? Who are the three people who most influenced your life? The three events? Each of the group then bares his or her soul; the talk is wrenching, heartbreaking—divorce, Vietnam, death. This builds a bond.

The retreat, indirectly, was Ben's doing. But can he live with the results?

Well before the big production crisis, Ben had begun feeling a need to tinker with the company and its structure. The company, he felt, should shore itself internally and, to do so, should simply stop growing. "I felt if we did not take the time to create an excellent organization, soon we would no longer have an excellent product." Ben himself wanted to put more power in the hands of lower management. He also wanted to make life at the company more enjoyable for the staff. "Everyone was paddling away madly, individually, trying to bodysurf on this big wave, the superpremium ice-cream wave; and we were all trying to stay in front of this wave so we would keep on getting carried along by it. And we were all going crazy. And I said, maybe it's time for us to stop trying to keep up with the wave, and take our time and build a boat. Once we had that boat built we could go anywhere we wanted."

This rekindled the great debate. Many managers believe the company has no choice in the matter: it must grow, both to survive and to fulfill its obligations. Says Kaufman: "My feeling is, the day the company went public, it committed itself to growth. The day it sold its first franchise, it committed itself to growth—because you're tying someone's future to how you do."

The company needs to grow to retain its position on supermarket shelves as competition increases. Richard Smith, for one, has no intention of halting the growth of Steve's Homemade while Ben & Jerry's considers the meaning of life in the '80s. Moreover, the market for superpremium ice cream is maturing. Last year, the market grew only

15%; in the four prior years, it grew between 25% and 30% annually. And there are upstart companies out there using the same maverick marketing tactics Ben and Jerry's used, for example, The Great Midwestern Ice Cream Co., based in Fairfield, Iowa. Before the Iowa caucuses, the company won nationwide publicity with its line of Presidential flavors, including Bush's Preppie Mint, Kemp's Quarterback Crunch, and Dukakis's Massachewy Chocolate.

"Growth can't be stopped," says Chico Lager. "You can't say you're going to grow to a certain level and that's it. It doesn't work that way, not in the real world." Growth by itself can't kill culture, he believes. "It's a convenient scapegoat. You can say we can't grow because we're not going to be the same company we used to be, and we're not going to be a family. I don't agree with that. I say you can be every bit as much the company you used to be as you grow, if—underline the word if—you pay attention to those issues and deal with them." 55

The board struck a compromise. Ben & Jerry's would continue to grow, but would devote a lot more effort to developing its internal organization. For this, the board hired a consultant, Philip Mirvis, a research fellow at Boston University's Center for Applied Science—in effect, an organizational therapist. His mission was to improve communications, help the board hammer out a statement of mission, and build a strong, unified cadre of managers. "The management team was fragmented all over the place," says Mirvis. "Everyone had very different perceptions of what Ben & Jerry's was and should be."

The retreat got Mirvis's program off to an unexpectedly fast start. By the end of the three days, the managers had traded dark secrets, gnawed the bones of long-dead skeletons. They'd acted in skits, one parodying Ben and his corporate philosophies. Rick Brown, Ben's opponent in The Great Belly Bounce, played Ben while a Greek chorus chanted, "Social responsibility." By design, Ben and Jerry stayed away—after all, they wanted to ease out of daily management. This would give the managers some elbow room and underscore the new separation of power. Ben and Chico were now members of the board, and Jerry was an unofficial member. All the others were management. Ben and Jerry, however, were invited to speak on the last evening, to pass the pipe of corporate culture—two plump shamans telling tribal tales to their adoring warriors.

Ben and Jerry sat back and told the usual stories: why Jerry had left the company, Ben's theories about corporate responsibility. It didn't sit right. This was not what the Hulbert group wanted to hear. Wedded by confession, they expected more of the same. Self-exploration. Honesty. Spilled tears might have been nice.

"We'd been incredibly honest with one another." says Brown. "When Ben and Jerry showed up, I guess we expected an openness with them that we'd had with one another." Instead, it seemed, Ben and Jerry were intruding. "For the hour or so we were listening, we couldn't keep the same emotion. It sort of broke the spell."

Director of sales and marketing Allan Kaufman spoke first. Even though the first day of the retreat had been his first day on the job, he already felt close to the other managers. If Ben & Jerry's is so socially responsible, he asked, why was this retreat forced on everybody—people worked hard enough without having to leave their families for three days. Chico remembers Kaufman's challenge of the company rhetoric: "Ben, you didn't invent charity." 60

Others jumped in, first about the family issue, then about other matters. The managers wanted something more than the same old stories; they felt good, empowered, and wanted a new business vision. "We couldn't just tra-la anymore," says Diane Cadieux, director of franchise marketing. "We could tra-la, but we had to do it with business in mind."

Ben told how he'd rather fail at something new than succeed at something old. Later, Chico rose and said—as Ben remembers it—"Ben, that statement scared the shit out of me."

Ben calls that night a positive experience. Nonetheless, it played on his fears about growth, the potential damage growth could do to the moral pilgrimage of Ben & Jerry's Homemade.

Back in Waterbury, the management group continued to coalesce rapidly. The board of directors planned meetings with all the departments, starting with the franchise department, to hammer out goals and discuss the strategic role of franchises. A snowstorm, however, led most of the board members to cancel. The franchise department went ahead and met anyway. Why not? The management group was supposed to be making decisions; holding the meeting without the board would underscore management's independence. For the first time, a department had settled down for some strategic planning. "It was a great meeting," says Chico. "Up until then, it was probably the best meeting I'd ever been to."

The management group spent two more months building goals for the other department clusters as well, the most concentrated planning the company had ever done. And the board had not been involved; Ben had not been involved. In April, the managers presented the board with working drafts of their plans, all so businesslike and attuned to the bottom line. 65

But where was the rakish funk of times gone by? The board—meaning primarily Ben, Jeff Furman, and Jerry, who holds a nonvoting membership—reacted in a way no one had expected. Afterward, the managers felt a keen, personal hurt.

Chico brought the news. A director as well as the senior officer of the management group, Chico straddles the divide and is said to have a "pronoun problem." When to use "we," when to use "they"? His sympathies, however, lie with management. The board, Chico reported, was concerned that management had not fully bought into the social agenda; that the company was becoming less creative, less ready to move on new ideas. Jerry, moreover, had suggested that perhaps Ben ought to have a separate budget so he at least could keep coming up with ideas. There was talk, too, of giving Jeff Furman a job as a kind of new-ideas czar. What the board was asking, Chico reported, distilling the board's own words, was, "Are you weird enough?"

Oh, rip out our hearts and grind them in the dust!

. . . But after the hurt came compassion. Controller Milly Badger says the board's reaction was not so surprising, if you put yourself in Ben's shoes: "You've brought the company to where it is, and all of a sudden we're saying, OK, you've done your job, now we'll do ours. We don't need you anymore."

Is Ben & Jerry's weird enough? By circumstance and necessity, the   70
company has grown more corporate. For example, when the company went public, it automatically encased itself in new restrictions and requirements. Milly Badger worries about the balance between the corporate and the weird. She cites the passing of the Cowmobile, a motor home painted Ben & Jerry's colors and decorated with cows. It made its last national scooping tour in September 1987. (A previous Cowmobile burst into flames and was destroyed just outside Cleveland in 1986.) Now, Badger says, with evident dismay, the Cowmobile is going to be a museum piece, set out in front of the Waterbury plant and used as an ice-cream kiosk. "What made us is Ben and Jerry going out there, being funky, being different," she says. "If we don't continue to do the things that made Ben & Jerry's, we're going to lose something."

What the company needs is to find a new balance. Diane Cadieux believes more structure will enhance the company's creativity, rather than dampen it, by giving people a break from fighting fires. The board and the management group just aren't that far apart, she says. "My feeling is we're all talking about the same stuff. I don't think we're spending enough time together. They're getting all this very cold paper laid out like a business plan, and they're not really getting the feeling behind it."

Jeff Furman, who shares Ben's concerns, says there is nothing to despair about. "This is living, it's an organic thing here. It's got a lot of fluidity. Right now, everybody's huddled in their corners. The organizational consultant [Phil Mirvis] wanted it that way. There's a 'we' and a 'they' because we haven't gotten together yet."

That process is underway now, with the management group and the board meeting and talking. It is clear, however, that Ben & Jerry's can't go home again, and that what will emerge, regardless of the weirdness of the next decade's ideas, will be a more mature business—the last thing in the world Ben and Jerry ever expected back in May 1978, the last thing, for that matter, they ever wanted.

Jerry has made his peace. He is sitting in a booth at the Waterbury Holiday Inn, half a mile from the plant. The music coming over a speaker is kind of sad, something from an old movie. Jerry smiles: "The idea, I think, is to maintain the values of your culture and yet bring it along with you. I mean, you don't want to stay stuck in the past. The gas station we started in was an amazing place, but it is there no longer. It's a parking lot. You can tell wonderful stories about the place—but tell me the wonderful story about what happened at the plant last month. I think our company will be changed. I think there's no doubt about that. It will be changed. We just have to make it a good change."

For anyone who's looking, there are plenty of symbols, meta- 75
phors, and artifacts to describe the evolution of Ben & Jerry's. The Belly Bounce, for example—Ben the visionary versus Rick the salesman. The T-shirt, designed to commemorate the company's 10th anniversary—"Be 10 again!" it cries.

And then there are the one-year hats.

It's Friday again, toward the close of the staff meeting, time for Chico to hand out Ben & Jerry's baseball caps to honor new employees who've completed their first year of work. Ben is absent, on an ice-cream mission to Thailand, so Chico calls for nominations for Ben stand-ins. He gets three, including Jim Rowe, who is wearing a tie and a trenchcoat and does not even have a beard. All three line up at the front of the room to the right of Jerry. Chico calls out the names of the one-year employees, and each comes forward to shake hands with Jerry and the stand-in Bens. The applause for each is loud, the cheers warm and joyous; one man curtsies to Jerry, bringing down the receiving bay with laughter. Then Chico calls out another name and scans the room; no one responds.

Now Chico is trying to make out what a few people are saying through the din. And in a sense they're telling him once again, as if he needed to hear it, how much times have changed, how large and unfamiliar this big family has become. One hundred and fifty people jam the floor in front of him; father Ben is off in Thailand; Jerry is smiling his benign, slightly lopsided grin.

Chico again calls the name of the honored employee. At last, someone shouts, "She quit." "Retired early," another says. And Chico did not know it.

❖ Focused Freewriting   Consider as possible focal points Ben's notion of "weird," the dilemma of growth versus social responsibility, or one of the topics you've identified in your journal.

❖ Guided Responses

1. Describing Ben as looking like "a chubby Central American guerrilla—Daniel Ortega Cohen," Larson calls the man a "capitalist guerrilla" (para. 5). How does Ben fit the description of a guerrilla? How do his methods of operation threaten the traditional concept of an American corporation? How serious is the threat?

2. Plant manager Jim Miller calls the 1987 underproduction crisis the one that "woke the sleeping giant" (para. 35). How does this story illustrate both the strengths and the weaknesses of Ben & Jerry's Way? Based on your reading of the article, do you think the company can alter its management style enough to prevent such crises in the future without sacrificing its social commitments? Explain your response.

3. Ben Cohen criticizes those who "feel the company's first goal is to make as much money as possible, and then spend it in a socially responsible way" (para. 45). How would he define "the company's first goal"? Would you agree with him? Why, or why not?

4. Chico Lager is quoted as saying, "Growth by itself can't kill culture. . . . It's a convenient scapegoat" (para. 55). Does growth seem to be killing the Ben & Jerry's culture? Do you think the company's attempts to deal with growth will remain successful? Explain your responses.

❖ Shared Responses   In your journal, argue for or against the five-to-one salary ratio in force at Ben & Jerry's. Consider issues such as corporate responsibility, company morale, recognition of individual achievement, and individual contributions to the company. In your group discussion, try to determine the beliefs about business that underlie individual responses.

Maude DeVictor

JOHN LANGSTON GWALTNEY

JOHN LANGSTON GWALTNEY *received a Ph.D. from Columbia University and has been a professor of anthropology at Syracuse University since 1971. His books include* The Thrice Shy: Cultural Accommodations to Blindness and Other Disasters in a Mexican Village *(1970) and* Explorations in Anthropology *(1973). In this chapter from* The Dissenters: Voices from Contemporary America *(1989), Maude DeVictor tells her own story. What begins as simple allegiance to her job propels DeVictor into a controversy that, at the time of this writing, has yet to be fully resolved. Through a tale that meanders back and forth in time amidst various apparent digressions, she impresses upon the reader the convictions that have made her a rather unwilling hero.*

Before reading the selection, write in your journal about your own sense of loyalty in a job. What would you do if your loyalty to your employer conflicted with your loyalty to a client or customer or with your own convictions? How would you respond if a position you took threatened your job?

As you make notes on your reading, you may want to focus on DeVictor's frequent digressions, her humor, or her dedication to her cause.

"Today's genocide is tomorrow's humanocide."

◆

If the minds of the people are impure, their land is also impure.
—NICHIREN

A FFABLE, CLEVER, WARY *Maude DeVictor and I were well met long before our first face-to-face meeting. She had consented to assist me in this inquiry in the fall of 1980, but it was not until the fall of 1982 that we actually shook hands at a conference in Chicago. Maude is an articulate improviser. She not only read her own fine paper but chaired the session when the person charged with that responsibility failed to appear. Subsequently she delivered a series of lectures at Syracuse University at my invitation.*

A number of seemingly contradictory elements are curiously combined in her personality. Military service and years of conferring and commiserating with veterans tends a directness just short of abruptness to her manner. More than occasional exposure to very hard times has made her a keen relisher of the better things of this life. I have yet to meet anyone who can extract more pleasure from both the essence and the aura of a champagne cocktail, a good conversation, or a noble dish than Maude does. She is inordinately fond of humanity in general and all but the most hidebound of that species tend to like her. She is an organic initiator of dialogues. She laughs often and her humor is most often prompted by wry reflection or by her strong inclination to disarm and teach.

Maude's formidable capacity for establishing genuine rapport is essentially being wasted now. Her decision to embark upon what was initially a one-woman crusade to publicize the dangers of dioxin poisoning has cost her dearly. After having been relegated to pushing papers at the Veteran's Administration's Chicago Regional Office and banned from doing what she does best—person-to-person counseling—Maude was finally fired in January of 1984, after eighteen years of service. At the time of this writing, she is instituting legal proceedings in an attempt to get her job back.

Maude has earned the cumbersome accolade of "Mother of Agent Orange." There is far more of commitment and courage in that awkward appellation than triteness. I have spoken to more than one Vietnam veteran who believes that Maude DeVictor should receive the Nobel Prize for her campaign to publicize the connection between exposure to Agent Orange and susceptibility to cancer and birth defects.

However jocularly she makes her points, Maude is serious and unswerving in her determination that the nation, indeed the world, shall know of the myriads of tragedies that spring from the decision to defoliate a sizable portion of the Indo-Chinese rain forest. Getting to know Maude lends appropriateness to the title, "Mother of Agent Orange," for there is a very real aspect of the maternal in the genuine solicitude she feels toward the causes and casualties she champions. 5

What happened was, in June of 1977 I was a VBC—Veterans Benefits Counsellor—and we have two assignments we do. We alternate between answering the phones and sitting at a desk and meeting the public. So I was at that point working in the phone unit doing telephone interviews and this woman called from the pay phone at the VA hospital in Chicago, distraught, saying that they'd just told her that her husband was going to die. He had cancer and there was nothing they could do to reverse his condition, it was just a matter of time. And she said she knew it was service-connected because he'd never been sick. In their marriage he had made two references to this situation. One was that he told her that if his death were ever due to cancer, it was due to the chemicals used in Vietnam. Now the other reference that he made was one time when they were coming into L.A. from the airport. It was the smog season and they could see this crud just hanging like a curtain, and he made a reference to her in the cab that that's just the way it is in Vietnam, only sometimes it's so bad you can't even see your hand in front of your face when they spray. She was always at home, she never traveled with him in his military career, which lasted, you know, for twenty-three or twenty-four years. He was a career air force man who has literally spoken from the grave. Charlie Owens was his name. Yes, he was black and you know, you're the first one who has ever asked me that? That's what I love about you, that's what I love about you! This is one of my themes I always get in, try to get in when the majority interviews me. Your two significant stories of the seventies have been what? Watergate and Agent Orange. Who were they found by? Blacks. Black federal employees. How were they found by blacks? In the course of their "routine" job assignments. And that says something about, you know, maybe if they would activate equal opportunity and let more of us rise to managerial positions, then a lot of this crap and waste and bullshit we have in the government we wouldn't have. And I have spent a lot of my energy so that I wouldn't wind up like that Watergate guard. Ah, where's Mr. Wills now, that's the key question. Where is he? Aha! He couldn't get a job parking cars last time I heard. Yeah, I give speeches, but I don't have a speaker's bureau like Haldeman and Ehrlichman.

So, anyway, at that point in time I had no idea whether they were puttin' saltpeter in his soup or giving him some kind of funny shaving cream. I didn't know anything—just "chemicals," Okay? And so I work with the attitude that the veteran knows, no matter how bad it sounds, even if it's syphilis off the toilet seat, or whatever. If that's what the guy says, that's what it is. I've found that there are two types of reality working at the VA. There is the official reality and the actual reality. And I can tell you best from this because I have interviewed vets who played cornet with John Philip Sousa. I have interviewed guys who were on the sub that brought MacArthur out of the Philippines. I've interviewed guys that were standing guard at the White House when Roosevelt was there. I'm not like a Ph.D. candidate, you know, I've been with the little guys who were bringing in the catsup and whatever, the ones who were putting the luggage aboard the sub, this kind of thing. I've really been at different points in history that are not available to the average person. So this is why I've always dealt with what the veteran says because he was there and he's seen the reality and he was there in the environment. In the setting. Reports are doctored in the wash, you know, depending upon who's contributing to somebody's campaign. I kinda go with the little people.

So what I did, I got in my car and drove to her home and filled out the papers with her because this woman had been doing this, you know, vigilance with the dying husband. Bags under her eyes, shaking. So I filled out the papers and got his discharge. This guy was a finance clerk—like a bank clerk in civilian life. His job at the terminal in Vietnam, when you came in country, was to take your American money and give you Vietnamese money. This man, although he was a finance officer, had gotten numerous awards for suggestions. With his own hands he had built a little thing to make it look like a bank. You might think, well what the hell, in a wartime zone, but he was trying to be efficient and professional, even as a finance officer, because he was an enlisted man. He had all kinds of awards for suggestions, you know. How to do this better, because you can imagine being in a war zone and having your paycheck messed up. This is something not tolerated! He was just a team man. He got all kinds of awards just for being a great finance officer. He got the Air Force Accommodation Medal because he was damn good. So even in his little square of the checkerboard of life, he had professionalism. 'Course he had been in the fighting too. So when I was there, she was crying, and showing me these awards and special letters from generals and stuff like that and so I filed it, Okay? I filed a claim for disability compensation. She called me back about a week or ten days later and said he had died.

He had been going to school. He had done his bit in the military, he was a full-time college student and he had a little job on the side. You know how men are, a little job on the side, and then all of a sudden this man died. Between the day that he went to the hospital till the day he died were 110 days. So this is a person who's never been sick. He was about fifty-three years old when he died. He had gotten a ten-thousand-dollar insurance policy from the Supreme Insurance Company. Now quite naturally when the insurance person comes to see a military retiree, there's no questions because they know he's in good health and it wasn't any fraud or anything because he had his discharge physical and all of that and they insured this man. So when it came time to collect, they refused to pay the policy, saying that he had known he had cancer and all this kind of crap. So that leads me to believe—and I heard of this from other insurance companies—that even though the government hasn't recognized or "validated the existence of Agent Orange by action," in terms of what would directly flow to the veteran, the insurance industry has sent up its antenna.

We have a VA reg that if a veteran dies before the claim is adjudi-   10
cated, the claim dies with the vet. So we have to come back in and file a form for the same benefit, but now for the surviving spouse. It took

'em three months to decide, "No." She just got the basic pension, that any wartime widow of a service veteran would get. It was a hundred and twenty-five bucks a month, substantially less than she would have gotten from the other claim. There were no children so she wasn't entitled to any kind of Social Security. She was a young woman, she wasn't gonna get Social Security for another ten years, something like that. And this was all the money she had because the insurance company hadn't kicked in the ten thousand and she had the funeral bill to pay and they were gonna give her a hundred and twenty-five bucks a month. That was all she had in the world. So, as always, when they deny your claim they give you notice of a right to appeal. And she say, "Well, I have this right to appeal, Maude, and I would like you to represent me on the case." Another one of my duties is to be an attorney-in-fact for a claimant in cases of appeal. So I said "Okay."

Now I said, "What do I know about this man?" Well, this guy was in the air force and he had like a twenty-four-year straight enlistment from World War II up until approximately seventy-three and Vietnam. And I said, "Anything he used, the air force would have, at the bottom line, had to have paid for or stored or transported." So anything that he came in contact with they would have had some kind of knowledge of. That at least started me on what became an odyssey. This man extended his enlistment at least six or seven times, Okay? And when he extended his enlistment he had to sign a document. Now when he signed that document he knew that there was a possibility of him dying, being shot, you know, crashing in a plane, stepping on a land mine, whatever. However, he had no indication of chemical contamination, you see, so consequently, when he signed his enlistment document, it wasn't an informed consent because they hadn't said, "Well, you know, we're using this and that and you might have some problem with it." So in theory, it wasn't informed consent. So I had all this beautiful theory thought out in my mind and I got my rap together, tightened my teeth, and called the JAG, which is the Judge Advocate General's office of the air force, where I was immediately told, "No, you're in the wrong ballpark, this is a health problem." And they transferred my call politely up to the office of the Surgeon General of the air force at the Pentagon. And of course the Surgeon General was out at one of those ever-present meetings and his assistant was there, so I told him what the deal was and he told me he himself was not aware of any kind of problem like this, but that he would alert the proper command element within the air force and have them call me back with complete information. So this guy called whose military rank was captain and whose civilian rank was a Ph.D. in plant physiology. He was also practicing the art of plant physiology in the air force. And before he opened his mouth, I knew immediately I was onto something because my old street rationale said, "What is a plant physiologist doing in the Air Force of the United States?" He himself said that he was the only plant physiologist on staff in the entire U.S. Air Force. I'm a military person myself and I know how you are always being kidded about how you never are able to do what you're trained to do in the military. You never hear of anybody doing that. Now he was a man academically trained, Ph.D. level, I mean, had *published* and was still publishing, pursuing the same occupation within the military. As I said, his military rank was captain, which is kinda low, right? Now since I've met that man, he's a major going up for colonel.

Anyway, that day he called, I thought, "They couldn't have that many potted ferns at the Pentagon to justify the need for a plant physiologist." And then I knew the lady wasn't lying, you know, the widow wasn't lying. So this guy called and he began to tell me the scientific name of the chemical. Want me to spell it for you? It's 2,3,7,8 Tetrachlorodibenzoparadioxin. Now he spelled that for me and you know what I mean, you don't get that at the A & P, right? He spelled it and he gave me the everyday routine name, Agent Orange. And he also stated that there were other chemicals used in Vietnam. Agent Orange, Agent White, Agent Blue, Agent Purple, all named for the color of the fog they produce. We decided on Agent Orange because it would kill you just as bad as the others, but in terms of the staff handling it, loading it, whatever, it was less toxic and less dangerous to handle for the American troops. But it would all kill you just as good as Agent Blue and White. Agent Purple was a little bit too much, a little bit too wild and so they quickly had to stop using Agent Purple. So Agent Orange was the poison of choice. He told me that it had been used on certain regions of Vietnam and, let me see, he told me that it was a teratogen, which is fetus deforming. He told me that it was a carcinogen, which means cancer producing, and that it was 150,000 times more toxic than—now I don't know my chemistry, I don't know if this is inorganic or organic—but it's more toxic than arsenic. I don't want to say the wrong thing because some chemistry professor would say there's an error in the article, so bullshit to the whole thing.

Okay, so I had to report to my immediate supervisor and he's a fantastic man and he immediately told me, "Hey, document it and call it in." We use a 1946 disability rating book at the VA and because this situation was not in our rating book, that meant it had to go all the way to Congress for approval of this disability. After all, we basically use taxpayers' money to pay disability benefits. The rating board at the VA is made up of trusted servants who have sat there and managed to stay awake for at least twenty years. So Congress has to approve this as an additional disability. We have the same problem with radiation exposure. They didn't have that in the book either. They just got thumbs and toes and ears, you know, the regular stuff, not the exotic stuff. My job was to call in all documented information, scientific papers, and not only scientific papers that said there was something wrong with it, no. *Anything*, every sheet of paper that I could get hold of. So that's what I did. And in the month of October I made 384 phone calls telling 'em that we had a claim and that we were attempting to get to the bottom of it. That's how it all got started. And at that point I was in a state of shock because I was the only one in the world that knew about it. I had to really get myself together. I couldn't sleep because my mind was still running. When the impact of the whole thing hit me, I can't tell you what a hard time I had. There were people who were just dealing with me as if it was business as usual. I had nobody on my job to talk to. All my son knew was that I was bringing all these papers home and my house began to look like a library, and that the phone was ringing constantly.

So I proceeded on with Agent Orange, and of course they denied her claim at the local level. Then they had me write a white paper on it. I've written about two of 'em, two or three. It's been so long, Doc, I'm sorry. In fact, I've lived and died a thousand times since. You know what I mean? Anyway, the regional director asked me to write a white paper, which was totally alien to me, my culture. Here this is a Kentucky colonel telling me to do a white paper and in my mind I'm saying, "What the hell is a white paper?" But I figured it out and just wrote it down verbatim long hand.

People were always coming to my desk, whether they had a   15
change of address, or they'd had a baby and had the birth certificate and I would take care of all that first, then I'd do my own number. I would ask, "Are you tired?" "Do you have numbness in your hands and feet?" "What you might call circulation problems?" "Has your wife or lady been pregnant and then something happened between the second and third month?" And they'd say, "Yeah, yeah, how do you know? I go to the VA hospital and they tell me I'm crazy. They tell me it's nothing to worry about." If they got eruptions on their skin, they'll give 'em something like Pacquins cold cream, which is like a basic dermatology solution. And when you get really bad they give you the kind of stuff that's like cornmeal inside, you know, calamine lotion bullshit. And then also there were the veterans who were having heart attacks, what they themselves thought were heart attacks. The emergency squad would come flying and get him to the emergency room, put him on the EKG machine, do a Code Three, you know, and they get a normal reading. They think, "This son-of-a-bitch,

here I was in the middle of lunch." They'll soothe him down and pat him on the head and give him some Librium or something. Then if it happens a second or third time, they send him up to the psychiatric ward, because they think he's just doing it to get attention. But he has the classic symptoms.

The VA has always noticed, especially the old-timers, that there was something funny about the Vietnam veteran. They had worked with returning guys from World War II, from Korea, but these Vietnam guys were a group separate and apart. They used to say, "Something happened over there." I knew that Agent Orange was the cause when the plant physiologist guy talked to me, but it's one thing to know something intellectually, and another to experience it. I guess my blood really ran cold when I began to see these children and these veterans. There was one guy who looked sixty years old, all wizened and bald. The interviewer asked him how old was he and he said, "Twenty-eight." He had cancer and I'll never forget. He died at Great Lakes and I called Great Lakes and asked them had they done a dioxin series on him, and the guy that did the autopsy said no, they didn't tell him to. He said, "You mean this kid had dioxin poisoning?" I said, "Yes." "Well," he said, "there's no mention on his records." So that was like a body that got away. I'm like Dracula, if I can't get 'em alive, I hunt the bodies.

You know, we have a Veterans Benefits Counsellor stationed at each hospital just to take care of the claims. When the regular VBC had a Christmas vacation, they needed somebody to cover the VA hospital. They needed somebody that was familiar with hospital procedure, and I had been a medic in the military, so they said, "Hey, we need somebody, Maude, you go over there." And, I might add, they haven't asked me to do it since! So I had all these people coming in with "DU tumor," "DU lump," which means diagnosis undetermined. I had a couple of World War II vets in there, but most of them were Vietnam veterans, and I had a case that just ripped my heart out. I had a little twenty-eight-year-old guy. His first name was William. He had two children, and his wife was getting ready to file for a divorce. He had fibrosarcoma, which is like a spiderwebby kind of cancer cell. It was growing in his left arm and it was choking off his circulation, Okay? Are you ready? This is a twenty-eight-year-old kid. They had to amputate right here by his breast bone, it came down angular, and all he could think of was, "How'm I gonna have sex?" You know, the old missionary position, right? He lived in the ghetto, on Forty-seventh Street in Chicago, and he said, "They'll kill me. I'll only have one hand." And he tried to commit suicide. And his amputation was so extensive until the prosthesis had to be approved by Central Office in

Washington. 'Cause usually when you amputate you go from the shoulder or something, but they had never had a case like that in the VA. He was up on the ledge trying to jump. He had one leg in and one leg out kind of thing, and he just couldn't deal with it. The nurse called me from downstairs. I was in my office and I ran upstairs and I said to him, "Well, it's not that bad." "*You* don't know," he said, "*you* ain't got—" blah blah blah, you know. So what I did, I reached in and pulled out my breast prosthesis—'cause I'm a cancer patient myself— and I said, "Hey, you ain't the only one with the bug, here I got it myself." So that kinda shocked him and he came back in. And I sat there with that man and I what we call talked him down until about nine-thirty, ten o'clock that night. And we had a very deep conversation and I've never forgotten that experience. That made me think about all these guys. They don't know what it's about, why they are suffering the way they are and nothing about Orange is being done. But this is the whole crime of Agent Orange. See, the doctor in Omaha, Nebraska, he's just treating it as a cancer case. He doesn't realize that there's a doctor in Denver, a doctor in Albuquerque that's got the same thing.

When did the worm turn? Okay, well, first of all, you gotta look at the VA in structure. This investigation was occurring because the regional director's attitude was that of the benevolent administrator who says, "One of my staff people found this problem and we're going to help the veteran and give her free rein, and this is gonna look good on my résumé and I'll soon be down there in Washington in the walnut room overlooking the Potomac" kind of thing. So they were encouraging me and telling me, "If you want to do it, fine." But then they sent the stuff into Washington, and it went to a higher level, and it got to the point of, "We can't afford to have this bullshit. Is this woman crazy? All these veterans out here—how many hours of biology does this woman have? Is she a doctor at the VA? No. What does she know? Well, if you want to retain your job, you put the lid on this in Chicago right now."

I guess since then my whole juices have been and my entire expertise has been geared toward survival at the VA. I didn't get in trouble with the VA, they got in trouble with me! I will say this: If it hadn't been for the Vietnam Veterans of America, I wouldn't have my job. If it hadn't been for the Office of Special Counsel of the Merit System Protection Board in Washington, I wouldn't have my job. See, what they did was, they called me into the office and they said I was going to be fired for insubordination. Doesn't that sound militaristic? Insubordination because I had the unmitigated gall to refuse to work in front of the computer terminals. Those things emit radiation and

I'm a cancer patient. I had told them this, and submitted a note from my doctor, but the VA told me that my employment was conditional upon me operating the machine.

I wasn't trying to organize the VA in a work stoppage—this is just my own body. So I told my boss, "Well, I've never been fired before from a job, do I leave now or do I work till the end of the day, or what?" And he said, "Oh no-no-no-no, it's just like the military, you have to go and sign out and I'll call personnel and have 'em get your papers ready." So what I did, I ran upstairs to the regional director's office and told him what my boss had said. "Well," he says, "you know everybody is exposed to radiation. Background sunlight, background lights." Then I got pissed off and I said, "Well, let me talk to your wife, because if it was something to do with the testicles and their potency you would never have taken it from the loading dock into the building!" He says—you know what he says? "You're right, Maude." I'm telling ya!

So they didn't fire me. The regional director stopped that and they put me on answering Congressionals. This is where they're pissed off and they write their Congressman. VA people answer those letters, send them back to the Congressman, the Congressman has his gals retype them for his signature. Now they've put me back on it. They asked me to go back to doing that about three weeks ago. They told me in one of those two o'clock Friday afternoon conferences. You know, so it will upset you for the weekend? Anyway, the first time they put me on those Congressionals was back in 1980. It was due to terminate December 31 of eighty. I was down with the flu, came back to work January the 5th and when I went to my little Congressionals desk they said, "That's not your work anymore. You gotta go back upstairs." I went back upstairs and they had put the damn computer thirty-three and a half inches from my desk, facing my bosom, all day long! I said, "I can't sit there, are you kidding? I'm not supposed to be in this area." "Well, it's part of your job, it's part of your job. You gotta—" I said, "I'm not working there." They just knew I was going to say, Take this job and shove it up your ass, but I didn't. I said, "Thanks but no thanks," got up and got my coat on and walked out of the VA. Went home and promptly called the Office of Special Counsel and told them about it. And of course the next day I had a letter from the VA saying, "Notice of Intention to Remove from the Federal Rolls." I sent that in to the Special Counsel. They were going to fire me like February twenty-seventh but the Office of Special Counsel flew an attorney out and all of a sudden the papers for me being fired could not be found. I had the only copy! The day I was due to be fired, that's the day the attorney showed up on their doorstep and they said, "What do you mean, Maude is one of our most qualified, dedicated

20

workers. See how thick her file is?" So they had to stop that. He took a deposition from the people and that immediately halted all firing action. I'm so glad because the following Tuesday I became deathly ill, close to dying in fact. I had gangrene in my gall bladder, plus a stone, and if they had fired me that Friday, I wouldn't have had any insurance that Tuesday and I would have literally died. So, when I became ill, that further cemented the stop-the-firing-of-Maude action, because it wasn't that I was refusing to report for duty, I was medically unable to work. Okay. So we had six weeks of grace. They told me, at the end of six weeks, "You should be back. Report to work such-and-such a date." You know, I had a little bag on me like a little pocketbook that I toddled around with so all this pus and gangrene and crap could drain out. And I told them, "No because I got this pocketbook draining off of me. I've got this crud. I've got to change dressings three and four times a day." And they said, "Oh you can do that right here in the bathroom." I said, "Wait! I'm not changing dressings in my *own* bathroom, what you talking about public-ass toilet?" I'm telling ya! And change dressings, you know. I might get something *else* in there! And I refused to go back to work.

No, they didn't go through with firing me because Special Counsel was there, though I didn't have a settlement, you know, as I should have. Their attorney, who is a fantastic man, is a cancer patient himself. He could understand what I'm talking about. It's a thing of healthy people trying to deal with people who have cancer. They don't understand about sitting in front of that machine. They don't know what it is to be married and you're pulling off your, you know, you go to the motel, you're young, well you can go off to the motel and pull off your wig; you may even can take out your teeth, but to take out your *bosom*? And put it on the dresser? Even your leg you can take off, you know, but the boob . . . ? So I wasn't going to do it. I told 'em, they'll bury me just as deep whether I die as a welfare recipient or as a trusted civil servant. And one thing, I *will* have my one breast. I did, I told 'em. And I said, you can't understand, you're a man. Here's my phone number. Have your wife call me. So now I'm in the Career Development Center, which is one of the few havens at the VA where there's no computer terminal. You see what I'm talking about? Shit. You know what I mean? I'm just trying to tell you. I don't know what it is but I figure I've got the survival streak in me. I think if I hadn't had that I'da just deep-sixed a long time ago.

So anyway, I'm to the point now where two weeks ago Friday, at one of those two o'clock Friday meetings they were telling me that they were going to change my duties again, and I told them, "Well I can't do that because I'm under a signed agreement. Until I confer with the attorneys I don't want to break the agreement and give you cause to not follow it. I'll deal with him and then I'll get back to you. But I tell you this, and I'm just giving you a statement, it's not a threat, that I'm not going to carry on a long campaign with you guys." I said, "I'm forty-two years old and at the point in life when I should be attending the Ebony Fashion Show and attending the Urban League Scholarship Awards Night and going down to Jamaica now and then for a little R and R. I'm Buddhist and I'm always expounding on the dignity of life—and I said, "When I was lying up in that hospital trying to get my health back, I made a decision that it's best for me to be in a federal prison walking around reading law books, writing letters to the editor, whatever, than to be laying somewhere watching blood drip into my body with oxygen going down my nose, or be physically crushed. I have made that determination." And I said, "This is not a threat. I'll tell you who Maude DeVictor is. If you cannot let me enjoy my healthy life on the outside, I will enjoy my healthy life on the inside. I'm not saying I want to kill you or anything like that. I'm saying I'm not going to be pushed anymore." They just kind of gaped. And then they had the Friday two o'clock meeting. It had kind of flipped on 'em and *they* went home shaky. Trying to restrategize and regroup.

I'm an only child and I never realized the value of companionship. Being raised as an only child I've always had an ability to keep myself occupied, but one of the things that was very devastating to me was the situation wherein no one would talk to me for like two or three, well, really for three years I ate lunch by myself. If people talked to me they would be told, "You were seen talking to Maude DeVictor. You realize she's under investigation? This is not going to be too good for you." I knew this because some of those people would call me at night and tell me. On the surface it was like business as usual, but at night they would call and tell me what happened. They would encourage me. They would say, "Maude you're doing a good job, no matter what." It wouldn't be openly. Out of the side of their mouths they would say, "Keep it up kid, we're with you." You know, that kind of thing. Or else they might walk past me and wink. Bottom line, they were afraid of the pressure and the control their supervisors have over them. When there's a job posted the supervisor must evaluate you on a scale A to E, A being the lowest, E being the highest. They evaluated me as being an average writer, average communication skills. And I know that's bullshit. I can make myself understood. I know a little sign language for when the hearing impaired come in. I know a few words of this, a few words of that and there's something about me that I can communicate with people, even people who have psychiatric illnesses. I can tell them, you know, I have done this many times and I wasn't taught this, but I tell them, "You can be crazy just as soon as you get up from my desk, you can resume your whatever. However, it's very important that I get the proper information so I can help you." And I say, "I won't tell that you were here sane as a judge." That might be the wrong analogy, and they come right out of it. They deal with me, they stand up, they go right back into it. So it's like a talent I have for communication. I don't know where I picked it up, I really don't.

What do I think most people think about principled dissent? Not   25
a damn! The current thing is not to rock the boat. But principled dissent is the foundation of this country. Principled dissent is primarily an individualistic thing. If it was mass action, then it would be revolution.

Agent Orange isn't a racial kind of thing. I'm out here speaking for whites, blacks, Hispanics, officers, *and* enlisted men. Even so, it was a black soldier who first mentioned it to his wife, and it was a black Veterans Benefits Counsellor that took the case, and this has come out of the minds and assessments of black people, Agent Orange has. 'Course it'll never be put in the paper of the United States, but I know he's a black soldier, I know his *wife* was black. I *know* I'm black. You know, people think niggers don't do nothing but get drunk and get welfare checks.

I think of myself as just a housewife living on the South Side of Chicago. Maybe I have an ability to speak and write the King's English and describe the black situation. That's the only thing that differentiates me from the black housewife who's on public aid and can't do it. Now others say I'm a spokesperson for this, a watchdog for that, a fabulous figure, and, just like Martin King said, a drum major for justice and all that. It's bullshit. I live payday to payday just the same as somebody who was a high school dropout. If I can keep Bell Telephone uptight, and the light company and the landlord, those are still my coordinates. One guy said I'm extraordinary—that has been a definition ascribed to me—but within the bowels of my life, I'm no different from anybody else. Like most blacks, I have never even envisioned a public life—that's for whitefolks and politicians. And those blacks who have been "accorded public life" have always had to cash in their life insurance.

Well, the reason why I participate is that I gave my word to Dad and people who cannot be here, Okay? I think that the beauty of the principled dissenter is that he's like a missionary walking into a house of ill repute, you know, to do recruiting. You know what I mean? He gets swept up in the activities of the evening. We don't start out to say, "I want to be a principled dissenter." I was raised to be an Eastern Star, a Link, a member of the National Black—what's that national black women's association? Maybe a Delta Sigma Theta, and all those other trappings. It's not as though I'm raised to do this. It's that when the situation presents itself something flies up in me and I take action and somewhere, somehow it comes out all right. It's not like my dad was a noted herbicide person, or my mom was a noted teacher, a philosopher, or anything like that. It was like I had all this mixture in me and if it hadn't been Agent Orange, it might have been something as mundane as getting a streetlight placed on the corner. But it's never planned. Just like Rosa Parks. She hadn't left home that morning saying, "Well, this is the last damned day, the hell with the back of the bus." No, she didn't. She was a little churchwoman, pillar of the community, just a little grandmotherly type. She was tired. You know what I mean? And that issue came up and she responded with the statement, "Well, hell, I'm gonna ride this horse till it stops. This is it. I'm through with it." But she didn't say in eighth grade when they asked, "What do you want to be, Rosa Parks?" "Well, forty-five years from now I want to be on a bus in Atlanta and I want to stop sitting in the back of the bus."

I would say all people do what they think is basically right, but they have a kicker. What is right for *them* as opposed to what is right for the population and humankind. I think we all do what is right, it's just that for some people the borders are narrower. Yeah, they know when they're behaving selfishly, but they don't want to know. I don't think it's a question of whether they can distinguish. They feel it's unnecessary to distinguish because, number one, they are dealing out of the self-orientated aspect. I'm just trying to say a lot of people are trying to, shall I say, follow the path of least resistance, so that they don't make waves and they will be able to get promoted, so they will be able to get the finer things in life. Because their universe is the here and now versus the there and then.

When I look back on my life, you know, I was in country clubs at age thirteen or so, and at that time the height of society was playing croquet on the country club lawn. I was doing all that kind of stuff in the fifties. I was playing golf, I was playing tennis. What I'm trying to say is, I had the highest level of living economically—and notice I said economically—and I acquired and became accustomed to that in my father's home. It has been downhill economically for me ever since. I was raised in all that stuff and so I don't pursue it because it's just shallow to me. What is profound to me is to be able—and I know I can say this because I've had experience, and I'm so grateful that you allowed me to have this experience again—to stand up in front of a class and watch the light bulb go on in somebody's mind. For me to be a "bearer of knowledge," to be a resource. What's profound to me is to be able to do that which is right, even though I know I can do wrong and get there quicker, but I can't stay as long. You know what I mean? It's just like check-out time.

I didn't realize I was so different from other people until people started interviewing me. I know I'm not *supposed* to be different from other people. I feel that I was raised very, very right. However, my parents did not realize that the world would go into such an acute level of mediocrity in such a fast time period!

My mother was seventeen years old when I was born. She's had such a hard life. She's not really working for a living now, she's on disability. She's an independent warrior. Not a mercenary. She's an independent warrior and she writes letters. That's where I get my letter-writing abilities from. She will write a letter to the White House, she will write a letter to Sears, she *will* write her letter. I think from my father I get love of people, interest in government and news, ability and desire to help people. My speaking ability, even though I'm trained. Respect for knowledge, love of government and the mystique of government. My daddy was always interested in politics but I couldn't talk to my father because he was behind the counter in the store all the time. I was in such a little world and I felt I had to get away from home, but not far enough away that I couldn't get back, so I went to a school called Ripon College in Ripon, Wisconsin, which is the birthplace of the Republican Party. That's where Lincoln was drafted for his presidency. That's where I first realized that I was black. Before, I thought I was a human being. I was raised in an all-black town named after Elijah P. Lovejoy, the abolitionist, and I've always known black fire chiefs, black principals, black doctors, black wineheads. We had about two white families in town. So I arrived at Ripon on an autumn day in September of fifty-seven. And when we started doing the old sorority rush bit, pledging, I had the nerve to participate. The unmitigated gall to participate. It was a general invitation to the freshman class, but I was supposed to have better sense than to act on this. I was supposed to have read the signs. Now to be part of that whole pledge psychodrama—you have no concept of this—I mean, you're walking around with the little tea and crumpets and you had to have white gloves. The last time I had white gloves on my hand was in Ripon in the spring of fifty-eight. And then people were taking you off to the corner and saying, "Well, Maude, you'd be an excellent pledge, however, we cannot risk having a colored pledge ('cause we were colored in those days) because we have applied to the National for acceptance into their organization and that might be a deterrent to our overall chances of being accepted." Yeah, they got me aside, it was just like going down a receiving line and it would be the president or something like that and they'd look me dead in the eye with those ice-cold blue eyes, you know, and I said, "Well, I'll plant my tree on another shore." So I became president of the Independent Dorm. You know, the cloak of leadership was still on my black shoulders!

And when we would go on the town on Saturday for a movie, you'd stop by the drugstore at bedtime and have a hamburger and a malt or something. Inevitably I was the fifth, the seventh, or the ninth in the group. And it was just hurting me and then that old Sigma Chi—that's another rock in my craw, Sigma Chi. "The girl of my dreams is the sweetest girl of all the girls I know, da dee da dee da." Okay, and they would let the girl out at night and the dorm lights were bathed on the triangle there and she would be pinned and smooched and all that shit. Now this is in fifty-seven. That Sigma Chi was created in the Civil War and I know what time that is, and I would be there with my little black ass just, OH! Just tears. Oh how romantic! And not even relate to the fact that that came from the Confederate battlefield. You know what I mean? That's where Sigma Chi fraternity originated. So I had to go through all that and it was just hell. It was just complete hell.

The only other time I found out I was black was when my grades went caput, you know, and I said the hell with it. But I had had that taste of freedom and I knew I couldn't go back to my daddy's house and be in every night at twelve and this and that and cooking and cleaning and all that, so I went into the navy.

Now I left from Polk Street Station, here in Chicago, and we rode   35
all night and we got off at Baltimore and took a bus. We were going into Bainbridge, Maryland, on the shores of the beautiful Susquehanna. So before you pull into the base at Bainbridge, there's a pit stop because that was before the advent of the toilets on the bus. That was in fifty-eight. September the tenth, in fact. So we pulled into a place called Perryville, Maryland, and that was the day I went from being a house nigger to a field nigger, at approximately 4:30 in the afternoon. What happened was, we come into Perryville, Maryland, and it's like a truck stop, or a bus stop, a way station and I'm the only black, but I don't even notice this, you know. I just wasn't raised that way. So I was the only "colored" girl, and I'm going in with the rest of 'em to go to the bathroom and they stopped me and said, "No, you can't come in this way." They made me go around the back and come in through a basement, stepping over crates. Now all I had to do was go to the bathroom. You know, I'm not trying to buy the place! Or come in there and try to order frog legs. All I wanted to do was go to the bathroom. And I was so gung-ho. Here I am, a representative of the United States Government, going to serve my country and they're doing me like this? And I said, "Well, I'll be damned!"

And there was one incident when I was in the navy, the drill team. I wasn't in the drill team, I was in the band. I said, what the hell, music is universal, I'll go that route. But the drill team went into Baltimore, Maryland, to participate in a parade or something and there was a black member of the drill team and they went into this restaurant to eat and of course they went up to the drill sergeant and said, "We can't serve the black member"; or the "colored" girl. So, the drill sergeant says, "Oh, that's okay." Oh, I guess it must have been eighty or ninety of those girls. The drill sergeant had 'em all to order their food and she told 'em they wanted to be served all at once because everybody had to leave together. So the waitress and the maitre d' said, okay, and brought all that food out there—and of course the poor black gal didn't have no food. The drill sergeant had 'em set it all in front of them and then she called attention and marched 'em straight out of there! And I have always respected that woman! She was a store-keeper, that was her rating in the navy and she was a tiny woman, about four feet ten, but boy she had a voice! I don't know her name. She was white.

Then I'm learning naval etiquette, right? Opposed to social etiquette. And of course one of the main subheadings of naval etiquette is flag etiquette. So one of the naval traditions is that when the flag goes down, if you're outside, they have a five-minute whistle to let you know in five minutes if you're outside and the flag is going down, you've gotta freeze or face the flagpole and salute while the flag is going down. So I was in the middle of what we called the grinder. It was like a huge parking lot and I was in the middle of that and I couldn't get across that damned thing. So, I had gone beyond the flagpole and of course they started the whole taps or whatever and I kept on walking, didn't turn around, kept right on walking and of course when I got to the door I was sent to the sergeant's office and she's like my company commanding officer and she says, "Elmore"— that was my maiden name—"you've committed an infraction. You were seen crossing the grinder when the flag was coming down and you were properly warned and you did not adhere to naval policy." And I made the mistake of saying, "That's not my flag." Now I'm nineteen years old in 1959. I didn't know nothin' about no red, black, and green. All I knew was the red, white, and blue. But I knew those son-of-a-bitches had made me go into the restaurant in the back door in Perryville. I couldn't put the generalities together, but I had the specifics down pat!

What happened when I said it was not my flag? Oh honey! They sent me over to the woman that was the head of the recruiting camp and she said, "How long have you had these views?" And I related to her the Perryville incident and she said she didn't know that had happened. I said, "Well, it did," and she says, "Well, be that as it may—" And when you hear that "Be that as it may" it's like, dee dee da da, the style, the tone is the same the world over. When you get that—"You know that's the flag of the United States of America, you are a member of the United States of America defense forces and that's a heavy responsibility and we must all"—and she didn't say be consistent, but "We must all act accordingly," blah blah blah blah. And she was white and right.

Yes, I've been described as the Mother of Agent Orange and that goes both ways. It's "mother" in the sense of the way we use it in the ghettoese and "mother" in the sense of the dominant culture in that I have been like a universal mother to these guys. I have nurtured, I have listened. It appears to be that I'm a black woman highly visible in a white movement, but that's not it. I'm just a concerned human female that's highly visible in an international movement. There are not too many minorities involved. Minorities many times view it as just another hassle. You know, I can't get no job, I can't get no promotion on the job I've got, and it's just another hassle, the frustration of it all. It's not as if they didn't use the chemicals. It's not as though you bought a raffle ticket and the prize was a year in Vietnam. So the two together, you were using this, this has this side effect, you sent me to this country, I was there, boom. There should be compensation.

This is how I met Paul Reutershan. He's the guy, you know, that   40 founded Agent Orange Victims International. I never actually met him, I just talked to him on the phone for hours and hours. Whenever someone calls and wants me there, Okay, that's the way I am and I just have to trust humanity. April of seventy-eight the phone rang and it was ABC News in New York and they wanted to talk to me and I figured I'd go big time! And they said, "Well, um, Miss DeVictor, we've got this veteran here whose name is Paul Reutershan, are you familiar with him?" I said, "No, never heard of him. Who?" You know. "Says that he's been contaminated by Agent Orange and before he dies everybody's going to know about it and you know our business is the news and we've *never* heard of this before." I said, "Whatever the veteran says is true." "Do you know the vet?" I said, "No, but have him call me tonight and reverse the charges," and I gave ABC my home phone number and Paul called me that night. The only time I saw him was on "20/20." I was on first and he was on behind me. That's how I saw him. And I cried, I was walking around my mother's house and tears were just coming out. My mother thinks I'm crazy. Paul made all of us take oaths, you see, I'm not just doing this. It's hard for people to understand. Paul made us all take oaths, we had to take oaths. Frank McCarthy and I, Roger Pappas, Victor Yannacone, we've all taken oaths that as long as, now I can't say what Victor's oath is, he's the attorney, Okay? About things like, "Don't back off the case," "Don't let 'em buy you off," you know, because Paul was dying. And I'll never forget Paul dying. Paul had his chin on his pillow and he called me and he says, "Maude, I'm dying. My body no longer does what my mind tells it to." And he says, "I don't want to be unconscious, I don't want to be in a coma, 'cause I want to have my wits about me. And I want you to promise me, Maude, you swear, swear to me that you will never let this go, because even though I won't be there, I'll know that you backed out of the deal! I have to depend on you because my body will be elsewhere. You and Frank and the other guys will have to do it 'cause I won't be able to function in this dimension. I won't be able to, so it's up to you guys. I don't care how hard it gets, because we're right."

That's why I look at the politicians and maybe I'm glad I haven't gotten any money out of this. Listen, the VA isn't worth shit. They're not studying the question. They try to romanticize it by having a Vietnam veteran as head of the committee, but they haven't recognized him. You know, why are you going to pay someone sixty thousand dollars a year to head a committee if we don't have an issue here? I mean, what about the guy that's somewhere in an oxygen tent now and is trying to file a claim, or some poor soul who's in jail and can't even file a goddamned claim? That's why I have this hidden rage, you know. I get tired of the bullshit because they're all depending on us to die. In fact, they're *banking* on it because we're all kinda sickly and frail. And that's why I don't want no flag, no American flag on me when I go. Paul lives, he lived, in Mohegan Lake, New York. In fact, he's buried in the cemetery at Mohegan Lake. The most beautiful gravestone I've ever seen. Upstate. Peekskill. *Reader's Digest* country. Whatever that is. Mohegan Lake, New York. He died December 14, 1978.

When I think of the veterans who have died, all of that concern, fighting to the last bit, it's something. Agent Orange has changed the law. I mean, they had to videotape these guys' testimony, the ones who had brain tumors. It's just something that you have to experience. Even in a courtroom you can just feel it. When you walk into that Agent Orange courtroom it's like you're going into an electric field. You think I'm kidding. When you walk into the courtroom your hair stands up on your arm. It's not tension, it's almost like a vibrator chair or foot vibrators, you know. It's a feeling. I'm not lying, I have done it. The hair just stands up on your arm because they are still there. Those guys are there. You can't see 'em, but they're there. People think we're crazy, but we're not. They're dead, but not dead. You can really sense their presence.

The government has already accorded these people special status because they put their bodies between the enemy and the shores of the United States. That alone entitles them to special programs. VA education, home loan insurance, you know, the whole bit. But now the government is taking a new stance, saying that it's too expensive to deal with Agent Orange, but that should be expanded. It's too expensive to be going to war. Something has got to be done. It has to come from the mothers of America. Something happens to you when you go to Washington. It's dangerous for your health. Something happens to human beings when they go to Washington.

You know, it used to be like you had Group A that tried to annihilate Group B and Group A lived to tell about it. And their children are there to tell about it now. Now with the advent of chemical warfare, they who are the perpetrators of genocide are the victims, just as the victims are, 'cause you cannot spray without you yourself being contaminated. So that's what I call humanocide because as South Africa is spraying in Namibia, and Egypt is spraying the Blue Nile for its hibiscus problem, the whole culture goes into the pits for a hibiscus. I mean by underdeveloped nations trying to increase their agriculture yield to feed their local populations, all of these genetic pools are becoming contaminated. So it's not just one group, it's humanity. That's why I call it humanocide.

No, I haven't done any more research because they haven't acted,   45 the sons-of-bitches, on the research I *have* done. I do not question authority, I support justice. We don't need any more wars, 'cause the fact is, we don't need any more veterans if we're not going to treat them right. You know, they crawl through the rice, they jump out the planes, they eat the K-rations, while somebody in Ashtabula, Ohio, is putting in their roses and their tomato plants or is sleeping at night while somebody is staying awake on a perimeter somewhere, trying to watch for the enemy. And that's the very person who says we can't afford to be paying for this. What you're saying is, you can't afford wars. Don't say you can't afford to pay the vet, say you can't afford to have wars and just leave it at that. 'Cause a veteran is as much an element of war as the cost of the bullets, the gas, the planes, the uniforms. But it's not viewed as that.

I would say I am a typical principled dissenter. The other dissenters I meet are just like sisters and brothers. They are sincere people, they don't have this phonyism of saying what you think a person wants to hear—it's just up and out. And when we get together it's no ego thing. We're not trying to out shout the other or anything like that. It's just like a warmth because it's just like, "Hey, I'm with the ugly ducklings."

Yeah, it was sort of like the Independent Dorm at Ripon. We had our own dorm, and I was the president of that group. These were like the leftovers, this is like the sludge and the dregs. You know, either the ones that kinda had the malfeasance of mind not to even bother with the bullshit or those who did not have affiliations elsewhere. That was a hell of an experience to have at an early age and I'm glad I had it.

My father, not to sound poetic, but my father, his word meant something to him. When you gave your word that meant something. That's the kind of way he lived. He had these little, I call 'em quotable quotes. He used to say, "Peace if possible, justice above all." He sort of lived it. He would just make these comments, you know. First of all, my father only had an eighth-grade education and then it wasn't an eighth-grade education as we would know it today because he lived in Mississippi where they would go to school in conjunction with the harvesting and planting. He lived in a place called Benton County and it's right outside Holly Springs, Mississippi. Our family's sort of entrenched in the soil in that area. My father went to Lovejoy, I guess, because he wanted to get out of that agriculture kind of thing. He didn't go off to war or anything like that because he worked in the stockyards in East St. Louis and he had the common sense to spill a cauldron of hot water on his foot, so therefore he was 4-F in World War II, but he did run one of the local groceries. He had these little quotes I'm thankful for now because the quotes come back, maybe not the situations, but certainly the quotes, because they were so repetitious. "Never forget the bridge that brings you across." I'll never forget that. One day he was sweeping the floor. My daddy had like three grocery stores at one time and he'd employ little cousins and nephews and 'course I had perpetual employment and I said, "Daddy, why are you sweeping the floor? You know you're the owner. We'll sweep the floors." He said, "You my little woman?" And I said, "Daddy, you the big man here." And my daddy said, "No, I purposely sweep the floor, Maude, so I will never forget the bridge that brought me across. I'll never get up too high where I'll forget to remember from whence I came." And that stuck with me. There was another thing. "There's only one right and the rest is wrong. And you just have to either deal with the right or various gradations of wrong." That's what he used to say.

As I look back, I probably wouldn't have been a principled dissenter if I had not had my particular religious conviction or persuasion. Why do I say that? And this is my third religion, Okay? I was born gut bucket Baptist, you know, the BTU and all that. I switched to Catholicism for a sophisticated, intellectual, cold, distant religion with the pageantry. Then I came into Buddhism when my ass was in a corner and I was suffering from cancer. One thing, I wouldn't have had a sense of mission. I wouldn't have had a sense of trying to work for world peace. I don't mean by working for world peace that "I-done-beat-the-shit-out-of-you-and-you-too-weak-to-deal-with-me." I don't mean that kind of peace. I mean a sense that when I'm happy, then I can work toward making my family happy. When I can work toward making my family happy, I can work toward making my community happy. There's a saying in volume ten of *The Human Revolution*, which is a book on Buddhism, that says, "One man by changing his destiny can change the destiny of the nation." I love Nichiren! I love Nichiren. He was a principled dissenter because he remonstrated with the Kamakura government and he strayed three times with the government, and when they don't take your advice, you leave the country, and he left and he stood tall.

I don't have a good method of seeing bullshit and not dealing with it. It's like the older I get the straighter my back grows. And I cannot bend. I cannot bend down low enough to kiss ass. I just try to do what's right. And right is very hard to do because I look up and I see somebody there that I have trained that is now my supervisor and of course that hurts. It can't help but hurt. I get tired, I get frustrated.

I could have ignored Agent Orange. I could have ignored the radiation and not made any waves. I might have survived the radiation from the computer and been making thirty, thirty-five thousand dollars now. Going to the Ebony Fashion Show, helping the United Negro College bit, know what I mean? They're worthy things to do, but the price I've got to pay to be able to do them!

I think the challenge is to *live* creatively for the issue rather than die for the issue. But it's still a death. There's nobody riding up with the Lady Pepperell sheets on 'em and yanking me out and trying to hang me from the nearest tree physically, but I died a thousand times since seventy-seven when I first started with Agent Orange. I'm just as far away from the end tonight as I was the day before Miz Owens called the VA. I don't know if the bill was signed if it would mean anything. It depends on what it contains, who sponsors it, and the temper of the country. I know I might not live to see it.

Well, I go on because, number one, the wheels of the gods grind so slow but they grind so fine. I'm not the only one in this world that can read. I'm not the only one that hasn't been dehumanized as much as some others. I'm not the only one that becomes enraged and seeks to contribute toward improving a situation. There will be somebody to pick it up. I've asked my son to pick it up, so there'll always be a DeVictor associated with it and to train his kids to deal with it. I've asked him that for when I'm gone across to the big VA in the sky. But even if he doesn't, I would hope that somebody would. I would hope that people will remember the issue. Since we have Agent Orange today, it'll be agent somethin' else in three years.

❖ Focused Freewriting   Consider as possible focal points the discrimination DeVictor suffered in her early life, the empathy she feels for her clients, her isolation at work, or one of the topics you've identified in your journal.

❖ Guided Responses

1. Early in her monologue, DeVictor says, "I've always dealt with what the veteran says because he was there and he's seen the reality. . . . Reports are doctored in the wash" (para. 7). Think about this statement in light of Gwaltney's choice to let DeVictor tell her own story, digressions and all. Why do you think he chose not to write anything beyond the initial sketch, or not to edit out material not directly relevant to the Agent Orange story? How would the effect of the piece be different had he decided differently in either case?

2. What is the significance of DeVictor's references to her own illnesses (paras. 17, 21–23)? How do they help to explain her empathy for the Agent Orange victims? What do they reveal about the Veterans' Administration?

3. In paragraph 28, discussing Rosa Parks's refusal to give up her seat on the bus (the action that sparked the Montgomery bus boycott and the national career of Dr. Martin Luther King, Jr.) DeVictor explains: "She was tired." About her own activism she says in the same paragraph, "it's never planned." What do these comments tell you about DeVictor's self-image as a hero? How does she perceive her role in the Agent Orange story? Do you agree with her self-assessment? Why, or why not?

4. DeVictor dismisses government claims that compensating veterans exposed to Agent Orange is too expensive, saying, "Don't say you can't afford to pay the vet, say you can't afford to have wars and just leave it at that" (para. 45). What is the logic of this statement? Do you agree with her that "a veteran is as much an element of war as the cost of the bullets, the gas, the planes, the uniforms"? Explain your response.

❖ Shared Responses   In your journal respond to DeVictor's father's admonition, "Never forget the bridge that brings you across" (para. 48). What do those lines mean to his daughter? What do they mean to you? As you discuss your responses in small groups, highlight the different ways in which group members interpret the quotation.

Napa, California

ANA CASTILLO

ANA CASTILLO, *a graduate of Northeastern Illinois University, is a reviewer and editor for* Third Woman Magazine *and teaches ethnic studies at Santa Rosa Junior College. Among her numerous publications are* Otro Canto *(1977) and* The Invitation *(1979), both collections of poetry, and the novels* The Mixquiahuala Letters *and* Sapognia *(1989). Castillo's poem, from her 1984 collection* Women Are Not Roses, *provides images of the lives of migrant grape pickers, juxtaposing the body-breaking, mind-numbing work with the pride and hope offered by their leader.*

Before reading the selection, explore in your journal your feelings about a life of hard labor. If you've worked at a physically demanding but monotonous, draining job, write about how it felt. If not, try to imagine what such a life would be like.

As you make notes on your reading, you may want to focus on the metaphors Castillo uses.

Dedicado al Sr. Chávez, sept. '75

> We pick
>   the bittersweet grapes
>   at harvest
>   one
>   by   5
>   one
> with leather worn hands
>   as they pick
>   at our dignity
>   and wipe our pride   10
>   away
>   like the sweat we wipe
>   from our sun-beaten brows
>   at midday

In fields   15
  so vast
  that our youth seems
  to pass before us
  and we have grown
  very   20
    very
      old
        by dusk . . .
        (*bueno pues, ¿qué vamos a hacer, Ambrosio?*
        ¡bueno pues, seguirle, comparde, seguirle!   25
        ¡Ay, Mama!
        Sí pues, ¿qué vamos a hacer, compadre?
        ¡Seguirle, Ambrosio, seguirle!)[1]
We pick
  with a desire   30
  that only survival
  inspires
While the end
  of each day only brings
  a tired night   35
  that waits for the sun
  and the land
  that in turn waits
  for us . . .

❖ Focused Freewriting   Consider as possible focal points the hopelessness of migrant work, the relationship between the workers and the land, or one of the topics you've identified in your journal.

❖ Guided Responses

1. In the second line of the poem, Castillo calls the grapes "bitter-sweet." In what ways, both literal and metaphorical, is this adjective appropriate?

2. How does this work "pick / at [the workers'] dignity / and wipe [their] pride / away . . . " (lines 8–11)? Why can't the workers take pride in what they do? Why is this work not dignified?

---

[1] Well then, what are we going to do, Ambrosio?
Well then, follow him, my good friend, follow him!
Mama!
Yes, well, what are we going to do, friend?
Follow him, Ambrosio, follow him!

3. Castillo sets off the dialogue in the poem by using parentheses, italics, and Spanish language. What is the effect, both visual and verbal, of this passage? How do all three techniques contribute to the meaning of the passage?

4. The poem ends with the land lying in wait for the workers, who "pick / with a desire / that only survival / inspires." How do you interpret this ending? Is it optimistic? pessimistic? a little of both? Explain your response in the context of the entire poem.

❖ Shared Responses   In your journal write what you know about either César Chávez or labor leaders in general. What kind of image do these leaders have with their followers? How does the rest of the public perceive them? What is your understanding of the contributions organized labor has made to American workers? As you discuss your responses in small groups, ask those who seem better informed to elaborate on their responses.

A Free Press Flourishes
Behind Bars

DAVID ARNOLD

DAVID ARNOLD *is a writer for* Time *magazine. His work often features traditional subjects served up with an unusual twist, as exemplified in this article, originally published in* Time. *Arnold describes here the work of a convicted murderer who has turned his life around while serving a life sentence. Robert E. Taliaferro spends much of his time in prison editing the* Mirror, *"the oldest continuously published newspaper in a U.S. prison."*

Before reading the selection, write in your journal your impressions of prison life. Is it possible to lead a productive life behind bars? How do you think inmates cope with the notion of spending the rest of their lives incarcerated? How useful is it to society to allow prisoners the right to perform meaningful work?

As you make notes on your reading, you may want to focus on what constitutes news in prison, how Arnold characterizes Taliaferro, or the nature of the editor's job.

SEVERE PENALTIES SOMETIMES THREATEN the editor of the *Mirror,* a tabloid published every other week behind the rock walls and accordion-wire fences of the maximum-security Minnesota Correctional Facility at Stillwater. The punishment is likely to come not from the warden or the guards but from any of the approximately 1,200 convicted car thieves, drug dealers, armed robbers, kidnapers, rapists, child abusers and murderers who may take issue with his editorial responsibility. "My editor wrote a story about how inmates were smuggling reefer in here in balloons," Taliaferro recalls. "I told him, 'You don't sit up here and put that stuff in the newspaper. You wanna get yourself killed?' "

A short time after that article circulated through the cellblocks, an irate inmate struck the editor across the head with a chair. The complaint triggered the editor's early retirement, leaving Taliaferro in charge of two secondhand IBM computers and a small staff working in an office the size of a large bathroom. But the prestige of the job is considerable.

The *Mirror* is the oldest continuously published newspaper in a U.S. prison, founded in 1887 by the likes of the notorious bank-robbing Younger brothers, who each served more that 20 years here after a badly planned bank job in Northfield, Minn. Coleman, the eldest, became prison librarian and printer's devil at the newspaper. In his second year Cole was named *Mirror* editor, and the paper's motto became—and remains—"It's never too late to mend."

Among the dark, walled fortresses of U.S. penology, Stillwater is considered a well-secured country club with a relatively mellow population. It is a kind of felon's Lake Wobegon where gangs do not rule and sex offenders outnumber those who have killed; a prison where only the guards wear uniforms and only four of them carry firearms. Other U.S. prisons are overcrowded, but each Stillwater resident has a cell of his own, a TV if he chooses to buy one, and ready access to a dozen phones mounted on the wall beneath the towering, barred windows of the cellblock walls. D cellblock, where Taliaferro and a few dozen other convicts cram at night for final exams in bachelor's and master's degree programs, is appointed with carpets, computers and hanging plants. The rest of Stillwater can earn up to $5 an hour making manure spreaders and birdhouses, or fixing school buses and highway patrol cars.

The *Mirror*'s pages read like a chapter from Tom Peters' *In Search*   5 *of Excellence*. In this place of punishment, achievement is possible and highly promoted. The newsmakers in a fall edition of the *Mirror* were Karta Singh and the other bonsai-club members, who practically blew away the civilian competition at the Minnesota State Fair. "I'm ecstatic about it," Singh told the *Mirror*. "Winning a blue ribbon motivates me even more, and I think it's a statement to the quality of instruction we're getting."

The newspaper sells no ads, and annual subscriptions are cheap: Free to residents, $10 outside the walls. The state pays for it, and the warden is publisher. But Taliaferro's best readers are the men inside, the line officers and inmates. "You've got to walk the line; you'd not believe how thin it is," Taliaferro says.

Keeping an editorial balance among publicity seekers, black culturalists, bonsai growers and softball teams complaining of favoritism is physically demanding. Taliaferro measures up to the job. "I'm 6 ft. 7 in. tall and weigh 200 lbs.," Taliaferro says. "I came out of other systems where you had to be tough." Readers and staff writers who disagree with the editor are sometimes invited to the prison gym to put on boxing gloves. "I'm not afraid to fight for my opinion, be it ever so humble," the editor says. "And I'm not afraid to be locked in the hole. I've been there."

Power in prison falls to those who gather it, and Taliaferro prefers to hire men who, like himself, were convicted of capital offenses and therefore face long prison terms. "Short-timers have an ax to grind. They never learn anything in here. They blame everyone else, and they just can't wait to get out and screw up again. Then they come back. I committed murder. Homicide. I put myself in here. I take that responsibility, and I will deal with that."

Taliaferro illustrates the theory that serious crime makes a good prisoner. A former drug addict who killed his wife, he has become a productive citizen of the Stillwater prison. He has almost completed his bachelor's requirements, and hopes to become a college professor someday.

Hovering over his keyboard, Taliaferro cradles the telephone re- 10 ceiver just above the monogrammed *RT* on his black jersey. Like the capable editor of a small-town newspaper, Taliaferro has the reader by the pulse. He is a leader of his captive constituency; vice president of the Jaycees' Star of the North prison chapter, a leader of a black-culture group and a big editorial voice inside these walls. "I'm a black redneck," he says with a casual smile. If he were free, he'd have voted for George Bush for President even though he thought his candidate didn't understand prison furloughs.

Taliaferro wanted to capitalize on his prison term and invested his time in the *Mirror*, where he's made big changes. He dropped "Prison"" from the masthead, gave the front page a *USA Today* look, and brought into the cellblocks a broader view of things, quoting frequently from such outside papers as the nearby St. Paul *Pioneer Press & Dispatch*.

The biggest change was an end to all the bad news. The *Mirror*'s readers will not read about gang rape, booze brewed in a toilet or how a man in C cellblock took a dive from the gym rafters and landed on a broom. Not even an obit for a lifer who died of natural causes. It's bad enough just being in here," Taliaferro says.

The *Mirror* casts a lighter, more positive reflection. Booster journalism promotes progressive activities. It includes poetry and several pages of basketball, handball and softball scores. Consumer stories criticize new prison regulations, meat fraud in the cafeteria, movies on the closed-circuit channel and such outside issues as exploitation of lab animals and the Federal Government's handling of the AIDS crisis.

The newspaper's changes have attracted attention. Three first-place American Penal Press awards received in the past four years and a row of plaques stretch around a newsroom occasionally cluttered with visiting journalists who've come to examine the prison news-room.

His publisher has noticed the company the *Mirror* has been keep-   15
ing. All the awards and publicity have helped give the *Mirror* a life of
its own, says warden Robert Erickson. The newspaper has a fourth-es-
tate status he would not like to challenge. And, after all, how could
Erickson mess with history? "Cole Younger would turn over in his
grave, with his six-shooter blazing," the warden says.

❖ Focused Freewriting   Consider as possible focal points the contribution made by prison newspapers, the question of prisoners'
rights to a free press, or one of the topics you've identified in your
journal.

❖ Guided Responses

1. What is the significance of Arnold's description of the *Mirror*'s
founding? What difference does it make that the paper has notorious
origins? How does the description affect the reader's perceptions of
Taliaferro?

2. Does it matter that "Stillwater is considered a well-secured
country club with a relatively mellow population" (para. 4)? Why, or
why not? How does this information alter your perception about
Taliaferro's accomplishments?

3. Taliaferro believes that prisoners facing long sentences make
the best workers, arguing, "Short-timers have an ax to grind. They
never learn anything in here. They blame everyone else . . ." (para. 8).
Do you find his argument convincing? How does his dedication to the
newspaper reflect his views?

4. Stating that "It's bad enough just being in here," Taliaferro
prohibits publication of any bad news, even obituaries (para. 12).
What other reasons might he have for focusing only on good news?
Do you think his decision is a sound one? Why, or why not?

❖ Shared Responses   In your journal explore the implications of
prison journalism. What advantages does an in-house newspaper
have for prisoners? for society? What are its disadvantages for both
groups? Should public money support such ventures? Explain your
responses. As you discuss your responses in small groups, highlight
the different reasons for individual responses.

On Dumpster Diving

LARS EIGHNER

LARS EIGHNER *attended the University of Texas at Austin, and worked in government service before becoming homeless in the late 1980s. His memoir,* Travels with Lizbeth, *was published by St. Martin's Press in 1993. Eighner's essay, which first appeared in* The Threepenny Review, *is a surprisingly dispassionate look at scavenging for a living. Covering such subjects as preferred locations, culinary analysis, etiquette, and territorial rights, Eighner offers a glimpse of a way of life wholly foreign to most people, for whom dumpsters are merely waste receptacles.*

Before reading the selection, list the things you throw out in the course of a week. Include food, household trash, worn-out items, packaging, and anything else that comes to mind. How might any of these items be useful to someone else?

As you make notes on your reading, you may want to focus on the various distinctions Eighner makes: between types of items found in dumpsters, between types of people who discard things, between types of dumpster divers, and the like.

LONG BEFORE I began Dumpster diving I was impressed with Dumpsters, enough so that I wrote the Merriam-Webster research service to discover what I could about the word "Dumpster." I learned from them that "Dumpster" is a proprietary word belonging to the Dempster Dumpster company.

Since then I have dutifully capitalized the word although it was lowercased in almost all of the citations Merriam-Webster photocopied for me. Dempster's word is too apt. I have never heard these things called anything but Dumpsters. I do not know anyone who knows the generic name for these objects. From time to time, however, I hear a wino or hobo give some corrupted credit to the original and call them Dipsy Dumpsters.

I began Dumpster diving about a year before I became homeless.

I prefer the term "scavenging" and use the word "scrounging" when I mean to be obscure. I have heard people, evidently meaning to be polite, use the word "foraging," but I prefer to reserve that word for gathering nuts and berries and such which I do also according to the season and the opportunity. "Dumpster diving" seems to me to be a little too cute and, in my case, inaccurate because I lack the athletic ability to lower myself into the Dumpsters as the true divers do, much to their increased profit.

I like the frankness of the word "scavenging," which I can hardly   5
think of without picturing a big black snail on an aquarium wall. I live from the refuse of others. I am a scavenger. I think it a sound and honorable niche, although if I could I would naturally prefer to live the comfortable consumer life, perhaps—and only perhaps—as a slightly less wasteful consumer owing to what I have learned as a scavenger.

While my dog Lizbeth and I were still living in the house on Avenue B in Austin, as my savings ran out, I put almost all my sporadic income into rent. The necessities of daily life I began to extract from Dumpsters. Yes, we ate from Dumpsters. Except for jeans, all my clothes came from Dumpsters. Boom boxes, candles, bedding, toilet paper, medicine, books, a typewriter, a virgin male love doll, change sometimes amounting to many dollars: I acquired many things from the Dumpsters.

I have learned much as a scavenger. I mean to put some of what I have learned down here, beginning with the practical art of Dumpster diving and proceeding to the abstract.

What is safe to eat?

After all, the finding of objects is becoming something of an urban art. Even respectable employed people will sometimes find something tempting sticking out of a Dumpster or standing beside one. Quite a number of people, not all of them of the bohemian type, are willing to brag that they found this or that piece in the trash. But eating from Dumpsters is the thing that separates the dilettanti from the professionals.

Eating safely from the Dumpsters involves three principles: using   10
the senses and common sense to evaluate the condition of the found materials, knowing the Dumpsters of a given area and checking them regularly, and seeking always to answer the question "Why was this discarded?"

Perhaps everyone who has a kitchen and a regular supply of groceries has, at one time or another, made a sandwich and eaten half of it before discovering mold on the bread or got a mouthful of milk before realizing the milk had turned. Nothing of the sort is likely to happen to a Dumpster diver because he is constantly reminded that most food is discarded for a reason. Yet a lot of perfectly good food can be found in Dumpsters.

Canned goods, for example, turn up fairly often in the Dumpsters I frequent. All except the most phobic people would be willing to eat from a can even if it came from a Dumpster. Canned goods are among the safest of foods to be found in Dumpsters, but are not utterly foolproof.

Although very rare with modern canning methods, botulism is a possibility. Most other forms of food poisoning seldom do lasting harm to a healthy person. But botulism is almost certainly fatal and often the first symptom is death. Except for carbonated beverages, all canned goods should contain a slight vacuum and suck air when first punctured. Bulging, rusty, dented cans and cans that spew when punctured should be avoided, especially when the contents are not very acidic or syrupy.

Heat can break down the botulin, but this requires much more cooking than most people do to canned goods. To the extent that botulism occurs at all, of course, it can occur in cans on pantry shelves as well as in cans from Dumpsters. Need I say that home-canned goods found in Dumpsters are simply too risky to be recommended.

From time to time one of my companions, aware of the source of   15
my provisions, will ask, "Do you think these crackers are really safe to eat?" For some reason it is most often the crackers they ask about.

This question always makes me angry. Of course I would not offer my companion anything I had doubts about. But more than that I wonder why he cannot evaluate the condition of the crackers for himself. I have no special knowledge and I have been wrong before. Since he knows where the food comes from, it seems to me he ought to assume some of the responsibility for deciding what he will put in his mouth.

For myself I have few qualms about dry foods such as crackers, cookies, cereal, chips, and pasta if they are free of visible contaminates and still dry and crisp. Most often such things are found in the original packaging, which is not so much a positive sign as it is the absence of a negative one.

Raw fruits and vegetables with intact skins seem perfectly safe to me, excluding of course the obviously rotten. Many are discarded for minor imperfections which can be pared away. Leafy vegetables, grapes, cauliflower, broccoli, and similar things may be contaminated by liquids and may be impractical to wash.

Candy, especially hard candy, is usually safe if it has not drawn ants. Chocolate is often discarded only because it has become discolored as the cocoa butter de-emulsified. Candying after all is one method of food preservation because pathogens do not like very sugary substances.

All of these foods might be found in any Dumpster and can be   20 evaluated with some confidence largely on the basis of appearance. Beyond these are foods which cannot be correctly evaluated without additional information.

I began scavenging by pulling pizzas out of the Dumpster behind a pizza delivery shop. In general prepared food requires caution, but in this case I knew when the shop closed and went to the Dumpster as soon as the last of the help left.

Such shops often get prank orders, called "bogus." Because help seldom stays long at these places pizzas are often made with the wrong topping, refused on delivery for being cold, or baked incorrectly. The products to be discarded are boxed up because inventory is kept by counting boxes; a boxed pizza can be written off; an unboxed pizza does not exist.

I never placed a bogus order to increase the supply of pizzas and I believe no one else was scavenging in this Dumpster. But the people in the shop became suspicious and began to retain their garbage in the shop overnight.

While it lasted I had a steady supply of fresh, sometimes warm pizza. Because I knew the Dumpster I knew the source of the pizza, and because I visited the Dumpster regularly I knew what was fresh and what was yesterday's.

The area I frequent is inhabited by many affluent college stu-   25 dents. I am not here by chance; the Dumpsters in this area are very rich. Students throw out many good things, including food. In particular they tend to throw everything out when they move at the end of a semester, before and after breaks, and around midterm when many of them despair of college. So I find it advantageous to keep an eye on the academic calendar.

The students throw food away around the breaks because they do not know whether it has spoiled or will spoil before they return. A typical discard is a half jar of peanut butter. In fact non-organic peanut butter does not require refrigeration and is unlikely to spoil in any reasonable time. The student does not know that, and since it is Daddy's money, the student decides not to take a chance.

Opened containers require caution and some attention to the question "Why was this discarded?" But in the case of discards from student apartments, the answer may be that the item was discarded through carelessness, ignorance, or wastefulness. This can sometimes be deduced when the item is found with many others, including some that are obviously perfectly good.

Some students, and others, approach defrosting a freezer by chucking out the whole lot. Not only do the circumstances of such a find tell the story, but also the mass of frozen goods stays cold for a long time and items may be found still frozen or freshly thawed.

Yogurt, cheese, and sour cream are items that are often thrown out while they are still good. Occasionally I find a cheese with a spot of mold, which of course I just pare off, and because it is obvious why such a cheese was discarded, I treat it with less suspicion than an apparently perfect cheese found in similar circumstances. Yogurt is often discarded, still sealed, only because the expiration date on the carton had passed. This is one of my favorite finds because yogurt will keep for several days, even in warm weather.

Students throw out canned goods and staples at the end of semes- 30
ters and when they give up college at midterm. Drugs, pornography, spirits, and the like are often discarded when parents are expected— Dad's day, for example. And spirits also turn up after big party week-ends, presumably discarded by the newly reformed. Wine and spirits, of course, keep perfectly well even once opened.

My test for carbonated soft drinks is whether they still fizz vigor-ously. Many juices or other beverages are too acid or too syrupy to cause much concern provided they are not visibly contaminated. Liq-uids, however, require some care.

One hot day I found a large jug of Pat O'Brien Hurricane mix. The jug had been opened, but it was still ice cold. I drank three large glasses before it became apparent to me that someone had added the rum to the mix, and not a little rum. I never tasted the rum and by the time I began to feel the effects I had already ingested a very large quantity of the beverage. Some divers would have con-sidered this is a boon, but being suddenly and thoroughly intoxi-cated in a public place in the early afternoon is not my idea of a good time.

I have heard of people maliciously contaminating discarded food and even handouts, but mostly I have heard of this from people with vivid imaginations who have had no experience with the Dumpsters themselves. Just before the pizza shop stopped discarding its garbage at night, jalapeños began showing up on most of the discarded pizzas. If indeed this was meant to discourage me it was a wasted effort because I am native Texan.

For myself, I avoid game, poultry, pork, and egg-based foods whether I find them raw or cooked. I seldom have the means to cook what I find, but when I do I avail myself of plentiful supplies of beef which is often in very good condition. I suppose fish becomes dis-agreeable before it becomes dangerous. The dog is happy to have any such thing that is past its prime and, in fact, does not recognize fish as food until it is quite strong.

Home leftovers, as opposed to surpluses from restaurants, are 35
very often bad. Evidently, especially among students, there is a com-

mon type of personality that carefully wraps up even the smallest
leftover and shoves it into the back of the refrigerator for six months
or so before discarding it. Characteristic of this type are the reused jars
and margarine tubs which house the remains.

I avoid ethnic foods I am unfamiliar with. If I do not know what
it is supposed to look like when it is good, I cannot be certain I will be
able to tell if it is bad.

No matter how careful I am I still get dysentery at least once a
month, oftener in warm weather. I do not want to paint too romantic a picture. Dumpster diving has serious drawbacks as a way of
life.

I learned to scavenge gradually, on my own. Since then I have initiated several companions into the trade. I have learned that there is a
predictable series of stages a person goes through in learning to scavenge.

At first the new scavenger is filled with disgust and self-loathing.
He is ashamed of being seen and may lurk around, trying to duck
behind things, or he may try to dive at night.

(In fact, most people instinctively look away from a scavenger. By   40
skulking around, the novice calls attention to himself and arouses
suspicion. Diving at night is ineffective and needlessly messy.)

Every grain of rice seems to be a maggot. Everything seems to
stink. He can wipe the egg yolk off the found can, but he cannot erase
the stigma of eating garbage out of his mind.

That stage passes with experience. The scavenger finds a pair of
running shoes that fit and look and smell brand new. He finds a
pocket calculator in perfect working order. He finds pristine ice
cream, still frozen, more than he can eat or keep. He begins to understand: people do throw away perfectly good stuff, a lot of perfectly
good stuff.

At this stage, Dumpster shyness begins to dissipate. The diver,
after all, has the last laugh. He is finding all manner of good things
which are his for the taking. Those who disparage his profession are
the fools, not he.

He may begin to hang onto some perfectly good things for which
he has neither a use nor a market. Then he begins to take note of the
things which are not perfectly good but are nearly so. He mates a
Walkman with broken earphones and one that is missing a battery
cover. He picks up things which he can repair.

At this stage he may become lost and never recover. Dumpsters   45
are full of things of some potential value to someone and also of
things which never have much intrinsic value but are interesting. All
the Dumpster divers I have known come to the point of trying to

acquire everything they touch. Why not take it, they reason, since it is all free.

This is, of course, hopeless. Most divers come to realize that they must restrict themselves to items of relatively immediate utility. But in some cases the diver simply cannot control himself. I have met several of these pack-rat types. Their ideas of the values of various pieces of junk verge on the psychotic. Every bit of glass may be a diamond, they think, and all that glitters, gold.

I tend to gain weight when I am scavenging. Partly this is because I always find far more pizza and doughnuts than water-packed tuna, nonfat yogurt, and fresh vegetables. Also I have not developed much faith in the reliability of Dumpsters as a food source, although it has been proven to me many times. I tend to eat as if I have no idea where my next meal is coming from. But mostly I just hate to see food go to waste and so I eat much more than I should. Something like this drives the obsession to collect junk.

As for collecting objects, I usually restrict myself to collecting one kind of small object at a time, such as pocket calculators, sunglasses, or campaign buttons. To live on the street I must anticipate my needs to a certain extent: I must pick up and save warm bedding I find in August because it will not be found in Dumpsters in November. But even if I had a home with extensive storage space I could not save everything that might be valuable in some contingency.

I have proprietary feelings about my Dumpsters. As I have suggested, it is no accident that I scavenge from Dumpsters where good finds are common. But my limited experience with Dumpsters in other areas suggests to me that it is the population of competitors rather than the affluence of the dumpers that most affects the feasibility of survival by scavenging. The large number of competitors is what puts me off the idea of trying to scavenge in places like Los Angeles.

Curiously, I do not mind my direct competition, other scavengers, 50 so much as I hate the can scroungers.

People scrounge cans because they have to have a little cash. I have tried scrounging cans with an able-bodied companion. Afoot a can scrounger simply cannot make more than a few dollars a day. One can extract the necessities of life from the Dumpsters directly with far less effort than would be required to accumulate the equivalent value in cans.

Can scroungers, then, are people who *must* have small amounts of cash. These are drug addicts and winos, mostly the latter because the amounts of cash are so small.

Spirits and drugs do, like all other commodities, turn up in Dumpsters and the scavenger will from time to time have a half bottle of a rather good wine with his dinner. But the wino cannot survive on these occasional finds; he must have his daily dose to stave off the DTs. All the cans he can carry will buy about three bottles of Wild Irish Rose.

I do not begrudge them the cans, but can scroungers tend to tear up the Dumpsters, mixing the contents and littering the area. They become so specialized that they can see only cans. They earn my contempt by passing up change, canned goods, and readily hockable items.

There are precious few courtesies among scavengers. But it is a   55 common practice to set aside surplus items: pairs of shoes, clothing, canned goods, and such. A true scavenger hates to see good stuff go to waste and what he cannot use he leaves in good condition in plain sight.

Can scroungers lay waste to everything in their path and will stir one of a pair of good shoes to the bottom of a Dumpster, to be lost or ruined in the muck. Can scroungers will even go through individual garbage cans, something I have never seen a scavenger do.

Individual garbage cans are set out on the public easement only on garbage days. On other days going through them requires trespassing close to a dwelling. Going through individual garbage cans without scattering litter is almost impossible. Litter is likely to reduce the public's tolerance of scavenging. Individual garbage cans are simply not as productive as Dumpsters; people in houses and duplexes do not move as often and for some reason do not tend to discard as much useful material. Moreover, the time required to go through one garbage can that serves one household is not much less than the time required to go through a Dumpster that contains the refuse of twenty apartments.

But my strongest reservation about going through individual garbage cans is that this seems to me a very personal kind of invasion to which I would object if I were a householder. Although many things in Dumpsters are obviously meant never to come to light, a Dumpster is somehow less personal.

I avoid trying to draw conclusions about the people who dump in the Dumpsters I frequent. I think it would be unethical to do so, although I know many people will find the idea of scavenger ethics too funny for words.

Dumpsters contain bank statements, bills, correspondence, and   60 other documents, just as anyone might expect. But there are also less obvious sources of information. Pill bottles, for example. The labels on pill bottles contain the name of the patient, the name of the doctor, and the name of the drug. AIDS drugs and anti-psychotic medicines, to name but two groups, are specific and are seldom prescribed for any other disorders. The plastic compacts for birth control pills usually have complete label information.

Despite all of this sensitive information, I have had only one apartment resident object to my going through the Dumpster. In that case it turned out the resident was a University athlete who was taking bets and who was afraid I would turn up his wager slips.

Occasionally a find tells a story. I once found a small paper bag containing some unused condoms, several partial tubes of flavored sexual lubricant, a partially used compact of birth control pills, and the torn pieces of a picture of a young man. Clearly she was through with him and planning to give up sex altogether.

Dumpster things are often sad—abandoned teddy bears, shredded wedding books, despaired-of sales kits. I find many pets lying in state in Dumpsters. Although I hope to get off the streets so that Lizbeth can have a long and comfortable old age, I know this hope is not very realistic. So I suppose when her time comes she too will go into a Dumpster. I will have no better place for her. And after all, for most of her life her livelihood has come from the Dumpster. When she finds something I think is safe that has been spilled from the Dumpster I let her have it. She already knows the route around the best Dumpsters. I like to think that if she survives me she will have a chance of evading the dog catcher and of finding her sustenance on the route.

Silly vanities also come to rest in the Dumpsters. I am a rather accomplished needleworker. I get a lot of materials from the Dumpsters. Evidently sorority girls, hoping to impress someone, perhaps themselves, with their mastery of a womanly art, buy a lot of embroider-by-number kits, work a few stitches horribly, and eventually discard the whole mess. I pull out their stitches, turn the canvas over, and work an original design. Do not think I refrain from chuckling as I make original gifts from these kits.

I find diaries and journals. I have often thought of compiling a 65 book of literary found objects. And perhaps I will one day. But what I find is hopelessly commonplace and bad without being, even unconsciously, camp. College students also discard their papers. I am horrified to discover the kind of paper which now merits an A in an undergraduate course. I am grateful, however, for the number of good books and magazines the students throw out.

In the area I know best I have never discovered vermin in the Dumpsters, but there are two kinds of kitty surprise. One is alley cats which I meet as they leap, claws first, out of Dumpsters. This is especially thrilling when I have Lizbeth in tow. The other kind of kitty surprise is a plastic garbage bag filled with some ponderous, amorphous mass. This always proves to be used cat litter.

City bees harvest doughnut glaze and this makes the Dumpster at the doughnut shop more interesting. My faith in the instinctive wisdom of animals is always shaken whenever I see Lizbeth attempt to catch a bee in her mouth, which she does whenever bees are present. Evidently some birds find Dumpsters profitable, for birdie surprise is almost as common as kitty surprise of the first kind. In hunting season all kinds of small game turn up in Dumpsters, some of it, sadly, not entirely dead. Curiously, summer and winter, maggots are uncommon.

The worst of the living and near-living hazards of the Dumpsters are the fire ants. The food that they claim is not much of a loss, but they are vicious and aggressive. It is very easy to brush against some surface of the Dumpster and pick up half a dozen or more fire ants, usually in some sensitive area such as the underarm. One advantage of bringing Lizbeth along as I make Dumpster rounds is that, for obvious reasons, she is very alert to ground-based fire ants. When Lizbeth recognizes the signs of fire ant infestation around our feet she does the Dance of the Zillion Fire Ants. I have learned not to ignore this warning from Lizbeth, whether I perceive the tiny ants or not, but to remove ourselves at Lizbeth's first pas de bourrée. All the more so because the ants are the worst in the months I wear flip-flops, if I have them.

(Perhaps someone will misunderstand the above. Lizbeth does the Dance of the Zillion Fire Ants when she recognizes more fire ants than she cares to eat, not when she is being bitten. Since I have learned to react promptly, she does not get bitten at all. It is the isolated patrol of fire ants that falls in Lizbeth's range that deserves pity. Lizbeth finds them quite tasty.)

By far the best way to go through a Dumpster is to lower yourself 70 into it. Most of the good stuff tends to settle at the bottom because it is usually weightier than the rubbish. My more athletic companions have often demonstrated to me that they can extract much good material from a Dumpster I have already been over.

To those psychologically or physically unprepared to enter a Dumpster, I recommend a stout stick, preferably with some barb or hook at one end. The hook can be used to grab plastic garbage bags. When I find canned goods or other objects loose at the bottom of a Dumpster I usually can roll them into a small bag that I can then hoist up. Much Dumpster diving is a matter of experience for which nothing will do except practice.

Dumpster diving is outdoor work, often surprisingly pleasant. It is not entirely predictable; things of interest turn up every day and some days there are finds of great value. I am always very pleased when I can turn up exactly the thing I most wanted to find. Yet in spite of the element of chance, scavenging more than most other pursuits tends to yield returns in some proportion to the effort and intelligence brought to bear. It is very sweet to turn up a few dollars in change from a Dumpster that has just been gone over by a wino.

The land is now covered with cities. The cities are full of Dumpsters. I think of scavenging as a modern form of self-reliance. In any event, after ten years of government service, where everything is geared to the lowest common denominator, I find work that rewards initiative and effort refreshing. Certainly I would be happy to have a sinecure again, but I am not heartbroken not to have one anymore.

I find from the experience of scavenging two rather deep lessons. The first is to take what I can use and let the rest go by. I have come to think that there is no value in the abstract. A thing I cannot use or make useful, perhaps by trading, has no value however fine or rare it may be. I mean useful in a broad sense—so, for example, some art I would think useful and valuable, but other art might be otherwise for me.

I was shocked to realize that some things are not worth acquiring, but now I think it is so. Some material things are white elephants that eat up the possessor's substance.   75

The second lesson is of the transience of material being. This has not quite converted me to a dualist, but it has made some headway in that direction. I do not suppose that ideas are immortal, but certainly mental things are longer-lived than other material things.

Once I was the sort of person who invests material objects with sentimental value. Now I no longer have those things, but I have the sentiments yet.

Many times in my travels I have lost everything but the clothes I was wearing and Lizbeth. The things I find in Dumpsters, the love letters and ragdolls of so many lives, remind me of this lesson. Now I hardly pick up a thing without envisioning the time I will cast it away. This I think is a healthy state of mind. Almost everything I have now has already been cast out at least once, proving that what I own is valueless to someone.

Anyway, I find my desire to grab for the gaudy bauble has been largely sated. I think this is an attitude I share with the very wealthy— we both know there is plenty more where what we have came from. Between us are the rat-race millions who have confounded their selves with the objects they grasp and who nightly scavenge the cable channels looking for they know not what.

I am sorry for them.   80

❖ Focused Freewriting   Consider as possible focal points the reasons behind Eighner's methodical analyses, his characterizations of people such as students and can scroungers, the pride he seems to take in his occupation, or one of the topics you've identified in your journal.

❖ Guided Responses

1. Calling himself a "scavenger," Eighner states, "I think it a sound and honorable niche" (para. 5). Given his account of the practice of scavenging, why do you think he feels this way? What support does Eighner offer elsewhere in the essay for his evaluation of scavenging?

2. Eighner offers a careful, detailed explanation of how pizzas are inventoried, why they're discarded, and how he determines their freshness (paras. 21–24). What is the effect of this detailed description? Based on this and similar descriptions elsewhere in the essay, why do you think Eighner presents his material in this way? What impression does he want to make on the reader?

3. In describing the early stages of learning to scavenge, Eighner strays from his objective tone and writes of the novice "filled with disgust and self-loathing," "ashamed of being seen," and incapable of erasing "the stigma of eating garbage out of his mind" (paras. 39, 41). Why do you think he abandons his air of objectivity here? How do these paragraphs influence your perception of scavengers? How do you react to the subsequent paragraphs describing how the novice becomes accustomed to dumpster diving?

4. Eighner concludes his essay with "two rather deep" lessons he has learned from scavenging, the first "to take what I can use and let the rest go by," the second "of the transience of material being" (paras. 74, 76). Explain what these lessons mean to you. How do they lead to his philosophical observation on the materialism of "the rat-race millions" (para. 79)? How does this ending differentiate Eighner's essay from other accounts of homelessness you've read?

❖ Shared Responses   In your journal respond to Eighner's lessons. How has his analysis of dumpster diving changed your view of what's expendable and what's worth saving? of the importance of material things? of the dignity of scavengers? As you discuss your responses in small groups, explain the reasons behind individual interpretations of Eighner's lessons.

❖ Generating Ideas   Reread all of your journals and annotations from the selections in this unit. Look for connections between selections or still unanswered questions. First, list those connections and questions as briefly as possible. Next, choose two or three to elaborate on. As you respond in more detail to the connections and questions, focus on one topic and consider how well it would serve you in an extended piece of writing. Then decide what kind of writing best suits your topic: Should you write a conventional essay, a poem, a short story, or a scene? Would your topic lend itself more to a letter to the editor or a personal letter? Might a proposal to solve a specific problem be a good choice? Possible topics:

1. the responsibilities of business to the larger community
2. workers' pride in their product
3. various definitions of the dignity of work
4. the relationship between employer and employee
5. the price of progress in business

❖ Focusing Responses   Choose one of your extended responses and formulate a statement of one or two sentences that captures its essence. Use this statement as a guide to organize your piece. (If you write an essay, letter, or proposal, the statement may actually appear as a thesis.)

❖ Guided Writing Assignments

1. Write an essay in which you compare and contrast Hamper's view of work with either Taliaferro's or Eighner's. Focus on such issues as the pride and satisfaction derived from the job, the significance of the job, the attitude of the employer and/or the outside world to the job, and anything else you consider relevant. What do you conclude about what makes work meaningful?

2. Imagine that you are Ben Cohen writing a review of Hamper's "At War with the Minute Hand." Use the review not only to pass judgment on the significance of the writer's accomplishments, but also to offer your own assessment of the operation of General Motors and your views on how the corporation might improve working conditions for its line operators. Make specific reference to both selections in composing your response.

3. Using material from Castillo and Roberts, write a letter to the editor of a major newspaper commenting on the failure of the American public to appreciate the work of groups such as American Indians

and Mexican Americans. Discuss the relative value placed on work done by these groups, the question of who benefits most from the work, the issue of job security and recognition, and any other issues you consider relevant. Suggest how these workers might be better served.

4. Reconstruct Maude DeVictor's story from the point of view of Erik Larson. As you compose your response, apply the journalist's critical assessment techniques to DeVictor's situation, decide which of her many anecdotes he would relate, and consider how he would open and close the story.

❖ Research Topics   As you consider how to expand your reading beyond the selections in this chapter, identify in your journal and notes questions that remain unanswered or topics you'd like to explore further. Or you may consider the following:

1. Research the role played by César Chávez and the United Farm Workers of America in organizing migrant workers. Investigate the relationship between growers and workers, the charisma of Chávez as a leader, the politics of the organization itself, and its methods for achieving its goals. You may want to focus your research on the question of whether or not the UFW has significantly improved the lives of migrant workers.

2. Create a profile of one of the organizations mentioned in this chapter. Depending on which organization you choose, focus your research on labor relations, origins, contributions to society, financial position, or another issue you find relevant. Use as sources books and articles about the company, reports issued by the company, and statements and speeches made by corporate personnel.

——— Chapter 7 ———

A Woman's Place

I N 1984, GERALDINE FERRARO, a congressional representative from New York, made United States electoral history when she became the first woman ever to appear on the national ticket of a major political party. Three years earlier, Sandra Day O'Connor became the first woman to sit on the Supreme Court. Since that time the number of women in visible government positions has grown steadily. But what of the ordinary woman? What strides has she made in the last decade? And how have attitudes toward women changed, if at all?

Since the women's liberation movement of the 1960s, the perception of a woman's place has undergone significant changes. With the mass entry of women into previously male-dominated fields came a sense of empowerment, but the price of that empowerment was a rift between employed women and homemakers. Some women see that rift as the product of male resistance to women's progress; others consider it an inevitable consequence of change and predict that we are entering an age in which any occupation, so long as it is the woman's own choice, reflects her new-found freedom.

Other issues that arose as women began to redefine themselves involved behavior toward them in the workplace, their treatment in the media, and reactions to their growing independence. As women changed, everyone who came in contact with women had to change as well.

In this chapter, the lives and images of women from Hollywood to the barrio are explored, revealing some progress, some setbacks, a few victories, and several defeats. Throughout the selections, however, the spirit of the women portrayed offers hope for the future of all women.

Nan Robertson, in "Promises," recounts the story of women's struggles for equality at the *New York Times,* not only for female staff, but also in regard to the treatment of women in the pages of the newspaper.

In "Teen Angels and Unwed Witches," Susan Faludi paints a scathing portrait of television producers as misogynists. Her account of the roles allotted women on television indicates backward rather than forward movement.

On the occasion of her daughter's second birthday, Anna Quindlen ponders the limitations still facing women. Despite gains made in the past two decades, Quindlen still sees "The Glass Half Empty."

Naomi Wolf's "PBQ: The Professional Beauty Qualification" provides a telling example of the problems still facing women as it examines the increased pressure put on professional women to present an attractive appearance. The cases Wolf cites indicate that physical requirements that were never considered when men dominated the work force have become routine as women make inroads into previously male professions.

In "Don't Tell," Laura Mansnerus takes the unpopular position of endorsing a woman's choice to remain silent about sexual discrimination and harassment. Her reasons, however, have more to do with survival than with ideology.

A more hopeful view of women's lives emerges with the everyday musings of a single mother of boys in Linda Sharron's poem, "This Spring (Mama Changes the Oil)." Contemplating her responsibilities while performing a "man's job," Sharron finds the link between the mechanical work she's doing and her role as a mother.

Finally, Mary Helen Ponce's "Enero" celebrates the strength of a Mexican-American woman whose energies are spent in the care of her family. As she contemplates the birth of her tenth child and the imminent death of her eldest daughter, this mother continues to provide for the needs of the rest of the family.

The selections in this chapter cover a wide variety of women's experiences. Mothers single and married, employed and at home; professionals content and frustrated with their positions; activists savoring victory and contemplating defeat—all of the women in these selections are familiar with struggle, and all have found a voice to speak out about that struggle.

Promises

NAN ROBERTSON

NAN ROBERTSON, *culture reporter for the* New York Times, *is a graduate of Northwestern University. She was awarded a Pulitzer Prize in 1983 for her article on toxic shock syndrome. Her best-selling book* The Girls in the Balcony *(1992), subtitled* Women, Men, and The New York Times, *focuses on a successful sex-discrimination lawsuit filed by women at the newspaper. This selection from* The Girls in the Balcony *recounts, through several stories, the advances and setbacks of women at the* New York Times *in the late 1980s and early 1990s. Appreciative of her superiors' motivations and intentions, Robertson nevertheless holds them fully responsible for their errors in judgment. Her characterization of the battles fought at the* Times *indicates that women's struggles are far from over.*

Before reading the selection, comment in your journal on your perception of the treatment of women in the press. Based on news stories you've read, do you think women are held to a different standard of behavior than men? Are their accomplishments given equal coverage? Are their private lives treated with equal respect? Explain your responses.

As you make notes on your reading, you may want to focus on Robertson's careful identification of each individual who plays a role in her story, her use of pointed comments and quotations, or the statistics she cites.

ABOUT A YEAR AFTER Punch made young Arthur[1] his deputy, the son began to gather groups of middle and senior management people together to hear what was called The Speech. Some in his audiences were upset by what they heard.

---

[1] Punch: nickname for Arthur Sulzberger, publisher of the *Times*. Young Arthur is his son. [ed.]

There was one statistic he gave them that he believed would have more impact on the future of *The New York Times* than any other: The U.S. Census had projected that by the end of the nineties, 80 percent of all new American employees would be women, minorities, or first-generation immigrants. That did not give the male, white *New York Times* much time to get its house in order. He said the company was not adequately prepared to deal with the changes that were certain to come.

He told his managers that the *Times* had to treat its own people as well as it tried to treat its public—to be fair, honest, open, and responsive. Too often, young Arthur said, the newspaper forced its employees to choose between their home life and their work life, rather than creating a balance between the two. The fundamental questions of parental leave, child care, and flexible scheduling, affecting mainly women, had to be addressed.

He said that the *Times*'s commitment to integrating women and minorities into the highest levels of management went to the very heart of what the newspaper stood for. He warned that managers would be judged more and more on the effectiveness with which they hired and encouraged a diverse work force. Finally, young Arthur put his listeners on notice that all of them, like himself, must reject what he called the "comfort factor" of promoting only white men, and must commit themselves to risk.

That is what he promised. It is one measure of the man who will run *The New York Times* in the years to come.

During my interview with him in 1990, young Arthur was eager to show how women's salaries were catching up with men's. He flipped through sheets of statistics, pointing out that new employees on every level—those hired within the last five years—were benefiting most.

In 1987 the average salary of men in the news division hired within the previous five years was $13,000 higher than the average salary of women hired during the same period; in 1990 there was no gap between the average starting salary of men and that of women in the division. In 1987 men in the business division with six to ten years of experience earned, on average, $25,000 more than women with the same experience. In 1990 the gap between the average starting salaries of men and women had narrowed to $7,000, and, young Arthur said, progress in this direction would continue until there was parity. It was the long-term women workers, those with twenty-one or more years of experience on the *Times*, who would never make as much as the men with equal seniority. One reason was that until very recently, women simply had not been given the chance to rise into the better-paid ranks of middle management, let alone the higher levels.

It gets Anna Quindlen's goat. On New Year's Day, 1990, at the age of thirty-seven, she became only the third woman to have a regular column on the Op-Ed page of the *Times*. But, she said, "every time guys like Max Frankel [the executive editor, who succeeded Abe Rosenthal in 1986] talk about the status of women, they should repeat four words: 'Look at the masthead. Look at the masthead.' "

The masthead, at the top of the editorial page, tells people where the real power lies within *The New York Times*. On the highest line is the name of the publisher, and just below is that of his son, and then there is a space, followed by sixteen names. By early 1991, only two women were listed there.

From the business side of the paper, there was Elise Ross, the senior vice president for systems, who runs the giant computers that run the newspaper. She is the only woman among the six vice presidents, who report directly to Lance Primis, the newspaper's president. (Primis has enlightened ideas about women and has done much to help them; he did not, however, hire Elise, a technical whizbang who came to the *Times* long before Primis became president in 1988.)

From the news side of the *Times*, there was Carolyn Lee, who began her job as the assistant managing editor for administration in 1990, on the same day that Anna Quindlen first appeared on the Op-Ed page. The two women are close. It is Carolyn—one of five assistant managing editors who report directly to Frankel, and the highest-ranking woman in the history of the news staff—who has the power to hire and encourage women and minorities in the ranks of reporters, photographers, and editors. She is using that power. She also possesses a rare gift: she speaks up, she speaks her mind, but with such grace and good humor that almost nobody takes offense.

The important women managers in the news division but *not* on the masthead in the winter of 1991 were the editor of the national desk, Soma Golden; the editor of the Sunday book review, Rebecca Sinkler; and the editor of the Sunday arts and leisure section, Constance Rosenblum. Nancy Newhouse was the Sunday travel editor, Angela Dodson the editor of the style department (traditionally a woman's post). Laurie Mifflin, a former deputy sports editor, was the education editor. Women were deputy editors on the Sunday magazine and in the business, science, photo, and graphic art departments. Four of the fifteen members of the editorial board early in 1991 were women: Diane Camper, who is black; Mary Cantwell; Joyce Purnick, formerly an excellent City Hall reporter, who is Frankel's second wife; and Dorothy Samuels.

The *Times* was certainly doing better by its women in 1990. The women knew that it was not yet nearly good enough.

Nancy Newhouse, who came to the paper in 1977 as editor of the new home section and became editor of the style department and then of the Sunday travel section in 1989, suggested laughingly, when I told her that I was writing a book about the women of the *Times,* that it be titled *The Kingdom of the Powerless*—a play on *The Kingdom and the Power* by Gay Talese, published in 1969. Gay's subtitle was *The Story of the Men Who Influence the Institution That Influences the World.* That was fitting, since Talese virtually ignored the women employees of the newspaper—with the notable exception of Charlotte Curtis, then in her heyday; and of Patricia Riffe, Clifton Daniel's secretary, whose beauty he chose to comment upon, as well as "that nice hip motion she has when she walks."

Newhouse is just one of an outspoken group of women managers   15
hired in the late seventies or eighties who acknowledge that they were beneficiaries of the women's lawsuit but believe that many male executives remain unliberated. This group broke through the "glass ceiling" only to find what one called the "interruption factor."

One day Nancy Newhouse was talking to David Jones, for fifteen years the national news editor and the first of his rank to hire significant numbers of women to edit copy on his desk. During their conversation, the interruption factor took hold of Dave. Nancy stopped him in his tracks. "You're not hearing what I'm saying," she told Jones. "You're reacting before I finish my thought."

"That conversation with Nancy set me thinking," Dave recalled. "I said to some of the other editors, 'You know, I think she's right. I wonder how much we do that?'

" 'Absolutely not!' cried one editor. 'I don't believe it!' said another."

A woman editor said managerial meetings on the news floor at the *Times* had given her anxiety attacks and sent her into therapy because "we are drowned out, not listened to, we are dismissed, passed over. It makes me crazy. The men running the *Times* now truly do not believe themselves capable of sexist feelings. They have serious wives. They help with the dishes. But they are still looking for, and are only comfortable with, people in their own image—in other words, other white men. They have a joking camaraderie together that walls us out." She sounded like young Arthur Sulzberger, only madder.

Another woman editor added, "We all face a more subtle form of   20
discrimination in meetings here. It's hard to make yourself heard in a roomful of men. They use sports metaphors, team language. We say things differently; our voices are higher pitched, and for some reason, men think we can't be serious. It's like women in broadcasting—it

took a long time before their voices were deemed 'important' enough
to deliver significant stories on the air." That very day, she attended a
meeting in which she offered an intriguing story idea about changes
in child care centers in New York. Her idea fell into a little pool of
silence. Then the assistant managing editor running the meeting said
repressively, "Let's get back to Iraq."

Carolyn Lee warned Frankel that the shutting-out of women in
high-level planning meetings was so bad that at least a couple of them
were keeping track of how many times they had been interrupted. She
gave specific examples; Max reacted with incredulity and then promised to do better in the future.

Carolyn has voiced her opinions under even the most daunting
circumstances. Shortly after she became the first woman assistant
managing editor, young Arthur Sulzberger invited about one hundred
and fifty of the paper's executives to a retreat-cum-brainstorming
session about the future of the *Times* at a country resort. Frankel,
whose style with women is ponderously gallant, told the assemblage
that he was pleased to welcome Carolyn Lee as the latest "adornment" to the paper's masthead. "Thank you," Carolyn said, "but I
have not worked so hard all these years to be called an *adornment*." A
woman editor who was there said, "The men gasped, they were scan-
dalized; the women were silently cheering." Max apologized on the
spot.

The incident brought to mind something that had happened to me
shortly after I won a Pulitzer Prize in 1983 for my story about an
attack of toxic shock syndrome that nearly took my life. Clifton
Daniel, by then retired, came by my desk. We embraced. He held me
at arm's length and he said with a smile: "What's a little bitty thing
like you doing winning the Pulitzer Prize?" I let him have it. Clifton
was a friend, but after the ordeal I had gone through I found his
remark thoughtless and patronizing. I deserved the prize, and I knew
it and I said it. When I told this story soon thereafter to a group of
newspaper editors and reporters in New Jersey, a murmur of understanding came from every woman in the room. The men there looked
utterly puzzled. "Aw, Daniel was just being affectionate," one said to
me. "Why don't you relax?"

Nancy Newhouse discovered that even when they died, women
were being ignored by the newspaper. One day she was browsing
through the obituary pages and noticed that among seventeen obituary articles, not one was of a woman. "I could not believe it," she said.
"I mean—women are not dying? Their lives are not worthy of notice?
I was livid and I was determined to bring it up in the next news
meeting. I knew I'd get dumped on." And she was. Editors laughed.
Frankel made a caustic remark. Allan Siegal, an assistant managing

editor, snickered and said, "You mean you want *more* women to die?" Finally Phil Boffey, then the science editor, came to Nancy's rescue. "It's true," he said, "that women in their seventies and eighties might not have had careers, but we should look into this." Nancy said that Siegal—who studies the paper as closely as if searching for devils on the head of a pin—"obviously was making mental notes, and from then on, there has been a woman on the obit page every single day."

Few male editors at the *Times* have seen more clearly than Dave Jones what it is that women can add to a newspaper. He brought so many women onto his national desk that he was known as "the Phil Spitalny of *The New York Times*." (Spitalny's "All-Girl" orchestra was a hit on radio in the thirties and forties.) Dave, now an assistant managing editor, is hardly the warm, fuzzy type—he has the deadpan manner of a Mississippi riverboat gambler. He said he was flattered that people thought he had helped women along, "but the fact is that the women did it themselves, on their own merit and ability." They have added real diversity and sensitivity to the daily report, he said, as well as material of interest to the large number of women readers. Whereas some men on the national staff tended to pass over or downplay such subjects as birth control or toxic shock, the women would say, "Wait a minute—this is a hell of a story."

Dave learned early how hard was the road for professional women. "Maybe it was my wife's experience decades ago," he said. "I think it changed my thinking decisively." Jones and his wife, Mary Lee, were both editors of the student newspaper at Penn State University in the early 1950s. After graduation and their marriage, Mary Lee Jones became a reporter at the Dayton *Journal Herald* while Dave served his stint in the Air Force at a nearby base. "She was making sixty dollars a week, and they would not give her a five-dollar raise," he said. "When I got out of the Air Force, I applied for a job at the same newspaper. I said I wanted a salary of one hundred dollars a week; they practically went white and then they offered me one hundred dollars a week and I said, 'Stuff it.' I was so angry at the way my wife had been treated, I've never forgotten it."

Jones remembered what Eileen Shanahan had told him about her first job interview back in 1962 with Clifton Daniel. Daniel asked Eileen what her ultimate ambition was, and although she had some thoughts about becoming an editor one day, she babbled eagerly, "Oh, all I ever want is to be a reporter on the best newspaper in the world."

"That's good," Eileen quoted Daniel as saying, "because I can assure you, no woman will ever be an editor at *The New York Times*."

By early 1991 in the newsroom, however, about a third of the copy editors were women. Twenty-seven percent of the photographers and photo editors were women; 30 percent of the employees in graphic

25

arts and on the desk that lays out the paper were women. Twenty-three percent of the reporters, correspondents, and critics were women—only 10 percent higher than in 1972, when the women of the *Times* began organizing. In 1990, the new hires of nonminority women reporters amounted to only 18 percent of the total.

While the paper's record shows improvement in important areas, it is nothing to crow about—considering that women compose half the population and that there are no longer any significant cultural or educational differences between white men and women in the United States. By 1990, however, the *Times* was hiring almost as many minority women reporters as minority men reporters.   30

The two persons presiding most closely over these changes on the news side have been Carolyn Lee and Max Frankel, her immediate boss. "Max may put his foot in his mouth about women and blacks, but look at his performance," Carolyn said. "Three-quarters of the women in management jobs on the news side have been put there by Max."

Frankel put his foot in his mouth twice in public in 1990. The first time he offended women. The second time he managed to offend both women and blacks. While trying to refute a charge that his paper had fewer stories by and about women on the front page than other major papers do, he told Eleanor Randolph of *The Washington Post*, "If you are covering local teas, you've got more women [on the front page] than *The Wall Street Journal*." The next day, dozens of women employees and a few males came to work sporting tea bags on their lapels; buttons showing a teapot crossed by a diagonal red line were worn soon thereafter by both women and men on the staff. New York's *Village Voice* commented: "Frankel's 19th-century relegation of women to wifely Darjeeling-and-scone duties would be objectionable from any editor, but when it comes from the head cheese of the paper that sets the world's news agenda, it's not just offensive, but dangerously stupid."

About fifty women of the *Times* met to protest, their biggest get-together since the 1988 Caucus reunion. This time the meeting was held right on the premises. What came out of it was a letter to Max, in which they asked, "Did you mean what you said? If not, what did you mean? ... It was painful to be contacted by colleagues across the country who suggested our executive editor did not value our contributions. And there is additional concern that this incident could impede efforts to recruit and promote women at *The New York Times*."

Max apologized handsomely, if somewhat obscurely. "I assure you that my sin was chronological, not ideological," he wrote back. "If I were 20 years younger, I surely would have found a better example" of an important women's activity than giving tea parties.

Six months later, he did it again. At a symposium on women and 35
the media at Columbia University's Graduate School of Journalism,
he said it was easier for him to fire women than blacks because there
were now more women in the newsroom. "We've reached a critical
mass with women," he explained. "I know that when a woman screws
up, it is not a political act for me to go fire them. I cannot say that with
some of our blacks. They're still precious, they're still hothouse in
management and if they are less than good, I would probably stay my
hand at removing them too quickly."

He later told black journalists that even though he had tripped
over his own "fat lips," the *Times* had no double standard. Rebecca
Sinkler, the Sunday book review editor, commented: "I think we're
lucky to have Max Frankel because he's so completely politically
incorrect—the man's well intentioned but antediluvian. He's not
hypocritical enough to mind his mouth—he shows us what really is
on men's minds. I thank him for that, for being unguarded, for getting
it all out there, because anything hidden under a mask of hypocrisy is
harder to fight."

"He does what Ed Koch [the former mayor of New York] does,"
another influential woman said. "He gives voice to certain bigoted
truths."

Still later, Frankel explained to me what he meant by his "critical
mass" statement:

"What I meant was that I as manager of this wonderful organization can afford to have a woman fail without having a political crisis
on my hands. I do aim for fifty-fifty [men and women on the staff].
Fortunately, enough women have already succeeded in high places
here so that we can also have them fail. What I was doing was revealing my own state of mind—really. When Branch Rickey recruited
Jackie Robinson, he had to say, 'Boy, this guy had better be great.' He
had to be better than anybody else. My mother used to say to me,
'Max, you're a Jew—you've got to be better than anybody else.' Now
major black ballplayers are routinely scolded, traded, kicked out, and
nobody calls it racism."

But the fuss kicked up over Frankel's "tea party" and "critical 40
mass" comments was as nothing compared with the outrage that
erupted against him among the employees of *The New York Times* in
April 1991. The anger focused on the paper's profile of the woman
who had accused William Kennedy Smith, Senator Edward Kennedy's nephew, of rape at the Kennedy estate in Palm Beach. Printing
the story, with its unsavory "she asked for it" tone as well as the
alleged victim's name, was Max Frankel's decision. It was the worst
decision of his career. It brought shame to the newspaper and those in
charge and scorching criticism from readers and periodicals across the

country. It pitted the staff against Frankel and his top editors in a confrontation that involved three hundred members of the newspaper, almost half of them male. The meeting in the ninth-floor WQXR auditorium—the only room in the *Times* building big enough to contain such a crowd—revealed as no other single event in memory how dramatically most staffers' perceptions of women had changed. It also revealed how Max Frankel's perceptions, and those of most of the men closest to him, had *not* changed.

The profile of Smith's accuser ran in the *Times* on Wednesday, April 17, on an inside page. An unidentified friend from high school mentioned that the woman had "a little wild streak," and there were details about her bar-hopping, her child born out of wedlock, her poor grades in school, her many speeding tickets; it was reported that her mother, once a secretary and a welder's wife, had moved up the social and financial ladder with her daughter after having an affair with a multimillionaire, who eventually married her. One *Times* reporter echoed the almost universal reaction by saying: "They made [Smith's accuser] look like a slut."

The morning the profile appeared, the *Times* building exploded. Becky Sinkler, the Sunday book review editor, was so incensed that she charged downstairs from her eighth-floor office and burst into Frankel's conference room, where a meeting was going on. John Lee, an assistant managing editor, looked up smiling and said, "Don't you think we had a terrific story this morning?" Becky snapped: "It's a disgrace! That's why I'm here." She said the faces of the men around the table "simply froze." Joe Lelyveld, the cool, disengaged managing editor, blurted out, "What do you *mean*?" Sinkler told them the story was an outrageous smear—sexist, class-ridden, a nasty piece of work riddled with negative quotes from anonymous sources, a violation of the paper's high journalistic standards. Frankel, overhearing the raised voices through an open door next to his office, rushed in to say to Sinkler in a voice thick with anger: "I woke up this morning so proud of that story. We had more reporting, more facts in that story than any other paper in the country."

By the next morning, it was obvious to Max and his associates that something was terribly wrong. Reporters and *Times* fans from all over the nation were calling, wondering what on earth had happened to the Good Gray Lady.

Young Arthur Sulzberger was privately appalled by the profile. The uproar and the bitter debate, inside and outside the *Times*, was also reaching a baffled Punch Sulzberger in London.

That Thursday morning, April 18, Allan Siegal, an assistant managing editor, who had watched the television news programs and   45

knew that "an enormous flap" was brewing over the *Times*'s performance, said to Frankel: "You know, we ought to call the staff together
and give them an opportunity to talk to us rather than talk around
us." He was concerned that their anger had no place to go, and that it
would leak, as always in the past, to eager ears at *New York* magazine
or *The Village Voice* or *Spy*. The WQXR auditorium was reserved for
early Friday afternoon.

Frankel, Siegal (the spokesman to the outside world for the
Times's news side), and Soma Golden, the national editor whose desk
had processed the Palm Beach profile, faced the staff from the platform. People poured in by the hundreds, filling the seats and packing the side aisles and the back. Fifty members of the Washington
bureau listened to the proceedings as they were piped down to the
capital on a speaker-phone. "They've got blood in their eyes," Al
Siegal said in an undertone to Max. He could "feel the anger radiating up off the auditorium like the heat radiating off a summer
highway."

What really radiates off the tape-recording of the next ninety
minutes is not so much anger as anguish and deep sadness, expressed
by both women and men speakers from the floor, about how the *Times*
had tarnished the very journalistic standards that they and the paper's readers had long admired. There are none of the "boos and
hisses" *Time* magazine later reported; nobody shouts or interrupts, the
reporters and editors ask tough questions without losing their dignity,
but their distress is palpable. What also comes strongly off the tape is
Max Frankel's total avoidance of responsibility, and his preoccupation
with the newspaper's image rather than his own values. Soma Golden
comes off no better. "It was not a damning portrait of somebody
asking for it," she says. "It was a portrait, period. . . . Everybody's
outraged. I don't understand that. . . . I can't account for every weird
mind that reads *The New York Times*." At this point a moan of revulsion
rises from the audience. Only Siegal, one of the most scrupulous
word-by-word readers of the paper, takes any blame. He confesses
that he read the profile "much too hastily," agrees with the objections
to the anonymous "wild streak" quotation, and speaks of how the
uproar has sensitized him to the emotions the delicate subject arouses.
Asked why there was not a profile of William Kennedy Smith, the
alleged rapist, Soma replies, "We're working on it." (A sympathetic
story ran May 12, almost a month later, the day after Smith was
indicted.)

Anna Quindlen, like many, felt betrayed by her own newspaper.
In the column she wrote for Sunday, April 21, she compared the
Times's discretion about the name of the victim in the 1988 Central

Park jogger case with the paper's current conduct in the Palm Beach affair. In the final paragraphs, her disgust sizzled off the page:

> In the face of what we did in the Central Park case, the obvious conclusion was that women who graduate from Wellesley, have prestigious jobs [the victim was an investment banker], and are raped by a gang of black teen-agers will be treated fairly by the press. And women who have "below-average" high school grades, are well known at bars and dance clubs, and say that they have been raped by an acquaintance from an influential family after a night of drinking will not.
>
> If we had any doubt about whether there is still a stigma attached to rape, it is gone for good. Any woman reading the Times profile now knows that to accuse a well-connected man of rape will invite a thorough reading not only of her own past but of her mother's, and that she had better be ready to see not only her name but her drinking habits in print. . . .

The day after the column appeared, young Arthur Sulzberger hugged and kissed his friend Anna in the middle of the newsroom, telling her, "It was brave of you to write that column." Thirteen of the highest-ranking women editors gathered soon thereafter in a supportive, females-only meeting in Frankel's conference room. A crestfallen Soma Golden was there, and was comforted. The women pushed Max to run an Editor's Note of apology. It ran Friday, April 26, along with a full and fair—and unprecedented—article summarizing the negative repercussions of the episode inside and outside the paper. Frankel was quoted as saying, "This is a crisis because many people feel The Times betrayed its standards."

The Editor's Note said in part: "The article drew no conclusions   50 about the truth of [the accuser's] complaint to the police. But many readers inferred that its very publication, including her name and detailed biographical material about her and her family, suggested that The Times was challenging her account.

"No such challenge was intended, and The Times regrets that some parts of the article reinforced such inferences."

Anna Quindlen told a friend: "First they blamed the victim. And then they blamed the reader."

I asked Al Siegal what lessons he had learned from all this. "I never thought that rape was something people took lightly," he replied, "but the power of the subject to provoke volcanic rage is a revelation to me, and the pain and the grief that women commonly experience about it is staggering. I knew how to handle sensitive material about Jews and Arabs, but not about this. Now I will be hypersensitive and cautious. I've heard a lot of screaming from the depths of people's souls, and I'll remember. That awareness alone could serve me as an editor."

There were other lessons. First, from beginning to end, it was the women of the *Times* who pushed and prodded and called the paper and its most powerful editors to account and insisted upon action. They received their staunchest support from younger male staff members. Second, the WQXR meeting would never have been called under Abe Rosenthal—who believed at the end that *he* was *The New York Times*—nor under any of his predecessors. (If the article had been run during Abe's regime, however, he almost certainly would have taken entire responsibility for it, because that was his nature and because he thought he and the *Times* were one and indivisible.)

Perhaps Max Frankel was born too soon to comprehend the   55
women of this generation, or those of his own generation, like myself, who were irrevocably changed by the modern women's movement. He has always given the impression of being a weighty thinker, but I sometimes wonder—as do many of those who work for him—if Max will ever understand us in his gut.

❖ **Focused Freewriting**   Consider as possible focal points the different perspectives of men and women on a given issue, the significance of women's advancement at the *Times*, one of Robertson's anecdotes, or one of the topics you've identified in your journal.

❖ **Guided Responses**

1. In paragraph 8 Robertson quotes Anna Quindlen's response to women's progress at the *Times*: "Look at the masthead. Look at the masthead." In light of the number of women in high positions at the newspaper, why should Quindlen feel that the masthead is so important? Do you agree with her? Why, or why not?

2. In describing their problems now that they have reached editorial positions, women interviewed by Robertson comment that their male colleagues "are still looking for, and are only comfortable with, people in their own image—in other words, other white men," and that it is "hard to make yourself heard in a roomful of men . . . ; for some reason, men think we can't be serious" (paras. 19–20). Given Robertson's accounts of life at the *New York Times*, do you agree with this assessment? How might the men referred to respond? Explain your response, drawing from your own relevant personal experience as well as the selection.

3. When Robertson tells her colleagues about Clifton Daniel's "little bitty thing" remark, one of the males responds, "Why don't you

relax?" (para. 23) How do you respond to her story? How is your response affected by Robertson's other anecdotes of insensitive remarks (paras. 22, 32, 35)? Taken together, do these remarks indicate a pattern of behavior among her male colleagues? Explain your response.

4. Robertson's final paragraph focuses on Max Frankel, perhaps implying that Frankel is representative of many men on the staff of the *Times*. What do you think Robertson means when she says that despite Frankel's reputation as "a weighty thinker," she wonders "if Max will ever understand us in his gut"? How might Frankel and others understand something intellectually that they can't comprehend on a "gut" level? Where in the selection can you find indications that in spite of men like Frankel, there is hope for women at the *Times*?

❖ Shared Responses   In your journal explain your reaction to the *Times* story about William Kennedy Smith's accuser. Given the information Robertson provides (and perhaps your own recollection of the controversy), do you agree that the newspaper "betrayed its standards" (para. 49)? How do you respond to Anna Quindlen's analysis, and to Max Frankel's justification of the story? As you discuss your responses in small groups, try to distinguish between responses that focus on journalistic standards and those that emphasize the story's impact on women.

—— ❖ ——

Teen Angels
and Unwed Witches

SUSAN FALUDI

Susan Faludi, *a 1981 graduate of Harvard University, is a freelance writer and former reporter for the* Miami Herald, *the* Atlanta Constitution, *and the* Wall Street Journal. *Her 1991 book* Backlash: The Undeclared War Against American Women *won a 1991 National Book Critics Circle Award. In this selection from* Backlash *Faludi analyzes the portrayal of women in popular television fare. Unflattering images of women, argues Faludi, are no accident but rather part of a "backlash," a negative reaction by television producers to strong women.*

Before reading the article, write in your journal about familiar female characters on television. Which of them could be characterized as strong role models for young women? Which characters reflect negative stereotypes? What is the ratio of strong, assertive women to weak, passive women?

As you make notes on your reading, you may want to focus on Faludi's choice of quotations, her characterization of television programmers, or her use of statistics to support her argument.

"Under no circumstances is this going to be the return of 'jiggle.' These aren't just girls who look good; they have actual personalities." Tony Shepherd, vice president of talent for Aaron Spelling Productions, puts his full weight behind each word, as if careful enunciation might finally convince the remaining skeptics in the Hollywood press corps. Thankfully, most of the reporters assembled at the Fox Television Center for the announcement of the network's new television series, "Angels '88," see things Shepherd's way; they reach across the buffet table's mountain of pastries to shake his hand. "Great work, Tony," says one of the guys from the tabloids, his mouth full of croissant. "Great work selecting the girls."

This May morning in 1988 is the grand finale of Fox's two-month quarter-million-dollar nationwide search for the four angels—a quest the company publicists liken to "the great search for Scarlett O'Hara" and "the glamour days of Old Hollywood." Shepherd has crossed the country four times ("I had to watch *Three Men and a Baby* five times on the plane"), personally conducted open casting calls in twelve of the forty-four cities, and eyeballed at least six thousand of the sixteen thousand women who stood in half-mile-long lines all day for one-and-a-half-minute interviews. Secretaries and housewives, he says, weathered 25-degree temperatures just to see him; one woman even passed out from hypothermia.

But a few journalists at this event can't resist asking: Isn't "Angels '88" just a reprise of Spelling's "Charlie's Angels," where three jiggle-prone private eyes took orders from invisible boss Charlie and bounced around in bikinis? "No, no, no!" Shepherd, the chain-smoking great grandson of Louis B. Mayer, exhales a fierce stream of smoke. "*They* didn't have distinct characters. They were just beauties." The characters in "Angels '88," he says, are more "advanced," independent women who won't even necessarily be fashion plates. That's why the network interviewed so many real women for the leading roles. These new angels "might not have perfect hair and be the perfect model types," he says. "In 'Angels '88,' you're going to find these girls sometimes wearing no makeup at all. Particularly, you know, when they are running around on the beach."

Just then, a Fox publicist takes the stage to announce the angels' imminent debut. No interviews, he warns the media, until the photographers finish their "beauty shots." The angels file on stage and the cameramen begin shouting, "Girls, over here, over here!" "Oh, young ladies, right here!" The angels turn this way and that, well-coiffed hair swinging around flawlessly made-up faces. The idle reporters leaf through their press kits, which offer large photographs and brief biographies of each star—Tea Leoni, "the 5'7" blonde beauty"; Karen Kopins, "the 5'8" brunette beauty"; and so on. Of the four, only Leoni was actually picked from the nationwide casting call. The others are models with minor acting backgrounds.

The angels spend a carefully timed five minutes with the press   5 before they are whisked off for a lengthy photo session for *Time.* The stage mike is turned over to Aaron Spelling, creator of some of the most lucrative programs in television history, a list ranging from "Love Boat" to "Fantasy Island." "How's this show going to be different from 'Charlie's Angels'?" a reporter asks. "These young ladies are on their own; they do not report to any men," Spelling says. "It's an entire ladies' show without guidance. It's a young ladies' buddy-buddy show is what it is." He turns a beseeching face on his audience.

"Why, why," he wants to know, would anyone think that he wants to bring back "the beautiful bimbos"? He shakes his head. "It's going to be a show of today's young ladies of today [sic], and we'll go into their personal lives, we'll treat today's issues, we'll treat the problems of their dating and sex and safe sex and sex of our time. It's going to be a very attractive show."

Later that same day in Santa Monica, screenwriter Brad Markowitz rolls his eyes as he hears the details of the press conference. A few months earlier, Spelling had hired Markowitz and his writing partner to script the series pilot. "Spelling made all these fine speeches to us about how 'the girls' would be more real," Markowitz recalls. "He talked a good game about how the show would be more representative of how women really are, as opposed to that idealized, frosted look." But when it came down to drafting a script, Markowitz says, Spelling instructed the screenwriters to open the episode with scantily clad angels wriggling to a rock video. Spelling was unhappy with their first draft, Markowitz recalls, because "we didn't have enough girls in bikinis"; he ordered them to add more bathing-beauty scenes. Spelling also insisted that the thirty-two-year-old police academy-trained detectives (their original status in "Charlie's Angels") be demoted to unemployed actresses in their early twenties who just fall into police work and bungle the job. Spelling, who later denies demanding these changes—"the script just wasn't good enough is all I know"—defended the alterations this way: "That's what makes the show funny—that they are supposed to be doing it by themselves and they can't! They are incompetent!"

After various delays and script battles, "Angels '88" was put on hold, then reformatted as a "telefilm," in which, Spelling says, the women will be even younger college "coeds." Meanwhile, for the 1988–89 season, Spelling applied his "young ladies' buddy-buddy show" concept to "Nightingales," an NBC prime-time series about five jiggly student nurses who prance around the locker room in their underwear. While they aren't independent, their boss is a woman, Spelling says proudly—as if a female head nurse represents nontraditional casting.

Anyway, as Spelling pointed out at the "Angels" press conference, at least his shows have women in lead roles. "Go and look at television today. Tell me how many shows outside of a few comedies are dominated by women. You'll find the answer is very few."

True enough. In the 1987–88 season, the backlash's high watermark on TV, only three of twenty-two new prime-time dramas featured female leads—and only two of them were adults. One was a sorority girl and another a nubile private eye who spent much of her time posing and complaining about the dating scene. (The title of that show, "Leg Work," speaks for itself.) In a sharp dropoff from previous seasons, 60 percent of the shows launched as series in this season had either no regular female characters or included women only as minor background figures; 20 percent had no women at all. And women over the age of consent were especially hard to find.

Women were also losing ground in the one television genre they   10
had always called their own: situation comedy. In a resurgence of the old "Odd Couple" format, bachelor buddies took up house together without adult women in one out of five new sitcoms, a list that included "Everything's Relative," "My Two Dads," "Trial and Error," and "Full House." In the single-parent household sitcoms that took over prime time that year, two-thirds of the children lived with dad or a male guardian—compared with 11 percent in the real world. "This season it's especially clear that TV writers are uncomfortable with the concept of working mothers," *New York Woman* observed. The magazine offered a quiz that starkly documented this discomfort; the "Moms at Work" puzzle invited readers to match each new prime-time show with the current status of the working-mother character. The correct answers: "A Year in the Life"—dead. "Full House"—dead. "I Married Dora"—dead. "My Two Dads"—dead. "Valerie's Family"—dead. "Thirtysomething"—quits work to become a housewife. "Everything's Relative"—show canceled. "Mama's Boy"—show canceled.

Women's disappearance from prime-time television in the late '80s repeats a programming pattern from the last backlash when, in the late '50s and early '60s, single dads ruled the TV roosts and female characters were suddenly erased from the set. By the 1960 season, only two of the top ten rated shows had regular female characters—"Gunsmoke" and "Real McCoys"—and by 1962 the one woman on "Real McCoys" had been killed off, too. The vanishing act eventually spread to domestic dramas, where the single father took charge of the household on "Bachelor Father," "My Three Sons," "Family Affair," and "The Andy Griffith Show."

In the '80s, women began to shrink and dwindle in the 1985–86 season, as a new breed of action-adventure series that included women only as victimized girls began crowding out more balanced fare. In this new crop of programs, as uneasy critics commented at the time, the viciousness of the assaults on the young female characters rivaled slasher films. On "Lady Blue," for example, teenage boys armed with scalpels eviscerate their female prey; on "Our Family Honor," a seventeen-year-old girl is slashed to death with a coat hanger. And that season, female characters who weren't under attack were likely to be muzzled or missing from action: An analysis of prime-time TV in 1987 found 66 percent of the 882 speaking characters were male—about the same proportion as in the '50s.

While the new male villains were busy pulverizing women, male heroes on continuing series were toughening their act. The "return of the hard-boiled male," *New York Times* television writer Peter Boyer dubbed it in an article on the phenomenon. In "St. Elsewhere," the affable Dr. Caldwell was recast as an unapologetic womanizer. In "Moonlighting," the immature hireling of the elegantly confident Maddie Hayes now overshadowed his boss lady—and cut her down to size. Network executives even instructed Tom Selleck to get more masculine on "Magnum, P.I." And the networks continued to boost their macho output; of the ten new dramas unveiled in the fall of 1989, five were about male cops or cowboys, with such self-explanatory titles as "Nasty Boys" and "Hardball." The latter show's premiere made it clear who would be on the receiving—and losing—end of this game. In the debut episode, a homicidal and evil female cop is beaten into submission by the male hero—a scene that reenacts the climactic confrontation in *Fatal Attraction*. (He holds her head under water in the bathroom and tries to drown her.)

If TV programmers had their reasons for bringing on the he-men, popular demand wasn't among them. In audience surveys, TV viewers show the *least* interest in police dramas and westerns. Nonetheless, Brandon Tartikoff, president of entertainment at NBC, asserted in the *New York Times* that the TV men were turning brutish because "the audience" was sick of male "wimps" and "Alan Alda-esque heroes who wore their sensitivity on their shirtsleeves"; as proof, he pointed not to real people but to the outpouring of macho movies—yet another case of the makers of one cultural medium invoking another's handiwork to reinforce the backlash. Glenn Gordon Caron, producer of "Moonlighting," admitted to more personal motives in an interview in the *New York Times:* "I very much wanted to see a *man* on television." He complained that the last decade of social change had elbowed his sex off the screen. "[For] a long time, men just sort of went away," he grumbled: one could only tell the gender of these ineffectual guys "because their voices were lower and their chests were flatter." Glen Charles, coproducer of "Cheers," was even blunter: he turned his show's bartender Sam into a chauvinistic womanizer because "he's a spokesman for a large group of people who thought that [the women's movement] was a bunch of bull and look with disdain upon people who don't think it was."

The backlash on television would to a degree follow the film 15 industry's lead. *Fatal Attraction* became ABC's "Obsessive Love" a year later; *Baby Boom* became a television series of the same name;

Working Girl, Parenthood, and *Look Who's Talking* all resurfaced as TV series; the western returned to the big screen and the small set. (And in keeping with the single-dad theme, bachelor cowboy Ethan Allan, the hero of TV's "Paradise," gets saddled with four orphans.) The same backlash trends were recycled: single women panicked by the man shortage dashed into the arms of a maniac on "Addicted to His Love." (The ABC TV movie even cited the Harvard-Yale marriage study's 20 percent odds for college-educated single women over thirty.) Career women swooned with baby fever and infertility on shows like "Babies." ("My biological clock is beginning to sound like Big Ben!" cries one of the empty-vessel heroines.) Even the "epidemic" of sex abuse at day care centers was turned into ratings fodder: In "Do You Know the Muffin Man?" a divorced working mother discovers her four-year-old son has been raped and contracted gonorrhea at nursery school.

But TV's counterassault on women's liberation would be, by necessity, more restrained than Hollywood's. Women have more influence in front of their sets than they do at the movies; women represent not only the majority of viewers but, more important, they represent the viewers that advertisers most want to reach. When the TV programmers tried to force-feed its cast of over-weening guys and wilting gals in the 1987–88 season, a devastating proportion of the female audience simply shut off their sets. None of the twenty-five new prime-time shows made it into the top twenty except for "A Different World," which was a spinoff of the "Cosby" show (and one of the rare new shows with a female lead). By December, the networks' prime-time ratings had plunged a spectacular nine points from a year earlier, an average loss of 3.5 million households a night and the lowest rated TV season ever. While the dropoff can be partly attributed to the phasing in of the "people meter," a more finely tuned measure of viewership, that technological change doesn't explain why the audience flight was so disproportionately female. Nor does it explain why, in subsequent backlash seasons, when the people meter was no longer at issue, a lopsidedly female exodus kept recurring. Moreover, the people meters were reputed to favor younger viewers more than the old "diary" methods of audience measurement had. But while younger men increased their weekly viewing time by more than two hours in the fall of 1987 over the previous year, younger women *decreased* their viewing time by almost an hour in the same period.

By the following season, the programmers backed off a bit to admit a couple of strong female leads to the prime-time scene. "Roseanne" and "Murphy Brown," both featuring outspoken women—and both, not coincidentally, created by women—became instant and massive hits: "Roseanne" was one of the most successful series launched in television history and held the number-one ratings slot season after season. But two strong women were seen as two too many. Independent women were "seizing control of prime time," *Newsweek* griped in a 1989 cover story. "The video pendulum has swung too far from the blissfully domestic supermoms who once warmed the electronic hearth." Behind the scenes, the network tried to make changes that amounted to "taking all the stuffing out of Murphy," the show's creator Diane English observed. The tart-tongued Roseanne Barr especially became a lightning rod for that rancor. While her penchant for mooning crowds and singing the national anthem off-key clearly warrants no Miss Congeniality prizes, the level of bile and hysteria directed at this comic seemed peculiarly out of proportion with her offenses. The media declared her, just like the *Fatal Attraction* temptress, "the most hated woman in America"; television executives savaged her in print; her former executive producer even took out a full-page ad in *Daily Variety* to deride the comedian; and, despite critical acclaim and spectacular ratings, "Roseanne" was shut out of the Emmys year after year after year. Outside the network suites, a chorus of male voices joined the Barr-bashing crusade. Sportswriters, baseball players, and news columnists damned her in print as a "bitch" and a "dog." Even George Bush felt compelled to issue a condemnatory statement; he called her "disgraceful." (And later he told the troops in the Middle East that he would like to make her a secret weapon again Iraq.) Businessman James Rees, the son of the former congressman, launched a nationwide "Bar Roseanne Club," soliciting members in the classified sections of *Rolling Stone* and *The National.* ("Hate Roseanne Barr?" the ad copy inquired. "Join the club.") In a few weeks, he had more than six hundred responses, almost all from men who thoroughly agreed with Rees's assessment of "old lard butt." She's "a nasty filthy ugly Jell-O-Bodied tasteless monster from the black lagoon," wrote one man. Another proposed, "Let's shish-Kebab [her]."

By the following season, prime time reverted to traditional feminine icons, as the new series filled the screen with teenage models, homemakers, a nun and—that peculiar prototype of the last TV backlash—the good suburban housekeeper witch. An updated version of the tamed genie of "Bewitched" reappeared in the ironically named "Free Spirit." By the next season, women were shut out of so many new shows that even comic Jay Leno joked about it at the Emmys. TV critic Joyce Millman, observing that the new offerings were "overloaded with adolescent boys and motherless households," asked, "Whatever happened to TV's 'Year of the Woman'? ... [I]t's back to

'Boys' Night Out' for the upcoming fall season." Only two of thirty-three new shows were about women with jobs; on the rest they were housewives, little girls, or invisible.

The lurching quality of television's backlash against independent women is the product of the industry's own deeply ambivalent affair with its female audience. TV prime-time programmers are both more dependent on women's approval than filmmakers and, because of their dependence, more resentful. To serve a female master is not why the TV men came west to Hollywood. (And most are men; more than 90 percent of television writers, for example, are white males.) They say they want shows that draw a large audience, but when those shows feature autonomous women, they try to cancel them. "Designing Women" and "Kate and Allie," both tremendously popular series, have fought back repeated network attempts to chase them off the set.

The modern network programmers find themselves in a situation   20
roughly analogous to that of the late Victorian clergymen. Like those leaders of the last century's backlash, TV executives watch anxiously as their female congregation abandons the pews—in the daytime for work and in the evening for other forms of electronic entertainment that offer more control and real choices. Women are turning to VCRs and cable offerings. In 1987, as the networks took their free fall in the ratings, prime-time cable viewership increased 35 percent and the proportion of TV households that owned VCRs rose from 19 to 60 percent in one year. The networks' audience shrank by more than 25 percent in the decade—and women contributed most to that shrinkage. By 1990, Nielsen was reporting that the percentage of decline in female prime-time viewers was two to three times steeper than male's. Women's desertion was more than an insult; it represented a massive financial loss. (A mere one-point drop in prime-time ratings equals a loss of more than $90 million in the network's revenue in one season.)

Not only do some programming executives personally want to expel the independent women from the American set; their advertisers, who still view the housewife as the ideal shopper, demand it. This puts TV programmers in an impossible bind: the message advertisers want the networks to promote appeals least to modern women. Female viewers consistently give their highest ratings to nontraditional female characters such as leaders, heroines, and comedians. But TV's biggest advertisers, packaged-foods and household-goods manufacturers, want traditional "family" shows that fit a sales pitch virtually unchanged in two decades. Advertisers prefer to reflect the housewife viewer because she is perceived as a more passive and willing consumer, because she is likely to have more children, and because they are simply used to this arrangement. Since its inception, television has been marketed as a family-gathering experience—the modern-day flickering hearth—where merchandisers' commercial messages can hit the whole clan at once.

As the '80s television backlash against independent women proceeded in fits and starts from season to season, a few shows managed to survive its periodic surges—"L.A. Law," "Designing Women," and "The Golden Girls" are some examples. But overall, it succeeded in depopulating TV of its healthy independent women and replacing them with nostalgia-glazed portraits of apolitical "family" women. This process worked its way through television entertainment in two stages. First in the early '80s, it banished feminist issues. Then, in the mid-'80s, it reconstructed a "traditional" female hierarchy, placing suburban homemakers on the top, career women on the lower rungs, and single women at the very bottom.

❖ Focused Freewriting   Consider as possible focal points the history of women on television, the attitude toward women reflected by Aaron Spelling and Brandon Tartikoff, or one of the topics you've identified in your journal.

❖ Guided Responses

1. Paragraph 1 ends with the image of "one of the guys from the tabloids" reaching "across the buffet table's mountain of pastries" to shake Tony Shepherd's hand and say, "Great work, Tony. . . . Great work selecting the girls." Given Shepherd's insistence that the characters in his new show will be fully realized women, how does this remark strike you? Why do you think Faludi chooses to close her introductory paragraph with the word "girls"?

2. Arguing that *Angels '88* will not signal the return of "the beautiful bimbos," Aaron Spelling states that the new program will "treat today's issues, . . . the problems of [the Angels'] dating and sex and safe sex and sex of our time" and argues that "what makes the show funny [is] that they are supposed to be doing it by themselves and they can't! They are incompetent!" (paras. 5–6) How do these lines underscore Faludi's argument that there is a "backlash" against strong women on television? How do you react to these words vis-à-vis Spelling's description of the program? Why do you think the program never made it to the air?

3. Faludi claims that "the level of bile and hysteria directed at [Roseanne Barr] seemed peculiarly out of proportion with her offenses" (para. 17). Given Faludi's observations on television produc-

ers, why do you think the reaction against Barr was so strong? How did you react to news stories about the comedian? Do you think your response was influenced by the tone of the stories? Why, or why not?

4. Faludi compares the television backlash of the eighties to the religious backlash of clergymen during the Victorian era who watched "anxiously as their female congregation [abandoned] the pews" (para. 20). In what way are network programmers like the ministers who used their pulpits to condemn early women's rights activists? What motivations do you think the ministers had? What were the motivations of the programmers?

❖ Shared Responses   In your journal, write an analysis of women's roles in your favorite television programs. After reading Faludi's selection, how do you react to these portrayals? Do you think they bear out her conclusions? Why, or why not? In your group discussion, use members' responses to try to determine the range of women's roles on television today.

The Glass Half Empty

ANNA QUINDLEN

Anna Quindlen graduated from Barnard College in 1974, after which she became a reporter for the New York Post. *In 1977 she joined the* New York Times, *where she is still a regular columnist. She has written several books, including* Living Out Loud *(1986) and* Object Lessons *(1991). In 1992 Quindlen won a Pulitzer Prize for commentary. In this column from the* Times, *she reflects upon how her perspective on women's progress has changed since the birth of her daughter. The glass she once saw as half full she now sees, in light of her child's prospects, as half empty.*

Before reading the selection, write in your journal about your impressions of the gains women have made in the past two decades. Do you think opportunities for women are equal to those for men? Have women achieved their goals? Explain your responses.

As you make notes on your reading, you may want to focus on the contrasts between Quindlen's sons' prospects and those of her daughter, or on the scenarios she envisions.

MY DAUGHTER is 2 years old today. She is something like me, only better. Or at least that is what I like to think. If personalities had colors, hers would be red.

Little by little, in the 20 years between my eighteenth birthday and her second one, I had learned how to live in the world. The fact that women were now making 67 cents for every dollar a man makes—well, it was better than 1970, wasn't it, when we were making only 59 cents? The constant stories about the underrepresentation of women, on the tenure track, in the film industry, in government, everywhere, had become commonplace. The rape cases. The sexual harassment stories. The demeaning comments. Life goes on. Where's your sense of humor?

Learning to live in the world meant seeing the glass half full. Ann Richards was elected Governor of Texas instead of a good ol' boy who said that if rape was inevitable, you should relax and enjoy it. The police chief of Houston is a pregnant woman who has a level this-is-my-job look and a maternity uniform with stars on the shoulder. There are so many opportunities unheard of when I was growing up.

And then I had a daughter and suddenly I saw the glass half empty. And all the rage I thought had cooled, all those how-dare-you-treat-us-like-that days, all of it comes back when I look at her, and especially when I hear her say to her brothers, "Me too."

When I look at my sons, it is within reason to imagine all the   5
world's doors open to them. Little by little some will close, as their individual capabilities and limitations emerge. But no one is likely to look at them and mutter: "I'm not sure a man is right for a job at this level. Doesn't he have a lot of family responsibilities?"

Every time a woman looks at her daughter and thinks "She can be anything" she knows in her heart, from experience, that it's a lie. Looking at this little girl, I see it all, the old familiar ways of a world that still loves Barbie. Girls aren't good at math, dear. He needs the money more than you, sweetheart; he's got a family to support. Honey—this diaper's dirty.

It is like looking through a telescope. Over the years I learned to look through the end that showed things small and manageable. This is called a sense of proportion. And then I turned the telescope around, and all the little tableaus rushed at me, vivid as ever.

That's called reality.

We soothe ourselves with the gains that have been made. There are many role models. Role models are women who exist—and are photographed often—to make other women feel better about the fact that there aren't really enough of us anywhere, except in the lowest-paying jobs. A newspaper editor said to me not long ago, with no hint of self-consciousness, "I'd love to run your column, but we already run Ellen Goodman." Not only was there a quota; there was a quota of one.

My daughter is ready to leap into the world, as though life were   10
chicken soup and she a delighted noodle. The work of Prof. Carol Gilligan of Harvard suggests that some time after the age of 11 this will change, that even this lively little girl will pull back, shrink, that her constant refrain will become "I don't know." Professor Gilligan says the culture sends a message: "Keep quiet and notice the absence of women and say nothing." A smart 13-year-old said to me last week, "Boys don't like it if you answer too much in class."

Someday, years from now, my daughter will come home and say, "Mother, at college my professor acted as if my studies were an amusing hobby and at work the man who runs my department puts his hand on my leg and to compete with the man who's in the running for my promotion who makes more than I do I can't take time to have a relationship but he has a wife and two children and I'm smarter and it doesn't make any difference and some guy tried to jump me after our date last night." And what am I supposed to say to her?

I know?

You'll get used to it?

No. Today is her second birthday and she has made me see fresh this two-tiered world, a world that, despite all our nonsense about post-feminism, continues to offer less respect and less opportunity for women than it does for men. My friends and I have learned to live with it, but my little girl deserves better. She has given me my anger back, and I intend to use it well.

That is her gift to me today. Some birthday I will return it to her, 15 because she is going to need it.

❖ Focused Freewriting   Consider as possible focal points Quindlen's litany of the remaining obstacles women face, the anger that infuses the selection, or one of the topics you've identified in your journal.

❖ Guided Responses

1. What do you think Quindlen means by the last two sentences of paragraph 2: "Life goes on. Where's your sense of humor?" Who is asking about a sense of humor? Of whom is the question asked? What would Quindlen's response to the question be?

2. Why does the birth of her daughter cause Quindlen to see "the glass half empty" (para. 4)? Why had she been able to live with inequity prior to her daughter's birth?

3. How do you react to the telescope metaphor in paragraph 7? How is it that Quindlen considers "a sense of proportion" as the opposite of "reality"? Do you agree with her assessment? Why, or why not?

4. Why does Quindlen consider anger a gift (paras. 14–15)? How do you think she intends to use this anger? Do you consider such anger a good or a bad thing? Explain your response.

❖ Shared Responses   In your journal respond to Quindlen's statement, "Role models are women who exist—and are photographed often—to make other women feel better about the fact that there aren't really enough of us anywhere, except in the lowest-paying jobs" (para. 9). Using your reading and your own experience, explain why you agree or disagree with this statement. As you discuss your responses in small groups, try to determine the influence of gender and personal experience on members' responses.

———— ❖ ————

PBQ:The Professional
Beauty Qualification

NAOMI WOLF

NAOMI WOLF *began studying beauty when she was at Oxford University on a Rhodes Scholarship. Her best-selling book,* The Beauty Myth: How Images of Beauty Are Used Against Women *(1991) developed from her thesis. After writing the book, Wolf claims, "I'm much less interested in the mirror than I used to be." In this selection, excerpted from* The Beauty Myth, *Wolf exposes the origins of what she considers a new requirement of physical attractiveness that has evolved as women enter traditionally male occupations. According to Wolf, standards of beauty previously reserved for "display professions" (e.g., dancers, models, escorts) are now being applied to women in most professions.*

Before reading the selection, explore in your journal your feelings about the emphasis on physical beauty in women. Do you think such an emphasis is a compliment to women? an insult? Do you think society applies a "double standard" of attractiveness to men and women? Explain your response.

As you make notes on your reading, you may want to focus on Wolf's use of statistics, her focus on a few prominent women, or her analysis of "beauty" as a concept.

WHERE DID THE PBQ BEGIN? It evolved, like the beauty myth itself, alongside women's emancipation, and radiates outward to accompany women's professional enfranchisement. It spreads, with women's professionalization, out of American and Western European cities into smaller towns; from the First World to the Third World; and West to East. With the Iron Curtain drawn back, we are due to see an acceleration of its effects in the Eastern bloc countries. Its epicenter is Manhattan, where many of the women who have risen highest in the professional hierarchies are concentrated.

It started in the 1960s as large numbers of educated middle-class young women began to work in cities, living alone, between graduation and marriage. A commercial sexualized mystique of the airline stewardess, the model, and the executive secretary was promoted simultaneously. The young working woman was blocked into a stereotype that used beauty to undermine both the seriousness of the work that she was doing and the implications of her new independence. Helen Gurley Brown's 1962 best seller, *Sex and the Single Girl*, was a survival map for negotiating this independence. But its title became a catchphrase in which the first term canceled out the second. The working single girl had to be seen as "sexy" so that her work, and her singleness, would not look like what they really were: serious, dangerous, and seismic. If the working girl was sexy, her sexiness had to make her work look ridiculous, because soon the girls were going to become women.

In June 1966 the National Organization for Women was founded in America, and that same year its members demonstrated against the firing of stewardesses at the age of thirty-two and upon marriage. In 1967 the Equal Employment Opportunity Commission began to hold hearings on sex discrimination. New York women invaded the Plaza Hotel's all-male Oak Room in February 1969. In 1970, *Time* and *Newsweek* were charged with sex discrimination, and twelve TWA stewardesses filed a multimillion-dollar action against the airline. Consciousness-raising groups began to form. Women who had been politicized as students entered the job market, determined to make women's issues, rather than antiwar and free speech issues, their priority.

Away from the ferment, but well informed by it, law was quietly being made. In 1971, a judge sentenced a woman to lose three pounds a week or go to prison. In 1972, "beauty" was ruled to be something that could legally gain or lose women their jobs: The New York State Human Rights Appeals Board determined, in *St. Cross v. Playboy Club of New York,* that in one highly visible profession, a woman's "beauty" was a bona fide qualification for employment.

Margarita St. Cross was a Playboy Club waitress fired "because   5
she had lost her Bunny Image." The club's employment standards ranked waitresses on the following scale:

1. A flawless beauty (face, figure, and grooming)
2. An exceptionally beautiful girl
3. Marginal (is aging or has developed a correctable appearance problem)
4. Has lost Bunny Image (either through aging or an uncorrectable appearance problem)

St. Cross's male counterparts who did the same work in the same place were "not subjected to appraisals of any kind."

Margarita St. Cross asked the board to decide that she was still beautiful enough to keep her job, having reached, she said, a "physiological transition from that youthful fresh, pretty look to the womanly look, mature." Hefner's spokesmen told the board that she was not. The board reached its decision through taking Hefner's word over St. Cross's—by assuming that the employer is by definition more credible about a woman's beauty than is the woman herself: that that evaluation was "well within the competence" of the Playboy Club to decide.

They did not give weight to St. Cross's expertise about what constitutes "Bunny Image." In ordinary employment disputes, the employer tries to prove that the employee deserved to be fired, while the employee tries to prove that he or she deserves to keep the job. When "beauty" is the BFOQ,[1] though, a woman can say she's doing her job, her employer can say she isn't, and, with this ruling, the employer automatically wins.

The Appeals Board identified in its ruling a concept that it called "standards of near perfection." In a court of law, to talk about something imaginary as if it is real *makes it real.* Since 1971, the law has recognized that a standard of perfection against which a woman's body is to be judged may exist in the workplace, and that if she falls short of it, she may be fired. A "standard of perfection" for the male body has never been legally determined in the same way. While defined as materially existing, the female standard itself has never been defined. This case lay the foundations of the legal maze into which the PBQ would evolve: A woman can be fired for not looking right, but looking right remains open to interpretation.

Gloria Steinem has said, "All women are Bunnies." The St. Cross   10 case was to resonate as an allegory of the future: Though "beauty" is arguably necessary for a Bunny to do a good job, that *concept* of female employment was adapted generally as the archetype for all women on the job. The truth of Steinem's comment deepened throughout the next two decades, wherever women tried to get and hold on to paid work.

In 1971 a prototype of *Ms.* magazine appeared. In 1972 the Equal Employment Opportunity Act was passed in the United States; Title IX outlawed sex discrimination in education. By 1972, 20 percent of management positions in America were held by women. In 1975, Catherine McDermott had to sue the Xerox Corporation because they

---

[1] "Bona Fide Occupational Qualification," a legal term. [ed.]

withdrew a job offer on the grounds of her weight. The seventies saw
women streaming into the professions in a way that could no longer
be dismissed as intermittent or casual or secondary to their primary
role as wives and mothers. In 1978 in the United States, one sixth of
the master of business administration candidates and one fourth of
graduating accountants were women. National Airlines fired stewardess Ingrid Fee because she was "too fat"—four pounds over the
line. In 1977 Rosalynn Carter and two former first ladies spoke at the
Houston convention of NOW. In 1979 the National Women's Business
Enterprise Policy was created to support women's businesses; that
very year a federal judge ruled that employers had the right to set
appearance standards. By the new decade, United States government
policy decreed that the working woman must be taken seriously, and
the law decreed that her appearance must be taken seriously. The
political function of the beauty myth is evident in the timing of these
case laws. It was not until women crowded the public realm that laws
proliferated about appearance in the workplace.

What must this creature, the serious professional woman, look
like?

Television journalism vividly proposed its answer. The avuncular
male anchor was joined by a much younger female newscaster with a
professional prettiness level.

That double image—the older man, lined and distinguished,
seated beside a nubile, heavily made-up female junior—became the
paradigm for the relationship between men and women in the workplace. Its allegorical force was and is pervasive: The qualification of
professional prettiness, intended at first to sweeten the unpleasant
fact of a woman assuming public authority, took on a life of its own,
until professional beauties were hired to be made over into TV journalists. By the 1980s, the agents who headhunted anchors kept their
test tapes under categories such as "Male Anchors: 40 to 50," with no
corresponding category for women, and ranked women anchors'
physical appearance above their delivery skills or their experience.

The message of the news team, not hard to read, is that a powerful   15
man is an individual, whether that individuality is expressed in asym-
metrical features, lines, gray hair, hairpieces, baldness, bulbousness,
tubbiness, facial tics, or a wattled neck; and that his maturity is part
of his power. If a single standard were applied equally to men as to
women in TV journalism, most of the men would be unemployed. But
the women beside them need youth and beauty to enter the same
soundstage. Youth and beauty, covered in solid makeup, present the
anchorwoman as generic—an "anchorclone," in the industry's slang.
What is generic is replaceable. With youth and beauty, then, the work-

ing woman is visible, but insecure, made to feel her qualities are not unique. But, without them, she is invisible—she falls, literally, "out of the picture."

The situation of women in television simultaneously symbolizes and reinforces the professional beauty qualification in general: Seniority does not mean prestige but erasure—of TV anchors over forty, 97 percent, claims anchorwoman Christine Craft, are male and "the other 3% are fortyish women who don't look their age." Older anchorwomen go through "a real nightmare," she wrote, because soon they won't be "pretty enough to do the news anymore." Or if an anchorwoman is "beautiful," she is "constantly harassed as the kind of person who had gotten her job solely because of her looks."

The message was finalized: The most emblematic working women in the West could be visible if they were "beautiful," even if they were bad at their work; they could be good at their work and "beautiful" and therefore visible, but get no credit for merit; or they could be good and "unbeautiful" and therefore invisible, so their merit did them no good. In the last resort, they could be as good and as beautiful as you please—for too long; upon which, aging, they disappeared. This situation now extends throughout the workforce.

That double standard of appearance for men and women communicated itself every morning and every night to the nations of working women, whenever they tried to plug in to the events of "their" world. Their window on historical developments was framed by their own dilemma. To find out what is going on in the world always involves the reminder to women that *this* is going on in the world.

In 1983, working women received a decisive ruling on how firmly the PBQ was established, and how far it could legally go. The thirty-six-year-old Craft filed suit against her ex-employers, Metromedia Inc., at Kansas City on the charge of sex discrimination. She had been dismissed on the grounds that, as Christine Craft quotes her employer, she was "too old, too unattractive, and not deferential to men."

Her dismissal followed months of PBQ demands made on her   20 time and on her purse in breach of her contract, and offensive to her sense of self. She was subjected to fittings and makeovers by the hour and presented with a day-by-day chart of clothing that she would not have chosen herself and for which she was then asked to pay. None of her male colleagues had to do those things. Testimony from other anchorwomen showed that they had felt forced to quit due to Metromedia's "fanatical obsession" with their appearance.

Other women were assigned to cover the trial. Craft was humiliated by her colleagues on camera. One suggested she was a lesbian; Diane Sawyer (who, six years later, when she won a six-figure salary, would have her appearance evaluated on *Time*'s cover with the head-line IS SHE WORTH IT?) asked Craft on a national news broadcast if she really was " 'unique among women' in [her] lack of appearance skills." Her employers had counted on going unchallenged because of the reaction such discrimination commonly instills in the victim of it: a shame that guarantees silence. But "Metromedia," she wrote defi-antly, "was wrong if they thought a woman would never admit to having been told she was ugly."

Her account proves how this discrimination seeps in where others cannot reach, poisoning the private well from which self-esteem is drawn: "Though I may have dismissed intellectually the statement that I was too unattractive, nonetheless in the core of my psyche I felt that something about my face was difficult, if not monstrous, to be-hold. It's hard to be even mildly flirtatious when you're troubled by such a crippling point of view." An employer can't prove an employee incompetent simply by announcing that she is. But because "beauty" lives so deep in the psyche, where sexuality mingles with self-esteem, and since it has been usefully defined as something that is continually bestowed from the outside and can always be taken away, to tell a woman she is ugly can make her feel ugly, act ugly, and, as far as her experience is concerned, *be* ugly, in the place where feeling beautiful keeps her whole.

No woman is so beautiful—by definition—that she can be confi-dent of surviving a new judicial process that submits the victim to an ordeal familiar to women from other trials: looking her up and down to see how what happened to her is her own fault. Since there is nothing "objective" about beauty, the power elite can, whenever nec-essary, form a consensus to strip "beauty" away. To do that to a woman publicly from a witness stand is to invite all eyes to confirm her ugliness, which then becomes the reality that all can see. This process of legal coercion ensures that a degrading public spectacle can be enacted at her expense against any woman in any profession if she charges discrimination by beauty.

The moral of the Christine Craft trial was that she lost: Though two juries found for her, a male judge overturned their rulings. She seems to have been blacklisted in her profession as a result of her legal fight. Has her example affected other women in her profession? "There are thousands of Christine Crafts," one woman reporter told me. "We keep silent. Who can survive a blacklist?"

Defenders of Judge Stevens's ruling justified it on the grounds   25 that it was not sex discrimination but market logic. If an anchor-per-son doesn't bring in the audiences, he or she has not done a good job. The nugget hidden here as it was applied to women—bring in audiences, sales, clients, or students *with her "beauty"*—has become the legacy of the Craft case for working women everywhere.

The outcome of the trial was one of those markers in the 1980s that a woman may have witnessed, and felt as a tightening around the neck, and knew she had to keep still about. When she read the summation, she knew that she had to distance herself from her knowledge of how much she was Christine Craft. She might have reacted by starting a new diet, or buying expensive new clothes, or scheduling an eyelift. Consciously or not, though, she probably reacted; the profession of "image consultant" grew eightfold over the decade. Women and work and "beauty" outside the sex professions fused on the day Craft lost her case, and a wider cycle of diseases was initiated. It will not, the woman might have told herself, happen to me.

It could and did continue to happen to working women as the law bolstered employers with a series of Byzantine rulings that ensured that the PBQ grew ever more resilient as a tool of discrimination. The law developed a tangle of inconsistencies in which women were paralyzed: While one ruling, *Miller* v. *Bank of America,* confused sexual attraction with sexual harassment and held that the law has no part to play in employment disputes that centered on it ("attractiveness," the court decided, being a "natural sex phenomenon" which "plays at least a subtle part in most personnel decisions," and, as such, the court shouldn't delve into such matters"), the court in another case, *Barnes* v. *Costle,* concluded that if a woman's unique physical characteristics—red hair, say, or large breasts—were the reasons given by her employer for sexual harassment, then her personal appearance was the issue and not her gender, in which case she could not expect protection under Title VII of the 1964 Civil Rights Act. With these rulings a woman's beauty became at once her job and her fault.

United States law developed to protect the interests of the power structure by setting up a legal maze in which the beauty myth blocks each path so that no woman can "look right" and win. St. Cross lost her job because she was too "old" and too "ugly"; Craft lost hers because she was too "old," too "ugly," "unfeminine," and didn't dress right. This means, a woman might think, that the law will treat her fairly in employment disputes if only she does her part, looks pretty, and dresses femininely.

She would be dangerously wrong, though. Let's look at an American working woman standing in front of her wardrobe, and imagine the disembodied voice of legal counsel advising her on each choice as she takes it out on its hanger.

"Feminine, then," she asks, "in reaction to the Craft decision?" 30

"You'd be asking for it. In 1986, Mechelle Vinson filed a sex discrimination case in the District of Columbia against her employer, the
Meritor Savings Bank, on the grounds that her boss had sexually
harassed her, subjecting her to fondling, exposure, and rape. Vinson
was young and 'beautiful' and carefully dressed. The district court
ruled that her appearance counted against her: Testimony about her
'provocative' dress could be heard to decide whether her harassment
was 'welcome.' "

"Did she dress provocatively?"

"As her counsel put it in exasperation, 'Mechelle Vinson wore
clothes.' Her beauty in her clothes was admitted as evidence to prove
that she welcomed rape from her employer."

"Well, feminine, but not too feminine, then."

"Careful: In *Hopkins* v. *Price-Waterhouse*, Ms. Hopkins was denied   35
a partnership because she needed to learn to 'walk more femininely,
talk more femininely, dress more femininely,' and 'wear makeup.' "

"Maybe she didn't deserve a partnership?"

"She brought in the most business of any employee."

"Hmm. Well, maybe a little more feminine."

"Not so fast. Policewoman Nancy Fahdl was fired because she
looked 'too much like a lady.' "

"All right, less feminine. I've wiped off my blusher."   40

"You can lose your job if you don't wear makeup. See *Tamini* v.
Howard Johnson Company, Inc."

"How about this, then, sort of . . . womanly?"

"Sorry. You can lose your job if you dress like a woman. In *Andre*
v. *Bendix Corporation*, it was ruled 'inappropriate for a supervisor' of
women to dress like 'a woman.' "

"What am I supposed to do? Wear a sack?"

"Well, the women in *Buren* v. *City of East Chicago* had to 'dress to   45
cover themselves from neck to toe' because the men at work were
'kind of nasty.' "

"Won't a dress code get me out of this?"

"Don't bet on it. In *Diaz* v. *Coleman*, a dress code of short skirts was
set by an employer who allegedly sexually harassed his female employees because they complied with it."

It would be funny if it weren't true.

❖ Focused Freewriting   Consider as possible focal points the contradictory images in paragraph 11, the importance of the Christine
Craft case, the psychological impact of the PBQ, or one of the topics
you've identified in your journal.

❖ Guided Responses

1. Wolf quotes Gloria Steinem as saying, "All women are Bunnies" (para. 10). Based on your reading of this selection, in what ways is this statement accurate? How does Steinem's statement underscore the significance of the female "standard of perfection" (para. 9)?

2. According to Wolf, "the paradigm for the relationship between men and women in the workplace" is the image of news co-anchors, "the older man, lined and distinguished, seated beside a nubile, heavily made-up female junior" (para. 14). Based on your familiarity with regional and national anchors, is Wolf's characterization of them accurate? Explain your response. In what ways does the news-anchor situation reflect male-female roles in the workplace?

3. Explain in your own words the psychological toll the PBQ can take on women (para. 22). Do you agree with Christine Craft that being publicly declared not attractive enough is psychologically "crippling"? Why, or why not?

4. The selection ends with an imaginary conversation between a woman and her attorney contemplating what the woman should wear to work. What is the effect of presenting this material in dialogue form? How would the impact change if Wolf had simply related this information as she did her other examples?

❖ Shared Responses   In your journal apply the PBQ to male news anchors. Prepare a list of qualifications based on age, physical attractiveness, dress, and other relevant factors. How many existing anchors would fit your requirements? As you discuss your responses in small groups, try to explain why the requirements for males and females in public positions are so different.

Don't Tell

LAURA MANSNERUS

LAURA MANSNERUS *is an attorney who writes on issues of education and law for the* New York Times. *She is particularly concerned with the status of women in the work force. In this essay, which originally appeared in the "Hers" column of the* New York Times Magazine, *Mansnerus argues that women who remain silent about sexual harassment are simply preserving their positions. For a woman to do anything else, says Mansnerus, could amount to professional suicide.*

Before reading the selection, write in your journal about your response to the Anita Hill-Clarence Thomas hearings. How did you respond to Hill's testimony at the time? Has your view changed with the passage of time? Explain your responses.

As you make notes on your reading, you may want to focus on the author's alternating between discussion of Anita Hill's case and generalizations about the appeals process.

SOMETIMES DISCRIMINATION ANNOUNCES ITSELF like pie in the face to the most wide-eyed young workers. I know this from a talk I had 18 years ago with the executive editor of the first newspaper I worked for. I made an appointment with the busy man and asked if he thought I could ever move from copy editing into a reporting job. He called for the results of the battery of tests I'd taken as a job applicant, he frowned over them and then he said no. A machine-scored personality profile, which he helpfully posed in front of me to let me see that science compelled his answer, showed that I was much too female a type to work as a reporter for him.

So much for my career plans. The news was a surprise (Nurturing and compliant? Me?), a non sequitur and an insult, and it looked like a violation of the employment-discrimination laws. So what did I do? I chatted up the editor at the press club. At parties, I pasted on a smile of rapt interest in his anecdotes. With my boyfriend of the moment, a protégé of the editor—bad coincidence—I went to dinner at the editor's apartment and surely said, "Wonderful to see you." The man was widely loathed, but no one, except the poor boyfriend, heard a word of grievance from me; I was as sweet as the test said I was. A year later, after I'd quit to take a job that then evaporated, I wrote the editor a warm, ingratiating letter asking him to take me back. His response left the door open, but fortunately another job materialized.

I demonstrated a complete failure of moral resolve. Nearly two decades later, having held many other jobs, having become a lawyer, having seen the sex-discrimination laws evolve and having watched the United States Senate recently consider an account of sexual harassment from the most impeccable witness that a plaintiff's lawyer could invent, I know I did the right thing.

Now, I haven't suffered degradation; the sexual advances I've received from superiors have consisted mostly of peculiar remarks from guys who were stranded in the era of pledge formals and hope chests. But I had plenty of answers for the senators and witnesses who demanded to know about Anita Hill: Why didn't she report these incidents? Why didn't she take notes? Why did she continue to speak highly of Clarence Thomas? Why did she follow him into another job?

One answer is that in trying to patch up the humiliations of daily life, you probably do not consult the rules of evidence, even if you're a lawyer, expecting that someday you'll have to explain any lapses in strategy to Senator Specter. Another is that your tormentor can also be your friend, which might or might not stop you from telling the truth if the F.B.I. comes around 10 years later to ask what it was like to work for him.   5

But the easiest answer is that a young woman who brings enthusiasm and hope to a job is going to try, sometimes with heartbreaking docility, to get along. And nobody likes a tattletale. We know now that the uglier the tale, the more savage the raking that the victim gets. But we knew all along that to squeal on one's mentor, or even one's boss, is an idiotic thing to do. (You'd think a senator wouldn't have any trouble understanding that proposition.)

A tattletale is by definition a weakling who asks for intervention, which is exactly what the grievance procedures available to workers are all about. The laws and company policies and sensitivity-training seminars are supposed to aid victims and whiners, and that's why the authorities are just as happy that they don't work.

Begin with the Equal Employment Opportunity Commission: last year it received about 33,000 sex-discrimination complaints and filed suit in 197 cases. For a woman who is somehow able to retain her own lawyer—and the plaintiff, incidentally, has typically already been fired—the odds are better, but not by much.

Legislated remedies are fine. They're absolutely necessary. And Congress is stunningly proud of itself for this year's Civil Rights Act, which liberalizes the rules in job-discrimination cases, in ways that a worker can understand if she is also a civil rights lawyer. But most people, civil rights lawyers included, can understand that sworn accusations, discovery motions and depositions are going to have a horrifying effect around the office. Even a discreet inquiry by the company's Human Resources Department will mark the complainer as, well, a complainer—and probably, eventually, as a loser too.

What of the view that the woman who speaks up is a fighter   10
rather than a whiner? Well, it's something you might believe if you're very young or extraordinarily aggressive. But fights take place between adversaries, not between the boss man and a pesky underling. That Anita Hill emerged from the hearings without looking like a perpetually kayoed cartoon character is testament to a dignity that most people don't have.

It's clear that the senators didn't view Professor Hill, who found none among them inclined to be combative on her behalf, as an actual challenge to Clarence Thomas. After all, they were themselves cowed by Clarence Thomas. Would anybody be cowed by Anita Hill? At best the senators were oily and patronizing.

At worst, of course, they blithely slandered her which is usually the case when the charge is the kind that would upset the accused's wife. Delusion and vindictiveness are handy explanations, easier and at the same time more cruel to the aggrieved woman than the traditional defense of calling her a slut.

So I look at my own little potential sex-discrimination case from 1973. Suppose I had lodged a complaint. I would not have been cross-examined by Orrin Hatch. I would not have had to watch some preening egomaniac I'd spoken to at a party appear on national television to accuse me of romantic fantasizing. No one would have suggested that I'd asked for whatever was said to me. Not at all. As a union member, I probably wouldn't have lost my boring job. But I wouldn't have got another one, at that newspaper or any other, and that seems like enough of a deterrent to me.

Anita Hill, law professor, said hesitantly to her questioners that in declining to invoke the legal process she might have used poor judgment. No, no, no. The 25-year-old who shut up proceeded with a recommendation and no muss or fuss to a university teaching job. Now she has tenure. Her judgment was dead on.

❖ Focused Freewriting Consider as possible focal points Mansnerus's characterization of the Senate Committee, the relevance of her own personal experience, or one of the topics you've identified in your journal.

❖ Guided Responses

1. How can Mansnerus call her decision to remain friendly with her editor at once "a complete failure of moral resolve" and "the right thing" to do (para. 3)? Do you agree with her assessment of the situation? Why, or why not?

2. Mansnerus's response to those who questioned Anita Hill's initial silence is tinged with sarcasm (para. 5). Why do you think the author phrased her response sarcastically instead of offering a straightforward answer? What does her tone indicate about her attitude toward Hill's questioners?

3. Workers with grievances often fail to go public, according to Mansnerus, because a "tattletale is by definition a weakling" (para. 7). Later, in paragraph 10, she characterizes a grievance as a fight "between the boss man and a pesky underling." In your opinion, how accurate is her assessment of the grievance procedure? Do bosses have such an advantage over subordinates that to file a grievance is "an idiotic thing to do" (para. 6)? Explain your response.

4. How convincing do you find Mansnerus's final paragraph? Why do you think she ends the piece with the words "dead on"?

❖ Shared Responses

In your journal respond to the following question: Where do you think Anita Hill would be today if she had filed and lost a grievance against Clarence Thomas? What difference would it have made had she won? In either case, would she have achieved the prestigious appointment she now holds? Explain your reasoning. As you discuss your responses in small groups, try to determine how far these have been influenced by individuals' attitudes toward Hill.

This Spring (Mama Changes the Oil)

LINDA SHARRON

LINDA SHARRON, *a 4.0 graduate of Fitchburg (Massachusetts) State College, won numerous prizes during her college career, including the Matti N. Antila Poetry Prize, the Massachusetts Women in Higher Education Achievement Award, and varsity letters in cross-country, indoor and outdoor track—all as a single parent of six young children. This poem won first prize in the 1992 spring poetry contest sponsored by the Lawrence, Massachusetts,* Eagle Tribune. *The deeply felt connection between family members is illustrated in Sharron's story of how the poem came to be finished: Stuck without an ending, she read the poem to her comatose father, whose subsequent smile inspired the opening lines of the last stanza. His recollection of her visit? He dreamed that an angel was asking him for help and laughed at the thought. He awoke from his coma the next morning, and a poem was born. (Sharron's father has since died of cancer.)*

Before reading the selection, write in your journal about your own sense of relationships between fathers and daughters, mothers and sons. What distinguishes these from other relationships?

As you make notes on your reading, you may want to focus on Sharron's use of ordinary images or her straightforward language.

The underbelly of this van splays above me
Like an open fish. My kids are scrimmaging in the sun—
What fun! But all I see is eye-level grass
(Most of it dead, but some straight as swords)
Little carriage-wheels and low-heeled shoes   5
I'm batting cleanup, with out-of-the-ballpark blues.

Ten years ago, this spring, I strolled around the park
With a nine-month tummy bulge. Where . . . ouch! There,

That's him running by—I recognize his stride.
His nut-brown little brother's still trying   10
To keep his line untangled long enough
To convince a carp that a gumdrop tastes good.

It should. It sure looks better than an oatmeal plug.
I shrug my body back to today's mess
But my arm aches from finagling the wrench   15
Around this stubborn bolt. "Just unscrew it,"
He said as he quit my life, "it's easy." Yeah,
It's always easy 'til you have to do it.

A gang of crows talks off to my left.
One coughs on a cigarette butt, kicks   20
The habit and buzzes off, startling a pair
Of smoochers from their blanket. My eyes fill
And my cheek smarts against the asphalt as
I release the greasy bolt with a final tug.

And the drain-plug clinks in the pit of the waiting pan.   25
Oil runs thick over my knuckles. Dark. Sweet.
Sudden as menses. Soon, from the corner of my eye
I see a fluttering, hear a yipe and know
It's my boy. From what I can see, he's
Bringing a fish into the world—a big one.   30

"Carpe carp!" I scuttle through the grit
For a good view, sunnyside up, where I see
The tops of things; the people atop those legs
Stop to crane with me at my kid's luck
He's smiling hard, distancing the line as the fish   35
Flops like it's already being pan-fried.

And I smile the same smile, my Daddy's smile
As I hoist the drain-pan high: to the future joy
Of blanket-kisses, a man who's truelove loyal
Of each spring day, bright as a brand-new toy   40
Of tummy bulges, ball games, easier oil
Changes, and that little fishing boy.

❖ Focused Freewriting   Consider as possible focal points the difficulties of a single mother's life, the pride the narrator takes in her boys, her self-sufficiency, or one of the topics you've identified in your journal.

❖ Guided Responses

1. Sharron's opening sentence is rather startling: "The underbelly of this van splays above me/Like an open fish." How do the images of belly, van, and fish function throughout the poem? How do you interpret the images individually? How do they work together?

2. How do you interpret the lines "Just unscrew it,"/He said as he quit my life, "it's easy"? What might be their literal meaning? How do they fit into the meaning of the poem?

3. When she finally unscrews the bolt, Sharron likens the flow of oil to menstruation. Later in the stanza, she refers to her son's "Bringing a fish into the world." Why do you think she uses these images of reproduction? How do they relate to other such images in the poem?

4. Describe in your own words what is happening in the final stanza. Why do you think Sharron chooses to list these particular images? How do they pull the entire poem together? Why do you think she's so optimistic at the end?

❖ Shared Responses   In your journal rewrite this episode in paragraph form, explaining images where necessary. What is gained in the translation? What is lost? How does this exercise help you understand poetic form? As you discuss your responses in small groups, highlight the different interpretations of images among group members.

❖

Enero

MARY HELEN PONCE

MARY HELEN PONCE, *whose real name is Merrihelen Ponce, has taught Chicana literature at the University of New Mexico in Albuquerque. She currently teaches in the Chicano studies program at the University of California at Santa Barbara. This story, written for her mother, was first published in* The Graywolf Annual Seven: Stories from the American Mosaic *(1990), edited by Scott Walker. In the story Ponce takes the reader through a day in the life of a proud, hard-working woman. While Constancia makes her way through the myriad household tasks that await her attention, she ponders the significance of the new life growing insider her, even as her first child lies dying in a sanatorium.*

Before reading the selection, discuss in your journal your perception of a homemaker's role. What are her responsibilities? How is her family dependent on her? Why is her work undervalued in this society?

As you make notes on your reading, you may want to focus on Constancia's many duties, the direction her thoughts take, or Ponce's description of her main character.

"THE BABY," *la doctora* said, her wide hands pressing lightly on Constancia's protruding belly, "will be born in January. Uh, *Ineerio?*"

"*Sí, Enero.*" Constancia smiled up into the pleasant face of *la Doctora* Greene, then slowly raised her thick body to an upright position. In the clean, uncluttered bedroom the window curtains danced in the morning breeze and cooled Constancia's warm brow. She adjusted her underclothes, smoothed the bedsheet, then sat quietly on a chair, waiting for Doctor Greene to leave.

Constancia felt tired, lethargic. But my day is only half over, she told herself, smoothing down her dark hair. She sat, watching Doctor Greene, who with her customary efficiency, packed the worn stethoscope into her scruffy black bag, jammed a brown felt hat atop her head, and then, in her sensible brown shoes with the wide heels hurried down the porch steps and to her car. Her crisp cotton dress crinkling at the waist, Constancia stood watching the dusty 1938 Dodge as it went past, Doctor Greene at the wheel. On sudden impulse she leaned over the porch railing, her swollen stomach straining, to snap off a pink rambling rose from a nearby bush. She held the dewy soft flower to her nose and inhaled. The sweet fragrance made her dizzy, yet happy. She thought back to what *la doctora* had predicted. *Enero*. It would be a winter baby after all! The first of her ten children to be born in January, during cold weather. The others, born in spring, summer, and early fall, she remembered, had had a chance to thrive before the mild California weather turned cold. She sighed: *Enero*, the first month of the New Year—a month full of promise. *Enero*, the month when winter roses bloomed.

Across the street Constancia spotted a neighbor and waved, the flower clutched in her hand. At thirty-eight Constancia was still a pretty woman. Her olive face was unlined; the black, wavy hair slightly gray. She, like other women in the Mexican neighborhood, spent her days cooking, cleaning, and caring for a large family. She washed on Mondays, ironed on Tuesdays, and each Sunday cooked a pot of stew for supper. Unlike some of her friends, Constancia was not overly religious, although she made certain the children attended catechism and Sunday Mass, and, during Lent, took part in the *Via Crucis*.

She took pride in her clean appearance, knowing that Americans 5 looked down on "dirty" Mexicans who lived in the barrio. She never left the house without first washing her face and combing her hair. She seldom wore an apron without washing it, and wore cotton stockings all year round, even in summer. She disliked wearing the maternity smocks stored in a box under the bed. Throughout her pregnancies she wore starched cotton dresses until her expanded waist literally burst the seams; then she retrieved the cardboard box under the bed, dusted the full-blown cotton smocks, and rinsed and ironed them. They hung in the small closet until the last months.

Constancia no longer tried to guess her unborn child's birth date—or sex. After the first two—a boy and a girl—it no longer mattered, or so she told herself. What did matter was that this baby be healthy, she conceded—healthy and strong enough to fight disease. She leaned against the railing, took a deep breath of the cool October air, pushed a lock of hair off her face, then went indoors.

In the roomy kitchen, Constancia pulled open a drawer where aprons lay next to snowy dish towels, took one, then slowly tied the flowered apron around her extended belly and began to work. She felt sleepy. The night before, the stirrings of the unborn baby, the rain that hit against the window, and thoughts of Apollonia, her eldest daughter, had kept her awake. Try as she might, she could not close her eyes without seeing the thin, pale face of her tubercular daughter.

The day before, a warm Sunday of blue skies and white clouds, had been busy. Getting the children washed, fed, and then dressed in their good clothes for the short walk to church was a chore. Gabriela, the baby, had fussed at being left behind by the older kids, and had to be held for a time. Aware of the children's disapproval, a stubborn Constancia had forgone Sunday Mass. I'm not in a mood to pray to alabaster saints, or sing hymns of hope and praise, she decided. Nor do I want to squeeze myself into my "good" maternity dress (bought at J. C. Penney). While Gabriela napped, Constancia prepared for the visit to Apollonia. Once the children returned she fed them the usual Sunday fare: *cocido,* stewing beef with carrots, potatoes, and onions. While the older girls washed and rinsed dishes, she packed a bar of Palmolive soap, chewing gum, and lemon drops into a small carton; then, with Justo at her side and Felicitas in the back seat, they drove to visit Apollonia. Later that evening, when they returned, Constancia felt tired and depressed.

But today is another day, she sighed, pushing aside the kitchen curtains to stare out the window, and I must finish my work. She rinsed the breakfast dishes left soaking in the sink, dried them, and put them away in the cupboard above the linoleum-covered counter. *Enero.* Three months left to visit at will the sanatorium where Apollonia, now almost eighteen, lay dying of tuberculosis. Three months to cope with the pain of knowing Apollonia would not live past Easter Sunday. Three months to make arrangements for the inevitable funeral—and to prepare for the child that was coming.

Apollonia, the serious, sulky child born to them in Mexico, had   10
been in the sanatorium close to three years. When in elementary school she was diagnosed with pleurisy, then later with tuberculosis. Soon after, she was sent to a nearby sanatorium. At first her condition had improved. Her youth, and the daily rest and medication, had arrested the fever, but the raspy, dry cough remained. The experimental surgery and the latest drugs have not helped my daughter, Constancia often thought, trying not to be bitter. Last month Apollonia had been moved to the infirmary reserved for critical cases. Two operations had failed to cure her; her weight had recently dropped. She was close to death.

The visit on Sunday had been especially trying. Constancia shivered as she remembered holding Apollonia's thin hands, squeezing fingers too weak to squeeze back. Long past visiting hours she had sat next to the sullen Apollonia, plying an embossed ivory comb through Apollonia's limp, curly hair, hoping to cheer her dispirited, pale daughter. But Apollonia, a bright and studious girl, knew she was not getting better, but worse. She refused to smile or eat the oatmeal cookies baked by Felicitas. Her dark eyes, like those of Constancia, shone bright, a sign not of good health but of the fever that was consuming her. When they left the sanatorium, which was surrounded by a grove of lemon trees, the sun was no longer visible. By the time they got home, a light rain was falling. Now, as she wiped the kitchen counter, Constancia thought once more about Doctor Greene's visit that morning. She sighed, thinking: I must prepare for life . . . And death.

Constancia hitched up her dress, then picked up the wicker basket near the zinc tubs in the washroom, *el llavadero*. The small cluttered room adjacent to the kitchen was a repository for dented tubs and empty glass jars. She walked outdoors, her steps slow yet firm, to the clothesline, where *calzones*, shirts, and pants flapped on the line. She laid the basket on the ground, pulled the clothespin bag toward her, then began to take down the clothes. Back and forth between the lines she moved, strong arms glistening in the sunlight. Constancia glanced up at the sky, never so blue, and at the birds darting here and there. With minimum effort she pulled, folded, and stacked the clean dry clothes inside the basket. Her pliant fingers released the wooden clothespins, then placed them in the faded cotton bag. The sun felt warm on her round face, in which the dark eyes, so like Apollonia's, blinked, then focused on a white cloud floating in the cobalt blue sky. *Enero.* In three months the clothesline would hold cotton diapers, and the *zapetas* would be folded in the trunk, Constancia knew. Once more I'll have a child and be forced to stay in bed for a month. One month without seeing Apollonia! How will I bear it? Constancia felt familiar tears sting her eyes. She took a handkerchief from her apron pocket, wiped her troubled eyes, then continued with her work.

It seemed to Constancia that most of her life had been spent caring for children. As a girl in Mexico, she had helped care for Rito and José, her mischievous younger brothers, a job she hated. The boys outshouted and outran her, slung mud and sticks at each other, and chased after the newborn calves. They refused to obey her and, during harvest time, hid in the haystacks piled along the road. She liked best to sit indoors embroidering linens, or to work in the rose garden that was her mother Martina's pride and joy, but she dared not disobey her parents. And now here I am, she thought, pulling at the clothesline, still caring for children, still chasing after boisterous boys who play with sticks and mud. Still, still. Except that unlike my mother, I have nine children who depend on me and, come January, one more baby to care for.

Constancia lingered by the clothesline, resisting the urge to reenter the confines of the house. She stood on tiptoe, her stomach straining from the effort, to inhale the pungent scent of the green leaves on the walnut tree. The tree, planted when they first moved to the roomy house, was as old as Apollonia. Unlike the sickly, pale girl, the walnut tree had taken root in the rich California soil. It now stood tall, with a thick, gnarled trunk and large branches that sprouted glossy, gray green leaves. Around its base small shoots were beginning to show.

By next year the tree would bear fruit, Constancia knew. Round,   15 meaty walnuts for the children to roast, and for the Christmas cookies baked by Felicitas. She inspected the tree, her strong hands caressing the veined leaves, unmindful of the laundry in the basket: socks rolled tight as baseballs, undershirts folded in three equal parts, khaki pants turned inside out—clothes ready for the hot iron. She stood silhouetted against the walnut tree, her stomach round as a watermelon, brown eyes fastened on the fluffy white clouds that drifted across the pale sky.

It was during fall that Constancia most missed her family in Mexico. She vividly remembered the sudden change in weather with the arrival of the harvest months, when she and her sisters worked alongside their mother. During the peak days of the *cosecha*, (the harvest), they cooked *cocido* in the huge cauldrons set atop open fires, and piled high the large wooden tables with steaming platters of frijoles, *sopa,* and baskets of hot tortillas. Each table held an enamel coffeepot which Constancia kept filled with *café,* the strong chicory-flavored coffee preferred by the ranchhands. Providing for the workers in Mexico was hard work, Constancia remembered, frowning slightly, as is caring for a large family. She sighed, looking up at the sky once more. And having to appear cheerful when I feel like crying is most difficult. But, I must persevere. She picked up the basket and heaved it onto her ample hip. I must not give in to misfortune, illness, or despair but persevere, like all the women in my family. At least until *Enero.* I must be strong, for the new baby . . . and for Apollonia.

Don Pedro, her father, was often on Constancia's mind. As *gerente* (general manager) of a large hacienda in Leon, Guanajuato, his job was to see that all went smoothly on the ranch. An intelligent, hard-working man, Don Pedro was responsible for the hiring (and firing) of workers, the harvesting of crops, and the replenishing of stock. More importantly, he kept all the business records and submitted monthly reports to the hacienda owner.

As Constancia folded a worn shirt into the laundry basket, she thought of her father and the many evenings he sat hunched over the kitchen table to enter numbers into the old, dusty ledgers kept on a shelf. With painstaking care he had dipped a quill pen in ink, then entered each transaction into the record. An astute, honest man, don Pedro was known throughout the area for his kindness and integrity.

Constancia sighed, her thoughts on the ranch in Mexico, then slowly picked a clothespin off the ground and put it inside the pin bag.

My mother, too, worked hard, Constancia recalled, pulling at her sweater—very hard. As the ranch manager's wife, doña Martina kept the large house allocated to the manager in perfect order; there was never panic or confusion in that busy household. In addition to caring for a family of seven, her mother, an expert with medicinal herbs, often assisted ranch women during childbirth. Doña Martina also supervised the women at numerous chores connected to the ranch: hauling water, making soap, and wrapping goat cheese in muslin squares. During harvest time when the ranch teemed with men, wagons, and oxen, she was at her best.

When older, Constancia was allowed to deliver lunch baskets to   20
the workers in the fields, where the warm sun and clean air beckoned. She enjoyed being outdoors with girls her own age, aware that the young men in the fields were potential *novios* (suitors). The older girls who already had beaus hid extra tortillas in the baskets for their men. Once lunch was delivered the girls, flushed from the long walk—and from being around the young men—were free to walk around at their leisure. Constancia had roamed the lima bean fields, staring up at the sky and clouds, wondering when Justo would return, when they would marry. She envied her sisters whose *novios* lived nearby, and who chided her for choosing to marry a man who wanted to live *en el otro lado*, "on the other side"—a man who would take her far from her family, her roots.

Yes, we women on the ranch worked hard, Constancia groaned, shaking a creamy yellow towel, and so do women in America. But at least I don't have to make stacks of tortillas every day, although Justo would certainly like that. Still, there's nothing wrong with white bread. The *Americanas* buy it, so why shouldn't I? And besides, she sighed, I've cooked enough in my lifetime. She pulled the laundry basket close, then yanked down a pair of socks with bunched toes, rolled them tight, and tossed them into the wicker basket, her mind still on Mexico.

Harvest time was fun too, Constancia remembered, folding a pillowcase into a perfect square. Large wooden tables were set beneath the cottonwoods that stood like sentinels next to the ranchhouse. There the workers were fed a tasty stew garnished with chiles grown on the ranch. Constancia and her sisters, giggling and smiling, had helped their mother prepare the food. She enjoyed the camaraderie among the workers; both the men and women relished hard work, and the knowledge that they would be well paid. She recalled how the men attacked the food with gusto . . . and smiles of appreciation. She especially liked being assigned to serve the younger men, many of whom shyly looked away when *la hija del patrón* (the boss's daughter) approached. But once Justo asked for her hand—and she accepted his proposal—she stayed behind to help her mother in the kitchen, trying not to pine over the tall, handsome boy she was to marry.

At eighteen, Constancia had married Justo de Paz, a man two years her senior. When seventeen, Justo had emigrated with an uncle to California, where for three years he worked the lemon groves that flourished in the damp, cold town of Ventura. He saved money, spending it only for room and board and an occasional sack of to-bacco. His plan was to return to Mexico, marry, then return to *el norte* accompanied by his bride. He often worked on Saturdays, too. Now and then he went to town with his uncle, but for the most part Justo remained at the ranch to read the Spanish newspaper. Soon he taught himself to write. He wrote to Constancia, the crude letters smudged across the lined paper bought at the five-and-dime. He regaled her with stories of the wonders of her soon-to-be adopted country.

Everyone here owns property, Justo wrote: land, a house . . . and an automobile! I earn more money in the lemon groves than I ever dreamed of. He also described what he perceived as "strange Ameri-can habits." Here everyone brings their lunch to work, he wrote, unlike in Mexico where a rancher feeds his workers. In this country they only give you water, and at times, very little of that. He told of buying a *lonchera* (a tin lunchpail) for his cold tacos. *Aquí todo es diferente*, he noted: "Everything is different." This strange custom, of not feeding workers, was to Constancia appalling; her parents, she knew, took pains to feed the ranchhands. But, Justo insisted, in Amer-ica each man provides his own work gloves, and his own lunch. He posted the letters, counting the days until his return.

When it was agreed she and Justo would marry, Constancia began   25
to make preparations. She accompanied her mother to Silao, a nearby town, to buy a bolt of muslin for the linens she would take to the new country. She and her sisters sewed tablecloths, *servilletas,* and a simple trousseau. Each afternoon they sat beneath the cottonwoods, assorted pins and needles at their sides, to embroider as a flushed Constancia read Justo's letters aloud. Her sisters were impressed with the reports written in large, round letters. Once read, the letters were stored in a cedar chest. The women all agreed: Justo de Paz was indeed a young man with a future. But that was long ago, Constancia now told herself . . . long ago.

Inside the house Constancia removed her sweater, then arranged the folded sheets inside the *patequilla* (the trunk) that years before had accompanied her from Mexico and now stood at the foot of her bed. In it, between sacks of potpourri, dried rose petals wrapped in faded lace, were sheets, doilies, and assorted baby clothes. At the bottom, wrapped in faded tissue paper, was Apollonia's baptism gown, now thin and worn but with the lace intact. Constancia bent down, took out the potpourri, and brought it to her face. The aroma of dusky roses filled the room. She sighed, thinking back to Sunday's visit to Apollonia.

That day, as a surprise for her sister, Felicitas had wrapped dried flowers in a muslin square, sprinkled it with eau de cologne, then tied a bright ribbon around it. When given the packet, Apollonia had plunged her nose into the fragrant flowers, then smiled happily at her mother, who smiled back. But Apollonia will never return to this house, Constancia reminded herself, nor will she walk in the rose garden. She stood, closed the trunk lid, then returned to the kitchen, the smell of roses in her hair.

On warm summer evenings while the older girls washed the supper dishes, Constancia retreated to the rose garden to snip roses and carnations left to dry outdoors next to bay and mint leaves. When ready, the mixture was crushed, then wrapped in pieces of muslin and stored in the linen closet. But, thought Constancia, as she relied her apron, come next year, when carnations bloom once more, Apollonia will be dead.

Now, as she set up the ironing board in the kitchen, Constancia felt the baby kick. She sat down, held a hand to her stomach, and waited, but the baby was quiet. She continued to sit, hoping once more to feel the child inside her. She pulled at her stockings, then slowly stood, spread a starched pillowcase across the board, and began to iron. As she worked, she thought again of what was uppermost in her mind: Apollonia, and, to a lesser degree, the baby due in *Enero*.

As she ironed Justo's shirt, Constancia recalled how upset she had 30
been to discover, early in May, she was once more pregnant. One time the doctors had cautioned her and other neighborhood women not to have so many children. "*No es* good for you!" the good doctor had said, her face agitated. "*No es* good!" And now here I am, Constancia sighed, pregnant with my tenth child. As she grew heavier, and the summer sun became unbearable, the visits to Apollonia tired her more and more. The drive to the sanatorium was neither bumpy nor long and, under different circumstances, it would have been pleasant, what with the orange groves and flowering oleanders along the highway. But Constancia feared catching tuberculosis, the highly contagious disease prevalent among Mexican families. Early on, the public health nurse had instructed her on what precautions to take when visiting Apollonia so as not to endanger the other children—and the unborn

baby. Thereafter, upon returning from the sanatorium, Constancia quickly changed her dress and stockings, washed herself carefully, then, prior to cooking, rinsed her hands with alcohol in a tin basin.

After this baby comes I must remain in bed for six weeks, sighed Constancia, spreading a checkered tablecloth across the ironing board, or at least for a month. And I must try to get someone to help with the children. Justo does his share, and the older girls help with the cooking, but I do not want to burden them with my work. Never will I keep Felicitas home from school to do housework. Never. Yet with each baby I feel more tired, and it takes longer to heal. But until *Enero* I'll visit Apollonia every Sunday, and take her lemonade and cookies.

Once the baby is born, Constancia swore, the iron steady in her hand, Justo and I will have to sleep apart again. It will be difficult for him, she admitted, as she slid the iron across the shirt yoke, but it has to be done. She often heard the neighbor women comment on Justo's slim form, his unwrinkled skin. But, she grumbled, bending to retrieve a fallen handkerchief, I shall insist. Surely Justo will understand how weary I am of childbearing.

Soon after Gabriela's difficult birth, Constancia had claimed the sunny bedroom that looked onto the rose garden as her own. Justo now slept alongside his sons in an adjoining room. In Mexico, Constancia knew, couples who wanted to limit their children followed this custom, one more difficult for men than for women, a thing that created strife in a marriage. And Constancia loved her kind husband, keenly aware that at forty, Justo was still a handsome, virile man.

As the afternoon wore on, Constancia continued with her housework; the pressed clothes covered the kitchen table. She looked out the window, thinking of her mother, and of the subject of birth control. It was rarely discussed on the ranch, even among married women. Her mother had made brief references to couples who slept apart, as did she and her husband. According to *la Iglesia,* doña Martina had intoned, her face a bright pink, any kind of birth control is a mortal sin. However, she concluded, one can always sleep apart. *That* the Church will condone. Constancia had heard her mother proudly note that her children, like those of her own mother, were born three years apart. Anything else was said to be *muy ranchero* (too low class).

Now, as she buttoned Justo's shirts, Constancia felt the baby kick again. She sat, waiting for the incessant kicking that often irritated her. She pressed down on her stomach, but the baby refused to move. With a weary sigh Constancia walked to the stove to stir the beans in the blue enamel pot, then returned to the iron. As she worked she thought back to her cousin Amador's last visit, a visit she sensed had contributed to her pregnancy.

Justo was not a drinking man, although he now and then bought a jug of dago red at an Italian market. The wine was stored in the pantry for company, or special occasions. Constancia hated the taste of alcohol, and stuck the jug behind the oatmeal. Like her mother before her, Constancia feared *el viscio*, the alcoholism said to afflict even the best of families. She remembered well her parents' pain when Lucas, her brother, moved to the city and took to the bottle. The shame still rankled. She knew her father approved of her husband because Justo, an anomaly among his friends, rarely drank. He drank only when her cousin, that rascal Amador, visited.

Amador was Constancia's first cousin, a well-built, fair-skinned, vain man who wore a white Panama hat in summer and a grey fedora in winter. He visited often, accompanied by his sour (and homely) wife and three robust sons. Amador liked to drink. He also liked for everyone else to drink. When he visited in his shiny Ford (with a rumble seat) he brought two things: a jug of wine, and roses for his cousin Constancia. As much as she protested his drinking, Constancia's eyes lit up at the sight of Amador, her handsome, flirtatious cousin who throughout the visit chided Justo for having married the boss's daughter. Within minutes of Amador's arrival, Constancia took to the kitchen to prepare his favorite dish of chicken *molé* while the men sat to talk—and drink dago red. By suppertime Amador's fair skin was flushed red, his caramel brown eyes slightly glazed. After the meal, if the weather was warm, the men sat in the small patio covered with palm fronds to eat *capirotada* (bread pudding made with brown sugar, garnished with raisins and almonds) and drink hot coffee. While Justo and Amador ate dessert and drank coffee from the flowered cups given free with Rinso soap powder, Constancia hid the wine in the pantry, a clear sign that all drinking had come to an end.

In early April Amador had visited and, as usual, polished off a jug of wine. Unable to drive, he asked to remain overnight. Much to Constancia's chagrin, he was given her husband's bed. A smiling Justo returned to the double bed. Soon after Constancia knew she was in the family way. A contrite Justo returned to his solitary bed. His loud snores, he carefully explained, made sleep impossible for his pregnant wife.

Inside the large kitchen a flushed Constancia stirred the beans cooking on the stove. By the time the famished children arrived home from school, she knew, the rosy, plump beans would be ready. The bean soup garnished with tomatoes and onions was especially tasty with hot tortillas, and was a favorite of the children, except for Gabriela, who hated onions.

Although she worked hard, Constancia knew enough to pamper herself. She napped most afternoons, and whenever possible, slept in.   40

She no longer cooked tortillas for each meal. She knew the younger children preferred Weber's bread, bought at the corner store. Lately she was too tired to cook even a few tortillas—Justo now ate bread, too. As she added a limp onion to the beans, Constancia stopped to gaze out the window at the graying sky. It will be cold in *Enero*, she sighed, cold and wet.

She was surprised to see birds darting back and forth outside, small twigs in their beaks. The birds are preparing for winter, Constancia thought—securing nests and storing food. Arms folded across her swollen stomach, she leaned on the window frame, gazing at the clouds.

Her habit of watching cloud formations often irritated Justo.

"Qué tanto miras en las nubes?" he often asked. ("What do you see in the clouds?")

"Nada. Solo me gusta ver para afuera." ("Nothing. I just like to look outdoors.")

The clouds remind me of the ranch in Mexico, she longed to say, and of the lazy summers when I played in the open meadows . . . of when I was free. On sudden impulse, she pushed aside the curtain. The sky above, she noted, was almost as blue as the Mexican sky that long ago hovered over her sisters and her as they walked across grassy meadows, kicking at dirt clods. Evenings at the ranch were spent telling stories, while the overhead sky turned a deep, purplish blue. When of late Constancia gazed at the sky, Justo said nothing.

Inside the large kitchen Constancia slowly moved, aware of the baby pushing against her ribs. She wandered outdoors, to the rosebush that bloomed from early summer to late fall, adjusted her cotton dress, then squatted on her bare knees. The soil felt cold and damp against her warm skin. She pulled the dry leaves off the rose plant, then bent low to get at the shoots sprouting at the base. This bush cannot grow with these small suckers, she grumbled, her hands coated with mud. They take the nourishment needed by the plant to grow. If I get rid of them the roses will bloom much bigger, and prettier. Still, I must cover them at night, or the frost will kill them. She remained in the quiet garden, her round form bent low, until Gabriela, in need of a bottle, called her; then she reluctantly went indoors.

Later that evening, as she cleared the crude table made years ago by Justo, Constancia noted the household repairs she wanted done before January. New linoleum would be nice, she murmured: blue with a red border. Two more clotheslines would help, too. And while it was not a priority, a yellow rose plant would be nice. She smoothed her crumpled apron, thinking of the one task she had so far ignored: the sorting of the baby clothes in the trunk, a job she found depressing. Still, I must do it while I have the time, Constancia reasoned,

45

pushing back her dark hair—before Apollonia gets worse . . . and before *Enero*, while I have the strength. She rinsed her hands, then walked to the bedroom that overlooked the rosebushes.

With each pregnancy Constancia added and discarded baby clothes: undershirts, flannel nightgowns, embroidered sweaters of soft, light colors. The worn diapers were used as cleaning rags and, when handy, by Justo to wipe oil off his hands. But Apollonia's clothes, worn by no one else, lay intact at the bottom of the trunk between yellowed sheets of tissue paper: smocked dresses trimmed in lace, crocheted caps braided with pink ribbons—each item too precious to discard. Each piece had been stitched by her mother and sisters in Mexico. Each buttonhole had been sewn when life had held such promise, such happiness! But now Apollonia is dying, Constancia sighed, fighting back tears. I have no reason to keep them.

In the dim bedroom Constancia pulled close the rocking chair. She heaved her ample body into the chair, then slowly pulled the dented trunk to her feet. She rummaged through the clothes that smelled of dust and roses; her fingers clutched a faded bonnet, then came to rest on a tiny gossamer dress. Constancia's dark eyes brightened at the sight of the silky dress, now a faded rose color. She pressed the tiny gown to her breast, then brought it to her face. Apollonia. *Hija mía*, she sighed, as warm tears streamed down her face to land on her breasts and stomach. I cannot bear to lose you.

In the evening shadows the rose plants visible through the windows shone a deep green, the blossoms closed tight for the night. Constancia sat lost in thought, the baby dress clutched in her hands. Perhaps the baby can wear Apollonia's dress, she decided, wiping her swollen eyes. Perhaps. She held the baptismal dress against her beating heart, leaned back in the rocker, and closed her eyes. She remained motionless for a time. Suddenly Constancia stood up, smoothed her dress, and took a deep breath. I *will* dress the coming baby in Apollonia's clothes, she vowed—in the dresses, booties, and crocheted jackets. I'll wash the baptismal dress and come next Sunday, I'll show it to Apollonia. Knowing her new brother—or sister—will be christened in this gown will make her happy, make her smile. She shook the clothes free of dust and closed tight the metal trunk; then, baby dress clutched in her hands, Constancia went out of the dark room and into the warm kitchen.

50

❖ Focused Freewriting   Consider as possible focal points the alternating senses of hope and despondency in the story, the pride Constancia takes in her work, her memories of girlhood, or one of the topics you've identified in your journal.

❖ Guided Responses

1. Constancia's tasks include making a stew with "carrots, pota-toes, and onions" (para. 8); folding clothes into the laundry basket: "socks, rolled tight as baseballs, undershirts folded in three equal parts, khaki pants turned inside out—clothes ready for the hot iron" (para. 15); stirring the "bean soup garnished with tomatoes and on-ions" (para. 39). Why do you think Ponce describes these activities in such detail? How does the detail contribute to her characterization of Constancia? How would the story's impact be affected if the details were eliminated?

2. Constancia frequently thinks back on her early life in Mexico. What effect do these reminiscences have on Constancia? How do they help the reader understand her? Choose one of the memories and explain its importance to the story.

3. At one point Constancia recalls the doctor telling the Mexican women in her neighborhood that they were endangering themselves by having so many children (para. 30). Later, she recalls her mother's admonition that birth control is a sin in the eyes of the Church (para. 34). How do these conflicting messages from authorities affect Constancia's life? How does she seem to react to the contradictions?

4. At the end of the story, Constancia makes a decision: "I *will* dress the coming baby in Apollonia's clothes . . . in the dresses, boo-ties, and crocheted jackets." Why is this decision so significant to Constancia? Of what significance is the last line of the story?

❖ Shared Responses   In your journal discuss your views on the roles mothers and fathers should play in their children's lives. Whose primary responsibility is it to bring up the children? to maintain the household? What factors should influence the division of labor in the house? As you discuss your responses in small groups, try to deter-mine how members' own home lives influence their responses.

❖ **Generating Ideas**   Reread all of your journals and annotations from the selections in this unit. Look for connections between selections or still unanswered questions. First, list those connections and questions as briefly as possible. Next, choose two or three to elaborate on. As you respond in more detail to the connections and questions, focus on one topic and consider how well it would serve you in an extended piece of writing. Then decide what kind of writing best suits your topic: Should you write a conventional essay, a poem, a short story, or a scene? Would your topic lend itself more to a letter to the editor or a personal letter? Might a proposal to solve a specific problem be a good choice? Possible topics:

1. media images of women versus the reality of women's lives
2. different expectations of men and women in the business world
3. achievements and remaining goals of the women's movement
4. the significance of her children in a woman's decisions
5. the power of male superiors over female workers

❖ **Focusing Responses**   Choose one of your extended responses and formulate a statement of one or two sentences that captures its essence. Use this statement as a guide to organize your piece. (If you write an essay, letter, or proposal, the statement may actually appear as a thesis.)

❖ **Guided Writing Assignments**

1. Three of the authors in this chapter (Quindlen, Sharron, and Ponce) refer specifically to the impact of children on women's lives. Drawing on at least two of these authors to support your observations, compose a letter to your son or daughter (real or imagined) in which you define yourself as a woman (real or imagined) and offer counsel on how your child should react to women's changing roles. Comment on the significance of the mother-child relationship, the impact a child has on his or her mother's view of the world, and the hopes and fears mothers have for their children.

2. Wolf and Faludi both point to unrealistic images with which real women are expected to compete. Referring to both selections, write an essay in which you argue that fictional media images of women, rather than realistically based images, are being used as models for women in business. In addition to offering evidence to support your view, show how these images are detrimental to women and

suggest reforms in both media and business that can lead to more realistic expectations for women workers.

3. Compose a conversation between Nan Robertson and Laura Mansnerus on the subject of women's responses to harassment and/or discrimination. Have each author refer to evidence from her selection to support her stand on whether women should challenge or silently submit to authority. If you wish, indicate your view on the subject by allowing one author to convince the other of the validity of her view.

4. Sharron and Ponce both celebrate a woman's role as mother. In a story or poem, present your vision of the relationship between a mother and her children. Using these authors' images as models, try to find familiar images of your own to illustrate your perceptions of the mother-child bond.

❖ Research Topics As you consider how to expand your reading beyond the selections in this chapter, identify in your journals and notes questions that remain unanswered or topics you'd like to explore further. Or you may consider the following:

1. Research the history of the women's rights movement of the late nineteenth and early twentieth century. Consider such issues as the origins of the movement, its reception by men in power, its goals, and its accomplishments. Consider also the contributions of women such as Carrie Chapman Catt, Susan B. Anthony, and Elizabeth Cady Stanton. If possible, identify some of the specific influences of the earlier movement on the contemporary feminist movement.

2. Trace the changes in female characters over the past twenty-five years on television or in the movies. First identify stages during which women were portrayed in a particular way; then examine the reasons for and the effects of these portrayals. Focus on two or three representative female characters from each stage you define in order to illustrate your conclusions.

—— Chapter 8 ——

Living on the Edge

——————————— ❖ ———————————

ALTHOUGH THE UNITED STATES is still widely considered the most affluent, tolerant, and egalitarian society in the world, not everyone shares
in its bounty. Some live on the fringes of society because of economic
conditions, some because of the status of their health, some because
of race, and some simply by their own choice.

In part because the media focus most of their attention on mainstream American society, we rarely have the opportunity to take a
close look at the lives of those who live on its periphery. While some
attention is paid to homelessness, the view provided is almost always
from a distance. And the living conditions of poor urban Americans
receive little if any attention. AIDS is often in the news, but its impact
on the everyday lives of people with the virus is a mystery to most
Americans. Similarly, relatively little is known about the lives of people who live in remote areas, either by circumstance or by choice. It
can do a society good occasionally to examine its edges.

This chapter performs such an examination. Since homelessness
represents the most visible example of living on the edge, two selections explore this phenomenon. In addition, the lives of the poor,
people with AIDS, recent immigrants, and self-proclaimed hermits
provide insights not only into the nature of living on the edge but into
mainstream society as well.

In "The Life of Johnny Washington," Grant Pick takes readers into the heart of the inner city to see what life is like for those who have none of the security of a middle-class existence. Members of what Pick calls "the underclass" struggle to find and keep employment at the same time that they struggle to stay alive in a dangerous environment.

In Jon D. Hull's "Slow Descent into Hell," an even more precarious existence is described. Facing assaults by thugs, police, and nature, homeless men on the streets of Philadelphia barely survive.

Cathy Stern, in "Those Places," offers a glimpse of life on the fringes of society from the physically comfortable but emotionally uncomfortable perspective of the middle class. The knowledge of homelessness cannot be erased, even when its victims are temporarily invisible.

A family with no desire to be a part of the mainstream culture is featured in Elizabeth Cook-Lynn's "A Visit from Reverend Tileston." When a Christian preacher literally invades the home of an extended Native American family, their response makes clear that they have no need of his prayers or salvation.

Richard Goldstein, in "AIDS and the Social Contract," discusses a population that has been forced to the edge. The danger of stigmatization, both to the targeted population and to society at large, is highlighted in this essay.

In "The Hopeland" K. Kam introduces a population currently on the margins but hoping to become part of the mainstream. Her work with Southeast Asian immigrant students gives Kam a unique perspective from which to view the promise of America.

Finally, in Sue Halpern's "The Place of the Solitaries," readers are introduced to a couple who have chosen to live far from society. Hermits Ned and Mae are quite content in their existence without electricity, newspapers, and other accoutrements of civilized life.

Many of the selections in this section provide a dismal view of American society. But some offer considerable hope, either because of their sympathy, their proposals for change, or their emphasis on the traditional American values of equality and tolerance.

The Life of Johnny Washington:
Notes from the Underclass

GRANT PICK

GRANT PICK, *a staff writer for the* Chicago Reader, *frequently recounts the stories of people living on the edge. This article was published originally in the* Chicago Reader *in April 1988 and reprinted in* Utne Reader *in November of that year. By the time the reprint went to press, Johnny Washington and Tricia Young had been evicted from their apartment, and he was living on the streets. (She and the children were with her parents.) In this article Washington reveals himself to be a concerned parent whose worries over the well-being of his children and the safety of his home reflect the concerns of average, middle-class Americans. His story is told primarily in his own words.*

Before reading the selection, write in your journal about your perceptions of the uneducated urban poor, whom Pick calls the "underclass." Do you think of them as essentially similar to or different from you? What do you think their values are? Why do you think they remain poor?

As you make notes on your reading, you may want to focus on Pick's descriptions, Washington's attitude toward his life, or the language Washington uses.

PROMPTLY AT 9:30 LAST FEBRUARY 18, Associate Circuit Court Judge John R. Ryan ascended the bench of his Chicago courtroom. Although sunlight cascaded down through skylights that run the length of the room, it failed to make Judge Ryan's court a cheery place. The atmosphere was heavy with purpose.

People come before Judge Ryan for only one reason. Whenever public aid is sought for a child born out of wedlock in Illinois, the Department of Public Aid and the local state's attorney are required by law to try to establish paternity. The father—if he's able—must help the state support his child. Ryan's caseload consists solely of mothers and alleged fathers who the state's attorney has summoned to court.

In his opening remarks, Ryan outlined the court procedure. A mother and alleged father would be summoned to the bench, and the man would be asked to affirm that he had fathered her child. If the man answered no, he could be required to submit to a blood test; if his answer was yes, he would receive a document acknowledging his paternity.

A court bailiff began to call the names of the men and women who now stood before Ryan. Most of the men acknowledged that they were fathers; the judge ordered those who were employed to pay small monthly sums—$20 or $40—but more often the fathers were unemployed and could contribute nothing. One of those men was 37-year-old Johnny Washington, who appeared before the judge wearing a black Nike sweatshirt. Yes, he was the father of Natasha Young, born on January 28, 1987. Yes, he was on public assistance.

And so it was done. Johnny put back on his worn cloth overcoat   5 with fake-fur collar and his blue stocking cap. Limping from an old gunshot wound, Johnny trudged to the back of the court and joined his common-law wife Patricia Young, who was waiting there with their two kids, 1-year-old Natasha and 2-year-old Chaqueeta. The family took the bus home to their basement apartment on Monroe Street near Western Avenue on the city's West Side.

It is possible to describe Johnny Washington entirely in terms of statistics. He was the defendant in one of approximately 38,000 paternity cases filed last year by the Cook County state's attorney, 98 percent of which involved welfare families, according to that office. His family is one of 120,000 Chicago households that the Census Bureau says exist below the poverty line. Until recently, he was among 90,000 Chicago men on general assistance. But these figures by no means explain the life of Johnny Washington.

The 2300 block of West Monroe is a dilapidated stretch of 19th century buildings. Some buildings have been torn down, others stand abandoned. Johnny's home is a two-flat building with a stone front that has been painted red. Under the broad wooden front steps at the edge of a dirt yard strewn with paper and empty liquor bottles, there's a door leading to the basement. Ring the doorbell once for the front tenant, twice for Johnny, who lives in back.

Washington's apartment consists of a living room and a kitchen. Chaqueeta and Natasha sleep together on the bottom of a bunk bed in one corner of the living room, under some porcelain sconces containing pink plastic flowers. Johnny and Tricia share a double bed across the room. Underwear and the girls' sleepers hang drying from exposed heating pipes. On one wall is a print of street lamps along a seawall.

Two television sets—a large color console and a small black-and-white—are flickering in the living room; the small set is silent, but it gives the family an idea of what's on another channel. "I like westerns and gangster movies." Johnny says. "I don't like soap operas, mainly 'cause I wonder what the big deal is. They're like everyday life, it seems to me."

The kitchen has a grease-caked, four-burner stove and a refrigera-   10
tor, topped with foil pans and a corn flakes box. A small shelf holds the seasonings—chili powder, garlic salt, black pepper—and assorted cups and glassware are neatly placed on a small table. Old clothes are stashed in a cardboard box. On the floor next to another couch are a child-size table, a rattle, and a toy phone. The walls are pea green; a bare bulb illuminates them.

For this—and a community bathroom down the hall—Johnny and Tricia pay $175 a month. The rent includes heat, but the radiators provide insufficient warmth, and they keep the stove burning in winter; even so, says Washington, "the kids come down with colds." Just the other day, Johnny finally plastered the holes in the kitchen ceiling and gave it a new coat of paint. The ceiling had been in such bad shape that there were places you could see up to the joists; but Johnny's landlord, who owns a nearby hardware store, was slow giving him the money to make repairs.

The community john "stays filthy," Johnny maintains, " 'cause there's nobody in the building who cares to keep it clean. The guy who lives in front leaves the front door unlocked, so people off the street use it all the time. Half of them leave their stool smeared all over the floor, and they urinate, too." To improve matters, Johnny has posted a sign: "When you take a bath, wash the tub out. And mop up the water. Do like Dad, not sis. Lift the lid before you piss."

Though Johnny does not have a job, his days follow a certain pattern. He usually rises around 5:30 a.m. and gets to work fixing his breakfast, which consists of two eggs done over easy, bacon, and coffee.

If the weather's cold, Johnny stays indoors; otherwise, by 7 o'clock he is off foraging on the West Side for discarded cans, copper and brass pieces, and old batteries, which he sells to a junkyard.

Washington skips lunch, but supper is a family meal shared some-   15
time after 6 o'clock. "We eat hearty," says Johnny, which means chicken or pork chops, mixed vegetables, and greens. At night they watch more television. Bedtime is 9 p.m. for the girls, 10:30 for Tricia

and Johnny, unless the TV watching is good, in which case Johnny stays up till the wee hours.

Until a few months ago, Johnny got $154 a month in General Assistance, a state subsidy for poor people who don't qualify for any other form of public aid. In addition, he gets $81 a month in food stamps. Tricia's food stamp allotment is $172, and she gets $342 a month in Aid to Families with Dependent Children (AFDC).

Johnny tries to bring in other income. He is a barber of sorts. "I cuts my own hair, and most everybody else's in the neighborhood," he says. The haircuts are given in the Washington kitchen, underneath a sign that reads: "Due to the increase in tax and the high cost of living, haircuts are $4 and up."

Money from odd jobs—painting, shoveling snow, cleaning out basements—also comes Washington's way, although he is usually rebuffed when he solicits work beyond his own block because strangers are suspicious of him. Johnny spends this extra money on milk and Pampers. He runs short on money toward the end of the month and has to borrow. Recently, he went on a frantic two-day search for money to buy a box of Pampers; the girls had a doctor's appointment, and Johnny wanted their hind ends properly covered when they were examined.

Tricia's welfare check arrives at the end of each month, and Johnny's comes on the ninth, which is when the family shops for food. Johnny pays a friend known as Papa Cool $10 to drive them to a discount supermarket and a meat market. "He doesn't ask for it, but I know gas doesn't run on air," Johnny explains.

"In canned goods, we buy a case of whole-kernel corn, a case of 20 cream-style, sugar, and lard," says Washington. "At the meat market, we get ground beef, 15 to 20 chickens, beef and pork liver, round steaks, pork chops, oxtail, neck bones, and things like salt and pepper."

For clothes, the family frequents budget stores. "And lots of stuff people throw away can be used," he says. Johnny got his topcoat and the art print in the living room from someone he did a job for. Johnny does the family laundry twice a week at a nearby laundromat.

Johnny has never taken a vacation. He finally scraped together the dollars to install a phone recently. He doesn't buy a newspaper. His major cash outlay in recent years was $219 for the color television, which he considers essential. Another must each week is *TV Guide*: "I make sure I get mine, if I have 75 cents to spend. I be at the newspaper stand up on Madison when it comes out on Wednesday, at 5:30 or 6 in the evening. If I wait until Thursday morning, the newsstand will be all out."

Johnny's spare moments are spent watching television or talking out front with friends and neighbors, often while enjoying one of the several cigarettes he smokes each day. He also loves to sketch; Johnny's specialty is faces, and he is quite good. "I guess I just have God-given talent," he figures. He once responded to an ad in *TV Guide* for a correspondence course in art. Soon a salesman stopped by, but the fee he quoted for the course struck Johnny as outrageous.

Johnny's greatest pleasure is his daughters. "When the weather is nice in the summer, I take them to the zoo, to the neighborhood park at Homan and Madison. I play with them, but I don't get rough with them. Ain't nothing but girls, you know. Sometimes Chaqueeta, she can get out of hand. She's the older one, and since Tasha's been born she wants to be the baby. But I explain to her that if I'm spending more time with Tasha I'm not neglecting her. She's a big girl; she has to look out for her sister. I don't treat them different, you understand. If I give to one, I give to the other. I love 'em, though, I love 'em. They are beautiful, beautiful—I wouldn't take nothing in the world for them."

Johnny Washington was born at Cook County Hospital on July 28, 1950. His mother, Ruth Washington, was 31 years old at the time. His father was Johnny Ivory. They both came from Mississippi, according to Johnny, and they had already had a son who died at birth. Johnny says his parents were married; he was given his mother's last name " 'cause I was with her and not with him."

Johnny Ivory "was around some, I guess," explains his son, "but you know how separations are. My father used to work, but at what I can't right tell you. He was the type who didn't stay at home very long. He drank," says Johnny, adding that he learned of his father's death when he went by the family's old apartment to show off baby pictures of Chaqueeta and was told Johnny Ivory had passed on.

About his mother, Johnny says, "She worked for a while, until she got sick with tuberculosis. Then she got her leg broke in a robbery. She was coming home from her sister's and three boys robbed her, breaking her leg in two places, 'bove the knee and below." The way the leg was set caused Ruth Washington's feet to turn inward.

"I never got a chance to graduate high school." Johnny says. "After my mother got hurt, of course, she wasn't able to work anymore. When she got her welfare check, I had to go cash it. I took care of the bills or whatever else I could do for her at a particular time. She had to have someone; she wasn't able to take care of herself. I cooked for her, bathed her, took her to the washroom; it fell to me to get all this done. This affected my work in school, so I had to stop. I dropped out two or three months before graduation."

For a time Johnny shouldered three jobs—grocery store clerk and usher at two movie theaters, the Imperial and the Four Star—and he was drawing $175 a week. That was a good wage, he admits, "but the strain that was on me in holding down three jobs was really tiresome.

25

I started losing sleep. I wasn't getting to work on time. Soon I let the jobs go." The grocery later burned in the riots that followed Martin Luther King's death in 1968, and the theaters soon closed. Johnny worked in a gas station until the owner died. "His wife shot him," Washington says.

Johnny was shot himself in 1970. He was on his way home to his mother's when two fellows stuck him up. He gave them what he had on him—$36—but it wasn't enough, and one of them fired at him. Doctors at Cook County Hospital removed the bullet; it left Johnny with a left hip filled with pins and clips, and a limp. In cold weather, says Johnny, "my hip aches somethin' awful." 30

Johnny lived with his mother until he was 27, when he ran afoul of her boyfriend. "He was using her for what he could get from her. He knew she had a problem with alcohol, and he'd get her full of liquor and take advantage of her, take a little money, a little check. Me and him got into it."

Johnny moved into an apartment building owned by a realty company for whom he did janitorial work in return for a small salary, free rent, and gas. The company eventually sold the building. He then went on General Assistance; Johnny forgets exactly when he became a welfare case, but it was "too long ago."

Johnny says his criminal career also ran its course long ago. He was arrested "on several occasions" for such offenses as disorderly conduct and theft and was convicted of both possession of marijuana and possession of stolen property. The stolen property, says Washington, was a portable TV and a camera that he didn't know were hot. He explains that because of his prior record he pled guilty, and he spent 10 months at Vandalia Correctional Center in southern Illinois.

I met Tricia through a friend," Johnny says, "and we started going out." A small, pretty, quiet woman of 28, Tricia graduated from Crane High School and later worked as a factory worker at the W. F. Hall Printing Company. She eventually quit because it was too difficult to get to work by bus and she could not afford a car. Around this time, five years ago, she met Johnny.

In large part because she is so quiet, it is hard to figure out the relationship between Johnny and Tricia. "Tricia's there when I need her," says Johnny. "When I'm upset, we sit down and talk you know, like couples do. And that is a big comfort to me." Is he faithful? "I try to be, though I can't say I'm 100 percent that way. Sometimes you get in that mood, you know." 35

Johnny doesn't drink or take drugs. "I don't go in for drinkin, 'cause I've seen what it did to my mother and other people. They so much as smell alcohol and they go craz-ee." Ruth Washington died of liver disease at Cook County Hospital a decade or so ago. "I don't know the name of the cemetery she's buried at," Johnny says. "I been there, but I don't like cemeteries."

If Johnny has any extended family, it is Tricia's folks, who live nearby. "I have a couple of aunties and a couple uncles, but we're not what you'd call close-knit," he says. "Once every four or five months I see this uncle who lives out by Adams and Bell, but the rest of my people put themselves above me. They got their own homes and everything. They're uppity; they look down on me. But I say, 'Hey, you can't make it all by yourself in this world. Someone's got to help you.' "

Tricia and the kids go to the Metropolitan Missionary Church; Johnny doesn't like to accompany them, because he prefers that some-one is at home at all times to protect it, but they all went to church together on Easter, the kids in new pink-and-blue outfits he'd bought them. "You can't go too far in this neighborhood, 'cause when you come back you can have nothing at all," Johnny says. He learned this truth the hard way. Two years ago, just before Christmas, burglars took the food, a color TV, blue jeans, boots, and Chaqueeta's sleepers.

Johnny knows he has to protect himself "I used to own a gun," he says, "a .32 revolver. It was really a hassle, though, with the quick temper I got. But, nope, I never shot it off." He didn't have a license: The gun was bought from someone nameless and sold the same way. Now a red-handled knife with a curved blade serves as Washington's defense. When he goes shopping Johnny tucks the knife in his pants.

The neighborhood has changed dramatically since Johnny's boy- 40
hood. His block is the turf of the Disciples street gang. A drug dealer operates out of a building at the end of the street. Johnny laments the new character of the neighborhood. "Young kids spend their lunch money to buy drugs from the junkie every morning. I tell 'em, 'Why do that? You should use your head for more than a hat rack.' Sad to say, that just goes in one ear and out the other.

"Last night this girl from the projects was out in the alley suckin' a man for drugs. 'Round here, you see everything. When the weather gets warm you see people screwing in the halls, in the doorways. For drugs—that's the only thing it can be for. You see prostitution out on Madison Street every day. These are young girls, 16 and 17 years old. You can't fault 'em. You have to fault their parents, their mothers, who encourage them. Why, there's venereal disease runnin' rampant, and half these girls don't know what a douche is.

"Sometimes Tricia gets mad at me for speaking up like I do. She says, 'Your mouth is too big—it's going to get you into serious trouble.' But if I see something wrong, I say so. Whether they listen to me or not, I let them know what I know.

"Like this kid the other day. He was no more than seven or eight. The kid was throwing bottles, and I told him to get his little butt out of there. I said, 'I'm going to tell your momma.' So he tells me, 'You black son of a bitch, shut up!' With that the kid lits off down the street, and, what do you know, back comes his momma. She says 'You know my son wouldn't say nothing like that.' I says, 'You can never say what your son or daughter will say when you ain't around. And I'm sure you'd rather have someone come and tell you what he's saying than someone come tell you that your kid's brains been blowed out.'"

Johnny believes in the idea of changing society through the ballot box. He votes strictly for Democrats, though if a Republican pleased him, he claims he could punch that number without a second thought. Information about the candidates comes to Johnny the way all news does: from the TV.

How often does he come into contact with a white person? "I'd   45
say every other day," Johnny replies. But whites seem uncomfortable when he's near. "The impression they give is that they are afraid, that they don't want to be bothered with me. Now I have no hard feelings toward anyone. In the Bible it says that we are sisters and brothers regardless of race. If we don't pull together to help one another, we are going to do more harm than good."

Johnny has recently suffered a number of medical problems. Last fall, a pain developed in his right side that he thought was a cold, but it lingered and he finally went to see a doctor at Cook County. He was hospitalized for six days with a diagnosis of pneumonia complicated by tuberculosis.

The family's hospital bills and other medical costs are covered by Medicaid. An orange card entitles them to treatment at Cook County Hospital.

Johnny maintains that his physical problems keep him from finding work. His gunshot wound, he says, "has affected me in that I'm off balance, so far as it comes to lifting; I can't put as much weight on my hip as I would like." Arthritis also afflicts the hip, Johnny claims.

But there isn't much public aid can do about Johnny's limp, which he's convinced has severely limited his ability to find work. "You go for a job interview, and they look at the way I walk and say, 'He can't work.' I'd rather be working. I'd take a job sweepin' and moppin', anything." This past winter he hunted for employment on the West Side and found nothing. He was either rejected without cause or was told there were no openings.

Johnny talks about his ambitions only grudgingly. He wants   50
Chaqueeta and Natasha to attend St. Malachy's Catholic School rather than his alma mater, Victor Herbert Public School. At St. Malachy's the

girls will receive "better training and a better outlook on life," he believes. "I would like to marry Tricia," he adds, "but I want it to be under much better conditions than this. This"—he motions around his living room—"just ain't going to cut it."

❖ Focused Freewriting   Consider as possible focal points the description of the neighborhood, Washington's history, his observations on the social problems he sees, or one of the topics you've identified in your journal.

❖ Guided Responses

1. Why do you think Pick describes the Washington apartment in such detail (paras. 8–12)? How do you react to the description?
2. The color television, the result of Washington's only "major cash outlay in recent years," is "essential" to him (para. 22) and occupies a prominent position in the apartment. Pick also comments that Washington gets all of his news from the television. Why do you think television is so important in Washington's life? What might it represent to him?
3. Washington describes his relatives as "uppity; they look down on me." His response to that attitude is, "Hey, you can't make it all by yourself in this world. Someone's got to help you" (para. 37). Based on your reading of the article, what kind of help do you think Washington has in mind? What kind of help do you think people need to "make it . . . in this world"?
4. In the last paragraph, Washington speaks "grudgingly" about his ambitions for his children, as well as for himself and Tricia. How realistic do such ambitions sound in general? How realistic are they in Washington's situation? What obstacles does he face in realizing his goals?

❖ Shared Responses   In your journal respond to Johnny Washington's belief "in the idea of changing society through the ballot box" (para. 44). How significant is the individual vote, in your opinion? How successful do you think political leaders have been in addressing inner-city problems? What kind of hopes do you have for political change? As you discuss your responses in small groups, try to determine to what extent political beliefs are reflected in members' responses.

Slow Descent into Hell

JON D. HULL

JON D. HULL *writes for* Time *magazine. While his subjects range from street gangs to smoking, he has written most extensively on Israel and the Middle East since becoming chief of the magazine's Jerusalem bureau. This article from* Time *(1987), the result of Hull's living for a week among the homeless in Philadelphia, presents a graphic picture of what it means to be homeless today in an American city. Focusing on the lives of several homeless men, Hull underscores the hopelessness these men face in their constant struggle to stay alive on the streets.*

Before reading the selection, enumerate in your journal the everyday problems you think homeless people face. Try to be specific, concentrating on the essentials of daily life—eating, washing, sleeping, and the like.

As you make notes on your reading, you may want to focus on Hull's use of quotations from homeless men or his physical descriptions of the men and their surroundings.

A SMOOTH BAR OF SOAP, wrapped neatly in a white handkerchief and tucked safely in the breast pocket of a faded leather jacket, is all that keeps George from losing himself to the streets. When he wakes each morning from his makeshift bed of newspapers in the subway tunnels of Philadelphia, he heads for the rest room of a nearby bus station or McDonald's and begins an elaborate ritual of washing off the dirt and smells of homelessness: first the hands and forearms, then the face and neck, and finally the fingernails and teeth. Twice a week he takes off his worn Converse high tops and socks and washes his feet in the sink, ignoring the cold stares of well-dressed commuters.

George, twenty-eight, is a stocky, round-faced former high school basketball star who once made a living as a construction worker. But after he lost his job just over a year ago, his wife kicked him out of the house. For a few weeks he lived on the couches of friends, but the friendships soon wore thin. Since then he has been on the street, starting from scratch and looking for a job. "I got to get my life back," George says after rinsing his face for the fourth time. He begins brushing his teeth with his forefinger. "If I don't stay clean," he mutters, "the world ain't even going to look me in the face. I just couldn't take that."

George lives in a world where time is meaningless and it's possible to go months without being touched by anyone but a thug. Lack of sleep, food, or conversation breeds confusion and depression. He feels himself slipping but struggles to remember what he once had and to figure out how to get it back. He rarely drinks alcohol and keeps his light brown corduroy pants and red-checked shirt meticulously clean. Underneath, he wears two other shirts to fight off the cold, and he sleeps with his large hands buried deep within his coat pockets amid old sandwiches and doughnuts from the soup kitchens and garbage cans.

Last fall he held a job for six weeks at a pizza joint, making $3.65 an hour kneading dough and cleaning tables. Before work, he would take off two of his three shirts and hide them in an alley. It pleases him that no one knew he was homeless. Says George: "Sure I could have spent that money on some good drink or food, but you gotta suffer to save. You gotta have money to get out of here and I gotta get out of here." Some days he was scolded for eating too much of the food. He often worked without sleep, and with no alarm clock to wake him from the subways or abandoned tenements, he missed several days and was finally fired. He observes, "Can't get no job without a home, and you can't get a home without a job. They take one and you lose both."

George had sixty-four dollars tucked in his pocket on the evening 5 he was beaten senseless in an alley near the Continental Trailways station. "Those damn chumps," he says, gritting his teeth, "took every goddam penny. I'm gonna kill 'em." Violence is a constant threat to the homeless. It's only a matter of time before newcomers are beaten, robbed, or raped. The young prey on the old, the big on the small, and groups attack lonely individuals in the back alleys and subway tunnels. After it's over, there is no one to tell about the pain, nothing to do but walk away.

Behind a dumpster sits a man who calls himself Red enjoying the last drops of a bottle of wine called Wild Irish Rose. It's 1 A.M., and the thermometer hovers around 20 degrees with a biting wind. His nickname comes from a golden retriever his family once had back in Memphis, and a sparkle comes to his eyes as he recalls examples of the dog's loyalty. One day he plans to get another dog, and says, "I'm getting to the point where I can't talk to people. They're always telling me to do something or get out of their way. But a dog is different."

At thirty-five, he looks fifty, and his gaunt face carries discolored scars from the falls and fights of three years on the streets. An upper incisor is missing, and his lower teeth jut outward against his lower lip, giving the impression that he can't close his mouth. His baggy pants are about five inches too long and when he walks, their frayed ends drag on the ground. "You know something?" he asks, holding up the bottle. "I wasn't stuck to this stuff until the cold got to me. Now I'll freeze without it. I could go to Florida or someplace, but I know this town and I know who the creeps are. Besides, it's not too bad in the summer."

Finishing the bottle, and not yet drunk enough to sleep out in the cold, he gathers his blanket around his neck and heads for the subways beneath city hall, where hundreds of the homeless seek warmth. Once inside, the game of cat-and-mouse begins with the police, who patrol the maze of tunnels and stairways and insist that everybody remain off the floor and keep moving. Sitting can be an invitation to trouble, and the choice between sleep and warmth becomes agonizing as the night wears on.

For the first hour, Red shuffles through the tunnels, stopping occasionally to urinate against the graffiti-covered walls. Then he picks a spot and stands for half an hour, peering out from the large hood of his coat. In the distance, the barking of German shepherds echoes through the tunnels as a canine unit patrols the darker recesses of the underground. Nearby, a young man in a ragged trench coat stands against the wall, slapping his palms against his sides and muttering, "I've got to get some paperwork done. I've just got to get some paperwork done!" Red shakes his head. "Home sweet home," he says. Finally exhausted, he curls up on the littered floor, lying on his side with his hands in his pockets and his hood pulled all the way over his face to keep the rats away. He is asleep instantly.

Whack! A police baton slaps his legs and a voice booms, "Get the   10 hell up, you're outta here. Right now!" Another police officer whacks his night-stick against a metal grating as the twelve men sprawled along the tunnel crawl to their feet. Red pulls himself up and walks slowly up the stairs to the street, never looking back.

Pausing at every pay phone to check the coin-return slots, he makes his way to a long steam grate whose warm hiss bears the acrid smell of a dry cleaner's shop. He searches for newspaper and cardboard to block the moisture but retain the heat. With his makeshift bed made, he curls up again, but the rest is short-lived. "This s.o.b. use to give off more heat," he says, staring with disgust at the grate. He gathers the newspapers and moves down the block, all the while muttering about the differences among grates. "Some are good, some are bad. I remember I was getting a beautiful sleep on this one baby and then all this honking starts. I was laying right in a damn driveway and nearly got run over by a garbage truck."

Stopping at a small circular vent shooting jets of steam, Red shakes his head and curses: "This one is too wet, and it'll go off sometimes, leaving you to freeze." Shaking now with the cold, he walks four more blocks and finds another grate, where he curls up and fishes a half-spent cigarette from his pocket. The grate is warm, but soon the moisture from the steam has soaked his newspapers and begins to gather on his clothes. Too tired to find another grate, he sets down more newspapers, throws his blanket over his head, and sprawls across the grate. By morning he is soaked.

At the St. John's Hospice for Men, close to the red neon marquees of the porno shops near city hall, a crowd begins to gather at 4 P.M. Men and women dressed in ill-fitting clothes stamp their feet to ward off the cold and keep their arms pressed against their sides. Some are drunk; others simply talk aloud to nobody in words that none can understand. Most are loners who stand in silence with the sullen expression of the tired and hungry.

A hospice worker lets in a stream of women and old men. The young men must wait until 5 P.M., and the crowd of more than two hundred are asked to form four rows behind a yellow line and watch their language. It seems an impossible task. A trembling man who goes by the name Carper cries, "What goddam row am I in!" as he pulls his red wool hat down until it covers his eyebrows. Carper has spent five to six years on the streets, and thinks he may be thirty-three. The smell of putrid wine and decaying teeth poisons his breath; the fluid running from his swollen eyes streaks his dirty cheeks before disappearing into his beard. "Am I in a goddam row? Who the hell's running the rows?" he swears. An older man with a thick gray beard informs Carper he is in Row 3 and assures him it is the best of them all. Carper's face softens into a smile; he stuffs his hands under his armpits and begins rocking his shoulders with delight.

Beds at the shelters are scarce, and fill up first with the old, the 15 very young, and women. Young men have little hope of getting a bed, and some have even come to scorn the shelters. Says Michael Brown, twenty-four: "It stinks to high heaven in those places. They're just packed with people and when the lights go out, it's everybody for themselves." Michael, a short, self-described con man, has been living on the streets three years, ever since holding up a convenience store in Little Rock. He fled, fearing capture, but now misses the two young children he left behind. He says he is tired of the streets and plans to turn himself in to serve his time.

Michael refuses to eat at the soup kitchens, preferring to panhandle for a meal: "I don't like to be around those people. It makes you feel like some sort of crazy. Before you know it, you're one of them." He keeps a tear in the left seam of his pants, just below the pocket; when he panhandles among commuters, he tells them that his subway fare fell out of his pants. When that fails, he wanders past fast-food outlets, waiting for a large group eating near the door to get up and leave. Then he snatches the remaining food off the table and heads down the street, smiling all the more if the food is still warm. At night he sleeps in the subway stations, catnapping between police rounds amid the thunder of the trains. "Some of these guys sleep right on the damn floor," he says. "Not me. I always use two newspapers and lay them out neatly. Then I pray the rats don't get me."

It was the last swig of the bottle, and the cheap red wine contained flotsam from the mouths of three men gathered in a vacant lot in northeast Philadelphia. Moments before, a homeless and dying man named Gary had vomited. The stench and nausea were dulled only by exhaustion and the cold. Gary, wheezing noisily, his lips dripping with puke, was the last to drink from the half-gallon jug of Thunderbird before passing it on, but no one seemed to care. There was no way to avoid the honor of downing the last few drops. It was an offer to share extended by those with nothing, and there was no time to think about the sores on the lips of the previous drinkers or the strange things floating in the bottle or the fact that it was daybreak and time for breakfast. It was better to drink and stay warm and forget about everything.

Though he is now dying on the streets, Gary used to be a respectable citizen. His full name is Gary Shaw, forty-eight, and he is a lifelong resident of Philadelphia and a father of three. He once worked as a precision machinist, making metal dies for casting tools. "I could work with my eyes closed," he says. "I was the best there was." But he lost his job and wife to alcohol. Now his home is an old red couch with the springs exposed in a garbage-strewn clearing amid abandoned tenements. Nearby, wood pulled from buildings burns in a fifty-five-gallon metal drum while the Thunderbird is passed around. When evening falls, Gary has trouble standing, and he believes his liver and kidneys are on the verge of failing. His thighs carry deep burn marks from sleeping on grates, and a severe beating the previous night has left bruises on his lower back and a long scab across his nose. The pain is apparent in his eyes, still brilliant blue, and the handsome features of his face are hidden beneath a layer of grime.

By 3 A.M., Gary's back pains are unbearable, and he begins rocking back and forth while the others try to keep him warm. "Ah, please God help me. I'm f—ing dying, man. I'm dying." Two friends try to wave down a patrol car. After forty-five minutes, a suspicious cop rolls up to the curb and listens impatiently to their plea: "It's not drugs, man, I promise. The guy was beat up bad and he's dying. Come on, man, you've got to take us to the hospital." The cop nods and points his thumb toward the car. As Gary screams, his two friends carefully lift him into the back seat for the ride to St. Mary Hospital.

In the emergency room, half an hour passes before a nurse appears with a clipboard. Address: unknown. No insurance. After an X ray, Gary is told that a bone in his back may be chipped. He is advised to go home, put some ice on it and get some rest. "I don't have a goddam home!" he cries, his face twisted in pain. "Don't you know what I am? I'm a goddam bum, that's what, and I'm dying!" After an awkward moment, he is told to come back tomorrow and see the radiologist. The hospital pays his cab fare back to the couch. 20

Gary returns in time to share another bottle of Thunderbird, and the warm rush brings his spirits up. "What the hell are we doing in the city?" asks Ray Kelly, thirty-seven, who was once a merchant seaman. "I know a place in Vermont where the fishing's great and you can build a whole damn house in the woods. There's nobody to bother you and plenty of food." Gary interrupts to recall fishing as a boy, and the memories prior to his six years on the street come back with crystal clarity. "You got it, man, we're all getting out of here tomorrow," he says with a grin. In the spirit of celebration, King, a thirty-four-year-old from Puerto Rico, removes a tube of glue from his pocket with the care of a sommelier, sniffs it and passes it around.

When the sun rises, Ray and King are fast asleep under a blanket on the couch. Gary is sitting at the other end, staring straight ahead and breathing heavily in the cold air. Curling his numb and swollen fingers around the arm of the couch, he tries to pull himself up but fails. When another try fails, he sits motionless and closes his eyes. Then the pain hits his back again and he starts to cry. He won't be getting out of here today, and probably not tomorrow either.

Meanwhile, somewhere across town in the washroom of a McDonald's, George braces for another day of job hunting, washing the streets from his face so that nobody knows where he lives.

❖ **Focused Freewriting**   Consider as possible focal points the observations the men make on their lives, their treatment by police, or one of the topics you've identified in your journal.

❖ Guided Responses

1. Characterize George in your own words. What are his values? How does he view himself? What circumstances have contributed to his condition? How would you compare your characterization with working people you know? Why do you think Hull opens the essay with George's story?

2. In describing Red, Hull makes several matter-of-fact observations: He sleeps with his hood "pulled all the way over his face to keep the rats away," he pauses "at every pay phone to check the coin-return slots," and he "searches for newspaper and cardboard to block the moisture but retain the heat" of a sidewalk grate (paras. 9 and 11). What is the impact of this dispassionate presentation? How would the effect be different if Hull had given readers his reaction to these sights?

3. How does the description of Gary (paras. 17–18) contrast with that of George at the beginning of the article? How is your response to the two men different? Are you better able to accept Gary's homelessness than George's? Why, or why not? Why do you think Hull leaves Gary's story until the end?

4. At the end of the article, Hull returns to the image of George washing himself in a public bathroom. Why do you think he chooses to close the piece with George? What commentary does this technique offer about homelessness in American cities?

❖ Shared Responses   In your journal return to your original list of everyday problems faced by the homeless. Based on your reading of this article, how accurate was your list? How would you revise it? In what way, if any, does your revision alter your perception of homeless people? As you discuss your responses in small groups, try to identify value judgments in members' responses.

Those Places

CATHY STERN

*C*ATHY *S*TERN *(biographical information on p. 312) reflects in this poem on how the sight of a young, homeless man etches itself on the mind of a comfortable, middle-class worker. Stern says of her poem's genesis, "I didn't want to see that man again. I drove that way early every morning and I kept thinking, Please God, don't let me see that man again, I cannot handle this."*

Before reading the selection, explore in your journal your own feelings when you see the reality of homelessness. How do you feel toward the person? toward yourself? Do you feel guilty? angry? frustrated?

As you make notes on your reading, you may want to focus on the details Stern uses to establish the reality of the situation.

It's early when I drive to work and thread
the final Main Street slot between the Texas
Historic Building and the XX Video Arcade,
Open 24 Hours, Ladies Free.

Each time I hope that I won't see the young   5
lost man again, with his dirty, white blanket,
carrying his life across the street.

He's put it down in a corner of my mind.
He's curled up there and he won't move
where I can't see him when I close my eyes.   10

Now the nights are cold. I've had to put
another blanket over him, or would
if I could find him anywhere
in all those places I tried to move him to.

❖ Focused Freewriting   Consider as possible focal points Stern's resistance to the image, her compassion, or one of the topics you've identified in your journal.

❖ Guided Responses

1. In the first stanza Stern mentions "the Texas / Historic Building and the XX Video Arcade." What effect does the naming of these specific places have on your reading of the poem? Why do you think Stern chose to highlight these two places? Why do you think she adds, "Open 24 Hours, Ladies Free"?

2. Stern calls the young man she sees "lost," and writes that he is "carrying his life across the street." What do you think she means by this phrasing? What do the lines tell you about the man? about Stern's reaction to him?

3. What has the young man "put . . . down in [Stern's] mind"? Why does this disturb her so? Do you think she presents herself honestly in this stanza? Is her self-image here sympathetic? Explain your responses.

4. What are "Those Places"? Why does Stern try to move the young man to them? Do you think she's speaking of real places in the final stanza, or is she still referring to her mind? Explain your response.

❖ Shared Responses   In your journal imagine yourself in Stern's place. Try to explain, in prose or poetic form, how you'd react to the sight of this young man. As you discuss your responses in small groups, distinguish between those responses based on actual experience and those based on imagination.

A Visit from Reverend Tileston

ELIZABETH COOK-LYNN

ELIZABETH COOK-LYNN *writes poetry and fiction and has taught Indian studies at Eastern Washington University. A founding editor of* The Wicazo sa Review, *a Native American studies magazine, she has also published a collection of short stories,* The Power of Horses and Other Stories *(1990), from which this selection is taken. In it Cook-Lynn presents a humorous tale of an encounter between cultures. As the Reverend Tileston and his disciples descend on the Family's house, their welcome is not quite what they would have expected—or wished for. The Family members are far too concerned with getting on with their lives to worry about the product the Reverend is selling.*

Before reading the selection, write in your journal about an encounter with someone who tried to impose his or her values on you. Perhaps you recall a persistent salesperson, a religious representative, a self-help guru, or some other proselytizer. How did you react to the attempt to convert you?

As you make notes on your reading, you may want to focus on Cook-Lynn's use of humor or her physical descriptions of characters and/or surroundings.

FIFTY MILES FROM THE NEAREST TOWN of any size, deep in the Bend of the Missouri River where the Dakotapi had made history for generations, lived the Family: Father, a first-born son whose eyes bore the immutable and unspoken agony of his generation, handsome and strong, a cattleman not so much from choice as from necessity; Mother, a fine quill artist, small boned and stout, a woman with one crooked elbow caused by a childhood accident, a good cook, accomplished at the piano, guitar and harmonica, talents she had learned at the government boarding school; Uncle, the Mother's younger brother, a truck driver sometimes, a drunk increasingly often whenever those inexplicable waves of grief washed over him; Grandmother, Grandfather and five children ranging in ages from 3 to 15 years. Uncle's son often lived with the Family as did the Grandmother's half sister and her husband and their two granddaughters. The Family was part of a small community which had reassembled itself at this place after the violent Diaspora and Displacement which was endured by this ancient tribe for several generations, the Family all the more closely knit because of this tragedy of recent history as well as the more practical problem of long distances to the few sparse surrounding towns settled a hundred years before by whites anxious to possess land and become rich. The year was 1935 and this was a place where strangers, though alien and undesirable, even called *to' ka*, were largely unthreatening and often ignored, and where strange events were witnessed with inexplicable but characteristic tolerance.

From the gravelled road which followed the course of the river, the small three-room frame house in which the Family now lived, built by the U.S. Government for Bureau of Indian Affairs employees in early reservation days and abandoned in later times, looked strangely remote and ageless. It seemed to stare listlessly toward the river's loop, and in winter its long-windowed eyes would be the first to catch a glimpse of the landing of the Canadian geese on the cold shores of the whitened, timeless river. It turned its back on the ludicrously inexpedient pyramid-shaped, steel-roofed ice-house which had once afforded Bureau employees from the East the luxury of iced drinks in the summer as they came to this blistering Dakotan prairie to work "in the Indian Service." The ice-house was abandoned now, also, too big and deep to be of any use to the Family except for the summer drying of the pounded meat and berry patties, *wasna,* which would be laid out upon its roof in the sun. During this drying process the children would be set to fanning the flies away with long willows, a task which held attention a surprisingly brief time. Bored, they would run off in pursuit of more imaginative pastimes only to be called back as soon as Grandmother discovered their absence.

Also at the rear of the house was a large tipi, the color of smoke at the top, streaked with rain, lined with cow hides, comfortable, shaded in late afternoon by the lone pine tree which was, itself, a stranger to the hot plains country of the Dakotan, itself a survivor of the days when Bureau employees lived there. The children imagined that the tree was brought there by a medicine man and was used in his cures but it was not a cedar, just a scraggly pine tree which had barely survived hard times. There was a tall hand pump set in the middle of the yard where Grandmother would kneel to wash the paunch during butchering times and also a corral set some distance away in the tall pasture grass at the foot of a small rise in the prairie landscape. A huge mound of earth covered a man-made cave which was complete with wooden steps and a slanting door which had to be picked up and drawn aside. A very large bull-snake often found refuge from the blistering sun under one of the wooden steps, stretching himself full length in the soft, cool black earth.

Just beyond the cave was the small white outdoor toilet, another survivor of former times, a product of imaginative Public Health Service officials who set about dotting Indian reservations with these white man's conveniences during the early part of the century. Across the road from the house a gray stuccoed Catholic church, St. Anne's, sat with a closed, tight-lipped visage as though shielding itself from the violent summer prairie storms which came intermittently, pounding the gravel and the stucco, flattening the prairie grass. To the rear of the church lay the remains of the ancestors in a cemetery which, years later, was said to be occupied by a den of rattlesnakes.

In summer evenings, the air was often still and quiet, heavy with 5 moisture. After a late meal, the quiet deepened. The only sound was Grandmother's soft footsteps as she went back and forth to the kitchen carrying dishes from the table. Her ankle length black dress hid her bowed legs and her head was covered, always, with a black scarf, her long white braids lying on her breast. Every now and then she stopped to wipe her smooth face with a white cloth, breathlessly.

"Grandmother, we should cook outside, tomorrow," said the Youngest Daughter, disheveled and hot, bearing a load too heavy for her to the kitchen.

The Mother simply sat, one arm outstretched on the table, the crooked one fanning her face and hair with a handkerchief. For her it had been a long day as she and her sister had spent the afternoon picking wild plums and buffalo berries along the river.

As the evening came on, the children could be heard outside running and chasing one another around the house and yard, trying to touch each other on the back, stretching away, laughing, now and again falling and crashing into the bushes near the pump. The dogs barked loudly. It was a game the boys never seemed to tire of even as the sun started to glow in the west and Uncle went outside to begin his nightly summer ritual of starting a smoke-fire, a smudge, to keep the mosquitoes away for the evening.

"*Hoksila kin tuktel un he?*" muttered Uncle as he looked around for one of his nephews to help him gather firewood. "He's never around when you need him."

"Go get some of that wood over there by the back porch," he 10 directed his voice toward the hapless Youngest Daughter who wrinkled up her nose, but went, dutifully, to get the wood. Uncle bent down on one knee to place the sticks and dead leaves just right to produce a heavy smoke. He carefully touched a match to the soft underbrush and as the smoke rose he watched, one thumb hooked in his belt. In a few moments smoke filled the air and members of the Family began to gather for the evening.

They might even see man-being-carried in the sky, thought Uncle, and then he could tell a story if the children felt like listening and could stay awake long enough for the stars to show themselves clearly.

When he straightened up, he was surprised to see a small black sedan some distance down the road, making its way slowly toward them. He kept his eyes on the road to see if he could recognize in the dusk who its occupants were. He stepped up on the porch and lit a cigarette, the match illuminating the fine, delicate bones of his deeply pocked, scarred face.

Holding the match close for a moment, Uncle said, to no one in particular, "A car's coming."

Cars were rarely seen here on this country road this late in the evening.

As Uncle stood watching, he heard church music, faintly at first, and later, blaring, and he realized after a few long moments that it was coming from the loudspeaker positioned on top of the sedan.

"On-ward, Christian so-o-o-l-diers," sang the recorded voices of an entire church choir into the quiet evening light as the car came slowly into the river's bend, "with the cross of J-e-e-e-sus going on before."

Uncle stood with the cigarette in his mouth, his hands in his pockets as his brother-in-law came out of the house and sat down on the porch step with a cup of coffee. They watched the car approach and listened to the music, now blaring loud enough to get the attention of the children who stopped running and stood gazing at the strange-looking vehicle.

They stood, transfixed, as the car approached slowly and came to a stop. The loudspeaker fell silent as the driver of the sedan parked the car on the side of the road near the mailbox and, with great cheer, stepped from the car, waving and smiling. He was a man of about forty with a broad, freckled face. He was perspiring heavily and he made his way down the short path from the road to the house. Behind him came two women dressed in blue white-flowered dresses, brown stockings and flat brown shoes; their faces, like pale round melons, were fixed with broad smiles. They all carried black leather-bound Bibles, the kind with red-tipped pages.

"Boy, it's hot!" said the fortyish, freckled man as he held out his hand in greeting. The Father did not look at him nor did he get up. He put the cup to his lips and sipped coffee quietly, ignoring the intrusion with sullen indifference. Uncle kept his hands in his pockets and with his tongue he shifted his cigarette to the other side of his mouth.

Ignoring what was clearly a personal affront by the two men on   20
the steps, the freckled man said, "Say, that's a good trash burning operation there," turning to the children standing beside the smudge. The children looked first at the smudge and then back at the perspiring man and, silently, they shook hands with him. Grasping the unwilling hand of the Youngest Daughter standing a few feet away, the man, in a loud voice asked, "Is your mommy home, honey?" Nearly overcome with embarrassment she said, "Yeh, she's in there," and gestured toward the door.

"Well," the man said as he turned and walked up the steps slowly, avoiding the Father and the Uncle still mutely positioned there, "we've come a long way with the message of hope and love we've got right here," and he patted the black leather-bound book be carried. As he tapped on the screen door, the Mother appeared and the freckled man quickly opened the door, stepped inside and held it open for the two smiling women who accompanied him to squeeze inside and in front of him.

"I'm Sister Bernice," began the plumper of the two women, "and this is Sister Kate . . . ?" Her voice trailed off as if she had asked a question. When there was no response, she turned to the freckled man and, putting her hand on his elbow she said, "And we're here with Reverend Tileston."

Taking a deep breath, the Reverend said to the Mother in his kindliest voice, "Ma-a'aam, we'd like to pray with you," and there in the middle of the room he knelt and began paging through his Bible, motioning for the women to join him as he knelt. His two companions quickly dropped to their knees and the plump one said to the Mother, "Please pray with us, sister," and the Mother, after a brief, uncertain moment, also knelt. Espying the Grandmother and her half sister peering at them curiously from the kitchen doorway, the Reverend quickly got up and led them to the middle of the room saying, "Come on with us, Granny, pray with us," and the two old women, too, with great effort, got to their knees. The Youngest Daughter, having followed the astonishing trio into the house, stood beside her Grandmother and looked expectantly at the perspiring freckled man as he fell to reading from the leather-bound book:

"With ALL our energy we ought to lead back ALL men to our most MER-ci-ful Re-DEEE-mer," he read. His voice rose:

"He is the Divine Conso-o-o-oler of the afflicted"; Youngest   25
Daughter hung her head, copying the attitude of the visitors.

"To rulers and subjects alike He teaches lessons of true holiness," the Reverend sucked in air:

"unimpeachable justice and,"
he breathed again,
"generous charity."
The Reverend's voice seemed to fill the cramped little room and Sisters Bernice and Kate, eyes tightly closed, murmured "Amen" louder and louder with each breath the minister took.

Youngest Daughter glanced first at her Mother, then her Grandmothers who were kneeling shoulder to shoulder, faces impassive, eyes cast to the floor. Then, the Reverend closed the book, raised his arms and recited from memory, PROVERBS:

"Hear, O Children, a father's instruction," he shouted. "Be attentive, that you may gain understanding! Yea, excellent advice I give you; my teaching do not forsake."

One of the dogs, hunching itself close to the screen door, began to whine.

The Reverend continued to shout: "When I was my father's child,   30
frail, yet the darling of my mother, he taught me, and said to me: 'Let your heart hold fast my words! Keep my commands, do not forget; go not astray from the words of my mouth.' "

His arms fell and his voice softened as he uttered the last phrase, opened his eyes and looked, unseeing, at the little girl, his gaze moist and glittering. The dog's whine became more persistent, his tone now pitched higher to match the Reverend's and he began to push his nose against the screen door, causing it to squeak loudly.

The Reverend Tileston looked into the passive faces of the Mother and the Grandmothers and he said, "The beginning of wisdom is: get wisdom; at the cost of ALL-L-L-L you have," his arm swung dangerously close to the unfortunate dog who flattened his ears and pushed himself closer to the door.

"Get understanding," Reverend Tileston urged. "Forsake her not and she will preserve you; love her, and she will safeguard you; extol her, and she will exalt you; she will bring you honors if you embrace her; she will put on your head a graceful diadem; a glorious crown will she bestow upon you."

The words seemed to roll from his tongue and Youngest Daughter imagined shining crowns placed upon the heads of her Mother and her Grandmothers still kneeling stiffly and impassively. She was thrilled with the sound of the English words though she knew she didn't comprehend their meaning. It was like the time when Felix Middle Tent, the well-known Dakotah orator, made his speeches at the tribal council meeting she sometimes attended with her father, when he used his most eloquent and esoteric Dakotah vocabulary, oftentimes derisively referred to by Uncle as "jawbreakers."

As the Reverend's hefty arm again swept the room, the whining   35
dog lurched backward and fell against a large pail of buffalo berries

which Mother had left on the porch that late afternoon. Terrified, the dog leapt into the second pail of plums, scattering them wildly, then he dashed under the porch where he set up a mournful howl. The boys who had been listening at the side window fled into the bushes, laughing and screaming.

The Mother and Grandmothers, surprised and shocked at this turn of events but bent upon retrieving the day's pickings, swept past the astonished, speechless minister, shouting abuse at the now thoroughly miserable dog, and the screen door slammed behind them. Youngest Daughter was left looking into the disappointed faces of the Reverend and his companions. She smiled.

Forced by these circumstances to admit that the spiritual moment was lost, the Reverend Tileston got to his feet and ushered Sisters Bernice and Kate out of the house, carefully picking a path through the berries covering the porch. He was relieved that the Father and Uncle were nowhere to be seen and he turned at the last step and made a final effort, saying, "Meditate, Mothers, on the Scriptures, have knowledge of them for they are the food which sustains men during times of strife."

The women, engrossed in saving the berries, didn't hear him.

His final proselytical gesture, the attempted distribution of printed pamphlets, was also ignored.

Their composure now completely shattered, the trio which bore   40
God's word into this obscure bend in the river found its way, falteringly, to the sedan, switched on the loudspeaker, and drove slowly away.

Youngest Daughter looked after them as they ventured deeper into the curve along the river and the faint echo of "With the Cross of Jee-e-sus . . . " rang in her ears. After a moment she went to find Uncle who would tell her a story about the star people and how the four blanket carriers once helped him find his way home from a long and difficult journey.

She hoped that the Reverend knew about the blanket carriers.

❖ Focused Freewriting   Consider as possible focal points the contrast between the visitors' enthusiasm and the Family's impassiveness, the characterization of Tileston himself, or one of the topics you've identified in your journal.

❖ Guided Responses

1. When describing the Family's house, Cook-Lynn uses *personification*, attributing to the dwelling human characteristics ("its long-windowed eyes," "It turned its back" [para. 2]). What is the effect of this technique? Why do you think she uses it to describe the house and

later the church ("tight-lipped visage" [para. 4])? How would the effect be altered had she used more conventional description?

2. What is the significance of the initial description of Reverend Tileston and Sisters Kate and Bernice (para. 18)? What do their words and actions indicate about their familiarity with Native American culture?

3. The departure of Reverend Tileston and his disciples contrasts starkly with their arrival. Why does the incident of the upset berry cans convince Tileston "that the spiritual moment was lost" (para. 37)? Why do the women of the Family ignore his departure? What does he realize about their reasons for kneeling with him?

4. The story ends with Youngest Daughter's hope "that the Reverend knew about the blanket carriers." Why do you think Cook-Lynn concludes the tale this way? What does the ending tell readers about the Family's spiritual life and needs?

❖ Shared Responses   In your journal compose a conversation between Reverend Tileston and the Sisters as they leave the Family's house. What would they say about the men's welcome? How would they interpret the change in the women's behavior? How would they feel about the success of their spiritual mission? As you discuss your responses in small groups, explain how your response is supported by what is revealed in the story.

AIDS and the Social Contract

RICHARD GOLDSTEIN

RICHARD GOLDSTEIN *graduated from Hunter College and Columbia University. A senior editor of the* Village Voice, *he has written extensively on social issues and popular culture. His books include* The Poetry of Rock *(1969) and* Reporting the Counterculture *(1989). In this essay, which first appeared in the* Village Voice, *Goldstein argues that we cannot allow the threat of AIDS to push certain groups to the fringes of society. Although it was written in 1987, the article still accurately describes the marginalization not only of people with AIDS but of those who belong to populations at risk for the disease.*

Before reading the selection, discuss in your journal your understanding of the term stigmatization. *What kinds of people are stigmatized? Why do people stigmatize others? What does fear have to do with stigma? How do moral values relate to stigmatization?*

As you make notes on your reading, you may want to focus on the distinctions between Goldstein's rational arguments and his emotional appeals.

THE FIRST GAY MAN I KNEW who died of AIDS did what no human being with a mortal sphincter should have done—or so I told myself. The second was an A-list achiever; he moved in "those circles"—no one who would ever pick me up. So it went. Every time I heard about another death, I would strain to find some basis for a distinction between the deceased and me: He was a clone, a Crisco queen, a midnight sling artist. Then Nathan died of AIDS, and Peter, and Ralph, to whom this piece is dedicated. When it moved in on my friends, the epidemic shattered my presumption of immunity. I, too, was vulnerable, and everything I thought and did about AIDS changed once I faced that fact.

Something like this process is going on in what the media call the "general public." There is a secret logic we apply to people with AIDS: they are sick because they are the Other, and they are the Other because they belong to groups that have always been stigmatized. Every now and then, we read about a woman or child with AIDS, but usually, they are black—another invitation to Otherness for the general public. The disease has brought all sorts of stigma to the surface, and made the fears that any deviance conjures up seen hyper-real. If anything, AIDS has made society less willing to confront those fears, because they suddenly seem so useful as a way to distinguish between people—and acts—that are "risky" or "safe." Rejecting partners who look like they run with junkies or queers is a lot less threatening than mastering the art of condoms. We would rather rely on stigma to protect us than on precautions that would force us to acknowledge that AIDS is not only among us, but of us.

The hot topic in AIDS discussions right now is how efficiently HIV virus can be transmitted during heterosexual intercourse. The medical answer is by no means clear: About a third of the sex partners of infected IV drug users have themselves become infected, but nearly all are women. To date, only six men in New York City have acquired the virus during heterosexual intercourse. Whether this ratio will change over time is anybody's guess. The point is that our sense of who is vulnerable to AIDS is based not on conclusive information about the disease, but on assumptions about its victims. Those who believe AIDS could permeate society tend to see carriers as ordinary people who were infected by specific practices. Any act that spreads the virus is potentially dangerous, regardless of its moral meaning. Those who are convinced the risk is low or nonexistent tend to see these acts, and the people who perform them, as isolated and perverse. Normal people don't do those things, and therefore, they will be spared. On the fringes of this scenario, AIDS is regarded as a natural process of eliminating the abominable.

Most of us are rationalists in the streets and moralists in the sheets. We look back on the past, when people flocked to their churches in times of plague, with pity and contempt for those who thought piety would spare them. Yet we act as if only corrupt acts performed by corrupt people can transmit AIDS. What's more, we proceed as if the corrupt and the virtuous never meet in bed. In this incantation of immunity, I hear echoes of my own denial. Every gay man alive is Ishmael, with a tale to tell about the infinite capacity of human beings to deny what they cannot feel or see. But the stigma that surrounds homosexuality makes it hard for heterosexuals to act as if my witness applies to them. Few of my straight friends are compelled to ponder the question that has haunted me ever since I saw it plastered on a wall in Greenwich Village: "Why him and not me?"

That question must always be asked in regard to the sick, and it is never easy to answer. As Susan Sontag has observed, illness is made infinitely harder to bear by its affinity for metaphor. We pity the afflicted and simultaneously shun them, regardless of the actual danger they pose. In times of plague, the entire range of stigma is called into play in the service of public safety, and one is reminded that the word itself first entered our vocabulary as a description of the marks and signs of illness. For medieval Christians, lepers and victims of bubonic plague were literally *stigmatized*. This diagnosis persists in the contemporary notion that many illnesses—from cancer to ulcers—are expressions of a character flaw.

If the sick are often stigmatized, they are also, in many cases, dispensable. In the best of times, the temptation to ignore the vital interests of some patients is why we have an elaborate code of medical consent. But when plague strikes, we discover that there are no rights so inalienable that they cannot be subordinated to the greater good. Isolating the infected, which began with leprosy in the Middle Ages, soon became a standard public health measure, and once the concept of latent infection gained acceptance, the quarantine expanded to include anyone who might have been exposed. The pages of Defoe are filled with the howls of those locked up in their homes—healthy people trapped with dying relatives or spouses. Finally, the entire city is stigmatized. Murder is not uncommon, as refugees wander the countryside in search of food and shelter. In the plague zone, all the amenities of death—the rituals of nursing, praying, and memorializing—are sacrificed to the imperatives of corpse disposal. Merrymaking is banned, and the stench of gunpowder and vinegar hangs in the air.

So far, our response to AIDS has been governed by the distinctly modern assumption that epidemics can be contained. The periodic demands to crack down on commercial sex notwithstanding, very little has changed about the quality of public life in New York. The suffering of the afflicted, the fear and loathing of the well, are artfully privatized. Visitors would hardly know that this city is in the grip of a health emergency. Partly, this response reflects the fact that AIDS is a plague in slow motion, and we are witnessing a protracted period of latency with no real idea of how far the infection will extend. But our obliviousness also derives from the conviction that AIDS is a disease of deviants. This image persists because, in America, the virus did initially appear to single out groups—and acts—regarded as contaminating. Many illnesses transform their victims into a stigmatized class, but AIDS is the first epidemic to take stigmatized classes and make them victims. Not even syphilis was so precise.

Worse still, AIDS is demonstrably infectious. So carriers are marked both by their Otherness and by the common humanity they are denied. They can infect anyone, though they themselves are infected because they are *not* just anyone. This paradox amplifies the fear and denial that always surround disease. AIDS is not just contagious; it is polluting. To catch this disease is to have your identity stolen; to be lowered, body and soul, into the pit of deviance. This is true even for an "innocent victim," since, once stigma attaches to an illness, it ceases to be about behavior. Anyone with AIDS becomes the Other. And since anyone can be otherized by this disease, deviance itself must be contagious. The most cherished components of personal identity can, irrationally and abruptly, be revoked. This may explain why, though a majority of Americans say they oppose discrimination against people with AIDS, 26 percent of those polled by Gallup last month still fear drinking from a glass or eating food prepared by an infected person. What people fear from casual contact is not so much the disease as its very real power to pollute.

Stigma is the reason an AIDS patient in North Carolina, being transferred from one hospital to another, arrived wrapped in a body bag with a small air tube protruding so he could breathe. Stigma is the reason a plane carrying demonstrators to the gay rights march on Washington was fumigated when the passengers departed. Stigma is the reason a social worker in the Bronx must regularly visit a healthy child whose parents have succumbed to AIDS, because no neighbor will comb her hair. All these incidents occurred within the last year— while, the polls tell us, people are becoming more "enlightened" about AIDS. What people are becoming enlightened about is transmission modes, but the impact of stigma remains poorly understood.

It is rarely mentioned in discussions of AIDS prevention, though the fear of being stigmatized is often the reason infected people have sex without revealing the danger to their partners. It is seldom raised in discussions of testing, though stigma plays a part in determining who will be screened—and why people resist screening in the first place. Stigma has always been a factor in mass detentions; the incarceration of Japanese-Americans during World War II had everything to do with their Otherness. Yet, opponents of proposals to isolate AIDS carriers often argue their case on the less contentious grounds of cost efficiency. To acknowledge that so much of what we fear stems from a conviction that AIDS is a disease of people with "spoiled identities" (Erving Goffman's phrase), would threaten the validity of these categories. So liberals try to separate AIDS the infection from AIDS the stigma, as if, by skirting the issue, they can transcend it. But in fact an unexamined stigma is free to expand.

Because it is not an objective condition, but a relationship between the normal and the deviant, stigma ripples out from the reviled to include their families, their friends, their neighborhoods, even the cities where they congregate. Whole zip codes have been marked by some insurance companies as AIDS zones, and when rumors about a famous fashion designer circulated, the concern was whether people would still be seen in clothing that bears his name. The stigma of AIDS has the capacity to reinvigorate ancient stereotypes, not just about sexuality but about race and urbanity. And no city in America is more vulnerable to this conjunction of biases than New York. Half its AIDS cases are among IV drug users, most of them heterosexual and non-white. Unless a treatment is found, the death toll in East Harlem and Bed-Stuy will eventually approach what it is today in Kinshasa. As the boundaries of infection extend, more and more of us will live in fear of being stigmatized. And in the end, it won't matter who is actually vulnerable. The entire city will bear the brand of AIDS.

And its cost. By 1991, the state health department estimates, one in 10 hospital beds in the city will be occupied by AIDS patients. Some administrators think that figure will be more like one in four—a prospect that terrifies them, since the city's hospitals are already operating at 90 percent of capacity. Moreover, because so many AIDS patients in New York are IV users, they stay in the hospital longer than people with AIDS in other cities, and their infections are more expensive to treat. These patients are already putting an enormous strain on scarce medical resources. As the gap between supply and demand becomes acute, some form of triage could well emerge, along with violations of privacy, autonomy, and informed consent—concepts of medical ethics that were codified at the Nuremberg trials. The mounting despair of physicians in the face of demands that cannot be met from patients who cannot be saved is bound to affect the practice of medicine for all New Yorkers. The burnout is already leading to an exodus of medical residents and interns—as has often happened in cities besieged by plague.

But New York is only the focal point of an epidemic that will soon make its presence felt in every American city. A recent study sponsored by the Centers for Disease Control predicts that, by 1991, the bill for AIDS will be $8.5 billion in medical costs alone—more money than is spent on any group of patients except for victims of automobile accidents. By 1991, the "indirect costs," in productivity, of a disease that kills people in their prime will be more than $55 billion—12 percent of the indirect cost of all illnesses. AIDS will be among the top 10 killers of Americans, and the leading killer of people between the ages of twenty-five and forty-four. "People don't seem to realize that, beyond compassion, there's a real self-interest in controlling AIDS, because we don't have the resources to handle this and all the other diseases," says medical ethicist Carol Levine, executive director of the Citizen's Commission on AIDS. "Everyone who gets sick will pay the price for thinking people can be separated."

Most of us still think AIDS is happening to someone else. It's not. AIDS is happening to some of us, and in some places, many of us. In the Bronx today, 6 percent of all women over 25 using a prenatal clinic, and 14 percent of all patients who had blood drawn in an emergency room, test positive for antibodies. Are they junkies? Are they faggots? Are they niggers? Are they us?

Where epidemics are concerned, the race, class, and sexuality of car- 15 riers has always played a major part in how they are cared for, and how dangerous they seem. Isolation, incarceration, the destruction of whole neighborhoods—all were public health measures practiced in this country, almost exclusively against poor, nonwhite, or sexually disreputable people. AIDS hysteria is a throwback to a politics of public health we thought we'd put behind us—the "purity crusade" that flourished in the early part of this century, constructing the reality of prohibition and the ideal of abstinence. It turns out that the hygiene police have been lying in wait for a crisis like this.

One has only to ponder the thundering silence in the Senate whenever Jesse Helms rises to rail about "safe sodomy" to understand that this most social disease has occasioned a most political response. Every plan for prevention, every push for treatment and research funds, is guided by ideological assumptions, not just about the disease but about those who are vulnerable to it. The image of a person with AIDS determines who we think is guilty or innocent, where we fix blame for the epidemic, and whether we support a policy of education and volition or one of regulation and repression. As with all issues that arise from sexual politics, AIDS exhorts the right to fire and the left to platitudes. But beyond these reflexes, it taps our capacity for empathy, and so, AIDS transcends conventional divisions of left and right. *In These Times*, a socialist weekly with a profamily agenda, calls the president's program of routine testing, "by no means unreasonable." Nat Hentoff, an avowed advocate of minority rights, sees AIDS almost entirely as a threat to the majority. Some black activists regard the distribution of condoms as a "genocidal" act. In each case, one could argue that sexual conservatism is the driving force behind a paranoid agenda on AIDS. But C. Everett Koop, a reactionary on abortion, is a progressive on AIDS. Cardinal Kroll of Philadelphia may echo Vatican orthodoxy when he calls this epidemic "an act of vengeance against the sin of homosexuality," but the same tradition can encompass Sister Patrice, director of patient support services of Saint Vincent's, for whom AIDS is "an especially important time to live out reverence of the human being."

Where we place ourselves in relation to the stigma surrounding this disease determines what we think is necessary to protect ourselves; whether we think laws are needed to identify, and if necessary, isolate AIDS carriers; whether "innocent" people ought to take risks on their behalf. It isn't the extent of risk but its source that made a judge in California recently rule that a teacher of deaf children could be removed from the classroom because he carries HIV antibodies. It's the image of the carrier that makes physicians and cops insist on taking extraordinary precautions. In both these cases, people who might ordinarily place themselves in considerable peril shrink from the relatively minor danger posed by those who carry the HIV virus. In some cities, police who risk their lives in pursuit of criminals wear rubber gloves during a gay rights demonstration. At some hospitals, surgeons who run a high risk of contracting hepatitis (a blood-borne virus that infects twenty-five thousand health workers—and kills three hundred every year) refuse to operate on people with HIV. There's not a single reported case of AIDS being transmitted in the operating room; only doctors and nurses who care for AIDS patients day after day, and lab technicians who are constantly exposed to live virus, have been infected in the line of duty. Nevertheless, Dr. Ronald M. Abel, who has emerged as a spokesman for surgeons refusing to operate on AIDS carriers, calls such "personal, voluntary" decisions into question because they commit not only the physician but "dozens of operating-room assistants . . . to a high degree of risk." Though no policeman has ever been infected by a suspect, Phil Caruso, present of the Patrolmen's Benevolent Association, urges his members to "do whatever is necessary to protect your life and health in any police situation, be it a shootout or the handling of an AIDS sufferer, each of which is a potentially lethal proposition."

Carol Levine calls this refusal to deal with the relatively manageable hazards of AIDS "a disjunction of risk." She maintains that "what people are afraid of is not dying, but what happens before." A cop who is killed rescuing a baby from the ruins of a collapsed building becomes a hero. A doctor who risks his life to treat a victim of radiation poisoning, as happened recently in Brazil, makes the news-weeklies. But the HIV virus invests all its hosts with stigma. Doctors carrying AIDS have lost their practices; a policeman with AIDS could well imagine his peers abandoning him—and his family. Parents told that a classmate with AIDS poses no threat to their children might reason that, even if the children's safety is not at stake, their normalcy is. They may become bearers of a secondary stigma, shunned by other children even more insulated. And for what? "When you voluntarily assume a risk, it fits your self-image," says Levine, "But this is a risk you didn't bargain for—and it's being brought to you by people you're not crazy about—so it's perceived as unacceptable."

Though AIDS has been dehomosexualized in the popular imagination, its origins as a "gay plague" continue to haunt the afflicted—and prevent us from acknowledging that, on a global scale, most people with AIDS are heterosexuals and their children. "What's the hardest thing about getting AIDS?" goes the joke among gay men. "Convincing your mother that you're Haitian." This is a nasty gag about the hierarchy of stigma, but few Haitians would be amused. Each stigma feels like the ultimate injustice, and each oppression seems unique. But the odium attached to race and sexuality actually reflects a single process, whose function is to organize and validate the norm. Anyone can fall prey to such a beast —the "innocent victim" along with the defiled. The irony about health workers demanding that their patients be tested for AIDS antibodies is that it will surely lead to a demand that doctors and nurses take the test—with penalties inevitable for those infected.

I was surprised by the anxiety testing provokes in heterosexuals, until I realized that nearly everyone I know has had a relationship with someone who might be infected. In any urban population, most people who take the test pass through a psychic rite that has less to do with fear of death than with the consequences of a positive result: guilt over the past, rage at the present, fear of the future. That fear must include not only the disease but disclosure—and the full range of rejection that might ensue. Yet it is seldom remarked that, for anyone in a vulnerable group, taking the test is an act of enormous courage. The only controversy is over whether such people should be forced to know their antibody status—and in this debate, the anguish of an AIDS "suspect" is easily subordinated to that great equalizer, the common good. Stigma determines whose interests are expendable. "You always assume the test will happen to someone else," says Levine. "Left to their own devices, most people don't want to know."

That may be wise. As *The New York Times* recently acknowledged, the potential for inaccuracy in the general population is high enough to make mass-testing a "treacherous paradox." Yet certain populations are expected to bear the uncertainty: soldiers, aliens applying for amnesty, Job Corps enrollees, and in some hospitals where state law permits, candidates for surgery. Just last month, at Jesse Helms's behest, the Senate voted to require all veterans' hospitals to "mandatorily offer" antibody testing—an interesting euphemism, since patients who refuse the offer would risk being treated like a person with AIDS. (Turning down the test is, in itself, a stigmatizing experience, because it implies that you have reason to suspect . . . you may have had sex with . . . or might even be . . . !) What these groups have in common is not the danger they might pose to others, but the fact that they depend on public institutions. In America, everyone who relies on the government must expect to forfeit some basic rights. As the debate over testing heats up—and it will, once AIDS enters the arena of presidential politics—we may see this psychodrama acted out on other populations stigmatized by their dependence, such as welfare recipients. An old adage must be dusted off in the current crisis: "If you prick us, do we not bleed?"

This is the classic response to bigotry. Yet it takes a leap of consciousness to see the connection between one stigma and another. Gay men and IV drug users face each other across a vast behavioral divide. But both cultures are based on behavior—indeed, an act of penetration—deemed illicit. Both deviate from the norms of ecstasy, and invest their deviance with enormous significance, using it to foster intimate bonds and a "lifestyle" with its own slang and gait. Both exist as distinct groups within every class, though the drug culture flourishes in the ghetto, as a gory symbol of its vulnerability, and gay culture is most militant in bourgeois society. Of course, shooting heroin has profound implications for one's health and security, while homosexuality, per se, does not. And the drug culture is a violent, haunted environment. But it is a culture, and though we need to keep its damage in mind, we also must wonder how much the antisocial behavior associated with IV use stems from stigma and from the stranglehold of dealers. Freed from both these sources of oppression, the IV user might emerge as a citizen, and we might have to think about what the word "junkie" really conveys.

"It seems that some real change in the cultural norms is going to be necessary," says Don Des Jarlais, a behavioral researcher at the State Division of Substance Abuse Services. "Society will have to make a decision that the chance of spreading this virus is so great, and drug users play so crucial a part in that spread, that we cannot simply allow them to die of AIDS, or make a rule that they must stop using drugs in order *not* to die of AIDS."

Rescuing the IV user may involve some of the same techniques that have worked in the gay community. The sharing of needles must be understood in the same context as anal sex—as an ecstatic act that enhances social solidarity. "Within the subculture, the running partner becomes the substitute for family," Des Jarlais writes. "It would be considered a major insult to refuse to use one's partner's works . . . [or] share one's own works. . . . It would undermine the teamwork and synchronicity of intense experience that are the bases of the run-

ning-buddy relationship." One answer is to provide the IV equivalent
of a condom: bleach kits or clean needles. Contrary to the assumption
that drug users are oblivious to AIDS, Des Jarlais reports that the
epidemic is "a topic of 'grave' concern among IV drug users" in
several cities, and that they "want to learn how to protect themselves
against exposure." Safe injection is as central to the humanistic AIDS
agenda as safe sex.

Des Jarlais has observed much more ambivalence among drug   25
users than among gay men about discussing AIDS prevention with
their sexual partners. It may not be narcissism but fear of abandonment that stands in the way of candor. "Most IV users have their
primary relationship with a non-drug-using partner," says Des Jarlais.
The dependence for food, shelter, and money—not to mention emotional security—can be intense. "When you have a pair like that,
there's no symmetricality of risk. To bring up the subject of AIDS
points to the disparity in the relationship. Half the time, the partner
using condoms gets abandoned by his female lover. So it's easier to
practice safe sex with a casual partner than in a long-term relationship." Surveys have found the same phenomenon among gay men,
but the likelihood that either partner could be carrying the virus
makes mutual safety part of their bond.

Most gay men have other advantages—not just race and class, but
organization. One has only to imagine what the response to AIDS
would be like if the gay rights movement did not exist. There is no
annual parade of drug users down Fifth Avenue, no press that circu-
lates among them, and their advocacy organizations, such as ADAPT,
are severely underfunded. This squad of former and current addicts
tours the shooting galleries, dispensing condoms and clean needles.
But they are hardly as effective as the *junkiebonden* (drug users' unions) of Holland, because in that country, the need to fight stigma with
community is imbedded in both the legal and social service traditions.
Organizing IV users may enable their culture to preserve its members
by altering the rituals of risk, much as gay men have altered theirs. It
may empower users to strike back at oppressive dealers and lobby for
access to meaningful treatment. But funding this liberation means
overcoming what Des Jarlais calls "an empathy barrier."

So far, the support system for people with AIDS has done more to
break down this barrier than any church or public agency. About a
quarter of the clients at Gay Men's Health Crisis are non-gay, and
many groups for "body positives" (as carriers now call themselves)
are integrated. But most gay men and IV users still cannot imagine
that each other's identities might spring from a shared perspective. As
Erving Goffman writes: "Persons with different stigmas are in an
appreciably similar situation, and respond in an appreciably similar

way." AIDS forces us to confront this commonality. The "innocent" black woman infected by her lover, the gay man whose class has always insulated him, the addict abandoned in a hospital ward—all were victims of stigma before they became victims of disease. And though they may live (and die) in utter contempt for each other's deviations from the norm, they are implicated in each other's fate. What happens to the prostitute can happen to the amateur; what they do to the junkie they can do to the fag.

In a hospital, everyone looks like the Other. An AIDS ward is no different, except that, in a public hospital, it might be filled with black people. I walked through one such ward on assignment, trying not to look too hard at the flesh bundles in the beds. Finally, I took a long peek at a black woman in her late thirties, propped up on pillows, surrounded by tissues and magazines. She had the gaunt intensity that people in the late stages of AIDS often get, as if her entire being were confined to the eyes. I stopped seeing her race and sex, both of which are, in some sense, alien to me. Instead, I saw my lover. She resembled him, not as he was but as he might be if he ever got AIDS. I walked on quickly, struggling to fight the welling up of tears.

That night, I dreamt I was leaving my apartment for work. There was a corpse outside the door.

"Love," writes Martin Buber, "is responsibility of an I for a thou." In 30 social terms, this suggests that the bond between citizens is as essential to human development as the bond between lovers, or between parent and child. The social contract is a codification of that bond—an agreement to form a government that sustains us. There is a corollary obligation to protect each other, discharged through duties and limits on behavior which we accept as a fair price for the welfare of the community. Without this compact no individual can survive.

When health crisis strikes, Buber's equation becomes demonstrable: the mutual obligation of the infected and the uninfected *is* the responsibility of an I for a thou. As we confront the limits of freedom, the ego becomes collectivized, and the community, an abstraction in ordinary times, becomes the tangible sum of its parts. An ethic of inclusiveness makes personal sacrifice not only bearable, but unremarkable. One simply does what is necessary, because, as Camus writes, "the only means of fighting a plague is common decency."

The gay community has gone through just such a process in the face of AIDS. It has reshaped itself to care for its own, and changed behavior once regarded as the mark of liberation. But the boundaries of the gay social contract are tightly drawn, for obvious reasons. The common good has always been enforced at their expense. For homosexuals, "public health" has been a euphemism for stigma. They are

among the usual suspects rounded up in panics over sexually transmitted disease. AIDS threatens to revive this tradition of hygiene
pogroms on a much more devastating scale. William Buckley's suggestion that people with AIDS be tatooed on the forearm and buttocks
to warn the uninfected shows how easily the technocratic imagination
can conjure up what Goffman calls a "stigma symbol." Every now and
then, someone hatches a gothic variation on Buckley's scheme; the
urge to literally stigmatize the infected will not die. A newly published tome called *AIDS in America: Our Chances, Our Choices* recommends
"discreet genital tatooing"—just outside the urethra for men, just
inside the labia minora for women. Such proposals are always
couched in the rhetoric of reason and equity, as if they would apply to
anyone who happened to be infected. But in reality, they can only be
enacted on people whose freedom is already precarious. IV users and
prostitutes are eminently detainable, and the parole granted homosexuals can easily be revoked.

It's a mark of my generation to regard the social contract as
fraught with bad faith. But AIDS can't be stopped without a compact
among citizens, enforced by the government. It demands that we
renegotiate the terms, infusing the contract with an expanded sense of
equity—and empathy. "Our best weapon against AIDS," writes Dan
Beauchamp, whose book, *The Health of the Republic*, will be published
next year [1988 Temple University Press],

> would be a public health policy resting on the right to be
> different in fundamental choices and the democratic commu-
> nity as 'one body' in matters of the common health. This new
> policy would mean the right of every individual to funda-
> mental autonomy, as in abortion and sexual orientation, while
> viewing health and safety as a common good whose protec-
> tion (through restrictions on liberty) promotes community
> and the common health.

Under a new social contract, we could talk about the limits on
personal freedom in a time of plague; the need for vulnerable people
to know their antibody status or act as if they are seropositive; the
duty to protect your partners and inform others at risk. But saving
lives also means setting limits on moralism: confronting the full range
of human sexuality, including its expression in the erotics of shooting
up; promoting the use of any implement—condoms, needles—that
slows the spread of AIDS (if anything, we will have to demand *better*
implements); breaking down barriers of sexism that dispose women
to infection and men to secrecy.

AIDS renders both the liberationist mentality and the moralistic   35
world view obsolete. But so far, only the sexual revolution has been

criticized—and in highly moralistic terms. The public health profession has beaten back the most savage proposals for dealing with AIDS, but it is neither powerful enough, nor militant enough, to stand up to political and social conservatism. Ethicists fill monographs with their vision of the social contract, while the usual bad bargain is forged by Church and state. And the epidemic goes on, as sexually transmitted diseases always have—stoked by shame and secrecy.

That's the usual progressive objection to stigma. But in the age of AIDS, social justice can't be promoted in purely pragmatic terms, It's too easy to imagine the majority protected by the erotic segregation that pervades American society. The danger is not that AIDS will wipe our species off the planet, but that it will wipe out people most of us already hate—and that is a moral as well as medical crisis. "My worst fear," says Beauchamp, "is not the concentration camps but a kind of paralysis, in which people will just be left to cope." As a professor of public health in Jesse Helms's home state, Beauchamp sees the epidemic not as an incarnation of the Holocaust (with which it is often wrongly compared), but as a "new civil war." The danger for him lies in "splitting off another chunk of the Republic," condemning millions of Americans to expendability. The wages of this sin is not only death, but "a kind of amnesia about who we are and who we want to be."

We are haunted by events that expose the gap between who we are and who we want to be. They may happen to other people, but they reveal us to ourselves. Hiroshima and Vietnam are watersheds in our culture because they were moral as well as military conflagrations. These two events shaped my generation. I believe AIDS will define the next.

❖ Focused Freewriting   Consider as possible focal points the relationship between AIDS and other plagues, the argument over identification of HIV-positive people, or one of the topics you've identified in your journal.

❖ Guided Responses

1. Early on in the essay Goldstein introduces the concept of Other, arguing, "There is a secret logic we apply to people with AIDS: they are sick because they are the Other, and they are the Other because they belong to groups that have always been stigmatized" (para. 2). What does the concept of Other mean to Goldstein? to you? In what circumstances does it become necessary for people to identify Others? What is accomplished by this tendency?

2. What point is Goldstein trying to make when he points up the irony of police "who risk their lives in pursuit of criminals [wearing]

rubber gloves during a gay rights demonstration" (para. 17)? How might the police explain their use of "extraordinary precautions" in these cases? To what does Goldstein attribute their actions?

3. Goldstein credits (at least in part) gay rights organizations for the increased public response to AIDS (para. 26). In what ways have such organizations helped gay HIV carriers? Based on Goldstein's article and your own experience, explain how activist organizations help both their own constituents and the public at large. Do your observations bear out Goldstein's assertions? Explain your response.

4. How does Goldstein explain the concept of the "social contract"? How does he use it to argue for a more compassionate and understanding approach to the AIDS epidemic? Do you find his argument convincing? Why, or why not?

❖ Shared Responses   In your journal discuss your perceptions of the public response to AIDS. Consider such topics as how communities support AIDS victims, as well as how they educate people about the disease. Do you find the current public response acceptable? Why, or why not? If you think the public response is inadequate, comment on what you would like to see changed. As you discuss your responses in small groups, try to determine the assumptions about AIDS and people with AIDS that underlie individual responses.

The Hopeland

K. KAM

*K. KAM immigrated to the United States from Hong Kong at the age
of two. She received an M.A. in journalism from Syracuse University and currently edits the magazine* California Tomorrow. *In
this essay from* Making Waves: An Anthology of Writing by and
about Asian American Women *by Asian Women United of California (1989), Kam reflects on the similar immigrant experiences of
her parents and her students. Fleeing wartorn countries to partake
of the hope offered by the United States, both generations receive a
mixed welcome. The dreams nurtured by this country are sometimes
tempered by its hostility toward foreigners, especially those who look
"different."*

*Before reading the selection, describe in your journal what you
think the United States offers non-European immigrants. Comment
not only on the opportunities afforded them, but also the obstacles
they face.*

*As you make notes on your reading, you may want to focus on
Kam's metaphoric language, her attempts to understand both her
parents' and her students' experiences, or her sense of responsibility
to both.*

My FATHER TURNED THE PAGES SLOWLY. His eyes shifted over several
photographs in the history book, then focused on a picture taken in
China during World War II. He stared at the black and white shot of
several limp bodies entangled on a stairway, the corpses of families
trampled in a stampede flight from a Japanese raid. Clothing had been
torn from some of the dead, perhaps by desperate villagers. Children,
necks bent awkwardly, were sprawled across the steps like discarded
toys. On the opposite page, a clean, neat title, black on white, read:
"1939–1941 Continuing Horror in China." Decades of hidden grief
began to line my father's face as he closed the book. He handed it back
to me, wordless, as he left the room. My father rarely talked about his
boyhood in China. He kept silent about the war. The photographs
spoke for him.

"Your father's youngest brother vanished during the war when he was nine," my mother confided later when I was sixteen. "Third Uncle and Fourth Uncle were inside a schoolhouse when the planes soared overhead. The children had no time to escape before the bombs exploded on them. When your grandmother heard the loud blasts and saw smoke and fire rising from the schoolhouse, she ran towards her children instead of taking cover. Later, she sifted through the rubble with the rest of the villagers, tearing her hands on jagged bricks, but she found only Third Uncle alive beneath the destruction. When you go to Hong Kong someday, ask him to show you the scars on his legs. As for Fourth Uncle, he simply disappeared in the blast. Your father's mother lost her youngest son in the war and there wasn't even a body left for her to bury. I tell you these things because you ask, but don't mention them in front of your father."

My mother has her own stories to tell, tales of fleeing to damp hillside caves for days whenever bomber planes, too small to be distinguished as ally or foe, were heard in the distance. Grabbing a handful of yams and a bottle of water kept ready for such emergencies, she bolted out the door, joining other villagers in a frenzied exodus as she wrapped the food inside an extra shirt, her only protection from the night chill. As a youngster in wartime, my barefoot mother collected leaves and boiled them, using the congealed sap to wash herself since no one had soap. Matches were a luxury, too. My grandmother would step outside and glance above the housetops before preparing a meager dinner of rice gruel. When she spotted a thin blue curl of smoke rising, she would shove my mother towards it with dry branches in hand to carry home the precious flame.

I try to imagine my mother as a young girl, small and frail with a quiet heart, shiny black hair cropped to prevent her from indulging in hours of vanity before the mirror. I laugh when she tells me some pranksters in her village filled a large vat with dung and lit a fire under it, boiling the smelly contents until they exploded.

But the funny stories are always followed by somber ones that 5 will not let me forget the horrors my parents must have endured. I hear only bits and pieces. My mother tells of drunken soldiers banging on the doors of houses nearby, dragging out screaming girls and raping them in the night. She watched an angry crowd of villagers haul a traitor to the top of a hill, where they hanged him for selling secrets to the enemy. There were the victims forced to kneel on broken glass and the hunted ones who chose suicide. During land raids, she stared mutely as soldiers smashed windows and shot down old women barricading doorways with their bodies to protect young ones inside. During one onslaught, she hid underneath a bed as a soldier entered her house and held a bayonet to her mother's throat.

I am disturbed, yet intrigued. I listen to the stories, casting the characters and writing the script, but my mental exercise is only a game. My parents' China still eludes me.

I wonder also what their first years in America were like. I was only two when we sailed across the ocean that separates me from an ancient and remote homeland.

As a young man, my father lived in Hong Kong. He had worked hard to come to America, taking English classes at night to improve his timid, halting speech. He postponed marriage until he was thirty-one, reluctant to take a wife when he might leave for America the following year. But after a decade of pursuing his dream, he decided to marry my mother in 1959. Three years later, America opened her arms to my father, willing to embrace him after years of snubbing. My mother, less eager, stood defenseless against the powerful charms of America.

My father rarely speaks any more of his deferred dreams. But I have plowed restless fingers through his bookshelves and stumbled upon Shakespeare readers tucked between the Chinese novels with their musty trunk smells, and then a series of English grammar texts, old and yellowed with blotches of tea stains on the pages. I've raided his bookshelves section by section and have found hidden delights each time—a Sinclair Lewis novel, a Tennessee Williams play, a book of poetry. It was impossible for me to imagine my father's thickly accented syllables wrapping themselves around the elegant words.

When he first came to this country, his dreams incubated in the 10
heat of a stuffy kitchen by day and pecked a little further out of their confining shells at night. Hard shells—language barriers, uncertainties, prejudices, fears—were chipped away bit by bit as he attended night school and struggled to become an educated man, a new success in a new land. Week after week, he sat under the glaring fluorescent lights of the classroom eking out gram-ma-ti-cal essays as English teachers with pleased smiles and small nods of approval assigned him book after book of "American reading."

But somewhere far in the past, my father stopped the weary tasks of "American reading" and writing assigned essays. He relegated his American books to the shelves and focused his energy upon the persistent questioning of his children, each of whom had gone off to college.

"What are you going to do next year when you graduate?"

"I'm not sure yet, Dad. I'm thinking of working for a couple of years, and then maybe I'll go back to school," answers his son, the one who studied economics.

"Why don't you become a dentist?" my father urges.

"It's not that easy, Dad. Besides, I don't want to become a dentist." 15

Once, when I worked for a group of attorneys in San Francisco, my father asked where all of them had attended law school. "Where do they go on vacations? Do they ski? Do they own houses up in the mountains?" I was reluctant to answer, not wanting to fan age-old disappointments. Before I could reply, he sighed, "You know, a very nice doctor comes into the restaurant all the time, and he always seems sad to me. I ask him what is wrong and he tells me his son is no good—uses too many drugs. Sells them, too. He asks me what my kids do and I tell him four are college graduates. He says that's beautiful, says I'm a lucky man."

His words startled me. When we had run home from grade school with near-perfect report cards, my father admonished us solemnly. "Never compare yourselves to those below you, only to those above you," he said year after year. My mother chided us, too. "You must study hard and make something of yourselves. When I was in China, I had to leave school at fourteen and start working as a seamstress in Hong Kong when I was sixteen. If I had been given the same opportunities you've received, I could have become anything I wanted— anything."

Their words seep into my blood and cause my muscles to pull taut. At times I am frustrated by the pressure to succeed, yet I am driven by guilt and sadness to redress my parents' lost dreams and regrets of an uneducated past.

Somehow, I owe another kind of debt because of their past, and so I, the American daughter, have sought jobs working with refugees in Chinatown legal clinics, resettlement agencies, and inner-city schools.

When I first started working at the high school where I am now a counselor, I would follow the Cambodian and Vietnamese refugee students with my eyes, listen for conversations about their pasts, alert myself to clues about them in their essays. I studied student transcripts that read "Birthplace: Vietnam, Year: 1969" and was astonished at the birth of tender, delicate children, all smooth flesh and soft hair, born amid bombing in the night. When I looked into the children's faces at school, their slow eyes and solemn gazes told of loss and loneliness. They opened their current distresses to me, but I remained on the periphery of their past hurts. In time, the silence of the children broke and the past poured forth.

A beautiful young girl with honeyed skin and trusting eyes sat in my office and told me of her childhood in a Khmer Rouge labor camp in Cambodia.

By day, she sat in the dirty, bleak schoolroom Pol Pot's soldiers had set up, mumbling answers, fearful that the simple-minded peasant teachers would catch a glimmer of too much intelligence in her eyes if she recited too readily or looked up too quickly. She had already seen too many bright people and their families slaughtered by the Khmer Rouge. "Never admit that your father was an engineer in Phnom Penh," her mother had warned her. "We must say he was a rice farmer."

In the fields, she cowered under the glares of the soldiers and wept, mouth shut, half starved, as she struggled to spread big pails of dung over the crops. Those around her collapsed dead from hunger, beatings, and exhaustion as they worked in the fields. When she saw them drop, she mourned for her parents, who had died within months of each other.

Not even a brother or a sister remained by her side. The soldiers had herded the biggest, strongest children, her sister among them, to another camp to build reservoirs to hoard the rainwater.

When my student watched young women in her camp forced to 25 marry Khmer Rouge soldiers who were deformed from the war—ugly, legless men with bulging stumps—she thought of her seventeen-year-old sister now digging trenches in the strong children's camp.

"Pol Pot's soldiers shouted 'enemy' at me all the time," she told me. "I don't know why they hated me. I never hated them before."

The stories differ in time and place and intensity, but this child's voice speaks to me of the pain when a parent or brother or sister is lost forever, when a homeland is ravaged—things I wish my father could tell me but I know he cannot.

Sometimes when I walk the corridors of the high school, I see many children who look so much like me—round faces, tilted eyes, dark hair—but who are not really like me at all. A few have become sad, quiet, and crazy because of the war.

Then I notice that some of the children who have walked through fire in Southeast Asia have emerged not destroyed, but tempered with strength, hope, and resilience. For these children, obstacles simply mean finding another way.

Daily I see these young ones contend with the rigors of their new 30 lives here. I overhear a willowy Vietnamese girl attempt to discuss a class project with her teacher, a ruddy-faced man with graying hair. Her speech stumbles along, then halts when she utters a phrase he cannot understand.

"Could you please say that last word again?"

Her eyes dart away from his face to the floor, and once more, the phrase tumbles out of her mouth in halting English. His eyebrows knit quizzically. She senses his confusion and blushes red, disgraced and flustered at not being able to make herself understood. But she tries once more. The teacher's face strains hard, trying to redeem the efforts of a nervous girl whose words hang suspended in the air between them.

I am reminded of my mother's frustrations. Once, when I was young, my mother came home weeping from the restaurant pantry where she worked. I overheard her telling my father that the loud, fat woman who sliced meats at a work station next to hers had berated her all morning until my mother felt her small voice explode within her and rise to the top of her throat like a ball of flame. She tried to yell back, but the words would not come out in English. I ran into my room and slammed the door furiously, wishing I could storm into that kitchen pantry and tongue-lash that big mean woman with all the scathing American words I knew.

When I hear tales of faceless, merciless youths who taunt refugee children, spit on them, shove them, and laugh at them as they read aloud in English classes, a bit of the same old childish rage starts to rise within me. I feel silly and impotent, like a little girl slamming doors again. Then I tell myself that my mother never really needed me to fight her daily battles for her. She waged them on her own, and now in her self-sufficiency she no longer needs her children to accompany her to stores, banks, and post offices.

As I follow these young refugees in their struggles to begin again   35
in a land of promise, I remember my father's youthful ambitions. From the clamor and filth of refugee camps, America still shines in her splendor—sweet, clean, free. "It was a dream, but it did come true," writes one Vietnamese student about coming to this country. "It was an eager wish, yet it was fulfilled as if by magic. When stepping on this hopeland, America, I knew that I had stepped forward to a future filled with faithful promises." Only three years ago, as a child of fourteen, she had crouched stealthily in a sampan headed for sea. On the waters, she fled from Thai pirates and endured the harshness of camp life in order to reach this new country.

One student told me, "Most of my life has been spent struggling, so now that I'm in a peaceful land, my energies will go towards moving ahead." These young people pour into my office with dreams of becoming doctors, bankers, engineers, computer scientists, and accountants. Many are eager and diligent, smart and capable. Some are conscientious to an extreme, recopying applications four times over before sending them to colleges that hold within their walls the promise of a bright future.

I see all the good things America has to offer these young refugees—peace, education, opportunity, food, warmth, a future, and a hope. They are free now. I am anxious to see them accomplish what they came here hoping to achieve, but I worry that some may see their dreams unfulfilled. I am afraid that some may not be given the jobs they deserve because of their sex or the slant of their eyes or the inflections in their speech. Some of them will be called "chinks" and "gooks" and may suffer physical beatings because they have entered a society that does not automatically make room for them. Not all of them will achieve the high goals for which they aim. If they fail, will they lament the missed opportunities? Will their dreams become their children's duties, legacies of guilt and regret?

New lives in America are not easily forged. One of my brightest students, a Vietnamese war orphan, awoke one morning, and shunning the soft radio music she relied on at the start of each day to soothe what the American teachers labeled "cultural adjustment," she wandered to a nearby lake and found a wizened Chinese man playing his flute on the shore. Out of the silver instrument floated sweet, holy, tremulous notes unlike anything the girl had heard except in Vietnam.

A few days later, she appeared in my office, her eyes looking sad and aged. She told me the story of the flute and of how she lingered on, listening until the old man went away. "Now I must confess to you, my counselor, that I do not have the same heart to be in this country. I do not fit well in this society. I do not like to compete all the time. I know it cannot happen, but often, I wish I could go back to Vietnam and become a simple person again."

The homeland will never be forgotten. But I remain buoyed in my   40 hopes for these children's futures when I recall their exuberance upon arriving in this new land. One child wrote: "I was overwhelmed by the friendly hospitality of some Americans who had given me an optimistic prediction for my next days in this country. At that moment, I had almost forgotten all the terribly dark times of my life. Wishing to fly to another promised land. . . . And now, the wish has come to reality, even though at first, I could not believe it was so. America has opened her arms and greeted us, the miserable birds struggling against the winter's coldness, with the warmest humanity."

Let it be so, I whisper. Like my parents, these children have come to the hopeland, and I celebrate them.

❖ Focused Freewriting   Consider as possible focal points the similarities between the experiences of Kam's parents' and those of her students, the immigrant's sense of belonging in America, or one of the topics you've identified in your journal.

❖ Guided Responses

1. In her first paragraph Kam writes, "My father rarely talked about his boyhood in China. He kept silent about the war. The photo-

graphs spoke for him." Why can't he talk about his childhood? What do the photographs and the other contents of his bookshelves tell his daughter about his youth and his early years in America?

2. Although Kam sometimes feels "frustrated by the pressure to succeed," she also admits to being "driven by guilt and sadness to redress [her] parents' lost dreams and regrets of an uneducated past" (para. 18). Why should she feel guilt over her parents' past? Why does she feel the need to make up for their lost dreams? How typical do you think such feelings are for American children?

3. Kam writes of the rage she feels when she "hears tales of faceless, merciless youths who taunt refugee children, spit on them, shove them, and laugh at them as they read aloud in English classes. . . . " But then she reminds herself that her mother, on whose behalf Kam felt similar rage, "never really needed me to fight her daily battles for her. She waged them on her own . . . " (para. 34). Do you think her students need her to wage their battles? Why, or why not? How does the analogy to her mother's battles help Kam understand her students' prospects?

4. Why do you think Kam includes the anecdote about the girl listening to the Chinese man playing his flute? Why is it important to remember that occasionally a refugee wishes that she "could go back to Vietnam and become a simple person again" (para. 39)? Does Kam believe that memories of the homeland can coexist with loyalty to the "hopeland"? Do you agree with her? Explain your response.

❖ Shared Responses   In your journal list ways in which institutions in your community might help refugees adjust to life in the United States. Consider their need for housing, language assistance, employment counseling, general education, cultural adjustment, and the like. As you discuss your responses in small groups, try to synthesize responses to form a comprehensive plan for assistance.

The Place of the Solitaries

SUE HALPERN

Sue Halpern *holds a doctorate from Oxford University, where she studied as a Rhodes Scholar. A prolific writer, her work has appeared in such diverse publications as* Granta, The New York Review of Books, Sports Illustrated, *and* Rolling Stone. *Interested in exploring "privacy as a quality of life, rather than . . . as a matter of rights," Halpern briefly entered the lives of a number of solitary people and wrote the critically acclaimed* Migrations to Solitude *(1992), from which this selection is taken. In this essay two hermits discuss the value of life away from the distractions of civilization. Ned and Mae are not only content to live apart from other people, but they revel in the peace their solitude brings them.*

Before reading the selection, describe in your journal your perception of what a hermit is. Record your notions about the appearance, living accommodations, habits, and values of people who deliberately separate themselves from society.

As you make notes on your reading, you may want to focus on Halpern's use of quotations, her attitude toward Ned and Mae, or her careful descriptions of their lifestyle.

To GET THERE you drive past the village of Severance and through the town of Paradox, names that make sense when you are going to visit hermits. Then you go five miles one way and nine and a quarter another, look for a stump between two blue spruces, walk half a mile through an open pine forest, turn at the forked birch, cross a stream on a slatted bridge, walk uphill another quarter mile, and listen for her ax or his shovel. Actually, this is not how you get there at all. They asked me not to tell. "Otherwise we wouldn't be hermits, would we?" the one I call Ned says. The other one, Mae, nods in agreement. She is just over five feet, and tough, like beef jerky. She wears blue jeans and a striped man-tailored shirt. Her hair is clipped short and shaped like a helmet. It is white. She is sixty-eight. She has been a hermit for forty years.

The same with Ned. He has merry blue eyes and a gap-toothed grin, and he's tall and as thin as a split rail. He is so thin, in fact, that his green cotton pants, which are held up by suspenders, look like waders. He's got on a plaid flannel shirt and work boots. He is seventy years old. He wears his clothes sincerely.

" . . . [W]e readily attribute some extra virtue to those persons who voluntarily embrace solitude, who live alone in the country or in the woods or in the mountains and find life sweet," the aspiring recluse John Burroughs wrote in a volume called *Indoor Studies*. "We know they cannot live without converse, without society of some sort, and we credit them with the power of invoking it from themselves, or else of finding more companionship with dumb things than ordinary mortals." But with Ned and Mae it is not this way, for they have each other. They are solitaries together, but solitaries nonetheless. They live deep in the forest in a house of their own construction. They are self-sufficient. They would prefer not to know you.

Ned and Mae were not born to this life. They had conventional up-bringings—as conventional as upbringings were during the Depression. After high school in Herkimer, New York, where they were sweethearts, Mae worked as a clerk in a five-and-ten-cent store and Ned strung lines for the telephone company. His health was bad, he had kidney disease, and a doctor suggested that a month or two in the woods would be restorative. If two months might help, the newly-weds reasoned, what about two years, or twenty-two? They quit their jobs and moved to the southwestern end of the Adirondack Park, where Ned's father, a lawyer, had been given a parcel of lakefront in exchange for legal work. There was a summer camp on the lake, and the two of them found work there as carpenters and caretakers. They started an egg and chicken route. Ned tied flies and sold them through the mail. But after a while the lake got "too busy," Ned says, and they decided to move.

"We took out a map of the Adirondacks and circled the places that 5 interested us," he recalls. In their spare time they visited each one, camping out or sleeping in their car in order to see it through varied grades of light. It took three years before they found the land they wanted. "B'gosh, we liked it over here," Ned says. They sold their house on the water and bought 175 acres of ridge and hill.

"He shouldn't be here," Mae says of Ned. "The doctor told his father he wouldn't see forty. That was fifty years ago. See what the Adirondack woods can do for you."

But it's not just Ned. The Adirondack woods have long been hospitable to hermits. In *Tales of Hamilton County*, local historians Ted Aber and Stella King devote page after page to the likes of Noah John

Rondeau, Ezra Bowen, Laramie Harney, and Adirondack French Louie—men who lived in the interior by their wits and the good graces of the land, eighteenth-century men born a century too late, men who would have been a century late no matter when they were born. Once, according to Aber and King, a consumptive city dweller came to spend the winter in French Louie's cabin in the hope of regaining his strength. As soon as he arrived he tacked a calendar to the wall near his bed. "It was the first thing that met the hermit's eyes when he reached the door. Instantly he snatched the offensive decoration from the wall and shoved it into the stove. 'If you stay with me, tomorrow will be just like today, and today just like yesterday—no different,' he pronounced."

It is time, as much as distance, that distinguishes the hermit's life. It is Thoreau sitting in his doorway from sunrise till noon. It is Rousseau, self-exiled on the island of Saint-Pierre, trading philosophy for flowers. ("Botany is the ideal study for the idle, unoccupied solitary," he writes; "a blade and a magnifying glass are all the equipment he needs for his observations. . . . This ideal occupation has a charm which can only be felt when the passions are entirely at rest. . . . ") It is Ned and Mae spending two years laying nine hundred feet of pipe by hand from a stream to their house. It is Ned and Mae spending an entire winter peeling the bark of the balsams, oaks, maples, and pines they felled in the warm seasons before. They brought these logs down without benefit of a chain saw or a skidder or horses. And they raised them up again to build their house without using a crane. Six years— that's how long it took them.

It is a playful corduroy house on a rise, with windows that open to every point of the compass, to tree and bird and sky and hill. Inside there is a root cellar' and a mud room, a bathroom, a bunk room, a kitchen and hearth on the first floor, and a bedroom, study, and sitting room on the second. The house has running water—hence the nine-hundred-foot pipe—some of which is left to bake in a holding tank off the kitchen, and an indoor toilet, a concession, they say, to their advancing ages, though Mae still prefers the outhouse. They built this hermitage when they were in their sixties.

Before this they lived in a similar two-story homemade dwelling, 10 but without plumbing. It is downwind from this one, overlooking a pond. They built the pond, too, clearing the half acre with picks and shovels, digging down six feet, prising the stones with their hands, using the stones to make a dam and a retaining wall and a walkway. They have built other things as well: a log garage, a summer kitchen, three garden plots, two wood-fired hothouses, a storage shed, a carpentry workshop, a composter, and three pavilions filled with enough split wood to keep them going for a year if need be.

Ned and Mae are off the power grid. They don't have electric lights, telephones, a toaster, or a washing machine. If they did, they wouldn't have anything to plug them into. "I guess most people would go crazy," Mae says. For them it is the other way around. The absence of electricity doesn't simplify things; it keeps them simple. Day begins at sunrise and ends with darkness. What do they do then? "We make popcorn every night in the winter," Ned says. "Well, that takes a lot of the evening. I guess it's what you'd call kind of a slow lifestyle."

When Emerson writes in "Self-Reliance," "The civilized man has built a coach but has lost the use of his feet," he suggests that people like Ned and Mae, who are fleet, are uncivilized, and this is true. Before everything else, civilized man (and woman) is a consumer. He lives in a market economy, he feels bound to do his part. Not Ned and Mae. They have taken a lien on nature's capital. They have a three-season refrigerator a few yards from their door—a galvanized tub sunk in a swift, cold stream—and a winter refrigerator indoors, which captures the frigid air of outdoors. They can't afford a "real" refrigerator; their income is three or four thousand dollars a year, about half the amount the state welfare office pays to individuals on home relief. In conventional, civilized terms they are dirt-poor. But poverty is a matter of desires as well as of means. Ned and Mae *would be* poor if they wanted a 16-cubic-foot white enamel frost-free refrigerator or a ten-cycle washing machine. What they want instead is to spend the afternoon in the sun, kneading their dirty clothes in a metal basin. What they want is to have as few clothes to wash as possible. And so they are not poor. Wood that you chop for fuel is said to warm you twice, first in the splitting, then in the burning. In the same way, Ned and Mae say that they are enriched by their wants.

A few years ago, on December 25, a neighbor hiked in on snowshoes to wish the hermits Merry Christmas and was treated to a sermon denouncing the holiday. Every day is a celebration, they grumbled. No day is a holiday if you have to work so hard at it, and so on. Chastened, the neighbor retreated. A few days later, walking in the woods, Ned and Mae found a small package, a gift, hanging from a tree. "I guess she was too scared to hand it to us," Ned says, laughing.

He can laugh. He takes himself seriously, but not grimly. He doesn't confuse their way of life with a religion and make it an orthodoxy or a mission. (He doesn't tell you their way is the true way because he probably doesn't think you are up to many of its truths.) Nor does he confuse religion with God. Religion is the creation of people—to Ned it is as artificial as electric light. God is the creator of the world he holds dear and *is* the light. In the poems Ned writes, this theme plays like a fugue. "High up in the mountains a fir tree stands/By a lakelet beneath a bright star—/The icy wind shivers its snow-laden hands,/Sparkling and glittering in light from afar. . . . /Other fir trees glory in tinsel and gold/For 'tis Christmastime all over the land,/But none are more loved in heaven above/Than this wildling cared for by God's own hand." The title of the poem is "God's Christmas Tree."

Most of Ned's poems and essays exalting the natural world and   15 lamenting its destruction, as well as his gardening tips, and Mae's too, can be found in a little index-card-sized magazine they put out on a hand-cranked mimeograph machine in the sixties and seventies called *Backwoods Journal*. ("We thought other people might be interested in doing what we were doing," Ned says. Or at least daydreaming about it.) It cost two dollars a year for six issues, and at its peak there were a few hundred readers across the country whose letters found their way to the hermits' post-office box to request a subscription. A typical issue had thirty-five articles spread over sixty pages, most of which were written by Ned and Mae, using six or seven pseudonyms. (Their real names never appeared in the publication.) Rhubarb, the dangers of lead shot, winter camping, and migrating geese were popular subjects. There were no ads, but there was a Personals column. (From a man in Greeley, Pennsylvania: "I'm looking for a Birthday Twin to correspond with and compare notes on our trail through life, a person who was born October 10, 1911, the same day as I. I was an only child as my Mother passed on shortly after my birth. I'm married to a wonderful wife.") Ned did all the artwork in the magazine—pen-and-ink portraits of pine martens and coyotes, sketches of waterfalls and mountains—and though he was not trained as an artist, it is clear that he has a gift for this, too. In another life he might have been able to parlay it into a career and consider himself blessed to be able to work at what he loved.

After they turned over *Backwoods Journal* to a couple of homesteaders who had been regular contributors, and the homesteaders found it harder to put out a magazine than to live in a tent in the mountains in winter and gave it up, Ned and Mae began to sing. Putting their poems to music, they recorded "Songs of the Wildwood" on a battery-operated, dual-head boom box, from which they then made a bunch of copies, one at a time. The album is dedicated to " . . . those folks everywhere who find inspiration in unspoiled wild lands." On it, Ned sings melody in a wobbly baritone and Mae joins in with a thin soprano, and the overall effect, which is to make you want to turn off the tape player and go for a strenuous hike, is probably what they wanted to accomplish anyway.

But why shouldn't they sing, and even sing badly, especially when they have something to say? ("When life becomes a weary thing, and each new day is hard to bear, take your burdens to the hills, and you will find them lighter there . . . " begins one song.) And why shouldn't they write poems? It is symptomatic of how civilized we have become that poetry must now be written by poets. But if poetry is left to the poets, it means that something else, picking apples, say, is left to the apple pickers, and not only don't we get good poems about harvesting apples, we get a society that believes that apple pickers can't write poetry—which is what we have. But not Ned and Mae. They have the society of each other, and they have poems, and they have fresh apples, and no one to tell them they can't.

When Thoreau went to Walden Pond to live for two years, it was a young man's experiment. When the time was up, he quit his cabin and moved back to Concord and got on with his life. Ned and Mae were about thirty when they settled on their land, and it was no more an experiment than tilling the soil is an experiment for a farmer. It's like the difference between dating and marriage, Thoreau's retreat and Ned and Mae's. The hermits are wedded to their life in the woods. It's a marriage that's not about what they don't have (central heat, news-papers, ice cream) but what they do (buffleheads on their pond, a pond), and it's not about what they have given up (children, light bulbs), but how to use what they have to make what they need.

Ned shows off his tomato plants, which are still bearing fruit in the late fall, and his cucumbers and lettuce. He mentions the filtration system he rigged up to collect leaves from the pond and points out a ground-floor skylight he built to illuminate trips to the root cellar. He seems genuinely surprised that the things he knows are not common knowledge. Maybe five or six people visit a year, mostly family. "My sister comes and wants to go shopping," Mae says. It's as if she had heard of the practice but can't quite picture it. They don't get out of the woods much. When they do, encounters with their own kind send them back to seek the fellowship of the wind and the whippoorwill. They are happy there. Not gleeful, get-out-the-noisemakers happy, but happy as larks, or buntings.

"We felt kind of funny at first, living this way," Mae says, "but not anymore." Forty years in the woods earning a life, not a living. "A lot of people, I think, wished they would have done it."   20

❖ Focused Freewriting Consider as possible focal points con-trasts between Ned and Mae's life and your own, the hard work involved in a hermit's life, or one of the topics you've identified in your journal.

❖ Guided Responses

1. After a meticulous description of the route to Ned and Mae's home, Halpern writes, "Actually, this is not how you get there at all. They asked me not to tell" (para. 1). What is the effect of this opening? Why do you think she chose to open this way, rather than simply stating that the hermits wished no one to know where they lived?

2. The essay is sprinkled with references to other writers: John Burroughs (para. 3), Ted Aber and Stella King (para. 7), Rousseau (para. 8), Emerson (para. 12), and Thoreau (paras. 8, 18). How do these references help readers understand the choices Ned and Mae have made? How would the impact of the essay be different if the references were eliminated?

3. Commenting on Ned and Mae's income of three to four thousand dollars a year, Halpern writes, "But poverty is a matter of desires as well as of means" (para. 12). What do you think she means by this statement? Do you consider Ned and Mae poor in any way? Explain your response.

4. How do you interpret Halpern's comment, "It is symptomatic of how civilized we have become that poetry must now be written by poets" (para. 17)? What is wrong with such a level of civilization, according to Halpern? Do you agree with her assessment? Why, or why not?

❖ Shared Responses   In your journal respond to Mae's final comment in the essay, "A lot of people, I think, wished they would have done it." After reading this account, what do you find attractive about the hermit's life? What do you consider unappealing about it? As you discuss your responses in small groups, try to distinguish between responses that romanticize the solitary life and those that appear more realistic.

❖ **Generating Ideas** Reread all of your journals and annotations from the selections in this unit. Look for connections between selections or still unanswered questions. First, list those connections and questions as briefly as possible. Next, choose two or three to elaborate on. As you respond in more detail to the connections/questions, focus on one topic and consider how well it would serve you in an extended piece of writing. Then decide what kind of writing best suits your topic: Should you write a conventional essay, a poem, a short story, or a scene? Would your topic lend itself more to a letter to the editor or a personal letter? Might a proposal to solve a specific problem be a good choice? Possible topics:

1. the difficulty of escaping from the cycle of poverty
2. middle-class attitudes toward marginalized groups
3. making the choice to remain outside society
4. support services for ostracized or deprived groups
5. the impact of marginalized groups on mainstream society

❖ **Focusing Responses** Choose one of your extended responses and formulate a statement of one or two sentences that captures its essence. Use this statement as a guide to organize your piece. (If you write an essay, letter, or proposal, the statement may actually appear as a thesis.)

❖ **Guided Writing Assignments**

1. Both Hull and Pick describe men who express a desire to work but are thwarted in their attempts to find employment. Write an essay in which you analyze the reasons for Johnny Washington's and George's inability to find or keep a job. Consider not only what the two men say about their respective situations but also what those words imply about their sense of control over their own lives. Consider also the stated and implied comments of the authors. If possible, conclude with suggestions for ways to help men like Washington and George escape the cycle of poverty and unemployment.

2. In Goldstein's and Kam's essays we see people who do live in society but are often viewed as Other. Write a poem or story that explores the notion of Other, considering questions such as the following: Why do people identify certain groups as Other? What comfort do people take in distinguishing themselves from the Other? What are the effects of this practice on those who ostracize and those who are ostracized?

3. Imagine yourself as Cathy Stern. Having just read Hull's "Slow Descent into Hell," you feel compelled to write a letter to *Time* magazine about your own haunted visions of the homeless. In the letter allude to the experience you describe in "Those Places" and discuss how Hull's account of living with homeless men has helped you understand your reaction to the man with the blanket.

4. Halpern and Cook-Lynn write about people with no desire to become part of mainstream society or to share its values. Using material from both selections, write an essay comparing the advantages and disadvantages of the choice to remain apart from civilization. Consider not only the tangible differences but also the psychological and spiritual differences between life in and out of society. You may want to use as your focal point the reasons that Ned and Mae and the Family choose to live as they do.

❖ Research Topics   As you consider how to expand your reading beyond the selections in this chapter, identify in your journals and notes questions that remain unanswered or topics you'd like to explore further. Or you may consider the following:

1. Homelessness has been a prominent problem in the United States for over a decade. Through library and field research, investigate several theories explaining the rise in homelessness during the past ten to fifteen years. Research books on the subject, as well as articles in popular and academic journals. Interview social science professors, political leaders, and officials of organizations devoted to serving the needs of the homeless. If possible, visit a shelter and speak with workers and residents about their perception of the origins of the problem. Based on your research, decide which of the theories offered you consider most credible. Explain your reasoning.

2. Research immigration trends in a community with which you are familiar. Identify the countries from which people emigrated, their reasons for coming here, and the type of reception they encountered on arrival. Consider the problems different immigrant groups faced, the contributions they made, and the extent to which they have been assimilated into the dominant culture. Try to draw conclusions from your research about experiences shared by most immigrant groups. If appropriate, also highlight differences in experiences between groups.

Acknowledgments continued from page ii

Stuart D. Bykofsky. "No Heart for the Homeless" from the Dec. 1, 1986 issue of *Newsweek*. Copyright © 1986 by Stuart D. Bykofsky. Reprinted by permission of the author.

Jean Seligmann. "The Medical Quandary" from the January 14, 1985 edition of *Newsweek*. Copyright © 1985 by Newsweek, Inc. All Rights Reserved. Reprinted by permission.

Frank Bentayou. "The New Chain Gangs" from the August 1992 edition of *The Progressive*. Copyright 1992 by The Progressive, Inc. Reprinted with permission from *The Progressive* magazine, 409 East Main Street, Madison, WI 53703.

Chapter Two

Michael Ventura. "Report from El Dorado" from *Shadow Dancing in the USA* by Michael Ventura. Copyright © 1985 by Michael Ventura. Reprinted by permission of The Putnam Publishing Group.

Ben Hamper. "Growing Up in Greaseball Mecca" from *Rivethead* by Ben Hamper. Copyright © 1991 by Ben Hamper. Reprinted by permission of Warner Books/New York.

Lorene Cary. "June 1989" from *Black Ice* by Lorene Cary. Copyright © 1991 by Lorene Cary. Reprinted by permission of Alfred A. Knopf, Inc.

Robert Coles. "The Children of Affluence" from the July 1977 issue of *The Atlantic*. Copyright 1977 by Robert Coles. Reprinted by permission of the author.

Itabari Njeri. "What's in a Name?" from the January 29, 1989 edition of the *Los Angeles Times*. Copyright © 1989 by the *Los Angeles Times*. Reprinted by permission of the *Los Angeles Times*.

David Mura. "Secrets and Anger" from the September/October 1992 issue of *Mother Jones*. Copyright © 1992 by the Foundation for National Progress. Reprinted by permission of Mother Jones.

Mickey Roberts. "It's All in How You Say It," from *Talking Leaves*, edited by Craig Lesley, is reprinted by permission of the author.

Elinor Langer. "The Chameleon." Excerpt is from an essay published in *The Nation*, "The American Neo-Nazi Movement Today" by Elinor Langer. Research for the essay was supported, in part, by grants from the Fund for Investigative Journalism and the Dick Coldensohn Fund. Copyright © 1990 by Elinor Langer. Reprinted by permission of Georges Borchardt, Inc., for the author.

Inés Hernandez. "Para Teresa" from *Con Razón, Con Razón, Corazon: Poetry* by Inés Hernandez. Reprinted by permission of the author.

Chapter Three

Lev Raphael. "Okemos, Michigan" from *Hometowns*, edited by John Preston. Copyright © 1991 by Lev Raphael. Reprinted by permission of the author.

Lorene Cary. "Welcome to St. Paul's" from *Black Ice* by Lorene Cary. Copyright © 1991 by Lorene Cary. Reprinted by permission of Alfred A. Knopf, Inc.

Richard Rhodes. "Cupcake Land," copyright © 1987 by *Harper's* Magazine. All rights reserved. Reprinted from the November 1987 issue by special permission.

Joseph L. White. "Black Family Life" from *The Psychology of Blacks: An Afro-American Perspective*. Copyright © 1984 by Joseph L. White. Reprinted by permission of Prentice Hall, Englewood Cliffs, New Jersey.

Virginia A. Huie. "Mom's in Prison" reprinted from the April 1992 issue of *The Progressive*. Copyright 1992 by Virginia A. Huie. Reprinted by permission of the author.

Wil Haygood. "The Remarkable Journey of Willie Edward Gary" reprinted from the May 24, 1992 edition of *The Boston Globe*. Reprinted courtesy of *The Boston Globe*.

Steven VanderStaay. "Ask a Homeless Person . . ." from *Street Lives: An Oral History of Homeless Americans* by Steven VanderStaay. Copyright 1992 by Steven VanderStaay. Reprinted by permission of New Society Publishers.

David Bradley. "Harvest Home" from *Family Portraits*, edited by Carolyn Anthony. Copyright © 1989 by David Bradley. Used by permission of Doubleday, a division of Bantam Doubleday Dell Publishing Group, Inc.

Chapter Four

Amy Tan. "Two Kinds" from *The Joy Luck Club* by Amy Tan. Copyright © 1989 by Amy Tan. Reprinted by permission of The Putnam Publishing Group.

Ana Castillo. "Napa, California" from *Women Are Not Roses*. Originally published by Arte Publico Press. Copyright © 1984 by Ana Castillo. Reprinted by permission of Susan Bersholz Literary Services, New York.

David Arnold. "A Free Press Flourishes Behind Bars" from the March 13, 1989 issue of *Time*. Copyright © 1989 by Time Inc. Reprinted by permission.

Lars Eighner. "On Dumpster Diving" first appeared in *The Threepenny Review*, Fall 1991. Copyright © 1991 by Lars Eighner. Reprinted by permission of the author.

Chapter Seven

Nan Robertson. "Promises" from *Girls on the Balcony* by Nan Robertson. Copyright © 1992 by Nan Robertson. Reprinted by permission of Random House, Inc.

Susan Faludi. "Teen Angels and Unwed Witches" from *Backlash* by Susan Faludi. Copyright © 1991 by Susan Faludi. Reprinted by permission of Crown Publishers, Inc.

Anna Quindlen. "The Glass Half Empty" from the November 22, 1990 issue of the *New York Times*. Copyright © 1990 by The New York Times Company. Reprinted by permission.

Naomi Wolf. "PBQ: The Professional Beauty Qualification" from *The Beauty Myth* by Naomi Wolf. Copyright © 1991 by Naomi Wolf. Reprinted by permission of William Morrow & Company, Inc.

Laura Mansnerus. "Don't Tell" from the December 1, 1991 edition of the *New York Times*. Copyright © 1991 by The New York Times Company. Reprinted by permission.

Linda Sharron. "This Spring (Mama Changes the Oil)" from the April 19, 1992 edition of the *Lawrence Eagle Tribune*. Copyright 1992 by Linda Sharron. Reprinted with permission of Linda Sharron, Fitchburg State College.

Mary Helen Ponce. "Enero" first published in *Graywolf Annual: Stories from the American Mosaic*. Reprinted by permission of the author.

Chapter Eight

Grant Pick. "The Life of Johnny Washington: Notes from the Underclass" from the April 8, 1988 issue of the *Chicago Reader*. Copyright 1988 by Chicago Reader, Inc. Reprinted by permission of the author.

Jon D. Hull. "Slow Descent into Hell" from the February 2, 1987 issue of *Time* Magazine. Copyright 1987 by Time Inc. Reprinted by permission.

Cathy Stern. "Those Places" copyright © 1987 by *Shenandoah: The Washington and Lee University Review*. Reprinted from *Shenandoah*, Volume 37, No. 4 (1987) by permission of the Editor.

Elizabeth Cook-Lynn. "A Visit from Reverend Tileston" from *The Power of Horses and Other Stories* by Elizabeth Cook-Lynn. Copyright © 1990 by Elizabeth Cook-Lynn. Reprinted by permission of Little, Brown and Company.

Richard Goldstein. "AIDS and the Social Contract" from the December 29, 1987 issue of *Village Voice*. Copyright © 1987 by Richard Goldstein. Reprinted by permission of the author.

K. Kam. "The Hopeland" from *Making Waves* by Asian Women United. Copyright © 1989 by Asian Women United. Reprinted by permission of Beacon Press.

Sue Halpern. "The Place of the Solitaries" from *Migrations to Solitude* by Sue Halpern. Copyright © 1992 by Sue Halpern. Reprinted by permission of Pantheon Books, a division of Random House, Inc.

Index of Authors
and Titles